SOURCEB(

Criminology

SECOND EDITION

MICHAEL DOHERTY
BA (Law), MA (Criminology)
Senior Lecturer in Law, University of Glamorgan

OLD BAILEY PRESS

OLD BAILEY PRESS
at Holborn College, Woolwich Road,
Charlton, London, SE7 8LN

First published 1998
Second edition 2002

© Michael Doherty 2002

All Old Bailey Press publications enjoy copyright protection.

All rights reserved. No part of this publication may be
reproduced or transmitted in any form or by any means,
electronic, mechanical, photocopying, recording or otherwise, or
stored in any retrieval system of any nature without either the
written permission of the copyright holder, application for which
should be made to the Old Bailey Press, or a licence permitting
restricted copying in the United Kingdom issued by the
Copyright Licensing Agency.

Any person who infringes the above in relation to this
publication may be liable to criminal prosecution and civil
claims for damages.

ISBN 1 85836 450 7

British Library Cataloguing-in-Publication Data

A catalogue record for this book is available from the British
Library.

Printed and bound in Great Britain

LLYFRGELLOEDD SIR DDINBYCH DENBIGHSHIRE LIBRARIES	
C4600000325601	
L B C	15/01/2003
364.0942	£11.95
	RU

Contents

Preface

The aim of this *Criminology Sourcebook* is to allow students to have convenient access to the most important thoughts of criminological writers. Lecturers implore students to acquaint themselves with such work and it can seem an impossible task as each writer may have produced several lengthy and difficult volumes. My hope is that by gathering and selecting these extracts this task becomes more manageable. The extracts focus on the United Kingdom, but where important contributions have been made by writers from other countries these have been included. This means in practice that there are a number of contributions from American sociologists which reflect their importance in the development of ideas about crime causation.

In terms of focus, the material is designed to reflect legal and sociological traditions of criminology. Since criminology is such a multi-disciplinary affair it is inevitable that other forms of thinking will also be reflected in some of the extracts. The process of selecting material was not an easy one as contrary forces were at work. The desire to be up to date conflicts, of course, with the need to include the classics. The extracts reflect what was available up to January 2002.

The intended audience for this text is those students who are following courses in law, criminology, criminal justice and deviance and who will, to a greater or lesser extent, have to tackle issues of criminology and criminal justice. For those who are making use of the *Criminology Textbook,* which is also published by Old Bailey Press, you will be pleased to find that the material is organised in a very similar fashion. The *Sourcebook* divides into two main parts – theories of crime and the criminal justice process. For theories of crime the chapter order largely reflects historical developments in criminological thought. The chapters on the criminal justice process are arranged in terms of the successive stages of that process – starting with crime prevention and finishing with imprisonment.

Michael Doherty
University of Glamorgan Law School
February 2002

Acknowledgements

The author and the publishers would like to thank all those whose work has been reproduced in this Sourcebook and to the copyright holders who have kindly granted permission for their material to be included. Every effort has been made to contact the owners of the copyright in each extract. If any of these has inadvertently been wrongly attributed, the publishers will be happy to make the necessary arrangements in order to rectify the situation.

The publishers would like to thank, in particular, the following for their kind permission to include material: the University of California Press; Allyn and Bacon; Oxford University Press; Taylor & Francis Books Ltd; Pluto Publishing Ltd; Professor Einar Kringlen; Odd Steffen Dalgard; Professor Howard Parker; Houghton Mifflin Company; the University of Pennsylvania Press and the University of Chicago Press.

Finally, we are indebted to the Controller of Her Majesty's Stationery Office for permission to reproduce Crown Copyright material.

Crown copyright is reproduced with the permission of the Controller of Her Majesty's Stationery Office.

1 Sources of Data

Though frequently criticised, the official criminal statistics are a very important source of data in relation to crime and the criminal justice system in England and Wales. The first extract provides some of the most important data that is to be found in these statistics.

Home Office (2001) *Criminal Statistics 1999*

An indication of the amount of crime during the year is the figure of 5.3 million notifiable offences recorded by the police in 1999. This was a rise of 3.8 per cent in comparison with the year before. There had previously been a run of six consecutive year on year reductions in the figure for notifiable offences. The current rate amounts to 10,100 offences per 100,000 of the population. In comparison the rate was as low as 1,100 per 100,000 in 1950. Property crime made up 83 per cent of the total in 1999 amounting to 4.4 million crimes. Between 1998 and 1999 the burglary rate fell by 5 per cent having also fallen by 5 per cent and 13 per cent in the two previous years. Violent crime rose by 16 per cent in 1999 having fallen by 6 per cent in the previous year. There were 761 homicides initially recorded in 1998. The recorded crime statistics do not tell the whole story. Figures from the British Crime Survey suggest that the number of offences committed is more than four times the number reported to the police and even if reported it seems that many are not recorded by the police.

The detection or clear up rate was 25 per cent in 1999, having been 29 per cent in the previous year. The rate was as high as 45 per cent in the 1960s. There were 1.3 million arrests in 1999. Of those arrested 23 per cent were under the age of 18. Where arrest was resorted to, in 30 per cent of cases this was for theft and handling, 17 per cent for offences of violence and 8 per cent for drug offences. 1.7 million people were found guilty or cautioned, this being a 4 per cent decrease on the year before in the figure for indictable offences, whilst for all offences the rate of decrease was higher at 5 per cent. In total 1,433,900 were found guilty whilst 287,900 were cautioned – a figure that includes reprimands and warnings. There was an 8 per cent reduction in the cautioning rate, compared to the previous year. Between police force areas, there were big differences in cautioning rates for indictable offences with Surrey at 51 per cent, Dyfed Powys 44 per cent and Gloucestershire 43 per cent having the highest rates. In contrast, Durham, Lincolnshire and West Yorkshire had a rate of less than 25 per cent. 4,256 juveniles were given reprimands and 2,051 final warnings.

In relation to court proceedings 1.88 million people were proceeded against at magistrates' courts, a 4 per cent decrease on the previous year. Inclusive of guilty pleas, convictions remained almost unchanged between 1992 and 1999 at 98 per cent of cases proceeding to a hearing in magistrates' courts. Convictions in the Crown Court remained almost unchanged between 1992 and 1998 at 90–91 per cent of cases proceeding to a hearing, inclusive of guilty pleas. Convictions following a plea of not guilty rose gradually from 56 per cent of contested hearings in 1992 to 60 per cent in 1997 but were back down to 57 per cent in 1998 and 1999. In the Crown Court 77,000 cases were tried, a reduction from the figure of 91,000 two years earlier. Of the 77,000 61 per cent pleaded guilty. For the remainder who pleaded not guilty as many as 65 per cent of them were acquitted.

A SUMMARY OF SOME OF THE MAIN STATISTICS FOR NOTIFIABLE OFFENCES

	(thousands)	
	1981	1999
Offences recorded by the police	2,794	5,300
Offences cleared up	1,056	1,325
Defendants proceeded against	2,373	1,957
Offenders found guilty and cautioned	2,259	1,722
Found guilty	2,105	1,434
Cautioned	144	288

PERSONS AGED 18 AND OVER PROCEEDED AGAINST AT THE CROWN COURT IN 1999

	(thousands)	
	Male	Female
Violence against the person	58.7	5.8
Sexual offences	6.8	0.1
Burglary	32.0	1.7
Robbery	5.8	0.4
Theft and handling stolen goods	110.7	27.8
Fraud and forgery	19.8	7.1
Criminal damage	12.4	1.3
Drug offences	46.6	6.3
Motoring offences	9.7	0.7
Other offences	68.0	9.4
Totals	370.5	60.5

This source of data provides more recent data than the full version of the criminal statistics in relation to criminal offences. It does not however provide such comprehensive coverage.

Povey D et al (2001) *Recorded Crime Statistics, England and Wales, 12 months to March 2001*

In the year to March 2001, 5.2 million offences were recorded by the police, a 2.5 per cent decrease on the previous year. Violence against the person showed a 3 per cent increase which was an improvement on the 16 per cent increase in the previous year. Robberies rose 13 per cent, an improvement in terms of the 26 per cent increase of the previous year.

NOTIFIABLE OFFENCES RECORDED BY THE POLICE

	12 months to March 2000	12 months to March 2001
Violence against the person	581,036	600,873
Sexual offences	37,792	37,299
Robbery	84,277	95,154
Burglary	906,468	836,027
Theft and handling	2,223,620	2,145,372
Fraud and forgery	334,773	319,324
Criminal damage	945,682	960,087
Drug offences	121,866	113,458
Other offences	65,671	63,237
Totals	5,301,185	5,170,831

The data provided in this report concerns the most common form of criminal behaviour: that committed by motorists. Given the huge amount of people with whom it deals it is clear that being an offender is a very common occurrence and provides further evidence to doubt the idea that the criminal is a category distinct from the law abiding.

Wilkins G et al (2000) *Motoring Offences England and Wales 1999*

The report notes that there were 9.5 million offences in 1999, a 3 per cent decrease on 1998. The number of speed limit offences was 1,015,000, a considerable change from 761,000 cases in 1996.

TYPES OF PROCEEDINGS FOR MOTORING OFFENCES 1999

	(millions)
Fixed penalty notices	3.1
Court proceedings	2.1
Penalty charge notices	4.0
Written warnings	0.1
VDRS notices	0.2
Total	9.5
Number of vehicles licensed	26.2

The penalty charge notices are issued by local authority parking attendants. The fixed penalty notices are issued by the police and traffic wardens. Written warnings are issued by the police. VDRS notices are vehicle defect rectification scheme notices. Six million of the offences, well over half of all offences, are obstruction, waiting and parking offences and over 20 per cent are licence, insurance and record-keeping offences. Roadside cameras provided evidence for 551,000 offences (a large increase from 319,000 in 1996), which included 49 per cent of speeding offences. Police forces vary in their use of court proceedings, the figure for Sussex being 23 per cent whilst for Staffordshire it was 52 per cent. This is largely a product of local circumstances such as the degree of urbanisation.

Valuable as the official criminal statistics are as a source of data, it is clear that they do not record all of the crime that is committed. One remedy for this is to carry out surveys of victims in order to discover crimes that may not have been reported to the police. This method is a valuable supplement to the official statistics and the *British Crime Survey* (BCS) is the most important of the surveys available. It is national rather than local, covering England and Wales. The extracts provide data on a number of issues, most importantly it demonstrates the fact that there is a lot more crime than the official statistics reveal. Also provided is an account of the methodology of how these crime surveys are undertaken.

Home Office (2000) *The 2000 British Crime Survey*

This is the eighth survey of people's experiences and perceptions of crime carried out on behalf of the Home Office – it measured crime that occurred in 1999. The first survey was carried out in 1982. In this latest survey, a representative national sample of 19,411 people over the age of 16 plus an ethnic boost of 3,874 was selected and 74 per cent of them were successfully interviewed. The ethnic boost was used to remedy perceived gaps in the data for such groups. The information from the British Crime Survey provides important insights into criminal behaviour. They certainly tell us that the official statistics do not portray anything like the whole story, though they may well reveal similar trends, as with the recorded fall in crime. The survey estimated that 14.7 million offences were committed against individuals and their property in 1999; the figure had been 16.5 million in 1997. Where comparisons can be made with categories used in the official statistics the survey estimated 11.3 million offences whilst the official statistics recorded 2.6 million offences. The survey data thus records more than four times the amount of crime than is the case with the official statistics.

For 1999, the amount of crime recorded is 39 per cent greater than in 1981 but 10 per cent less than in 1997. There was a fall recorded for nearly every offence that is measured with the exceptions being theft from the person (a 4 per cent increase) and robbery (a 14 per cent increase). Of the decreases, burglary saw a 21 per cent reduction and vehicle thefts a 15 per cent reduction. Better security on recent makes of car is certainly making a difference and the reduction is a success for the promoters of crime prevention strategies. There were still nearly 3 million vehicle-related thefts. As many as 13 per cent of vehicle-owning households had a vehicle related theft. On the issue of violence it is still the case that the source of this is likely to be an acquaintance (36 per cent of cases) or because of a domestic (another 23 per cent) rather than a stranger.

Where comparisons can be made only 13 per cent of the BCS crimes ended up in police records. This is because only 35 per cent were reported to the police and only about 38 per cent of those that were reported ended up being recorded as a crime. The British Crime Survey asked victims why they did not report incidents to the police. The most common reason was that the incident was not serious enough or involved too small a loss (46 per cent of cases). Other common reasons were that the police would be unable to do much about it (30 per cent), or that the incident was considered a private matter and was dealt with by the victim (22 per cent). Vandalism, thefts from vehicles and attempts were likely not to be reported because they were considered not serious enough. For violent crime, the reasons for not reporting were rather different: more were not reported because victims felt the matter was private or they had dealt with it themselves. This was particularly true of domestic violence.

These surveys are also very valuable as a source of information on risk of being a victim of crime. The BCS estimates that 30 per cent of adults in 1999 were victims of at least one of the crimes that the survey records, this being a fall from 39 per cent in 1995 and 34 per cent in 1997. Risks of crime are highest for certain groups such as youngsters, unemployed people, single parents, private renters, inner city dwellers and those living in areas of high physical disorder. Specifically on violence: 4.2 per cent had been victims with a higher rate of 20 per cent for 16–24 year old males. The 1998 and 2000 sweeps of the BCS included a question to try to assess to what extent fear of crime had an impact on people's quality of life. Respondents were asked on a scale from 1 to 10 to what extent their own quality of life was affected by fear of crime. In 2000, just over a half (55 per cent) of those asked felt that fear of crime had a minimal impact (scores 1 to 3) on their quality of life and a further 38 per cent said it had a moderate impact (scores 4 to 7). Only 6 per cent considered that their quality of life was greatly affected (scores 8 to 10). In 1998, significantly more were greatly affected (8 per cent). The following groups were most likely to say fear greatly affected their quality of life – women aged 60 plus, Asians, those in poor health, people in low income households, people living in council or Housing Association accommodation and those living in areas with high levels of physical disorder. For the future, there are plans to move to an annual survey rather than one every two years. It is also intended to improve the quality of the data by doubling the number of interviews that are conducted.

A further method of supplementing the official statistics is to carry out local crime surveys. The Islington Crime Survey is the most famous of these and an extract from one of its reports is provided below. A particular feature of this work is the attention that it has brought to the issue of fear of crime. These local surveys are one of the aspects of the work of the left realists who also provide the last two extracts in Chapter 7.

Jones T, Maclean B and Young J (1986) *The Islington Crime Survey*, p201

We have shown that crime is perceived by the people of Islington to be a problem of major dimensions. Indeed, crime and vandalism are seen as the second greatest problems in the Borough after unemployment, on par with poor youth and children's facilities and housing – and way ahead of schools and public transport.

The impact of crime is considerable and it is far from a rare event. Thirty-one per cent of households in Islington had a serious crime committed against them in the last year – and it shapes their lives. For example, over a quarter of all people in Islington always avoid going out after dark because of fear of crime and this rises to over one-third in the case of women. We have here a virtual curfew of the female population. Yet it is frequently suggested that such fears are fantasies, part of some moral hysteria fanned by the newspapers and television. Thus it is often suggested that it is paradoxical that women have a higher fear of crime than men given the supposedly lower rate of crime against them. We have shown that this is simply not true: women have a higher victimisation rate than men, they suffer to a greater extent from particular crimes, sexual assault obviously but also crimes like street robbery, and they suffer from a much greater rate of sub-criminal harassment. And all this is in the context of a much greater level of precautions taken. Their fears, therefore, are realistic. Similarly, we find that the degree of criticism of the police in terms of unfairness between groups and the use of excessive violence and other malpractices varies with people's actual experiences. The virtue, then, of a crime survey is that it provides us with a more realistic mapping of the impact of crime and policing, and it also reminds us that we should take seriously people's knowledge of

crime. Successful police work depends on the police tapping such knowledge and the various other social agencies acting upon such a public information stock, whether it is providing suggestions as to who is committing racist attacks, which kids are the local vandals, why such an architectural blindspot is dangerous at night and what are the problems of their area.

It is clear then that there are a variety of different sources of data on crime and the criminal justice system. What is required is that they be used with an awareness of their particular strengths and weaknesses. The text by Coleman and Moynihan is valuable as a source of material on these strengths and weaknesses and the extract provided concentrates on victim surveys.

Coleman C and Moynihan J (1996) *Understanding Crime Data*, pp88–89

Victim studies

It was originally thought that victimisation survey data, like self-report data, would allow criminologists partially to quantify their long-held obsession; these new forms of data would, it was hoped, eat into the dark figure of unrecorded crime, exposing both its size and nature. This process is sometimes pictured as a series of concentric circles; as new research methods are put into practice, so the dark figure is progressively revealed. However, the real picture is more complex than this.

Official crime statistics are concerned with recorded crime and known offenders; self-report studies, being offender-based, provide us with information on the wider population of both known and unknown offenders; victimisation surveys are offence-based and provide information on those crimes which have been recorded by the police, those reported to the police but not recorded by them, and those which are not reported. Not only are the three data sets measuring different things, they are taking these measurements from three very different perspectives: those of the police, the offender and the victim, three perspectives which are unlikely to be congruent.

Many of the incidents which are captured by self-report studies and victimisation surveys are the very types of crime which are most likely to enter the official statistics, while others tend to evade capture by any of these methods of data collection. Self-report studies and victimisation surveys concentrate upon their own universe of crimes; self-report studies are good at counting offenders of a 'trivial' nature, while victimisation surveys are suited to collecting data on 'ordinary' offences. Both are of limited use in collecting data on crimes of the powerful or white-collar crime; neither can tell us anything about homicide-successful murderers (or rather, those who remain undetected) who are unlikely to confess their sins even for the benefit of research and their victims would be difficult to include in a survey sample.

Victimisation survey data have a complex and overlapping set of relationships with both officially recorded crime data and that generated by self-report studies, relationships which need to be fully appreciated before such data are put to any use. However, the data produced by these surveys have outgrown their original purposes and can, in many instances, stand alone without the need for comparisons with other forms of crime data. Their silence with regard to certain crimes and largely on the nature of offenders can be excused – once it is understood – as they provide us with a vital piece of the criminological jigsaw.

One method that can be used to tackle the dark number of crime and to provide a supplement to the official statistics is self-report studies. The extract provides data in relation to a recent example of the use of this technique. The material relates to both juvenile and adult offenders.

Flood-Page C, Campbell S, Harrington V and Miller J (2000) *Youth Crime: Findings from the 1998/99 Youth Lifestyles Survey*, ppv–x

This report discusses the extent of self-reported offending by 4,848 people aged between 12 and 30 living in private households in England and Wales. It is based on the Youth Lifestyles Survey (YLS) carried out between October 1998 and January 1999. The YLS focused on 27 offences including arson, theft, burglary, shoplifting, and buying and selling stolen goods. Four types of fraud offences were asked about (tax evasion, benefit fraud, and making false expenses and insurance claims). Violent offences ranged from threatening someone with a weapon to fighting and assault. This is the second sweep of the YLS. The first took place in 1992/93 and was reported by Graham and Bowling (1995). The second YLS includes a wider age group than the first. Together with a larger sample size, this allows us to gain a more complete picture of the extent and nature of youth crime and also to test whether the findings of the first YLS still hold.

Offending by 12- to 30-year-olds

Some kind of offending is common among young people – almost half of 12- to 30-year-olds admitted committing at least one of 27 offences at some point in their lives (57 per cent of men and 37 per cent of women). However, as people get older, they will have had more time to commit crime and new opportunities will have presented themselves, such as workplace theft or fraud. For this reason, this report concentrates on offending in the 12 months prior to interview which offers the best indication of recent offending levels. Almost a fifth (19 per cent) of 12- to 30-year-olds admitted one or more offence in the last 12 months. Women were less likely to have offended (11 per cent had done so) than men (26 per cent). When they offended, about half (48 per cent of men and 59 per cent of women) had committed only one or two offences. Taking all offences, those aged 14 to 21 committed most, whereas those in the youngest (12 to 13) and oldest (26 to 30) age groups committed least. The average age at which offending began was 13-and-a-half for boys and 14 for girls. Rates of offending are highest among men aged 18 – the peak age of offending. (This falls to 15 if one excludes those who only committed either fraud or workplace theft.) Among women, the peak age of offending is 14. (This is unchanged if fraud and workplace theft are excluded.)

At ages 12 and 13 there is little difference between boys and girls in offending (or indeed in drug use or regular drinking). After age 14 however, the difference between men and women becomes more marked. Over the age of 17, male offenders outnumber women offenders by a ratio of around 3:1.

Those sanctioned
Overall, three per cent of all 12- to 30-year-olds (4 per cent of men and 1 per cent of women) said they had been cautioned or taken to court in the last 12 months on at least one occasion. (Respondents may have included formal and informal cautions when answering.) Among offenders, 12 per cent had been cautioned or taken to court at least once. The figure was higher for male offenders (14 per cent) than females (9 per cent), and slightly higher for those under 18 (14 per cent) than those older (11 per cent). Among persistent offenders (ie, those who had offended on three or more occasions) almost a fifth (18 per cent) said they had been cautioned or taken to court. More generally, the police had some contact with the majority of offenders. Two-thirds (68 per cent) of persistent offenders had been stopped, told to move on or been visited at home by the police in the past year.

Serious and/or persistent offenders
Eight per cent of 12- to 30-year-olds (12 per cent of men, 4 per cent of women) were classified as serious and/or persistent offenders because they had either committed at least

three offences during the past year or else had committed one or more serious offences such as violence, burglary, theft of a car or motor bike, pickpocketing or robbery. The most prolific 10 per cent of offenders were responsible for nearly half of the crimes admitted by the sample. They represented 2 per cent of men and less than 1 per cent of women in the entire sample.

Prevalence of offending
There are marked differences in the nature of crime committed by men and women at different ages.

AMONG WOMEN
The most common offences committed by girls under 16 were criminal damage, shoplifting, buying stolen goods and fighting. Over the age of 16, girls committed less criminal damage and shoplifting, although they were increasingly involved in fraud and buying stolen goods.

Over 21, all types of offending fell: fraud or buying stolen goods were most often admitted.

AMONG MEN
Comparatively high rates of offending by 14- to 15-year-old boys reflected their involvement in fights, in buying stolen goods, 'other theft' and in criminal damage. Roughly one in eight boys of this age admitted to each. 16- to 17-year-old boys showed a similar pattern of offending but were less involved in buying and selling stolen goods, 'other theft' and criminal damage. Over a third of offences committed by this age group involved fighting. The highest levels of offending were among 18- to 21-year-old men. At this age, fighting increased sharply although shoplifting and criminal damage declined. Involvement in fraud and workplace theft began. Buying and selling stolen goods continued at a similar rate to 14 to 15-year-olds. Generally offending declined after the age of 21. However, the fall is sharper, and occurs earlier, for criminal damage and violence. The proportion of men admitting property offences

was fairly constant between the ages of 18 and 25 and only fell after 25. (To this extent, this supports the finding of the first YLS that men do not grow out of property crime before their mid-20s.) However, the type of property crime committed during the 20s changes from shoplifting and 'other theft' to workplace theft. Fraud also increases in the late 20s. More than half of male offenders aged 26 to 30 had only committed fraud and/or workplace theft in the last year. Put another way, only eight per cent of men aged 26 to 30 admitted to offences other than fraud or workplace theft compared to 20 per cent of 22 to 25-year-olds and 31 per cent of 18 to 21-year-olds.

Volume of offences
Overall, nearly three-quarters of all offences committed were property offences (55 per cent) or fraud (16 per cent). Buying stolen goods accounted for a quarter (26 per cent) of offences admitted by women and 18 per cent of offences by men. Shoplifting made up another 18 per cent of women's offences but only 6 per cent of men's crimes. Violent offences accounted for one in five of men's crimes and one in ten of women's crimes.

Area differences in offending
There was little difference between different types of areas in terms of the proportion of men who admitted committing any offence in the past year. However, men who lived in inner-city areas were twice as likely as those living in rural areas to be serious and/or persistent offenders.

Employment and offending
The YLS indicated that the unemployed were more likely to offend than those in employment or further education although the difference was not statistically significant. However, unemployed men were nearly twice as likely to be serious and/or persistent offenders as those who were either in education or work.

Risk factors for serious and/or persistent offending
Whilst data is only available in relation to males it is thought that similar factors will operate in relation to females.

12- TO 17-YEAR-OLD BOYS
The factors most strongly associated with serious and/or persistent offending included family, school and lifestyle choices. Using drugs in the last year was the strongest predictor of serious and/or persistent offending: the odds of offending were nearly five times higher for boys who had used drugs in the last year compared with those who had not. School also exerts a strong influence, with boys who were disaffected from school or who were persistent truants being more at risk. Those who were excluded from school were more likely to offend, although this was not among the best predictors of offending. Families and friends have an important influence on offending. Boys who were less highly supervised by their parents were more at risk. Having friends or acquaintances who had been in trouble with the police was also highly predictive of serious and persistent offending. Boys who hung around in public places were more likely to be offenders than those who did not, even controlling for other factors.

18- TO 30-YEAR-OLD MEN
Drug use remains influential at an older age: using drugs at least once a month was the most predictive factor of serious and/or persistent offending. Heavy drinking (ie on at least five days a week) was also important for older men. The influence of school and friends also continued to be important after the age of 18: the second most important predictor was leaving school without any educational qualification. Those who had been excluded from school were also at greater risk.

Men with delinquent friends or acquaintances had almost four times the odds of being a serious and/or persistent offender as others.

One feature of research into the victim perspective is that the data gathered can be used to sharpen up the focus of policy making. The present research tackled the difficulties of estimating the economic and social cost of crime.

Brand S and Price R (2000)
The Economic and Social Costs of Crime

Every day decisions are made by policy makers and managers in the criminal justice system which reflect implicit judgments about the relative seriousness of different crimes, or about the benefits of pursuing one approach to reducing crime rather than another. This study represents a first step towards making such judgments more explicit and in making sure they better reflect the available evidence on the impacts on society of different types of crime. Cost of crime estimates can play an important role in helping the Government to achieve the greatest impact on crime for the money spent. They can be used in both appraisal and evaluation of crime reduction policies, such as those in the Government's evidence-based Crime Reduction Programme. They can help us to prioritise, focusing scarce resources on policies that have the biggest impact on harm caused by crime, rather than simply the number of crimes.

'Costs of crime' refers to the full range of impacts of crime (within the notifiable offences category), expressed where possible in monetary terms – though this does not suggest that it is either straightforward or always right to reduce the consequences of any crime into purely financial terms. Costs are incurred in anticipation of crimes occurring (such as security expenditure and insurance administration costs), as a consequence of criminal events (such as property stolen and damaged, emotional and physical impacts and health services), and responding to crime and tackling criminals (costs to the criminal justice system). Costs were measured using surveys of victims, such as the British Crime Survey and Commercial Victimisation Survey, and estimates of industry turnover and costs, such as the security and insurance industries. Resource cost estimates for the criminal justice system have been derived from a model developed by the Home Office to track flows and costs through the criminal justice process. Emotional and physical impacts of crime are, for the time being, estimated using figures for people's willingness to pay to avoid road traffic accidents, but work is underway to derive better estimates reflecting more accurately the impacts of crime on victims.

Average costs of crime vary widely between offence categories. The most costly property crimes are theft of vehicles, costing around £4,700 per incident. Burglaries cost an average of £2,300, and criminal damage around £500. Personal crimes are far more costly on average than property crimes. Homicides have been estimated to cost at least £1 million, with other violence against the person costing on average £19,000 per incident.

Robberies incur costs of almost £5,000 on average. Common assault is the least costly personal crime, with an average cost of around £500 per offence. The total cost of crime to England and Wales in 1999/2000 is estimated at around £60 billion, although this figure is still far from comprehensive, as it does not include important costs such as fear of crime or quality of life impacts. Around £19 billion of the total cost of crime is the cost of property stolen or damaged. Nearly £18 billion of the total is the direct emotional and physical impact on victims of crime, with a little over £14 billion of this incurred as a result of violent crime. The response to crime by the criminal justice system constitutes around 20 per cent of the total cost of crime, at around £12 billion. Identifiable costs in anticipation of crime – security expenditure and insurance administration costs – come to over £5 billion, the bulk of this being security expenditure.

One example of how such data can be applied in practice will be provided. The relative importance of violent crime in comparison with other, property crimes is marked. When we focus on the volume of offences violent crimes come to around a quarter of the total. When we focus on the cost of those offences, rather than the volume, violent crimes constitute nearly three-quarters of the total cost. This finding is one example of the way in which cost of crime estimates can help illuminate potential areas where gains may be made by new policies or the switching of resources from one area to another.

Race as a factor in the criminal justice system is an issue that is regarded as requiring particular attention in terms of statistical monitoring. The data in this report relates mainly to 1999–2000 though some of the data reflects earlier time periods.

Home Office (2001) *Statistics on Race and the Criminal Justice System*

Data indicates that 2 per cent of the population aged 10 and over in England and Wales were of black ethnic origin, 3 per cent of Asian origin and 1 per cent other non-white ethnic groups. A total of 800,000 stops and searches were recorded by the police under a range of legislation, including the Police and Criminal Evidence Act (PACE) 1984, of which 8 per cent were of black people, 4 per cent Asian and 1 per cent other non-white origin. Police forces varied widely in their rates for recorded stops and searches. Compared with 1998/99, the number of stops and searches fell by 41 per cent for white people and Asians and 35 per cent for black people in the Metropolitan Police area (MPS). In England and Wales (excluding the MPS) the falls were less with an average fall of about 14 per cent for white people and Asians and 10 per cent for black people.

Police recorded 2,003 homicides in 1997/98, 1998/99 and 1999/2000 (provisional figures) of which 10 per cent were of black people, 6 per cent Asian and 3 per cent other non-white ethnic origin; 15 homicides were recorded as being racially motivated over this three year period. The police were statistically less likely to identify suspects for homicides involving black victims than for white or those from other ethnic groups, but differences in the type (ie the method of killing) of homicide involved may play a part here.

There were 1.3 million arrests for notifiable offences, of which 7 per cent were of black people, 4 per cent Asian and 1 per cent other non-white origin. Black people were four times more likely to be arrested than white or other ethnic groups. White people showed a higher likelihood of being arrested for burglary and criminal damage, black people for robbery and both black people and Asians for fraud and forgery and drugs. The police cautioned about 180,000 persons for notifiable offences of which 6 per cent were of black people, 4 per cent Asian and 1 per cent other non-white ethnic origin. Relative to the number of persons arrested, the cautioning rate was slightly higher for white people (16 per cent) and Asians (15 per cent) than for black people (11 per cent). An offender's eligibility for a caution depends upon a number of factors including the circumstances of an offence and whether they will admit to the offence. Information collected from five pilot areas on magistrates' court decisions indicated that, excluding those defendants committed to the Crown Court for trial, white defendants were more likely to be convicted (65 per cent) than black or Asian defendants (both 56 per cent). There was no clear evidence of substantial differences in the use of custody at the magistrates' court although black defendants were more likely to be sentenced to a community sentence and less likely to be fined or given a conditional discharge.

In June 1999, ethnic minorities accounted for 18 per cent of the male prison population (12 per cent black, 3 per cent Asian and 3 per cent other) and 25 per cent of the female prison population (19 per cent black, 1 per cent Asian and 5 per cent other). This included foreign nationals who made up 8 per cent of the male prison population and 15 per cent of the female population. Black and Asian prisoners tended to be younger than white prisoners and white and Asian prisoners tended to be serving shorter sentences than black prisoners.

Estimates from the British Crime Survey suggests that although racist incidents fell by 27 per cent from 1995 to 1999, there was a general fall of 22 per cent in all incidents both racial and non-racial over this period. Racist incidents recorded by the police rose by 107 per cent to 47,810 in 1999/00; this is likely to reflect better recording of such incidents by the police. During the first full year of recording for the new racially aggravated offences 21,750 offences were recorded (one half were offences of harassment which included the public order offences of threatening or disorderly behaviour), of which one third were detected. 3,815 defendants were prosecuted for these offences and 1,073 convicted at magistrates' courts with a further 990 defendants committed for trial to the Crown Court. 9 per cent of complaints made against the police in 1999/2000 were from black people, 6 per cent from Asian and 2 per cent from other ethnic minority groups. Ethnic minorities are underrepresented in all grades as employees in the police service, prison service and in senior posts in all the criminal justice agencies. There have been some small improvements in this representation, compared to earlier years, in most criminal justice agencies.

REPRESENTATION OF ETHNIC GROUPS AT DIFFERENT STAGES OF THE CRIMINAL JUSTICE PROCESS (PERCENTAGES)

| | Ethnicity | | | | | |
	White	Black	Asian	Other	Not known	Total
Population						
(aged 10 and over)	94.5	1.8	2.7	1.1	0.0	100
Stops and searches	85.2	8.2	4.4	0.9	1.3	100
Arrests	87.0	7.3	4.0	0.8	0.9	100
Cautions	87.2	5.7	4.1	1.0	2.0	100
Prison receptions	86.0	8.5	2.5	2.9	0.0	100
Prison population	81.2	12.3	3.0	3.4	0.1	100

This Home Office research provides data in relation to the criminal convictions of people born in the following years: 1953, 1958, 1963, 1968, 1973 and 1978. This reveals for example that 33 per cent of males and 9 per cent of females born in 1953 had been convicted of at least one 'standard list' offence before the age of 46. Two-thirds of all court appearances where a conviction occurred before the age of 46 for males born in 1953 were attributable to about one-quarter of offenders, or 8 per cent of the male population.

Prime J, White S, Liriano S and Patel K (2001) *Criminal Careers of Those Born between 1953 and 1978*

Population with a conviction

Males

Thirty-three per cent of men born in 1953 had at least one conviction for a 'standard list' offence before the age of 46. The percentage of the population with at least one conviction increases with age, rising from 7 per cent before the age of 15, to 19 per cent before the age 20, 28 per cent before the age of 30, and 31 per cent before the age of 40. Most offenders are first convicted of an offence between the ages of about 13 and 20. The number of new offenders tails off with increasing age and only 2 per cent of the population are first convicted of an offence in their late thirties to mid forties.

There are differences between the six birth cohorts in the percentage of the population with a conviction. Before the age of 15, males born in the later cohort years are less likely to have been convicted of an offence than males born in 1953. The difference is slight for males born in 1958 (when 6.8 per cent had a conviction before the age of 15 compared to 7.4 per cent of males born in 1953), and also for males born in 1963; however the difference increases steadily through the remaining cohorts (only 1 per cent of males born in 1978 had a conviction before the age of 15). After the age of 15, males born in 1958 and 1963 are more likely to have been convicted of an offence, with 20 and 21 per cent respectively convicted of an offence before the age of 20 compared to 19 per cent of the population born in 1953. After the age of 16 the 1968 cohort shows a similar trend to that of the 1953 cohort and by the age of 19, 18 per cent had been convicted. Males born in 1973 and 1978 are much less likely than males in the earlier cohorts to have been convicted; only 14 per cent of those born in 1973 and 12 per cent of those born in 1978 had been convicted of a 'standard list' offence before the age of 20. The lower proportion of males born in 1973 and 1978 convicted of an offence is probably due to changes in the way offenders are dealt with by the police rather than any change in behaviour. From the late 1960s to the early 1970s and again throughout the 1980s and early 1990s the use of the caution as a means of dealing with an offender, particularly a young offender, increased. In the 1960s only about 10 percent of offenders were dealt with by means of a caution whereas by the 1980s that proportion had increased to 20 per cent, and increased further still during the 1990s to over one third of all offenders. This has had the effect of reducing the proportion with a conviction for the population born in the later cohort years, since those offenders are likely to have been given a caution rather than to have been sent to court. A survey in 16 police forces of persons arrested in late 1995, published in Home Office Statistical Findings Issue 2/96, 'Police disposals of notifiable offences cleared up following arrest or report' reveals evidence to suggest that there may also have been an increase in the police use of informal cautions for young offenders. The increased use of informal methods helps to explain the substantial fall in the number of juvenile males (particularly males aged 10–14) found guilty or cautioned since the mid 1980s. Males born in 1953 had a cautioning rate of 0.7 per cent at the age of 15 whereas males born in 1978 had a much higher rate of 4.3 per cent. This change has contributed to the reduction of the population with a conviction in the more recent cohorts.

Females

Nine per cent of women born in 1953 had been convicted of a 'standard list' offence before the age of 46. At the younger ages the percentage of the female population with a conviction is only between a eighth and a twentieth of the percentage of the male population with a conviction, but by the time the population were in their late thirties and early forties the percentage of women convicted is about a quarter of the percentage of men convicted. The differences between the six birth cohorts are very similar to those observed for males. As for the male population, cautioning rates for young female offenders are much higher for the later cohorts. Whilst this bulletin analyses the criminal behaviour of persons born in six particular years, it is possible to estimate from the cohort files the proportion of the general population currently aged under 46 who have a criminal conviction. By comparing the cohort proportions with the current estimated population in England and Wales, the figures reveal that 27 per cent of males and 6 per cent of females currently aged 18 to 45 have a criminal conviction. The following table shows similar estimates for other age breakdowns.

PROPORTION OF PERSONS ESTIMATED TO HAVE A CRIMINAL CONVICTION: 1999

Age band	Males	Females
10–17	2 per cent	– per cent
18–20	12 per cent	2 per cent
21–45	28 per cent	6 per cent
10–45	22 per cent	5 per cent
18–45	27 per cent	6 per cent

Offenders desisting

In this bulletin an offender is defined as a 'desister' if he or she has had a conviction, but was not convicted of a subsequent crime for at least five years. This is a measure of the proportion who have not been reconvicted rather than a measure of those who have not reoffended, which we cannot estimate directly.

MALES BORN IN 1953

The likelihood of someone desisting increases as the age of the offender increases. The proportion of males convicted at the age of 10 who were not convicted of a further offence was only 19 per cent. This figure is an over-estimate of the proportion who have desisted from committing a crime since not all offenders will have been caught by the police and some who have been caught will have been dealt with by a caution rather than by sentence at court. The desistence rate increases steadily with age, reaching one third by the age of 19, 43 per cent by the age of 25 and around one in two between the ages of 34 and 40. This is not necessarily an indication that offenders are less likely to commit crimes as they get older: it could be that they become better at avoid-

ing detection as they get older, or that they switch to crimes with lower detection rates, or that because they are more likely to contest cases at court they are more likely to be found not guilty. This conclusion was also drawn by Graham and Bowling in Home Office Research Study 145, 'Young People and Crime'. The desistence rates for the other five birth cohorts show a similar pattern to that of the 1953 cohort.

FEMALES BORN IN 1953

The desistence rates of female offenders born in 1953 show a very different pattern to those of male offenders. The proportion of offenders desisting is much higher than for males, and the rate hardly changes with age. The average desistence rate for all ages is 65 per cent, ranging from 52 per cent to 71 per cent.

Criminal activity

A person is defined here as being 'criminally active' at age X if: they are convicted at age X, or they have two or more convictions and age X is between their first and last recorded conviction.

MALES

The proportion of the male population born in

1953 known to be 'criminally active' increases rapidly with age to a peak of 11 per cent at age 19. The known criminally active proportion of the population tails off gradually after that age to reach 3 per cent at age 40. The pattern is similar for the later cohorts (not shown here), with the highest proportion of the population known to be involved in criminal activity at the ages of 18 and 19. The level of known criminal activity of the 1973 and 1978 birth cohort appears to be lower than that of the earlier cohorts, partly because these offenders have not been followed up for so long, but mainly because offenders born in the 1970s are more likely to have been cautioned than offenders in earlier years.

FEMALES

The proportion of the female population known to be 'criminally active' is much lower than for males, with the proportion peaking at 1.1 per cent between the ages of 20 and 26, with small variations between the six cohort years.

Type of offence at first court appearance

Table A shows the distribution of the type of offence at each offender's first court appearance resulting in a conviction, for offenders born in 1953. In cases where there was more than one conviction at this court appearance, the offence attracting the most severe sentence has been counted.

MALES

Nearly half of male offenders born in 1953 received their first conviction for theft and handling stolen goods. Violence against the person, burglary and criminal damage were also relatively common offences at first con-

TABLE A: PERCENTAGE WITH PRINCIPAL OFFENCE AT FIRST CONVICTION IN EACH OFFENCE GROUP, 1953 COHORT

Offence Group	Males	Females
Violence against the person	9.6	7.3
Sexual offences	2.7	0.1
Burglary	12.9	3.2
Robbery	0.5	0.1
Theft and handling stolen goods	48.6	67.7
Theft of a vehicle	9.0	1.5
Theft from a vehicle	3.1	0.3
Theft from shops	8.2	38.7
Other theft and handling	28.3	27.2
Fraud and forgery	4.2	8.9
Criminal damage	10.1	3.6
Drug offences	3.4	3.2
Other indictable	2.0	1.8
Other summary	3.3	1.9
Motoring	1.9	2.2

viction, with between 10 and 13 per cent of offenders being first convicted of each of these offences.

FEMALES

Two-thirds of female offenders born in 1953 were first convicted of theft and handling stolen goods. Fraud and forgery was also relatively common at 9 per cent, followed by violence against the person at 7 per cent.

Whilst it is difficult to make comparisons of crime rates across jurisdictions, some guidance is provided by the following material in relation to homicide.

Barclay G, Tavares C and Siddique A (2001) *International Comparisons of Criminal Justice Statistics*

NUMBER OF HOMICIDES AND HOMICIDES PER 100,000 OF THE POPULATION IN URBAN AREAS 1997–1999

City	Number of Homicides	Homicides per 100,000 population
Canberra	6	0.64
Ottawa	24	1.04
Tokyo	420	1.17
Rome	97	1.22
Athens	52	1.49
Paris	139	2.21
London	539	2.36
Belfast	45	5.23
New York	2,074	9.38
Copenhagen	50	11.23
Moscow	3,863	18.2
Pretoria	1,512	27.47
Washington	802	50.82

2 Biological Theories

In this work Lombroso considered numerous possible influences upon criminal behaviour and also possible remedies for crime. Even at this late stage of his writing he still thought that there was an important role to be played by genetic factors and the extract concentrates on this. Note well that you are thus reading the most sophisticated version of Lombroso's work. The numerous medical terms are likely to be beyond most of us but the basic themes are clear enough. Whilst some of this seems very peculiar and unacceptable to us now, full credit must be given to Lombroso for his pioneering work and his attempt to put Criminology on a scientific footing. Further insight into Lombroso's thinking is provided by the extract in Chapter 8, Lombroso and Ferrero, which deals specifically with female offenders.

Lombroso C (1918) *Crime – Its Causes and Remedies*, pp365–366, 368

The born criminal shows in a proportion reaching 33 per cent numerous specific characteristics that are almost always atavistic. Those who have followed us thus far have seen that many of the characteristics presented by savage races are very often found among born criminals. Such, for example, are: the slight development of the pilar system; low cranial capacity; retreating forehead; highly developed frontal sinuses; great frequency of Wormian bones; early closing of the cranial sutures; the simplicity of the sutures; the thickness of the bones of the skull; enormous development of the maxillaries and the zygomata; prognathism; obliquity of the orbits; greater pigmentation of the skin; tufted and crispy hair; and large ears. To these we may add the lemurine appendix; anomalies of the ear; dental diastemata; great agility; relative insensibility to pain; dullness of the sense of touch; great visual acuteness; ability to recover quickly from wounds; blunted affections; precocity as to sensual pleasures; greater resemblance between the sexes; greater incorrigibility of the woman; laziness; absence of remorse; impulsiveness; physiopsychic excitability; and especially improvidence, which sometimes appears as courage and again as recklessness changing to cowardice. Besides these there is great vanity; a passion for gambling and alcoholic drinks; violent but fleeting passions; superstition; extraordinary sensitiveness with regard to one's own personality; and a special conception of God and morality. Unexpected analogies are met even in small details, as, for example, the improvised rules of criminal gangs; the entirely personal influence of the chiefs; the custom of tattooing; the not uncommon cruelty of their games; the excessive use of gestures; the onomatopoetic language with personification of inanimate things; and a special literature recalling that of heroic times, when crimes were celebrated and the thought tended to clothe itself in rhythmic form.

… We may add that the atavism of the criminal, when he lacks absolutely every trace of shame and pity, may go back far beyond the savage, even to the brutes themselves. Pathological anatomy helps prove our position by showing in the case of the criminal a greater development of the cerebellum, a rarer union of the calcarine fissure with the parieto-occipital, the absence of folds in the passage of Gratiolet, the gutterlike shape of the nasal incisure, the frequency of the olecranial foramen, extra ribs and vertebrae, and especially the histological anomalies discovered by Roncoroni in the cortex of the cerebrum of criminals, that is to say, the frequent absence of granular layers, and the presence of nerve cells in the white matter, and immense pyramidal cells. In seeking for analogies beyond our own race we come upon the explanation of the union of the atlas with the occipital bone, the prominence of the canine teeth, the flattening of the palate, and the median occipital fossa, occurring among criminals as with the lemurs and rodents; as also the prehensile foot, the simplicity of the lines of the palm, motor and sensory left-handedness. We recall also the tendency to cannibalism even without desire for vengeance, and still more that form of sanguinary ferocity, mingled with lubricity, of which examples are furnished us by Gille, Verzeni, Legier, Bertrand, Artusio, the Marquis of Sade, and others, with whom atavism was accompanied by epilepsy, idiocy, or general paralysis, but who always recall the pairing of animals, preceded by ferocious and sanguinary contests to overcome the reticence of the female or to conquer rivals.

These facts prove clearly that the most horrible crimes have their origin in those animal instincts of which childhood gives us a pale reflection. Repressed in civilised man by education, environment, and the fear of punishment, they suddenly break out in the born criminal without apparent cause, or under the influence of certain circumstances, such as sickness, atmospheric influences, sexual excitement, or mob influence.

Lombroso had many followers in the tradition of attempting to discover biological and hereditary factors in criminal behaviour. Dalgard and Kringlen provide an account of a variety of studies of the twin study method of investigating a possible hereditary factor in criminal behaviour. They also provide an excellent critique of such studies and of the method generally.

Dalgard O S and Kringlen E (1976) 'Criminal Behaviour in Twins', *British Journal of Criminology*[1], 16: 213–232

Particularly in the psychiatric literature it has been maintained that genetic factors play a central role in the etiology of crime, but during the last 20 to 30 years, with increasing delinquency and violence in the Western countries, there has been a weakening of the genetic hypothesis in criminology. A significant number of investigations have shown how delinquency and criminal behaviour are related to psychological, social and cultural factors. However, even though today one is apt to stress psychosocial factors in the etiology of crime, it is nevertheless common to suppose that hereditary factors play a role, at least in certain types of criminal behaviour. For instance, it is reasonable to assume that typical juvenile crime, which varies in accordance with social conditions, is largely environmentally determined, whereas more serious crime, such as grave violence and sexual assaults, is more individually determined and perhaps even genetic in origin. Crime is a cultural and legal concept and accordingly what is considered crime varies to some extent from country to country. In order to entertain the idea that crime could have a genetic origin, one has ... to assume that crime is linked to certain personality characteristics, such as aggressive tendencies or deficient ego control.

The study of the relative contributions of genetic and environmental factors in human behaviour can best be carried out by the classic twin method. This method is based on the existence of two types of twins: *monozygotics* (MZ) and *dizygotics* (DZ). Whereas MZ twins are supposed to be identical in hereditary endowment, DZ twins are no more alike genetically than common siblings. Thus all differences in MZ have to be attributed to the environment in the widest sense of that term, whereas differences in DZ, on the other

[1] Copyright © 1976 *British Journal of Criminology* and contributors. Used by permission.

hand, may be due to both hereditary and environmental factors.

Through a comparison of concordance figures in MZ and DZ with regard to certain traits, one might arrive at an impression of the relative significance of hereditary and environment for the trait in question. A pair is called *concordant* if both twins ... harbour the same trait or illness, *discordant* if they are dissimilar, for instance if one twin is criminal and the other is not. Significantly higher concordance figures in the group of identical twins have usually been regarded as evidence in support of a hereditary background of the traits concerned. Conversely, if a characteristic is chiefly environmentally determined, one would expect similar concordance rates in MZ and DZ. In the case of epidemics where genetic differences are far less important than environmental ones, one would expect clustering in families but no marked difference in concordance rates for MZ and DZ. The same would be true for criminality in the case of environmentally causative origin.

We shall not here discuss methodological problems but we would like to draw attention to a few common sources of error in twin research and make some general statements with regard to interpretation of data.

The results of twin studies are debatable if the following requirements are not fulfilled:

a) The sampling must be based upon complete series of twins. Cf Rosenthal's (1962) theoretical discussion and Kringlen's (1967) empirical research in the field of schizophrenia.

b) The separation of MZ and DZ same-sexed twins must be reliably carried out. Particularly in small samples is blood- and serum typing necessary.

c) The concept of concordance must be clearly defined and the method of computing [it] given, since there are different measures of concordance (Allen et al, 1967).

Higher concordance figures in MZ than in DZ have usually been regarded as proof of hereditary disposition for the trait concerned. Such an interpretation is, however, based on the following assumptions:

a) The environmental conditions are in general similar for MZ and DZ pairs. This assumption is obviously not true. Zazzo (1960) and others have shown that the environment of MZ pairs is more likely to be closely similar than the environment of DZ pairs.

b) The frequency of the trait concerned is not higher in MZ than in DZ pairs. Christiansen's (1968) data threw doubt on this assumption with regard to criminality since he found that MZ twins were more frequently imprisoned for crime than DZ twins.

Table I gives a summary of previous twin studies, along with the present one, with regard to concordance in crime.

Lange (1929) studied 30 pairs of same-sexed (male) twins and observed that 10 of 13 MZ were concordant, whereas only two of 17 DZ displayed concordance. Concordance was defined as offences which lead to imprisonment. Lange obtained his sample of criminal same-sexed twins from prisons, from registered convicted psychopaths, and from his own psychiatric hospital. In addition to the 13 MZ and the 17 DZ of the same sex he learned by chance of ten opposite-sexed twin pairs. The zygosity – monozygotic or dizygotic – was determined by means of somatic measurements, photographs and fingerprints. As a rule the author himself examined personally both twins in a pair. In his monograph Lange gives a fairly detailed description of all the MZ pairs. He concluded his famous study by stating that heredity plays a major role in crime under contemporary conditions.

LeGras (1933) found that all four of his MZ were concordant whereas the five DZ were discordant with regard to criminality. He investigated both psychotic and criminal twins and collected his sample by writing to heads of asylums, prisons, state working colonies and correctional institutions as well as by a search of the university psychiatric-neurological department in Utrecht. Where the twin pairs were similar in appearance they were investigated by means of the Siemens' method

TABLE I

PAIRWISE CONCORDANCE FOR CRIMINALITY IN PREVIOUS AND PRESENT TWIN STUDIES (a)

	MZ		DZ-same sex		DZ-opposite sex	
	No of pairs	% con-cordance	No of pairs	% con-cordance	No of pairs	% con-cordance
Lange 1929, Germany	13	76.9	17	11.8	10	10.0
LeGras 1933, Holland	4	100.0	5	0.0	-	-
Rosanoff et al 1934, USA	37	67.6	28	17.9	32	3.1
Kranz 1936, Germany	31	64.5	43	53.5	50	14.0
Stumpfl 1936, Germany	18	61.1	19	36.8	28	7.1
Borgstrom 1939, Finland	4	75.0	5	40.0	10	20.0
Yoshimasu 1961, Japan	28	60.7	18	11.1	-	-
Tienari 1963, Finland	5	60.0	-	-	-	-
Christiansen 1968, Denmark	81	33.3	137	10.9	226	3.5
Dalgard and Kringlen 1976, Norway (b)	49	22.4	89	18.0	-	-
	31	25.8	54	14.9	-	-

(a) Only concordance rates for adult criminals are included in the table. Some studies include female same sex twin pairs, ie Rosanoff, Kranz, Stumpfl and Christiansen.
(b) Broad and strict concepts of crime, respectively.

(Siemens, 1924), whereas in cases of dissimilarity they were considered dizygotic and investigated further by mail only.

Rosanoff et al (1934) obtained their relatively large sample of twins both from mental and penal institutions. The sample was divided into three groups: criminal adults, ie persons 18 years or over who had been sentenced by a criminal court; juvenile delinquents, ie boys and girls who had been placed on probation or had been committed to a cor-rectional institution; and children with behaviour disorders who had not been in conflict with the law. It is unclear to what degree the twins were personally seen by the research team. Concordance for the adult group was 67.6 per cent in MZ and 17.9 per cent in same-sexed DZ, whereas only 3.1 per cent of the opposite-sexed DZ were concordant. Concordance rates in juvenile delinquents were 93 per cent in MZ. and 80 per cent in DZ of the same sex, and 20 per cent in DZ opposite-sexed. Concordance in children was 87 per cent in MZ, 43 per cent in same-sexed DZ and 28 per cent in opposite-sexed DZ.

Kranz (1936) sampled from several prisons and thus obtained 552 pairs of twins. However, the majority had to be excluded, 127 pairs because they were in fact not twins, 202 pairs because one of the partners had died, and 97 pairs because of uncertain zygosity diagnosis or uncertain concordance. The author combined Siemen's similarity method with blood testing in determining the zygosity of the remaining same-sex subject twin-pairs and Kranz himself investigated most of the twins personally. Concordance in MZ and DZ of the same sex was 64.5 per cent and 53.5 per cent respectively, whereas the concordance figure for opposite-sexed DZ was considerably lower, namely 14 per cent. In his comprehensive monograph Kranz discusses the zygosity diagnosis of several pairs in detail, and he gives a thorough description of the life histories of both MZ and DZ pairs.

Stumpfl (1936) collected his sample from several prisons as well as from the register of 'biological criminals'. Zygosity was determined by photographs and physical measurements. The author investigated most of the twins personally and supplemented his data by information from relatives and official sources. The concordance rates of this study fall into the same pattern as we have observed for the Rosanoff and Kranz studies, concordance figures being highest in MZ (61.1 per cent) and lowest in opposite-sexed DZ (7.1 per cent) with the same-sexed DZ falling in between (36.8 per cent).

Borgstrom (1939) reported that three of his four MZ pairs were concordant compared with two out of five DZ same-sexed pairs. Only two out of ten opposite-sexed DZ pairs were concordant.

Yoshimasu (1961) studied 46 same-sexed (male) twin pairs and observed that 17 of 28 MZ and two of 18 DZ were concordant. The author was aware of the significance of representative sampling but could not obtain a complete series because of no access to a twin register. Zygosity was based on various measures, and on blood-typing. We have not been able to obtain Yoshimasu's original report.

Tienari (1963) in his large-scale twin study of various types of psychopathology reported that six of 15 MZ pairs were concordant with regard to psychopathic behaviour, and three of five MZ were concordant with respect to manifest criminal behaviour.

Christiansen (1968) based his study on the Danish twin register, which includes virtually all twins born in Denmark between 1870 and 1910. Nearly 6,000 pairs of twins where both twins had survived the age of 15 were checked against the central police register and/or the local police registers. Zygosity diagnosis was based on a modified similarity test which previously had been controlled by a thorough blood and serum testing. In his 1968 paper the author reported that 35.8 per cent of the 67 male MZ pairs were concordant, ie both twins had been recorded in the official penal register, in contrast to 12.3 per cent concordance in 114 male DZ pairs. In the female group the concordances were 21.4 per cent in 14 MZ pairs and 4.4 per cent in 23 DZ pairs. In the group of opposite-sexed DZ pairs the concordance was 3.5 per cent.

The studies reviewed above consistently show a higher concordance for MZ than for DZ twins, a finding which supports the genetic hypothesis. However, the differences in concordance figures in MZ and DZ are in some studies slight and statistically not significant. Furthermore one also observes a difference in concordance between same-sexed DZ and opposite-sexed DZ, a finding which indeed emphasises the significance of environmental factors. Finally, the 1968 study and the results of the present one deviate considerably from the general pattern previously reported. Not only is the difference in concordance for MZ and DZ small in these last studies but the concordance in MZ is considerably lower than reported earlier. In fact discordance is more pronounced than concordance.

We shall now present some findings from our own study, reverting later on to these other studies. We shall then try to explain the observed differences in concordance figures and will argue that the recent studies which show that genetic factors play a minimal role in the etiology of crime are more reliable, essentially due to improved sampling.

The aim of this investigation was first of all to arrive at 'true' or representative concordance figures for MZ and DZ twins with regard to criminality in order to elucidate the relative contributions of heredity and environment in antisocial behaviour. In addition, we wanted to study in more detail the developmental histories of MZ twin-pairs discordant for crime in order to throw light on individual predisposing factors. Finally, our aim was to study nosological aspects of behaviour. Given an MZ criminal twin, what spectrum of behaviour can one observe in the MZ co-twin? In order to reach our aim, the investigation was from the start planned in two steps. To begin with, we wanted to study the total sample of twins in a crude manner. Afterwards we intended to carry out a more intensive study of a sub-sample focusing attention on discordance. In this selection we shall report our methods and findings regarding the first part of the study and accordingly address ourselves to the problem of concordance figures.

The sample
A twin register comprising all twins born in Norway between 1900 and 1935 had previous been compiled by one of the authors (Kringlen, 1960). This register contains the names and dates of birth of approximately 66,000 twins, ie 33,000 pairs. In the present investigation the names of all male twins born in the period 1921 to 1930 were checked against the national criminal register at December 31, 1966. We thus obtained a sample of 205 pairs of twins who had passed the main risk period for serious crime: 42 pairs where one twin had died before age 15 were excluded from the sample. In addition, 24 pairs were excluded for other reasons (cf Table II). Female twin-pairs and opposite-sexed twins were not included in the investigation because the low frequency of reported crime for women would have required an

unusually large basic twin population to afford a sufficient sample, and hence considerable secretarial work. Thus we are left with a sample of 139 twin-pairs where according to the national criminal register one or both of the twins had been convicted. Local directories enabled us to ascertain the addresses of the subjects, whereupon the twins were approached personally for blood test and interview.

The zygosity diagnoses were in most cases based on blood and serum typing. The following systems were employed: ABO, MN, CDEce Hp, Gc, PGM, K, SP, and C3. Identicalness on all these systems was considered evidence of monozygosity. The dizygotics were classified as such when only dissimilar on at least two factors. All pairs were thus not tested on all systems. By such a thorough testing, the zygosity diagnosis is rendered almost 100 per cent correct (Juel-Nielsen et al, 1958). In case it was not practically possible to have blood samples taken from both twins, the zygosity diagnosis was determined by comparing the twins with regard to such physical categories as similarity of external appearance, colour of eyes and hair, shape of face, and height. Finally, in all cases we obtained information with respect to identity confusion as children. Research has shown that simple questions such as 'Were you mixed up as children? Were you considered alike as two drops of water?' can determine the zygosity correctly in over 90 per cent of cases (Cederlof et al, 1961). Accordingly, even though blood tests were not available in all cases, there is no reason to believe that many if any twin pairs have been misclassified. Table III gives the zygosity diagnosis of the sample.

General discussion
In a sample obtained from the Norwegian criminal register we have observed very slight differences in concordance rates in MZ and DZ twins with regard to crime. Since MZ twins experience a more similar upbringing and an identity with each other stronger than

TABLE II
SURVEY OF THE SAMPLE

Number of original twin pairs		205
Excluded from original sample due to		
death of one twin prior to age 15	42	
Unknown address	10	
Other reasons	14 (a)	66
Number of pairs in final sample		139

(a) Six pairs by death of both twins, two pairs due to their living in the most northern part of the country, two pairs were in fact not twins, two pairs could not be located, two pairs were living abroad.

TABLE III
ZYGOSITY DETERMINATION OF SAME-SEXED (MALE) TWIN PAIRS

Zygosity diagnosis	Blood-tested	Not blood-tested	Total
MZ	33 pairs	16 pairs	49 pairs
DZ	49 pairs	40 pairs	89 pairs
Unknown	-	1 pair	1 pair
Total	82 pairs	57 pairs	139 pairs

that of DZ twins, we have compared groups of monozygotic with dizygotic twin pairs who by and large have experienced this same close twin relationship and report the same type of upbringing with regard to dressing and treatment by the parents. In such a comparison the difference in concordance between MZ and DZ practically disappears altogether. These findings lead us to conclude that the significance of *hereditary factors in registered crime is* non-existent.

One could, of course, object that by focusing attention only on registered crime one misses the unreported and unconvicted crime. Could it not be that several of the co-twins of registered criminals in fact are also criminals and accordingly the reported concordance figures are minimum figures? Obviously our figures are minimum figures in this respect. However, in our interviews we tried to obtain information with regard to criminal behaviour in the co-twin, and furthermore there is no reason to believe that we should have missed disproportionately more MZ co-twins than DZ co-twins with criminal records. Thus even if one accepts the possibility that the real figures should be higher, there is no reason to believe that the relative difference in concordance rates between MZ and DZ is affected by this source of error.

Conclusion
Our data and review of the literature suggest that previous studies of criminal twins probably observed too great a difference in concordance rates between MZ and DZ due to sampling errors and unreliable zygosity diagnosis. Here we would like to emphasise the fact that the number of twin pairs of different zygosity is in most previous studies relatively

small and, accordingly, a shift of two or three cases from one group to the other would produce different concordance rates. An unsystematic, uncontrolled sampling procedure will include disproportionately more concordant than discordant cases, and zygosity determination without blood and serum grouping tends to classify MZ pairs as DZ.

Compared with previous investigations the present study and Christiansen's have been able to collect large samples and avoid sources of error due to deficient sampling and zygosity diagnosis. Accordingly the results of these studies probably give a better picture of the relative significance of heredity and environment in crime than did previous studies.

The concordance rates in the Christiansen study were 33.3 per cent in MZ and 10.9 per cent in DZ of the same sex. In our study the difference between MZ and DZ is still smaller, namely 22.4 per cent in MZ and 18.0 per cent in DZ, when a broader concept of crime is employed, and 25.8 per cent and 14.9 per cent when a more strict concept of crime is used. These differences between MZ and DZ are not impressive compared with previous twin studies, but are still clear-cut. Since MZ pairs usually are brought up more similarly than DZ, this slight difference in concordance rates could be partly explained on these grounds. In our study we have been able to show that the difference in fact disappears almost completely when this 'twin relationship factor' is controlled for. In other words, the difference in concordance rates between MZ and DZ is partly due to environmental factors. The consistent difference in concordance rates between same-sexed and opposite-sexed DZ also supports this conclusion (cf Table I).

Summary

In an unselected sample of 138 pairs of same sexed male twins, age 40–50 years, who were obtained through the national twin and criminal registers of Norway, concordance with respect to registered crime was slightly higher in monozygotic (MZ) than in dizygotic (DZ) twins. Employing a broad concept of crime including violation of the motor vehicle law and treason during World War II-concordance was 11/49 or 22.4 per cent in MZ and 16/89 or 18.0 per cent in DZ. With a more strict concept of crime, concordance was 81/31 or 25.8 per cent in MZ and 81/54 or 14.9 per cent in DZ.

However, since MZ pairs experience a more similar upbringing than DZ pairs, we compared groups of MZ and DZ who by and large had been exposed to the same type of environmental influences in childhood and adolescence. In such a comparison the difference in concordance almost completely disappears. These findings support the view that hereditary factors are of no significant importance in the etiology of common crime.

These observations and conclusions are at variance with most of the earlier twin studies in criminality. However, it has been demonstrated by a review of the older literature that previous studies in this field, owing to various sources of error, gave results in which the genetic factor was over-estimated. The present study seems to have avoided the pitfalls of unrepresentative sampling and uncertain zygosity diagnosis and has therefore arrived at considerably lower concordance figures in MZ with respect to crime.

Bibliography

Allen G, Harvala B and Shields J (1967) 'Measures of Twin Concordance', *Acta genet*, Basel, 17: 475–481.

Borgstrom C (1939) 'Eine Serie von Kriminellen Zwillingen', *Arch Rass ges Biol*, 33: 334–343.

Cederlof R, Friberg L, Jonsson E and Kaij L (1961) 'Studies on Similarity Diagnosis in Twins with the Aid of Mailed Questionnaires', *Acta genet*, Basel, 11: 338–362.

Christiansen K (1968) 'Threshold of Tolerance in Various Population Groups Illustrated by Results from Danish Criminological Twin Study', A V S de Reuck (ed), *The Mentally Abnormal Offender*, Boston: Little Brown.

Juel-Nielsen A and Hauge M (1958) 'On the Diagnosis of Zygosity in Twins and the Value of Blood Groups', *Acta genet*, Basel, 8: 256–273.

Kranz N (1936) *Lebensschicksale Krimineller Zwillinge*, Berlin: Springer.

Kringlen E (1967) *Heredity and Environment in the Functional Psychoses*, Oslo: Universitetsforlaget and London: Heinemann, 1968.

Lange J (1929) *Verbrechen als Schicksal. Studien an Kriminellen Zwillingen*, Leipzig: Thieme.

LeGras A M (1933) 'Psychose und Kriminalitat bei Zwillingen', *Z ges Neurol Psychiat,* 144: 198–222.

Rosanoff A J, Handy L M and Plesset I R (1934) 'Criminality and Delinquency in Twins', *J Crim Law Criminol*, 24: 923–934.

Rosenthal D (1962) 'Problems of Sampling and Diagnosis in the Major Twin Studies of Schizophrenic Twins', *J Psychiat Res, 2:* 116–134.

Siemens H W (1924) *Die Zwillingpathologie, Ihre Bedeutung, ihre Methodik, ihre bisherigen Ergebnisse*, Berlin: Springer.

Stumpfl F (1936) *Die Ursprunge des Verbrechens, dargestellt am Lebenslauf von Zwillingen*, Leipzig: Thieme.

Tienari P (1963) 'Psychiatric Illness in Identical Twins', *Acta Psychiat Scand, 39:* suppl 171.

Yoshimasu S (1961) 'The Criminological Significance of the Family in the Light of the Studies of Criminal Twins', *Acta Criminol Med leg jap*, 27: 117–141, cited after Excerpta Criminologica, 2: 723–724, 1962.

Zazzo R (1960) *Les Jumeaux, Le Couple et la Personne*, Paris: University of France Press.

Shah and Roth provide a review of studies of links between the premenstrual syndrome and criminal behaviour. The evidence is such that you have to say that there is a strong indicator of a biological factor in criminal behaviour.

The great problem is what can society do about this? To what extent, if at all, should this condition operate so as to remove or limit criminal responsibility?

Shah S A and Roth L H (1974) 'Biosocial and Psychophysiological Factors in Criminology', in Glaser D (ed), *Handbook of Criminology*, pp124–125

The premenstrual syndromes and some behavioural correlates

It is clinically well known that fluctuations of mood in women frequently occur in association with the menstrual cycle. Indeed, *premenstrual tension*, as this phenomenon has been called, seems to be the most common of minor endocrine disorders. It has been estimated that about 25 per cent of all women suffer in moderate or severe degrees from this syndrome, and that possibly as many as 40 per cent of all women experience some degree of distress during the premenstrual and menstrual periods (Green & Dalton, 1953; Coppen & Kessel, 1963; Dalton 1964: Mandell & Mandell, 1967; Hamburg et al, 1968; Wetzel et al, 1971).

The symptoms more commonly experienced, although in markedly varying degrees, include: tension and nervousness, irritability, fatigue and exhaustion, headaches, depressed moods, abdominal bloating and pain, muscle stiffness and cramps, various autonomic reactions (such as dizziness, cold sweats and nausea), and other symptoms (see, eg Moos, 1969). Studies have also indicated that there is no single or uniform aspect to the premenstrual or menstrual syndrome: rather, a variety of subtypes have been indicated by factor analytic studies (Moos, 1969).

The various symptoms associated with the premenstrual and menstrual periods appear to be related to the imbalance between oestrogen and progesterone levels; in particular, to the deficiency of progesterone during the premenstrual period. An interesting common feature of premenstrual distress and postpartum psychiatric disorders is that both occur at a time when circulating progesterone is at a very low level.

The importance of premenstrual and menstrual symptomatology is appearing in new light with the increasing accumulation of evidence that a large proportion of suicides or suicide attempts, admission for psychiatric illness or acute medical and surgical reasons, as well as involvement in criminal acts by women appear to occur during these periods. For example, Dalton (1964) found that the four premenstrual and four menstrual days accounted for 45 per cent of the sick calls by female industrial employees, 45 per cent of acute psychiatric admissions, 49 per cent of acute surgical and medical admissions, and 52 per cent of emergency accident admissions. Also, it was during these eight days that 49 per cent of women prisoners had committed their crimes.

Morton et al (1953) studied 249 volunteer prisoners at a state penal farm and found that 51 per cent of the prison population suffered from premenstrual tensions. In a more detailed study of 58 women who had committed crimes of violence (murder, manslaughter, and assaults), it was found that 62 per cent of this group had committed their crimes during the premenstrual period, and another 17 per cent had committed their crimes during the menstrual period. It is rather significant that 79 per cent of these crimes had occurred during the premenstrual and menstrual periods.

Similarly, Dalton (1961) studied 386 newly convicted prisoners and found that of those who were menstruating regularly (74 per cent), nearly half (49 per cent) committed their crimes during the premenstrual and menstrual periods. Assuming an equal distribution across the menstrual cycle, only two-sevenths (or 29 per cent) of all crimes would be expected during this eight-day period. The probability of obtaining the actual distribution (49 per cent) by chance would be less than one in a thousand.

Dalton (1961) also studied 94 regularly menstruating prisoners who had received reports for rule-violating behaviour, and dis-

covered that 51 (or 54 per cent) had been disorderly during their premenstrual or menstrual periods. Among the 54 prisoners who had been reported only once, the misbehaviour was associated with menstruation in 43 per cent of the cases. However, among the 40 women who had been reported for misconduct more than once, 70 per cent of the incidents were associated with menstruation.

The relationship between the premenstrual and menstrual syndrome and low levels of circulating progesterone is further confirmed by the finding of Greene and Dalton (1953) that treatment with a progesterone was almost invariably successful.

These studies suggest a highly significant relationship between certain periods of the menstrual cycle and emotional and behavioural distress, especially for women with certain subtypes of premenstrual or menstrual symptoms. It would appear that, for a number of women, hormonal changes resulting in irritability, tension, nervousness and related symptoms markedly increase the probability of committing crimes. However, during these periods women law-violators could be more likely to be detected, since slower reaction time, lethargy and fatigue are also experienced by many women at these times. Nevertheless, premenstrual and menstrual symptoms resulting in tension and irritability could facilitate crimes of violence.

It must be emphasised, however, that endocrinological factors contribute to deviant behaviours in conjunction with other factors; it is not suggested that the endocrine imbalance by itself determines these behaviours. Indeed, Coppen and Kessel (1963) found that women who complained of irritability during premenstrual and menstrual periods were more likely to be irritable at other times too. These investigators concluded that premenstrual and menstrual symptoms were an exacerbation of certain personality traits.

Bibliography
Coppen A and Kessell N (1963) 'Menstruation and Personality', *British Journal of Psychiatry*, 109: 711–721.

Dalton K (1961) 'Menstruation and Crime', *British Medical Journal*, 2: 1752–1753.

Dalton K (1964) *The Premenstrual Syndrome*, Springfield, Ill: Thomas.

Greene R and Dalton K (1953) 'The Premenstrual Syndrome', *British Medical Journal*, 1: 1007–1014.

Hamburg D, Moos R H and Yalom I D (1968) 'Studies of Distress in the Menstrual Cycle and the Postpartum Period', in R P Michael (ed), *Endocrinology and Human Behaviour*, New York: Oxford University Press.

Moos R (1969) 'Typology of Menstrual Cycle Symptoms', *American Journal of Obstetrics and Gynaecology*, 103: 390–402.

Morton J H, Additon H, Addison R G, Hunt L and Sullivan J J (1953) 'A Clinical Study of Premenstrual Tension', *American Journal of Obstetrics and Gynaecology*, 65: 1182–1191.

Wetzel R D, Reich T and Mc Clure J N (1971) 'Phase of the Menstrual Cycle and Self-referrals to a Suicide Prevention Service', *British Journal of Psychiatry*, 119: 523–524.

As this extract indicates it is not necessary or indeed desirable to choose between nature and nurture in the search for causes of crime. It has to be admitted that biology has some role to play, though the major influence is likely to be nurture. The two extreme views referred to in the text are aspects of the debate: free will and determinism.

Fishbein D (1990) 'Biological Perspectives in Criminology', *Criminology*, pp29–30

'Few behavioral scientists today adhere to either of these extreme views. A consensus has been emerging over the past 10 to 15 years that the "truth" lies somewhere in between a "nature plus nurture" perspective (see Plomin, 1989). Although the nurture perspective has dominated fields such as criminology for the past few decades, substantial biological findings can no longer be ignored. Several studies on alcoholism, temperament, criminality, depression, and mental illness have established a solid role for genetic and biological. Even though behavioural scientists have yet to determine precisely the separate, relative contributions of biology and social learning to behaviour, their findings are particularly relevant to the criminologist, who should play an instrumental role in their evaluation given the potential impact on policy. Evidence for an interaction between nature and nurture comes from both animal and clinical studies, which demonstrates the strength and importance of the dynamic link between biological and acquired traits. One example of this interaction is that aggressive behaviour in monkeys can be elicited by stimulating certain areas of the brain with implanted intracerebral electrodes (see Carlson, 1977: 442–9). The final behavioural result depends on the hierarchical structure of the monkey colony. Dominant monkeys will exhibit aggressive behaviour with electrical stimulation of the brain in the presence of a submissive monkey. The same monkeys will suppress aggressive behaviour, on the other hand, if another dominant monkey is present. An example of this interaction in humans is illustrated by recent reports that gender differences in cognitive ability are decreasing (see Geary, 1989). Cognition, however, is fundamentally influenced by neural processes that operate during an individual's development (ontogeny). In an effort to explain changing trends in a seemingly immutable biological process, researchers are discovering that cultural and experiential conditions directly influence the developing pattern of cognitive abilities. For example, activity patterns (eg, frequency of rough and tumble play) may alter cognitive ability (eg, spatial skills) by modifying processes of brain development. These illustrations remind us that as evidence for a substantial genetic influence grows we must be cautious not to replace environmental explanations with biological deterministic views. Instead, a more accommodating, balanced approach will carry more empirical weight.

3   Psychological Explanations

By far and away the most likely figure from psychology that you may be called upon to study is Eysenck. For this reason I have provided quite a long extract for you to examine. Whilst his ideas were controversial they do deserve to be taken seriously. Like many other theorists, insight into the causes of crime comes as much from the critique that the theory inspires as from the theory itself.

Eysenck H J (1977) *Crime and Personality*, 3rd ed, pp114–116, 118–119, 130–133

We may illustrate the way in which we consider conditioning to work in the production of a conscience by looking briefly at a very famous experiment carried out by Professor J B Watson, one of the originators of the behaviourist school of psychological thought shortly after the first World War. He was concerned not with criminal behaviour but rather with the genesis of neurotic disorders, particularly the unreasoning fears or phobias which are so frequently found in neurotics. His hypothesis was that these neurotic fears are essentially conditioned fear reactions and he attempted to demonstrate it in the following manner. He selected a boy of eleven months of age, called Albert; little Albert was particularly fond of white rats and often played with them. Watson tried to inculcate in Albert a pathological fear of rats. He proceeded to do this by standing behind Albert with a metal bar in one hand and a hammer in the other. Whenever Albert reached out for the rats to play with them, Watson would hit the bar with the hammer. In this situation, the rat constitutes the conditioned stimulus, very much as the bell does in Pavlov's experiments with the salivating dogs; the very loud noise produced by the hammer striking the bar constitutes the unconditioned stimulus which produces a reaction of fear, withdrawal, whimpering and crying. By always associating the conditioned and the unconditioned stimulus over a given period of time, Watson argued that in due course he would produce a fear reaction to the conditioned stimulus when presented alone. This is precisely what happened. He found that after a few pairings of the two stimuli Albert would begin to cringe when the rats were introduced, would try to crawl away, cry, and show all the signs of a strong fear of these animals. This fear response persisted for a long period of time and even extended, as we would have expected it to, on the principle of stimulus generalisation discussed earlier, to other furry objects, such as rabbits and a teddy bear. Thus Watson showed that, through a simple process of Pavlovian conditioning, he could produce a strong phobic reaction in little Albert. Before we go on to show how Albert's phobic reaction may be extinguished, let us see for the moment how much light this experiment sheds on the possible growth of a conscience.

Consider the case of the very young child. He has to learn a great number of different things, by means of trial-and-error. As we have pointed out before, there is no real difficulty in accounting for this, because all correct responses tend to be rewarded immediately and incorrect ones, not being rewarded, will tend to drop out; gradually his performance will improve, and he will learn whatever he wishes to. But there are also many other behaviour patterns which he has to acquire, not so much because he wants to, but because society insists that he should. He has to keep clean, he has to learn to use the toilet, he has to refrain from overt aggressive and sexual impulses, and so on. The list of these socially required activities is almost endless. Clearly, learning, as defined earlier, does not come into this very much, because the child is not usually rewarded for carrying out these activities: quite the contrary. He is rewarded, in a sense, for not carrying them out, because in that case carrying them out is what he wishes to do. If somebody annoys him, he wants to punch them in the nose; if he feels like it, he wants to defecate and urinate wherever he happens to be without interrupting his game to go to the toilet. In other words, reinforcement follows immediately upon his disregard of these social mores, the patterns of behaviour which are desirable from the point of view of society. How, then, can the individual ever become socialised?

Suppose now that our little boy misbehaves. Immediately his mother will give him a smack, or stand him in the corner, or send him off to his room, or inflict one of the many punishments which have become customary with parents over the centuries. In this case, the particular asocial or antisocial activity in which he has been indulging is immediately followed by a strong, pain-producing stimulus and we have exactly the same situation as we had in the case of little Albert. The conditioned stimulus is a particular kind of activity in which the child has been indulging; the unconditioned stimulus is the slap, or whatever constitutes the punishment in this case, and the response is the pain and fear produced in the child. By analogy with the experience of little Albert, we would expect conditioning to take place, so that from then on this particular type of activity would be followed by a conditioned fear response. After a few repetitions, this fear response should be sufficiently strong to keep the child from indulging in that type of activity again, just as little Albert was prevented from indulging in his customary play with the white rats. ...

Let us continue with our analysis of the conditioning of moral and social responses. How does our account differ from one that posits a process of learning, and regards the intervention of the policeman and the magistrate and the possibility of prison or a fine as the essential feature of social behaviour? The first and most obvious difference, of course, is the difference relating to the time-interval which elapses between crime and punishment. A crime is committed; it takes a long time before the police are notified, before the culprit is detected, brought before the magistrate, sentenced, and finally sent to prison. All of this may take several months or, in some cases, even several years but clearly the immediate gain of the crime is not outweighed by the gaol sentence which ultimately comes, possibly at the end of several years. The autonomic anxiety and fear reaction which is aroused by the crime happens immediately, however, and precedes any possible gain that the criminal might derive from his action. Time, therefore, is on the side of the angels in this case; the severity of the unpleasant reaction produced by the crime is enhanced by the immediacy of this reaction, whereas the gain may be delayed. Under these conditions, therefore, the autonomic reaction, even though it may not be terribly strong, has a powerful advantage over the ordinary legal process. Conscience can make cowards of us all!

The second difference is that the punishment of crime, in the ordinary legal sense, is a very haphazard affair. It may or may not happen and in the usual case, indeed, it does not happen. Certainly far less than half of all crimes are reported, detected, and brought home to the criminal. The autonomic reaction, on the other hand, is not only immediate but also inevitable. Whenever an individual commits a crime, the autonomic reaction will occur. The inevitability of this occurrence makes it a far stronger threat to the criminal than haphazard processes of law.

A third important difference is that the punishment, in the ordinary sense, always follows the crime; the autonomic fear-anxiety reaction, however, precedes the crime. It follows upon the very conception of the crime or its preparation and may, therefore, be very influential in keeping the crime from being committed at all. Consider the youth who has been reasonably strictly brought up and who has developed very strong autonomic reactions to the thought of overt sexual relations. Imagine that one day he decides to go to a prostitute, which he has never done before in his life. The very thought produces an immediate, intensely unpleasant autonomic reaction and the closer he comes to the place where the prostitute is situated, the greater his reaction will become. It acts, therefore, as a powerful deterrent long before he has a chance to indulge in the particular immoral and antisocial activity which he is contemplating. As a deterrent, therefore, we must consider that the autonomic reaction, the conditioned conscience, of the criminal ... has it all the way over the forces of law and order.

In the next chapter we will attempt to show that it is the person who fails to develop conditioned moral and social responses, due to his low conditionability and his extraversion, who tends to become the psychopath and the criminal. We will also try to show that a high degree of emotionality or neuroticism is a very important influence in this process, in the sense that it provides a higher drive for the person concerned to carry out his crimes. ...

We have now propounded our theory, that it is conscience which is, in the main, instrumental in making us behave in a moral and socially acceptable manner; that this conscience is the combination and culmination of a long process of conditioning; and that failure on the part of the person to become conditioned is likely to be a prominent cause in his running a-foul of the law and of the social mores generally. We must now turn to a consideration of the evidence which may be in favour of, or counter to, this hypothesis, and we must also discuss some of the consequences which follow from it. Let us first have a good look at the evidence.

Now there are several deductions which we can make from our theory. In the first place, we would expect conditioning experiments to show that psychopaths and extraverts generally manifest less conditioning in these

experimental situations than do normal people or dysthymic neurotics. Similarly, if we studied groups of criminals, we would also expect to find that they would be more difficult to condition than non-criminals. We have already noted, in a previous chapter, that extraverted people, both neurotic and normal, are indeed more difficult to condition than are introverted neurotics and normals. It will be remembered that, on the eyeblink conditioning test for instance, it was found that extraverts condition only about 50 per cent as well as introverts, and roughly similar results have been found with other types of conditioning. When we turn to psychopaths specifically, we find that, here too, there is a distinct tendency for such people to show poor conditioning. ... The evidence on conditioning then, as far as it is available, tends to favour our hypothesis. It should be noted, however, that the amount of work that has been done is far from conclusive. Many more studies, involving thousands of criminals, both diagnosed as psychopaths and others, will be required before we can assert that our theory does in fact accord with reality. In particular, it will be necessary to try out a great many different types of conditioning experiments. It will be necessary to vary the parameters we mentioned before, such as the strength of the unconditioned stimulus, the length of time elapsing between the conditioned and the unconditioned stimulus, the spacing of the trials, and so forth. Furthermore, it will be necessary to distinguish between different types of criminals.

Hare has summarised the research which has been done in this field since the first appearance of this book; he concludes as follows:

'It appears that psychopaths do not develop conditioned fear responses readily. As a result, they find it difficult to learn responses that are motivated by fear and reinforced by fear reduction. The fact that their behaviour appears to be neither motivated nor guided by the possibility of unpleasant consequences, particularly when the temporal relationship between behaviour and its consequences is relatively great, might be interpreted in this way. There is some evidence that psychopaths are also less influenced than are normal persons by the relationship between past events and the consequences of their present behaviour. This is in good accord with our theory.'

Hare also summarises evidence on arousal and the attenuation of sensory input which we have hypothesised in previous chapters to be characteristic of criminals and psychopaths. On arousal, he writes:

'Several lines of research and theory suggest that psychopathy is related to cortical under-arousal. As a result, the psychopath actively seeks stimulation with arousing or 'exciting' qualities. In the process, however, he may be unaware of, or inattentive to, many of the subtle cues required for the guidance of behaviour and for adequate social functioning.'

He also states that the evidence indicates that psychopathy may be related to a general tendency to attenuate sensory input. ... Besides a general tendency to attenuate sensory input, it is possible that psychopaths may be able to 'tune out' or at least greatly attenuate stimulation that is potentially disturbing. The result would be that threats of punishment and cues warning of unpleasant consequences for misbehaviour would not have the same emotional impact that they would have for other individuals. Paradoxically, this would mean that cues that are a source of emotional (and cortical) arousal for normal persons would not have the same function with psychopaths, the very ones who are most in need of this arousal.

On the two crucial deductions from our general principle, then, an independent observer concludes positively and he also supports the validity of the general principle. The principle is that psychopaths are characterised by low cortical arousal; the deductions that they condition poorly and that they seek excitement. This accounts for their being subject to temptation (arousal seeking) and having less conscience to save them from temptation (poor conditioning of social mores). Proof is certainly not conclusive (indeed, followers of Popper will realise that conclusive proof in science does not exist), but the results do make it seem likely that this whole line of reasoning is likely to lead to the discovery of worthwhile new facts.

... another deduction from our theory, is of course, the more general one that the people who commit crimes and other antisocial or asocial acts would, on the whole, be more extraverted than people who refrain from carrying out such acts. Here the evidence is fortunately more extensive, indeed so extensive that we can look at only a few typical studies. Let us begin by looking at the problem of traffic accidents and violations of traffic rules. In an earlier chapter, we mentioned the fact that severe violation of the traffic laws tends to be the responsibility of people who have also run afoul of the law in many other ways. What about less severe violations of the traffic code? There is an interesting study carried out by Bernard J Fine of the U S Army Research Institute of Environmental Medicine, which was planned specifically to test this hypothesis. As subjects, he used 993 male freshmen in the general college of the University of Minnesota, who had been administered a personality questionnaire. For each of these students information was available regarding the date, type, number, and place of occurrence of traffic accidents and traffic violations. On the basis of the questionnaire responses, Fine grouped his subjects into the most extraverted, the most introverted, and an intermediate group, each constituting roughly one-third of the total group. He found that the extraverts had significantly more accidents and were also guilty of more traffic violations than were the intermediates or the introverts.

Personality tests have been one method by which thinking by psychologists has been applied to criminal behaviour. Williams provides a good account of these.

Williams K (2001) *Textbook of Criminology*, 4th ed, pp203–207

Psychologists are still searching for a general explanation of human personality. Over the years almost every aspect of human personality has been studied – emotions, temperament, morals and ethics as well as specific traits such as aggression, conformity, self-esteem and timidity. The types of tests and the ways of conducting them have been numerous and include self-administered questionnaires (such as the MMPI, see later), performance tests, free association tests and the Rorschach test (a test designed to show intelligence, personality and mental state, in which the subject interprets ink-blots of standard type). Despite extensive study, the human personality is still an enigma.

Many researchers have tested the difference between criminal and non-criminal personalities. Schuessler and Cressey (1950) carried out a comparison of 113 studies which used 30 different types of personality tests, all of which sought to detect a personality difference between criminals and non-criminals. They found that 42 per cent of the 113 studied showed differences in favour of the non-criminal, whilst the remainder were indeterminate. These links were too tenuous to conclude that personality traits were consistently and systematically linked to criminality.

Seventeen years later, Waldo and Dinitz (1967) carried out a similar comparison of some 94 studies which had been undertaken during the intervening years. They claimed that the comparisons they made were more accurate because they were methodologically more sound, involved larger sample groups, made better use of control groups and had taken account of other variables which might affect criminality, especially the environmental variables. In 76 of the studies (81 per cent) they found a difference between criminals and non-criminals. Although these tests seemed to provide evidence of a personality difference between criminals and non-criminals, Waldo and Dinitz felt that the findings were far from

conclusive. Thus they too concluded that no personality traits were consistently and systematically linked to criminality. In order to comprehend this conclusion it is necessary to understand the main personality test: the MMPI.

MMPI test

Between the 1950 and 1967 comparative studies a new, and allegedly more reliable, test became more widely operative as a test for assessing the criminal personality. This test was called the Minnesota Multiphasic Personality Inventory, or the MMPI for short. It consists of 550 items which were developed to assist the diagnosis of adults who sought psychiatric help. The subjects decide whether the 550 statements are true or false when applied to themselves. There are a number of checks included in the questionnaire in order to catch untruthful answers. The test is split into ten scales and the subject is given a score on each scale; there is no overall score. The individual's full personality is then constructed from a score profile obtained by entering the scores from each scale onto a graph. The ten scales indicate an assessment of hypochondria; depression; conversion hysteria or disorder (where unexplained physical symptoms are assumed to be linked to psychological factors); psychopathic personality; masculinity-femininity; paranoia; neurosis; schizophrenia; hypomania (a condition marked by over-excitability) and introversion. As the MMPI is now used for the assessment of the personalities of normal individuals, the scales do not usually bear any names but are usually only identified numerically, eg scale 1, scale 2, scale 3 etc.

The items which the study by Waldo and Dinitz had found most often distinguished the criminal from the non-criminal lay in the Psychopathic personality, Pd scale, or scale 4 of the test. However, rather than simply accepting the findings, they looked behind them and discovered that this pan of the test could produce a systematic bias because it included a number of items which were most likely to be answered differently by a criminal. The most obvious was: 'I have never been in trouble with the law.' Other questions which appeared in this scale and to which the delinquent is more likely to answer differently from the non-delinquent were: 'I liked school'; 'My relatives are nearly all in sympathy with me'; 'I often was in trouble in school, although I do not understand for what reasons.' In the studies where personality differences were said to be found, this was based on the different answers given to only four questions out of 50. The small differentiation resulted in a significant difference between criminals and non-criminals in the final statistical analysis. In any event, an explanation could be found in the different environments or situations of the two groups, rather than personality differences.

It is unsurprising that the delinquent scores higher on this Pd scale, as it was designed specifically to differentiate delinquents from other groups, a factor which Waldo and Dinitz seem to have ignored. The more surprising fact is rather that the score differences on this scale were not greater. But its utility for identifying delinquents is weakened because it has been found to predict characteristics besides delinquency. For example, those who drop out of school have been found to have a higher Pd score than others, as have those who are less shy, particularly if they are more aggressive. Professional actors also have high Pd scores and so do those who have 'carelessly' shot someone in a hunting accident (Gleitman, (1986, p616). Used as a predictor, one would expect those who scored high on this scale to drop out of school, be outgoing, possibly more aggressive, become professional actors and be involved in hunting accidents. It would seem that what is being measured is not a predictor of action but rather something which indicates a disposition towards a certain type of personality. And the personality tendencies involved (the significance attached to what other people think of them) are too slight to point to any direct link to criminality. The practical application of such tests in criminology is thus severely limited.

Interpersonal maturity tests

A further level of tests which came out with very similar results was based on the social maturity levels of individuals. These are often called 'interpersonal maturity' tests or 'I-Level' tests. In these studies, individuals are tested for their social and interpersonal skills and they are then placed on one of several levels of maturity. These levels are simply given numerical values, but each of the numerical levels is also linked with descriptions of the person's 'core personality'. Both Warren (1970) and Palmer (1974) discovered that most convicted delinquents appeared in levels 2, 3 and 4 and all were socially immature. Level 2 personalities are asocial, aggressive and power-orientated, which is very similar to the descriptions found in the MMPI tests. Individuals on level 3 are characterised by their conformity to the delinquent group, which bears marked similarities to claims by Hewitt and Jenkins (1947), and those on level 4 are often called neurotic. They claimed that 90 per cent of delinquents fell into one or other of these three levels.

Assessment of personality tests

The MMPI tests and the I-Level studies all suggest that there is a link between criminality and assertiveness, hostility, resentment of authority, dynamic personalities and psychopathy. However, while in the first two of these research studies the findings were statistically significant, their actual sizes were small. This has given rise to doubts about their reliability, and they have been questioned by later researchers. Each study compares delinquents or criminals (those who have been officially convicted) with non-delinquents or non-criminals (a group of those who have not been officially convicted but a number of whom may have committed acts which are as unacceptable or criminal). Some of the personality traits found in the criminal group could derive from their treatment by the justice system, rather than from something inherent in their characters. Such a reaction might be natural and normal, especially if they know of other people, possibly friends, who have committed similar crimes but have not been caught. A hostile reaction would in those circumstances be understandable, as would a feeling of injustice and resentment of authority. The small personality differences found in these studies may not have been there prior to their contact with police or courts, and they might be the result of those encounters rather than the reason for them.

Conceptually, it would be better to begin testing at a very young age and follow the children through to adulthood. Ideally, the tests should cover not only personality and official criminality but also self-reported criminality. The researcher would then be better able to assess whether their personalities were inherent or were the result of a brush with the criminal justice system. The proposed method of assessment might also show whether these personality types actually commit more crime or whether they are just more likely to be caught. There would still be problems: the perceived personality traits may be the result of earlier conflict with figures of authority such as teachers.

In any event, it seems that the personality trait will not determine the criminal behaviour, but will only predict a certain type of behaviour, of which criminality is but one example. Some even doubt whether there is any real personality trait, claiming instead that the way each individual acts depends rather upon the situation they are in. They point out that a person who is said to have a more aggressive personality will not be generally aggressive; the trait will only show in certain situations. Thus they may be aggressive on the sports field, or whilst driving and at work but be very gentle in their personal relationships. The argument is that it is the situation, not the individual's personality, which decides their behaviour. For example, if a police car is behind you it would not cause you to stop although it might cause you to drive with more care, but if the blue light on the police car starts flashing, you would stop. The situation of the blue light brought about the behaviour, not any personality attribute of the individual – the same behaviour would have occurred whether you were dominant or submissive, sociable or unsociable. But in a different situation you might not stop. If, for example, you had just committed a crime other than a driving offence, you might try to escape. This is not to deny any influence to personality, but rather to say that reactions may depend on a number of factors. For example, the behaviour of a person in a school depends partly on their position – head teacher, teacher, secretary, caretaker, prefect, pupil or parent; partly on the situation – classroom, sports field, parents' evening, disciplinary, social; and partly on the personality of the individual. It might also be affected by the pressures of a peer grouping or by the values of the community.

Bibliography

Gleitman H (1986) *Psychology*, New York, Norton.

Hewitt L and Jenkins R (1947) *Fundamental Patterns of Maladjustment*, Springfield: State of Illinois.

Palmer T (1974) 'The Youth Authority's Community Treatment Project', *Federal Probation*, 38: 3.

Schuessler K and Cressey D (1950) 'Personality Characteristics of Criminals', *American Journal of Sociology*, 55: 476.

Waldo G and Dinitz S (1967) 'Personality Attributes of the Criminal', *Journal of Research in Crime and Delinquency*, 4: 185.

Warren M (1970) 'The Case for Differential Treatment of Delinquents', in H Voss (ed), *Society, Delinquency and Delinquent Behaviour*, Boston: Little Brown.

4   Social Ecology

Shaw and Mc Kay were two of the main figures in the Chicago School of Human Ecology. This group operated mainly in the inter-war years and they were, of course, based in Chicago. They were influential both academically and in relation to the development of measures designed to deal with the problem of crime. They saw crime as being very largely the result of environmental factors. They isolated factors concerned with the characteristics of certain sectors of cities as being criminogenic. They were the first major figures in American sociology theorising about crime causation. A good number of the extracts that appear later in this book are from theorists and researchers who have followed traditions established by Shaw and McKay. You will of course find in the course of your studies that their ideas of social ecology have been subjected to criticism. This, of course, is true of all theories of crime causation. The purpose of the extract is to allow you to have access to some important pioneering ideas.

Shaw and McKay examined the crime rate for different groups over time. One of the features of their work was to divide Chicago into 140 different square mile areas and to see what the crime rate was for each of these areas. This revealed that there are wide differences between areas, and that the number of areas with low rates is much greater than the number where they are high. The areas with the highest rates are located directly south of the central business district, and the areas with the next highest rates are north and west of the Loop. At the extreme, low rates of delinquents were found in many of the outlying areas. Most of the areas characterised by high rates of delinquents, as well as by a concentration of individual delinquents, are either in or adjacent to areas zoned for industry and commerce. This is true not only for areas close to the central business district but also for outlying areas, such as those near the Stock Yards, the South Chicago steel mills, and other industrial sections. On the other hand, the areas with low rates are, for the most part, those zoned for residential purposes. They also presented data that showed that these findings remained constant over time.

Whilst Shah and McKay represented the first thoughts in social ecology, in the next extract Bottoms and Wiles are very much a look to the future. Over the years social ecology also started to be known as environmental criminology. The message in this extract is that there are fundamental economic and social changes taking place that will significantly affect the nature and patterning of crime. Bottoms and Wiles offer a summary of those main areas of change which seem to have criminological implications

Bottoms A E and Wiles P (1997) 'Environmental Criminology', in Maguire M et al (eds), *The Oxford Handbook of Criminology*, 2nd ed, pp349–354

So far this chapter has been concerned to summarise (with, we hope, a friendly but critical eye) the existing literature on environmental criminology. Now we turn to the future research agenda of environmental criminology. Our starting point is a recognition that the economically more advanced countries of the world are, in our view, at the present time undergoing some quite fundamental economic and social changes that will significantly affect the nature and patterning of crime. Environmental criminology needs to under-

35

stand these transformations in order to explain crime in the future: to use the language we have been using so far, we need to understand these macro changes in order to offer explanations at the meso and micro level. The macro changes we are referring to are usually designated as the change from 'modernity' (basically) the social formations which emerged out of industrialisation) to 'late modernity' or alternatively, 'post-modernism' (1). Many writers have discussed these changes, and whilst, as will by now have become apparent, we find Giddens's work particularly useful (see Giddens, 1990 and 1991), for present purposes we do not want to adopt a particular theoretical view but instead to concentrate on the empirical nature of the transformations.

Within the length of this chapter we can do no more than summarise those main areas of change which seem to us to have criminological implications, but for a fuller treatment see Bottoms and Wiles (1995) (2).

First, business and the flows of capital have become increasingly transnational and have created their own transnational orders. The ability of nation states to control this transnational capital and business is not very great, precisely because they do not operate solely within the territory of a nation state (3). The result is that effective power is being increasingly either exercised at the transnational level or alternatively with the decline of state power at the local level (4), leading to what is often described as the 'hollowing out' of power at the state level. Yet during modernity the nation state has been the prime location for the making of laws against crime and the control and policing of crime. If the state is being hollowed out in this way then the main definers of crime in the modern period will cede this power both upwards (to transnational capital and political organisations) and downwards (to local areas). We have already seen within Europe the EU taking such a role, and local campaigns and programmes against crime are increasingly common.

Secondly, manufacturing industry is now a declining proportion of total economic activity

and business decisions are, as a consequence, less determined by the supply of raw materials for manufacture than by new considerations, such as the availability of highly skilled labour, or a pleasant environment to attract such labour. The wealth and prosperity of a city are thus no longer determined by its location relative to the physical resources of material production, and indeed nearness to such resources may result in environmental degradation which makes it less attractive to highly skilled labour. The result is that cities, or regions, can have very uneven and different economic development – for example, one of us works in a 'rustbelt' city (Sheffield) which is trying to overcome the problems of de-industrialisation, and the other in a 'sunrise' city (Cambridge) which has developed new hi-tech industries. The economic structures, which (as we have seen) provide the macro framework for the routine activities which pattern crime, are therefore increasingly uneven and varied. On the one hand, declining traditional industries can leave environmentally blighted areas of cities, including residential areas originally built to provide labour for those industries, with high unemployment rates and having lost their most entrepreneurial residents. On the other hand, new information-based industries may flourish in semi-rural locations with 'homeworking' blurring the more traditional home/work divide.

Thirdly, recent technology means that neither time nor space is the fixed framework of our routines. Quite apart from virtual realities we commonly shift time (by videoing television programmes to watch later), or space (by working on the move with mobile phones, computers, etc). The result can be globalised cultures, no longer fixed in time or space, from which we can choose and indeed make a series of different choices. Television representations based on the culture of Australia or west coast America have taken on an autonomous existence and may be as 'real' to some British youth as anything else. Yet geographically localised cultures, in the sense of 'community' and spatially fixed institutions, such as churches and families, have been regarded by much criminological theory as the main defences against crime: hence the Chicagoans' concern with community 'disorganisation' and crime (5). Furthermore, a market culture of consumer choice depends on the financial ability of participants and may encourage crime by those who do not possess the (legitimate) resources to exercise such choice in the new global market place.

Fourthly, in our new social world we are increasingly dependent upon reflexively acquired social knowledge rather than tradition (6), yet this new form of knowledge becomes ever more specialised and, in practice, forces us to take on trust the expertise of others, and the efficacy of abstract systems. For example, unless we are specially trained we have to trust the expertise of environmental scientists about, for example, radiation or pollution levels. The problem is that we are regularly presented with grounds for doubting whether we should grant such trust (it is not difficult to recall examples of environmental 'knowledge' being proved wrong) and so we increasingly suffer from insecurities which can compound each other into an overall and generalised sense of ontological insecurity. This ontological insecurity embraces everything, from the long-term sustainability of the planet to anxieties about day-to-day living. One response to doubts of, the latter kind is the creation of 'security bubbles' deliberately designed to calm our insecurities and encourage our trust, many of which (such as women-only hotels, CCTV systems, gated residential estates, or well protected shopping malls) particularly focus on the insecurities associated with crime or disorder.

Fifthly, our new social world has developed new forms of social differentiation ranging from changes in gender roles to increasing economic polarisation. From a criminological point of view these new forms change the context of the routine activities relating to crime (for example more working women can mean less occupied and guarded homes during the day: Cohen and Felson,

1979). Most importantly, increased economic polarisation and the decline of traditional manufacturing industry, and the disappearance of many jobs through technological or other restructuring, have led to an apparently irreversible increase in the long-term unemployment of the unskilled. This has created an increasing social exclusion of some subgroups of the population from effective participation in key areas of social life (ranging from jobs to education and leisure facilities). Where particular groups experience multiple exclusion then the operation of the housing market may well concentrate them in particular residential areas (see Wiles, 1992). In the contemporary United States this has especially happened to poor blacks and produced the black ghettos of American rustbelt cities, such as Chicago or Detroit. The ghettos have alarmingly high offence and offender rates, and this has produced a generalised (although statistically largely misplaced) fear of the danger they may represent to the rest of the city, which mirrors the nineteenth century Victorian concerns about the dangerous classes (see Morris, 1994). An acrimonious debate has ensued about the reasons for such high ghetto crime rates. Both sides of the debate agree that in such areas social exclusion (especially from the labour market) goes together with distinct forms of neighbourhood culture and social organisation, but they disagree about why this is the case and how it relates to crime. On the one hand, it has been argued that an 'underclass' has been created by poor, but welfare-dependent blacks being allowed to make irresponsible cultural choices not to support social institutions, such as two-parent families, which are capable of successfully socialising the young into non-criminal values and controlling any attempted deviance (see eg Murray, 1994). On the other hand, it has been argued that the culture and social organisation of the ghetto and its crime is an adaptation by a people who have been systematically excluded and disadvantaged by the wider society (see Wilson, 1987 and 1996). The arguments from this American debate about the 'underclass' have since been borrowed to try and explain high crime and lawlessness in some British council estates (see Murray, 1990, 1994). More generally, the Canadian criminologist John Hagan (1994: chapter 3) has argued persuasively that the economic changes of late modernity, and especially growing economic polarisation, have created the need for a 'new sociology of crime and disrepute' to replace some of the now less relevant sociologies of crime. Central to this new approach, Hagan argues, will be the study of the 'criminal costs of social inequality' (ibid: 98).

These changes, of course, are not uniform either within, or between countries – indeed, that is one of the characteristics of late modernity. Nevertheless, they seem to affect all late modern societies to some degree. Future research in environmental criminology will have to try and understand how these changes are affecting the distribution of crime in space and time. Clearly our cities, their surrounding hinterlands, and rural areas are being physically re-modelled by these processes, but this is happening in different ways in different places. The housing tenure map of Britain, for example, is being transformed, and we have already seen how important housing markets have been in environmental criminological explanations. The new housing markets will change crime patterns, but how is not yet clear: a shrinking public housing sector could produce increasing residualisation of public housing and, at its most extreme, mirror the American problem of ghettos (see Wiles, 1992), but alternatively a more varied housing market could encourage a new social discipline, enforced by housing managers and the civil courts, which reduces residential area crime rates in at least some areas (cf NACRO, 1996). The development of out-of-town shopping centres and leisure facilities is creating attractive new crime targets away from traditional city centres, but, because these are often legally privately owned places, they are more likely to be rigorously and privately policed, though in an unobtrusive style that most of the public approve of (see Beck and

Willis, 1995). The decline of time or space as a fixed framework for our lives could reduce the commitment to geographical neighbourhood and so reduce social control at the local level. On the other hand, these changes could mean that we learn successfully to base local control increasingly on the *public* rather than *parochial* level, or that residential areas become less important and parochial control is instead exercised in the locations where we choose to pursue our varied interests. Increasing social differentiation combined with the creation of security bubbles could lead to increased segregation and the exclusion of deviant or threatening groups (eg the exclusion of groups of young people from shopping malls) and the collapse of a public civic society into a series of private realms (eg private places with their own private police forces effectively enforcing their private law). Alternatively, increasing lifestyle choices may freely and spatially separate social groups with different interests (eg by lifestyle activities being provided at different places or in the same place at different times), and so reduce the potential for inter-group conflicts which produced crime in traditional city centres, especially at weekends.

We can be certain that changes in the geographical patterning of routine activities will alter the pattern of crime, but this will be modified by the differential use of social control, such as new technology (eg CCTV, flash card entry control, etc) or manned security services. Since such changes in routine activities are most commonly the outcome of a large number of uncoordinated individual market decisions, the resulting changes in crime patterns will not be easy to predict. At the time of writing the consequences of the changes of late modernity for the patterns of crime in space and time are not clear – indeed, some evidence for all the above examples could be found. To some extent this is because we will have to await the results of new empirical research, but also because there is unlikely to be a single set of crime outcomes from the changes of late modernity. This is partly because (as already stressed) late modernity is itself an uneven process, although of itself that might simply suggest a limited number of different crime outcomes: for example, we could try to model the crime outcomes in 'rustbelt' cities compared to 'sunrise' cities. Some commentators seem to believe that is all that is involved; on this view, the forces of late modernity are global, and neither resistible nor manageable by political choices made by an increasingly weakened state. However, there is at present still clear evidence of national differences in the effects of late modern changes (see Lash and Urry, 1987), and also that broad historical differences, combined with very broad political choices as to the desired relationship between economic forms, individual freedom, and forms of social ordering can still produce very different social orders (compare, for example, contemporary Japan and the USA). Some of the alternative crime outcomes suggested above would therefore be influenced by these kinds of political choices, although the most important ones will increasingly be just as likely to be made at either the transnational or local level, as by the state.

The environmental criminology of the future will therefore need to continue to study crime patterns at local levels, but it will necessarily have to situate its explanations within a macro-level understanding of the emerging forces of late modernity. Some of the preoccupations of traditional environmental criminology will thus have to change – but there is every indication that this will remain an exciting and vibrant sub-specialisation within criminological studies in the future.

References
1. Post-modernism in the hands of some writers has had methodological links with epistemological relativism, an intellectual position we reject, and so we would prefer 'late modernity' in order to focus on the empirical transformations presently taking place.
2. For a general, historical account of how the processes of change can create new crime and social control patterns in a city see also Mike Davis's (1990) study of Los Angeles.
3. Witness, for example, the British government's problems in dealing, with recent sterling crises in which it had, in the end, to admit defeat at the hands of currency speculators and international capital markets. Nation states have attempted to respond by themselves trying to create supranational institutions for control, such as the European Union or the General Agreement on Tariffs and Trade. However, nation states, by their nature, find it difficult not to pursue their own narrow interests, and so such institutions are very much more difficult to create successfully than the transnational institutions of business and capital – witness the problems of the two examples just given.
4. Not only has the state ceded power to the transnational level but some services must respond to increasingly differentiated local demands and the state is much less able to provide such services effectively than locally based institutions and organisations. Hence the state's ability to govern is being attacked from both above and below.
5. Of course, this does not mean that local place-based community factors are no longer important in people's lives – they clearly are, but alongside the more globalised influences.
6. In earlier societies guides to action (from parents, company directors, or community leaders, etc) tended to be based on maxims relating to the past ('tradition'): for example, 'we've always done things this way'. In contemporary societies, the reference point is decreasingly the past and increasingly the future ('lets have your projections for 2010'; 'let's do it this way, try it out and see if it works', etc).

Bibliography
Beck A and Willis A (1995) *Crime and Security: Managing the Risk*, Leicester: Perpetuity Press.

Bottoms A E and Wiles P (1995) 'Crime and Insecurity in the City', in C Fijnaut, J Goethals, T Peters, and L Walgrave (eds), *Changes in Society, Crime and Criminal Justice in Europe*, The Hague: Kluwer (2 vols).

Cohen L E and Felson M (1979) 'Social Change and Crime Rate Trends: A Routine Activities Approach', *American Sociological Review* , 44: 588–608.

Davis M (1990) *City of Quartz: Excavating the Future of Los Angeles*, London: Vintage.

Giddens A (1990) *The Consequences of Modernity*, Cambridge: Polity Press.

Giddens A (1991) *Modernity and Self-Identity*, Cambridge: Polity Press.

Hagan J (1994) *Crime and Disrepute*, Thousand Oaks, Calif: Pine Forge Press.

Lash S and Urry J (1987) *The End of Organised Capitalism*, Cambridge: Polity Press.

Morris L (1994) *Dangerous Classes: The Underclass and Social Citizenship*, London: Routledge.

Murray C (1984) *Losing Ground*, New York: Basic Books.

Murray C (1990) *The Emerging British Underclass*, London: Institute of Economic Affairs.

Murray C (1994) *Underclass: The Crisis Deepens*, London: Institute of Economic Affairs.

NACRO (1996) *Crime, Community and Change: Taking Action on the Kingsmeade Estate in Hackney*, London: NACRO.

Wiles P (1992) 'Ghettoisation in Europe?', *European Journal on Criminal Policy and Research*, 1: 52–69.

Wilson W J (1987) *The Truly Disadvantaged*, Chicago, Ill: University Press.

Wilson WJ (1996) *When Work Disappears: The World of the New Urban Poor*, New York: Alfred Knopf.

The data in the following Home Office research relates to the geography of crime. It explores the extent to which offenders are prepared to travel in order to commit offences. Whilst greater mobility may have suggested that the distances involved should have increased over time, the data reveals that there is a considerable unwillingness on the part of criminals to stray far from home. This suggests that crime prevention strategies in the vicinity of the breeding grounds of offenders may be plausible.

Wiles P and Costello A (2000) *The 'Road to Nowhere': The Evidence for Travelling Criminals*, pp1–4, 43–49

The geography of crime is increasingly important to the work of both the police and criminologists. This is so for two reasons. First, in contemporary societies people are increasingly mobile. Such mobility could create new patterns of crime either because offenders can maraud over greater distances, or because victims travel to areas of greater risk or are more vulnerable as travellers. We need to understand, therefore, how offenders and victims come together in time and space for a crime to occur. Second, the digital technology of geographical information systems (GIS) will allow us to examine such questions much more routinely. The data to examine offender and victim movement has long existed but the methods available for doing so were laborious and expensive (see, for example, Baldwin and Bottoms (1976). The police are very significant collectors and holders of data, but analysing and releasing the added value from that data has so far been primitive and limited. As for analysing police-held data against that held by other agencies, the variations in administrative boundaries has often made this difficult. The new generation of computer analysis methods are capable of radically transforming this situation. Bringing together and interrogating large data sets is now technically routine. GIS as one new method will allow us to analyse data on spatial patterns but may also be the means for linking together different data sets at local level. These advantages will only be realisable as new computer systems become commonplace in public agencies. In the meantime the present report is an early attempt to explore how such methods may be used.

It is often assumed that because travel has become much easier in the contemporary period then offenders must be taking advantage of this fact and travelling further to commit their crimes. There is a widely held view within police forces, especially rural and urban fringe ones, that a considerable amount of high volume crime is committed by travelling, often urban, offenders taking advantage of increasingly easy mobility. Many detectives have ready stories of travelling offenders invading their areas. Recently rural forces have been arguing that an increasing amount of their crime is committed by outsiders and that, since the police funding formula is largely driven by resident population, then they are not being properly resourced to deal with the problem. Furthermore, many forces have used the evidence of cross-police force border crime to argue that travelling offenders are now a widespread phenomenon.

The present report examines these beliefs and attempts to identify the extent to which there is evidence to support them. It is based on research into what police recorded crime statistics and DNA records can tell us about offender travel patterns. The research mainly focuses on 'volume crime', which for this purpose was defined as burglary, and TWOC (TWOC hereafter includes: Taking Without the Owner's Consent, Aggravated Taking Without the Owner's Consent, and Theft of a Motor Vehicle).

Previous empirical research

Most travel-to-crime research has been conducted in the United States, one important exception being the Home Office report *Tackling Cross Border Crime* (Porter, 1996). This looked at the evidence for cross-border crime in the UK; that is, crime which crossed police force boundaries. Its main findings were: the majority of police forces experienced difficulty in quantifying cross-border crime; 10 per cent of detected crime appeared to be cross-border, mostly inter-force (i.e. between adjoining forces); rates of cross border crime differed between forces – forces adjoining or close to large metropolitan forces and forces attracting large numbers of tourists saw rates of cross-border offending of up to 23 per cent of all detected crime.

Whilst the issue of offender travel is under-researched, a number of broad findings have emerged from earlier research, particularly that conducted in North America. The most general and consistent is the fact that offenders do not appear to travel very far. With regard to burglary and car crime the following distances have been found:

Auto theft			
White	(1932)	3.43 miles	Indianapolis
Phillips	(1980)	1.15 miles	Lexington-Fayette, Kentucky
Gabor and Gottheil	(1984)	1.24 miles	Ottawa

		Burglary	
White	(1932)	1.76 miles	Indianapolis
Reppetto	(1974)	0.5 miles	Boston and a nearby small city
Pyle residential	(1974)	2.48 miles	Akron, Ohio
Pyle non-residential	(1974)	2.34 miles	Akron, Ohio
Phillips	(1980)	1.05 miles	Lexington-Fayette, Kentucky
Rhodes and Conly	(1981)	1.62 miles	Washington DC
Gabor and Gottheil	(1984)	0.35 miles	Ottawa

The general trend is for distances to be relatively short and this does not appear to vary by time of day or time of year. It is also worth noting that Pyle (1974) found travel to burglary the longest of the offences they examined whereas Gabor and Gottheil (1984) found it to be the shortest. Another general finding has been that travel-to-crime increases with the age of the offender (Phillips, 1980; Baldwin and Bottoms, 1976; Davidson, 1984; Reppetto, 1974; Reiss and Farrington, 1991). With regard to gender and distance most studies have concentrated on male offenders and so there are no clear findings with regard to gender and distance. Much of the research carried out in the US has been interested in the issue of race. The general finding is that black offenders travel shorter distances than white offenders and that offending is intra-, not inter-racial (see, for example, Rand, (1986); Rengert and Wasilchick, (1985); Phillips, (1980) and Carter and Hill, (1979).

Reasons for travel

Explanations of the movement patterns identified by empirical research have been dominated by the issue of 'rationality'. In simple terms this focuses on whether we explain travel-to-crime as a consequence of instrumentally rational searching by highly motivated offenders, or as a result of affectually rational, opportunistic behaviour committed whilst 'potential' offenders are pursuing their day-to-day routine activities. This simple dichotomy is complicated by the possibility that the same offender may at different times straddle the categories. Furthermore, it could be that, say, domestic burglary is generally committed following instrumentally rational reasoning, whilst TWOC is mainly carried out for affectually rational reasons. Even within a single crime category, such as car theft, there could be different travel-to-crime explanations for 'joyriding' and stealing a car to 'ring' or 'chop'.

The theories produced by previous research do not point to one single explanation of offender mobility: for a fuller review see Bottoms and Wiles, (1999). The problem with the existing studies is that although they suggest explanations these are often simply hypotheses which appear to fit the facts plausibly, but are not always backed up by empirical research findings. Furthermore, such hypothecated explanations are often embedded in broader master theories of criminal or general social action. For example, instrumental explanations of offenders' travel are embedded in broad theories of rational choice and have been related to crime prevention notions of target hardening. There is nothing wrong with such an approach (indeed, it is a necessary aspect of explanations which operate at different levels of generality), except that sometimes empirical investigation has been limited within a broader theory and so is not capable of arbitrating between explanations which belong to different master theories.

In spite of this limitation there are a number of central issues which emerge for further examination:

To what extent do offenders instrumentally travel as part of a search pattern for suitable targets?

To what extent do offenders travel as part of their routine non-criminal activities and then within those patterns commit crimes?

Are there any systematic differences in travel-to-crime patterns between different types of offender or different types of offences?

Are there different travel-to-crime patterns for different types of geographical area?

How do all of these relate to victims' travel-to-crime patterns?

Answers to these questions will provide better grounded explanations of offenders' travel and also hold out the possibility of providing models of offender and victim mobility which can be used for crime pattern analysis for the management and prevention of crime.

Conclusion

On the basis of the evidence gathered a number of conclusions can be drawn about the offender movement patterns involved in high volume crimes. Firstly, the vast majority of offender movements are relatively short: for Sheffield-based offenders (regardless of offence location) police recorded crime data shows that over a third of crime trips are less than one mile; over half consist of less than two miles, and only 11 per cent involve travel greater than 10 miles. There has, however, been some small increase in travel-to-crime distances over the last 30 years. Whilst data is not available on Sheffield commuting-to-work, it is likely that it would involve greater distances than journeys to crime and has probably increased more over the last 30 years. In general it is probably the case that persistent offenders travel less (whether to offend or for other reasons) than the rest of the population. Recent Department of Environment, Transport and the Regions research (DETR, 1999) supports our argument in that it shows

the better-off travel much more than the poor. In 1995/97 the average distance travelled per annum for the top 20 per cent of the population (in terms of income) was about 11,000 miles, but for the bottom 20 per cent it was only around 3,500 miles. Journeys for work or leisure average around 8 miles, whereas journeys for education or shopping average only 2.75 and 3.75 miles respectively. The interviewees were little involved in journeys to work and their leisure travel was largely short-range. Furthermore, even for shopping and education it is likely to be the wealthier groups in society who are more likely to travel to a 'better' school or an out of town shopping facility. This finding is not surprising given the short travel-to-crime journeys found in earlier research in more mobile North American cities. The Sheffield findings are confirmed by those from the city of York, where the vast majority of burglary and TWOC offenders live locally and, if anything, travel even shorter distances to offend, and by the analysis of the national DNA data.

Secondly, the research indicates that much travel associated with crime is not primarily driven by plans to offend. The offenders interviewed did not travel to the offence location in order to offend in the majority of instances (70 per cent for burglary and 62 per cent for TWOC). Offending appeared to be much more dependent upon opportunities presenting themselves during normal routines, rather than as a result of instrumental, long-range search patterns. This is further supported by the fact that the strongest correlation found was between offence location and the current residence of the offender.

Thirdly, when offenders do travel to offend it is overwhelmingly local in nature. Indeed, of all trips over three miles by Sheffield-based offenders, 55 per cent were wholly within the city. Even when offending crossed local authority borders most offence locations of Sheffield-based offenders had strong connections with the city. Forty per cent of Sheffield offender movements out of the city ended up in either Rotherham or North

East Derbyshire, both places with strong work, leisure and family ties to the city and lengthy and often indistinguishable boundaries. This pattern was confirmed by the interviews with the offender sample, where the places they visited for non-crime reasons were by and large the same as those recorded when Sheffielders offended outside the city. If anything the pattern of offender movements into Sheffield was even more restricted with almost half (46 per cent) of offender movements originating in the adjoining town of Rotherham. The findings from the city of York confirm these findings with 94 per cent of burglary and 84 per cent of TWOC offender movements originating within the city.

Fourthly, even when longer-range travel was involved in offending elsewhere, this was mainly in places which had strong traditional connections with Sheffield (such as Skegness) or were obvious leisure trips (such as southern seaside resorts or London).

Overall there was little evidence that offenders' travelling to offend was significantly increasing compared with the past or that new travel opportunities were changing traditional travel patterns used by offenders. Indeed, an overwhelming impression was just how traditional the travel behaviour of the offenders was. Theories of late modernity, or post-modernism, have argued that various global forces are undermining traditional social structures and culture and this will ultimately affect crime patterns (see for example Bottoms and Wiles, 1995). As far as the travel patterns of the offenders were concerned there is little sign of such changes. Given what is known generally about persistent and repeat offenders, then these limited travel patterns are not surprising. Long-range travel, like much other human activity, requires knowledge, confidence, skills and resources. However, the risk factors associated with offending are either the lack of such skills or are closely correlated with them. Offenders generally do not travel long distances because they are drawn from those groups in the population who lack the personal and material

resources to learn to travel and sustain such travel thereafter. Whilst these findings were confirmed by interview data, the general patterns could all be identified from police recorded crime data. This is important because police recorded crime data is already available for the whole country and does not require the additional cost and difficulty of interviewing offenders. However, police data tends to over-estimate travel. This is because using home address and offence location to measure travel distance produces noticeably larger figures than using offence location, and where the offender spent the night prior to the offence. Again this finding illustrates that offender travel is not primarily about offending, but is mainly related to routines such as staying at a friend's or girlfriend's house; thus the location of the offence is not determined by instrumental search patterns except over short ranges. Earlier research has discussed the extent to which patterned routine activities produce 'anchor points' (such as home, place of work or place of leisure) around which offending is carried out. In this study, persistent offenders had little contact with a world of regularised work and lacked the resources for stable leisure pursuits. The one clear anchor point which emerged, therefore, was their home. However, since their lives were largely irregular, spontaneous and unstructured, then alternative and temporary 'anchor points', such as a girlfriend's home, came and went although always within a limited number of the city's neighbourhoods.

The behaviour of the known offenders who committed high volume crimes is dominated by opportunistic offending during routine and limited travel patterns. However, this is not to deny that there may be 'professional travelling criminals'; just to deny they are responsible for much high volume crime. An attempt was made to examine this possibility in the research by interviewing a small group of offenders who had been identified by the police as 'professionals'. However, the sense of 'professional' used by the police was 'persistent' and their travel patterns were not distinct. Future research could well examine other senses of 'professional' perhaps by investigating particular types of crime. For example, country house rather than council estate burglaries might be one starting point, or the theft of valuable cars where joyriding does not seem to be the prime motive might be another.

Given the foregoing and other research we have conducted into crime patterns, particularly in Sheffield, we feel confident in asserting that generally, high volume crime is a highly localised phenomenon, especially for offences such as domestic burglary and criminal damage. Residential areas with high offence and victimisation rates are generally found on poorer social housing estates, and some mixed inner-city areas. We can suggest this highly localised pattern holds for a number of reasons:

1. Even poor areas contain plenty of suitable targets such as videos, televisions and cars. Recent Home Office research into car crime, for example, appears to support the notion of localised victimisation, as it shows the highest rates of theft for older cars of the type that predominate in poorer areas of Britain (Houghton, 1992).

2. Offenders tend to live in these areas and also, on the whole, tend to offend close to home rather than conduct long-range instrumental searches across a city. The Sheffield interviewees generally lived in a restricted number of the poorer social housing areas of the city – what we have termed 'impacted crime areas'.

3. The other areas the offenders knew (other than the city centre) were similar in character to the one they currently lived in, and usually they had either lived in them previously or had friends or family in the area. The result is that even if offending is

carried out away from home it tends to be in areas where offenders have contacts, not unknown middle-class parts of the city.

These factors mean that a city's broad crime patterns tend to be stable and predictable in the short-term. High offence and victim rate areas are the parts of a city where offenders tend to live and are generally the parts of a city which are considered least desirable in terms of residential location. Such patterns will be self-reinforcing through mechanisms such as the housing market and allocation systems, unless other macro policy or market factors disrupt them.

The result, in the case of Sheffield, has been that even in the long term some aspects of crime patterns appear to be fairly stable. Some of the areas with 'impacted' crime patterns in the 1960s – see Baldwin and Bottoms, (1976) – appear to be the same today, and the broad geographical crime pattern of Sheffield is little changed over 30 years. However, it is not the case that all patterns of crime remain static, and important changes in the fabric of the city have had an impact upon crime patterns. In Sheffield these have included: the redevelopment of once private rental areas of the city; the growth of a new private rental sector catering for the growing number of students; the demolition of unpopular areas of public housing which has changed the relative unpopularity of the remaining areas; the development of out of town retailing (such as Meadowhall shopping mall), which has seen the city centre's share of all offences decline from 25 per cent in 1966 to 10 per cent in 1995; and changes in the demographic profiles of neighbourhoods which have shifted their community crime careers. It is likely that a similar mixture of stability and change would be found in other British cities.

5   Class, Culture and Subculture

Merton, an American sociologist, applied Durkheim's notion of anomie, or normlessness, to crime. This work was to have a massive influence within Criminology. As Downes and Rock observed:

'It was something of a sociological counterpart to the cosmological Big Bang … it has been reincarnated again and again. It has an anonymous presence in Jock Young's essay in labelling theory, "The Drugtakers". It is the invisible prop to the Birmingham Centre for Contemporary Cultural Studies' radical work on class, youth, and deviance in Britain … Extensive echoes of the Big Bang will be discerned in any sensitive reading of the contemporary sociology of deviance.'

(Downes D and Rock P (1995) *Understanding Deviance*, Oxford: Clarendon Press, pp117–118.)

The first extract allows Merton to speak for himself. In your consideration of Merton's work it is important to be fair to him, and specifically you should note carefully the provisos (particularly in the last paragraph) that Merton made in relation to his work. It is very easy to lose sight of these amidst the avalanche of criticism that his ideas attracted. The second extract, by Clinard, offers a summary of many of these criticisms.

Merton R (1957) *Social Theory and Social Structure*[1], pp131–160

Patterns of cultural goals and institutional norms

Among the several elements of social and cultural structures, two are of immediate impor-

[1] Reprinted with the permission of The Free Press, a Division of Simon & Schuster. Copyright © 1957 The Free Press; copyright renewed 1985 by Robert K Merton.

tance. These are analytically separable although they merge in concrete situations. The first consists of culturally defined goals, purposes and interests, held out as legitimate objectives for all or for diversely located members of the society … Involving various degrees of sentiment and significance, the prevailing goals comprise a frame of aspirational reference. They are the things 'worth striving for'. …

A second element of the cultural structure defines, regulates and controls the acceptable modes of reaching out for these goals. Every social group invariably couples its cultural objectives with regulations, rooted in the mores or institutions, of allowable procedures for moving toward these objectives. … In all instances, the choice of expedients for striving toward cultural goals is limited by institutionalised norms. …

Types of individual adaptation

We here consider five types of adaptation, as these are schematically set out in the [above] table, where (+) signifies 'acceptance', (-) signifies 'rejection', and (+/-) signifies 'rejection of prevailing values and substitution of new values'. …

1 CONFORMITY

To the extent that a society is stable, adaptation type 1 – conformity to both cultural goals and institutionalised means – is the most common and widely diffused. Were this not so, the stability and continuity of the society could not be maintained. …

2 INNOVATION

Great cultural emphasis upon the success-goal invites this mode of adaptation through the use of institutionally proscribed but often effective means of attaining at least the simulacrum of

A TYPOLOGY OF MODES OF INDIVIDUAL ADAPTATION

Modes of adaptation	Culture goals	Institutionalised means
1. Conformity	+	+
2. Innovation	+	-
3. Ritualism	-	+
4. Retreatism	-	-
5. Rebellion	+/-	+/-

success – wealth and power. This response occurs when the individual has assimilated the cultural emphasis upon the goal without equally internalising the institutional norms governing ways and means for its attainment. From the standpoint of psychology, great emotional investment in an objective may be expected to produce a readiness to take risks, and this attitude may be adopted by people in all social strata. From the standpoint of sociology, the question arises, which features of our social structure predispose toward this type of adaptation, thus producing greater frequencies of deviant behaviour in one social stratum than in another? ...

But whatever the differential rates of deviant behaviour in the several social strata, and we know from many sources that the official crime statistics uniformly showing higher rates in the lower strata are far from complete or reliable, it appears from our analysis that the greatest pressures toward deviation are exerted upon the lower strata. ...

Of those located in the lower reaches of the social structure, the culture makes incompatible demands. On the one hand, they are asked to orient their conduct toward the prospect of large wealth – 'Every man a king,' said Marden and Carnegie and Long – and on the other, they are largely denied effective opportunities to do so institutionally. The consequence of this structural inconsistency is a high rate of deviant behaviour. The equilibrium between culturally designated ends and means becomes highly unstable with progressive emphasis on attaining the prestige-laden ends by any means whatsoever. Within this

context, Al Capone represents the triumph of amoral intelligence over morally prescribed 'failure', when the channels of vertical mobility are closed or narrowed in a society which places a high premium on economic affluence and social ascent for all its members. ...

In societies such as our own, then, the great cultural emphasis on pecuniary success for all and a social structure which unduly limits practical recourse to approved means for many set up a tension toward innovative practices which depart from institutional norms. But this form of adaptation presupposes that individuals have been imperfectly socialised so that they abandon institutionalised means while retaining the success-aspiration. Among those who have fully internalised the institutional values, however, a comparable situation is more likely to lead to an alternative response in which the goal is abandoned but conformity to the mores persists. This type of response calls for further examination.

3 RITUALISM
The ritualistic type of adaptation can be readily identified. It involves the abandoning or scaling down of the lofty cultural goals of great pecuniary success and rapid social mobility to the point where one's aspirations can be satisfied. ...

4 RETREATISM
Just as Adaptation 1 (conformity) remains the most frequent, Adaptation 4 (the rejection of cultural goals and institutional means) is probably the least common. People who adapt (or maladapt) in this fashion are, strictly speaking,

in the society but not of it. Sociologically, these constitute the true aliens. Not sharing the common frame of values, they can be included as members of the society (in distinction from the population) only in a fictional sense.

In this category fall some of the adaptive activities of psychotics, autists, pariahs, outcasts, vagrants, vagabonds, tramps, chronic drunkards and drug addicts. They have relinquished culturally prescribed goals and their behaviour does not accord with institutional norms. ...

This fourth mode of adaptation, then, is that of the socially disinherited who if they have none of the rewards held out by society also have few of the frustrations attendant upon continuing to seek these rewards. ...

5 REBELLION
This adaptation leads men outside the environing social structure to envisage and seek to bring into being a new, that is to say, a greatly modified social structure. It presupposes alienation from reigning goals and standards. These come to be regarded as purely arbitrary. And the arbitrary is precisely that which can neither exact allegiance nor possess legitimacy, for it might as well be otherwise. ...

Concluding remarks
It should be apparent that the foregoing discussion is not pitched on a moralistic plane. Whatever the sentiments of the reader concerning the moral desirability of coordinating the goals-and-means phases of the social structure, it is clear that imperfect coordination of the two leads to anomie. In so far as one of the most general functions of social structure is to provide a basis for predictability and regularity of social behaviour, it becomes increasingly limited in effectiveness as these elements of the social structure become dissociated. At the extreme, predictability is minimised and what may be properly called anomie or cultural chaos supervenes.

This essay on the structural sources of deviant behaviour remains but a prelude. It has not included a detailed treatment of the struc-

tural elements which predispose toward one rather than another of the alternative responses open to individuals living in an ill-balanced social structure; it has largely neglected but not denied the relevance of the social-psychological processes determining the specific incidence of these responses; it has only briefly considered the social functions fulfilled by deviant behaviour; it has not put the explanatory power of the analytical scheme to full empirical test by determining group variations in deviant and conformist behaviour; it has only touched upon rebellious behaviour which seeks to refashion the social framework. It is suggested that these and related problems may be advantageously analysed by use of this scheme.

One of the first attempts to develop Merton's anomie theory was the addition to it by Cloward and Ohlin of the dimension of opportunity. The following extract provides a good account of their thoughts and they illustrate the importance of the various types of subculture that may be present or indeed absent in the social structure.

Cloward R and Ohlin L (1961) *Illegitimate Means and Delinquent Subcultures*, pp151–152

The concept of differential opportunity structures permit us to unite the theory of anomie, which recognises the concept of differentials in access to legitimate means, and the 'Chicago tradition', in which the concept of differentials in access to illegitimate means is implicit. We can now look at the individual, not simply in relation to one or the other system of means, but in relation to both legitimate and illegitimate systems. This approach permits us to ask, for example, how the relative availability of illegitimate opportunities affects the resolution of adjustment problems leading to deviant behaviour. We believe that the way in which these problems are resolved may depend upon the kind of support for one or another type of illegitimate activity that is given at different points in the social structure. If, in a given social location, illegal or criminal means are not readily available, then we should not expect a criminal subculture to develop among adolescents. By the same logic, we should expect the manipulation of violence to become a primary avenue to higher status only in areas where the means of violence are not denied to the young. To give a third example, drug addiction and participation in subcultures organised around the consumption of drugs presuppose that persons can secure access to drugs and knowledge about how to use them. In some parts of the social structure, this would be very difficult; in others, very easy. In short, there are marked differences from one part of the social structure to another in the types of illegitimate adaptation that are available to persons in search of solutions to problems of adjustment arising from the restricted availability of legitimate means. In this sense, then, we can think of individuals as being located in two opportunity structures – one legitimate, the other illegitimate. Given limited access to success-goals by legitimate means, the nature of the delinquent response that may result will vary according to the availability of various illegitimate means.

When students come to a discipline like Criminology for the first time they tend to be taken in by the ideas that they find in the theories that they are exposed to. Merton's ideas in particular are often declared to be convincing. It falls to writers such as Clinard to deliver the bad news – that each successive attempt at explaining crime has met with criticism. After Clinard has finished you might begin to wonder what you ever saw in the application of anomie to crime causation.

Clinard M (1964) 'The Theoretical Implications of Anomie and Deviant Behaviour', in Clinard M (ed), *Anomie and Deviant Behaviour*[2], pp54–56

A number of extensions and reformulations of Merton's theory of anomie have been made, including Talcott Parsons' broader theory of interactions analyses, Robert Dubin's extension of innovation and ritualism, Richard Cloward's addition of illegitimate means and opportunity structures, and Albert Cohen's emphasis on the need for more adequate consideration of social interactive processes. In addition, increased efforts have been made to measure the relation of the social structure to anomie and anomia, a quality of the individual. The results have been somewhat contradictory, although, in general, tending to support the existence of anomie and anomia. Some sociologists have come to use the term alienation, rather than anomia, for the subjective aspect of what Merton termed anomie. In the concluding paper of this volume, Merton further elaborates his formulation of anomie by attempting to clarify the important problem of the relationship of anomie to anomia. As another facet of the strain toward anomie, he discusses more fully the role that social interaction plays in the theory, indicating that there is a particular need for the study of the interaction between deviant and conforming members of collectivities with differing degrees of anomie.

There is a common tendency in sociology to accept intriguing and well formulated theories in advance of adequate empirical support, through research or the incorporation of other relevant conceptual frameworks. This has been true of the relation of anomie to deviant behaviour. Despite reformulations there have been a number of specific objections to this theory: (1) It is claimed that the theory conceives of an atomistic and individualistic actor

[2] Reprinted with the permission of The Free Press, a Division of Simon & Schuster. Copyright © 1966 The Free Press.

who selects adaptations to the social system, and in so doing fails to stress the importance of interactions with others, who serve as reference groups for the actor. The actions of significant others affect the response and adaptation of the actor. (2) The deviant act is seen as an abrupt change from the strain of anomie to deviance, rather than as an event which has been built up through the interactions process. (3) Many deviant acts can be explained as part of role expectations rather than disjunctions between goals and means. (4) The dichotomy of cultural goals and institutional means, basic to anomie theory, may be so artificial as to have little meaning, since both are so linked in reality. (5) It is difficult to identify a set of values or cultural goals which could be considered universal in most modern, complex, industrial societies. The ends sought grow out of multi-value claims made on individuals participating in diverse groups. (6) The concept of anomie best explains deviant behaviour in societies where status is achieved; a different explanation may be needed where status is ascribed. (7) There is doubt that deviant behaviour is disproportionately more common in the lower class as the theory of anomie maintains. More studies of the incidence and prevalence of deviant behaviour are needed before what is assumed by theory can be stated as fact. (8) Even if it is assumed that there is a higher rate of deviation in the lower class, there is the further question of why the bulk of the lower class uses conformity to achieve prescribed goals. (9) The theory stresses the importance of position in the social structure and ability to reach cultural goals. Such factors as subcultures, urbanisation, and, especially, the role of group or collective adaptations are not normally taken into account. Short has pointed out in his paper that among lower class gang boys, middle class values are appreciated, but status is linked with more immediate contexts (being a male or a member of a gang) and immediate ongoing processes rather than ultimate ends. (10) At the level of social control an important theoretical problem in explaining deviation is

how deviant behaviour originates and how certain deviations lead to symbolic reorganisation at the level of self-regarding attitudes and roles while others do not. The societal elements isolating and reacting to deviants are largely disregarded. (11) Finally, the adaptation of retreatism has been challenged, particularly as an explanation of drug addiction, as lacking precision and as an over-simplification of the process of self-evaluation.

The continuing influence of Merton's ideas is seen in the attempts that are being made to adapt and develop it. The work of Agnew looks for strain in different manifestations of the social structure than was the case in the past. This work also represents a continuing interest in the development of a single theory of crime – quite unfashionable, as much of the theoretical impetus has moved towards integrative approaches.

Agnew R (1992) 'Foundation for a General Strain Theory of Crime and Delinquency', *Criminology*, p74–75

Much of the recent theoretical work in criminology has focused on the integration of different delinquency theories. This paper has taken an alternative track and, following Hirschi's (1979) advice, has focused on the refinement of a single theory. The general strain theory builds upon traditional strain theory in criminology in several ways. First, the general strain theory points to several new sources of strain. In particular, it focuses on three categories of strain or negative relationships with others: (1) the actual or anticipated failure to achieve positively valued goals, (2) the actual or anticipated removal of positively valued stimuli, and (3) the actual or anticipated presentation of negative stimuli. Most current strain theories in criminology only focus on strain as the failure to achieve positively valued goals, and even then the focus is only on the disjunction between aspirations and expectations/actual achievements. The disjunctions between expectations and achievements and just/fair outcomes and achievements are ignored. The general strain theory, then, significantly expands the focus of strain theory to include all types of negative relations between the individual and others. Second, the general strain theory more precisely specifies the relationship between strain and delinquency, pointing out that strain is likely to have a cumulative effect on delinquency after a certain threshold level is reached. The theory also points to certain relevant dimensions of strain that should be considered in empirical research, including the magnitude, recentcy, duration, and clustering of strainful events. Third, the general strain theory provides a more comprehensive account of the cognitive, behavioural, and emotional adaptations to strain. This account sheds additional light on the reasons why many strained individuals do not turn to delinquency, and it may prove useful in devising strategies to prevent and control delinquency. Individuals, in particular, may be taught those non-delinquent coping strategies found to be most effective in preventing delinquency. Fourth, the general strain theory more fully describes those factors affecting the choice of delinquent versus non-delinquent adaptations. The failure to consider such factors is a fundamental reason for the weak empirical support for strain theory.

Most of the above modifications in strain theory were suggested by research in several areas outside of traditional criminology, most notably the stress research in medical sociology and psychology, the equity/justice research in social psychology, and the aggression research in psychology. With certain exceptions, researchers in criminology have tended to cling to the early strain models of Merton (1938), A. Cohen (1955), and Cloward and Ohlin (1960) and to ignore the developments in related fields. And while these early strain models contain much of value and have had a major influence on the general strain theory in this paper, they do not fully exploit the potential of strain theory.

At the same time, it is important to note that the general strain theory is not presented here as a fully developed alternative to earlier theories. First, the macro implications of the theory were only briefly discussed. It would not be difficult to extend the general strain theory to the macro level, however; researchers could focus on (1) the social determinants of adversity (for an example, see Bernard, 1990, on the urban underclass) and (2) the social determinants of those factors that condition the effect of adversity on delinquency. Second, the theory did not concern itself with the non-social determinants of strain, such as illness. It seems doubtful that adversity caused by non-social sources is a major source of delinquency because, among other things, it is unlikely to generate anger (see Averill, 1982). Nevertheless, non-social sources of adversity should be investigated. Third, the relationship between the general strain theory and other major theories of delinquency must be more fully explored. As hinted earlier, the relationship is rather complex. While the general strain theory is clearly distinct from control and differential association theory, strain may lead to low social control and association with delinquent others. Further, variables from the three theories may interact with one another in producing delinquency. Individuals with delinquent friends, for example, should be more likely to respond to strain with delinquency. The general strain theory, then, is presented as a foundation on which to build.

After Merton's work the next major development was Sutherland's proposition that crime was best explained as normal learned behaviour. This is commonly known as differential association theory. The ideas were developed over time with his first thoughts being presented in 1934 and the first substantial attempt appearing in 1939. Cressey became a co-author as the years went by and the version presented here is a late version of their work. As with a number of the authors of previous extracts Sutherland and Cressey were American sociologists.

Sutherland E and Cressey D R (1966) 'A Sociological Theory of Criminal Behaviour', *Principles of Criminology*, 7th ed, pp80–82

The following statement refers to the process by which a particular person comes to engage in criminal behaviour.

1. Criminal behaviour is learned. Negatively this means that criminal behaviour is not inherited.
2. Criminal behaviour is learned in interaction with other persons in a process of communication.
3. The principal part of the learning of criminal behaviour occurs within intimate personal groups.
4. When criminal behaviour is learned the learning includes: (a) techniques of committing the crime, which are sometimes very complicated, sometimes very simple; (b) the specific direction of motives, drives, rationalisations, and attitudes.
5. The specific direction of motives and drives is learned from definitions of the legal codes as favourable or unfavourable.
6. A person becomes delinquent because of an excess of definitions favourable to violation of law over definitions unfavourable to violation of law. This is the principle of differential association.
7. Differential associations may vary in frequency, duration, priority, and intensity.
8. The process of learning criminal behaviour by association with criminal and anti-criminal patterns involves all of the mechanisms that are involved in any other learning.
9. While criminal behaviour is an expression of general needs and values, it is not explained by those general needs and values since non-criminal behaviour is an expression of the same needs and values.

The extract by Parker provides a first-hand account of a group of adolescents growing up in Liverpool. It is an attempt to provide evidence in relation to subcultures in England. The image that comes across is how normal their behaviour is in the context of their situation. It fits in well with the account of juvenile groups in Chicago as portrayed by Thrasher in his classic work: Thrasher F (1947) *The Gang*, Chicago: University of Chicago Press. It also fits in with the work of Matza: Matza D (1964) *Delinquency and Drift*, New York: Wiley, for whom an extract is provided in Chapter 6. The 'catseyes' that Parker refers to are a particular type of car radio whilst 'the busies' are the police.

Parker H (1994) *The View from the Boys*, pp62–63, 76–77, 116–120

To Authority in particular and outsiders in general, The Boys don't exist. The members of the network are merely downtown adolescents who look much alike, who live in a 'high delinquency area' and if the facts be known are 'persistent offenders'. By the end of Year Three, taking 25 members of the network, only one had no form of criminal record. The average number of indictable offences was just over three, with several of The Boys scoring six and seven convictions. Many had run the gauntlet of 'warnings' – probation, fines, attendance centres, more fines, approved schools, detention centres, borstals. The Boys, taking any official measure one likes, are viewed as severely delinquent, and consequently fit to receive the connotative definitions and degrading labels saved for their type.

During a six-month period starting at the end of Year Two, The Boys as a group almost certainly reached the peak, in terms of intensity of misdemeanour, of their delinquent 'careers'. For a while they became the Catseye Kings. Amongst other things this chapter deals with their rise and fall. Depending on where you are standing this is a story with many morals. As far as The Boys are concerned there are only two sides, theirs or Authority's. The sociologist involved in this contest must take sides, whether he likes it or not: every time he records an incident and leaves another buried, every time he quotes an actor and ignores another, he is taking sides. He not only reconstructs the action but then further interprets, by 'writing up' his own version of his original perceptions. By writing a lengthy chapter on The Boys' 'delinquency' there is a tendency to imply to the reader that illegal behaviour is a serious preoccupation of The Boys. Having spent two years of fairly close observation in this group who as individuals at least are regarded as highly delinquent and 'persistent offenders', I know The Boys in fact are not persistent in their rule-breaking at all. Indeed, put in the context of a wider society full of deviancy at all social levels and in all social classes, The Boys' 'delinquency' is mundane, trivial, petty, occasional and very little of a threat to anyone except themselves. Yet this is not seen as relevant to their disposal; instead they are 'dealt with' as if they were different from everybody else.

When society defines certain people as outsiders, it needs to emphasise the ways in which these people are different from the insiders, those who are normal. Thus criminals are not just people who have broken the law but are also generally dangerous and not to be trusted (1).

Hence The Boys are regarded by some, most of whom wield power, as malicious, thoughtless, devious, wild, vandalistic, with a chip on their shoulder and coming from 'a jungle'. The Boys' life-style, if all its aspects were known to our typecasters, our 'highly respected' citizens, would be stigmatised as depraved and damaging to the well-being of society. With minimal appreciation of their situation, The Boys would be earmarked. They are heavy drinkers, spending a great deal more time and money in pubs and clubs than they should. They take short cuts wherever possible, showing no self control and ability to defer gratification. ...

For over a year, Joey and Fatch, under the supervision of Joey's older brother, took several catseyes from cars in the area. One dinner-time they came onto the Corner rather pleased with themselves because the night before they had broken into two Rover cars and removed radios. The others already knew this. Joey announced: 'We've just got paid, fellers, lots of lovely poke. Come on you cunts, you don't deserve it but we'll get a few bevvies in.' About six of us went down to 'The Turk', where for the next couple of hours the lager flowed freely. Everyone was happy and full of friendly jibbing.

During the next couple of weeks there was much talk about Rovers and catseyes. Rover 2000 models were the main target for the ensuing 'attacks', because the plastic casing housing the speaker could be removed with one hefty boot up on to the dashboard. The holding brackets were then easily accessible and the radio could be taken quickly. That these cars were the most expensive and luxurious around town was a coincidence, though not without consequence as we shall see.

It was about 9.30 pm when we walked down the hill towards the centre. Colly had just seen 'a real beaut' in a Rover parked on waste ground in William Street. Although I was regarded as a friendly spectator I was briefed to keep look out, 'dixy', at the top end of the line of cars. A two-tone whistle, not unlike a police siren, was always used as a warning of possible trouble. Colly had a 'punch' with him, a spring-loaded centre punch used in the leather industry. Several of The Boys used these to break car quarter-light windows. Tonight the window shattered at the second attempt, and the door was opened quickly. Joey, who had on the correct footwear, put the boot in accurately. Colly did the rest, unscrewing the brackets and yanking the radio away, so snapping the connecting wires. The door was shut and Joey went off down the hill with the radio under his jacket. Colly joined me, concealed his punch and we walked back up the hill. I admitted to a certain amount of elation and a great deal of relief. Joey would make his way back to the Block and then meet us in the pub. 'We take it in turns to carry the radio, coz if you get caught with it on you you've had it. There's no point in everyone getting done for it, so the one who's got the radio goes off on his own.'

Colly remarked on how smoothly things had gone this night compared with the evening before. 'I really shit myself last night. I was in this Rover when these fuckin' headlights went on. I thought it was the busies. Joey pushed the door shut with me inside and just stood outside leaning on the car with me ducking down. He said "It's only someone going off."'

The catseyes capers spread. By the end of January at least 20 of the network were screwing cars, some regularly, others occasionally. A dialogue built up amongst The Boys and other regular faces who were interested in the knock-off business. Who was screwing cars, on the catseyes, or simply on the cars were important topics for the conversation culture. During the daytime wandering around the area, 'pipe-ing', looking over a car, became a regular practice, even if merely to pass the time: did it have a radio, was it the right kind to bring a high price at the fence, was the car door locked, was there an alarm, was it in a safe place to screw? Pipe-ing eventually had to become very subtle; the outsider, particularly the lurking plain clothes policeman, should not to be able to realise a couple of boys were pipe-ing a car at all as they walked past it. Talk during February centred around the techniques of removing radios from the dashboard without detection or damage to it, the problematic part of the exercise; expertise was scarce initially. At this time some radios were having to be sold at a reduced rate owing to damaged buttons. Walking down to the dole one morning with Titch and Fosser an innovation was born. We stopped to look at an open sports car which was somewhat novel at that time of the year. Titch recognised its radio as being of the same make as one he had damaged in taking it out of a car the week before. He yanked off the control buttons hastily and we were walking down the hill again in seconds. 'They'll fit great. That'll be a few quid for tonight.' ...

It is now time we turned to look at those things the down-town adolescent values and strives for. Until we can grasp the significance of the good times and the meanings of leisure time we cannot put The Boys' delinquency into perspective. For as Matza reminds us: 'A delinquent is a youngster who in relative terms more warrants that legal appellation than one who is less delinquent or not so at all. He is a delinquent by and large because the shoe fits, but even so one must never imagine he wears it very much of the time' (2). We must look at the other shoes The Boys wear and enjoy wearing.

In trying to explain The Boys' life style and the ethos of their neighbourhood, two main sorts of problems arise for solution. Firstly, are the subjects of study observably different in their attitudes, behavioural patterns and relationships, and in whose terms? Secondly, assuming there are some differences, what explanations can be offered for these diversities, what structures and motivators are at their root? These latter problems tend to lead us past observation into constructs and inference in our search for solutions.

A whole variety of quantitative explanations are offered by physical circumstances. Roundhouse as a predominantly unskilled manual working neighbourhood is solidly stuck in the mud of the Registrar General's occupational classes IV and V, the groups which also receive least of the economic cake. In terms of a social-malaise survey of official agency definitions of 'core problems', Roundhouse also comes out as 'different' by being at 'the bottom end'. So in terms of facility, employment, housing, health and hygiene, Roundhouse is seen, along with other down-town areas, as decidedly different, that is 'deprived' of certain life chances and living standards.

Explaining behavioural differences regarded as deviant is a more controversial matter. Dispute arises when behavioural styles other than those overtly and obviously related to local living conditions are looked at. Members of the unskilled working class who live in down-town areas, according to the statistics, are the most delinquent and criminal. They, it appears, are the not-so-lame ducks who rather than 'get up off their arses' take short cuts to things other people have to work for. Down-town Roundhouse also appears to produce more than its share of 'naughty' boys; indeed it breeds a host of those stereotyped delinquents, described at the beginning of the last chapter, according to some 'learned' and 'respected' men of city and societal influence. Once people accept these sorts of prejudices and stereotypes, then questions and answers become blurred and those people with less become those who deserve less. The deprived become the depraved. The down-towners become for the Corporation official with 'an open mind' and 'liberal' views, 'a ghetto of the less able' and for the so-called sympathetic documentary-film producer 'The Dead End Lads'.

This chapter looks more closely at the male adolescent milieu and its 'conversation culture' – the themes it articulates and concentrates on. The Roundhouse adolescent talks about more than 'robbing' and does a lot more than screw cars. Indeed, seen in the context of what he does with his day, his week and his year, the down-town adolescent's delinquency, and all that it is *meant to* imply according to 'respectable' society, is only one of several major concerns. For every delinquent act one of The Boys has committed, depending at what stage of his adolescence we are referring to, days, weeks or months can pass before the next. The last chapter concentrated on that period of The Boys' lives when they were (and as boys probably ever will be) at their most law-breaking, uncompromised and 'reckless'. Arguments which can explain this behaviour without descending to 'depraved' stereotypes and socialised robot models stand on relatively firm ground.

For exactly the same reasons this chapter will again come to terms with The Boys at their worst in 'typecaster' terms. Can the down-town adolescent's 'other' controversial activities (eg, heavy drinking, fighting) be

shown in terms of necessary style, a style which in fact deserves no 'attentions' and pointing fingers at all? If we remember The Boys spend most of their time as 'straight guys', sleeping, eating, playing and watching football, working, drinking in the local, listening to music, talking politics, etc, and then analyse the few times when they *break out,* we have a 'natural' test situation. If the break-outs prove to be explicable in terms that are normal, normative, rational, understandable, etc, then it is a matter of 'case proved'. Put less dramatically, do The Boys, their depressed situation apart, behave in the same way as other non-stigmatised adolescents, from the middle classes for instance? Is it a question of style related to their situation, or of a malicious, thoughtless, hedonistic 'depraved' ideology their kind live by ?

There has been extensive sociological theorisation about this area of 'working-class culture' and life style. Subcultural and 'culture-of-poverty' type explanations have rested heavily on the transmission of tradition, whereas a radical critique of this perspective suggests the whole cultural milieu of least well-off working-class life is no more than an on-going structural adaptation by a population that finds itself at the bottom of a highly stratified society. The question of tradition cannot be ignored – it is always a thorn in the sociologist's flesh. If tradition is defined as the transmission of knowledge or belief from one generation to another, it is no small problem to untangle what is tradition and what is functional adaptation and innovation in a stable neighbourhood. Yet tradition is one of the main ways the Roundhouse male explains much of his style: why he drinks so much and in the same old pubs, why he spends so much money in the same old way, why he fights and has 'always been a robber'. Tradition is epitomised in the everyday answers to the question why: 'That's why'; 'Coz I did'; 'I'm one of The Boys, aren't I?'; 'It's always been like that round here'; 'They just copy other kids'; 'There's always been fighting round here'.

His other explanation is that he is forced to

be the person he is because he has to react as best he can to the pressures around him. 'You've got to rob'; 'You need a few bob in your pocket'; 'I'd go nuts if I didn't go downtown for a night out'; 'You can't let somebody make a cunt out of you, you've got to fight sometimes'; 'I'd rather be on the dole than working in that place.' Although The Boys rarely put both explanations together, the implications that the two should be combined are there if their actions are compared with their beliefs. This personal diagnosis of their situation implicit in many dozens of conversations is one of the clearest messages that has come from the fieldwork.

References
1. Cohen S (1968) 'Vandalism: Its Politics and Nature', *New Society*, 12 Dec 1968.
2. Matza D (1964) *Delinquency and Drift*, New York: Wiley, p26.

The purpose of the extract from Hobbs is to provide an account of contemporary American gang research. It can be seen that, in contrast to earlier studies, the issue of race is now a crucial factor and the notion of the underclass is also being utilised. What has remained constant is the need to stress variation, diversity, and flexibility.

Hobbs D (1997) 'Criminal Collaboration', in Maguire M et al (eds), *The Oxford Handbook of Criminology,* 2nd ed, pp813–815

Since the 1970s, gangs have established themselves as a major social problem whose activities have altered in accord with shifts in the fortunes of the nation's urban economies. As for the extent of the problem, Miller estimates that 83 per cent of America's largest cities had gangs, along with 27 per cent of cities with a population of 100,000 or more, and 13 per cent of cities with populations of 10,000 or more (Miller, 1982). Similar findings were reported by Neddle and Stapleton (1983). More recent work supports the thesis that the

larger conurbations are more prone to gang formation (Curry et al, 1994), although ethnographic work in compact social settings indicates that they are also likely to produce their own gangs (Hagedorn, 1988; Vigil, 1988). It would appear that the harder researchers look, the bigger the gang problem becomes (Institute for Law and Justice, 1994), for eliciting numerical data on a subject that is ill-defined and dominated by law enforcement agencies which will often have an interest in inflating the phenomenon can be a problematic exercise (see Spergel, 1994: 26–42; Hagedorn, 1990: 240–59, for interesting discussions of the validity of different methods of gang research).

Modern gang researchers have explicitly located race as a major feature of youth gangs, which highlights the manner in which groundbreaking studies such as Thrasher's (1927) took race for granted, by placing the emphasis on immigration and the subsequent process of culturation. For instance Moore's (1978) work stresses the way in which, excluded from the mainstream of economic life, informal Chicano culture is supported by prison gang culture (cf Camp and Camp, 1985) to form neighbourhood gangs that were territorially based, segregated by age, and were violent and drug-orientated. Moore's later work (1991) further emphasised the role of the broader political economy in changing the function of the gang, making it a form of alternative neighbourhood government in the absence of legitimate institutions.

Central to the theme of change that is so apparent in these new gang studies, and accompanying the emphasis on race, is the location of gangs within an urban underclass (Hagedorn, 1988; Vigil, 1988; 1991). The term underclass was initially expressed by Wilson as a predominantly non-white urban American problem (Wilson, 1987), claiming that economic changes within urban America have produced transformations in class structure that effectively exclude those at society's rump. The British debate has been largely dominated by Murray's (1990) 'moral turpitude' (Westergaard, 1992) use of the term, and is fiercely contested in the British context (cf McNichol, 1993; Mann, 1992) where it has been drained of both its liberal roots and its empirical grounding (cf Leviatas, 1996). However, common to both countries is the perception of a working-class mutation, no longer active in the workforce, violent, and dependant on welfare. The notion of such a monster emerging from the swamp of late twentieth-century capitalism wearing a reversed baseball cap, intent on apparently ignoring the Mertonian (1938) concept of upward mobility upon which American society is grounded, constitutes rather more of a threat in the United States than in Britain, where such a myth has hardly been a central societal prop.

However, such fears may be unfounded, for there has in these new studies been a marked shift towards understanding gangs in terms of the adoption of market prerogatives within traditional territorial frameworks. The destruction of established territories that were based upon racially defined working-class neighbourhoods is associated with a decline in traditional male employment; the drugs trade offers an alternative sphere of enterprise, and the structure of the gang is an ideal adaptive device for entrepreneurial engagement. As a consequence violent conflict is as likely to be market, as opposed to turf, driven. This is crucial as it locates gangs not, as in the classical sense described by Thrasher, as interstitial, but as part of mainstream economic and social life.

However, in the post-industrial age the notion of territory becomes more problematic, for in the light of the destruction of those traditional working class areas that formed the basis for gang affiliation, gangs, despite having become quasi-institutions (Fagen, 1990; Moore, 1991), would appear to be relying upon increasingly artificial or symbolic territorial boundaries (Katz, 1988: 146), although localised variations are, in the form of community and neighbourhood variables (Skolnick et al, 1993), central to the process of deindustri-

alisation and globalisation (Robertson, 1995). Gang activity does appear to be an increasingly rational activity (Sanchez-Janowski, 1991), and for contemporary youths suffering 'multiple marginality' (Vigil, 1988), the gang offers opportunities to redefine the youth problem in terms of entrepreneurial imperialism via the drugs trade (Taylor, 1990). Most crucially the mainstream presumption of upward mobility has been eroded (Hagedorn, 1988), and as the shift from the formal to the informal economy is compounded, and traditional forms of working-class organisation are made redundant, gangs can represent one of the few traditional strategies that retain the potential to adapt to the market, and are elevated to the forefront of the practical consciousness of youth, and to the cutting edge of entre-preneurial strategy (see Davis, 1990: chapter 5). This emulation of organised crime has led Hagedorn (1990) to pose some crucial questions that can only be answered by future generations of researchers. Is this entre-preneurial shift typical? Are there different types of gang-related economic organisations? Do these new *gangs* resemble contemporary small businesses with a high rate of failure and their employees working part-time for less than subsistence wages? And do these new gangs have any non-economic functions? (Hagedorn, 1990: 243).

Empirical evidence for this shift varies, some researchers reporting well organised drug distribution operations (Skolnick, 1990; Taylor, 1990; Padilla, 1992), while others question this portrayal (Waldorf and Lauderback, 1993), and the issue of local variations on collaborative criminal strategies is central to the overall thesis of this chapter. The point is that entrepreneurial trends in inner city life have led to the formation of strategies that should not be regarded as totally separate from the influences of mainstream society. For the demands of the American dream, according to Horowitz (1983), also implicitly mandate an affiliation to competing demands of 'honour', which within the gang, with its emphasis upon character and self respect, constitutes a subcultural solution. Such a mandate allows for diversity (Fagen, 1989), and trends that are driven by the political economy can be located within a historical context, for gangs based upon entrepreneurship as a central ethos (Padilla, 1993) show close similarities with the street *gangs* of the early part of the twentieth century, who on developing rudimentary organisational structures based upon race, class, and territory, evolved via the Volstead Act into America's principal organised crime groups (Lacey, 1991: chapter 3; Stuart, 1985: chapters 2, 3, 4; Ianni, 1972). Nearly 80 years on, old and new youth gangs, both acquisitive and non-acquisitive, can be seen as rational attempts at discovering solutions to, and acquiring insulation from, their economic, ethnic, and class marginality via the construction of identity around a form of 'local patriotism' (Sanchez-Jankowski, 1991: 99) that has essentially ambiguous symbiotic relationships with its host communities.

Summary
To summarise, the early gang studies charted the emergence of youth gangs from poor disorganised urban neighbourhoods. Arranged around race and territorial imperatives, American theories of status frustration and alienation resulted in subcultural theories organised around strain and conflict. British studies questioned the application of American research to British society, and suggested that delinquent groups are organised around dissociation, locating delinquent subcultures within the broader parent culture, and stressed the inherited quality of the problems to which delinquent subcultures are a response, perceiving the emergence of subcultures as an attempt to solve ideological and economic contradictions within the parent culture. Contemporary American studies locate gangs as a segment of a racialised urban underclass, and stress variation, diversity, and flexibility.

Bibliography
Camp G and Camp C G (1985) *Prison Gangs: Their Extent, Nature and Impact on Prisons*, Washington, DC: US Department of Prisons.

Curry G D, Ball, R A and Fox R J (1994) *Gang Crime and Law Enforcement Record Keeping*, Washington DC: National Institute of Justice.

Davis M (1990) *City of Quartz*, London: Verso.

Fagan J (1989) 'The Social Organisation of Drug Use and Drug Dealing among Urban Gangs', *Criminology*, 27, 4: 633–669.

Fagan J (1990) 'Social Processes of Delinquency and Drug Use among Urban Gangs', in C R Huff (ed), *Gangs in America*, Newbury Park: Sage, pp183–219.

Hagedorn J (1988) *People and Folks: Gangs, Crime and the Underclass in a Rustbelt City*, Chicago, Ill: Lake View.

Hagedorn J (1990) 'Back in the Field Again: Gang Research in the Nineties', in C R Huff (ed), *Gangs in America*, Newbury Park: Sage, pp240–262.

Horowitz R (1983) *Honor and the American Dream: Culture and Identity in a Chicano Community*, New Brunswick, NJ: Rutgers University Press.

Ianni F A J (1972) *A Family Business: Kinship and Social Control in Organised Crime*, New York: Russell Sage Foundation.

Institute For Law and Justice (1994) *Gang Prosecution in the United States*, National Institute of Justice, Office of Justice Programs, US Department of Justice, August.

Katz J (1988) *Seductions of Crime*, New York: Basic Books.

Lacey R (1991) *Little Man*, New York: Little Brown.

Levitas R (1996) 'The Concept of Social Exclusion and the New Durkheimian Hegemony', *Critical Social Policy*, 16, 1: 1–20.

Mann K (1991) *The Making of an English 'Underclass'?* Milton Keynes: Open University Press.

Miller WB (1982) *Crime by Youth Gangs and Youth Groups in the United States*, Report prepared for the National Youth Gang Survey,

Washington, DC: Office of Juvenile Justice and Delinquency Prevention.

Moore J W (1978) *Homeboys: Gangs, Drugs and Prison in the Barrios of Los Angeles*, Philadelphia, Penn: Temple University Press.

Moore J W (1991) *Going down to the Barrio: Homeboys and Homegirls in Change*, Philadelphia, Penn: Temple University Press.

Murray C (1990) *The Emerging British Underclass*, London: Institute of Economic Affairs.

Needle J A and Stapleton W V (1983) *Police Handling of Youth Gangs*, Office of Juvenile Justice and Delinquency Prevention, National Institute for Juvenile Justice and Delinquency Prevention.

Padilla F (1992) *The Gang as an American Enterprise*, New Brunswick, NJ: Rutgers University Press.

Robertson R (1995) 'Globalisation: Time-Space and Homogeneity-Heterogeneity', in M Featherstone, S Lash and R Robertson (eds), *Global Modernities,* London: Sage.

Sanchez-Jakowski M (1990) *Islands in the Street: Gangs in American Urban Society*, Berkeley, Calif: University of California Press.

Skolnick J H (1990) 'The Social Structure of Street Drug Dealing', *American Journal of Police*, 9: 1–41.

Spergel I (1995) *The Youth Gang Problem*, New York: Oxford University Press.

Stuart M (1985) *Gangster*, London: W H Allen.

Taylor C S (1990) *Dangerous Society*, East Lansing, Mich: Michigan State University Press.

Thrasher F (1927) *The Gang*, Chicago, Ill: University of Chicago Press.

Vigil J D (1988) Barrio Gangs: *Street Life and Identity in Southern California*, Austin, Tex: University of Texas Press.

Waldorf D and Lauderback D (1993) *Gang Drug Sales in San Francisco: Organised or Freelance?*, Alameda, Calif: Institute for Scientific Analysis.

Westergaard J (1992) 'About and Beyond the "Underclass"', *Sociology,* 26, 4: 575–587.

Wilson W J (1987) *The Truly Disadvantaged*, Chicago, Ill: University of Chicago Press.

6   Control Theory, Interactionism and Labelling Theory

David Matza, in this extract, provides a critique of previous overly deterministic theoretical propositions. The positive criminology that he refers to is not just the work of biological determinists – he also sees psychological and sociological theories as having been overly deterministic. Matza is an American sociologist.

Matza D (1964) *Delinquency and Drift*, pp21–22, 26–30

An embarrassment of riches
Positive criminology accounts for too much delinquency. Taken at their terms, delinquency theories seem to predicate far more delinquency than actually occurs. If delinquents were in fact radically differenciated from the rest of conventional youth in that their unseemly behaviour was constrained through compulsion or commitment, then involvement in delinquency would be more permanent and less transient, more pervasive and less intermittent than is apparently the case. Theories of delinquency yield an embarrassment of riches which seemingly go unmatched in the real world. This accounting for too much delinquency may be taken as an observable consequence of the distorted picture of the delinquent that has developed within positive criminology. ...

Just as the frequency of maturational reform may indicate that current theories of delinquency predict far too much delinquency over lifetimes, so too the frequency of the delinquent's conformity to both conventional and unconventional standards may suggest that these same theories predict too much delinquency even during the period of optimum involvement. Delinquency is after all a legal status and not a person perpetually breaking laws. A delinquent is a youngster who in relative terms more warrants that legal appellation than one who is less delinquent or not at all so. He is a delinquent by and large because the shoe fits, but even so we must never imagine that he wears it very much of the time. Delinquency is a status and delinquents are incumbents who intermittently act out a role. When we focus on the incumbents rather than the status, we find that most are perfectly capable of conventional activity. Thus, delinquents intermittently play both delinquent and conventional roles. They play, or act well in both situations. The novice practitioner or researcher is frequently amazed at 'how like other kids' the delinquent can be when he is so inclined. ...

Delinquent drift: an alternative image
An alternative image of the delinquent can be developed by accepting the implications of soft rather than hard determinism. One effect of restoring choice to man is to render feasible a joining of classical with positivist assumptions. I wish to maintain the spirit of positive inquiry but to suggest certain modifications of its picture of the delinquent. These modifications consistently follow lines implicit in the classic criminological view.

Some men are freer than others. Most men, including delinquents, are neither wholly free nor completely constrained but fall somewhere between. The general conditions underlying various positions along a continuum from freedom to constraint may be described. Viewed in this way, determinism loses none of its heuristic value. We may still act as if all were knowable, but we refrain at least temporarily from an image of the delinquent that is tailored to suit social science. The image of the delinquent I wish to convey is one of drift; an actor neither compelled nor committed to deeds nor freely choosing them; neither different in any simple or fundamental sense from the law abiding, nor the same; conforming to certain traditions in American life while partially unreceptive to other more conventional traditions; and finally, an actor whose motivational system may be explored along lines explicitly commended by classical criminology – his peculiar relation to legal institutions.

The delinquent is casually, intermittently, and transiently immersed in a pattern of illegal action. His investment of affect in the delinquent enterprise is sufficient so as to allow an eliciting of prestige and satisfaction but not so large as to 'become more or less unavailable for other lines of action' (1). In point of fact, the delinquent is available even during the period of optimum involvement for many lines of legal and conventional action. Not only is he available but a moment's reflection tells us that, concomitant with his illegal involvement, he actively participates in a wide variety of conventional activity. If commitment implies, as it does, rendering oneself presently and in the future unavailable for other lines of action, then the delinquent is uncommitted. He is committed to neither delinquent nor conventional enterprise. Neither, by the canons of his ideology or the makeup of his personality, is precluded.

Drift stands midway between freedom and control. Its basis is an area of the social structure in which control has been loosened, coupled with the abortiveness of adolescent endeavour to organise an autonomous subculture, and thus an independent source of control, around illegal action. The delinquent *transiently* exists in a limbo between convention and crime, responding in turn to the demands of each, flirting now with one, now the other, but postponing commitment, evading decision. Thus, he drifts between criminal and conventional action.

To be loosened from control, conventional or delinquent, is not equivalent to freedom, and, thus, I do not propose a free or calculating actor as an alternative to constraint. Freedom is not only the loosening of controls. It is a sense of command over one's destiny, a capacity to formulate programmes or projects, a feeling of being an agent in one's own behalf. Freedom is self-control. If so, the delinquent has clearly not achieved that state. The sense of self-control, irrespective of whether it is well founded, exists to varying degrees in modern man. Those who have been granted the potentiality for freedom through the loosening of social controls but who lack the position, capacity, or inclination to become agents in their own behalf, I call drifters, and it is in this category that I place the juvenile delinquent.

Drift is motion guided gently by underlying influences. The guidance is gentle and not constraining. The drift may be initiated or deflected by events so numerous as to defy codification. But underlying influences are operative nonetheless in that they make initiation to delinquency more probable, and they reduce the chances that an event will deflect the drifter from his delinquent path. Drift is a gradual process of movement, unperceived by the actor, in which the first stage may be accidental or unpredictable from the point of view of any theoretic frame of reference, and deflection from the delinquent path may be similarly accidental or unpredictable. This does not preclude a general theory of delinquency. However, the major purpose of such a theory is a description of the conditions that make delinquent drift possible and probable, and not a specification of invariant conditions of delinquency.

In developing an alternative picture, it should be obvious that not all delinquents correspond to the drifter here depicted. By hypothesis, most delinquents, although perhaps not most criminals, approximate the model. The delinquent as drifter more approximates the substantial majority of juvenile delinquents who do not become adult criminals than the minority who do. Some delinquents are neurotically compulsive and some in the course of their enterprise develop commitment. These flank the more ordinary delinquent on either side, and during situations of crisis perhaps play crucial leadership roles. Partially because he is more sensational and dramatic, the extraordinary delinquent has received greater attention in both mass media and criminological theory. The mundane delinquent is the exemplary delinquent in that he personifies, more fully than the compulsive or the committed, the spirit of the enterprise. The delinquent drifter is less likely to command our attention and we have partially ignored him. However, the drifter is no less a problem than the compulsive or committed delinquent even though he is far less likely to become an adult criminal. Though his tenure is short, his replacements are legion. Though his ideology does not make violations of personal and property rights mandatory, under certain conditions it condones them. Thus, what follows is not a plea for the delinquent but a plea for a reassessment of his enterprise.

Reference
1. William Kornhauser (1962) 'Social Bases of Commitment: a Study of Liberals and Radicals', in Arnold M Rose (ed), *Human Behavior* and *Social Processes*, Boston: Houghton Mifflin, pp321–322.

The vast majority of the earlier extracts have looked at either individual/ biological factors or the impact of environmental factors upon individuals or groups in the search for causal factors in criminality. Becker, an American sociologist, makes it clear that it is also of vital importance to understand the role of law makers and law enforcers in what is a process of becoming a criminal. The message is that breaking the law is not enough to become a criminal, a reaction by society is required. Indeed, the breaking of the law itself is not even essential if you are falsely accused and falsely convicted.

Becker H (1963) *Outsiders: Studies in the Sociology of Deviance*[1], pp1–8, 9

All social groups make rules and attempt, at some times and under some circumstances, to enforce them. Social rules define situations and the kinds of behaviour appropriate to them, specifying some actions as 'right' and forbidding others as 'wrong'. When a rule is enforced, the person who is supposed to have broken it may be seen as a special kind of person, one who cannot be trusted to live by the rules agreed on by the group. He is regarded as an outsider. ...

Deviance and the responses of others

The sociological view I have just discussed defines deviance as the infraction of some agreed-upon rule. It then goes on to ask who breaks rules, and to search for the factors in their personalities and life situations that might account for the infractions. This assumes that those who have broken a rule constitute a homogeneous category, because they have committed the same deviant act.

Such an assumption seems to me to ignore the central fact about deviance: it is created by society. I do not mean this in the way it is ordinarily understood, in which the causes of deviance are located in the social situation of the deviant or in 'social factors' which prompt his action. I mean, rather, that *social groups create deviance by making the rules whose infraction constitutes deviance,* and by applying those rules to particular people and labelling them as outsiders. From this point of view, deviance is not a quality of the act the person commits, but rather a consequence of the application by others of rules and sanctions to an 'offender'. The deviant is one to whom that label has successfully been applied; deviant behaviour, is behaviour that people so label (1).

Since deviance is, among other things, a

---

[1] Reprinted with the permission of The Free Press, a Division of Simon & Schuster. Copyright © 1963 by The Free Press; copyright renewed 1991 by Howard S Becker.

consequence of the responses of others to a person's act, students of deviance cannot assume that they are dealing with a homogeneous category when they study people who have been labeled deviant. That is, they cannot assume that these people have actually committed a deviant act or broken some rule, because the process of labelling may not be infallible; some people may be labelled deviant who in fact have not broken a rule. Furthermore, they cannot assume that the category of those labelled deviant will contain all those who actually have broken a rule, for many offenders may escape apprehension and thus fail to be included in the population of 'deviants' they study. ...

References

1. The most important earlier statements of this view can be found in Frank Tannenbaum (1951) *Crime and the Community*, New York: McGraw-Hill and E M Lemert (1951) *Social Pathology*, New York: McGraw-Hill. A recent article stating a position very similar to mine is John Kitsuse 'Societal Reaction to Deviance: Problems of Theory and Method', *Social Problems*, 9: 247–256.
2. Malinowski B (1926) *Crime and Custom in Savage Society*, New York: Humanities Press.
3. James Davis P (1952) 'Crime News in Colorado Newspapers', *American Journal of Sociology*, 325–330.
4. Cohen A K and Short J F Jr (1966) 'Juvenile Delinquency', in R K Merton and Nisbet, *Contemporary Social Problems*, New York: Harcourt, Brace and World.
5. See Harold Garfinkel (1949) 'Research Notes on Inter- and Intra-Racial Homicides', *Social Forces, 27:* 369–381.
6. Sutherland, E H (1940) 'White Collar Criminality', *American Sociological Review*, 1–12.
7. Vincent C (1961) *Unmarried Mothers*, Free Press of Glencoe, pp3–5.
8. Rose A M and Prell A C (1955) 'Does the Punishment Fit the Crime? – a Study in Social Valuation', *American Journal of Sociology*, 247–259.

The material from Rozenburg makes it clear that the labelling process is such a powerful one, that there is no need at all for the person to have committed the offending behaviour in question – it is quite sufficient that a person is successfully falsely accused.

Rozenberg J (1992) 'Miscarriages of Justice', in Stockdale E and Casale S, *Criminal Justice under Stress*, pp91–92

Anyone who still has any illusions about the ability of the criminal justice system to rectify miscarriages of justice should look up a statement made by the then Home Secretary Douglas Hurd in the House of Commons on 20 January 1987. In it he announced his conclusions on three cases which had recently been reviewed by his department.

Mr Hurd began with the case of the Maguire family. There was no new evidence, he said, which cast doubt on the safety of their convictions for handling explosives. He could see no grounds for referring the Maguires' case to the Court of Appeal.

On 26 June 1991 the Court of Appeal quashed their convictions.

Mr Hurd then dealt with the Guildford pub bombings. Again, there were no new points of substance. Again Mr Hurd could find no grounds to justify referring the case of the Guildford Four to the Court of Appeal.

On 19 October 1989 the Court of Appeal quashed their convictions.

Mr Hurd turned finally to the case of the Birmingham Six. He was satisfied that there was new evidence to justify referring their murder convictions to the Court of Appeal. But on 28 January 1988 the Court of Appeal decided not to allow their appeals.

On 14 March 1991 the Court of Appeal changed its mind and quashed their convictions.

To justify his refusal to re-open the cases of the Maguire family and the Guildford Four, Mr Hurd circulated two detailed memoranda in January 1987. Written by C3, the Home Office department responsible for investigating miscarriages of justice, they put forward eminently plausible arguments for not referring these two cases to the Court of Appeal – on the evidence then available. But as events were to prove, there was sufficient new evidence to clear all these defendants, if only somebody in authority was prepared to look for it.

The extract that follows came from the United States some years ago but it manages to convey very well the dangers involved in labelling.

Wheeler S and Cottrell L (1969) 'The Labelling Process', in Cressey D and Ward D, *Delinquency, Crime and Social Process*, p611

Every effort should be made to avoid the use of a formal sanctioning system and particularly the official pronouncement of delinquency. Such a position is justified on grounds of the potentially damaging effects of the labelling process. The primary reason for use of the official sanctions should be the seriousness of the conduct and its potential damage to the community.

A concomitant effort must be devoted to developing new forms of controlling youthful misbehaviour without relying on the traditional agencies that usually process deviants. If the school system, for example, can develop programmes for truants and potential dropouts, it might be possible to avoid the potentially negative effects of processing offenders by the police and courts. Further, if cases normally coming before the courts can be handled by police referral to family and neighbourhood institutions and child welfare agencies, a similar benefit may result. Currently, about one-fourth of all cases handled by the juvenile courts are youth offences that have no parallel in adult crime: curfew violation, running away from home, ungovernability, and related types of activity. Many of these activities, and perhaps many of the more minor forms of delinquency, could be handled without official court contact.

The aim in all such cases would be to avoid a possibly premature labelling of a young person as delinquent or deviant, except in cases where the action is so repetitive or so clearly dangerous to the community that really major efforts are required. Adherence to such a policy would considerably reduce the number of cases that now come before the juvenile courts. It would clearly be necessary, for at least many of such cases, to provide supportive services at the family and neighbourhood level. The goal of all such services would be to keep the juvenile functioning in the family and community as long as possible without recourse to the official sanctioning systems.

The same logic should apply at each point in the process of delinquency control. If it is necessary to take official actions, efforts should first be made to leave the offenders in the community. The burden of proof, any time official intervention occurs, must be on the side of those who feel that the intervention is clearly necessary for the safety of the community and the welfare of the juvenile.

The next extract is intended to start you thinking about the complexity of the factors involved in labelling.

The President's Commission on Law Enforcement and Administration of Justice (1969) 'White-Collar Crime and the Criminal Process', in Cressey D and Ward D, *Delinquency, Crime and Social Process*, pp218–219

There is strong evidence that many white-collar offenders do not think of themselves as criminals. Cameron's study of middle-class shoplifters who had stolen from a large department store in Chicago gave some indication of the potential educative effect of the use of criminal sanctions. Shoplifters generally do not think of themselves as thieves, Cameron points out, and:

> 'even when arrested, they resist strongly being pushed to admit their behaviour is theft. Again and again store people explain to pilferers that they are under arrest as thieves, that they will, in the normal course of events, be taken in a police van to jail, held in jail until bond is raised, and tried in a court before a judge and sentenced.'

Interrogation procedures at the store are directed specifically and consciously toward breaking down any illusion that the shoplifter may possess that his behaviour is merely regarded as 'naughty' or 'bad'.

> 'In the course of this investigation, it becomes increasingly clear to the pilferer that he is considered a thief and is in imminent danger of being hauled into court and publicly exhibited as such. This realization is often accompanied by a dramatic change in attitude and by severe emotional disturbance' (1).
>
> 'Because the adult pilferer does not think of himself, prior to his arrest, as a thief and can conceive of no in-group support for himself in that role, his arrest forces him to reject the role and is in itself sufficient to cause him to redefine his situation' (2).

And Cressey found that:

> 'among the violators interviewed, the accountants, bankers, business executives and independent businessmen all reported that the possibility of stealing or robbing to obtain the needed funds never occurred to them, although many objective opportunities for such crimes were present' (3).

Application of criminal sanctions in this area raises some of the most delicate and perplexing problems confronting the criminal justice system. The sensitivity of successful members of society to the threat of criminal prosecution is indicative not only of the potential success of criminal sanctions in deterring misconduct, but of their potentially destructive effect upon the offenders. Criminal sanctions may help to educate the public to realise the seriousness of misconduct which is not on its face abhorrent, yet their indiscriminate use in areas where public opinion has not crystallised may seriously weaken the condemnatory effect of the criminal law.

References

1. Cameron M (1965) *The Booster and the Snitch*, New York: Free Press, p162.
2. Ibid, p165.
3. Cressey D (1953) *Other People's Money*, Glencoe: Free Press, p102.

Mankoff presents a powerful critique of the labelling perspective. He raises a number of important issues and in his conclusions he makes suggestions for further research.

Mankoff M (1971) 'Societal Reaction and Career Deviance: A Critical Analysis'[2], *The Sociological Quarterly*, vol 12, no 2, pp204–206, 215–217

In recent years the societal reaction or labelling perspective of Tannenbaum (1935), as elaborated by Lemert (1951), Erikson (1962), Becker (1963), and Scheff (1966), has become well known and seemingly widely accepted in one form or another by sociologists studying social deviance. Whether Tannenbaum and others *intended to* expound a general theory of deviance (Gibbs, 1966), particularly career deviance, is not nearly as important as the fact that the work of these sociologists has been perceived by many to form a fairly coherent body of thought on the subject. Accordingly, a great deal of research has been generated by, using some central concepts associated with the labelling per-

---

[2] Reprinted by permission of the *Midwest Sociological Society*. Copyright © 1971.

spective (ie, primary and secondary or career deviance and societal reaction) to examine many forms of rule-breaking.

The bulk of the research growing out of this tradition has succeeded in demonstrating that social labelling is not randomly applied throughout the population of rule-breakers (Cicourel, 1965; Piliavin and Briar, 1964). While not wishing to belittle the importance of such documentation and its implications for social theory (and social justice), one must point out that to date there has not been a systematic examination of one of the labelling perspective's most profound derivative 'theories'; that is, *rule-breakers become entrenched in deviant* roles *because they are labelled 'deviant' by others and are consequently excluded from resuming normal roles in the community* (Lemert, 1951:75–79; Becker, 1963: 316; Scheff, 1966). Much of the documentation of the discriminatory use of labelling is based on the belief that labelling is the primary determinant of career deviance. It is worthwhile, therefore, to examine the validity of this position. Without validation of this central notion, the research on the labelling process loses a great deal of its significance.

Among labelling theorists there are, of course, subtle disagreements concerning whether the labelling process is merely a necessary condition, or approaches a necessary and sufficient condition for the development of secondary or career deviance. Lemert (1967), for example, is extremely sensitive to the indeterminacy of the interaction between rule-breakers and other social actors and is even willing to exclude certain forms of rule-breaking from the general societal reaction model. Yet in focusing on the variety of paths rule-breakers travel he does not develop any explicit formulation of the conditions under which the societal reaction model is most applicable to the phenomena at hand.

The failure of those whose work falls within the boundaries of the labelling tradition to develop typologies that indicate which particular kinds of social deviance can be most

fruitfully understood by using the concepts of labelling theory is a serious shortcoming which prevents evaluating the significance of their research. While labelling theorists may think they are only applying the principles of the labelling perspective to one form of deviation, their incidental endorsements of generalisability to other forms of deviant behaviour make the critic wary, of 'straw men' arguments when he attempts to project the implications of specific research for general theory. Those who write about deviance from the labelling perspective, whether they feel they are being general theorists or not, should welcome an attempt to consider the limits of their model for explaining career deviance.

Given the above-mentioned confusion, it is the primary intention of this exploratory paper to examine critically some empirical studies bearing on the validity of labelling theory and to provide some tentative answers to the following queries:

1. Is societal reaction to rule-breaking a necessary and sufficient condition for career deviance?

2. Is societal reaction to rule-breaking equally significant in the determination of career deviance for all kinds of rule-breaking phenomena, or is it best applied to a limited number of rule-breaking phenomena?

3. What are the most serious obstacles to an adequate assessment of the theory?

I shall consider two distinct types of rule-breaking phenomena, ascriptive and achieved, which should illuminate the limitations of the labelling perspective when it addresses itself to the source of career deviance (1). *Ascribed* rule-breaking occurs if the rule-breaker is characterised in terms of a particular physical or visible 'impairment'. He does not necessarily have to act in order to be a rule-breaker; he acquires that status regardless of his behaviour or wishes. Thus, the very beautiful and the very ugly can be considered ascriptive rule-breakers. By contrast, *achieved* rule-breaking involves activity on the part of the rule-breaker, regardless of his positive attachment to a deviant 'way of life'. The embezzler who attempts to conceal his rule-breaking act, no less than the regular marijuana user who freely admits his transgression, has had to achieve rule-breaking status, at least to some extent, on the strength of his own actions (2) …

Conclusion

This paper has been concerned with the empirical validation of one of the most significant 'theories' derived from the labelling perspective, namely, rule-breakers become entrenched in deviant roles because they are labelled 'deviant' by others and are consequently excluded from resuming normal societal roles. By dividing rule-breaking phenomena into two major types, ascribed and achieved rule-breaking distinguished by the necessity of rule-breaking *activity* on the part of the rule-breaker, the paper has attempted to demonstrate that the utility of this theory is severely limited.

Ascribed rule-breaking, because it involves a passive rule-breaker almost totally dependent upon the whims of social labellers exemplifies the kind of rule-breaking phenomena for which the labelling model is most applicable. Even in this case, however, while social labelling may be a necessary condition for career deviance, it is probably not a sufficient condition for such a development. Variations in power, socio-economic status, the acquisition of compensatory skills, and defence mechanisms, may permit some labelled ascribed rule-breakers to avoid career deviance. Nevertheless, collective attempts to change social values, beliefs, and institutions are probably necessary to end ascribed deviance in the face of the dependence of ascribed rule-breakers upon prevailing community ideology and behaviour.

In the case of achieved rule-breaking, the labelling model is extremely inadequate in providing an explanation for the genesis of career deviance. Labelling theorists ignore the possibility of genuine commitment on the part of the rule-breaker to achieved career deviance. This failure of analysis stems from an underestimation of the importance of social and psychological factors other than labelling in generating deviant careers. Finally, labelling theory underestimates the possibilites for successful social control through labelling. The evidence suggests that while the labelling process may play a significant role in the development of career achieved deviance it is neither a necessary nor sufficient condition for such an outcome.

Besides considering the particular strengths and weaknesses of the labelling model in regard to the generation of career ascribed and achieved deviance, the paper has also discussed some of the major dilemmas pertaining to theory and research which must be faced by those who may wish to assess labelling theory in the future. Among the theoretical problems are the previously stated failure to consider the continuing effects of the social structural and psychological sources of initial rule-breaking in the development of career deviance, the lack of concern with the vulnerability of certain rule-breakers to self-labelling processes which may reduce the significance *of objective* labelling practices in determining deviant careers, and the related omission of any serious analysis of the types and severity of actual social sanction which facilitate 'successful' labelling. Ultimately students of deviance will have to reconsider the mechanistic assumptions of labelling theory when applied to achieved and to a lesser degree ascribed rule-breaking. The implicit notions of human passivity, so characteristic of behaviourism, seem out of place in a sociological tradition that has been founded upon penetrating observations of the creative potential of human beings. Researchers will have to learn to control the effects of the sources of initial rule-breaking and sensitivity to self-labelling and particular types of societal reaction. Only in this way can they demonstrate the power of actual labelling processes by community members in determining career deviance.

Finally, because of the observation that the

empirical research of labelling theorists has often provided evidence which contradicts the labelling model of career deviance the paper has briefly explored some of the ideological and social sources of this model. It has suggested that the model arises out of a tension between the reformist ideological orientations of most sociologists of deviance, the conservative bias of American sociology derived from European conservative social theory, and the pressures arising from the sources of political and financial support for the American sociological profession. These three factors have permitted some sociologists to become advocates of a theoretical perspective which resolves the tensions which are rooted in the conflict between ideology, professionalism, and political and financial pressure. Unfortunately, the inadequacy of the labelling perspective leads to ideological, scientific, and political bankruptcy. It is suggested that sociologists of social deviance concern themselves more with macro-sociological analysis in the future, focusing primarily on the institutional sources of career deviance. This focus may lead to greater understanding of the nature of career deviance, although it may result in shifting ideological, political and professional orientation for those who undertake this task.

In conclusion, this paper has left many problems unresolved, particularly the difficulties involved in the conceptualisation and operationalisation of 'societal reaction' and the development of a viable research programme designed to test the labelling model adequately. Nevertheless, directing attention toward some of the outstanding weaknesses of the model as it currently stands will hopefully lead to more productive attempts to grapple with the problems associated with the phenomenon of career deviance.

References
1. For discussion of the utility of typological analysis with specific focus on typologies of criminal behaviour, see Clinard and Quinney (1967:1–19), cf McKinney (1966). The particular types under analysis in this paper were drawn from Parsons'

(1951) consideration of role relationships. The element of reciprocity and the possibilities for active role-making rather than passive role-accepting implicit in achieved roles, as opposed to ascribed ones, were felt to be in contrast to the lack of autonomy characteristic of the ideal-typical rule-breaker in the labelling perspective. By exploring the implications of Parsons' distinction as it applies to types of rule-breaking, it is possible to see how the labelling perspective is dependent upon a passive actor whose rule-breaking is ascribed.

2. In the case of both ascribed and achieved rule-breaking, it is, of course, possible that persons are falsely accused of rule-breaking (Becker, 1963:20). Nevertheless, the above distinctions hold because the falsely accused ascribed rule-breaker is thought to be someone, whereas the falsely accused achieved rule-breaker is felt to have done something.

Bibliography
Becker H S (1963) *Outsiders: Studies in the Sociology of Deviance*, New York: The Free Press.

Becker H S (1967) Whose Side Are We On?', *Social Problems*, 14: 239–248.

Cicourel A (1968) *The Social Organisation of Juvenile Justice*, New York: Wiley.

Clinard M and Quinney R (1967) *Criminal Behavior Systems: A Typology*, New York: Holt, Rinehart, and Winston.

Erikson K (1962) 'Notes on the Sociology of Deviance', *Social Problems*, 9: 307–314.

Erikson K (1966) *Wayward Puritans: A Study in the Sociology of Deviance*, New York: Wiley.

Gibbs J (1966) 'Conceptions of Deviant Behavior: the Old and the New', *Pacific Sociological Review*, 9: 9–14.

McKinney J C (1966) *Constructive Typology and Social Theory*, New York: Appleton-Century-Crofts.

Parsons T (1951) *The Structure of Social Action*, New York: McGraw-Hill.

Parsons T (1951) *The Social System*, New York: Free Press.

Piliavin L and Briar S (1964) 'Police Encounters with Juveniles', *American Journal of Sociology*, 69: 206–14

Scheff T (1966) *Being Mentally Ill: A Sociological Theory*, Chicago: Aldine.

Tannenbaum F (1938) *Crime and the Community*, Boston: Ginn and Co.

Vagg provides a commentary on an alternative approach to the problem of social control, one in which attempts are made to increase rather than to undermine social ties. This approach was promoted by John Braithwaite in his 1989 text, 'Crime, Shame and Reintegration'. These ideas offer a positive response to the dilemma of social control causes crime, as portrayed within labelling traditions.

Vagg J (1998) 'Delinquency and Shame', *British Journal of Criminology*, pp247–248

One of the most promising explanations of crime to have been presented in recent years is Braithwaite's (1989) syncretic model. This links control theory, labelling theory, and sub-cultural theory, and suggests that while factors that could reasonably be subsumed under the heading of 'lack of social control' influence initial entry into delinquency, labelling factors and the presence of a sub-culture of delinquency are likely to lead to a vicious circle of 'disintegrative shaming' and further delinquency. Braithwaite's model was made with a purpose, which was to argue that social control processes currently result in delinquents losing their 'stake' in conformity – a concept not dissimilar to Laub and Sampson's notion of 'social capital'. The implication is that delinquents who are 'processed' have decreasingly pressing reasons to conform at least until some way into adulthood. This led Braithwaite to hypothesise that if the current 'disintegrative' shaming processes could be replaced with 'reintegrative' ones that created, or at least did not damage, a stake in conformity, the result would be a reduction in recidivism.

This hypothesis raises the question of whether examples of 'reintegrative' shaming processes exist. Braithwaite argues that Japanese society provides such examples. In Japan, he claims, there is a high level of interdependency between family members, and between workers and employers; a high level of communitarianism in terms of a willingness to place the community above individual interests, and a willingness of groups to accept collective responsibility for actions committed by individual members. These lead to a widely shared commitment to the maintenance of social norms, strong incentives for deviants to conform and for social groups to re-accept them, and ultimately to low crime rates. Braithwaite contrasts this with western cultures, in which there tend to be fewer factors pushing towards communitarianism and many individualist doctrines, fewer checks on deviance, and a disarticulation of shame and punishment. Higher crime rates are one result of this situation.

7   The New Criminology and Left Realist Criminology

Taylor, Walton and Young developed ideas similar to labelling theory with a large input of ideas derived from the writings of Karl Marx. These ideas operated as a critique of earlier and indeed contemporary criminological approaches. The law is seen as a product of societal, particularly economic, forces. The bad guys are those who are able to seize and use power with the person who breaks the law being recast as a victim in it all. These writers are British, though similar ideas were also developed in America and elsewhere.

Taylor I, Walton P and Young J (1975) 'Critical Criminology in Britain: Review and Prospects', in Taylor I, Walton P and Young J (eds), *Critical Criminology*, pp44–46, 56–57

Materialist criminology: methodology, crime and law

A people's statute book is its Bible of Freedom (Karl Marx) (1)

Throughout this chapter, we have argued that criminology and deviancy theory can only advance as radical theory and practice. But we have also suggested that the only radical approach which does not degenerate merely into moralising is a materialist one. There are, therefore, two questions, which we have let pass until now, but which we shall now address. What is a materialist approach? And in what manner is it radical? The answers to these questions are interconnected, for they both turn upon the purposes informing the way in which we examine society. Our pur-

poses in examining society are quite explicit: since, both in this essay and in *The New Criminology* (2), we have argued for a criminology which is normatively committed to the abolition of inequalities in wealth and power. And we have strongly argued also that any theoretical position which is not minimally committed to such a view will fall into correctionalism (ie individual rehabilitation or tangential social reform). We hope that we were successful in *The New Criminology* in demonstrating that correctionalism (no matter how liberal its aims or formulations) is irretrievably bound up with the identification of deviance with pathology, or that, where it is not, it collapses (like contemporary phenomenological approaches) into a mindless relativism. The task we have set ourselves, and other criminologists, is the attempt to create the kind of society in which the facts of human diversity are not subject to the power to criminalise.

We erected our position in this way not out of any desire to shock or enrage (though we seemed to have had that effect anyway), but because we believed that these are the central questions facing any criminology which sets out to be anything other than an adjunct of the forces of social control, under existing social arrangements. If criminology is to advance as a science, it must be free to question the causes not only of crime, but also of the norms which, in a primary sense create crime – that is, legal norms. The unquestioning acceptance of a given legal system and given legal norms has been the general tendency in positivist criminology, and the result has been disastrous for criminology's claim to scientificity (3). Ignoring or displacing the propertied nature of crime, criminologists unwilling or unable to confront the facts of inequality in ownership of property have been driven back to individualistic explanations of the differences between criminals and conformists – a task which has proven (not surprisingly) to be unilluminating and inconclusive. Those criminologists who have begun their analysis with an examination of society itself, however, have been led to a normative position which, even in the case of a conservative thinker like Durkheim, leads logically to the demand for a free division of labour untramelled by inequalities of inherited wealth (4). The analysis of particular forms of crime, or particular types of criminal outside of their context in history and society has been shown, in our view, to be a meaningless activity; and the analysis of propertied crime without reference to the demands placed by a propertied society on its members especially diversionary. We have ourselves been forced, logically, to turn for such an analysis (and such a criminology) to Marx.

The superiority of Marx's work lies not in his individual genius but rather in his method. In part, this method rests on a refusal to separate out thought from society. Thus, for Marx, theoretical reflection is either obfuscation or an exercise in practical reasoning (a fact that ordinary language philosophers and ethnomethodologists, in our own time, conveniently ignore) (5). Marx insists upon two features of any properly social analysis. Firstly, he says that 'to be radical is grasp things at the root. For man the root is Man himself' (6). Second, he observes (necessarily, given some alternative views) that man is inseparable from society. It follows (if these premises are accepted) that to analyse crime, for example requires that we examine man's position in society. We would claim that the implications of these methodological imperatives have been poorly grasped even in the best of contemporary radical criminology. This shows up notably in the absence of any historical dimension in contemporary work. We are not dealing with a criminology that could possibly be true for all societies, but with a criminology

that is specific to societies in a given historical period, and societies of a particular type. In our period, the contours of the advanced societies are heavily shaped by their relationship to the world market; and any criminology which ignores this historically specific feature of its subject-matter cannot be regarded as fully social. Rather, inasmuch as it ignores the historicity of the 'social', it aspires to an ahistorical criminology which it assumes (or asserts) to be valid eternally.

In suggesting that criminologists have to make judgments about the kind of society in which they live, we are arguing simply that criminologists must understand (and analyse) the social forces which shape their 'science'; and that criminologists who refuse to do this because of the unpleasant political implications involved, are obstructing the development of criminology. Social problems become individual problems in an ahistorical criminology; and the task of criminology is reduced to the examination of 'the causes of crime' largely in terms of individualistic explanations, with the occasional dash of social factors or determinants. Much of modern criminology continues to operate in ignorance or avoidance of the essence of crime – that, above all else, it is a breaching of a legal norm - and that legal norms, like any other social norm, can be outmoded or obsolete. The reconstruction of criminology requires a re-examination of the ways in which such legal norms are constructed, their function, and the extent to which they are appropriate and relevant 'categorical imperatives' at all levels in the social structure and at all points in culture and time. ...

Materialist criminology must set about the task of seeking to explain the continuance, the innovation or the abolition of legal and social norms in terms of the interests they support, the functions they serve to particular material arrangements or production in propertied societies, realising that the legal norms in question are inextricably connected with the developing contradictions in such societies. At a time when the law (especially industrial law – but also law and order in general) becomes a subject for constant dissension in major political debate, it is clear that the powerful social forces in our society (ultimately, those of capital and labour) are coming into conflict – and that the *legal* expression of these conflicts has no power in itself. The mystification of social conflict in legal expressions is no new phenomenon, and it was Marx himself defending himself against a charge of conspiracy in the Cologne Trials of 1849, in a speech which won over the jury, who made the case which should win over radicals to the understanding of law, and the creation of a materialist criminology (7):

> 'Society is not based on law, that is a legal fiction, rather law must be based on society; it must be the expression of society's common interests and needs, as they arise from the various material methods of production, against the arbitrariness of the single individual. The *Code Napoleon,* which I have in my hand, did not produce modern bourgeois society. Bourgeois society, as it arose in the eighteenth century and developed in the nineteenth, merely finds its legal expression in the Code. As soon as it no longer corresponds to social relationships, it is worth no more than the paper it is written on. You cannot make old laws the foundation of a new social development any more than these old laws created the old social conditions. ... Any attempted assertion of these old laws created the old social conditions. ... Any attempted assertion of the eternal validity of laws clashes with present needs, it prevents commerce and industry, and paves the way for social crises that break out with political revolutions.'

References

1. Karl Marx (1842) 'The Proceedings of the Sixth Rheish Parliament', *Rheinische Zeitung*, 10–14 July 1842, reprinted in D McLellan (ed) (1971) *Marx's Grundrisse*, Oxford: Blackwell, pp64–69.
2. Taylor I, Walton P and Young J (1973) *The New Criminology*, London: Routledge and Kegan Paul.

3. Cf Taylor, Walton and Young (1973), chapters 2 and 3.
4. Cf Taylor, Walton and Young (1973), chapter 4.
5. A new statement of this position, continuing to confuse these issues, is Coulter J (1974) 'What's Wrong with the New Criminology?', *Sociological Review*, 22: 1, 119–135.
6. Marx K (1971) *Critique of Hegel's Philosophy of Right*, ed with an introduction by J O'Malley, Cambridge: Cambridge University Press, p137.
7. Marx K 'Speech in His Defence', reprinted in D McLellan (1973) *Karl Marx: His Life and Thought*, London: Macmillan, pp215–216.

In the last extract the role of the state and of the law were subjected to criticism from a left-wing perspective. Later within left-wing thought there developed a set of ideas called left realism. This carried with it a realisation that crime is a problem and that something needs to be done about it. The perspective of the victim becomes problematic in criminological thought as a result. Lea and Young presented an agenda for what they thought should be done about crime. This was an early statement of such a position. Clearly the extract only covers part of what they had to say. For example, as well as suggesting that crime had to be taken seriously they also developed related themes, such as the need to take crime control seriously and to be realistic about policing. The extract that follows this one contains a later statement of such a position.

Lea J and Young J (1984) *What is to Be Done about Law and Order?*, pp262–265

We have attempted in this book to outline a realistic strategy about crime and policing from a socialist perspective. In doing this we have heeded the appeal made by Ian Taylor (1) to transform the vacuum in left-wing thinking on the matter. Under the impact of the Women's Movement socialists quite correctly began to realise the problems of violence against women and their sexual harassment. The struggle against fascism galvanised particularly by the Anti-Nazi League and continued by numerous monitoring groups brought home to the Labour movement the extent and severity of racist attacks. But concern about crime stopped at these points. There was a schizophrenia about crime on the left where crimes against women and immigrant groups were quite rightly an object of concern, but other types of crime were regarded as being of little interest or somehow excusable. Part of this mistake stems, as we have noted, from the belief that property offences are directed solely against the bourgeoisie and that violence against the person is carried out by amateur Robin Hoods in the course of their righteous attempt to redistribute wealth. All of this is, alas, untrue. Indeed, the irony is that precisely the same kids who break into the next-door neighbour's flat sit around the estates wearing British Movement badges and harassing Asians.

But in adopting a realistic perspective on crime we must avoid finding ourselves in the ranks of the law-and-order lobby; a correct perspective is needed, but is extremely difficult at present. There is the story of a seminar in North London where one week the students, reeling from the impact of a description of the deplorable results of imprisonment on inmates, decided to abolish prisons. But then the next week, after being, quite correctly, informed by a speaker from the Women's Movement of the viciousness of many anti-female offences, decided to rebuild them!

An important corollary of the breakdown of community is decrease in accurate knowledge about crime. In a tight-knit social setting not only is there more unanimity of communal interest and an ability to stigmatise offenders, there is also greater knowledge about what is going on and what deviance is about. As social splintering occurs there is a decrease in direct knowledge about crime, but, although the quality of information declines, the actual

quantity increases. As has been well documented, one of the key selling-points of Western mass media is its coverage of crime and social problems (2). A commercially oriented media bent on maximising sales and audience ratings supplies news coverage which, although based on a rational kernel of public fear, has few curbs on its excesses of sensationalism. The only limits on this process are good taste and the limited knowledge that journalists have of crime. Thus we come to the crux of the matter. To recapitulate, in our time, relative deprivation and hence discontent have increased. This, combined with unemployment and community breakdown, has not allowed such discontent to be channelled into political forms. Instead, the most obvious solution is that of crime. Meanwhile, community breakdown facilitates crime by drastically undermining the informal process of social control. The same forces which make for the increase in crime fuel a moral panic about crime. That is, the real fear about crime is intimately related to the moral hysteria about crime. It not only provides a rational kernel for alarm, but its genesis lies at the same source; and the mass media serve and exaggerate such public fears. The demand for crime news is great; the media reporting of crime and policing foments and exaggerates this appetite. This atmosphere carries with it a corresponding politics, but the law and order campaigns, such a familiar monopoly of the right, are an area in which the left has had very little to say except when it is on the defensive.

Thus, at precisely the time when there is the greatest need for a rational approach to crime, the greatest level of irrationality occurs. Just at the time when there is a need for a humane and realistic political intervention from the left, such a movement is lacking. Let us conclude by spelling out the basic premises of left realism in the areas of crime and the police.

Crime really is a problem

In contrast to the beliefs of left idealists, working-class crime really is a problem for the working class. This is not to deny the impact of crimes of the powerful or indeed of the perfectly legal social problems created by capitalism. Rather, left realism notes that the working class is a victim of crime from all directions; that one sort of crime tends to compound another, as one social problem does another; and furthermore, that crime is a potent symbol of the antisocial nature of capitalism and is the most immediate way in which people experience other problems, such as unemployment or competitive individualism.

Left realism examines the problem of crime seriously; it does not enter into the moral panics of the mass media or the blatant denial of left idealism. It clearly separates out moral panic from moral realism, and moral indignation from material conflict. With this in mind, it assesses the impact of crime on different victims and sections of the population. Furthermore, it carefully appraises the impact of crime, materially, politically and ideologically, on the maintenance of capitalism. For fear of street crime helps the disintegration of the working-class community and thus engenders a breakdown in the ability to fight back. It divides the poor against the poor both in a real sense and in the distorted ideological sense repeated by the mass media that the real enemy is crime and not the inequitable nature of our society.

References
1. Taylor I (1982) *Law and Order Arguments for Socialism*, London: Macmillan.
2. Cohen S and Young J (1973) *The Manufacture of News*, London.

This extract provides a recent statement of the left realist perspective. Intervention is clearly seen as being desirable, with a clear message that it is very important to ensure there is some evidence to support particular interventions and appraisal of interventions that are undertaken. There is still a desire to transform society coupled with a realisation that action is needed in the interim. Also incorporated is an application of the ideas of post-modernism which has been utilised by a number of the authors in this text.

Young J (1997) 'Left Realist Criminology', in Maguire M et al (eds), *The Oxford Handbook of Criminology*, 2nd ed, pp491–494

Being tough on crime means being tough on criminal justice

We must reject the notion of 'nothing works', the prevalent slogan of the 1980s; our problem is that we do not know exactly what works, for what offences, with regard to which offenders. The problem is both the level of explanation and the level of monitoring. We must stop asking what works and begin to look at how things work. And once we have set up interventions based on reasoned analysis rather than folk wisdom, we must halt the flood of badly maintained projects whose main theme is self congratulation. If one-tenth of the projects which claimed success were half as successful as they claim, we would have 'solved' the crime problem. Part of our predicament is that the number of scientifically monitored interventions in crime control is surprisingly small, part that such monitoring is much more difficult than is usually supposed. There is a certain innocence about such interventions. Legislators expect that laws, once enacted, will both be satisfactorily implemented and, once implemented, effect these stated aims. Hallowed police practices, such as large-scale stop and search, are maintained in all their costly arbitrariness despite the fact that research shows 'yield' to be small and the resulting alienation of innocent individuals likely to be not merely ineffective but counterproductive (see Young, 1994). The problem is naiveté, rooted in common sense notions of obviousness. There is no reason to suppose that successful intervention in the social world is less difficult than in the natural world. Yet scientific interventions in the physical world are the result of a wealth of experiment and validation whilst the actual product, whether it be a bridge, aeroplane, or motor car, is a function of incessant research and development. Common sense did not create the space shuttle: why on earth should common sense dictate intervention in the much more complicated systems of social reality? It is this conception of the social as simple which beguiles the nature of criminal justice interventions and precludes adequate monitoring of effects. Furthermore, it is facile to assume a simple linear relationship between the quantity of an intervention and the amount of effect: for example, more police equal less crime or more punishment means greater deterrence. We must be aware of the declining marginal returns of any particular intervention and of the notion of 'too much' as well as 'too little'. For example, saturating an area like Brixton with police officers may start a riot and produce crime statistics greater than or equal to those of no policing whatsoever. We must look for the particular set of circumstances which produce effective policing. To do so requires us to examine what works, and, more importantly, to discover the causal mechanisms by which successful (and unsuccessful) policing occurs (Sayer, 1984).

Such an analysis indicates that it would be false to generalise from the present combination of effective, ineffective, and downright counterproductive parts of the criminal justice system. Some things work; some things do not work, some things possibly work in certain situations and not in others. None of this is to suggest that the criminal justice system is, or feasibly could be, the dominant mode of crime control. No manner of reform and change would achieve this. What it does suggest is that the present contribution of the criminal justice system could be raised but that to do so requires a more circumspect level of design and monitoring. Research, design, evaluation: all of these processes make sense, particularly if we take into account the vast sums we spend on the criminal justice system. But such vigorous examination must be matched by a determination to change practices and shift resources when something palpably does not

work. Being tough on crime must include being tough on the criminal justice system.

For realism, the control of crime involves interventions on all levels: on the social causes of crime, on social control exercised by the community and the formal agencies, and on the situation of the victim. Social causation is given the highest priority. Formal agencies, such as the police, have a vital role, yet one which has been greatly exaggerated. It is not the 'Thin Blue Line', but the social bricks and mortar of civil society which are the major bulwark against crime. Good jobs with a discernible future, housing estates that tenants can be proud of, community facilities which enhance a sense of cohesion and belonging, a reduction in unfair income inequalities, all create a society which is more cohesive and less criminogenic.

Realist strategies: short-term gain, long-term transformation

Realism seeks both immediate intervention and long-term fundamental change. It is, first of all, a radical discipline which sets itself against an establishment criminology intent on standing in the way of change and which believes that crime is a mere hitch in the social system which can be corrected by disparate, unconnected, piecemeal measures. But it is also critical of that sort of radicalism which, believing that nothing much can be done short of fundamental transformations, focuses defensively on the inequities of the criminal justice system in a series of one-off campaigns. Vital as such activities are, it is necessary fully to enter the debate about law and order and to suggest immediate policies which will ameliorate the impact of crime and disorder upon wide sections of the population (Scharf, 1990; Hansson, 1995). This involves reform of the criminal justice system in terms of aims and effectiveness, but it is vital to note that immediate interventions in terms of social improvements may be just as effective in their impact.

Such immediate reforms cannot be seen as separate from the problem of long-term social change (Cohen, 1990). Indeed, such measures improve the morale of the community and thus facilitate the capacity for change. Moreover, they are unlikely to be successful if not couched in terms of long-term goals of social justice (Matthews, 1988; Lowman, 1992; Loader, 1997). For crime is about social justice gone wrong. Its solution is not order divorced from justice, but an order that springs out of a just society. We live in an era where there has been a widening division between those in secure employment and those who are insecure, a chasm between those in work and those who are structurally unemployed. The days of the inclusive society of full employment and secure careers are over. The meritocratic racetrack on which all are supposed to run and gain prizes proportionate to our effort has become more and more exposed for what it always was, a dream. The tracks separate out to a fast lane and a slow lane, with a substantial section of the population allocated to the role of spectators (the losers) watching the glittering prizes doled out to the successful (the winners). Relative deprivation abounds, matched by a rise in economic precariousness and insecurity. A rampant individualism, itself a spin-off of market values, adds to this and creates a society which is crimogenic, and self-destructive. Crime becomes a normality of life, incivilities part of the fabric of everyday existence. The problems are most pressing amongst the growing body of people excluded from full citizenship, but they occur at all reaches of society and indeed within the family, the basic building block of liberal democracy. The motor of disorder thus lies at the heart of the system in the inequalities of merit and reward, which grow more evident as we enter the twenty-first century, and in the values of individualism which break down the acceptance of the status quo which was necessary for it to function smoothly.

Establishment criminology eschews all talk of social injustice. Its first response is actuarial, its second nostalgic. Most immediately there arises a criminology which is about the management of risk (Feeley and Simon, 1994; van Swaaningen, 1997; Young, 1994).

It is an actuarialism where the calculating criminal confronts the calculating public: the risk maker meets the risk taker, with no element of justice, indeed moral judgement, in the picture. As crime becomes a normal part of everyday life and the trouble-free management of the growing imprisoned population becomes more and more necessary, the task of the administrative criminologist becomes that of designing barriers, evaluating surveillance, and calculating the risk of disturbance – the protection of property, public space, and the management of prisons. A flourishing evaluation industry develops much of which is of little scientific validity, with few bothering to ask whether all the cost is worth it to maintain a system which is at basis fundamentally flawed. Establishment criminology evokes the unthinking order of the control theorists where basic values are drilled into the child from infancy, and morality is 'caught not taught' (Hirschi and Gottfredson, 1995). It attempts to revive the strong family (itself a prime site of crime and violence) where authority is unquestioned, and to rekindle a community which prioritises order and certainty over justice and equality (Etzioni, 1993). These are lost causes: they are attempts to bolt nostalgia onto the fast changing world in which we find ourselves. Such nostalgia has, of course, attractions to politicians of both left and right (indeed their policies become increasingly indistinguishable) but there is no going back. For, as Marshall Berman evocatively puts it, 'our past, whatever it was, was a past in the process of disintegration; we yearn to grasp it, but it is baseless and elusive; we look back for something solid to lean on, only to find ourselves embracing ghosts' (1983: 333). Any realism worthy of its name must go with the rapid changes which late modernity brings upon us (Hofman, 1993; Lippens, 1994). We must argue for work, but we must not deceive ourselves that it will support the graduation-to-grave careers of yesteryear. We must argue for strong support for child rearing, but take note that the nuclear family for life is becoming a dwindling option. We must build strong communities but not expect them to resemble the soap operas we so avidly watch. If we are to construct a social democracy for the next century, we must use new building blocks. Work, family, and the community will all be transformed, yet the demand for citizenship and justice will be even greater. Only in this direction can we realistically talk of a programme which reduces crime and moves towards a social order which will be in the interests of the majority.

Bibliography

Berman M (1983) *All that is Solid Melts into Air*, London: Verso.

Etzioni A (1993) *The Spirit of Community*, New York: Crown Publishers.

Feeley M and Simon J (1994) 'Acturial Justice: The Emerging New Criminal Law', in D Nelken (ed), *The Futures of Criminology*, London: Sage.

Hansson D (1995) 'Agenda-ing Agenda: Feminism and the Engendering of Academic Criminology in South Africa', in N Rafter and F Heidensohn (eds), *International Feminist Perspectives in Criminology*, 43, Milton Keynes: Open University Press.

Hofman H (1993) 'Some Stories of Crime Prevention', paper given to the Common Study Programme in Criminal Justice and Critical Criminology, University of Gent, 2 November.

Lippens R (1994) 'Critical Criminologies and the Reconstruction of Utopia, Some Residual Thoughts from the Good Old Days', Erasmus Common Study Programme in Criminal Justice and Critical Criminology, University of Bari.

Loader I (1997) 'Criminology and the Public Sphere: Arguments for Utopian Realism', in P Walton and J Young (eds), *The New Criminology Revisited*, London: Macmillan.

Lowman J (1992) 'Rediscovering Crime', in J Young and R Mattthews (eds), *Rethinking Criminology*, London: Sage.

Matthews R (1988) 'Review of Confronting Crime', *Contemporary Crisis*, 12: 81–83.

Sayer A (1984) *Method in Social Science: a Realist Approach*, London: Hutchinson.

Scharf W (1990) 'The Resurgence of Urban street Gangs', in D Hansson and D Van Zyl Smit (eds), *Towards Justice? Crime and State Control in South Africa*, Cape Town: Oxford University Press.

Von Swaaningen R (1997) *Critical Criminology: Visions from Europe*, London: Sage.

Young J (1994) *Policing the Streets*, London: London Borough of Islington.

8 Female Crime and Feminist Criminology

The main message that the criminal statistics deliver is that a much higher proportion of males than females become subjects of the criminal justice process.

Home Office (2001) *Criminal Statistics 1999*

INDICTABLE OFFENCES IN 1999 (THOUSANDS)

Males

	All ages	10–14	15–17	18–20	21 and over
Cautioned	126.1	22.0	28.7	22.7	52.7
Found Guilty	291.7	8.9	35.1	52.6	195.0
Total	417.8	30.9	63.8	75.2	247.7

Females

	All ages	10–14	15–17	18–20	21 and over
Cautioned	44.5	9.9	9.3	5.7	19.6
Found Guilty	49.0	1.4	5.2	7.6	34.7
Total	93.5	11.3	14.5	13.3	54.3

One of the issues for researchers is the position of women in the criminal justice system. The data in this report relates to 1999. This publication brings together the key results from recent research and statistics that focus on the treatment of women by the criminal justice system.

Home Office (2000) *Statistics on Women and the Criminal Justice System*

Criminal statistics show that, in 1999, only 17 per cent of known offenders were women. Over the age of 17, male offenders outnumber female offenders by a ratio of around three to one. Women 'grow out of crime' – they are most likely to desist from offending in their late teens. The peak age of reported offending for girls was 14. Fifteen per cent of those arrested are women but the proportion is higher for fraud and forgery (28 per cent) and theft and handling (21 per cent). Research suggests that following arrest, women are more likely than men to be cautioned and are less likely to have no further action taken or be charged. This partly reflects the fact that women are more likely than men to admit their offences and to be arrested for less serious offences. According to official statistics, female offenders are also more likely to be cautioned for indictable offences.

Although women are less likely than men to be remanded in custody or committed for trial, this mainly reflects differences in offending history and type of offence. Women on remand make up nearly a quarter of the female prison population. Women remanded in custody spend less time in custody than men. In relation to sentencing, women are more likely than men to be discharged or given a community sentence for indictable offences and are less likely to be fined or sentenced to custody. The top seven offences for women sentenced to custody in 1999 were: theft from shops (2,100 women sentenced to custody), fraud (470), wounding (440), production, supply and possession with intent to supply a class A controlled drug (360), summary motoring (350), handling stolen goods (350) and burglary (340). In terms of community penalties, women accounted for 12 per cent of those supervised by the Probation Service in 1998. Women were less likely than men starting community orders to have previous convictions to have served a custodial sentence.

There were, on average, 3,250 women in prison in 1999. They made up only 5 per cent of the total prison population. Between 1993 and 1999 the average population of women in prison rose by over 100 per cent as against 43 per cent for men. Theft and handling accounted for 39 per cent of sentenced receptions of women in 1999, drug offences for 14 per cent and violence against the person for 12

per cent. Among the population of sentenced female offenders, the main offence groups are drug offences (37 per cent at June 1999), violence against the person (18 per cent) and theft and handling (17 per cent). Over 200 women were sent to prison for fine default in 1999 but as the average stay is only five days, the average number of fine defaulters in the prison population was just five. In mid-1999, ethnic minority groups made up 25 per cent of the female prison population compared to 18 per cent of the male prison population. An estimated 55 per cent of all women in prison have a child under 16 and over a third of mothers in prison have a child under five. An estimated 20 per cent of women in prison had experienced some time in care. Over 40 per cent of sentenced women prisoners and over 50 per cent of women on remand have reported being dependent on drugs in the year before coming to prison. A recent healthcare assessment of prisoners found women reported more health problems and visited doctors more often than their counterparts in the general population. In 1999–2000, female prisons provided inmates, on average, with more time out of their cells and on education and skills training. Female prisoners have a higher rate of offending against prison discipline than men. A survey of released female prisoners found only 25 per cent were in employment when interviewed five to nine months after discharge.

In relation to data on victimology, 3.3 per cent of adult women and 5.3 per cent of adult men had been the victim of at least one violent crime in 1999. Just under 40 per cent of violent incidents against women were domestic; 33 per cent of homicide victims in 1998/99 were female. One third of women homicide victims, compared with only 8 per cent of men, were killed by a current or former partner. According to a study of rapes reported in 1996, nearly 90 per cent were committed by acquaintances or intimates. Just 9 per cent of suspects charged with rape offences were convicted of rape or attempted rape, mainly due to problems with evidence. Women are more likely to be stalked (defined as persistent and unwanted attention) than men. The risk is greater for younger women. An evaluation of the Protection from Harassment Act revealed that stalking is most likely to be perpetrated on someone known to the offender – usually an ex-partner. Figures suggest that, throughout the criminal justice system, women are well represented as practitioners, though not in senior management positions. Women practitioners make up more than 50 per cent of probation officers, CPS lawyers, magistrates' and Crown Court staff as well as Home Office, Forensic Science Service and CICA staff. They are underrepresented in the police, as judges, at the bar and as prison officers.

Earlier in the text you were offered a general account of Lombroso's biological determinism. This item offers a similar form of thinking in the context of female criminality. The emphasis on biology has lasted much longer, and been more intense, in relation to the study of female crime than has been the case in relation to male criminality. As odd as these ideas might seem it is important to note that the authors did not claim that all female criminals could be characterised in terms of biological factors.

Lombroso C and Ferrero W (1895) *The Female Offender*, pp88–90, 103–104, 147, 187, 192

Among the most ridiculous of the prohibitions obtaining in Italy, or rather in the Italian bureaucracy, which is certainly not the first in Europe, is the absolute impossibility of measuring, studying, or photographing the worst criminals once they have been condemned. So long as there is a presumption of innocence, so long as these persons are only suspected or accused, one can discredit them in every way, and hold them up to publicity by recording their answers to their judges. But once it is admitted beyond question that they are reprobates, once the prison doors have closed for good upon them – oh, then they become

sacred; and woe to him who touches, woe to him who studies them! Consumptive patients, pregnant women, may be manipulated, even to their hurt, by thousands of students for the good of science; but criminals – Heaven forfend!

When one of the writers wished to publish photographs of male criminals in his 'Uomo Delinquente', he was driven to the German prison 'album'; and the difficulties thrown in his way by the Italian authorities were doubled in the case of female offenders and prostitutes, whose sense of shame it was considered necessary to respect in every way.

In Russian prisons Madame Tarnowsky was afforded every facility, and after making a complete study of the body and mind of the delinquents, she forwarded us their photographs.

Female criminals

We will first take five homicides, of whom the two first have the true type of their class.

The first, aged 40, killed her husband with reiterated blows of a hatchet, while he was skimming the milk, then threw his body into a recess under the stairs, and during the night fled with the family money and her own trinkets. She was arrested a week later and confessed her crime. This woman was remarkable for the asymmetry of her face; her nose was hollowed out, her ears projecting, her brows more fully developed than is usual in a woman, her jaw enormous with a lemurian appendix.

No 2, aged 60. Was constantly ill-treated by her husband, whom she finally joined with her son in strangling, hanging him afterwards so as to favour the idea of suicide.

Here again we have asymmetry of the face, breadth of jaw, enormous frontal sinuses, numerous wrinkles, a hollowed-out nose, a very thin upper lip, with deepset eyes wide apart, and wild in expression.

No 3, aged 21. Was married against her will, ill-treated by her husband, whom she killed, after a night altercation, with a hatchet while he slept.

In her we find only a demi-type. Her ears stand out, she has big jaws and cheek-bones, and very black hair, besides other anomalies which do not show in the photograph, such as gigantic canine teeth and dwarf incisors.

No 4, aged 44. Strangled her husband by agreement with her lover, and threw him into a ditch. She denied her crime. Hollowed-out nose, black hair, deep-set eyes, big jaw. Demi-type.

No 5, aged 50. A peasant. She killed her brother at supper, so as to inherit from him. She denied her guilt persistently. Was condemned, together with her hired accomplices, to 20 years penal servitude. She had black hair, grey eyes, diasthema of the teeth, a cleft palate, precocious and profound wrinkles, thin lips, and a crooked face. Demi-type.

The criminal type in women and its atavistic origin

More instructive than a mere analytical enumeration of the characteristics of degeneration is a synthesis of the different features peculiar to the female criminal type.

We call a complete type one wherein exist four or more of the characteristics of degeneration; a half type that which contains at least three of these; and no type a countenance possessing only one or two anomalies or none.

Out of the female delinquents examined 52 were Piedmontese in the prison of Turin, and 234 in the Female House of Correction were natives of different Italian provinces, especially from the South. In these, consequently, we set aside all special characteristics belonging to the ethnological type of the different regions, such as the brachycephali of the Piedmontese and the dolichocephali of the Sardinians.

We studied also from the point of view of type the 150 prostitutes whom we had previously examined for their several features; as well as another 100 from Moscow whose photographs Madame Tarnowsky sent us.

And we classified under the same heads the various data furnished by Marro, by Grimaldi, and by Madame Tarnowsky, so as to compare the results obtained by all three. ...

The subjects we examined in the House of Correction resemble those we saw in prison; nor do our results differ much from the averages of the other observers, allowance being made for the personal equation or individual divergences in the mode of regarding the same peculiarity.

The results of the examination may be thus summarised:

1. The rarity of a criminal type in the female as compared with the male delinquent. In our homogeneous group (286) the proportion is 14 per cent, rising, when all other observations are taken into account, to 18 per cent, a figure lower almost by one half than the average in the male born criminal, namely, 31 per cent. In normal women this same type is only present in 2 per cent. All observers agree as to the rarity of the criminal type. Marro records the absence of the type in 58.7 per cent, Madame Tarnowsky in 55 per cent, we found it wanting in 55.9 per cent of the cases in the House of Correction, and in 55.8 of those in prison; so that altogether the criminal type results as wanting in 57.5 per cent of delinquents.
   …

The born criminal

The analogy between the anthropology and psychology of the female criminal is perfect.

Just as in the mass of female criminals possessing few or unimportant characteristics of degeneration, we find a group in whom these features are almost more marked and more numerous than in males, so while the majority of female delinquents are led into crime either by the suggestion of a third person or by irresistible temptation, and are not entirely deficient in the moral sense, there is yet to be found among them a small proportion whose criminal propensities are more intense and more perverse than those of their male prototypes.

'No possible punishments', wrote Corrado Celto an author of the fifteenth century, 'can deter women from heaping up crime upon crime. Their perversity of mind is more fertile in new crimes than the imagination of a judge in new punishments.'

'Feminine criminality', writes Rykere, 'is more cynical, more depraved, and more terrible than the criminality of the male.'

'Rarely is a woman wicked, but when she is she surpasses the man' (Italian Proverb). ...

Synthesis

In general the moral physiognomy of the born female criminal approximates strongly to that of the male. The atavistic diminution of secondary sexual characters which is to be observed in the anthropology of the subject, shows itself once again in the psychology of the female criminal, who is excessively erotic, weak in maternal feeling, inclined to dissipation, astute and audacious, and dominates weaker beings sometimes by suggestion, at others by muscular force; while her love of violent exercise, her vices, and even her dress, increase her resemblance to the sterner sex. Added to these virile characteristics are often the worst qualities of woman: namely, an excessive desire for revenge, cunning, cruelty, love of dress, and untruthfulness, forming a combination of evil tendencies which often results in a type of extraordinary wickedness.

Occasional criminals

The born offender is more completely and intensely depraved than any other, but the case is quite different with the occasional criminals who form the large majority of female delinquents. In them perversity and vice are of a milder form, and there is no want of the higher virtues of the sex, such as chastity and maternal love.

1. Physical characteristics. The first thing to be observed is the absence of any characteristics or features denoting degeneration. As we saw already 54 per cent of female offenders are absolutely normal in these respects, and even as regards the special senses they show no peculiarity, 15 per cent having fineness of taste, and 6 per cent fineness of smell.

2. Moral character. The same may be said of

their moral equipment. Guillot unconsciously described the occasional criminal exactly when recording his observations on female prisoners, in the following words: 'The guilty woman, with a few exceptions in which all vices are combined, is more easily moved to penitence to men, recovers the lost ground more quickly, and relapses into crime more frequently.'

It was noted in relation to the previous item that the emphasis on biology has lasted much longer, and been more intense, in relation to the study of female crime than has been the case in relation to male criminality. This extract from Pollak offers proof of this. It is a marvellous example of women being treated as objects who are largely understandable through their sexual characteristics. Other disciplines were doing rather better, for example by 1969 spacecraft had been developed sufficiently to permit a successful moon landing.

Pollak O (1950) *The Criminality of Women*[1], pp157–161

Causative factors in female crime

Thus alerted by the comparatively high criminal liabilities of women in the brackets of childbearing age and of married women independent of age, we turned to an investigation of the biological and social factors which seem to have a causative influence on female crime. Throughout the investigation of these two types of factors, we had to keep in mind that the human being is first a biological organism, but one who can never be studied outside a social environment. The individual being born into society cannot be thought of as separated from it.

The correlation between the incidence of female crime and the period of childbearing age indicated from the start that the biological phenomena which characterise this age period in women deserve our attention. Actually

---

[1] Copyright © 1977 O Pollak.

from this angle, menstruation, pregnancy, and the menopause have to be considered of central research interest in this respect. The student of female criminality cannot afford to overlook the generally known and recognised fact that these generative phases are frequently accompanied by psychological disturbances which may upset the need and satisfaction balance of the individual or weaken her internal inhibitions, and thus become causative factors in female crime. Particularly because of the social meaning attached to them in our culture, the generative phases of women are bound to present many stumbling blocks for the law-abiding behaviour of women. Menstruation with its appearance of injury must confirm feelings of guilt which individuals may have about sex activities which they have learned to consider as forbidden. As a symbol of womanhood, it must also, because of its recurrent nature, aggravate any feeling of irritation and protest which women may have regarding their sex in a society in which women have had, and still have, to submit to social inequality with men. In both instances, it must lead to a disturbance of the emotional balance of the individual and thus become potentially crime promoting. Pregnancy in a culture which frowns upon illegitimacy and fosters in large sectors of society limitation in the number of children or even childlessness must become a source of irritation, anxiety, and emotional upheaval in many instances. The menopause in a society which makes romance and emotional gratification the supreme value in a monogamous marriage system must be experienced, at least by married women, frequently as a threat to the basis of their emotional security if not to their general marital existence. In view of these cultural implications of the generative phases and their psychological consequences, it is difficult to understand why the existing literature contains so little discussion of their possible crime-promoting influence. Only the sex taboos which dominate our culture seem to furnish an explanation of this phenomenon. Still, we have been able to find some statistical

corroboration which supports the foregoing analysis. Thefts, particularly shoplifting, arson, homicide, and resistance against public officials seem to show a significant correlation between the menstruation of the offender and the time of the offence. The turmoil of the onset of menstruation and the puberty of girls appears to express itself in the relatively high frequency of false accusations and – where cultural opportunities permit – of incendiarism. Pregnancy in its turn is a crime-promoting influence with regard to attacks against the life of the foetus and the newborn. The menopause finally seems to bring about a distinct increase in crime, especially in offences resulting from irritability such as arson, breaches of the peace, perjury, and insults.

In the social sphere proper, we have found two groups of factors which seem to be of specific crime-promoting influence upon women. In the first group belong the double standard of our sex morality with its discrimination against women, our modern sales promotion methods in the retail trades with their concentration on the female shopper, and the specific female occupation of domestic employment with its many irritations and frustrations. In the second group belong the special opportunities which the traditional cultural roles of women in our society offer for the commission of crimes.

The general sex repression which characterises our culture is particularly strict with regard to women. Violations of sex morality meet with much stronger disapproval if they are committed by women than if they are committed by men. This double standard adds therefore to the burden of frustration of the sex urge, the burden of discrimination. It is only natural that women should protest against the situation, and they seem to do so in various ways. On the surface they appear to demand only the equal enforcement of our sex morality for the members of both sexes. More deeply, however, they seek other expressions of this protest, which frequently seem to lead them into crime. The vicarious flights into fantasy through which unmarried women seek to compensate for their sex repression and sex discrimination are well known, but it is not sufficiently recognised how often these fantasy experiences may lead them into false accusation with sexual content. Only too seldom do our law-enforcement officers realise how often the accusation of an unmarried woman against a man may indicate an experience which she consciously fears and abhors but unconsciously desires, and how often the mental conflict between desire and social restraint may lead her into false accusations of a sexual character and thus to perjury. On the other hand, married women seem to resort more frequently to overt protests against the double standard by criminal attacks against errant husbands, or if they do not dare to do so, against scapegoats in the persons of their children or their neighbors. This seems to explain why women who have committed a crime against the person of their husband or lover do not feel morally guilty although they recognise that their behaviour is technically a violation of the law. From their own point of view, they consider themselves as administrators of a higher justice, a mechanism which is always present in actions motivated by a desire for protest and revenge.

Next to the double standard, modern sales techniques with their exploitation of the female role of shopper create desires which may lead women into crime more frequently than they do men. With almost uncanny ingenuity the display of the merchandise is so organised that visual temptations are put in one's way before one can reach the objects originally intended for purchase. Of course, men are as much impressed and motivated into such unintended purchases as are women, but women shop more frequently and more regularly than do men. The former are, therefore, more exposed to this creation of desire for goods which may not be needed or at least may not be within their financial reach.

Revenge desires are created by the female occupation of domestic service. This occupation exposes many women to the frustration of

a daily experience of difference between their own standard of living and the living standards of their employers. Such a situation exists in hardly any other line of work. To see what other people have, and what she herself does not have, can almost be called the essential job experience of the domestic servant. In our time of class antagonism and in our country of race antagonism in which domestic workers are frequently coloured or at least members of another ethnic group than their employers, the situation is psychologically mined. Logically, it must lead to a tremendous amount of pent-up resentment which cannot help but create a desire for aggressive compensation.

Our culture, however, not only creates all these specific frustrations for women but also surrounds them with opportunities to respond to them by unlawful behaviour. Each of the social roles which women perform in our culture furnishes such opportunities. Marriage in itself delivers a whole array of possible objects of attack for crimes against the person, practically defenceless into the hands of the potential woman offender. Compared with the ease with which the preparer of meals, the child-rearer, and the nurse of the sick can direct an attack against physical well-being or life, the task of the male killer in our society is difficult indeed. Compared with the lack of economic restraint which the average housewife enjoys in our society, the pressures which force the wage earner into complying behaviour are overwhelming. It need not surprise, therefore, that married women participate to a higher degree in crime, and particularly crimes against the person, than do single women.

Similarly, the accessibility of objects of theft to the woman offender who either is or poses as a shopper or domestic must appear almost as the criminal's dream to our male burglars and robbers who have to struggle with the formidable array of defence mechanisms which our technological advances have put in their way.

In summary, then, we are forced into the

conclusion that the amount of female crime has been greatly underestimated by traditional opinion. At least in our culture, women are particularly protected against the detection of criminal behaviour on the one hand and exposed to a wealth of irritations, temptations, and opportunities which may lead them to criminal behaviour on the other. Therefore, meaningful differentials between male and female crime must be looked for, not in any appreciable and validly demonstrable difference in the crime volume, but in the ways in which women commit their crimes and in the causes of their criminal behaviour. They must be looked for in the interplay between biological and cultural determinants which distinguishes this behaviour from that of man. In short, the criminality of women reflects their biological nature in a given cultural setting.

This work by Adler is very different to the two previous extracts with the emphasis here being on social rather than sexual or biological factors. Adler's work is an example of the 'female liberation causes crime' hypothesis. The suggestion is that increased female liberation has led to an increase in both the proportion of women committing crimes and the range of crimes that women commit. It is an early example of feminist thought being applied to the subject of female criminality. The extract that follows this one provides a later view and contains material that suggests that the 'liberation causes crime' hypothesis should be challenged.

Adler F (1975) *Sisters in Crime*, pp25–30

In the early sixties, civil rights actions swirled across the country with the fervour of a revitalisation movement, challenging Americans to reaffirm their commitment to equality before the law, and redefining that equality to include those previously alienated by colour or age or sex. Man's characteristic tendency to assign other people – whether they were Asians, blacks, young, poor or women – to a subhuman status which barred them from equal protection under law was the real issue of the civil-rights movement, and women were now ready to recognise their stake in it. Why this moment was propitious for recognition is difficult to say. The theme of women as a suppressed social class had been carefully documented in 1953 by Simone de Beauvoir in her book *The Second Sex*, but it failed to develop as a serious national concern until the mid-sixties. America of the mid-sixties was rife with disillusionment and ripe for change. We were fighting what Omar Bradley called 'the wrong war at the wrong place at the wrong time, and with the wrong enemy' – liberals were adding, 'for the wrong reason'. In this climate of disillusionment with leadership that was white, male and over thirty, change was inevitable, and the seeds of liberation rooted in fertile soil. By the decade's end, large numbers of American women in all walks of life had begun to see themselves as Betty Firedan had portrayed them in *The Feminine Mystique*: a systematically and subtly suppressed majority whose real security lay in the strength of their own right arm, and whose time of delivery had arrived.

Many of these believers gravitated to organisations such as NOW, the National Organisation for Women, which has a current membership of 18,000 in 255 chapters in 48 states (1). The women's liberation movement suffered several distortions in the press and, at the same time, added a few bruises to its own image via the actions of a few of its more outspoken members. Hence, 'women's lib' came to designate – perhaps for the majority of Americans – organised groups of women who were primarily shrill-voiced witches with clenched fists and slovenly, unloosed breasts. Not so today.

There was, and is, more to women's lib. Much more. And the portrait is changing. The organisation and it goals are becoming separated from its rights which is perhaps best described as the 'new feminism'. The new feminism is not an organised movement, it does not hold meetings or press conferences. It is an all-pervasive consciousness which has permeated to virtually every level of woman-hood in America.

The new feminism pertains to the women who may deny any sympathy for the for-malised action, but who have recently secured their first job since marriage or decided to go back to school. It applies to the women who staunchly defend their 'right to be feminine', and their right to define 'feminine' as a variety of human rather than as a complement of mas-culine. They are standing up and speaking without apology at parent-teacher meetings, they are organising demonstrations, walking picket lines, and influencing decisions at all levels of their community. It includes the nuns who are asking for rights more closely aligned with the rights which priests enjoy, and the housewives who have come to expect their husbands to share more of the duties of the home. It also means sexually honest women who expect the same orgasmic satisfaction as men, and who are requiring that men do some-thing about it. And most relevant to our subject, it describes the women who have con-cluded that prostitution and shoplifting are not their style: embezzlement, robbery, and assault are more congenial to their self image.

'You wouldn't catch me doing no boost-ing', said one female inmate in New York who was somewhat offended by the inference that she might have been a shoplifter. The woman – in her late twenties – found the idea of shoplifting or 'boosting' undignified. She did not like 'small stuff'. Records say she was involved in robbery of a large movie-theatre ticket office. Other inmates privately related that the same woman was nearly killed in recent underworld warfare which broke out when she was thought to have 'ripped off' a local heroin dealer for a few thousand dollars worth of his product. The others spoke of her escapades with envy and obvious admiration.

The entrance of women into the major leagues of crime underscores the point that the incidence and kinds of crime are more closely associated with social then sexual factors. This is so for at least three reasons. First, while cupidity may be universal, ability and oppor-tunity are less evenly distributed. Housewives might pilfer from the supermarket while doing the grocery shopping, but could not embezzle from a corporation unless they work out of the executive office. Secondly, since a crime is a transgression as socially defined by the group in power, authorities are prone to overlook upper-class practices and lean a bit too heavily on the lower class. 'The law', declared Anatole France, 'forbids the rich as well as the poor from sleeping under bridges and stealing bread in the marketplace.' Arrests for prostitution are a pertinent example. If sex on the open market is an illegal commodity, then penalties should fall on the buyer as well as the seller, particularly if it can be established that the buyer understood the nature of the transaction and was a material participant. But such is not the case. While prostitution contin-ues to be a crime for which significant number of women are arrested every year, the number of males arrested for consorting with prosti-tutes is so small that it does not even merit a special category in the Uniform Crime reports. The third reason why kinds of crime are more closely linked with social roles then sex has to do with mental sets. According to the group-system hypothesis (2), behaviour is directed by a largely conscious desire to please one's own significant groups, and by a predominantly unconscious tendency to conform to an early ingrained set of attitudes. So decisive is this set for the way we think and feel and act that few people breach its bound-aries, even in imagination, even in deviance. We go crazy and we go criminal along the well-worn paths that our 'mazeway' has con-structed for us. Running amuck is not some-thing that Bostonians do, nor do sex-kittens rob banks – they peddle their bodies as untold generations of sex-kittens before them have done. How else can we understand the female (or, for that matter, male) offender except in the context of her social role? The mother becomes the child-beater, the shopper the shoplifter, and the sex-object the prostitute.

Adolescent girls have a particularly difficult task because they are attempting to negotiate puberty with nowhere near the spatial and sexual freedom of males. That they often deviate outside their narrow confines is understandable.

In the emergence of women as a socially rising group, we are witnessing an interesting phenomenon which has implication for other upwardly mobile groups. As they become more visible in positions of prestige and power, they receive more attention from the media, and are thus further bolstered in their rising achievement. Old mental sets of devaluation and self-contempt gradually yield to new ones of pride, and sometimes an overcompensating arrogance. Black shifts from denigration to beautiful. Sexually active bachelor women are no longer 'ruined' but 'free' or, at the very least, 'the ruined Maid', as Thomas Hardy described her, exacts no small tribute of envy from the raw country sister. How quaint seem the fallen women of literature – the Charlotte Temples and Hester Prynnes and Catherine Barkleys – who earned red letters or died in childbirth to mark well for generations of women the evils of extramarital sex. They are quaint because women are increasingly imitating men's attitude toward sex rather than submitting to one he designed for her, and they are quaint because sex is no longer the best road out of the female ghetto. In her education, in her jobs, and in her crimes she has found much faster routes to travel. The journey, relatively speaking, has just begun. While the rate of increase of major crimes for women is surpassing that for males, the data (3) still provides some justification for the epithet 'fair sex' in that men continue to commit the majority of crimes, and that the highest proportion of females are still arrested for larceny, primarily shoplifting (4).

However, even here a comparison of figures for 1960 and 1972 shows an unmistakable across the board trend. Females are cutting themselves in for a bigger piece of the pie in every category but murder and, in a few – like the subtotal for major crimes, forgery

and counterfeiting, and fraud and embezzlement – that piece is 80 to 100 per cent bigger than it had been 12 years before.

In summary, what we have described is a gradual but accelerating social revolution in which women are closing many of the gaps, social and criminal, that have separated them from men. The closer they get, the more alike they look and act. This is not to suggest that there are no inherent differences. Differences do exist and will be elaborated later in this book, but it seems clear that those differences are not of prime importance in understanding female criminality. The simplest and most accurate way to grasp the essence of women's changing patterns is to discard dated notions of femininity. That is a role that fewer and fewer women are willing to play. In the final analysis, women criminals are human beings who have basic needs and abilities and opportunities. Over the years these needs have not changed, nor will they. But women's abilities and opportunities have multiplied, resulting in a kaleidoscope of changing patterns whose final configuration will be fateful for all of us.

References
1. For a history of the National Organisation for Women, see Jo Freeman (1973) 'The Origins of the Women's Liberation Movement', *American Journal of Sociology*, 78: 792–811.
2. Herbert M Adler, MD, and Van Buren O Hammett, MD (1973) 'Crisis, Conversion and Cult Formation: an Examination of a Common Psychological Sequence', *American Journal of Psychiatry*, 138:861–864; and Herbert M Adler, MD, and Van Muren O Hammett, MD (1973) 'The Doctor-Patient Relationship Revisited', *Annals of Internal Medicine*, 78: 595–598.
3. Figures calculated from data of Uniform Crime Reports, United States Department of Justice (1972) Washington, DC: US Government Printing Office, p124.
4. For a comprehensive discussion of shoplifting, see Mary Owen Cameron

(1964) *The Booster and the Snitch*, New York: The Free Press. See also, T C N Gibbens and Joyce Prince (1962) *Shoplifting*, London: The Institute for the Study and Treatment of Delinquency.

Heidensohn offers an update of a whole range of ideas in relation to gender and crime. She also makes it clear how these ideas have been applied to the treatment of women within the criminal justice system. These latter issues are picked up in the final two extracts in this chapter.

Heidensohn F (1997) 'Gender and Crime', in Maguire M et al (eds), *The Oxford Handbook of Criminology*, 2nd ed, pp784–791

Theorising women and crime

One summary of work in feminist criminology divided its conceptual concerns into the *gender gap* and the *generalisability* problem. Some theorists have attempted to deal with these issues; however, the most significant work of feminist theorists is to be found *in explanations of female criminality*. Partly however, because of problems in developing such approaches and also because of wider difficulties and developments there is another, and growing, category of criminological *feminist sceptics* who proffer no answers but ask further and profounder questions.

The gender gap and generalisability

We have already noted the main contributors to theories about the gender gap: the so-called 'liberation causes crime' theorists (Adler, 1975; Simon, 1975) and the consequent debates about their views. This approach is one of the few perspectives on female crime to have been subjected to thorough empirical testing, to have been disproved (Box, 1983; Box and Hale, 1983; Austin, 1981; Smart, 1979; Steffensmeier, 1980). Strictly speaking the 'liberation hypothesis' was not a single coherent theory; indeed Adler and Simon

differ in key aspects of their approaches, although both see increased equality for women as a key variable in causing their patterns of criminal behaviour.

However, Adler contended that the battle to emancipate women had been won by the mid-1970s, and thus male and female behaviour were converging, with females resembling males more and more by becoming aggressive and violent. Simon, on the other hand, suggested an opposite situation and outcome. Women's opportunities had not yet expanded very much; when they did so, their violence would diminish and their property crimes increase with their growing opportunities. Both approaches fail when tested because they do not fit statistical trends, because criminal women are amongst those least likely to be affected by feminism (and those most affected by it, middle-class white women, are the least likely to be criminal), and because criminal women tend to score highly on 'femininity' scores whereas 'masculine' scoring women are less delinquent (Naffine, 1987). These ideas are not supported, then, by the evidence. 'Yet ironically it is around this theme that a considerable debate has focused, putting female criminality into mainstream discussion' (Heidensohn, 1989: 95).

Much of the initial critique of criminology's failure to address the issues of gender and of women was directed at the limits of conventional theories. They could not for the most part account for the gender gap and broke down when applied to women as well as men, usually because they overpredicted female crime. Some critics went on to suggest that some criminological theories could be applied to women with success if only they were developed or modified (Leonard, 1982; Morris, 1987). Indeed this was a criticism Greenwood (1980) made of feminist criminologists: that they merely wished to add women back in. In practice it is hard to find examples of this, although Smith and Paternoster (1987) have suggested that 'gender-neutral' theories of delinquency should be developed and try to do this in a study of marijuana use. They take factors from classic theories of male delinquency and conclude 'factors that influence participation decisions and the frequency of marijuana use are similar for males and females' (1987: 156).

This does not, however, explain the differences in recorded or self reported narcotic offences. Nor does it explain why many other researchers find gender specific theories important in just such areas (Auld et al, 1986; Rosenbaum, 1981).

Gender theories

In the early days of work on women Carol Smart issued a warning: 'In the movement towards developing a feminist perspective a critique of sexism is vital, but in itself a critique alone cannot constitute a new theoretical approach. ... In particular more research is needed in the area of women and crime' (1977: 183). This has in fact turned out to be the agenda for most of those who have contributed to this field. Once more it will be helpful to adopt a taxonomy within which we can group the work we are reviewing. This would include studies of patriarchy, of social and economic marginalisation, of control, and finally there is a group of feminosceptics who have focused particularly on epistemological issues.

Patriarchy

Patriarchy is simply the rule of fathers, but defining it and using it as a concept has not proved at all simple for feminists, who have none the less used it frequently. Many writers have tried to define and refine it (Mitchell and Oakley, 1986; Walby, 1989) and subjected it to rigorous criticisms (Pollert, 1996). Quite often it appears to signify the rule of men or the power of men, and especially the use of these against women. On the whole patriarchy, or male power, are not used very much as direct explanations of female crime. The concept is employed nevertheless in at least two important ways: to explain women's experience of the criminal justice system, and

the gendered nature of much criminal victimisation, especially from violence and abuse within the home.

Indeed, it is from concern about women's treatment as victims in the processes of the criminal justice system and their experience of 'family law' that much of the evidence comes which has led, as Dobash and Dobash put it, to 'some feminist activists and scholars (arguing) that it is impossible to use the law and legal apparatus to confront patriarchal domination and oppression when the language and procedures of these social processes and institutions are saturated with patriarchal beliefs and structures' (1992: 147). Victims and victimisation are topics covered fully elsewhere in this volume. It is only the elision of the issues which I wish to discuss here. Susan Edwards, whose earlier work did emphasise sexist aspects of criminal justice (1984 and 1989) puts this view forcefully:

'A consideration of patriarchy has been central to an understanding of sex/gender division within the law ... the criminal justice process ... and policing ... it is the precise juncture of bourgeois and male interest which constitutes the corner-stone of women's experience and corresponding oppression. In everyday experience women's need for protection, women's voice as victims of crime, as criminal offenders and as victims of the law has been totally eclipsed' (1989: 13).

Carol Smart (1989) has gone furthest in arguing that 'it is important to think of non-legal strategies and to discourage a resort to law as if it holds the key to unlock women's oppression' (1989: 5). Boldly she concludes:

'A main purpose of this book has been to construct a warning to feminism to avoid the siren call of law. But of equal importance has been the attempt to acknowledge the power of feminism to construct an alternative reality to the version which is manifested in legal discourse' (1989: 160).

Howe has extended Smart's discussion and insisted on its relationship with Carlen's apparently more pragmatic approach (1994:

213–15 and *passim)*. In the 1980s there was widespread discussion of the work of Carol Gilligan (1982, 1987) who argued that men and women differ in approaches to moral questions, with men stressing 'justice' as an independent concept while women focus more on a relational notion of caring.

I used Gilligan's dichotomy as the basis of an ideal-type model of two types of justice system: the *Portia,* rational, judicial, and masculine, and the *Persephone,* relational, informal, and feminine, and explored what the effects of using such an alternative system might be. The conclusion was that such approaches had been adopted at certain times and had not always been beneficial (1986). Daly, in a review of this and other applications of Gilligan's difference discourse, disagrees with this approach and concludes

'... in canvassing feminist scholarship for ways to rethink the problem of justice for men and women accused of crime, I find little guidance. ... I would like to see a feminist conception of criminal justice which maintains a focus on women's lives and on redressing harms to women, but which does not ignore those men who have been crippled by patriarchal, class and race relations'(1989).

These comments could serve as the basis for the whole of this series of perspectives. What these studies amount to is a sophisticated critique of the administration of justice and the structures in which it operates. Clearly, there are certain gender-specific forms of discrimination rife within it. However, as Gelsthorpe (1989: 137–145) goes to great lengths to point out, it is impossible to try and demonstrate the existence of a conspiracy behind such practices. It is even more difficult to relate them, aetiologically to women's crime, since although women can be shown to be more socially and economically oppressed than men, their experience of the system as perpetrators, rather than victims, is far less. Where links can be made is through social construction theories which actually deconstruct the meanings of concepts such as

rape (Rafter, 1990) or, as in Zedner's work quoted above, those of 'inebriation' and 'feeble mindedness' as applied to women. As Zedner's studies show, redefinitions of female deviance can diminish their apparent deviance or increase it (1991). This is not, of course, solely due to the operation of the criminal justice system. On the contrary, many other features of the Zeitgeist contribute: culture, values, changes in medical science. Politics and the media have also played crucial roles in such developments, as Young, for example, shows in her analysis of the media reactions to the women protesters at the Greenham Common Airbase in Britain in the 1980s. She argues that the criminal justice system and the media rely on each other's definition of deviance (1990).

This set of approaches informs much writing on women and crime. It leads us to question some of the most basic assumptions about law, justice, and punishment in our society and to raise queries about unstated 'patriarchal' values. However, it is also then essential to question all the other implicit parts of the system and we are likely, as Daly points out, to need to raise at least as many points about what happens to men, especially if they are young, poor, and come from minorities as we do about women.

Marginalisation

Economic explanations of criminal behaviour go back at least as far as Bonger and, albeit implicitly, to Marx as well (Taylor et al, 1975). More recently, critical criminologists insisted on the criminogenic capacities of capitalist societies (ibid). *Critical Criminology* omits all consideration of gender, yet this is surely a crucial test for such theories since women are generally poorer than men in most, especially capitalist, societies and have suffered more in modern recessions (Millar and Glendinning, 1989). Some writers researching female crime have put forward a variation of such approaches in arguing that deviant women are an especially marginalised group.

Part of the purpose of proposing this perspective is to counteract the liberation hypothesis discussed earlier. Chapman (1980) stressed that the rise in female property crime was due to women's poverty, and especially to the problems of single mothers, a growing proportion of the poor. In an empirical study Jurik (1983) found support for such findings. A series of studies undertaken by Carlen in Britain elaborate on this theme (Carlen, 1983, 1985, 1988). She concludes:

> '... the analyses presented here claim only to indicate that, under certain, relatively rare *combinations* of otherwise general economic and ideological conditions, some women are more likely than not to choose to break the law and/or be imprisoned. Such analyses do not assume or imply that the women involved have no choice' (1988: 162, original emphasis).

Recent work from Europe (Pitch, 1995; Platek, 1995) and elsewhere (Hansson, 1995) suggests parallel concerns and has also focused much more fully on women of colour (eg the special edition of *Women and Criminal Justice*, 1995). Obviously, as Carlen suggests, poverty can be an important factor in the choice of women's criminal careers. It then often reinforces such choices by limiting others. Yet, as Daly showed in her study cited above, other factors, such as abuse in childhood and marriage or relationships with men with associations with drugs, are also important. None of these offender based, somewhat positivist approaches can answer certain important queries however, namely are the situations of those not convicted of crimes necessarily different? In short do these explanations fulfil necessary and sufficient conditions of theorising; or have they, perhaps, not addressed the right questions?

Control and conformity

A quite different approach has been adopted by a number of other writers who have sought to understand female criminality. So called 'control theory' was developed originally by Hirschi and his colleagues (1969) who sought to explain delinquency by the failure of social bonding processes. The emphasis shifted from deviance and what caused it to conformity and what impaired it. Hirschi's work has been much criticised, notably for its weak theoretical base, although it appears to have empirical support from large survey studies (see Downes and Rock, 1988, for a review).

In various modified forms, control theories have been applied to women because 'an examination of female criminality and unofficial deviance suggests that we need to move away from studying infractions and look at conformity instead, because the most striking thing about female behaviour ... is how notably conformist to social mores women are' (Heidensohn, 1996:11). In the same book I suggested that women were subject to a series of pressures and rewards to conform to which men were not. Informal sanctions discourage women and girls from straying far from proper behaviour: parents will disapprove or impose sanctions, as will gossip, ill-repute, and male companions. Fear of crime, harassment, and stigma all aid this process. A range of other commitments – to children, family, community, etc – occupy women much more fully than they do men. Finally, public images and culture encourage daring deviance in men, but suggest that deviant women are punished (1996: chapters 5 and 9). Hagan and colleagues have also offered gender-specific versions of their general control theory, arguing that girls are much more subject to controls within the family than are boys (1979). Extensive empirical testing of various related hypotheses produced somewhat inconclusive results. Hagan found more informal control of girls, more formal of boys, in his Canadian study, and some predictive value for his hypothesis. Others found, however, that while greater social bonds among girls (and women) explained some of the sex crime ratio differences, they did not do so fully (Smith, 1979; Mawby, 1980; Shover et al., 1980). Further, some of the differences were not in the expected direction. Thus girls who were 'masculine' in their identification in the last study were less delinquent than indeterminate or 'feminine' girls (Norland et al, 1981).

These approaches do at least try and account for the gender gap and to present a generalisable theory of a kind, even though it seems only to have limited explanatory power, since the operation of the bonds is not fully theorised. (Although Hagan does attempt this in another text, 1990.) Naffine is especially critical of such approaches because they depict females as essentially passive (1987: 68–70) whereas male delinquency is glorified as active and defiant. She misses, I think, the rising tide of comment on women's own contribution to social control, especially of their own sex. In *Women and Crime* I discussed it at some length, noting women's higher investment in conformity and stability. More recently a spate of studies have focused on women's role as social control agents both historically (Carrier, 1988; Boritch and Hagan, 1990; Daly, 1988) and in modern times (Zimmer, 1986; Martin, 1980 and 1989; Jones, 1986; Heidensohn, 1989 and 1992). In a complex analysis, Worrall has suggested that women offenders do act within the criminal justice system to alter their own fates, although they are able to do so only because, as women, they confront two systems of social control.

'They are effectively offered a contract which promises to minimise the consequences of their criminality by rehabilitating them within the dominant discourses of feminity (that is, domesticity, sexuality and pathology). Despite these programmes of feminisation, such women it is argued, attempt to resist such construction by exploiting the contradictions of official discourses' (1990: 163).

Almost all the empirical testing of control theories has been conducted with juvenile subjects. Measures of delinquency often include relatively minor infractions such as truancy and under-age drinking. This does limit the value of such studies where adults and more serious crimes are concerned. Gender specific social control is, nevertheless, a widely cited

component of most efforts to discuss women and crime. There is also clearly scope within such an approach to ask about many further issues: the control of males, for instance, or the role of women in control.

In reviewing theories of female criminality advanced in recent times, Pollock Byrne makes a succinct if gloomy point. 'Unfortunately feminist criminology has not offered any comprehensive theory to supplement those it has criticised' (1990: 25). It is hard to disagree with this. Despite a considerable body of work; in the field, theoretical crocks of gold have still failed to appear. What has developed is a much more sustained and sophisticated critique and several important conceptual contributions which still have some scope in application. For the most part, the debate is still with older and existing theories and with the development of second-order constructs. This does not merely reflect poverty of imagination, indeed it is truer to say that something of an epistemological crisis has affected social science and feminism and studies of crime are implicated. There are, however, pitfalls in these approaches, as I have argued in a review of my own research experiences with 'deviant' women (1994b).

Feminist sceptics

Much modern feminist debate in social science has focused on methodological issues. How should women be studied? What is feminist analysis? Numbers of articles and books have sought to respond to these questions and several scholars have particularly applied the answers to the study of gender and crime. These debates are complex, subtle, and sometimes arcane, and are beyond the scope of these chapters. What I do wish to do is to draw attention to the proposals made by several scholars who have tackled the epistemological crisis. What characterises them all, to some degree, is their scepticism about either the past of this field or its future. Smart (1990) mounts the most devastating attack on criminology 'It is very hard to see what criminology has to offer feminism' (ibid: 84). This contrasts with what she sees as the value and influence of feminist post-modernism on analyses of women's experiences (1990: 83). It is also in contrast to other possible approaches such as feminist empiricism and what is termed 'standpointism' (Harding, 1986). The latter is based in experience and on the argument that only a shared perspective with the subject gives research adequate insight and knowledge. Smart favours the deconstruction of everything, insisting that no meanings should be taken for granted.

Cain in the same volume tries also to describe what she calls the 'successor science' and lays down criteria for its operation (1990:125–140). Somewhat confusingly, she calls her approach 'realism'.

Rafter (1990) also advocates a ruthless deconstruction of all laws, concepts, etc, as does Bertrand (1992). Once again, the source of this continuing critique is outside criminology, although in these examples it is debates within feminism itself which have fuelled these developments. *La lutte continue,* no doubt, without resolution of the issues, although these developments suggest yet further room for growth and dynamism as advocated by Klein in her spirited call for new approaches to justice (1995).

Conclusions

Alice in Wonderland and *Through the Looking Glass*

An intelligent enquirer who has followed the growth of this topic during the late twentieth century may feel that she has moved from the world of *Alice in Wonderland* to that of *Through the Looking Glass.* It is possible to construe all the modern work on women and crime as a great heap of glistening treasure. There is diversity, great range, rich material. It is possible to find the answers to many questions. There are still many puzzles and absurdities, but it is even possible to use key concepts to explain the studied world. Yet one of the main lessons which recurs throughout all the texts, articles, and reports is simple yet stunning in its implications. That is that Alice should be in the other strange place, through the glass where everything is reversed or upside down.

Then it becomes clear that we have to ask different questions. Not what makes women's crime rates so low, but why are men's so high? Such questions are being asked in a few places (Kersten, 1991; Newburn and Stanko, 1993), but they are the crucial ones, intellectually and politically. There is already a new *policy* agenda for law and order which highlights the gendered nature of much personal crime: domestic violence, rape, child abuse etc. It is in the impact of such studies that its effect should be found.

There has been a significant shift in the study of crime because of feminist perspectives on it. New ideas have been developed. The most important contribution of all, however, was to see the centrality of gender to crime and to press for that. We know a vast amount about women and crime viewed through the prism of gender. Research on masculinity and crime is a fast developing area (Messerchmidt, 1993 and 1995; Newburn and Stanko, 1994; Jefferson and Carlen, 1996) and is likely to provide some very challenging ideas to both criminology and to feminist perspectives on crime. As Nelken has suggested, it is with just such a reflexive synthesis that the futures of criminology are likely to be pre-occupied (1994).

Bibliography

Adler I (1975) *Sisters in Crime*, New York: McGraw Hill.

Auld J, Dorn N and South N (1986) 'Irregular Work, Irregular Pleasures: Heroin in the 1980s', in R Matthews and J Young (eds), *Confronting Crime*, London: Sage.

Austin R L (1991) 'Liberation and Female Criminality in England and Wales', *British Journal of Criminology*, 21, 4: 371–374.

Bertrand M A (1991) 'Advances in Feminist Epistimology in the Field of Social Control', paper delivered to the American Society of Criminology.

Boritch H and Hagan J (1990) 'A Century of Crime in Toronto: Gender, Class and Patterns of Social Control, 1859–1995', *Criminology*, 20, 4: 567–599.

Box S (1983) *Power, Crime and Mystification*, London: Tavistock.

Box S and Hale C (1983) 'Liberation and Female Criminality in England and Wales', *British Journal of Criminology*, 23, 1: 35–49.

Carlen P (1983) *Women's Imprisonment*, London: Routledge and Kegan Paul.

Carlen P (1985) *Criminal Women*, Oxford: Polity Press.

Carlen P (1988) *Women, Crime and Poverty*, Milton Keynes: Open University Press.

Carrier J (1988) *The Campaign for the Employment of Women as Police Officers*, Aldershot: Avebury/Gower.

Chapman J (1980) *Economic Realities and the Female Offender*, Lexington: Lexington Books.

Daly K (1988) 'The Social Control of Sexuality: A Case Study of the Criminalisation of Prostitution in the Progressive Era', *Research in Law, Deviance and Social Control*, 9: 171–206.

Daly K (1989) 'Rethinking Judicial Paternalism: Gender, Work-Family Relations and Sentencing', *Gender and Society*, 3, 1: 9–36.

Dobash R E and Dobash R P (1992) *Women, Violence and Social Change*, London: Routledge.

Downes D and Rock P (1988) *Understanding Deviance*, Oxford: Oxford University Press (2nd ed).

Edwards S (1984) *Women on Trial*, Manchester: Manchester University Press.

Edwards S (1989) *Policing Domestic Violence*, London: Sage.

Gelsthorpe L (1989) *Sexism and the Female Offender*, Aldershot: Gower.

Gilligan C (1982) *In a Different Voice*, Cambridge, Mass: Harvard University Press.

Gilligan C (1989) 'Moral Orientation and Moral Development', in E Kittay and D Meyers (eds), *Women and Moral Theory*, NJ: Rowman and Littlefield.

Greenwood V (1981) 'The Myth of Female Crime', in A Morris and L Gelsthorpe (eds), *Women and Crime*, Cambridge: Cropwood Conference Series No 13.

Hagan J, Simpson J H and Gillis A R (1979) 'The Sexual Stratification of Social Control: a Gender-based Perspective on Crime and Delinquency', *British Journal of Sociology*, 30.

Hansson D (1995) 'Agenda-ing Gender: Feminism and the Engendering of Academic Criminology in South Africa', in N Rafter and F M Heidensohn (eds), *Engendering Criminology: the Transformation of a Social Science*, Buckingham: Open University Press.

Harding S (1986) *The Science Question in Feminism*, Ithaca, NY: Cornell University Press.

Heidensohn F (1985) *Women and Crime*, London: Macmillan.

Heidensohn F (1989) *Crime and Society*, Basingstoke: Macmillan.

Heidensohn F (1992) 'Danger, Diversion or a New Dimension?', paper delivered at Seminar on Women and Violence at University of Montreal, Quebec.

Heidensohn F (1994) 'From Being to Knowing. Some Reflections on the Study of Gender in Contemporary Society', *Women and Criminal Justice*, 6, 1: 13–37.

Heidensohn F (1996) *Women and Crime*, Basingstoke: Macmillan (2nd ed).

Hirschi T (1969) *Causes of Delinquency*, Berkeley, Calif: University of California Press.

Howe A (1994) *Punish and Critique towards a Feminist Analysis of Penality*, London: Routledge.

Jefferson T and Carlen P (1996) 'Masculinities, Social Relations and Crime', *British Journal of Criminology*, 36, 3, Special Issue.

Jones S (1986) *Policewomen and Equality*, London: Macmillan.

Jurik N (1983) 'The Economics of Female Recidivism', *Criminology*, 21, 4: 3–12.

Kersten J (1991) 'A Cross-Cultural Debate of Crime and Its Causes in Australia, Germany and Japan', paper presented to Australian and New Zealand Criminology Conference.

Klein D (1995) 'Gender's Prism: Towards a Feminist Criminology', in N Rafter and F M Heidensohn (eds), *Engendering Criminology: the Transformation of a Social Science*, Buckingham: Open University Press.

Leonard E B (1982) *A Critique of Criminology Theory: Women, Crime and Society*, New York and London: Longman.

Martin S E (1980) *Breaking and Entering*, Berkeley, Calif: University of California Press.

Martin S E (1989) *On the Move – the Status of Women in Policing*, Washington, DC: Police Foundation.

Mawby R (1980) 'Sex and Crime: the Results of a Self-Report Study', *British Journal of Sociology*, 31, 4: 525.

Millar J and Glendinning C (1989) 'Gender and Poverty', *Journal of Social Policy*, 18, 3: 363–383.

Mitchell J and Oakley A (eds) (1986), *What Is Feminism?*, Oxford: Basil Blackwell.

Morris A (1987) *Women, Crime and Criminal Justice*, Oxford: Basil Blackwell.

Naffine N (1987) *Female Crime*, Sydney: Allen and Unwin.

Nelken D (ed) (1994) *The Futures of Criminology*, London: Sage.

Newburn T and Stanko E (eds) (1994) *Just Boys Doing Business: Masculinity and Crime*, London: Routledge.

Norland S, Wessel R C and Shover N (1981) 'Masculinity and Delinquency', *Criminology*, 19, 3: 421.

Pitch T (1995) 'Feminist Politics, Crime, Law and Order in Italy', in N Rafter and F M Heidensohn (eds), *International Feminist Perspectives in Criminology*, Buckingham: Open University Press.

Platek M (1995) 'What It's Like for Women: Criminology in Poland and Eastern Europe', in N Rafter and F M Heidensohn (eds), *Engendering Criminology: the Transformation of a Social Science*, Buckingham: Open University Press.

Pollert A (1996) 'Gender and Class Revisited; or the Poverty of "Patriarchy"', *Sociology*, 304: 639–659.

Pollock-Byrne J (1990) *Women, Prison and Crime*, Belmont, Calif: Wadsworth.

Rafter H N (1990) 'The Social Construction of Crime and Crime Control', *Journal of Research on Crime and Delinquency*, 27: 376–389.

Rosenbaum M (1981) *Women on Heroin*, New Brunswick, NJ: Rutgers University Press.

Simon R (1975) *Women and Crime*, London: Lexington.

Smart C (1979) *Women, Crime and Criminology*, London: Routledge.

Smart C (1989) *Feminism and the Power of Law*, London: Routledge.

Smart C (1990) 'Feminist Approaches to Criminology or Post Modern Woman Meets Atavistic Man', in L Gelsthorpe and A Morris (eds), *Feminist Perspectives in Criminology*, Buckingham: Open University Press.

Smith D and Pasternoster R (1987) 'The Gender Gap in Theories of Deviance: Issues and Evidence', *Journal of Research on Crime and Delinquency*, 24:140–172.

Steffenmeister D J (1980) 'Assessing the Impact of the Women's Movement on Sex-Based Differences in the Handling of Adult Criminal Defendants', *Crime and Delinquency*, 26: 344–357.

Taylor I, Walton P and Young J (1975) *Critical Criminology*, London: Routledge.

Walby S (1989) 'Theorising Patriarchy', *Sociology*, 23, 2: 213–214.

Worral A (1990) *Offending Women*, London: Routledge.

Young A (1990) *Femininity in Dissent*, London: Routledge

Zedner L (1991) *Women, Crime and Custody in Victorian England*, Oxford: Oxford University Press.

Zimmer L (1986) *Women Guarding Men*, Chicago, Ill: University of Chicago Press.

Hedderman and Gelsthorpe report on research that was carried out in relation to the sentencing of women. They make it clear that there should be parity between the sexes, and they also warn that assumptions should not be made. From the evidence in the report it is clear that women do receive different sentences to men. It also seems clear that this is not the result of discrimination – instead the differences are explainable by reference to other variables. For example, it is clear that differences in offences committed is an important factor. However, other factors are also at work, such as the offender's appearance and behaviour in court. Suggestions are made as to how the use of such problematic factors as appearance can be removed from the sentencing scene.

Hedderman C and Gelsthorpe L (1997) *Understanding the Sentencing of Women*, Home Office Research Study 170, pp55–59

Conclusion

TOWARDS AN UNDERSTANDING OF THE
SENTENCING OF WOMEN

The topic of sex discrimination is one on which people often hold such strong (and usually fixed) opinions. Up to this point, therefore, we have endeavoured to present the findings of this research quite straightforwardly and with only minimal interpretation. This conclusion, however, reflects the four authors' shared interpretations of both the statistical exercises described in Part I and the interviews carried out in Part II. We summarise what the research findings mean and how they feed into our understanding of the sentencing of women.

Few people would seriously contest the notion that the criminal justice system should dispense justice fairly, regardless of sex, race, class or any other improper influence. No one is more aware of this need than the magistracy, who already spend a proportion of their training on such (human awareness) issues. But what exactly does fairness consist of in this context? In our view, it lies in consistency of approach rather than uniformity of outcome. In other words, it involves asking the same questions about factors such as employment status, family responsibilities and financial circumstances regardless of the offender's sex, rather than presuming that certain questions will only apply to males or females. From this perspective, to criticise sentencing practices on the grounds that the official statistics show different sentencing patterns would be unfair and, in any case, a futile exercise. These patterns may simply reflect the fact that the men and women who come to court differ across a wide range of factors which sentencers take into consideration when determining an appropriate sentence. In order to look at whether there is disparity in sentencing decisions, one needs therefore to look at the characteristics of those coming to court and at how sentencers say they weigh these and other factors in their decision-making. This research set out to do both these things.

In our view, neither the statistical analysis described by Dowds and Hedderman nor the interviews Gelsthorpe and Loucks carried out support the contention that differences in the way men and women are sentenced by magistrates is a consequence of anything as simple as deliberate discrimination. If that were true one would expect the statistical exercise to show women consistently receiving different sentences to men. But they do not. For example, they stood an equal chance of going to prison for a first violent offence, whereas among repeat offenders, women were less likely to go to prison. And among drug offenders, women recidivists were as likely as men to be imprisoned, but first timers were not.

In fact both parts of this study suggest that sentencing decisions are the outcome of the interactive effect of a number of factors. The most important of these is the nature of the offence. However, the offender's circumstances, the way other participants in the courtroom portray the offence and offender, the offender's appearance and behaviour in court, and how the members of each bench interact are also influential. Together these factors shape the court's perception of an offender as essentially troubled or troublesome, and this in turn determines whether help or punishment is at the heart of the court's response.

Women were more likely to be defined as troubled than men. From interviews with magistrates there seem to be a number of reasons for this. First, five out of every six of the offenders magistrates routinely deal with are male and most are under 30 years of age. Perhaps because of their sheer numbers, young men are likely to be seen as troublesome and are only very rarely viewed as troubled. As we know from the statistics, the majority of the women offenders magistrates try and sentence are charged with shoplifting. Again, from the interviews with magistrates in Part II of this study, we know that magistrates generally believe that such women steal through need rather than greed, they often have sole care of young children, and they are usually living on benefits or are dependent on a partner's income. So how are these perceptions of women translated into sentencing? The most striking consequence is that, as the analyses presented in Part I show, magistrates are reluctant to fine women. Even if this difference was found to be inspired by a desire not to financially penalise a woman's family, it carries the risk that, skipping a step on the sentencing ladder this time round, will lead to an even more severe sentence being imposed in the event of a subsequent conviction. To use probation where a fine would have been appropriate is also an ineffective use of resources (Moxon et al, 1990).

Both parts of the study show that magistrates appear to favour probation or discharges for women. The interviews carried out in Part II suggest that these measures are used with the intention of assisting rather than punishing women. Unless sending women to prison was unavoidable because of the seriousness of their offending, it was usually ruled out on the grounds that it would adversely affect their children.

We know from previous research that female offenders do indeed describe themselves as stealing through need and having responsibility for dependent children (see, for example, Carlen 1988 and Morris et al, 1995). However, neither those studies nor the current research show whether they differ from men in either respect. Examination of court records to see if male and female offenders are matched in these ways has proved difficult because records do not hold such information consistently. This is certainly an issue worth examining in future research, however, as the magistrates interviewed in Part II of this study revealed that, when considering mitigation, they were not simply responding to the fact that women and men appeared in different circumstances. Thus, for example, having family responsibilities was less central to decisions about male offenders, and being employed carried less weight when the offender was a woman. Even when a man is considered to be more troubled than troublesome, this does not necessarily have the same consequences as for a woman. On the occasions when magistrates believed that male offenders merited assistance, this tended to take the form of employment training through Community Service Orders or help with alcohol or drug addiction. These findings are strikingly similar to those reported by Farrington and Morris (1983) and Mary Eaton (1983, 1986). A key difference is that they reflect sentencing in the mid-1990s rather than the mid-1980s and occur in a period when a great deal of attention has been given to notions of fairness and justice and to race and gender issues in the delivery of justice.

Turning to the offender in the courtroom, while some magistrates recognised that body language is open to misinterpretation, most stressed the importance of seeing the offender in court, and a number were confident that they would not themselves misinterpret non-verbal cues. The research also indicated that, based on perceptions of body language and appearance, men – ethnic minority men in particular – may come across as having less respect for the court, while women are generally perceived to be inexperienced, deferential and (therefore) honest.

The internal politics of the courtroom also seem to shape magistrates' decision-making. The same information could be viewed quite differently according to which courtroom player provided it – most weight was accorded to information from prosecutors or the Clerk, who were regarded by magistrates as being impartial. Not only defence solicitors but probation officers were seen as siding with the offender.

Interaction between magistrates was also important, with experience weighing; more heavily than training. Moreover, virtually all the magistrates mentioned 'common sense' or 'gut feelings' at some stage of their assessment as to who was respectful or rebellious, remorseful or rancorous; and 'common sense' was what magistrates used to explain any decision that seemed to have no other explanation or, at least, no easily expressed explanation. Yet notions of what is 'common sense' and what are reliable indicators of honesty and remorse differed among magistrates.

Taken as a whole, these findings suggest that there remains a risk that some magistrates will resort to their 'common sense' (and a gendered 'commonsense' at that) as the best arbiter of what is right, despite the fact that new magistrates receive training designed to inform them of the inherent dangers of making decisions on the basis of stereotypes and on the dangers of relying on non-verbal cues.

The difficulty to be addressed is one of finding ways to challenge stereotypical pictures of men and women, without ignoring the fact that they often (but not always) do have different needs and responsibilities (and these are often precisely the needs and responsibilities which fuel the stereotypes). It may also be that the time to recognise such differences is in the shape and content of particular sentences rather than in the choice between different levels of sentence, but discussion of this is beyond our remit. A number of changes may be helpful here:

Increased emphasis on gender issues in training to counteract the fact that so many magistrates have comparatively little experience of dealing with women in the courtroom. This is probably best accomplished through the 'human awareness' element of magistrates' training which encourages them to reflect on how cultural and gender specific stereotypes inform their practices and perceptions in the courtroom in ways which could lead to unfair sentencing. Currently, such training tends to focus on race issues and it would be unfortunate if combining race and gender in this way masked the importance of either issue. It is also important to note that while 'human awareness' training is popular, it does not appear to have been subject to any large scale or systematic evaluation.

Training on gender (and race) should be made available to all magistrates rather than to new magistrates alone so as to ensure that resistant or reluctant magistrates are exposed to the issues as a matter of routine.

Where magistrates may feel that their sentencing options are constrained by a (male or female) offender's childcare responsibilities, the Probation Service should use PSRs to draw attention to the fact that suitable childcare arrangements can be made.

Increased feedback on sentencing patterns in each court particularly patterns relating to men and women, may also assist magistrates in the general task of achieving consistency in approach.

Finally, we would suggest that there are

at least three questions which require further exploration and discussion:

1. To what extent does training help to address the tendency to use gender-stereotyping in sentencing?
2. To what extent do gender, race and other factors have an interactive effect on sentencing?
3. Are the decisions of professional sentencers subject to the same influences as those of lay magistrates?

Bibliography

Carlen P (1988) *Women, Crime and Poverty*, Milton Keynes: Open University Press.

Eaton M (1983) 'Mitigating Circumstances: familiar rhetoric', *International Journal of the Sociology of Law*, 11, 385–400.

Eaton M (1986) *Justice for Women? Family, Court and Social Control*, Milton Keynes: Open University Press.

Farrington D P (1983) 'Sex, Sentencing and Reconviction', *British Journal of Criminology*, 23, 229–248.

Morris A, Wilkinson C, Tis A, Woodrow J and Rockley A (1989) *Managing the Needs of Women Prisoners*, London: Home Office.

Moxon D et al (1990) *Deductions from Benefit for Fine Default*, London: Home Office.

The extract provided from this report is intended to give an account of the characteristics of female prisoners. The picture that emerges is of people who have a background of multiple disadvantage, who generally are not hardened criminals and who do not regard prison as a positive experience. One feature of this report that can be noted is that a separate prison system for women is argued for on the basis that the population has sufficiently different needs to the male population to justify this. This view can be contrasted with the argument for equality in the treatment of males and females that was presented in the previous extract.

Women in Prison: A Thematic Review by HM Chief Inspector of Prisons (1997), pp12–16

The women's population

To augment other data we conducted detailed interviews, lasting up to an hour, with 234 women prisoners who were selected at random. The main findings of the survey are set out below.

MOTHERS

Nearly two-thirds of women interviewed were mothers with the majority having at least one child aged under 16. The average number of children which each of these women had was just under three. Approximately 4 per cent had their child with them in prison, all these children were under 18 months old. Only a quarter of the children were being cared for by either their biological father or their mother's current partner. The main carers were the women's own mothers (27 per cent) and/or family and friends (29 per cent). More than one in ten of the women had children either in Local Authority care, fostered or adopted. Only a third claimed that the present caring arrangements for these children were permanent or likely to become so.

ACCOMMODATION

Over 70 per cent of the women were living or had been living in rented premises of which half was either council owned or housing association accommodation. Nearly one in ten of the women claimed to have been homeless before coming to prison.

EMPLOYMENT

As many as 70 per cent of the women said they had had no previous employment before coming to prison. Over a third of the women said they were in debt. The majority survived on state benefits augmented, in many cases, by criminal activity or casual work. Over 10 per cent of the women said they survived by crime alone. Only 3 per cent reported having turned to prostitution in order to make ends meet.

PREVIOUS CUSTODIAL EXPERIENCE
The majority (71 per cent) said they had not received a prison sentence before: nearly half reported having no previous convictions.

EDUCATION
Thirty-six per cent of the women reported having had serious problems at school.

LOCAL AUTHORITY CARE
Twenty per cent of the women said they had experienced time in care: in comparison the figure in the general population is 2 per cent.

ABUSE
Nearly half the women said they had been abused. A third of these reported both physical and sexual abuse, a third said they had been sexually abused and the remainder reported physical abuse. Of those who had been abused, 40 per cent had been under 18 at the time with a further 22 per cent having been abused both as a child and as an adult. In the majority of cases the abuser was male and well known to the woman (for example, father or partner).

SUBSTANCE ABUSE
Two-thirds of the women reported having used illegal drugs at some point in their lives. A third asserted that this usage was limited to experimental, recreational or occasional use. However, over a quarter reported poly-drug misuse and 40 per cent reported heavy use or addiction. Of this group, over half used heroin with one in five admitting to intravenous drug use. More than a quarter had used cocaine and/or crack. Nearly 20 per cent used amphetamines with one in ten of these women reporting she had injected. One in ten said they had been dependent on tranquillisers. One in four of the women with drug dependency admitted that they were still taking drugs in prison and would continue to do so when released.

SELF HARM
Over 40 per cent of the women interviewed reported that they had harmed themselves intentionally and/or attempted suicide. Their reasons ranged from histories of physical and/or sexual abuse, family and relationship problems, depression and stress.

Some issues arose from the women's imprisonment and these are set out below.

FAMILY
For over 25 per cent of the women, lack of contact with their children and other family members was their greatest concern. Other related issues of importance were a desire to be in a prison nearer to home, worries about the health of relatives, worries about the possibility of their children being taken into permanent care and financial issues.

BULLYING
Over 70 per cent of the women reported having come into contact with bullying in prison; a third of these said that they had been bullied. However, 87 per cent of the women reported feeling safe from bullying.

PERSONAL OFFICERS AND
SENTENCE/CUSTODY PLANNING
Over half the women reported that they did not know the name of their Personal Officer. Of those who said they had a Personal Officer the vast majority (90 per cent) described their relationship with him or her as ' all right'. The majority of sentenced women reported that they had not experienced sentence planning at all.

EFFECTS OF IMPRISONMENT
Over half the women interviewed (55 per cent) reported receiving no help in prison. Three-quarters of self-confessed drug misusers reported that they had received no help (other than, in some cases, light medication) to assist with drug problems. Only one in ten of these said they had received some drugs counselling. Over 70 per cent felt that prison had had a negative effect on them; reasons included becoming more criminally sophisticated as well as more angry and depressed.

WHAT WOULD PREVENT FUTURE
RE-OFFENDING?
All interviewees were asked what they

thought would help them not to reoffend. The majority felt that they were unlikely to re-offend anyway. (This is not an uncommon comment among prisoners generally and should be seen in that context.) Of the many who felt themselves to be at risk, their needs following release were likely to be: employment, stable relationships, accommodation, and proper help and support. ...

These are striking findings about the nature of the women's prison population. They have evident policy and practice implications for the Prison Service. Information about women prisoners should be the starting point for policy and planned use of resources. There should be an on-going assessment of the needs of women prisoners which can be identified from their characteristics.

Examples of their ideas on the regime
Except in special circumstances, all women should be given the opportunity of taking their meals in association with other prisoners.

PHYSICAL EXERCISE AND EDUCATION
PE staff should be made available to supervise activities in the evenings and at weekends in all women's establishments.

REGIME
Normally, sentenced women should be required to work as full a day as possible and there should be suitable work activities available.

More vocational training courses in manual skills should be provided.

The educational and vocational needs of women prisoners should be assessed and a policy identifying the role of education services developed.

The budgets for education in women's prisons should be based on assessment of needs and priorities.

There should be greater co-ordination and co-operation on educational matters by prisons holding women.

There should be more educational activities at weekends.

More use should be made of the skills of prisoners to teach other prisoners with the support of staff.

More art, drama and yoga should be provided in the education curriculum.

Reports by HM Chief Inspector of Prisons provide both an excellent and a frank source of information in relation to the operation of the prison system. In this case both good and bad practice are revealed in relation to the female part of the prison system.

HM Chief Inspector of Prisons (2001) *Report of an Inspection of HM Prison and YOI New Hall*, pp3–5

I hope that this report will be read with care and attention by all those with any responsibilities for the treatment of and conditions for females in prison. It contains yet more repetition of items that I have been reporting on and recommending over the past five years, that are still in need of urgent managerial attention, if Governors and staffs are to be enabled to carry out their functions. I do not mean so much a lack of resources but of co-ordinated and clear direction. The report discloses all that has been achieved since our last inspection, and also all that is yet to be achieved. Knowing the recently arrived Governor, I am sure that she will make best use of our recommendations, and continue to exert her influence that is already apparent. But she and her staff can only do what they can with what they are given, and much of what is needed is beyond their ability to provide. I find it depressing that I should have to be saying all the same old things over and over again, not only in connection with New Hall but also with other prisons. I continue to be amazed that good practice is not spread around the female prison estate, and consistency of delivery demanded by line management. I sincerely hope that the penny will drop one day, and that those in authority will realise that improvements in the treatment of and conditions for prisoners mean improvements not only in the prison in which they are highlighted, but in all those holding similar types of prisoner. Matters affecting prisoners are matters affecting people, not commodities, which means management in person and not by paper, which too is a lesson that must be read, marked, learned and inwardly digested.

My first concern is about the way in which management consultancy services (MCS) approach their task. I do not question the need for efficiencies and efficiency savings, but rather the MCS's method of examination and imposition, as I have done many times before. I have now come across countless examples of where their recommendations take no account of their impact on regimes and the treatment of and conditions for prisoners, only on making specific staff and other savings. In the case of New Hall their recommendation included the following supposition:

Bail and legal staffs should not be permanently allocated, but regarded as 'flexible', meaning that they can only give attention to bail and legal duties as and when time is available. This is nonsense. Bail and legal staffs must be selected and trained and available within 24 hours of each new reception's arrival and following any request from prisoners so that prisoners can have access to what is called 'due process' at all times. This is particularly true of a diverse population such as that at New Hall. To use MCS's own definitions, bail and legal aid work should be regarded as partly flexible, not as flexible. This example confirms, yet again, to me that MCS are in need of careful and well-thought out direction to ensure that their recommendations are conditioned by their impact on outcomes for prisoners as well as the need to make budgetary savings.

The need for more offending behaviour programmes is, again, mentioned. I am concerned that, by concentrating solely on high level accredited programmes, needed by and appropriate for only a small number of prisoners, the Prison Service is ignoring the needs of the vast majority who require no more than medium level intervention, and all who need low level intervention, such as ensuring that

prisoners have a home and a job to go to. Programmes suitable for juvenile, young and adult women are different from those designed to meet the needs of juvenile, young and adult men, and it is high time that the value of medium and low level intervention was recognised. Above all, these require delivery by staff, more and more of whom want and are motivated to do this work. Attention must be paid too to the specific needs of female substance users. What is required is not funding of individual programmes in individual prisons, but an integrated policy, based on equality of opportunity wherever a female prisoner is held, and continuity of treatment between prisons and on release.

I am very concerned at the continued lack of implementation of the policy for the treatment and conditions of juveniles as detailed in PSO 4950. The YJB has not yet funded the custody of those awarded detention and training orders (DTOs). There are no policies in place regarding child protection procedures, nor is there any training in them for managers and staffs. Despite earlier recommendations, there are still no social workers to look after the interests of children. There is no continuity in the post of manager of the Juvenile Unit. All these are things that would have been demanded by a regulator, and all that I can do is recommend, which I do again, as strongly as I am able.

I remain concerned at the absence of any specific mental health strategy for the female population, both young and adult. I have recommended many times that someone should be appointed to be responsible for health care in the women's estate, because of their special needs. That so many of the young girls and women are emotionally disturbed is glaringly obvious to anyone seeing them in prison, which confirms the need for a coherent assessment and treatment policy. Despite the strategic improvements about which I have recently been briefed by the Lifer Unit, there still is no proper regime for women lifers, whose numbers are, regrettably, on the increase.

These examples may make it seem that

New Hall is not a healthy prison, when, in fact, that is not so. The report draws attention to good practice, such as the excellent sentence planning unit, but it too is bedevilled by lack of continuity amongst its staff. The commitment of the governor and her staff are obvious, and prisoners feel both safe and respected. But HMP and YOI New Hall is a prison in need of Prison Service assistance if it is to achieve its potential, and fulfil its multiplicity of roles with its very varied population. I hope that urgent attention will be paid not only to its needs, but also, in parallel, to similar needs in every other women's prison in England.

9 Crime Prevention

The first four extracts provide information on quite specific practical examples of attempts at crime prevention. There seems to be some merit in tackling particular problems by means of strategies that have the specific characteristics of those problems in mind.

Ekblom P and Simon F (1988) *Crime and Racial Harassment in Asian-run Small Shops: The Scope for Prevention*, Crime Prevention Unit Paper 15, pp23–25

Crime suffered by Asian keepers of small shops (and probably, those in all ethnic groups) is a problem worthy of attention; the racially-offensive behaviour associated with it further heightens its significance. Fear of shop crime may in some areas be a problem worth tackling in its own right.

Crime Prevention Officers and others addressing the problem might adopt a strategic view, setting shop crime and racially offensive behaviour in shops in the broader social context in their local area; and could gather information, eg through surveys or visits to shops, to complement the picture available from officially reported crime. Effort to increase the reporting of crime, etc should proceed in parallel. Joint working between a force's crime prevention department and its community involvement department (which are often under the same overall command) may be useful in all these respects.

The strategy might involve giving priority to harder-hit shops and to some outreach work, involving visits or the distribution of leaflets, rather than waiting for shopkeepers to seek help and then operating purely on a demand-led, 'first-come-first-served' basis.

To begin with shops selling alcohol, or shops in isolated positions, could be approached.

The advice given to shopkeepers both nationally and locally could be extended to include ways of avoiding assault and avoiding or containing disputes or harassment. It may be worth exploring the market for producing leaflets in Asian language versions.

Shopkeepers suffering a fairly high rate of trouble should be encouraged to keep a simple log of incidents containing information on the nature of the offence, timing, method, etc. This could be initiated with the help of a CPO, kept over a month or two and then jointly considered as a basis for devising preventive measures targeted on the requirements of the individual shop.

It may be worth setting up local self-help groups of shopkeepers whose aim would be to identify particular local problems, develop and implement ways of preventing them, and offer mutual support – perhaps in the context of Business Watch organisations or chambers of commerce. The police and other agencies could participate on an advisory or supporting basis. There may be some benefit from running such a scheme as a national demonstration project.

These measures could help to increase shopkeepers' confidence in their ability both to cope with racial hostility and to prevent crime motivated from other sources. Because small shops are often focal points for their neighbourhoods, both socially and economically, the effects of better relationships and increased confidence could spread.

The results of this study suggest that some of the offensive behaviour suffered by Asian shopkeepers can be seen as having closer connections with materialistic crimes and disputes than might have been assumed. Some scope therefore exists for prevention by conventional means such as target hardening or changes in business practices.

Whilst many of the strategies that are used to tackle the problem of crime, such as the use of imprisonment, have had generally poor results the field of crime prevention and some of its highly specific experiments can claim to have succeeded. The account of the experiment in keeping drinkers off the streets in Central Coventry, detailed below, is one such success story.

Ramsey M (1990) *Lagerland Lost? An Experiment in Keeping Drinkers off the Streets in Central Coventry and Elsewhere*, Crime Prevention Unit Paper 22, pp23–25

Summary and conclusions

The 'alcohol-free zones' established in Coventry and six other places constituted a novel experiment. Developments in Coventry, the flagship for this initiative, were monitored closely by the Home Office. Only to a lesser extent did the Home Office enquire into the impact of the other six byelaws.

In Coventry, two large surveys of members of the public were carried out, involving visitors to the city centre, before and then a year after the introduction of the byelaw. These showed that:

Prior to the implementation of the byelaw, many of those interviewed were worried about falling victim to crime and disorder in the city centre. More than half sometimes made a point of avoiding certain people (or streets). In particular the sight of public drinkers triggered feelings of fear on the part of many members of the public. Together, 'drunks, winos and tramps' constituted the most commonly avoided category of person.

Comparing the findings of the 'before' and 'after' surveys, there was a modest but clear reduction in fear, to judge by various behavioural indicators. This reduction could

plausibly be attributed to the successful enforcement of the byelaw. Smaller proportions of the interviewees said that they sometimes avoided certain sorts of people, or that they felt it necessary to take a companion with them. In addition, visitors to central Coventry were less often exposed to incivilities – specifically, to insults by strangers (besides the sight of public drinkers) – following the introduction of the byelaw, and apparently as a result of it.

The surveys also revealed high levels of knowledge about the Coventry byelaw, which was enormously popular locally both on the eve of its implementation and, still more strongly, a year later. In the 'before' survey, 89 per cent of those interviewed claimed to be aware of the byelaw, a figure that subsequently rose to 93 per cent. Similarly, 86 per cent of the survey respondents felt initially that the byelaw was 'a good idea overall', while later that also increased to 93 per cent.

Interviews carried out with police officers responsible for patrolling central Coventry showed that enforcement had been achieved without too much difficulty. Such contraventions of the byelaw as did occur were generally resolved informally, on the spot: there were hardly any prosecutions.

Consequently, from a legal standpoint, the enforcement of the byelaw in Coventry can only be said to have been subjected to the mildest of testing. Some of the officers there (and indeed elsewhere) foresaw situations where difficulties might arise.

However well the byelaw worked – in ideal circumstances – in Coventry, its success was not without limits. Although incivilities were reduced, the surveys and the data assembled by the local police both indicated that crime proper stayed at much the same level as before the introduction of the byelaw. And a minority of those interviewed – over one in five – continued to feel that public drinking was a problem in the city centre, one year on from the introduction of the byelaw.

Information provided by the local authorities responsible for the other six places suggested that, while the introduction of their byelaws had in the main proceeded smoothly and successfully, some important questions over enforcement remained unresolved – for instance, the length of time for which individuals remained bound by any warning, or whether (and how) the alcoholic content of beverages needed to be proved, in the event of a prosecution. Notwithstanding any such difficulties, the byelaws had been generally well received in these other six locations, although for the most part this particular conclusion was not based on detailed research such as was carried out in Coventry. Also, it is worth emphasising that these six places were all relatively small ones where, broadly speaking, the prospects for the byelaw were reasonably favourable. Even then, enforcement led on occasion to conflict or controversy, while it may also be worth noting that in one area (Aldershot and Farnborough) scarcely half of those members of the public interviewed in the course of research carried out by the local authority were aware of the existence of the byelaw, let alone of any positive effects.

The main findings of this report, based on the in-depth research carried out in Coventry, raise a variety of issues. A particularly crucial one concerns the striking of a balance between the individual's right to consume alcohol out in the open and the evident desire of a good many people to avoid encountering public drinkers. (And, to be more specific, one is sometimes talking about the rights of those who are homeless and lack the money to drink in pubs.) It is interesting that, even in Coventry, 30 per cent of those interviewed before the byelaw came into effect believed that it did indeed represent an infringement of the freedom of the individual. Subsequently – when it had become apparent that the byelaw was working so effectively – that figure dropped to 19 per cent, in the second survey. At least in Coventry, the byelaw undoubtedly proved its acceptability to the public, in practice as well as in theory.

Precisely because of the strong appeal inherent in the claims of freedom from fear, it is worth emphasising that the byelaw experiment in Coventry took place in exceptional circumstances: there is a need for a degree of caution in interpreting an undoubted success story. Coventry's situation was a special one, in several important ways:

The area involved was limited in size, so that no-one was ever more than ten minutes walk from an unrestricted area to which they could go, or be moved on, to resume their interrupted drink.

The 'alcohol-free zone' was also extremely clearly demarcated, by the central ring-road, so that, effectively, anyone who was aware of the byelaw knew where it did and did not apply. Additionally, there were numerous warning notices.

Coventry had no tradition of open-air drinking, not even at chairs and tables outside pubs and restaurants. (Here it differed especially from Bath, where the byelaw has encountered critics in various quarters.) The byelaw formed just one element – albeit a particularly important one – in a package of strategies aimed at tackling a problem of alcohol related disorder; and this problem was one widely perceived by local people as needing serious attention.

Coventry's opinion formers – including the local media – were virtually unanimous in their support for the byelaw. (Here again, there is a contrast with Bath, where there has been political disagreement over the byelaw within the Council.)

Together, all these factors ensured that the byelaw was in large measure self policing in central Coventry, and that on the limited number of occasions when the police did have to tackle a contravention they were able to do so informally and effectively (albeit sometimes adhering slightly loosely to the precise format of the byelaw).

This extract provides an account of a crime prevention measure which has been used in

South Wales. It is called Vehicle Watch and it operates by means of members of the public putting a sticker on the back of their car requesting the police to stop the car if it is being used between certain night-time hours. This should reduce its desirability as a target for car thieves during those hours, as they would run the risk of being stopped by the police.

Honess T and Maguire M (1993) *Vehicle Watch and Car Theft: An Evaluation*, Crime Prevention Unit Paper 50, pp23–25

The study set out to address four distinct questions relating to Vehicle Watch schemes. The findings in relation to these are summarised below and overall conclusions are presented.

Assessment of effect in key areas:

Does Vehicle Watch appear to have any effect upon the overall level of vehicle theft (including unauthorised taking) in the areas studied?
There was a dip in car theft in Gwent in the first few months after the introduction of Vehicle Watch in September 1991. However, several other police forces also recorded a decline at this time. Moreover, theft rates in Gwent rose steeply at the beginning of 1992. Hence, nothing conclusive can be drawn from crime figures alone.

Does membership of Vehicle Watch improve an individual's chances of avoiding becoming a victim of vehicle theft in comparison with non-members?
This is apparently a simple question, but reliable data are difficult to collect. A questionnaire-based study of car theft during a three-month period in the county of Gwent suggested that the proportion committed against Vehicle Watch members was 16 per cent. The study did, however, suffer from a low response rate (44 per cent). Allowing that members may be more likely than non-members to respond to the questionnaire, a

speculative 'best estimate' of 11 to 12 per cent for car theft against Vehicle Watch members was subsequently produced. This compares favourably with an average membership of Vehicle Watch of 21 per cent within Gwent during the three months in question. If the best estimate of victimisation rates was correct, the risk to Vehicle Watch members appears to have been about one-half less than to the population at risk as a whole. However, the low response rate to the questionnaire means that this conclusion must be treated with considerable caution.

Does the Vehicle Watch scheme attract individuals who are anyway less vulnerable to vehicle theft?
In addition, does membership of the scheme have any impact upon the security behaviour of those who join?
A street survey revealed a number of important differences between the two groups. For example, the Vehicle Watch members were older, they were more likely to garage their cars overnight and during the day they were more likely to leave their car where they could keep an eye on it.

Thus, Vehicle Watch members do differ in a number of ways to non-members and these differences together indicate that the members may be a less vulnerable population both before and after joining.

What do members, non-members and police officers see as the main benefits and the main disadvantages of the scheme?
Vehicle Watch was well received by members and non-members alike. The most common response from Vehicle Watch members was that the scheme made them feel more secure and 55 per cent of the non-members indicated that they would consider joining. The main suggestion for improving the scheme was that the police should take more interest in it and should stop cars with Vehicle Watch stickers more regularly. In summary, Vehicle Watch appeared to be a popular scheme which encouraged members' confidence and was welcomed as a sign that the police were active.

Police officers who had experience of the scheme varied in their attitudes towards it. Officers who had been involved in the pilot scheme on the Bettws estate and had witnessed a very high rate of enrolment in their community, with a simultaneous drop in car theft, were enthusiastic supporters. Those officers working out of an urban centre were more cautious, some believing that its importance was likely to wane for a variety of reasons. For example, if publicity were not sustained or if the numbers joining increased appreciably and made policing the scheme less viable.

It was also clear that police could not fulfil the commitment to stop all cars carrying Vehicle Watch stickers which were active during curfew hours. The sticker was at best a contributory factor in a decision on whether to stop a vehicle. Other policing commitments (eg attending a call to an incident) always took priority and suspicious behaviour (eg driving dangerously, age of driver, type of car) tended to be regarded as more important than the presence of a sticker, which was not always easy to see. In summary, police attitudes were relatively cautious and suggested that the scheme was most likely to be effective in clearly defined communities with a high level of vehicle crime.

Overall conclusions

Although no definite statement can be made about the protective benefits of Vehicle Watch membership, the findings do indicate that Vehicle Watch members are less likely than non-members to become victims of car theft. However, how much this is due to membership of the scheme per se is less clear, as members – independent of the fact of joining the scheme – constitute a less vulnerable population. The primary advantages of the scheme are likely to be similar to those of Neighbourhood Watch: it makes people feel more secure and is potentially a good avenue for facilitating police/public relations. This, in turn may have pay-offs in encouraging better security habits. Finally, if the scheme is effective in protecting members' cars, it is likely to have more impact in clearly identifiable local communities rather than relatively open urban areas.

The research reported by Spenser provides a good example of how some depth of knowledge of offenders can lead to a variety of different strategies designed to tackle specific aspects of a crime problem, such as car crime involving young people.

Spenser S (1992) *Car Crime and Young People on a Sunderland Housing Estate*, Crime Prevention Unit Paper 40, pp22–24

This research has revealed a number of important, and perhaps alarming aspects of young people's involvement in car crime. The school survey found that over half of the 11–16 year olds in the sample knew others who were involved in car crime. This is particularly significant in view of the findings from offender interviews, that first involvement in car crime is usually through contact with more experienced offenders. Indeed, the school survey found that 32 per cent of the sample had been present when property had been stolen from a car.

The interviews with known offenders showed how a career in car crime could evolve from just being something exciting to do, to financial dependence on the sale of stolen cars or car parts. First involvement in car crime can begin as young as ten years old. Initially, the younger boys might act as lookouts, and be passengers in stolen cars. In this way the skills and techniques required were learned from the more experienced offenders. Young people are very concerned with status. The older offenders impressed the younger boys in Pennywell, and acted as role models providing the means by which the younger youths could also achieve status in their own peer groups. Concern for achieving status influenced their choice of car to steal which they claimed was always the fast sporty models. Many stolen cars were driven around local housing estates at high speeds, especially when they have managed to steal a particularly high status model of car. This was a way of 'proving themselves' to their peers. Peer pressure often encouraged the youths to be more daring in their exploits than they would otherwise have been, for example driving faster than they wished. In this way youngsters were 'sucked in' to what appears to be accepted by these youths as 'normal' behaviour for the young males in Pennywell.

Cars also provided the opportunity to make money and the financial rewards from selling stolen cars or parts sustained car crime activity when the initial thrill and sense of adventure had waned. For the majority of these youths stealing cars had progressed to being primarily profit motivated and they had come to rely on the money that their offending behaviour provided. There appeared to be a thriving local black market in cars and car parts. Without exception, all the offenders had 'contacts' in Pennywell who would buy what they had to sell. As well as this, people would ask the youths to steal specific makes of radio cassette, or car parts for them. Clearly, the ease with which stolen property could be sold encouraged and sustained the offenders' criminal activity.

Implications for preventative action
The majority of offenders suggested that the availability of more leisure facilities in the area might have prevented them from getting involved in car crime in the first place. They stressed the importance of targeting young boys aged ten years who were not yet involved in car crime but were in imminent risk of becoming so. They recognised that, once involved in car crime it would be very difficult to divert offenders away from it, especially if offenders have grown to depend on the financial rewards. ...

Clearly, car crime fulfils some very funda-

mental needs of young people, in the first instance for excitement and status, then progressing to the need for money. Any strategy designed to divert offenders away from car crime towards more law abiding activity must compete with these powerful attractions. For young boys, it must provide excitement and the possibility of achieving status in the eyes of their peers. This is at least a realistic objective for such projects. However, they are unlikely to be the most effective way of dealing with the financial attractions of car crime. In this respect, the local market for stolen cars and spare parts would seem to be a more appropriate target, by removing it or at least frustrating it so that it was more difficult to dispose of stolen goods. This suggests a more conventional policing strategy.

The need to 'show off' stolen cars and driving ability is also an important behavioural aspect of car crime which suggests another preventive approach. Introducing changes to the local roads might make it difficult to drive cars in this way and so remove another attraction. For example, eliminating long straights would prevent the build up of car speed and reduce the drama of hand brake turns.

The complex nature of car crime suggests that the most effective preventive approach is to target a number of different aspects of the problem. The findings from this research indicate the need for offender oriented measures – diversionary activities aimed at the very young; for situational measures to frustrate displays of daring driving and for the police to remove the black market for stolen goods.

Pease provides an account of two important matters in relation to crime prevention. Firstly, and in more detail, the need to understand the issue of displacement and then, secondly, he points to the need to improve both central and local government use of available funding.

Pease K (1997) 'Crime Prevention', in Maguire M et al (eds), *The Oxford Handbook of Criminology*, 2nd ed, pp978–980

Primary crime prevention: the declining years?

Given its frequent success, and incorporation into current policy (Garland, 1996), why has primary crime prevention not permeated our thinking more fully? There is a schizoid feeling about it. On the one hand there is a literature enumerating prevention techniques, largely directed at the private sector's techniques of self protection, in which there seems little or no obligation to demonstrate prevention success. The sense of the techniques is deemed self-evident. The most comprehensive example of this is Lawrence Fennelly's *Handbook of Loss Prevention and Crime Prevention,* which has now gone into its third edition (Fennelly, 1996). This excellent reference book assumes the efficacy of situational prevention and does not feel the need to cite rigorously evaluated success. The Fennelly volume will be the primary reference source of security managers charged with protecting their organisations against crime. To them, the effectiveness of primary prevention is not at issue.

In contrast to the Fennelly self confidence, criminologists and police crime prevention officers face inertia and scepticism about claims of efficacy when attempting to make crime prevention a feature of public policy. Before going on to explore the contrast between public- and private-sector prevention, the problems typically encountered by advocates of primary crime prevention will be rehearsed and commented upon. In brief, they are:

1. The claims of crime displacement, whereby crime is moved around rather than prevented, haunts the subject. If total, displacement could be held to render primary crime prevention useless.
2. The lack of imagination which characterises the public sector in its attempts to translate crime prevention policy into practice.
3. The dominance in local authorities of those who find primary prevention unappealing.

Crime displacement: conventional views

There is little point in the policy-maker investing resources and effort into situational (crime) prevention if by doing so he merely shuffles crime from one area to the next but never reduces it. For this reason, the possibility of displacing crime by preventive intervention is a crucial issue for the policy-maker (Heal and Laycock, 1986: 123).

This 'crime shuffling' is what is *conventionally* meant by displacement. Displacement can induce a 'paralysing extreme case pessimism' (Cornish and Clarke, 1986: 3). This is because of the practical limitations upon the measurement of displacement. One can show complete displacement to have occurred, but one can never show complete displacement not to have occurred. The prudent researcher of domestic burglary prevention will examine rates of the same offence in areas contiguous to a project area, to see whether crimes prevented in the project area have simply moved outside it. She may even look at the rate of the offence more generally in the police force area of interest. It is less likely that she will look at other property offences in contiguous areas, still less in the police force area as a whole. The probability that she will look still wider is effectively zero, since she is operating within a budget. Even if money were unlimited but displacement were to diverse offences and places, the effect would disappear into the normal variation in crime rates. Thus if some burglars turn to robberies close to home, some to robberies far from home, some to cheque fraud, some to drug-dealing, and so on, even total displacement would be undetectable. Total displacement is always something with which the extreme case pessimist can taunt the researcher, and never something that can be gainsaid. Whatever the truth, the sceptic can always add 'Ah but …'.

In the above, the *conventionality* of the definition of displacement was stressed. The best-known classification of displacement was devised by Reppetto (1976) and is set out below as modified form by Hakim and Rengert (1981). The classification is:

> 'temporal: committing the intended crime at a different time; spatial: committing the intended crime to the planned type of target in another place; tactical: committing the intended crime using a different method; and crime type/functional: committing a different type of crime from that intended.'

Perpetrator displacement is a category added by Barr and Pease (1990). This occurs where a crime opportunity is so compelling that even if one person passes it up, others are available to take their place (as in stealing by finding, or drug supply).

There is an obvious overlap of these categories. For instance, spatial displacement must always be temporal displacement too. No one can be in two places at once! That apart, they strike the writer as an extraordinarily unimaginative categorisation of the circumstances under which offenders change their minds, or have circumstances change their minds for them. This is not a criticism of Reppetto, who laid the foundation, but of those of us who came after and failed to develop the classification. Some space will be devoted to such a development, since it is of crucial importance for the assessment of crime prevention programmes.

Crime displacement or crime deflection?

Perhaps the most fundamental flaw in the literature on crime displacement is its failure to consider how crime patterns arise. Before crime gets displaced, it must get placed. Why is the pattern of crime as it is? In England and Wales, the 10 per cent of parliamentary constituencies with the highest crime incidence suffer 35 times the amount of crime as the 10 per cent with the lowest incidence, and the patterns can be more extreme depending on areal unit and crime type chosen (Trickett et al, 1992, 1995). These patterns do not emerge

by chance, but are a function of both attractive and repulsive forces.

Traditionally, displacement has been seen as a process of repulsion, whereby an initiative leads crime to go elsewhere. Stenzel (1977) noted that developments in an area can attract as well as repel crime, a point developed by Barron (1991a, 1991b), and by Block and Block (1995). The analogy of a force field in which repulsion and attraction interact should be the starting point for understanding crime (dis)placement. The neglect of Stenzel's point for so long illustrates how one-dimensional the perception of crime displacement has been. Crime is where it is because of the balance of effort and advantage for the offender currently built in to social and physical arrangements. There are two things which may happen when a crime is prevented. It may re-emerge as another crime (displacement). It may also prevent other crimes indirectly (the free-rider, or diffusion of benefits effect). If an offender does not know which places or people are protected and which are not, he or she may generalise from the decision not to commit crime against protected targets to decide not to commit crimes against other targets nearby. In this way the benefits of prevention are diffused. Research shows that the free-rider effect can be substantial (see eg Miethe, 1991; Hesseling, 1995). The fact that displacement has been long debated, and that diffusion of benefits has been so neglected suggests that displacement is dominant not because it reflects a real attempt to understand crime flux, but because it serves as a convenient excuse for doing nothing ('Why bother? It will only get displaced').

A second crucial flaw in considering displacement has been to judge the movement of crime from one setting to another as necessarily a failure. This is mistaken. Barr and Pease (1990, 1991) preferred the word 'deflection' over 'displacement'. Deflection may be a success. Displacement is never referred to as a success. Crime deflection is benign when the deflected crime causes less harm and misery than the original crime. It is also benign when there are good reasons for concentrating crime in particular locations. An obvious instance is prostitution. A distinct red-light area in cities away from residential areas offers the possibility of avoidance. Clearly located areas for drug-dealing offer similar, albeit more contentious, benefits. In short, the view that all displacement/deflection is bad and that all patterns of crime are equally desirable is naive. Displacement/deflection should be seen as a tool of policy rather than as an unmitigated evil.

None of the above should be taken to concede that displacement really is total. The most recent review suggests that it is not (Hesseling, 1995). There are good reasons for believing that review. Crimes are often closely distributed around an offender's home (Forrester et al, 1988), or around a particular purpose (like theft of a means of transport; see Mayhew et al, 1979), or around a particular criminal method, and this plausibly reduces the type and location of crime which should be scrutinised for displacement effects. Where that has been done, displacement has been shown to be far from total.

Prevention in practice
The examples of successful crime prevention cited earlier were intelligently conceived and implemented. However, perfect implementation by government and local practitioners cannot be relied upon. There are probably fundamental political reasons for this, and many of the references to the relevant debate were listed earlier in the chapter. In what follows, the discussion primarily concerns perceptions of how crime prevention should work and competence in its implementation, but there is a blurred boundary between these concerns and the wider political themes alluded to earlier. Let us take the Home Office as an example. Several steps have been taken to improve the status of primary prevention over the last few years. For example, the publications from the Police Research Group of the Home Office disseminate good practice. The Crime Prevention Centre, which trains police

officers as crime prevention officers, has been moved from portable buildings behind Staffordshire Police Headquarters to more prestigious premises in North Yorkshire. However, government expenditure on crime prevention represents only 3 per cent of expenditure on crime and criminal justice matters (Barclay, 1995). Within specifically Home Office expenditure on crime prevention, some 78 per cent goes on CCTV schemes (Koch, 1996). The way the money is dispensed is interesting. Local authorities are invited to submit proposals for appropriate CCTV schemes. They are not asked to submit proposals for maximally effective local schemes for prevention. In other words, whatever the crime problem, 78 per cent of the answer is assumed by Home Office ministers to lie in CCTV.

The bank robber Willie Sutton, when asked why he robbed banks, is alleged to have replied 'Because that's where they keep the money.' If one asks a local authority why it bids for a CCTV system, the same answer applies. The emphasis on CCTV invites local agencies to be cynical, to get money in, and spend it in ways which are of greatest local use and which can be reconciled to Home Office requirements for report. The process whereby local politics and expedience shape expenditure on crime is well documented (Gilling 1994a, 1994b; Buck 1997). In short, good primary prevention requires a clear crime focus, an objective analysis of the presenting problem, and a choice of means from among those available.

Bibliography
Barclay G (1995) *Information on the Criminal Justice System in England and Wales*, London: Home Office.

Barr R and Pease K (1990) 'Crime Placement, Displacement and Deflection', in N Morris and M Tonry (eds), *Crime and Justice: A Review of Research, vol 12*, Chicago, Ill: University of Chicago Press.

Barr R and Pease K (1991) 'A Place for Every Crime and Every Crime in Its Place: An

Alternative Perspective on Crime Displacement', in D J Evans, N R Fyfe and D T Herbert (eds), *Crime , Policing and Place: Essays in Environmental Criminology,* London: Routledge.

Barron J M (1991a) 'Shuffling Crime around: Offender Responses to Preventative Action', unpublished MA thesis, University of Manchester.

Barron J M (1991b) 'Repulsive and Attractive Displacement', paper presented to the American Society of Criminology, San Francisco.

Block R L and Block C B (1995) 'Space Place and Crime: Hot Spot Areas and Hot Places of Liqueur-related Crime', in J E Eck and D Weisburd (eds), *Crime and Place*, Monsey, NY: Willow Tree Press.

Buck W (1997) 'Crime Prevention on Merseyside', unpublished PhD thesis, Manchester University.

Clarke R V (1991) 'Deterring Obscene Phone Callers: the New Jersey Experience', in R V Clarke (ed), *Situational Crime Prevention: Successful Case Studies,* New York: Harrow and Hewston.

Cornish D B and Clarke R V (eds) (1986) *The Reasoning Criminal: Rational Choice Perspectives on Offending*, New York: Springer-Verlag.

Fennelley L J (1996) *Handbook of Loss Prevention and Crime Prevention*, Boston, Mass: Butterworth-Heinemann (3rd ed).

Forrester D P Chatterton M R and Pease K (1988) *The Kirkholt Burglary Prevention Demonstration Project*, Crime Prevention Unit Paper 13, London: Home Office.

Garland D (1996) 'The Limits of the Sovereign State: Strategies in Crime Control in Contemporary Society', *British Journal of Criminology*, 36: 445–471.

Gilling D (1994a) 'Multi-agency Crime Prevention: Some Barriers to Implementation', *Howard Journal*, 33: 109–126.

Gilling D (1994b) 'Multi-Agency Crime

Prevention in Britain: The Problem of Combining Situational and Social Strategies', in R V Clarke (ed), *Crime Prevention Studies 2,* Monse, NY: Willow Tree Press.

Hakim S and Rengert G F (1981), *Crime Spillover*, Beverly Hills, Calif: Sage.

Heal K and Laycock GK (1986) *Situational Crime Prevention: from Theory into Practice*, London: HMSO.

Hesseling R B P (1994) 'Displacement a Review of the Empirical Literature', in R V Clarke (ed), *Crime Prevention Studies 2*, Monse, NY: Willow Tree Press.

Koch B (1996) 'National Crime Prevention Policy in England and Wales 1979–1995', unpublished D Phil thesis, Cambridge: Institute of Criminology.

Mayhew P M, Clarke RV, Hough J M and Winchester S W C (1979) 'Natural Surveillance and Vandalism to Telephone Kiosks', in P M Mayhew, R V Clarke, J N Burrows, J M Hough and S W C Winchester, (eds), *Crime in Public View*, Home Office Research Study No 49, London: HMSO.

Miethe T D (1991) 'Citizen-Based Crime Control Activity and Victimisation Risks: an Examination of Displacement and Free Rider Effects', *Criminology*, 29: 419–440.

Reppetto T A (1976) 'Crime Prevention and the Displacement Phenomenon', *Crime and Delinquency*, 22: 166–177.

Stenzel W W (1977) 'Saint Louis High Impact Crime Displacement Study', paper given at the National Conference on Criminal Justice, February.

Trickett T A, Ellingworth D, Hope T and Pease K (1995) 'Crime Victimisastion in the Eighties: Changes in Area and Regional Inequality', *British Journal of Criminology*, 35: 343–359.

Trickett T A, Seymour J, Osborn D and Pease K (1992) 'What Is Different about High Crime Areas?', *British Journal of Criminology*, 2: 81–90.

The government in the following report adopts the philosophy of horses for courses as a remedy for the problem of criminal behaviour. There is a realisation that there is a need to target the minority of offenders who are responsible for a disproportionate amount of crime. Similarly it is clear that particular crimes may require particular solutions. As part of this thinking the 'what works' approach is to be implemented.

Home Office (2001) *Criminal Justice: The Way Ahead*, pp20–25

Targeting offenders

Recent research suggests that a small group of hard core, highly persistent offenders, probably no more than 100,000 strong – about 10 per cent of all active criminals – may be responsible for half of all crime. Yet the CJS is often slow and ineffective when dealing with these, the very people who should be fast tracked through the courts and subject to the most rigorous supervision.

1. Four out of five offenders coming to court with more than five previous convictions behind them and who are given a prison or community sentence will be back in court within two years to be convicted and sentenced for further offences. These offenders are returning to court again and again without seeing an appreciable increase in the severity of punishment they receive.
2. Although this hard core group has a high probability of being caught and convicted only about 20,000 will be in prison at any one time.
3. Follow-up is weak. Enforcement of community sentences by the probation service has not been as rigorous as required (though it has improved considerably in recent years). Those receiving short prison sentences get no post-release supervision, so too often return quickly to a lifestyle of drug abuse and crime.

Recent research has given us a clearer picture of the most persistent offenders. The 100,000 share a common profile. Half are under 21. Nearly two-thirds are hard drug users. Three-quarters are out of work – with only 22 per cent working full time– and they make most of their income from crime: three in ten are making over £500 a week from crime. More than a third were in care as children. Half have no qualifications at all and 45 per cent were excluded from school. They are also a highly fluid group: this year's 100,000 will not be the same as last year's 100,000 or indeed next year's. Perhaps a fifth of them will stop offending each year, though a fresh cohort of criminals graduating from intermittent to highly persistent criminality will soon take their place.

The Government's approach starts with prevention. Remedying extreme social exclusion, reinforced over many years, is very difficult. It is far better to keep someone in school and educate them properly the first time around than to have to do it on a prison wing 10 or 15 years later. And it is far better to stop a 12- or 13-year-old experimenting with hard drugs than have to break the vicious circle of heroin addiction and crime 10 years and hundreds of offences later. That is why we are directing resources across Government to tackling the underlying causes of crime. We will equip the CJS better to target persistent offenders. Within the CJS, the police have the key role to play. Using all the tools available to them – extra resources, new technology and new techniques – the police will give priority to serious and persistent offenders. The whole active criminal population will be on the DNA database by 2004, the national intelligence model will be applied in every police force, and there will be a CJS-wide target to increase by 100,000 the number of recorded crimes where an offender is brought to justice.

But getting to grips with recidivism goes beyond the police. The lessons of our radical reform of the youth justice system suggest that to tackle persistent offending, we need an approach which systematically:

1. targets offenders and the risk factors that underlie their offending;
2. concentrates on the outcome of preventing offending, rather than the process; and
3. deploys intensive, coordinated programmes based on 'what works' to tackle offending behaviour.

The Government wants to see a new sentencing framework for all offenders based around crime reduction as well as punishment, and taking account of what works to deliver these. Persistent offending should lead to increased severity of punishment, and offenders' progress during sentence should be monitored, with sanctions and incentives to encourage them to change their behaviour. To reduce re-offending we must combine new sentences and increased community supervision with work to resettle offenders and change the behaviours that make them more likely to re-offend. We will build on the good progress made by prison and probation services and consolidate cooperation from non-CJS agencies to develop an holistic approach that includes health, education, employment and housing. To this end, following the 2000 spending review, the Government is providing an additional £689 million funding for the Prison Service over the next three years. Of this, some £211 million will be directed to preventing re-offending through enhanced drug treatment, accredited programmes addressing offending behaviour, and enhanced healthcare. The Prison Service is also investing part of this – £30 million over the next three years – in a new programme to get more prisoners into a job and accommodation on release and so help them stop committing crimes. We will also target the hard core of persistent offenders after their release from prison. The police and probation services will cooperate closely in supervising serious or persistent offenders during community programmes or on release from prison, including the investment of £45million over the next three years in a new Intensive Supervision and Surveillance Programme.

Targeting different types of crime
Different types of crime require different types of response. Over the past four years we have been developing dedicated strategies to prevent vehicle crime, burglary and certain sorts of violent crime. There is an increasing need for specialisation in the CJS. Already, judges handling the most complex, organised crime cases must be appropriately trained. We will ensure that judges continue to have the necessary training and experience to handle complex cases. They will be joined by a specialist cadre of highly trained Crown Prosecutors focusing on the most difficult cases. And we will examine the scope for special review hearings to deal with, for example, drugs or domestic violence.

Targeting crime hot spots
Much crime is highly concentrated – by location, time, perpetrators and victims. Where you live has a large influence on your chances of being victimised. The concentration of crime means our strategic response should be:

1. *targeted* where it will have greatest impact, on the basis of evidence of 'what works'; and
2. *holistic* – working across agencies and with local communities to tackle the multiple problems deprived areas face.

CONCENTRATING EFFORTS
The Government's crime reduction programme, established after the comprehensive spending review, is funding and evaluating a range of interventions to reduce crime. The next phase will be to use the evidence gathered so far to get to grips with crime in the highest crime neighbourhoods across England and Wales. It is not just in the locations and among perpetrators of crime that we find a high concentration – but among the victims too. Twenty per cent of those burgled in 1999 were burgled again within the year and over a third of victims of violent crime were repeat victims within the year. Reducing repeat victimisation not only helps those who have experienced disproportionate suffering, it

helps target persistent crime itself. The police will continue to map victims, crime and fear of crime hotspots in their areas and will promote strategies through their crime and disorder reduction partnerships explicitly to tackle these patterns.

HOLISTIC SOLUTIONS

The National Strategy Action Plan for neighbourhood renewal aims to reverse the 20-year spiral of decline in the poorest parts of the country where crime is typically concentrated. When crime takes hold people, shops and employers leave and, as people move out, the opportunities for crime, vandalism and drug dealing increase. People from ethnic minorities are over-represented in deprived areas and so suffer disproportionately. The neighbourhood renewal strategy requires partnership between Government departments and agencies. And the wider communities and business must use their local knowledge to devise effective local solutions to put more people in work, to cut crime, and to improve skills, health, housing and the physical environment. Partnership and the involvement of local people is crucial and should encompass not just the formal branches of the CJS, such as the police, courts and probation service, but also individuals and organisations in the voluntary sector. The Government has continued to support community and voluntary engagement – best exemplified by Neighbourhood Watch (NW) and Victim Support.

Rational choice on the part of law breakers is a key feature of recent thought on crime prevention. The main idea is that if the pay-off is made more difficult and thus less attractive it will not be chosen as an option and the crime will be prevented. What Akers offers is insight as regards the earlier criminological traditions as to how choices are made by deviants. The suggestion is that much could have been learnt from these sources and that the danger at the moment is that we are reinventing the wheel in criminological terms.

Akers R (1990) 'Rational Choice, Deterrence and Social Learning Theory in Criminology', *Journal of Criminal Law and Criminology*, pp675–676

Assumptions about the level of rationality in criminal acts do not distinguish rational choice from current criminological theories. The basic ideas and central propositions of deterrence and rational choice theory as currently applied in criminology have already been captured in the social learning approach to deviant and criminal behaviour. Specific measures and application of these principles in research on rational choice models may be different; the concepts are not. In some of the most recent rational choice literature, such as Paternoster's, even the empirical measures do not differ. Social learning theory incorporates concepts and processes which the narrow rational choice models do not. When broader models of rational choice have been developed, they begin to take on the appearance of social learning models.

By the time that rational choice models began to take hold in criminology, there already had developed a rich body of theory and research on crime and deviance within the social behaviourist tradition, a tradition which already had incorporated the central proposition of rational choice theory. Yet, none of that tradition was consulted by proponents of rational choice theory. Rather, economic theory was imported and modified as rational choice models of crime. These models then were referred to in modifying the deterrence doctrine in criminology, as if none of the behavioural tradition existed.

One may wish to propose that what seem to be obvious theoretical links disappear upon closer examination, and that rational choice offers a brand new approach with concepts and propositions that differ significantly from anything in social learning or other extant criminological theory. Such an argument would be difficult to sustain, however, and no-one has yet attempted it. Instead, the issue is simply ignored. The links of deterrence and rational choice explanations to social learning principles are clear and cannot be explained away. Social learning is an established, well developed, and well researched theory widely known in criminology. Therefore, it is incumbent upon rational choice theorists to show how their 'new' models do or do not relate to it. They should also examine carefully other existing criminological theories instead of relying on blanket characterisations of 'traditional criminology.' Reinvention of the wheel should be avoided even in criminological theory.

10 Police, Cautioning, Prosecution and Bail

This chapter is largely concerned with the pre-trial stage of the criminal justice system and the first extract provides an introduction to the Government's perception of the issues that arise. A general theme is partnership, as in relation to these issues the expectation is that the causes of crime are at least partly structural; thus numerous Government departments and indeed the community at large have a role to play in tackling crime.

Home Office (2001) *Criminal Justice: The Way Ahead*, pp5–8

Introduction

There never has been a golden age when everyone in our society has been able to live their life free from crime, and free from the fear of crime. But, over much of the last quarter of a century, crime has had an increasingly pervasive – and corrosive – effect on our society. It restricts basic civil liberties and undermines the social bonds integral to strong communities. The factors which led to the rise in crime are complex. But there can be little doubt that contributory factors include the collapse of employment opportunities especially for unskilled men, an explosion in hard drug abuse, a great rise in the availability of higher value consumer goods, and widespread changes in social attitudes. Confronting these issues and creating a more responsible society is a task beyond the criminal justice system alone. It requires concerted action across Government, in local communities, in schools and homes. But an effective, well-run criminal justice system (CJS) can obviously make a significant difference to levels of offending and crime. Such a criminal justice system must be:

1. effective at preventing offending and re-offending;
2. efficient in the way it deals with cases;
3. responsive at every stage to the needs of the victims and the law abiding community; and
4. accountable for the decisions it takes.

In other words, a criminal justice system which delivers justice for all.

A great deal of work has already been made to secure effective cooperation between the police and local communities; to target those crimes of particular public concern; and to bring the often disparate criminal justice agencies together to work as part of a single, more coherent system. But radical reform of the CJS is a long-term project. So, the Government has given early priority to reforming those parts of the system in most urgent need of change. Profound improvement is already underway. Following an inquiry under Sir Iain Glidewell, the Crown Prosecution Service (CPS) has been restructured, its areas made coterminous with police force areas, with more local Chief Crown Prosecutors, and with a greater focus on its core business of prosecuting cases. After years of under-investment, a 23 per cent real term rise in funding for 2001–02 is enabling the CPS to begin the recruitment of scores of extra prosecutors. The youth justice system is also being transformed. The establishment of a national Youth Justice Board, and a network of local youth offending teams, is coordinating effort against youth crime as never before. Repeat cautioning of juveniles has ended, and new final warnings are providing effective early intervention to divert youngsters from crime. Graduated court sanctions are helping to ensure that young offenders, and their parents, take greater responsibility for their behaviour, and allow for the active involvement of the victims in the process. Statutory crime and disorder reduction partnerships between the police, local councils, the health service and voluntary organisations have been established across the country to ensure that everyone plays their part in reducing crime. They are benefiting from a three-year crime reduction programme– including the biggest ever expansion of CCTV this country has seen – to help drive crime down at a local level. New anti-social behaviour orders are bringing peace and quiet to many neighbourhoods, while more than 1,100 successful prosecutions have taken place for new offences of racial violence and racial harassment.

The Probation Service has been reorganised into a single national service beginning in April 2001, again with 42 areas, coterminous with the police. From the same date, magistrates' courts will also be reorganised into the same 42 coterminous areas. The Prison Service is investing large sums into drugs prevention, accredited offending behaviour programmes and better education and training. A range of programmes across Government is helping to tackle the underlying causes of crime, from Sure-Start for pre-school children, the new Connexions programme and the Children's Fund, Welfare to Work, through to substantial programmes within and outside the CJS to tackle drug abuse. These changes – and many more – are bearing fruit. The British Crime Survey (BCS) is the largest and most authoritative survey of overall levels of crime. It showed a 10 per cent drop in crime between 1997 and the end of 1999. This included big falls in the targeted crimes of burglary and car crime (21 per cent and 15 per cent respectively). This recent success is a testament to the dedication of those who work in the CJS, and to the many thousands of volunteers and community

groups who play such a crucial role in making our society safer.

Yet crime is still far higher than it was 20 years ago. And, although the BCS suggests that violent crime overall has fallen, robbery and street crime have risen. Moreover, the demands on the police – not least from increasing public expectations and easier communications (such as mobile phones) – are rising. Alongside all this, the nature of crime is constantly evolving. We know that a substantial proportion of property crime is fuelled by drugs misuse, while evidence suggests that a hard core of about 100,000 offenders are responsible for about a half of all crime. Crime is also increasingly becoming more organised and international in character, and the continuing advances in communications technology will provide further opportunities for criminal behaviour. Over the last 20 years the chances of an offender being brought to book for his or her crimes have fallen dramatically. Less than a quarter of crimes recorded by the police now end in an offender being brought to justice. Four-fifths of persistent offenders are reconvicted within two years of finishing a prison sentence or starting probation supervision. The formal system of justice needs to reflect the common sense all of us share about the best way to deal with wrong-doing in our everyday lives, like the importance of laying down clear and unambiguous rules; responding immediately and consistently if those rules are broken; and making sure that the punishment fits the criminal as well as the crime and gets more demanding if misbehaviour persists. Nothing does more damage to people's confidence in the CJS than a perception that criminals are getting away with their crimes. Why report a crime if there is little prospect of seeing a criminal convicted? Why come forward as a witness if the system cannot protect your interests as well as those of the defendant?

We are therefore committed to raise further the performance of the CJS and, in doing so, raise the confidence of the public, and of those who work in the CJS.

Fundamental to achieving this are two key components: fundamental reform and large-scale investment. Last year we announced the biggest investment in the CJS for 20 years. These resources, which come on stream from April 2001, will allow for the recruitment of hundreds more prosecutors and thousands more police and probation officers, as well as meeting a challenging list of Public Service Agreement (PSA) targets. But we will not get the full value of that investment if those new staff still have to operate within old systems and old ways of thinking, which stifle initiative and breed delay and inefficiency. We must ensure that new investment leads to real change: real increases in the numbers of criminals convicted; real reductions in the number of crimes committed; real improvements in the confidence of victims and witnesses that justice is being delivered. With the resources we have committed to tackling crime and reforming the CJS and through the major reforms outlined here, we aim to deliver by 2004:

1. 100,000 more crimes where a victim sees an offender brought to justice;
2. a 30 per cent reduction in vehicle crime; and a 25 per cent reduction in domestic burglary by 2005; and significant reductions in robbery in our principal cities – on track to meet our target of a 14 per cent reduction by 2005;
3. a five per cent reduction in re-convictions by those under probation supervision – it is estimated that 200,000 crimes might be avoided each year through 30,000 offenders completing accredited programmes; and
4. a 50 per cent increase in the number of qualifications achieved by prisoners in custody and double the number of prisoners going into jobs on their release.

How will all this be achieved? Our strategy has three core components. First, a coordinated attack across Government on the causes of crime. Other departments including the Department for Education and Employment (DfEE), Department of Health (DH) and Department of the Environment, Transport and the Regions (DETR) are now spending billions each year on programmes which will have a direct impact in the short, medium and long term on crime rates: initiatives like Sure Start to improve the life chances of pre-school children; or the £600 million that DfEE is spending on tackling school truancy and exclusion; or the £900 million DETR is investing in turning around England's most deprived neighbourhoods, for whom high crime is one of the worst problems. Second, a clear focus on the types of crime which most concern the public. By encouraging the police and local authorities to target domestic burglary and vehicle crime over the past four years we have made tremendous progress. Now we intend to apply that focused approach to other types of offence – in particular violent crime where we now have a clear strategy in place to make real inroads into offences like street robbery and alcohol related disorder. Third, a comprehensive overhaul of the CJS to lever up performance in catching, trying, convicting, punishing and rehabilitating offenders. Partly, this requires changes in process and method. But none of this will achieve its aim unless it is accompanied by a change in the culture of the whole system in which the particular responsibilities of each of the criminal justice professions are informed by the overriding social purpose of securing a more peaceful life for our citizens by delivering justice and reducing crime.

This document focuses on the third element of this strategy – reform of the CJS. It draws on two key insights:

1. first, that to get to grips with crime, we must get to grips with the 100,000 most persistent criminals who are estimated to commit half of all crime; and
2. second, that as crime and criminality change, so too must the CJS.

By tackling both of these key challenges head on we aim to:

1. close the 'justice gap' and bring more criminals to justice. By targeting persistent offenders and by investing in more staff

and better skills, greater court and prison capacity and new technology we should catch and convict more persistent offenders, more often;

2. ensure that punishments fit the criminal as well as the crime – with a clear message to all persistent offenders that they should reform or expect to stay under supervision. A new sentencing framework would ensure that short as well as long-term prisoners are supervised after release and by investing in drug treatment and more intensive support and surveillance for convicted offenders, we will get re-offending down;

3. put the needs of victims and witnesses more at the centre, not at the periphery of the CJS. We propose new victims' rights to ensure they get the service and support they deserve and we will make reporting crime and finding out about case progress much easier.

Getting crime down is central to the Government's vision of a society at one with itself, where all can prosper and everyone can enjoy reciprocal rights and responsibilities. Achieving such a vision however takes time; there is no quick fix. We have made a good start – but there is much more to be done if we are to restore people's faith in the ability of the criminal system to deliver justice and help reduce crime. This document maps out the way ahead, a route map towards a safer society.

The suggestion is made in this Home Office report that an integrated approach to the criminal justice system, based on the 'what works' philosophy, is desirable. If this is the case and it seems to be a reasonable proposition, then we need to take the message on board at the start of our consideration of the criminal justice system and carry it with us through to the end.

Nuttall C, Goldblatt P and Lewis C (1998) *Reducing Offending: An Assessment of Research Evidence on Ways of Dealing with Offending Behaviour*

The purpose of this study was to try and identify from existing research the best interventions where the aim is to reduce crime. The available evidence suggests the need for an integrated package of best practice developed and delivered consistently over time. For example, prevention programmes for young people should target risk factors affecting all aspects of a child's life. Strategies can and should be developed for particular timescales and particular situations and places. It is clear that some of the best ideas require a wait for the pay-off. The aim should be to have 'what works' considerations in mind – schemes should be well thought out, well delivered and evaluated. This will allow us to learn for the future.

From the report it seems that the following are valuable ideas for an integrated strategy:

1. intensive interventions among children and families at risk;
2. increasing informal social control and social cohesion in communities and institutions that are vulnerable to crime, criminality, drug usage and disorder;
3. intervention in the development of products or services vulnerable to crime so as to make them less so;
4. incentives to individuals and organisations to reduce the risk of crime;
5. targeting situational prevention measures on hot spots and areas of high risk generally;
6. reducing repeat victimisation;
7. placing greater emphasis on problem oriented policing;
8. extending the range of effective interventions with offenders and drug users;

Specifically, on effective policing, it seems that some things such as random patrols are ineffective in reducing crime. Also, it is clear that formal systems of processing juve-niles for minor crimes lead to re-offending. It is equally clear that some tactics do work such as targeting high profile repeat offenders, tar-geting repeat victims, having police patrols directed at places and times where crime is known to occur (hot-spots) and targeting drink-driving. As to sentencing options the following points can be noted. Custody is no more successful at preventing recidivism and is expensive. Clearly at times there is no other option. In 1994 it was estimated that a 20 per cent increase in the prison population was needed to produce a 1 per cent fall in crime. This does not seem like good value. There is evidence that curfew orders with tagging are being seen as a genuine alternative to custody. Community service seems to achieve rehabili-tative goals with some offenders, if focused on practising positive social behaviour and new skills. Some probation programmes can have an impact on offending whilst many do not. Use of the best ideas for probation for fewer offenders and a fine for the rest may be best, though this may move some a step closer to prison. Reconviction rates for fines compare favourably with community penalties. Although this largely reflects their selective use, there is no evidence that the switch from fines to community penalties that has occurred over the past 20 years has achieved anything by way of crime reduction.

Data is provided on an annual basis as regards police numbers and change over time. Females remain under represented at ranks above constable. In contrast there has been some success in the attempts that are being made to recruit officers from ethnic minori-ties.

Povey D and Nguyen K (2001)
Police Service Personnel England and Wales, as at 31 March 2001

There were 125,519 police officers as at 31 March, which was 1.1 per cent more than a year before. This is the largest increase in police strength since 1989. Of these 123,313 were on ordinary duty in the 43 police force areas, and 2,206 officers were on secondment to bodies such as the National Criminal Intelligence Service. Within the service, 21,174 police officers were female, which was 17 per cent of the total; 2,975 or 2.4 per cent of officers were from an ethnic minority group, a rise of 8 per cent over the last year. In the year, 7,415 officers were recruited which was 64 per cent more than in the previ-ous year. The number leaving the police service was 5,849 officers.

POLICE STRENGTH BY RANK AND GENDER

Rank	Male	Female	Total	% Female
Chief Constable	43	3	46	7%
Assistant Chief Constable	136	13	149	9%
Superintendent	1,149	73	1,222	6%
Chief Inspector	1,440	111	1,551	7%
Inspector	5,612	394	6,006	7%
Sergeant	16,770	1,790	18,560	10%
Constable	76,988	18,790	95,778	20%
All ranks	102,139	21,174	123,313	17%

The outcomes as regards those who are arrested are investigated in this Home Office research. The report highlights the importance of the Crown Prosecution Service in relation to the discontinuance of cases and charge reduction. The public are also identified as being very important in their role as complainant.

Phillips C and Brown D (1998)
Entry into the Criminal Justice System: A Survey of Police Arrests and Their Outcomes

The study developed out of a desire to provide information as to the 1.75 million people who are arrested by the police every year in terms of their characteristics, the eventual outcome of the arrest up to conviction and the influences upon the outcomes. It proceeded by examining a sample of over 4,000 cases. A third are arrested for relatively minor offences usually concerned with public disorder. Most are arrested for intermediate offences with burglary, motor crimes and shop-lifting being important examples. Most arrests are not the result of proactive policing but rather calls upon the police by the public. In most cases the evidence relied upon by the police is eyewitness evidence. As many as 6 per cent of arrests are for domestic violence. The arrest population is not typical of the population as a whole. Largely male, 13 per cent black and 6 per cent Asian, 75 per cent under 30 and over 60 per cent have previous convictions. It can be noted that blacks make up 1 per cent of the population and Asians 3 per cent. Arrests are not always in relation to an offence that has just taken place and can indeed be a means to protect vulnerable people. As to the main outcomes, conviction was the outcome for 40 per cent of the sample of those arrested and in all 51 per cent were charged. Many of those convicted had pleaded guilty and only 2 per cent of cases involved a contest. A further 17 per cent were cautioned by the police, 20 per cent were no further action, 12 per cent were other

police disposals whilst 7 per cent of cases were terminated by the CPS. The CPS played an important role in terms of charge reduction particularly in relation to certain offence types. For example over a third of cases of violence and nearly a quarter of fraud cases were so affected. The reasons offered for this were most commonly to reflect the available evidence, to get a guilty plea and to end up dealing with an offence with fewer problems as to intent.

This early American study is instructive as it shows the power that the police have in the criminal justice process. It provides an account supportive of the labelling perspective and it demonstrates how certain groups can become over-policed.

Piliavin I and Briar S (1964) 'Police Encounters with Juveniles'[1], *American Journal of Sociology*, p213

It is apparent from the findings presented above that the police officers studied in this research were permitted and even encouraged to exercise immense latitude in disposing of the juveniles they encountered. That is, it was within the officers' discretionary authority, except in extreme limiting cases, to decide which juveniles were to come to the attention of the courts and correctional agencies and thereby be identified officially as delinquents. In exercising this discretion policemen were strongly guided by the demeanour of those who were apprehended, a practice which ultimately led, as seen above, to certain youths (particularly Negroes and boys dressed in the style of 'toughs') being treated more severely than other juveniles for comparable offences.

But the relevance of demeanour was not limited only to police disposition practices. Thus, for example, in conjunction with police

---

[1] Reproduced with the permission of The University of Chicago Press. Copyright © 1964 by the University of Chicago.

crime statistics the criterion of demeanour led police to concentrate their surveillance activities in areas frequented or inhabited by Negroes.

Reiner's account offers a contemporary British rendition of the unfairness of patterns of policing that results from the phenomena of police discretion.

Reiner R (1997) 'Policing and the Police', in Maguire M et al (eds), *The Oxford Handbook of Criminology*, Oxford: Clarendon Press, 2nd ed, pp1010–1011

Police discretion has often been lauded as not only inevitable but wise and desirable. The central premise of the policing philosophy advocated by Lord Scarman in his report on the 1981 Brixton disorders (Scarman, 1981) – which has become the conventional wisdom of the police elite (Reiner, 1991: chapter 6) – was that public tranquillity should have a greater priority than law enforcement if the two conflicted. Discretion, 'the art of suiting action to particular circumstances', was the better part of police valour.

The problem is that research on police practice has shown that police discretion is not an equal opportunity phenomenon. Some groups are much more likely than others to be at the receiving end of the exercise of police powers. A general pattern of benign under-enforcement of the law disguises the often oppressive use of police powers against unpopular, uninfluential, and hence powerless, minorities. Such groups have been described graphically as 'police property' (Cray, 1972; Lee, 1981: 53–4). The social powerlessness which makes them prey to police harassment also allows the police to neglect their victimisation by crime. They tend to be over-policed and under-protected.

The main grist to the mill of routine policing is the social residuum at the base of the social hierarchy (Brogden, Jefferson, and Walklate, 1988: chapter 6). Those who are stopped and searched or questioned in the street, arrested, detained in the police station, charged, and prosecuted are disproportionately young men who are unemployed or casually employed, and from discriminated against ethnic minorities. The police themselves recognise that their main business involves such groups and their mental social maps delineate them by a variety of derogatory epithets: 'assholes' (Van Maanen, 1978), 'pukes' (Ericson, 1982), 'scum', 'slag' (Smith et al, 1983: vol IV, 164–5), 'prigs' (Young, 1991). In turn public attitude surveys show that such groups have the most negative views of the police (Smith et al, 1983: vol I, 314–15, vol IV, 162–8; Jones and Levi, 1983; Hough and Mayhew, 1983, 1985; Kinsey, 1984; Jones et al, 1986; Crawford et al, 1990; Skogan, 1990, 1996).

The basic organisation and mandate of the police in an industrial society tend to generate this practical concentration on policing what has currently come to be known as the underclass (Dahrendorf, 1985: 98–107). Most police resources are devoted to uniformed patrol of public space (over 65 per cent according to Tarling, 1988: 5). It has long been recognised that the institution of privacy has a class dimension (Stinchcombe, 1963). The lower the social class of people, the more their social lives take place in public space, and the more likely they are to come to the attention of the police for infractions. People are not usually arrested for being drunk and disorderly in their living rooms, but they may be if their living room is the street. Detective work – the next most important concentration of police resources (about 15 per cent according to Tarling, 1988) – largely involves processing those handed over by uniform patrol. Even when it does not, detectives' clientele is still largely the same police property group of 'rubbish' or 'toe-rags' (Maguire and Norris, 1992: 9–11) whose comparative lack of the rights conferred by the institutions of privacy exposes them more easily to detection.

The end result is that most of those handled by the police are from the 'police property' groups. The overwhelming majority of people arrested and detained at police stations are economically and socially marginal. One study of prisoners in custody found that over half (55 per cent) were unemployed. Most of the rest (a third overall) were in manual working-class jobs, predominantly unskilled ones. Only 6 per cent of the sample had non-manual occupations, and of these only one-third (ie 2 per cent overall) were in professional or managerial occupations. Most detainees were young (59 per cent under 25), 87 per cent were men, and 12 per cent were black (Morgan, Reiner, and McKenzie, 1990). The weight of adversarial policing falls disproportionately on young men in the lowest socio-economic groups.

Bibliography

Brogden M, Jefferson T and Walklate S (1988) *Introducing Policework*, London: Unwin.

Crawford A, Jones T and Woodhouse T (1990) *The Second Islington Crime Survey*, London: Middlesex Polytechnic Centre for Criminology.

Cray E (1972) *The Enemy in the Streets*, New York: Anchor.

Dahrendorf R (1985) *Law and Order*, London: Sweet and Maxwell.

Erickson R (1982) *Reproducing Order: a Study of Police Patrol Work*, Toronto: University of Toronto Press.

Hough M and Mayhew P (1983) *The British Crime Survey*, London: HMSO.

Jones S (1986) 'Caught in the Act', *Policing*, 2, 2: 129–140.

Jones S and Levi M (1983) 'The Police and the Majority: The Neglect of the Obvious', *Police Journal*, 56, 4: 351–364.

Kinsey R (1984) *The Merseyside Crime Survey*, Liverpool: Merseyside County Council.

Lee J A (1981) 'Some Structural Aspects of Police Deviance in Relations with Minority Groups', in C Shearing (ed), *Organisational Police Deviance*, Toronto: Butterworth.

Maguire M and Norris C (1992) *The Conduct and Supervision of Criminal Investigations*, London: HMSO.

Morgan R, Reiner R and McKenzie I (1990) 'Police Powers and Policy: a Study of Custody Officers', unpublished Final Report to the Economic and Social Research Council.

Reiner R (1991) *Chief Constables*, Oxford: Oxford University Press.

Scarman Lord (1981) *The Brixton Disorders*, Cmnd 8427, London: HMSO.

Skogan W (1990) *The Police and Public in England and Wales: A British Crime Survey Report*, London: HMSO.

Skogan W (1996) 'Public Opinion and the Police', in W Saulsbury, J Mott and T Newburn (eds), *Themes in Contemporary Policing*, London: Police Foundation/Policy Studies Institute.

Smith D, Gray J and Small, S (1983) *Police and People in London*, London: Policy Studies Institute.

Stinchcombe A (1963) 'Institutions of Privacy in the Determination of Police Administrative Practice', *American Journal of Sociology*, 69, 2: 150–160.

Tarling R (1988) *Police Work and Manpower Allocation*, Research and Planning Unit Paper 47, London: HMSO.

Van Maanen J (1973) 'Observations on the Making of a Policeman', *Human Organisation*, 32, 4: 407–418.

Young M (1991) *An Inside Job*, Oxford: Oxford University Press.

This work by Sanders concentrates upon the degree to which, and the ways in which, the police use of discretion is controlled. Data is also provided in relation to the crime control and due process models of criminal justice systems.

Sanders A (1997) 'From Suspect to Trial', in Maguire M et al (eds), *The Oxford Handbook of Criminology*, 2nd ed, pp1054–1058

Discretion

Discretion is at the root of criminal justice practice. Police officers necessarily exercise discretion in deciding whether to stop and search and arrest. Some people look less 'suspicious' than others, and multitudes of actual or likely offences have to be prioritised. Minor offenders (prostitutes, unlicensed street traders, and so forth) are often simply ignored (Smith and Gray, 1983). Arrest is less frequent than formal action even for relatively serious violence (Clarkson et al, 1994; Hoyle, 1997). Similarly, when officers are able to be proactive (as compared to their usual reactive mode) they have to use discretion about the offences or offenders in which to invest scarce time. Discretion is also created as a consequence of the way offences are defined. Most offences require *mens rea (a* 'guilty mind') which, broadly, amounts to intent. Thus breaking someone's leg by tripping them up would be a crime if done deliberately, but not if done accidentally. A police officer could make an arrest if she reasonably suspected the former, but not if she suspected the latter. However, since intent is so difficult to assess, officers have ample scope to arrest or not according to their preference. So, stop-and-search and arrest decisions are constrained only loosely by law: the powers themselves, based on reasonable suspicion, are ill-defined and subjective, the offences for which the powers are exercised are similarly ill-defined, and the police set their own priorities.

If discretion is not structured primarily by law is it exercised arbitrarily or is it structured by something else? Research on policing suggests four levels at which discretion is structured. First, there are general policing goals. To say that a prime function of the police is to maintain order, control crime, and catch criminals may be trite, but it identifies a fundamental conflict between policing goals and the due-process model. In so far as that model is an obstacle course it can only get in the way of policing goals. To expect the police to abide by due process standards voluntarily – without coercion through 'inhibitory' rules – is therefore unrealistic. The second level is force policy. In the United States, in particular, this can vary considerably from locality to locality (Meehan, 1993). Walmsley (1978) analysed arrest and prosecution figures for homosexuality offences before and after the 1967 Sexual Offences Act (which partially legalised adult male homosexuality). Arrests were considerably higher after the Act than before. This was despite the fact that, assuming no change in the level of homosexual activity, the level of homosexual offences must have gone down as a result of the legal changes. It is likely that police forces were reluctant to arrest and prosecute while the law was the subject of debate, but no longer felt constrained under the new law. Then there is 'cop culture' (see Chan, 1996; Reiner, this volume). Its elements of sexism and racism, and its stereotyping of people and groups of certain types (on 'rough' estates, with certain lifestyles, etc) affect the way officers view society. Take the Code of Practice's reference to 'wary' actions and what is normal for certain 'times and places'. How one views these matters depends on one's culture and individual officers' own ways of mediating that culture. The final level, then, is that of the individual. Police officers are not representative of the population. They tend to be from social strata 'C1' and 'C2', to be more conservative than the average, and to be white and male. The homogeneity of this group, coupled with police training and socialisation processes, enables 'cop culture' to be easily reproduced.

Patterns of bias and police working rules

Research has found that the weak constraints imposed on discretion by law allow considerable scope for bias in policing. Prior to the implementation of PACE in the mid-1980s study after study produced similar findings (eg Stevens and Willis, 1979; Turk and Southgate,

1981; Field and Southgate, 1982; Smith and Gray, 1983; Willis, 1983). Smith and Gray, for example, found that there was no 'reasonable suspicion' in one-third of all stops which they observed, and Willis found that stop-and-search was often based on the suspects' 'movements'. 'This category', Willis remarked, 'covered stops on grounds which police officers find it hard to specify.' This would be consistent with the crime-control model if officers relied on intangible but reliable 'instinct' or 'experience', but the arrest rate (which was generally low at perhaps 10 per cent of all stops) was particularly low in the 'movements' cases. However, as stop-and-search is useful for intelligence-gathering (Brogden 1985; McConville et al, 1991), a low arrest rate is not inconsistent with crime control goals. It certainly appears that due-process standards, even the minimal requirements of 'reasonable suspicion', were rarely adhered to. These findings are, of course, consistent with research in the United States (see, for instance, Piliavin and Briar, 1964; and, generally, Reiner, 1992), which has similar rules on stop-and-search and arrest. Stops were often based on classic stereotypes leading to patterns of bias on lines of class, gender, and race (discussed by Reiner and by Smith, from a different perspective, this volume).

The introduction of PACE in the mid-1990s was intended to make some difference. For although PACE gives more, not less, power to the police, it also incorporates more controls than operated hitherto. These include requirements to tell suspects why they are being arrested or stop-searched and to make records of the incident. However, stop-and-search and arrest decisions are of intrinsically low visibility (Goldstein, 1960). Thus written records can be constructed after the event (McConville et al, 1991: chapter 5). No longer are stops recorded as 'movements', but the reason for stops could be unchanged. As one officer put it to McConville et al (1991), he would stop a suspect 'instinctively and then think about how he would satisfy a disinter-

ested third party' (field notes). This suggests that the Code has altered the way officers *account* for their exercise of discretion, but not the way they *actually* exercise it. Accounts of incidents can correspond as much with legal expectations as with the reality of the incidents (Scott and Lyman, 1968; Ericson, 1981). Moreover, few stops are recorded at all. But this is only a breach of PACE if PACE powers are actually exercised (that is, if the stop is not consensual) and if there is a search or arrest (Sanders and Young, 1994: chapter 2). Predictably, research has not found the control and accountability mechanisms in PACE to be effective. Norris et al (1992) observed 272 stops in one London borough, of which 28 per cent were of black people despite only 10 per cent of the local population being black. The effect is continued at the arrest stage: black people constituted 16 per cent of all Metropolitan Police arrests in 1987, but comprised only 5 per cent of the capital's population (Home Office, 1988). In Leeds in 1987, 6 per cent of arrests were of black people, who comprised just 3 per cent of the population (Jefferson and Walker, 1992). Black people, Brown concluded in a review of PACE research, are more likely to be stopped than white people or Asians, more likely to be repeatedly stopped, more likely (if stopped) to be searched, and more likely to be arrested (1997: chapters 2 and 4; see also NACRO, 1997). How far race in itself leads to this disproportionate attention from the police and how far it stems from other sociodemographic factors (namely, class, gender, and location) is not known. It may be that crime is disproportionately prevalent among young black males, but this is a crime-control justification which should not be accepted without evidence. As it happens, although more stops lead to more arrests, the proportion of stops which lead to arrest decreases as the number of stops rises. This predictable consequence of the crime-control approach can be observed in most years since 1986 as the number of stops has increased fivefold since 1986 yet the proportion leading to arrest declined from 17 per cent in 1984 to 12 per cent in 1986 (see Sanders and Young, 1994: chapter 2; Brown, 1997: chapter 2). In other words, it is rare for police suspicions to be borne out by evidence on which to base an arrest.

McConville et al (1991) identify several 'working rules' which structure police decision-making. The first is 'previous' (ie being known to the police). Sometimes this 'bureaucratic' mode of suspicion (Matza, 1969) is sufficient on its own. As an arresting officer told McConville et al: 'When you get to know an area, and see a villain about at 2.00 am in the morning, you will always stop him to see what he is about' (1991: 24). The second concerns disorder and police authority. Dealing with disorder is a prime police task. Although Shapland and Vagg (1988) found that the police do not usually arrest when they intervene in disorderly incidents, arrests are usual if the disorder does not cease even when it is trivial and only the police are involved (Brown et al, 1994). This is in part because of the challenge thereby presented to police authority, even if no specific charge fits the facts. Hoyle (1997) found the same in relation to domestic violence incidents. Other working rules include consideration of types of victims and their wishes, 'information received', and workload. But perhaps the most important working rule is 'suspiciousness'. This entails the suspect 'being in the right place at the right time', or being 'out of the ordinary' or 'uncooperative', or keeping the wrong company, or its being 'just a matter of instinct' on the officer's part, 'something undefinable' (all these phrases are from officers quoted in McConville et al, 1991: 26–28).

Bibliography
Brogden M (1985) 'Stopping the People: Crime Control versus Social Control', in J Baxter and L Koffman (eds), *Police: the Constitution and the Community*, Abingdon: Professional Books.

Brown D (1997) *PACE 10 Years On: A Review of the Research*, London: Home Office.

Chan J (1996) 'Changing Police Culture', *British Journal of Criminology*, 36: 109.

Clarkson C et al (1994) 'Criminalising Assault', *British Journal of Criminology*, 34: 15.

Ericson R (1981) *Making Crime*, London: Butterworths.

Field S and Southgate P (1982) *Public Disorder*, London: Home Office.

Goldstein J (1960) 'Police Discretion Not to Invoke the Criminal Process: Low Visibility Decisions in the Administration of Justice', *Yale Law Journal*, 69: 543.

Home Office (1988) *Criminal Statistics*, London: HMSO.

Hoyle C (1997) *Policing Domestic Violence: the Role of the Victim*, Oxford: Oxford University Press.

Jefferson T and Walker M (1992) 'Ethnic Minorities in the Criminal Justice System', *Criminal Law Review*, 83–85.

McConville M et al (1991) *The Case for the Prosecution*, London: Routledge.

Matza D (1969) *Becoming Deviant*, New York: Prentice Hall.

Meehan A (1993) 'Internal Police Records and the Control of Juveniles', *British Journal of Criminology*, 33: 504.

NACRO (1997) *The Tottenham Experiment*, London: NACRO.

Norris C et al (1992) 'Black and Blue: an Analysis of the influence of Race on Being Stopped by the Police', *British Journal of Sociology*, 43: 207.

Piliavin I and Briar S (1964) 'Police Encounters with Juveniles', *American Journal of Sociology*, 70: 206–214.

Reiner R (1992) *The Politics of the Police*, Brighton: Wheatsheaf.

Reiner R (1997) 'Policing and the Police', in M Maguire et al (eds), *The Oxford Handbook of Criminology*, Oxford: Clarendon Press (2nd ed).

Sanders A and Young R (1994) *Criminal Justice*, London: Butterworths.

Scott M and Lyman S (1968) 'Accounts', *American Sociological Review*, 33: 46–62.

Shapland J and Vagg J (1988) *Policing by the Public*, London: Routledge.

Smith D, Gray J and Small S (1983) *Police and People in London*, London: Policy Studies Institute.

Smith D (1997) 'Ethnic Origins, Crime, Criminal Justice', in M Maguire et al (eds), *The Oxford Handbook of Criminology*, Oxford: Clarendon Press (2nd ed).

Stevens P and Willis C (1979) *Race, Crime and Arrests*, London: HMSO.

Tuck M and Southgate P (1981) *Ethnic Minorities, Crime and Policing*, London: HMSO.

Walmsley R (1978) 'Indecency between Males and the Sexual Offences Act 1967', *Criminal Law Review*, 400–407.

Willis C (1983) *The Use, Effectiveness and Impact of Police Stop and Search Powers*, London: HMSO.

The author had six months access to Kilburn police in London. The information he gathered suggests that some form of rethink may be required as regards prevailing views on policing.

Rose D (1996) *In the Name of the Law*, p230

It is not possible to be categoric. But on the evidence of my own eyes, I do not believe that the usual bleak descriptions of police or canteen culture deserve their current blanket status. They are becoming an anachronism. I caught one straw in the wind, appropriately enough, on an early visit to the Kilburn police canteen. There, in easy earshot of her colleagues, a PC of five years' service told me: 'I've been "out" as a lesbian since I joined the job, and it's not been a problem. My team come to the house I share with my partner. Even the older ones just accept it.' She was not the only 'out' lesbian in the division. Later, when another female constable began a relationship with an officer from another station, it became an item of interested gossip – but in such unpejorative terms that I did not realise for some time that the object of her affections was also a woman. Until his promotion a few months earlier, the division had also included an 'out' gay man: he was recalled by his colleagues as a 'good copper'.

Some of this tolerance is down to good management. Euan Read of Thames Valley said: 'If you make clear as a shift inspector what standards you expect, and what you will tolerate, they will follow you. If two of your officers beat someone up, and you do nothing, then the rest will follow that lead. I had a gay woman on a shift and she had had a bad time from my predecessor. She ended up inviting me and some of her colleagues to her gay wedding.'

There is already a Gay and Lesbian Police Association, which mounted a recruitment stand at the 1994 Gay Pride conference. I compared notes with Mariecca Coulson, who joined the Metropolitan Police in the late 1970s, and now works as a lawyer. 'Fifteen years ago, all this would have been unthinkable,' she said. 'There was once a girl who happened to be gay who made the mistake of confiding in her skipper one night when she was drunk. It went round the station overnight and her life was made a misery.'

The persistence of racism within the police service is so well documented that any optimism must be tempered with strong caution.
...

Insight into the powers and duties of the police was provided when a private citizen decided to try and obtain an order against a police force that would have compelled the force to enforce the law on gaming. The case was heard by the Court of Appeal.

R v *Commissioner of Police of the Metropolis, ex parte Blackburn* [1968] 1 All ER 763 at 765–777 Court of Appeal (Lord Denning MR, Edmund Davies and Salmon LJJ)

Lord Denning MR

Mr Blackburn, the applicant, moves for a mandamus against the Commissioner of Police of the Metropolis, the respondent. He says that it was the commissioner's duty to enforce the law against gaming houses, and he has not done it. He seeks an order to compel the commissioner to do it. This motion, thus made, raises questions of constitutional significance. I will deal with them separately.

1. THE LAW AS TO GAMING HOUSES

The common law of England has always condemned gaming-houses. This is not because gambling is wicked in itself, but because of the evils attendant on it. Hawkins in his Pleas of the Crown (Book I, c75, s6, 1716 ed p198) says ...

'... all common gaming houses are nuisances in the eye of the law, not only because they are great temptations to idleness, but also because they are apt to draw together great numbers of disorderly persons, which cannot but be very inconvenient to the neighbourhood.'

The statute law of England has likewise condemned gaming-houses. As early as 1541 in the time of Henry VIII (33 Hy 8 c 9, para 11) Parliament enacted that no person should for his gain keep a gaming-house. The reason then was because gambling disturbed the military training. It distracted the young men from practising archery which was needed for the defence of the country. Several statutes have been passed since. All of them condemned gaming houses because of the mischiefs attendant on them.

When roulette was first introduced over 200 years ago, Parliament tried to stop it. A statute of 1744 (18 Geo 2, c34), recited that the 'pernicious game called roulet, or roly-poly' was practised. It prohibited any person from keeping any house for playing it.

But all those statutes proved of no avail to prevent the mischief. Blackstone (Commentaries, Book IV, c13, s8, 8th ed, 1778, pp171, 173) said that the legislature had been careful to pass laws to prevent 'this destructive vice,' but these laws had failed to achieve their object. The reason for the failure was because the gamblers were too quick-witted for the law to catch them. He said (Commentaries, Book IV, c13, 8th ed, p173) that '... the inventions of sharpers being swifter than the punishment of the law, which only hunts them from one device to another.' So much so that by the beginning of the 19th century gaming-houses were a scandal. The Victorian legislation, aided by the Victorian judges in *Jenks* v *Turpin* (1884) 13 QBD 505, D.C. reduced the evil but did not exterminate it.

History has repeated itself in our own time. Parliament made an attempt in 1960 to put the law on a sound footing. It had before it the Report (1949–1951) of the Royal Commission (Cmd 8190) on the subject. The report drew a clear distinction between promoters who organised gaming for their own profit (which was an evil) and those who arranged gaming for the enjoyment of others without making a profit out of it themselves (such as gaming in a members' club, which was innocent). The Royal Commission (Cmd 8190, p125, para 412) thought that 'the main object of the criminal law should be to prevent persons being induced to play for high stakes for the profit of the promoter'. They recommended legislation to achieve this object. The draftsmen set to work and produced the Bill which became the Betting and Gaming Act, 1960, since re-enacted in the Betting, Gaming and Lotteries Act, 1963. The old common law was abolished. The old statutes were repealed. New sections were enacted with the intention of ensuring that promoters did not make high profits out of gaming, either in clubs or elsewhere.

These sections have lamentably failed to achieve their object. Just as in Blackstone's time, so in ours. The casino companies have set up gaming houses and made large profits out of them. They always seem to be one device ahead of the law. The first device they used after the Act of 1960 was to levy a toll on the stakes. They used to promote roulette without a zero and demand sixpence for themselves on every stake. That device was declared unlawful in *Quinn* v *Mackinnon* [1963] 1 QB 874; [1963] 2 WLR 391; [1963] 1 All ER 570, DC. Next, they claimed that they could take sixpence from every player on every spin of the wheel. That device too was held to be unlawful in this court in *Allan (J M) (Merchandising) Ltd* v *Cloke* [1963] 2 QB 340; [1963] 2 WLR 899; [1963] 2 All ER 258, CA. Then they claimed that they could charge every player 10 shillings for every 20 minutes. That too was found to be unlawful in *Kelland* v *Raymond* [1964] 2 QB 108; [1964] 2 WLR 662; [1964] 1 All ER 564, DC.

But one of their devices at this time succeeded. It was in chemin-de-fer. The promoters charged every player £5 for every 'shoe' which took about 35 minutes. This was held to be lawful in *Mills* v *Mackinnon* [1964] 2 QB 96; [1964] 2 WLR 363; [1964] 1 All ER 155, DC. I must say I doubt that decision. I should have thought that £5 for every 35 minutes was worse than 10 shillings every half hour. At any rate, it is more profitable.

After those cases, the casino companies thought out a new device which proved to be far more profitable. They promoted roulette with a zero. This is a game in which the chances over a long period mightily favour the holder of the bank. Under this new device, the organisers so arranged things that they themselves nearly always held the bank. But they claimed it was lawful because the croupier every half hour 'offered the bank' to the players. Very rarely, if ever, was the offer accepted, for the simple reason that it may be ruinous to hold the bank for only a few spins of the wheel. It is only worth holding if you can hold it for a long time, such as a week or a month. Nevertheless the organisers claimed that this 'offer of the bank' rendered the

gaming lawful. They were supported, we were told, by the opinion of some lawyers in the Temple, but there were conflicting views. At any rate, this device was highly profitable. For a time it was surprisingly successful, provided it was skilfully worked. It was not worked very skilfully in the first two cases, and the casino companies were convicted, one in *Blackpool, Casino Club (Bolton) Ltd* v *Parr* (1966) 64 LGR 155, DC and the other in *Southend, Kursaal Casino Ltd* v *Crickitt* [1966] 1 WLR 960; [1966] 2 All ER 639, DC. But this device was worked skilfully in the third case, and the casino company was acquitted in the Divisional Court in *Kursaal Casino Ltd* v *Crickitt (No 2)* [1967] 1 WLR 1227; [1967] 3 All ER 360, DC. That case has, however, recently been overruled by the House of Lords, [1968] 1 WLR 53; [1968] 1 All ER 139, HL (E). The device of 'offering the bank' will no longer work.

But the casino companies do not seem to be unduly worried. They have not stopped their gaming. They have put on their thinking-caps and brought out another device. They do not trouble now to 'offer the bank' to a player. They give a winner two kinds of chips, ordinary chips on which he collects his winnings, and special chips which he throws back. No doubt they hope that the same will happen with this device as with the others. It will have to be tested in the courts. Meanwhile they expect to carry on with their gaming. If this is then held to be unlawful, they will try to think of another device. and so on ad infinitum: at least they may think so.

What are the consequences? They were stated with striking clarity by the Secretary of State for Home Affairs, Mr Roy Jenkins, in 'The Times' newspaper of September 13, 1966. He is reported as saying:

'The Betting and Gaming Act, 1960, has led to abuses, particularly in the field of gaming clubs, which were not foreseen by its promoters. This country has become a gambler's paradise, more wide open in this respect than any comparable country. This has led to a close and growing connection between gaming clubs and organised crime, often violent crime, in London and other big cities. The fat profits made by proprietors (often out of the play itself and quite contrary to the intention of the 1960 Gaming Act) made them sitting targets for protection rackets. In addition, gaming on credit, with gaming debts unenforceable at law, means that strong-arm methods are sometimes used to extort payment from those who have gambled beyond their means.'

Mr Blackburn says that this state of affairs is due to the failure of the police to enforce the law and seeks to compel them to do it.

2. THE STEPS TAKEN BY MR BLACKBURN

In 1966 Mr Blackburn was concerned about the way in which the big London clubs were being run. He went to see a representative of the Commissioner of the Police of the Metropolis and told him that illegal gaming was taking place in virtually all London casinos. He was given to understand, he says, that action would be taken. But nothing appeared to be done. On March 15, 1967, Mr Blackburn wrote a letter to the commissioner in which he again stated that illegal gaming was taking place. He asked the commissioner to assist him in prosecuting several London clubs. Following that letter he was seen by Mr Bearman on behalf of the commissioner. Mr Bearman explained to him that there were difficulties in enforcing the provisions of the Act. He added that the way in which police manpower was used was a matter for the discretion of the commissioner; and that it was felt that, as the gaming law stood, there were higher priorities for the deployment of police manpower. He also stated that it would be contrary to a policy decision for him to promote or assist in the promotion of a prosecution for breach of section 32 of the Act of 1963.

Mr Blackburn was dissatisfied and made application to the Divisional Court for a mandamus directed to the commissioner requiring three things: (1) to assist him and others to prosecute gaming clubs; (2) to assist him in a particular complaint against a named club; and (3) to reverse the policy decision. The Divisional Court rejected his application. He appeals in person to this court.

Mr Worsley, for the commissioner, took an objection to the jurisdiction of this court. He argued that this was an appeal from a judgment of the High Court 'in a criminal cause or matter,' and that an appeal did not lie to the Court of Appeal, see section 31 (1) (a) of the Supreme Court of Judicature (Consolidation) Act, 1925. He referred us to several cases on the subject, particularly *Provincial Cinematograph Theatres* v *Newcastle-upon-Tyne Profiteering Committee* (1921) 27 Cox CC 63; 37 TLR 799, HL, in the House of Lords. I think there might perhaps have been something in this objection if Mr Blackburn had persisted in his first two requests. They might be said to be steps in a criminal matter. But Mr Blackburn withdrew those two and confined himself to the third, ie, requiring the commissioner to reverse his policy decision. It seems to me that this is not a step in any 'criminal cause or matter.' Mr Blackburn can appeal, I think, to this court on the matter. So I turn to it.

3. THE POLICY DECISION

The policy decision was a confidential instruction issued to senior officers of the Metropolitan Police. Mr Bearman exhibited it in his affidavit in these proceedings. It was dated April 22, 1966, and was in effect an instruction to take no proceedings against clubs for breach of the gaming laws unless there were complaints of cheating or they had become haunts of criminals. The actual terms of the instruction were as follows:

'Confidential instruction. Gaming in registered or licensed clubs. For the time being all applications for authority for an inside observation in licensed or registered clubs for the purpose of detecting gaming are to be submitted to A1 branch for my covering approval.'

Mr Bearman explained in his affidavit that the reason for the instruction was:

'In view of the uncertainty of the law, the expense and manpower involved in keeping gaming observations in such clubs were not justified unless there were complaints of cheating or reason to suppose that a particular club had become a haunt of criminals.'

It appeared in evidence before us that this policy decision was made under a misapprehension. It was thought that *Kursaal Casino Ltd* v *Crickitt* [1966] 1 WLR 960, was going to the House of Lords, in which event the law would be settled about the 'offer of the bank.' But in point of fact that case was not going there, and the commissioner's officers do not seem to have known of it. I do not know that that misapprehension would have made much difference. The commissioner got to know later that that case was not going there, and he did not revoke the policy decision even then. It was the Southend police who took action, as they had done before. The Metropolitan Police did not take action: it was the enterprising Superintendent Crickitt of Southend.

At any rate, the result of the policy decision of April 22, 1966, was that thenceforward, in this great metropolis, the big gaming clubs were allowed to carry on without any interference by the police. We were told that in one or two cases observations had previously been started: but after this policy decision they were discontinued. No prosecutions were instituted in the metropolis against these clubs. That is what Mr Blackburn complains of. He says that the policy decision was erroneous and that it was the duty of the commissioner to prosecute. To this I now turn.

4. The Duty of the Commissioner of Police of the Metropolis

The office of Commissioner of Police within the Metropolis dates back to 1829 when Sir Robert Peel introduced his disciplined force. The commissioner was a justice of the peace specially appointed to administer the police force in the metropolis. His constitutional status has never been defined either by statute or by the courts. It was considered by the Royal Commission on the Police in their Report in 1962 (Cmnd 1728). But I have no hesitation in holding that, like every constable in the land, he should be, and is, independent of the executive. He is not subject to the orders of the Secretary of State, save that under the Police Act, 1964, the Secretary of State can call upon him to give a report, or to retire in the interests of efficiency. I hold it to be the duty of the Commissioner of Police of the Metropolis, as it is of every chief constable, to enforce the law of the land. He must take steps so to post his men that crimes may be detected; and that honest citizens may go about their affairs in peace. He must decide whether or no suspected persons are to be prosecuted; and, if need be, bring the prosecution or see that it is brought. But in all these things he is not the servant of anyone, save of the law itself. No Minister of the Crown can tell him that he must, or must not, keep observation on this place or that; or that he must, or must not, prosecute this man or that one. Nor can any police authority tell him so. The responsibility for law enforcement lies on him. He is answerable to the law and to the law alone. That appears sufficiently from *Fisher* v *Oldham Corporation* [1930] 2 KB 364; 46 TLR 390, and *Attorney-General for New South Wales* v *Perpetual Trustee Co Ltd* [1955] AC 457; [1955] 2 WLR 707; [1955] 1 All ER 846, PC.

Although the chief officers of police are answerable to the law, there are many fields in which they have a discretion with which the law will not interfere. For instance, it is for the Commissioner of Police of the Metropolis, or the chief constable, as the case may be, to decide in any particular case whether inquiries should be pursued, or whether an arrest should be made, or a prosecution brought. It must be for him to decide on the disposition of his force and the concentration of his resources on any particular crime or area. No court can or should give him direction on such a matter. He can also make policy decisions and give effect to them, as, for instance, was often done when prosecutions were not brought for attempted suicide. But there are some policy decisions with which, I think, the courts in a case can, if necessary, interfere. Suppose a chief constable were to issue a directive to his men that no person should be prosecuted for stealing any goods less than £100 in value. I should have thought that the court could countermand it. He would be failing in his duty to enforce the law.

A question may be raised as to the machinery by which he could be compelled to do his duty. On principle, it seems to me that once a duty exists, there should be a means of enforcing it. This duty can be enforced, I think, either by action at the suit of the Attorney-General or by the prerogative writ of mandamus. I am mindful of the cases cited by Mr Worsley which he said limited the scope of mandamus. But I would reply that mandamus is a very wide remedy which has always been available against public officers to see that they do their public duty. It went in the old days against justices of the peace both in their judicial and in their administrative functions. The legal status of the Commissioner of Police of the Metropolis is still that he is a justice of the peace, as well as a constable. No doubt the party who applies for mandamus must show that he has sufficient interest to be protected and that there is no other equally convenient remedy. But once this is shown, the remedy of mandamus is available, in case of need, even against the Commissioner of Police of the Metropolis.

Can Mr Blackburn invoke the remedy of mandamus here? It is I think an open question whether Mr Blackburn has a sufficient interest to be protected. No doubt any person who was adversely affected by the action of the commissioner in making a mistaken policy decision would have such an interest. The difficulty is to see how Mr Blackburn himself has been affected. But without deciding that question, I turn to see whether it is shown that the Commissioner of Police of the Metropolis has failed in his duty. I have no doubt that some of the difficulties have been due to the lawyers and the courts. Refined arguments have been put forward on the wording of the statute which have gained acceptance by some for a time. I can well understand that the commissioner might hesitate for a time until those dif-ficulties were resolved; but, on the other hand, it does seem to me that his policy decision was unfortunate. People might well think that the law was not being enforced, especially when the gaming clubs were openly and flagrantly being conducted as they were in this great city. People might even go further and suspect that the police themselves turned a blind eye to it. I do not myself think that was so. I do not think that the suggestion should even be made. But nevertheless the policy decision was, I think, most unfortunate.

The matter has, I trust, been cleared up now. On December 19, 1967, the House of Lords in *Kursaal Casino Ltd* v *Crickitt (No 2)* [1968] 1 WLR 53, made it quite clear that roulette with a zero was not rendered lawful simply by the 'offer of the bank'. Following that decision, on December 30, 1967, the commissioner issued a statement in which he said: 'It is the intention of the Metropolitan Police to enforce the law as it has been interpreted.' That implicitly revoked the policy decision of April 22, 1966; and the commissioner by his counsel gave an undertaking to the court that that policy decision would be officially revoked. We were also told that immediate steps are being taken to consider the 'goings-on' in the big London clubs with a view to prosecution if there is anything unlawful. That is all that Mr Blackburn or anyone else can reasonably expect.

5. CONCLUSION

This case has shown a deplorable state of affairs. The law has not been enforced as it should. The lawyers themselves are at least partly responsible. The niceties of drafting and the refinements of interpretation have led to uncertainties in the law itself. This has discouraged the police from keeping observation and taking action. But it does not, I think, exempt them also from their share of the responsibility. The proprietors of gaming houses have taken advantage of the situation. By one device after another they have kept ahead of the law. As soon as one device has been held unlawful, they have started another. But the day of reckoning is at hand. No longer will we tolerate these devices. The law must be sensibly interpreted so as to give effect to the intentions of Parliament; and the police must see that it is enforced. The rule of law must prevail.

Salmon LJ

The chief function of the police is to enforce the law. The Divisional Court left open the point as to whether an order of mandamus could issue against a chief police officer should he refuse to carry out that function. Constitutionally it is clearly impermissible for the Secretary of State for Home Affairs to issue any order to the police in respect of law enforcement. In this court it has been argued on behalf of the commissioner that the police are under no legal duty to anyone in regard to law enforcement. If this argument were correct it would mean that insofar as their most important function is concerned, the police are above the law and therefore immune from any control by the court. I reject that argument. In my judgment the police owe the public a clear legal duty to enforce the law – a duty which I have no doubt they recognise and which generally they perform most conscientiously and efficiently. In the extremely unlikely event, however, of the police failing or refusing to carry out their duty, the court would not be powerless to intervene. For example, if, as is quite unthinkable, the chief police officer in any district were to issue an instruction that as a matter of policy the police would take no steps to prosecute any housebreaker, I have little doubt but that any householder in that district would be able to obtain an order of mandamus for the instruction to be withdrawn. Of course, the police have a wide discretion as to whether or not they will prosecute in any particular case. In my judgment, however, the action I have postulated would be a clear breach of duty. It would he so improper that it could not amount to an exercise of discretion.

Mr Worsley has argued that the discretion is absolute and can in no circumstances be challenged in the courts. He instances the policy decision not to prosecute, save in exceptional circumstances, young teenage boys who have had sexual intercourse with girls just under the age of 16. But this, in my view, is an entirely different and perfectly proper exercise of discretion. The object of the Criminal Law Amendment Act, 1885, which made it a criminal offence to have sexual intercourse with girls under 16, was passed in order to protect young girls against seduction. Unfortunately, in many of the cases today in which teenage boys are concerned, it is they rather than the girls who are in need of protection. These are not the kinds of cases which the legislature had in mind when the Criminal Law Amendment Act, 1885, was passed. Moreover, experience has shown that if young boys are prosecuted in such circumstances, the courts usually take the humane and sensible course of imposing no penalty. The object of the statute which made housebreaking a crime was quite simply to prevent housebreaking in the interests of society. Similarly, the object of sections 32 to 40 of the Betting, Gaming and Lotteries Act, 1963, and the corresponding provisions of the Betting and Gaming Act, 1960, which the statute of 1963 replaced, was quite simply to protect society against the evils which would necessarily follow were it possible to build up large fortunes by the exploitation of gaming. The statutes of 1960 and 1963 were designed to prevent such exploitation and would have been entirely effective to do so had they been enforced. Regrettably they have not been properly enforced. As a result, and entirely contrary to the intention and contemplation of Parliament, an immense gaming industry, particularly in London, has been allowed to grow up during the last seven years. This has inevitably brought grave social evils in its train – protection rackets, crimes of violence and widespread corruption. There are no doubt a few large establishments which are respectably run and from which these evils are excluded. But for every one of these, there are scores of others. As long as it remains possible for large fortunes to be made by the private exploitation of gaming, the evils to which I have referred will grow and flourish until they threaten the whole fabric of society. Since large fortunes can be made out of the exploitation of gaming, naturally a great deal of ingenuity has been exercised to devise schemes for the purpose of evading the law. With a little more resolution and efficiency, these schemes could and should have been frustrated.

In the present case we are concerned chiefly with the game of roulette played with a zero. For the reasons which appear in the evidence before us, so long as the odds offered against any one number are no more than 35 to 1, the chances favour the bank by 3 to 10 per cent, according to the way the bets are laid. If the house holds the bank, the house in the long run is bound to win. It follows that this contravenes section 32 (1) (a) and (b) of the Act of 1963, for the 'chances in the game are not equally favourable to all the players' (of whom the bank is one) (subsection (1) (a)), and the 'gaming is so conducted that the chances therein are not equally favourable to all the players' (subsection (1) (b)). We have all heard of the very old song 'The Man who Broke the Bank at Monte Carlo'. The bank could, of course, have a very bad run of luck during one evening and lose heavily. It could perhaps have a very bad run of luck for days and even for weeks, but month in and month out, it is bound to win. This, amongst other reasons, is why the house which holds the bank month in and month out is bound to be more favourably placed than any player who may hold it sporadically for comparatively short periods of time.

In *Kursaal Casino Ltd* v *Crickitt* [1966] 1 WLR 960, which was decided in the Divisional Court on March 23, 1966, the justices had held that for the house to hold the bank contravened the law. The point taken by the prosecution, which to my mind was manifestly a good point, was that whoever held the bank was ex hypothesi a player and accordingly the game could not be equally favourable to all players and was therefore illegal. It would, therefore, make no differ-

ence that the house went through the motions of offering the bank to the players and that very occasionally the offer was accepted for short periods of time. The defence had argued that as the bank was offered at regular intervals to all the players, the chances were equal for all. The justices convicted. Incidentally, they also held that as there must be very many players who could not afford to take the bank, the offer, therefore, was in any event neither genuine nor realistic. The Divisional Court, [1966] 1 WLR 960, upheld the conviction and concluded that there was ample evidence to support the finding that the offer of the bank was neither genuine nor realistic. It is perhaps a pity, if this was regarded as a test case, that the prosecution were not advised to call evidence, which could easily have been supplied by any actuary or anyone conversant with the game, that whatever the means of the players or however their liability might be limited, it would be quite impossible to offer the bank on any conceivable terms which could possibly result in the gaming being so conducted that the chances therein would be 'equally favourable to all the players'. This does not depend on questions of fact or degree or the circumstances of any particular case. It is something which is inherently impossible – as the House of Lords in *Kursaal Casino Ltd* v *Crickitt (No 2)* [1968] 1 WLR 53 subsequently decided. The Divisional Court certified, [1966] 1 WLR 960, a point of law of general public importance but refused leave to appeal to the House of Lords.

On April 22, 1966, after the time for applying for leave to appeal to the House of Lords had expired, the then assistant commissioner issued the following written confidential instruction:

'For the time being all applications for authority for an inside observation in licensed or registered clubs for the purposes of detecting gaming are to be submitted to A1 branch for my covering approval.'

According to the affidavit of Mr Bearman, the assistant secretary of the A1 branch, the then commissioner 'considered that, in view of the uncertainty of the law, the expense and manpower involved in keeping gaming observations in such clubs were not justified unless there were complaints of cheating or reason to suppose that a particular club had become a haunt of criminals.'

This, I think, can only mean that, save in the circumstances postulated, no steps were to be taken to bring any prosecution in respect of roulette or other games in which the bank held an advantage: that is to say, there should be no prosecution in respect of games contravening section 32 as such.

The affidavit continues as follows:

'At the time when this decision was taken, the *Kursaal* case [1966] 1 WLR 960 was believed to be going to the House of Lords on the point certified by the Divisional Court. Had this been decided in favour of the prosecution, it was felt that roulette and other games where the bank had an advantage would have been clearly illegal and would therefore have come to an end in any reputable club' – mark these words – 'or have been very easy to detect and prosecute.'

This can only mean that if the decision of the Divisional Court stood, there would have been no difficulty in the way of prosecution, but that the law was thought to be still uncertain because the *Kursaal (No 1)* case, [1966] 1 WLR 960 was believed to be going to the House of Lords and therefore no step should be taken meanwhile. No-one has or could possibly impugn the good faith of the assistant commissioner. It is, however, a very great pity that he apparently did not even take the trouble to discover that the time for asking the House of Lords for leave to appeal (which had been refused by the Divisional Court) had already expired by the date of his confidential instruction of April 22, 1966, and that therefore there was no possibility of any appeal to the House of Lords. Every month which went by added tens or perhaps hundreds of thousands of pounds to the profits made from illegal gaming, and, as the Secretary of State for Home Affairs said on September 13, 1966,

the connection between gaming clubs and organised crimes continued to grow.

In the meantime the Kursaal casino devised a scheme under which the bank was offered to the players in circumstances supposed to ensure that they could limit their liability to any sum they liked to name. The Kursaal continued playing roulette under this new scheme. They were prosecuted again by the vigilant Superintendent Crickitt of Southend and duly convicted on December 2, 1966: that is to say, more than seven months after the confidential instruction. During this period nothing had been done to enforce the law in London, apparently because of the belief that there was to be an appeal to the House of Lords in *Kursaal Casino Ltd* v *Crickitt* [1966] 1 WLR 960. This is the appeal that never was and which the slightest enquiry would have revealed never could have been at any time after April 20, 1966.

The inactivity after the conviction in *Kursaal Casino Ltd* v *Crickitt (No 2)* [1967] 1 WLR 1227 on December 2, 1966, is sought to be excused in Mr Bearman's affidavit by the fact that it was known that that conviction was to be tested in the Divisional Court, [1967] 1 WLR 1227. No steps, however, were taken (since no inside observations were kept) to see whether the London gaming houses offered the bank to the players under conditions which allowed the players to limit their liability. There was thus no reason to suppose that the London gaming houses had even the defence open to them which had failed before the justices in *Kursaal (No 2)* [1967] 1 WLR 1227.

Another seven months went by before *Kursaal (No 2)* [1967] 1 WLR 1227, was decided in the Divisional Court on July 10, 1967, in favour of the defence. Apparently still no steps were taken to ascertain on what terms, if any, the bank was being offered to players in London and still the gambling empires were left undisturbed. Then on December 19, 1967, the decision of the Divisional Court in *Kursaal (No 2)* [1967] 1 WLR 1227 was reversed by the House of

Lords [1968] 1 WLR 53. We have been told that that decision and its implications are being carefully studied. The study should not take long. Lord Pearson's speech, p61, in which all the other law lords concurred, made the law pellucidly clear. In no circumstances can roulette be legal when played with a zero and when the odds are 35 to 1 or less against any one number turning up. The correct odds are, of course, 36 to 1, since including zero there are 37 numbers on the roulette wheel.

According to the evidence before this court, however, most of the gaming houses in London, in direct defiance of the law as laid down by the House of Lords, are still playing roulette, unmolested, in exactly the same way (save for one immaterial variation to which I will refer) as they were doing prior to December 19 last. The variation is as follows: If the number backed by a player for, say, one chip turns up, he receives 35 ordinary chips and one special chip of a different colour. He is not allowed to play with this chip or to exchange it for an ordinary chip. The normal practice is for the players to toss the special chips back to the croupier. Clearly the players are under no illusion. They realise that these special chips are but a hollow sham devised to deceive the exceptionally gullible into thinking that the odds being paid out are 36 to 1 when in reality they are 35 to 1. If anyone with a special chip chooses (and very few of them do) to take it to the cash desk to be cashed, it is duly cashed but the player concerned has to pay a fee, for example, of £10 in the Golden Nugget Casino Club and £50 in the Victoria Sporting Club. It may be that gamblers are reluctant to cash the chips because they do not like paying the fee or because, rightly or wrongly, they fear they may be barred – and most gamblers would rather sacrifice a shade of odds than lose the chance of gambling.

However that may be, it is obvious that in reality the odds on the overwhelming number of bets remain at the rate of 35 to 1 against a single number turning up. What otherwise could be the object of having a different coloured chip to make the odds up to 36 to 1 and charging a fee for cashing it? At most it amounts to giving a player an option either to pay a fee or to play in a game in which the chances are not equally favourable to all players. There is certainly nothing here for a test case. This could only serve to give the gaming houses a further breathing space for another long spell, at the end of which no doubt an equally transparent ruse would be devised. What is now urgently needed is that energetic steps should immediately be taken to prosecute a substantial number of major London gaming houses in which the law is being defied. It may be that even when very heavy fines are imposed, they will be ineffective, in which event the Attorney-General would no doubt consider the advisability of bringing relator actions to restrain the present abuses by injunction.

Mr Blackburn has abandoned the first two parts of his application: only the third part remains which asks for an order of mandamus requiring the commissioner to reverse the policy decision that the time of police officers will not be spent in enforcing the provisions of the Act of 1963. Mr Worsley, on behalf of the commissioner, has given an undertaking to this court that the confidential instruction of April 22, 1966, will be immediately withdrawn and the whole matter referred to the Director of Public Prosecutions. Moreover, he has given an assurance that since December 19 last, the policy decision referred to in Mr Bearman's affidavit has been reversed and that observation has been kept on many of the principal gaming houses in London, including those referred to in the affidavits filed by Mr Blackburn. Had it not been for this undertaking and assurance, I should, I think, have been in favour of making an order.

I am not impressed by the argument that Mr Blackburn has an equally effective and equally convenient remedy open to him and that, therefore, the order of mandamus should in any event be refused in the court's discretion. It seems to me fantastically unrealistic for the police to suggest, as they have done, that their policy decision was unimportant because Mr Blackburn was free to start private prosecutions of his own and fight the gambling empires, possibly up to the House of Lords, single-handed. Nor, as at present advised, do I accept the argument that this is a 'criminal cause or matter' and that therefore, by reason of the Supreme Court of Judicature (Consolidation) Act, 1925, section 31(1)(a), no appeal lies to this court from the Divisional Court. No doubt the words 'criminal cause or matter' must be given a very wide construction, but I am not convinced that they relate to proceedings in which neither party is at risk of being prosecuted as a result of the order sought or made (see *Amand* v *Home Secretary* [1943] AC 147. I would prefer to keep that point open as it does not directly arise for decision. The only doubt I should have had would have been as to whether Mr Blackburn had a sufficient personal interest in order to obtain an order of mandamus. As it is, no order is necessary and I agree that, accordingly, none should be made.

Before parting with the case, I would, however, like to say that I entirely agree with the observations made by Lord Denning MR in regard to *Mills* v *Mackinnon* [1964] 2 QB 96. That was a decision which rested on some very special facts found in that case. Should there be another prosecution in relation to chemin-de-fer and the prosecution were to call a number of respectable people who thoroughly understood the game, I should be surprised if the decision were the same.

Edmund Davies LJ
It would be difficult to exaggerate the importance of these proceedings. If there are grounds for suspecting that a grave social evil is being allowed to flourish unchecked because of a set policy of inaction decided upon by a pusillanimous police force, public confidence must inevitably be gravely undermined. We have ranged far and wide in this case – both chronologically (from Anglo-Saxon times to the present day) and geographically (from Las Vegas to the Edgware Road) – but we have not travelled an inch beyond

that made necessary by the urgency and importance of the issues raised.

It is, to say the least, singularly unfortunate that, the conviction in *Kursaal Casino Ltd* v *Crickitt* [1966] 1 WLR 960 having been upheld by the Divisional Court on March 23, 1966, and the time for applying to the House of Lords for leave to appeal having expired, the assistant commissioner issued on April 22 the 'confidential instruction' regarding 'gaming in registered or licensed clubs,' to which Lord Denning MR and Salmon LJ have already referred. What prompted it has been one of the disturbing questions raised by these proceedings. This court was given no answer to that question directly emanating from its author, the assistant commissioner, but it appears from the affidavit of Mr Bearman of the administration department of New Scotland Yard that the assistant commissioner

'... considered that, in view of the uncertainty of the law the expense and manpower involved in keeping gaming observations in such clubs were not justified unless there were complaints of cheating or reason to suppose that a particular club had become a haunt of criminals.'

In other words, no steps were to be taken to investigate whether breaches of the Betting, Gaming and Lotteries Act 1963 as such were being perpetrated, and it is conceded by Mr Worsley for the respondent that in consequence observation in some of the biggest gambling clubs in the West End was immediately stopped. Small wonder, then, that on January 2 last 'The Times ' newspaper boldly asserted that,

'It is now clear that the Act has failed to achieve its purpose not so much because it could not be enforced as because the police failed to do so.'

The timing of this directive was as maladroit as the reasons given to this court for its publication. It prevailed for nearly two years after *Kursaal Casino Ltd* v *Crickitt* [1966] 1 WLR 960, notwithstanding that Mr Bearman in his affidavit stated in effect that, as long as that decision remained undisturbed, it rendered 'roulette and other games where the bank had the advantage ... clearly illegal.' As long as the directive remained operative, it has understandably created perturbation in the minds of many, and the fact that it apparently continued in force even after *Kursaal Casino Ltd v Crickitt (No 2)* [1968] 1 WLR 53, was decided on December 19 last, served to perpetuate that anxiety. Indeed, it was only on the penultimate day of this hearing that Mr Worsley, in answer to a direct question by a member of the court, intimated that oral instructions have been spread around that the directive no longer remains operative.

But a more satisfactory stage was reached when, in the concluding stages of his address, Mr Worsley undertook on behalf of the respondent that the criticised directive will be expressly and immediately withdrawn and replaced by a new directive emphasising the intention of the Metropolitan Police to enforce the law against 'roulette with zero and all other forms of gaming where the bank has an inherent advantage over players. ...' The main object sought to be attained by the applicant in these proceedings was that by mandamus the respondent be required 'to reverse or procure the reverse of the policy decision ... that the time of police officers will not be spent on enforcing the provisions of the Act of 1963.' The undertaking now given to this court has for all practical purposes secured for the applicant the relief he sought and accordingly no grounds remain in respect of which it would any longer be proper to consider granting mandamus.

That is the practical outcome of these proceedings, and from the public standpoint a very useful outcome it is. But how stands the law? Lord Denning MR and Salmon LJ have already dealt with it in extenso, and I propose to deal quite briefly with but some of the points raised by the respondent.

I deal first with jurisdiction. It is urged that these proceedings relate to 'a criminal cause or matter' and that accordingly an appeal from the Divisional Court lies directly to the House

of Lords and not to this court – see section 31(1)(a) of the Supreme Court of Judicature (Consolidation) Act 1925. I need not again go through the long line of cases relied upon in this connection by the respondent, beginning with *Ex parte Alice Woodhall* (1888) 20 QBD 832, CA. In my judgment they have no bearing upon the quite general application now made that the commissioner be compelled to reverse a policy directive regarding the enforcing of a statute. Such an application has no reference to any particular criminal cause or matter, and is not even a remote step in relation to a criminal cause or matter, but is designed simply and solely to ensure that the police do not abdicate, in consequence of a policy decision, their functions as law enforcement officers. I therefore agree with my lords in holding that this court has jurisdiction to hear and determine the present appeal. But it is necessary to add that I am persuaded so to hold by reason of the abandonment of all but the last portion of the motion, for the earlier parts (and particularly that which related to the prosecution of a specific named club) seems to me truly open to the objection as to jurisdiction raised by the respondent. In this context, I am not for the present prepared, with respect, to adopt the view expressed by Fletcher-Moulton LJ in *R v Governor of Brixton Prison, ex parte Savarkar* [1910] 2 KB 1056, 1065, CA, that –

'if any portion of an application or order involves the consideration of a criminal cause or matter, it arises out of it, and in such a case this court is not competent to entertain an appeal.'

Be that as it may, nothing there said can, in my judgment, apply to a case (such as the present) where the applicant for relief abandons those parts of his motion which offend, or may offend, against the rule, and I see no reason why this court should thereafter be prevented from adjudicating upon the validity of that which remains.

So far, so good, from the applicant's point of view. But even so it is said that he could not in any event have succeeded in these proceedings. In this context Mr Worsley has addressed to the court an elaborate and learned argument in support of the bald and startling proposition that the law enforcement officers of this country owe no duty to the public to enforce the law. Carried to its logical limit, such a submission would mean that, however brazen the failure of the police to enforce the law, the public would be wholly without a remedy and would simply have to await some practical expression of the court's displeasure. In particular, it would follow that the commissioner would be under no duty to prosecute anyone for breaches of the Gaming Acts, no matter how flagrantly and persistently they were defied. Can that be right? Is our much-vaunted legal system in truth so anaemic that, in the last resort, it would be powerless against those who, having been appointed to enforce it, merely cocked a snook at it? The very idea is as repugnant as it is startling, and I consider it regrettable that it was ever advanced. How ill it accords with the 17th-century assertion of Thomas Fuller that, 'Be you never so high, the law is above you.' The applicant is right in his assertion that its effect would be to place the police above the law. I should indeed regret to have to assent to the proposition thus advanced on behalf of the respondent, and, for the reasons already given by my Lords, I do not regard it as well founded. On the contrary, I agree with them in holding that the law enforcement officers of this country certainly owe a legal duty to the public to perform those functions which are the raison d'etre of their existence. How and by whom that duty can be enforced is another matter, and it may be that a private citizen, such as the applicant, having no special or peculiar interest in the due discharge of the duty under consideration, has himself no legal right to enforce it. But that is widely different from holding that no duty exists, enforceable either by a relator action or in some other manner which may hereafter have to be determined.

It was further urged that, assuming jurisdiction in this court and even assuming that the respondent is under the duty which this

court now unanimously holds he does owe, nevertheless the applicant should be denied the relief sought inasmuch as it is open to him to lay an information or apply for a voluntary bill of indictment. The law is, as I believe, that relief by way of a prerogative order will not be granted if there is available any other legal remedy, equally convenient, beneficial and appropriate. Having regard to the course these proceedings have taken, no final consideration of this submission is called for, and I content myself with the simple observation that only the most sardonic could regard the launching of a private prosecution (a process which, incidentally, is becoming regarded with increasing disfavour in this country) as being equally convenient, beneficial and appropriate as the procedure in fact adopted by this appellant.

I began by saying that these are important proceedings. They have served useful public purposes (a) in highlighting the very real anxiety which many responsible citizens manifestly entertain as to the adequacy of the steps hitherto taken to exterminate a shocking and growing cancer in the body politic; and (b) in clarifying the duty of the police in relation to law enforcement generally. Accordingly, while, for the reasons given by my Lords, there must be a formal dismissal of this appeal, it may well be that the applicant and his supporters will nevertheless feel as they leave this court today that in truth theirs has been the victory.

The next extract is concerned with the issue of cautioning and it contains an account of the 1994 Home Office Circular on the matter. In most respects, the guidance in the 1994 circular and in the revised national standards for cautioning which accompany it are similar to those contained in Circular 59/1990 which it supersedes. The police are described in the Home Office Annual Report for 1995 (Cm 2808), presented to Parliament in March 1995, as having 'discretion whether to charge an offender or formally to caution him or her'. It goes on to say that cautioning, properly used, is an effective deterrent to those who have committed minor offences or who have offended for the first time. However, it states that 'multiple cautioning can lead to an offender becoming an habitual criminal before even coming to court', suggesting that those who abuse the chance offered by a caution should generally be prosecuted. In March 1995, new guidance was issued to the police aimed at curbing the inappropriate use of cautioning. The use of cautioning is now ruled out for 'the most serious offences' and repeat cautioning was strongly discouraged.

Home Office Circular 18/1994 *The Cautioning of Offenders*

The aim of the circular is to provide guidance on the cautioning of offenders and in particular:

1. To discourage the use of cautions in inappropriate cases, eg offences which are triable on indictment only.
2. To seek greater consistency between police force areas.
3. To promote the better recording of cautions.

The purpose of a formal caution

A formal caution is intended to:

1. deal quickly and simply with less serious offenders;
2. divert such offenders from the criminal courts;
3. reduce the chances of their re-offending.

The circular emphasises that a formal caution is not the only alternative to prosecution. For example, in certain cases it will be appropriate for the police to give an offender an informal warning, or for them to take no further action.

The criteria to be met before cautioning

Several conditions must be met before a caution can be given:

1. The evidence must be sufficient to give a realistic prospect of conviction. If the evidence is insufficient, cautioning is ruled out.

2. The offender must admit the offence. The admission must be clear and reliable. If the offender's mental health or intellectual capacity were in doubt, a caution would not be appropriate but prosecution would not be inevitable in such a case – the police might take no further action or consider referral to another agency which could help the offender.
3. The offender (or in the case of a juvenile his parent or guardian) must consent to a caution being issued. Consent should not be sought until a decision has been made that a caution is the appropriate course of action – in other words it is not possible to offer a caution as an inducement to admit the offence. When consent is sought, the offender (or parent/guardian) must have the significance of the procedure explained to him:

   a) a record of the caution will be kept;
   b) if the person offends again, the caution may influence the decision whether to prosecute for the new offence;
   c) if the person is convicted of another offence in the future, the caution may be cited in court.

The public interest

If the first two of the above conditions are met, consideration should be given to whether a caution is in the public interest. The factors which should be taken into account are:

1. The nature of the offence. Cautions must never be given for the most serious indictable-only offences. Their use for other indictable-only offences will only be appropriate in exceptional circumstances. A caution will not be appropriate when the victim has suffered significant harm or loss. The term 'significant' is to be construed with reference to the circumstances of the victim. In cases of doubt, the assistance of the CPS should be sought.
2. The likely penalty if the offender were to be convicted by a court. The circular refers to the Code for Crown Prosecutors which

suggests that prosecution may not be appropriate where the offence is not particularly serious and the probable sentence would be an absolute or conditional discharge. The likelihood of a more substantive penalty being imposed does not mean that a caution could not be given.

3. The offender's age and state of health. The circular retains a presumption in favour of not prosecuting the elderly or infirm and people suffering from a mental illness or a severe physical illness. It goes on to state that the presumption against prosecution should be extended to other groups of adults where the criteria for cautioning are met.

4. The offender's previous criminal history. An offender's previous record is important but is not decisive on its own. The existence of a previous caution or conviction does not rule out a further caution if other factors exist which suggest that a caution would be appropriate. For example, there might have been an appreciable lapse of time since the last offence, the previous and most recent offences might be different in character and seriousness, or a previous caution might have had a noticeable effect on the pattern of offending. However, the circular suggests that a caution should not be given when there can be no reasonable expectation that it will curb the recipient's offending.

5. The offender's attitude to the offence. Two factors are to be considered. The first is the wilfulness with which the offence was committed. The second is the offender's subsequent attitude. A demonstration of regret, such as apologising to the victim or an offer to put matters right, are features which might support the use of a caution.

The views of the victim

The circular suggests that before a caution can be given the victim should normally be contacted to assess such factors as:

1. His view of the offence.

2. The extent of any damage or loss. The significance of the loss or damage should be considered in relation to the victim. The effect of the caution should be explained to the victim.

3. Whether there is any continuing threat from the offender. Although cautioning might otherwise be appropriate, in some cases a prosecution may be necessary in order to protect the victim from the future attentions of the offender.

4. Whether the offender has paid any compensation or made any form of reparation. The police must not become involved in negotiating over the making of reparation or the provision of compensation. The consent of the victim to a caution is desirable but not essential.

McConville et al note some of the general problems of the system of cautioning and provide a concrete example from their research.

McConville M et al (1991) *The Case for the Prosecution*, p78

For the police the caution is essentially a let-off, having few if any adverse consequences for the subject. From the police point of view the utility of the caution is in identifying individuals who will be suitable for prosecution should they re-offend, and as a means of warning a juvenile about undesirable conduct and associations. Thus, for the police there is no pressing need to apply rigorous standards of proof in caution cases, and the caution is seen as having utility not only for offenders but also for their associates or those on the periphery of crime. The consequence of this is that where cases are processed with a view to caution, exculpatory remarks short of a flat claim to innocence are routinely ignored as being irrelevant to the caution decision.

AH-J33 – J33 had been named by another boy as having been involved with a group of children who had stolen a bicycle. In interview

J33 described how the bicycle had been stolen by another boy who had then shown it to him. J33 did not admit having ridden it or even having touched it. J33 was cautioned for the offence of taking a vehicle without consent.

Ashworth makes it clear that people may feel pressure to admit an offence. This renders of little value the due process notion that a caution will not be appropriate where a person does not make a clear and reliable admission of the offence.

Ashworth, A (1998) *The Criminal Process*, p158

If the suspect denies knowledge of a certain fact, he or she might wish to decline a caution and have the point adjudicated in court; and yet the disincentives to taking that course are so great (delay, risk of not being believed, risk of conviction) that acceptance of the caution is likely. The National Standards state that 'a caution will not be appropriate where a person does not make a clear and reliable admission of the offence'; but there is the additional problem that the police may not fully understand the relevant law, such as the mental element required for the crime or the possible defences. In effect, whenever a person knows or believes that there will be a choice between accepting a caution and risking a prosecution, there is bound to be pressure to accept the caution. The disadvantages of this must be minimised by ensuring, as far as possible, that cautions are only offered if the conditions are strictly met. This would require far greater supervision within the police, or the provision of legal advice, or the transfer of the function to the Crown Prosecution Service.

Evans and Wilkinson suggest ways in which discretion could be better regulated in relation to cautioning practices. Of course the variation in policies and practices around the country makes understanding and reform of the system difficult.

Evans, R and Wilkinson, C (1990) 'Variations in Police Cautioning, Policy and Practice in England and Wales', *Howard Journal of Criminal Justice*, pp174–175

… by defining tight criteria for judging the seriousness of offences in terms of monetary values or degrees of violence scale, by subjecting individual decisions to consistent gatekeeping or by centralising decision making. Perhaps for guidance to be effective in producing uniform approaches to cautioning in practice greater attention needs to be given to this level of detail and to the question of enforcement. Finally, our research suggests that another potential source of a lack of a uniform approach to juvenile cautioning concerns consultation arrangements. These vary both between and within forces. For a major plank in cautioning policy surprisingly little is known about the effect of different systems on outcomes or about how discretion is exercised by the various professional interests involved, although our findings, like other recent research, suggests that difference professionals may have very different agendas.

The system of cautioning for youngsters was criticised for the repeated use of cautioning and this led to the introduction of a system of reprimands and warnings. These involve more than an interview with a police officer and there is a clear desire to operationalise ideas of restorative justice – more on which in the next chapter.

Home Office (2000) *The Final Warning Scheme – Guidance for Youth Offending Teams*, pp3–4

Introduction
PURPOSE OF THE FINAL WARNING SCHEME
1. The principal aim of the youth justice system, established by s37 of the Crime and Disorder Act 1998 (the 1998 Act), is to prevent offending by children and

young people. Final warnings are a crucial link in the chain of interventions designed to stop offending at an early stage. The scheme is designed to:

a) end repeat cautioning and provide a progressive and meaningful response to offending behaviour;

b) ensure appropriate and effective action to help prevent re-offending;

c) ensure that juveniles who do re-offend after a warning are dealt with quickly and effectively through the courts.

2. The key to the effectiveness of the scheme will be ensuring that young offenders participate in effective interventions made in support of warnings. The role of the youth offending team is to ensure that effective interventions are organised and delivered. Parallel guidance to the police sets out how to maximise the likelihood of the young person successfully engaging in such interventions, in particular by:

a) asking the youth offending team to carry out an early assessment of the young offender, before the decision whether or not to warn, to explore their attitude to intervention and to encourage their future engagement in any rehabilitation programme. The assessment will also provide an early opportunity for youth offending teams to consider what form of rehabilitation programme might follow.

b) encouraging the young offender where appropriate to participate in a restorative process for the delivery of the warning.

Restorative justice

3. The impact of a warning on a young offender can be significantly enhanced by delivering it as part of a restorative conference involving the young offender, his or her parents, any other influential adults and, where appropriate and willing, the victim and any others affected by the offending behaviour (both within the victim group and the offender group). If the victim does not want to take part, similar principles can be applied by giving a restorative warning. Delivery of a warning as part of a restorative process makes the young offender confront the consequences of his or her offence. It also provides a forum in which those affected by the offence – primarily the victim and the victim's supporters but also the offender's parents and supporters – can express their views.

4. Detailed guidance on the restorative approach is provided in Annex B, but its three underlying aims are as follows:

a) Responsibility – the young offender taking responsibility for the consequences of his or her offending behaviour;

b) Restoration – for the young offender to apologise or give something back to the person or community he or she has offended against;

c) Re-integration – for the young offender to be re-integrated into the law-abiding community.

5. The use of the term 'restorative conference' throughout this guidance does not preclude the use of other methods which are based on restorative principles. The important elements are the principles, and appropriate training in restorative processes as well as in victim sensitivity and awareness. Other restorative methods used must be robust and those using them must be able to demonstrate the same standards of practice as those outlined in the guidance.

6. A training package which is designed to equip people to facilitate both restorative conferences and restorative warnings is being made available by the Youth Justice Board. Areas which are already operating restorative processes will have their own training schemes in place. In order to ensure that all training programmes meet the required standards the Youth Justice Board will establish a mechanism for approving such programmes.

7. It is recognised that the use of restorative justice in the delivery of reprimands and warnings has resource implications for police forces and (where they are involved) youth offending teams. It will not always be appropriate or possible for the full range of restorative justice processes to be available for every young offender. However the overriding presumption must be on delivering reprimands and warnings in a way that will be most effective in preventing re-offending and in considering the views of victims. Local protocols should be established between police and youth offending teams to cover practice in relation to facilitating restorative conferences and warnings.

Children/young persons involved in prostitution

8. Young persons under the age of 18 who come to notice as being involved in prostitution should be dealt with in accordance with the (draft) joint Home Office/Department of Health guidance on the issue. That guidance emphasises that males and females under 18 who are involved in prostitution are primarily victims of abuse who do not consent freely to prostitution. As such, they should if at all possible be diverted away from prostitution without recourse to the criminal justice system. However, the (draft) guidance makes it clear that in exceptional cases, where diversion has repeatedly failed, the police may, after consultation with others in the multi-agency group, take criminal action against a person under the age of 18 for loitering, soliciting or importuning. Where the offence is admitted, the young person can be dealt with under the final warning scheme. The final warning scheme replaces all cautions for young people which means that a prostitute's caution can no longer be issued by the police to females under 18.

As with the last extract attention is focused on the need to go beyond simple cautions as such. The possibilities of caution plus are explored in terms of ideas of reparation and mediation with reference being made to international examples of such practices.

Crawford A (1996) 'Alternatives to Prosecution: Access to, or Exits from, Criminal Justice?', in Young R and Wall D (eds), *Access to Criminal Justice*, pp325–327

The future of mediation and reparation in criminal disputes

Mediation and reparation is still in its infancy. However, it has developed an established place on the international criminal policy agenda, as witnessed by its prominent inclusion within the 1995 UN Conference on Crime Prevention. There continues to be an expansion of experiments in North America and across Europe. Further, lessons from other countries, particularly in relation to young people, in New Zealand, Germany and Norway, show the potential (and pitfalls) of placing mediation and reparation schemes on a legislative footing. At a national level, despite the limited number of mediation and reparation schemes and their relatively small case-loads, their attraction for policy-makers remains evident. Perversely the fluctuations and U-turns in cautioning policy have opened up new spaces for mediation and reparation to fill and exploit. While the practice of cautioning is unlikely to go away, the present Government's unease with simple cautioning appeals to more intensive and interventionist forms of disposal short of prosecution. Leading academics and practitioners have come to advocate mediation and reparation as a part of 'caution plus' schemes as representing the ideal, or at least the best available, means of meeting many of the normative and administrative failings of the present (court-based) criminal justice process. Like others, David Faulkner, a former leading civil servant in the Home Office, has recently called upon the Government to (re)consider the options available through mediation and reparation. The original concerns which attracted the Government to mediation and reparation in the mid-1980s – the cost of criminal prosecutions, the belief that mediation may provide a cheaper means of disposing with certain criminal cases, and the problematic role of victims – have not diminished. However, the research evidence is ambivalent as to whether mediation offers real cost savings. The danger is that if a centrally driven expansion in mediation and reparation were to occur, the administrative and cost considerations would dominate over any normative and reparative potential.

However, the other important benefit of mediation and reparation attached to 'caution plus' schemes relates to the role of the victim. Victims are not disadvantaged in the same way as they are through 'simple' cautioning, where the possibility of financial compensation is precluded. A common criticism of 'simple' diversion is that it is often perceived by victims, and those who seek to champion them, as serving the interests of the criminal justice system and the offender while ignoring victims' own needs. Further, mediation can provide important information for victims that they would otherwise be denied, about the offence, the offender and their processing through the criminal justice system. Mediation, therefore, can (and does) draw support from, and connect with (although not unproblematically), increasing concerns in relation to the rights, needs and treatment of victims. In this way it is in accord with the rhetoric of the Government's Victim's Charter, if not its practice. Indeed, some of the pioneering mediation schemes, like the Leeds service, have developed their work to include the provision of pre-release enquiry reports in relation to life sentence prisoners. Mediators interview, give a voice and provide information to, the relatives and families of victims of life prisoners in the run-up to their release on licence. This work, on behalf of the probation service, is undertaken in fulfilment of probation's requirements under the Victim's Charter.

This extract deals with problems of the prosecution system with suggestions being made that there is evidence that the prosecution process does not always adhere to the formal rules that are designed to control it. This can lead to the continuation of cases that should have been discontinued. This extract should be compared with the one that follows it, as a counter argument is presented there – the central theme being that there has been a retreat from prosecution. What is certainly true in what Sanders has to tell us is that the Crown Prosecution has no meaningful role in relation to cautioning – in particular, there is no check to see if cases are being cautioned that should not be.

Sanders A (1997) 'From Suspect to Trial', in Maguire M et al (eds), *The Oxford Handbook of Criminology*, 2nd ed, pp1073–1075

The Royal Commission on Criminal Procedure (1981) realised that, left to their own devices, the police would not consistently apply the guidelines on evidential sufficiency and cautioning. To secure consistency, and to counterbalance extra police powers, it recommended establishing the Crown Prosecution Service (CPS). Apart from organisational and accountability matters, the government followed the Royal Commission's recommendations in the Prosecution of Offences Act 1985 and built the CPS around the pre-existing system. The police continue to charge, summons, caution, and NFA as before. Once charged or summonsed, though, the accused becomes the responsibility of the CPS, which decides whether to continue the prosecution. The CPS is headed by the Director of Public Prosecutions (DPP), whose office had previously been responsible for national prosecutions of particular importance and for the prosecution of police officers. The Code for Crown Prosecutors provides guidance on prosecution decisions in almost identical terms to those discussed before on evidential sufficiency and cautionability, so that poor police decisions can be corrected by the CPS.

McConville et al (1991) found, from research in three police-force areas, that the CPS rarely dropped cases which were evidentially weak, and that when they did so this was usually on the initiative of the police and/or only after several court appearances. There were three main reasons for this: policy (the furtherance of police working rules, shared by both prosecutors and police officers); the chance of a freak conviction (because verdicts are so hard to predict); and guilty pleas (just because a case is evidentially weak it does not follow that the defendant will contest the case; weak cases are continued in the often correct expectation of a guilty plea). If the CPS is passive in relation to weak cases where case failure is a measure of institutional efficiency, it is not surprising to discover that it is even more passive in relation to cautionable cases. McConville et al (1991) found no cautionable cases at all being dropped on grounds of cautionability alone, despite many similar cases being cautioned by the police. Again, where police working rules point to prosecution, the CPS is reluctant to stop the case (Gelsthorpe and Giller, 1990). In more recent years there has been a significant rise in discontinuances, both on evidential and 'public interest' grounds, although the former outnumber the latter by two to one (Crisp and Moxon, 1994). However, many 'public interest' discontinuances are of trivial cases, and are made on cost grounds. That there is scope for far more diversion by the CPS has been confirmed by Crisp et al (1994), who found that cases which went through experimental 'Public Interest Case Assessment' (PICA) schemes were far more likely to be discontinued than normal. Despite this, many cases which were assessed as cautionable were not discontinued

and yet received nominal penalties. McConville et al's argument that the police and CPS insist on prosecuting when they have extraneous reasons for so doing would appear to hold firm. Similarly, the findings of Cretney and Davis (1996) and Sanders et al (1997) that the police and CPS prosecute weak cases with victims of domestic violence and with vulnerable victims because they believe in the guilt of the suspect despite the probability that problems concerning the victims' testimony will lead to acquittal, supports this argument in relation to the evidential strength issue.

The CPS is in a structurally weak position to carry out its ostensible aims primarily because of police case construction. The CPS reviews the quality of police cases on the basis of evidence provided solely by the police. This is like the problem of written records, where those who are being evaluated write their own reports. Cases being prosecuted are usually presented as prosecutable; the facts to support this are selected, and those which do not are ignored, hidden, or undermined. Thus weaknesses or cautionable factors, whether known by the police or not, often emerge only in or after trial (Leng, 1992). This situation is exacerbated when the CPS relies on police summaries, which are very selective indeed (Baldwin and Bedward, 1991). Moodie and Tombs (1982) and Duff (1997) in Scotland (Duff in relation to psychiatric cases), and Gelsthorpe and Giller (1990) in England cite prosecutors who agree that the police present them only with what seems relevant to them as prosecutors (as distinct from neutral intermediaries). Similarly, when the police seek advice from the CPS, they can obtain the advice they want by carefully selecting the information they present (Sanders et al, 1997). This is why PICA schemes, which present prosecutors with information from non-police sources, lead to increased numbers of discontinuances.

Attempts to resolve problems of due process and disparity in cautioning by using the CPS suffer another structural problem. Although cautionable cases which are prosecuted are in theory reviewable by the CPS, prosecutable (and NFA-able) cases which are cautioned are not. If the police decide to caution the case ends with them. However able or willing the CPS may be to deal with cases which should be cautioned, they cannot deal with cases which should not have been cautioned. This means that disparity will continue, and the violations of due process inherent in police cautioning procedures remain untouched by the CPS. That the CPS is primarily a police prosecution agency is hardly surprising in an adversarial system, but it does suggest that suspects cannot rely on the CPS, as presently constituted, to protect them. Prosecutors could become adequate reviewers of either evidence or public interest only if placed in an entirely different structural relationship with the police. This would require fundamental changes in the adversarial system, and might even then be unsuccessful, if such impressionistic evidence as we have of continental systems is anything to go by (Leigh and Zedner, 1992; Field, 1994).

Bibliography
Baldwin J and Bedward, J (1991) 'Summarizing Tape Recordings of Police Interviewing', *Criminal Law Review*, 671–679.

Cretney A and Davies G (1996) 'Prosecuting Domestic Assault', *Criminal Law Review*, 162.

Crisp D and Moxon D (1994) *Case Screening by the Crown Prosecution Service*, London: HMSO.

Duff P (1997) 'Diversion from Prosecution into Psychiatric Care', *British Journal of Criminology*, 37: 15.

Field S (1994) 'Judicial Supervision and the Pre-Trial Process', in S Field and P Thomas (eds), *Justice and Efficiency?*, Oxford: Blackwell.

Gelsthorpe L and Giller H (1990) 'More Justice for Juveniles: Does More Mean Better?', *Criminal Law Review*, 153–164.

Leigh L and Zedner L (1992) *A Report on the Administration of Criminal Justice in the Pre-Trial Phase in France and Germany*, London: HMSO.

Leng R (1992) *The Right to Silence in Police Interrogation*, London: HMSO.

McConville M et al (1991) *The Case for the Prosecution*, London: Routledge.

Moodie S and Tombs J (1982) *Prosecution in the Public Interest*, Edinburgh: Edinburgh University Press.

Royal Commission on Criminal Procedure (1981) *Report*, London: HMSO.

Sanders A et al (1997) *Victims with Learning Disabilities: Negotiating the Criminal Justice System*, Oxford: Centre for Criminological Research.

The year 1998 saw a major report on the system of prosecution and its proposals were the basis for further reform of the system. In what was a detailed document there is valuable material on both the past and the future. Numerous themes are developed including the police –prosecution interaction and the problems of shortage of resource in the early days of the Crown Prosecution Service.

Home Office (1998) *The Glidewell Report on the Crown Prosecution Service*

The formation and history of the Crown Prosecution Service

1. The origins of the Crown Prosecution Service (the CPS) are to be found in the report of the Royal Commission on Criminal Procedure, chaired by Sir Cyril Philips, which was published in 1981. The report concluded that it was undesirable for the police to continue both to investigate and to prosecute crime, and that the wide differences in prosecution practice throughout England and Wales required a major change in the prosecution process. Philips advised that the functions of investigation and of deciding whether to charge

a person with an offence should remain with the police, but that from then onwards the conduct of the prosecution should be the responsibility of a new 'locally-based prosecuting service with some national features'. The Government at that time accepted in principle the recommendations for a new prosecuting service, but not the proposal that the service should be locally accountable. Government therefore opted for the establishment of 'a national prosecution service headed by the Director of Public Prosecutions and under the superintendence of the Attorney-General', which would not be accountable to any local body.

2. This concept was embodied in the Prosecution of Offences Act 1985 which created the Crown Prosecution Service. The CPS started to operate in 1986.

3. The new service found itself occupying a position between the police and the courts. The police continued to be responsible for deciding on the charge and for preparing a case file for the CPS. The CPS had a new role, that of reviewing cases passed to it after the police had charged a defendant in order to decide whether the evidence justified the charge. If the reviewing lawyer decided that the evidence was not sufficient he could decide to discontinue or to charge a lesser offence. The exercise by the CPS of this new power created tensions between CPS lawyers and the police. In contrast it does not seem that the establishment of the CPS greatly affected the working of the courts. To add to the initial problems, the CPS was certainly understaffed at first. Moreover, many of the staff had inadequate training and preparation, particularly in London.

4. The CPS was originally organised into 31 areas, each with a Chief Crown Prosecutor. Almost from the start it entered the cycle of internal review and reorganisation which has marked its history so far. In 1987, four Regional

Directors were appointed to assist with the running of the 31 areas but only two years later were found to have added an unnecessary layer of management and were removed. In 1993, following an internal report, the present structure of 13 areas was adopted. The enlarged areas became responsible for the performance and management of the branches. At the same time a headquarters organisation very similar to that which currently exists was put in place. The DPP took over the chief executive duties formerly exercised by the Deputy DPP whose post was put into abeyance.

5. Before and at the time of the formation of the CPS concerns were expressed in the Philips Report and in Parliament that a national prosecution service could become too centralised and bureaucratic. We believe that this has happened since 1993. We heard conflicting opinions as to whether at that time a proper balance between a national prosecution framework and a reasonable degree of local autonomy had been achieved. Some people said it had; others told us that inconsistencies were growing between the areas in the application of national policies and standards and that there was a gulf in communications between national HQ and the 31 areas. The 1993 reorganisation was intended to solve these problems. It did so by devolving the actual casework to the branches while vesting many of the powers of management in the new 13 area headquarters. There was devolution in the sense that many of these powers were transferred from Central Headquarters to the areas but that was where devolution of management ceased. In our view it was and is proper to regard the 13 areas as in effect branches of headquarters. If that is correct the reorganisation resulted in a greater degree of control and authority being vested in headquarters than had previously been the case. We agree that the 1993 reorganisation did have the effect of

welding the CPS into the national organisation which it is today and that this was a considerable achievement. Nevertheless, we believe that the price paid in the over-centralisation of management was too great. With the benefit of hindsight we conclude that, however good its intentions, the 1993 reorganisation was on balance a mistake.

6. When it started the CPS was grossly under-staffed. At the end of the first six months it had fewer than 3,500 staff, of whom 1,250 were lawyers. The shortage was worst in London. Recruitment at first proved difficult, but became easier, so that by 1993 there were over 6,000 staff in post, including over 2,000 lawyers. The greatest numbers were in 1995 (6,400 total staff, 2,200 lawyers). Government expenditure curbs have led to a reduction since then: the numbers are back down to under 6,000 total staff and fewer than 2,000 lawyers. As to finance for the CPS, the pattern has been similar. The CPS budget, in real terms, rose to about £320 million in 1992/93. It then remained steady for four years, but has been reduced to about £300 million in the present year. This contrasts with a total expenditure of £682 million on criminal legal aid for defendants.

The CPS today

7. During its short life the CPS has been the subject of many reviews and investigations which have made it difficult for it to settle down. Nevertheless, the first 12 years of the CPS have seen some real achievements. The CPS is now established as a national and independent organisation operating in accordance with a code for Crown Prosecutors and contributing to the formulation of Government policy on criminal justice.

8. The CPS now employs about 6,000 people of whom some one-third are lawyers. They deal with more than 1.3 million cases annually in the magistrates' courts

and about 120,000 in the Crown Court. Much of the work is routine and involves minor offences but at the other end of the scale CPS staff are responsible for handling complex and serious cases which often attract considerable public interest. The CPS has little control over its workload. The case files arrive from the police who have already agreed the date of the first hearing with the court. Both the quality and the timeliness of production of the files received from the police are sometimes a cause of concern to the CPS and in the relationship between the police and the CPS there is a tendency for one to blame the other for weaknesses in performance. In its relationship with the courts the CPS has no say in the listing of cases to be heard in the magistrates' or Crown Courts.

9. The CPS Headquarters offices in London and York manage the 13 areas which control the network of 93 branches which are the key operating units of the organisation, plus Central Casework in London. The area offices are very much an extension of headquarters. The CPS has adopted a concept known as 'whole case management'. Until this was applied the preparation of all Crown Court work was handled by a unit separate from that which dealt with the magistrates' courts. The whole case management concept has led to the introduction of 'teamworking'. Each branch is headed by a branch Crown Prosecutor and is normally organised into two or more teams of lawyers and lay caseworkers who share the work arising from prosecutions in both courts. The introduction of teamworking, which was accompanied by the introduction of open plan offices, has resulted in a great degree of dissatisfaction amongst the staff. We see much merit in the concept of teamworking, particularly in the removal of the division between lawyers and caseworkers. However, it is the particular form of teamworking and the way it was intro-

duced which have caused much resentment.

10. The prosecution process is essentially local in nature and whilst senior managers claim to have devolved management to a local level we discovered that the branches feel closely controlled and are required to operate in highly standardised ways. Until recently there were small groups of special caseworkers, who dealt with the more complex cases in each area. These lawyers have been dispersed; apart from those cases which are remitted to Central Casework the branches are expected to deal with all cases, from the most minor to the most serious. Attempts in recent years to introduce computer-based systems to assist in casework and case management have not been successful.

11. Until recently, an increasing proportion of the CPS budget was spent on accommodation and some headquarters functions. In the last few years this trend has been reversed and the staff at headquarters has been reduced in size. There has also been a drive to allocate work to staff at a lower level of experience than formerly and there is no doubt that some very experienced people have left the CPS since 1992. Although the number of cases has fallen overall, until a recent upwards trend, the workload per case has increased and become more difficult as a result of factors such as changes to the law on disclosure, Charter initiatives, internal monitoring and the increasing incidence of more serious crime. Overall we have found that at branch level the CPS has more work to do and fewer experienced people to do it.

12. Teamworking has not resulted in the more experienced lawyers spending more time on the serious cases; the CPS is still focused on the high volume work in the magistrates' courts. Furthermore, the most senior lawyers are now expected to devote the majority of their time to management. We estimate that the top 400 lawyers in the CPS spend less than a third of their time on casework and advocacy. We think this is undesirable The CPS requires more staff in its operating units. Our recommendations aim to ensure that the resources of the CPS are redistributed so as to be devoted to its core activity, the conduct of prosecutions.

How the prosecution process works at present

13. In order to present the case for the prosecution in court the CPS needs to have a file containing the evidence and other relevant information, including any criminal record the defendant may have. While it is for the police to obtain the evidence as part of the process of investigation, in our view the assembly of the file is part of the conduct of the proceedings for which the CPS is, or should be, responsible. Until now, however, the police have continued to compile prosecution files in a special unit often called an Administrative Support Unit (ASU). The most critical point in the flow of case papers between the investigating officer and the CPS prosecutor in court is at the interface between the ASU and the CPS branch office.

14. Another cause of discord between the police and the CPS stems from the power of the CPS to discontinue a prosecution. One of a CPS lawyer's most important tasks is to review the evidence in the file in order to decide whether it justifies the charge laid by the police, applying criteria set out in the 'Code for Crown Prosecutors'. If the evidence is not sufficient, the lawyer may either substitute a lesser charge ('downgrading') or discontinue the prosecution altogether. The exercise of this power, which was newly-given in 1986, was resented at that time by some police officers, but most now recognise and accept that it is a valuable provision which should ensure that only those prosecutions proceed to court in which there is an appropriate chance of a conviction in accordance with the code. This is a safe-

guard not only for defendants who should not have been charged but also for the public purse.

How the CPS has performed

15. Our terms of reference require us to 'assess whether the CPS has contributed to the falling number of convictions for recorded crime'. One thing is clear: the CPS is not concerned with the vast majority of recorded crime. The CPS is responsible for the conduct of all criminal proceedings after there has been a charge by the police or a summons. In 1996, of the crimes recorded by the police (nearly 5 million), only 1 in every 9 (576,000) resulted in a charge or summons. Recorded crimes do not include the large number of motoring offences, so the CPS is concerned with only one out of nine recorded crimes.

16. From there onwards our task becomes more difficult. To carry out such an assessment we have had to examine the available statistics, which has not proved an easy matter. The Home Office, the Court Service and the CPS each produce statistics relating to criminal prosecutions and often the figures within apparently similar parameters are inconsistent with each other. It was to be expected that when the CPS came into existence convictions would fall as a proportion of total cases simply as a result of the CPS properly exercising their new power to discontinue some cases. However, figures produced by the CPS have shown that in recent years the proportion of cases in the Crown Court resulting in conviction has increased, but this trend differs from that shown by the figures published in the Judicial Statistics produced by the Court Service, which show a decline in convictions over the period 1985 to 1996. We have tried but failed to find an explanation for the disparity in the two sets of statistics. We cannot therefore say that the CPS figures are wrong. We have recommended

that attempts are made to agree one set of figures.

17. Overall the CPS discontinues prosecutions in, on average, 12 per cent of cases where the police have charged. The CPS Inspectorate have found, in their consideration of branch performance, few decisions to discontinue which they considered wrong. However, there is some evidence that the average rate of discontinuance varies greatly between types of offence, with the highest discontinuance rates being for charges of violence against the person and criminal damage, and the lowest for motoring offences. This is clearly a matter for concern, the reasons for which must be investigated.

18. We have been specifically asked to comment on the proposal in the Narey Report that the CPS should no longer have the power to discontinue cases on certain public interest grounds, namely that the court is likely to impose a nominal penalty, or that the loss involved is small. We have recommended that the proposal should not be adopted but that the incidence of discontinuance on these grounds should be rare. To that end we have also recommended a small amendment to the code for Crown Prosecutors.

19. Charges are sometimes downgraded and such few statistics as are available seem to show that this happens most frequently with those which relate to serious crime, public order offences and road traffic accidents causing death. We have no evidence which proves that downgrading happens when it should not. Nonetheless, we suspect that inappropriate downgrading does occur and have recommended that cases of downgrading are specifically examined by the Inspectorate during visits to CPS Units. Both the police and the CPS are helped by the existence of guidance in the form of charging standards and whilst we approve their existence we have raised questions about the content of some of the standards. More information is needed

about the reasons why charges are down-graded. We have recommended research to consider both this matter and discontin-uance.

20. The CPS figures show that the proportion of those pleading not guilty in the Crown Court who were convicted increased between 1991–92 and 1996–97 to about 40 per cent. We have, however, given par-ticular consideration to the statistics relat-ing to acquittals in the Crown Court. Both the CPS statistics and judicial statistics agree that in 1996 less than half of these were acquittals by a jury. In other words, more than half of all acquittals in the Crown Court resulted from an order or direction of the judge. There are often good reasons why such an order or direc-tion should be made – a vital witness may not appear to give evidence or may prove unreliable in the witness box – but never-theless the statistic is a cause for concern. In our view, when the CPS has decided to proceed with a case after review, it is rea-sonable to expect that, unless a major witness is absent, the case will be strong enough to be put before a jury. We con-clude that the performance of some parts of the CPS in this respect is not as good as it should be, and improvement is needed.

21. The overall conclusion from this study of the available statistics is that in various respects there has not been the improve-ment in the effectiveness and efficiency of the prosecution process which was expected to result from the setting up of the CPS in 1986. Where the statistics show a recent improvement, that is often a recovery from a deterioration which took place in the years immediately after 1986. We do not place responsibility for this sit-uation wholly on the CPS; in large part it stems from the failure of the police, the CPS and the courts to set overall objec-tives and agree the role and the responsi-bility of each in achieving those objec-tives.

22. Also under the heading 'How the CPS has performed' the report contains a chapter describing the present state of the relation-ships between the CPS and the other agen-cies with whom it works and to whom it relates in the criminal justice system. The tensions between the police and the CPS which existed in the early years have been greatly eased, but in some places have not disappeared. There is still a tendency for each to blame the other if a prosecution file is incomplete or some other essential document missing, and, as a result, a case has to be adjourned. In order to establish their independence from the police after 1986, many in the CPS became isolation-ist, creating a rift in communication. In addition, many police ASUs are not func-tioning as effectively as they did when they were first created. As a result the CPS finds that it has to duplicate some of the work the ASU staff have done, in order to prepare a satisfactory prosecution file. It is important to seek a remedy for both prob-lems.

23. There are frequent complaints by both magistrates and judges of inefficiency in case preparation or delay on the part of the CPS. Often the CPS is not the cause of the delay, but sometimes it properly has to accept the blame. Part of the problem lies with court listing practices, into which the CPS at present has no input. Timeliness is a most important aspect of the fair and effective prosecution of crime, but at present the magistrates' courts and the CPS have different, and often inconsistent, performance indicators for timeliness.

24. In the Crown Court, all cases are at present prosecuted by members of the Bar. Both judges and the Bar raised several issues on which action, either by the CPS or by Government departments, is needed. They include a considerable disparity between the higher fees paid to defence Counsel under the Legal Aid Scheme and those paid to prosecuting counsel briefed by the CPS; the issue of briefs being returned by

counsel; problems arising from a shortage of CPS staff in the Crown Court, and a difficulty in counsel obtaining fresh instructions while in court. These are all matters we address.

25. Finally in this part of the Report we consider the proper role of the CPS in relation to victims and witnesses, particularly its obligations arising out of the Victim's Charter.

26. Our assessment of the CPS is that it has the potential to become a lively, successful and esteemed part of the criminal justice system, but that, sadly, none of these adjectives applies to the service as a whole at present. If the service – by which we mean all the members of its staff – is to achieve its potential, it faces three challenges. Firstly, there must be a change in the priority given to the various levels of casework; the 'centre of gravity' must move from the bulk of relatively minor cases in the magistrates' court in order to concentrate on more serious crime, particularly the gravest types, in the Crown Court. Secondly, the overall organisation, the structure and the style of management of the CPS will have to change. Government has started this process by deciding that the CPS should in future be divided into 42 areas, each headed by a Chief Crown Prosecutor. Each of these CCPs should be given as much freedom as possible to run his area in his own way, and he should support his staff to enable them to get on with the core job of prosecuting. Thirdly, the CPS must establish more clearly its position as an integral part of the criminal justice process. It is no longer the 'new kid on the block'.

The future of the CPS in the criminal justice system

27. The role of the CPS within the criminal justice system has not until now been spelt out and put into the context of its key objectives and related performance indicators. Nor have the relationships with the police and the courts been properly defined. At present neither the police nor the CPS have overall responsibility for the preparation of the case file. We have therefore recommended that the CPS should take responsibility for:

a) the prosecution process immediately following charge;

b) arranging the initial hearing in the magistrates' court;

c) witness availability, witness warning and witness care.

28. We believe that the police should remain responsible for the investigation of offences and for charging as well as for the preliminary preparation of case papers. Very often some part of the investigation will take place after the charge has been put but by then the CPS should have taken responsibility for the conduct of the prosecution and be putting together the case file. Our major recommendation is that there should be a single integrated unit to assemble and manage case files, combining the present police ASU and those parts of the CPS branch which deal with file preparation and review. In this way we intend to bridge the gulf between the police and the CPS to which we have referred.

29. We do not wish to be prescriptive about the precise form of these units, which will need to take account of local circumstances. However, we propose as a model a 'Criminal Justice Unit' in the charge of a CPS lawyer with mainly CPS staff, although many of these might be the civilian police staff at present employed in ASUs. Such a unit will need to be able to call on the police to take action in obtaining more evidence and so a senior police officer will need to be part of the unit, which would be housed in or near the relevant police station. The unit would deal with fast-track cases in their entirety and with simple summary cases, that is, with both the file preparation and the necessary advocacy. The CPS should primarily be

responsible in the Magistrates' Courts for the timely disposal of all cases prosecuted by its lawyers and share with the court one or more performance indicators related to timeliness. These will involve the other main part of the CPS at the local level where we have recommended the formation of trial units to deal with advocacy in some trials in the Magistrates' Courts and the management and preparation of all cases in the Crown Court. Such a unit would be staffed both by lawyers and caseworkers, not mainly by non-lawyers as was the case in the past.

30. We hope that these changes will lead to a shift in the centre of gravity of the CPS towards the Crown Court. In return we hope that the Crown Courts will work more closely with the CPS over listing to allow for the proper preparation of cases and assembling of witnesses and evidence.

31. No doubt as a result of financial stringency, CPS staff have increasingly been withdrawn from the Crown Court. We wish to reverse this trend. We recommend that a CPS lawyer should be present at each major Crown Court Centre and that there should be more CPS caseworkers or administrative staff available to support counsel in the Crown Court. We also make proposals to alleviate some of the other problems in the relationship between the CPS and the Bar to which we have already referred, especially the disparity in the fees paid to the Bar for prosecution and defence work, returned briefs, and the difficulty of counsel obtaining fresh instructions when he is in court.

32. CPS lawyers have recently been granted limited rights of audience in the Crown Court. We are keen for them to take the opportunity to exercise these rights as soon as they can, probably starting with plea and directions hearings, which we see as a key to greater efficiency and fewer adjournments.

33. We recognise that the police and the courts are aware of the difficulties presented by their current organisation and working relationships with the CPS and have put in place a number of groups and initiatives to help to resolve them. We do not agree that all these have practical value but their existence shows a welcome willingness to attempt to work together. We should like to see one joint body at local level representing all the relevant criminal justice agencies, to achieve the necessary unity of purpose and harmony in approach.

Central casework
34. The role of Central Casework in the CPS is absolutely vital. It deals with a wide variety of work which, by reason of its difficulty, importance or sensitivity, cannot properly be dealt with in the areas. Moreover, the importance and difficulty of its work is likely to increase, partly because serious international crime is increasing and partly because the incorporation of the European Convention on Human Rights into United Kingdom legislation is bound to create a considerable amount of extra work for the CPS. There are justified concerns about the functioning of and management systems in Central Casework in recent years. These need to be addressed, and indeed the CPS has various changes in hand. We are strongly in favour of Central Casework continuing to exist in much its present form, but as far as possible with its capability enhanced. We make recommendations to this end, including some about its structure.

Special casework
35. Those who were, until fairly recently, Special Casework lawyers, have for reasons which the CPS has explained to us, been distributed amongst the branches if they are still employed by the CPS. We believe that the necessity to deal with serious crime and difficult cases around the country, particularly the demands of the newly formed National Crime Squad,

are such that the groups of Special Casework lawyers which previously existed should be reconstituted, but in a new form. We recommend that there should be five or six such groups, each containing a number of Special Casework lawyers with support staff, throughout the country, probably located conveniently for the offices of the National Crime Squad and the judicial circuits. We have considered how they should be managed and have decided that the best pattern would probably be that they should be part of headquarters. This would mean that there would be a head of Special Casework with a small staff in headquarters. We have also considered, and have some observations to make, about the management of fraud cases within the CPS. We believe that instead of being distributed between Central Casework and Special Casework as hitherto, complex cases should now be dealt with by Special Casework lawyers with a special unit handling 'City' and large international fraud. This would not disturb existing arrangements which direct the most serious cases to the SFO.

The future organisation of the CPS

36. On coming into office in 1997 the Government announced that the CPS was to be reorganised into a structure of 42 areas, each to be coterminous with a police force. Our terms of reference include that reorganisation as the basis for our work. It would be possible to make a change to a 42-area structure with minimal disturbance to the current branch and headquarters organisation. However, this would not achieve the devolution which we believe is essential. Our view is that the reorganisation should be taken as an opportunity for a genuinely new start, building on the achievements of the past twelve years but creating a form of management at both national and local levels which is different in both structure and style.

37. The objectives of the changes that we propose are to:

a) Set up a 'decentralised national service' through the genuine devolution of as much responsibility and accountability as possible to the CCPs in the new areas;

b) Redefine the role of the headquarters organisation;

c) Ensure that all but the most senior lawyers in the CPS, including CCPs, spend much more of their time prosecuting;

d) Improve the career structure for all staff;

e) Give each CCP responsibility for managing the administrative support and services in his area, subject only to the constraints of nationally based accounting and data processing systems.

f) Reduce the bureaucracy by prioritising the information flows and limiting the headquarters support functions to a few key advisory services.

38. We see the decision to restructure the CPS into 42 areas not as increasing the number of areas from 13 to 42 but as:

a) Removing completely a layer of management by disbanding the 13 areas, and

b) Ensuring that in most areas, if not all, the area itself becomes the key operating unit instead of the branch, of which there are 93 at present.

39. In deciding on the functions of the new areas, we have thought of the CPS as analogous in some respects to a very large legal firm specialising in criminal prosecution and operating from 42 separate offices of greatly differing sizes. The local CCPs will be bound by central policies and procedures but will have a large degree of autonomy in carrying out their professional duties and managing their local offices.

The local structure

40. This may vary between areas. Thirty-two out of the 42 new areas have at present only one or two branches which often serve mainly one Crown Court. For them a useful model might be that there should be a series of criminal justice units throughout the Area, each serving one or more police divisions and one or two magistrates' courts, together with one trial unit for the area dealing with all Crown Court cases and the summary trials which have not been dealt with in the CJU. The trial unit would be located in the area office.

41. The remaining 10 larger areas may need different arrangements. We would expect there to be several trial units related to the Crown Courts. The location of the new CJUs would be a matter for the CCP.

42. The position of the new CCPs is clearly one of great importance. The competence, integrity and personality of the men and women who are appointed to these roles will be vital to the success of the move to a decentralised national service. What is important is that even in the smallest area, the CCP will have the ability and authority to negotiate and co-operate with the judiciary, the Chief Constable and the senior representatives of other bodies and agencies.

43. We propose that below the CCP the functions of the new area headquarters should be divided between legal operations on one hand and the management of process and administration on the other. We recommend that the latter function will be the responsibility of an area business manager. He will have two main fields of responsibility:

   a) The administration of the area, including being accountable to the CCP for planning, budgeting and financial control; and

   b) Working to improve the efficiency of the prosecution process.

   The area business manager would report directly to the CCP and would have a small staff.

44. The conduct of prosecutions would be under the direct control of the CCP. The heads of the CJUs and trial units would in most of the areas report directly to the CCP, but in the largest areas it might be desirable for them to report to an Assistant CCP, who would be in charge of one of the trial units.

National headquarters

45. The headquarters of the CPS should have two main functions: setting the national framework for prosecution, and resourcing and monitoring the areas. The one function requires top quality legal professionalism, and the other, high calibre managerial skills. The DPP clearly has to be a lawyer whose main concerns should be with the very considerable legal responsibilities that go with the position. The management of the process and administration and control of the organisation as a whole should, we recommend, be entrusted to a chief executive. He would be the second most senior officer in the headquarters organisation and be directly responsible to the DPP who would be relieved of the great bulk of administrative work.

46. The chief executive need not – and probably would not – be a lawyer by profession. He would be the Principal Establishment and Finance Officer (PEFO) for the CPS and would have working to him two divisional heads; one, the Head of Finance and the other the Head of Personnel, as well as other functional managers responsible for strategic planning and IT. He would have a functional link with the area business managers.

47. The DPP, freed to concentrate largely on the prosecution and legal process, would be immediately supported by a Director, Central Operations. He, in turn, would, we envisage, have three divisions under him, each with a head who would deal with policy (broadly, the functions of the present Casework Services); Central Casework; and Special Casework.

48. We propose that there should be no intermediate layer of management between the DPP and the CCPs in the 42 areas. We recognise that this is a much wider span of management control than is often thought appropriate. We discuss in the report how, in the circumstances, we believe it can be achieved.

London

49. London is different. It is by far the largest of the present 13 areas, employing nearly 1,000 staff and accounting for more than a sixth of the total CPS budget. The problems of the CPS as a whole tend to be writ large in London, and it also has some problems of its own. The latter are largely related either to the greater problems in co-ordinating the work of the police, the CPS, and the courts, or to the difficulties, which were there from the beginning, of maintaining standards of performance in a much more demanding environment.

50. The Attorney-General has already agreed with the DPP that there will continue to be a single Chief Crown Prosecutor for London. This fits in well with the organisation of the Metropolitan Police, where the Commissioner has designated one of his Assistant Commissioners to be functionally responsible, from the police standpoint, for the smooth running of the criminal justice process. There are five Assistant Commissioners, each responsible for a Metropolitan Police Area. We recommend that the CPS mirrors this organisation by appointing five Assistant Chief Crown Prosecutors.

51. Although London is in some respects significantly different from the rest of the country, we nonetheless see no reason why the organisation which we have suggested for the other large conurbations should not also work perfectly well in London. Thus we envisage a number of trial units, linked with the main Crown Court centres, and a related network of criminal justice units. The appointment of a single business manager responsible for the whole of London will be critical, but we see many advantages in retaining a single administrative centre, rather than creating a precedent by setting up administrative structures at sub-area level.

52. We also regard it as particularly important that London should have an effective body to co-ordinate the work of all the main criminal justice agencies. Currently the CPS chairs the TIG Strategic Board for London. We recommend that this body, or its successor, is given the necessary status to play an effective part in the delivery of criminal justice in the capital.

Management and people: management of the CPS

53. The concept of a national framework for the CPS involves central accountability for the management of the process and of the resources. However, the nature of the process in which the CPS is involved demands that the areas need to be granted as much autonomy as possible, if they are to deliver an effective and efficient local service. Whatever the intention, the freedom of action able to be exercised at operational level is, at present, very limited. We have concluded that the CPS is still too bureaucratic despite recent moves that are designed to move the organisation in the right direction. The result has been the effective withdrawal from prosecution of many senior lawyers, the demoralisation of others and a negative impact on the effectiveness of prosecution.

54. We have concluded that the management functions of the CPS Headquarters need to be contained and concentrated, specifically on:

   a) Policy formulation;
   b) The planning and budget cycle;
   c) Performance monitoring;
   d) Control of key appointments and associated personnel activities;
   e) Information systems and technology;
   f) Internal inspection and audit.

55. The move to 42 areas, the changes that will follow from the implementation of the fast-track provisions of the Crime and Disorder Bill, and the changes resulting from our own proposals, will together mean that almost everyone in the CPS will be asked to carry out his job rather differently in the future. It will also necessarily mean a change in the way the CPS is managed. We hope that what will emerge will be a more collegiate management style which, having devolved genuine power and responsibility to the areas, continues both to encourage and support local and individual initiative. Combined with this, as an inevitable counterbalance, is the requirement for a rigorous and effective system of accountability, for which we make proposals.

People in the CPS

56. As an organisation the CPS ought to be a showcase for the legal profession, providing attractive career opportunities for young and competent lawyers and caseworkers. This is not the current perception but we hope that, in time, it could become so. It is certainly our belief that overall the CPS as an organisation and the people who work for it are currently under too much pressure. We were also made aware of the fact that many of the staff were concerned at what they saw as limited career possibilities within the CPS and about the inadequacy of their training. The latter applied particularly to the caseworkers, and to the lawyers who had moved into management.

57. The CPS is no different from any other organisation in that the aspirations of its employees cannot always be met particularly when sometimes the aspirations are unrealistic. Nonetheless, until now there have been a number of constraints, both internally and externally imposed, particularly on the career options for CPS lawyers. Recent developments such as the granting of limited rights of audience in the Crown Court, and the changes which will inevitably follow from the Crime and Disorder Bill enabling the DPP to confer on lay staff powers of review and presentation, provide scope to both lawyers and non-lawyers to take on new and more interesting work. We believe that many of our proposals will serve the same cause.

58. There is already a need for more training of CPS staff. Carrying our proposals into effect will make that need greater, so that people may feel and be properly equipped to face the challenges of their new or altered jobs. We make proposals for the enhancement of staff training in all areas, but for administrators and business managers as a first priority. There will be a cost for this, which we have taken into account in our financial estimates referred to below.

Information systems and technology

59. Attempts by the CPS to introduce an effective IT-based case management system have not been successful. Implementation of the system (SCOPE) which has been introduced into about half the branches has been halted and work is in hand to devise a programme to introduce new systems and a communications infrastructure as soon as possible. Hitherto all the agencies in the criminal justice system have tended to take a very parochial view of their IT systems requirements despite the efforts of inter-departmental groups to foster a unified approach to computerisation. Now, however, steps are being taken to improve the management of IT in the criminal justice system and it is to be hoped that this work will enable swift action to prevent the initiatives of individual departments from impeding the development of consistent and where possible integrated systems. It is important that the CPS does not act in isolation and we have therefore recommended that it joins with the police IT organisation to implement a new integrated system under the auspices of the

new IT organisation for the criminal justice system.

60. We therefore welcome the emergence of an over-arching criminal justice IT organisation but are concerned that, unless it has a significant budget and powers of its own, it will be no more effective than its predecessors.

Accountability

61. The DPP is by statute accountable to the Attorney-General and to Parliament. The nature and extent of her accountability is a subject of some complexity; we discuss it in the report, but cannot summarise what we say without losing the argument. One point, however, we can properly make here. It has become apparent that there is a difference of opinion between us and senior CPS management as to the rigidity of the constraints imposed on the DPP by her accountability. We are confident that genuine devolution of power – the power to make decisions – to the new areas will bring benefits in better casework and more efficient management. The devolution must, however, carry with it some risk that somewhere, sometime, somebody will make a wrong decision. In our view the potential benefits far outweigh the risk. CPS management seem to take the view that, unless that risk is minimal, the DPP's accountability does not allow her to take it, even though this would sacrifice the benefits of devolution. We cannot and do not accept this interpretation, nor do we believe that it is currently accepted by Government. Sir Humphrey has moved on.

62. The CPS as a whole, being a national service, is not and should not be accountable to any local body, but we believe it should add to the steps it has taken in recent years to inform people about its work generally, and to respond to public concerns in each of the areas. We discuss this subject under the heading of Answerability, and suggest a possible forum in which from time to time local CPS representatives could be answerable for the general conduct and policy of their Area, though not for the detail of any individual case.

63. In the past two years the CPS has established an inspectorate, which publishes reports both on standards of casework in areas or branches, and on specific themes. We are impressed by the quality of these reports, but we believe and recommend that the inspectorate should be made more independent by having a lay chairman appointed by the Attorney-General and a number of lay members, and that its remit should be widened. We make proposals to achieve these aims.

Funding

64. Our terms of reference require us to cost our 'recommendations taking account of the need to operate within existing provision'. We devote a chapter of the report to explaining how in our view this can be achieved.

The way forward

65. We referred earlier to the three key respects in which the CPS needs to change. Firstly it needs to give greater priority to the more serious cases. Secondly it must have a new organisation, structure and style of management. Thirdly, it needs to establish firmly its proper role in the criminal justice process.

66. If our recommendations are adopted, the staff of the CPS, at all levels, must accept the desirability of and understand the aims of those changes. New working practices and a new culture will be necessary if the CPS is to thrive and find its rightful place in the criminal justice system.

67. Moving the emphasis from the less serious to the more serious cases, while continuing to give proper consideration to each prosecution, will require not only change in the CPS but also in the police and the courts. We are confident that at the local

level the staff of the CPS will, when they understand the nature of the change required of them, be able to take the CPS forward in the way we have recommended. We are also confident that the staff of the courts and the police will give the CPS their support.

68. On one issue we are quite clear. In its short life the CPS has been subjected to a whole series of reviews, external and internal. Some have resulted in major changes in the structure and staffing of the service or parts of it, others in considerable changes in working practices. The present 14 area structure has only lasted for five years. We repeat that, whether all or any of our other recommendations are adopted, the move to 42 areas is inevitably another major reconstruction. We are not, of course, suggesting that the decision by Government to set in train that reconstruction was wrong; indeed, as we have said earlier, we agree with it, and our proposals are based upon it and are designed to produce the most benefit from it. Nevertheless, constant change is inevitably unsettling for all staff, and for a time must affect their performance. If the recommendations of this review are accepted and when they have come into effect, the CPS must be given the opportunity to settle down and make the new systems work. No doubt there will be initial problems, and mistakes will be made. Some fine tuning of the machinery may prove necessary. But our firm recommendation is that when the new structure and procedures are in place, there should be no further major changes to, nor review of, the CPS or any major part of it for a considerable period of time. As a body, the members of the Crown Prosecution Service must be allowed to regain their pride and achieve their potential – in a word, get on with the job. We believe that together they can do so. We wish them well.

It is a cause for concern when cases fail, but the real issue is why they fail and what can be done about it. The empirical material in the next extract puts the focus on the problems that can be experienced with witnesses.

McConville M and Baldwin J (1981) *Courts, Prosecution and Conviction*, p41

The commonest factor that explains ordered and directed cases in the Crown Court is, according to our analysis, that key witnesses for the prosecution either fail to appear at court or, if they do appear, give their evidence in an unsatisfactory manner. Sometimes a case is destroyed because the witnesses have disappeared, but more frequently cases collapse because a key witness gives his evidence in an unconvincing or unreliable way. Where the poor performance of a witness is unexpected, there is little the prosecution can do. But it is worth noting that often no surprise was occasioned by what had happened: indeed, in as man as four out of 10 cases in this category, the police feared from the outset that prosecution witnesses would present difficulties. In such cases, the prosecution is more open to criticism since it can be argued that a prosecutor should take into account the credibility of witnesses in deciding whether or not to institute charges. If a prosecution hinges upon the word of an untrustworthy or unreliable witness, there are strong reasons for not proceeding. The variety of problems that the prosecution faces is illustrated in the following quotes:

Case 63 (London) (A key witness was a man serving a lengthy prison sentence)

Police officer: There were no witnesses other than (the man in prison) and only formal police evidence. I expected an acquittal from the beginning as he was not reliable at all. I wasn't surprised at all but we had to charge (the defendant). But it would have been unsafe to let the case go on.

Case 122 (London) (A cashier at a supermarket disappeared after a fellow employee had been charged with theft)

Police officer: We couldn't produce the girl as a witness. She had left home and disappeared. We had been to the Crown Court on three previous occasions and the judge eventually gave us no more time to find her.

Cases 36–7 (Birmingham) (A case of car theft)

Judge: The prosecution was not in a position to go on, because an essential witness was not there. The matter had been adjourned before. I did not feel that any more public money should be wasted so I refused the prosecution's application for an adjournment.

Whilst there have been complaints about a failure to prosecute, at the same time a major problem of the present system of prosecution has been acquittals. Some further insight into acquittals is provided by Block, Corbett and Peay who examined a sample of acquittals.

Block B, Corbett C and Peay J (1993) 'Ordered and Directed Acquittals in the Crown Court: A Time of Change?', *Criminal Law Review*, p100

Of the sample of 100 non-jury acquittals, there were 71 ordered acquittals, 28 directed acquittals and one mixed acquittal, where there were two indictments and one was acquitted by order and one by direction. Although fewer than half of ordered acquittals were considered definitely or possibly foreseeable, three quarters of directed acquittals were so classified. This supports our view, derived from the study, that directed acquittals result largely from weak cases that should have been discontinued, whereas ordered acquittals often

result from unforeseeable circumstances. This may be considered to challenge Zander's (1991) assertion that ordered acquittals represent an even weaker category of case than where the judge directs an acquittal. Our study shows that in fact there are at least two categories of ordered acquittals: those weak cases that are spotted by the Crown Prosecution Service immediately after committal, and others – seemingly good cases – which weaken unpredictably before committal or trial. Of all ordered acquittals in our sample (71), 14 were listed for mention (the former category) and 37 weakened nearer or on the day of trial (the latter category). Use of the term weak cases implies criticism of the Crown Prosecution Service, but this is misleading. The real basis for criticism is the distinction between predictably weak cases which the Crown Prosecution Service fails to spot and unpredictably weak cases. Of fundamentally weak cases, the Crown Prosecution Service may be held responsible for those resulting in ordered acquittals that should have been spotted even before committal, and for those ending in directed acquittals due to weaknesses not spotted at all. Any analysis of the national statistics which is used as a basis for assessing the performance of the Crown Prosecution Service needs to take account of these distinctions.

The extract from Rose examines the operation of the Crown Prosecution Service. The main message that Rose tries to get across is that there has been a retreat from prosecution. Much of the material is an indictment of the Crown Prosecution Service. The extract deals with the criteria in the CPS Code which allow cases to be withdrawn by the CPS.

Rose D (1996) *In the Name of the Law*, pp134–135

'Are there matters which might be properly put to a witness by the defence to attack his credibility?' amounts in practice to an invitation to abandon cases because a witness happens to have a criminal record. In rape and sex assault prosecutions, it opens the way to drop cases because the victim is a prostitute, was promiscuous, or had a previous relationship with her assailant. The CPS wants its crime victims and witnesses to be middle-class and squeaky clean. This section of the Code concludes: 'The Crown Prosecutor must be prepared to look beneath the surface of the statement. He must also draw, so far as is possible, on his own experience of how evidence of the type under consideration is likely to "stand up" in court before reaching a conclusion as to the likelihood of a conviction.' One could put this another way: having read the case file, the prosecutor should act on a hunch. In 1994, the CPS 'discontinued' 160,000 cases, about 11 per cent of the total. This represented an increase of about 50 per cent since the year of its foundation in 1986. Of the prosecutions dropped, 43 per cent were abandoned because there was thought to be insufficient evidence.

The second principal criterion set out in the Code requires an even bolder judgment than the prediction of how witnesses will react in giving evidence. Having been satisfied that there is a realistic prospect of conviction, the prosecutor must decide if proceeding is 'in the public interest'. Cases which failed to cross this hurdle amounted to 28 per cent of the total in 1994.

What is public interest? The Code adopts the definition of this somewhat elusive concept given by Lord Shawcross when he was Attorney-General in 1951. It had never been the practice in Britain that criminal offences would be prosecuted automatically, he said. One had to take into account 'the effect which the prosecution, successful or unsuccessful as the case may be, would have upon public morale and order, and with any other considerations affecting public policy'.

It is difficult to believe that the 2,000 salaried solicitors and barristers who make up the ranks of the CPS spend much time

dwelling on lofty notions of 'public morale and order'. The pre-eminent public interest here is not justice, but cost.

It is apparent from the following Government report that the problem of stretched resources in relation to the Crown Prosecution Service is now appreciated. The report outlines five key improvements that are on the agenda. Also covered in some detail is the workload and organisation of the Crown Prosecution Service. Finally, examples are provided of the manner in which links have been developed between the Crown Prosecution Service and the local community.

Home Office (2001) *Criminal Justice: The Way Ahead*, pp50–54

The CPS will play a key part in delivering the Government's commitment to improving radically the likelihood of offenders being brought to justice. The CPS must also play its central part in improving the effectiveness of the criminal justice system. At a time when crime and criminality is changing, the CPS must be adequately resourced, trained and deployed to be able to respond intelligently and flexibly to such changes. The CPS was created by the Prosecution of Offences Act 1985 and started work the following year. The Act followed a key recommendation of the 1981 Royal Commission on Criminal Procedure – that there should be a nationally consistent policy towards prosecutions and that the prosecution function should be separated from the police. But the commission's recommendations on the structure and organisation of the CPS – that the service should be 'locally based with some national features' not 'centrally directed' – were not adopted. Indeed the re-organisation of the CPS in 1993 (which changed the number of areas from 31 to 13) actually increased the centralisation.

In 1997 the Government commissioned a thorough review of the CPS by Sir Iain Glidewell. Reporting in 1998, the Glidewell

Review found a service that was over-centralised and grossly understaffed at its inception. Overall, Sir Iain Glidewell found that senior CPS lawyers were not able to spend enough time on casework as they were dealing with management matters. Moreover, at its inception, insufficient resources were allocated to the CPS. By 1998, Glidewell found fees for defence counsel had outstripped those for prosecuting counsel in the same case. The combined effect of an inappropriate national structure, over-stretched staff and under-funding depleted morale and contributed to under-performance in the CPS. It affected the service's ability to work with the police and to engage sufficiently with victims and the wider public, including within minority ethnic communities. Public confidence in the CJS has been damaged by a drop in conviction rates – that is to say, the proportion of crimes that result in a conviction– over the last 20 years. The reasons for the drop in the conviction rates are complex. But one contributory factor was an under-resourced and under-powered CPS. The challenge now is to rebuild that confidence by reversing the decline in the number of offenders brought to justice, whilst ensuring that the innocent are properly identified. This will depend, crucially, on police and CPS effectiveness in bringing offenders to court with good evidence; on the courts operating with increased effectiveness; and on fair, simple criminal procedures to ensure just outcomes.

A firm footing for the Crown Prosecution Service

The CPS continues to face great challenges. With approximately 5,800 staff (about one-third lawyers and two-thirds caseworkers and administrative support) the service has to deal with 1.4 million cases each year in the magistrates' courts and a further 125,000 in the Crown Court. On an average day, each CPS lawyer in inner London magistrates' courts can expect to be handling upwards of 50 remand cases and two or more summary trials.

The CPS is now well placed to meet these challenges. Great strides have been made to raise performance. Better co-ordination and joint working with the police has been achieved through its reorganisation, following Glidewell, into 42 local areas, coterminous with police force boundaries. Joint police/CPS Criminal Justice Units have been established to ensure closer working – improving the quality of cases and efficient use of resources, and Joint Performance Management provides a valuable basis by which the police and CPS can together drive up performance. Each CPS area is now headed by a local Chief Crown Prosecutor (CCP) with a strong degree of local autonomy to implement national policies in the light of local circumstances. The creation of the CPS Chief Executive post in 1998 and area business managers has freed up senior lawyers to do what they are skilled in – prosecuting difficult cases. As a nationally organised but locally delivered service, with short chains of command and strong local leadership, the CPS could be at the forefront of CJS modernisation. It has a particular role to play in offering a better service to victims and with local residents, being accountable for the difficult decisions made on behalf of those communities. The Lord Chancellor and Attorney-General were concerned that the difference in fees between defence and prosecution might lead to inequality of representation and therefore announced in July 2000 a unified fee scheme. This will cover all cases in the Crown Court of up to 25 days in length and will provide a considerable increase in prosecution fees in shorter cases. In order to finance these increases, defence fees will be subject to reduction.

Building on these foundations

The Government is taking action to deliver five key improvements:

1. a better resourced, better performing CPS, more effective in prosecuting crime and preparing good quality cases for court;
2. closer and earlier cooperation between

CPS and police and between CPS and courts to reduce duplication of effort and delays;

3. a greater sense of public accountability through closer involvement with local criminal justice system partners and communities;

4. moves towards simple, fair rules of criminal procedure and new rights of appeal to ensure just outcomes; and

5. an enhanced role for the CPS in explaining difficult or controversial prosecution decisions.

A stronger, more effective Crown Prosecution Service

The CPS is developing a framework for more effective prosecutions by focusing skilled and experienced senior lawyers on the most serious and difficult cases, persistent offenders and crimes that are particularly socially corrosive (for example racist crimes and domestic violence). The CPS will also be looking at widening the remit and number of designated caseworkers to cover a wider range of cases in order to release lawyers for more complex cases and achieve greater flexibility for listing. Trials Units will be established to work with case progression officers in the Crown Court to improve case management by April 2002. The CPS has set targets to improve its delivery of timely and efficiently prepared prosecution cases. It is crucial for public confidence that the CPS gets prosecution decisions right – this often requires difficult judgements, weighing the strength of evidence, the seriousness of the offence and the duties under Code for Crown Prosecutors – and an important target has been set here too. The CPS will also be exploring with the police how to develop a nationally consistent approach to the provision of earlier and better pre-charge assistance to the police (including out-of-hours). This will help to improve the quality of investigations, increase the number of prosecutions and reduce the number of cases that fail. Where necessary (for example in relation to serious

crime or particularly complex cases), this may need to involve greater clarity of the circumstances in which the police should seek advice from the CPS. This might involve greater use of protocols between CPS and police forces, building on current good practice. The central Casework Directorate of the CPS was established to handle the most important, sensitive and complex cases, such as those relating to terrorism and serious fraud as well as references and appeals to the Court of Appeal and House of Lords. The directorate will be expanded from two to three sites by end 2001 to complement the geographical spread of the National Crime Squad, maximising effective joint working and casework performance. Where it would help to improve whole system performance, the CPS should also contribute to local management decisions, for example by having a greater input to court listing arrangements.

Building expertise

Since 1997, the CPS has been developing a cadre of higher court advocates (HCAs) to exercise at first limited and now unrestricted rights of audience in the higher courts. HCAs have attracted a favourable reaction from the judiciary for their advocacy skills and thoroughness of case preparation. The CPS intends to deploy more HCAs. One hundred training places for new HCAs are being provided annually in the years 2001–03 with plans for as many as 460 operational by 2003–04. A central plank of CPS reform is to shift the centre of gravity towards the more serious casework in the Crown Court. More regular exposure to Crown Court practice and procedure, coupled with the stimulus of appearing before a Crown Court judge, and against experienced independent barristers, will develop CPS lawyers' experience and expertise, leading to improved standards of preparation and presentation. The ability of the CPS to attract high calibre staff will be boosted with a new pay and reward structure, to be in place by August 2002. The CPS will increase to 10 per cent by March 2004 the proportion of advocates whose performance is significantly above normal requirements. A Prosecutors' College will also be established to keep prosecutors and caseworkers up to date with law, practice and modern techniques and to encourage joint training with the police.

Provide closer links between the Crown Prosecution Service and communities

The CPS is well placed to adopt a central role in local criminal justice arrangements, to raise public confidence; to respond to the needs of victims and witnesses; and provide a focal point for local accountability. Local Chief Crown Prosecutors will have a strengthened local role and give a more visible lead to the vigorous and fair prosecution of offenders. CCPs' pay will reflect their enhanced role and their performance. CCP appointments should generally be the subject of open competition in a phased programme from April 2002.

Examples include:

1. CPS Nottingham has taken part in a Channel 4 programme on the workings of a magistrates' court.
2. The CCP Durham spent 24 hours in local casualty unit observing the pressures and problems of NHS staff who become involved with the CJS as witnesses to – or sometimes victims of – crime.
3. CPS Gwent has briefings with local crime reporters to update them on current and upcoming high profile cases. They have also had a series of school visits and held open days at local libraries in Gwent.
4. CPS Nottinghamshire's annual report was translated into five languages to help local communities understand its work and performance.
5. CPS South Wales has arranged for members of staff to have mentors from local minority ethnic communities.
6. The CPS in west London is working with local community groups and the voluntary sector to improve domestic violence prosecutions.
7. The CCP Suffolk is an active member of the Suffolk Multi-Racial Forum Against Racial Harassment and meets with local community groups to explain the role of the CPS. Local staff vacancies are specifically brought to the attention of minority ethnic communities throughout the county.

Since 1997 the Government has placed new responsibilities on local authorities and the police to consult local communities about local priorities. It is important that the CPS also has productive dialogue with local people so that local crime fighting priorities may be considered alongside national objectives and targets. The Government will encourage CCPs to develop stronger relationships with local communities to promote CPS accountability and public confidence. The prosecution process must be responsive to the varying requirements of different people and communities, delivering justice equally to all social and ethnic groups. The composition of CPS staff should reflect the diverse communities that they serve. The CPS is committed to ensuring that the fair and effective prosecution of crime is not hampered by discriminatory barriers and like all key criminal justice agencies, will be subject to the new duty to promote race equality contained in the Race Relations (Amendment) Act 2000. To achieve this, the CPS will ensure that cases with a racial element are prosecuted effectively by: taking forward the recommendations of the Stephen Lawrence Inquiry Report; and maintaining the CPS Racist Incident monitoring scheme and publishing annual results.

___

In the extracts provided the problems of the bail system are explored in the light of empirical evidence in relation to the system. The prospects for reform of the system are also explored.

Doherty M and East R (1985) 'Bail Decisions in Magistrates' Courts', *British Journal of Criminology*[1], vol 25, pp251–252, 255–257, 262–263

Not all criminal cases that are brought before a magistrates' court can be disposed of at the first hearing. For example, the prosecution or the defence may require time to prepare their case or the court may require reports on the defendant prior to sentence. These and other matters involve remands and the court has to decide if the remand should be on bail or in custody. The system of bail decision-making has received critical comment and some degree of statutory reform (most notably by the Bail Act 1976) in the period since the early 1960s. A major problem has been that the quality of decision-making is suspect. The system does not facilitate informed discretion and consistency in its use. A particular criticism has been that the limited amount of information made available to the courts has mainly been provided by the police and that the courts are too willing to adhere to the police viewpoint. One implication of such a system is that defendants, often unconvicted, may be unnecessarily remanded in custody. Such an injustice can be increased in several ways. First, defendants may be subsequently acquitted or declared unsuitable for a custodial sentence. Secondly, whilst in prison awaiting trial a defendant may find his ability to prepare for trial impaired. Thirdly, defendants remanded in custody are most likely to plead guilty and to receive custodial sentences. Other adverse effects of custody may materialise in relation to a defendant's family, employment and abode. For the penal system unnecessary detentions before trial add to the pressure on prisons. Finally, it is also possible that defendants who would be best remanded in custody are being released on bail to pose a threat to the operation of the criminal justice system and the community

generally. In this article the findings of an investigation into the workings of the bail system after the Bail Act 1976 are presented and considered in the light of some of the concerns about bail. ...

The study undertaken was of bail decisions in Cardiff magistrates' courts over a six months' period (August 1981– January 1982). A total of 496 hearings were observed and bail was granted in a total of 396 (80 per cent) of them. ...

A common finding of previous studies has been the importance of the police viewpoint. Bottomley observed that 'in the great majority of their decisions to grant or refuse bail the magistrates seemed to act in accordance with the implicit or explicit recommendations of the police' (Bottomley, 1970, p59). Similarly, Bottoms and McClean remarked that 'magistrates everywhere generally accept the police view' (Bottoms and McClean, 1976, p196). King suggested that 'magistrates, particularly lay magistrates, still rely very heavily on the police's opinion as to whether or not bail ought to be given' (King, 1971, p45). He also suggested that magistrates should enquire more thoroughly into police objections to bail (ibid, p46) and that the bail rate would not improve 'so long as members of the judiciary continue to follow blindly advice given by the police' (ibid, p94). In contrast to these earlier studies there was less evidence in our study of the police view being dominant. ...

In many cases the possibility of a remand in custody was never raised. This occurred in 345 cases (288+57), 70 per cent of those observed. This highlights the importance of the basic legal provisions in the bail process. The importance of the police and defendant's representatives is consequently limited to that extent. In only 101 (20 per cent) cases did the police make a positive contribution. Within these figures it can be seen that the police objected to bail in only 18 per cent of the cases. This is the lowest figure recorded in a research project and is considerably lower than some of the previous findings. Bottomley (1970, p59) in his study of the records of an

[1] Copyright © 1985 *British Journal of Criminology* and contributors. Used by permission.

urban court reported a figure of 64 per cent, and in his observation study of an urban court and three rural courts a figure of 55 per cent (ibid p44). Other findings were 50 per cent by Bottoms and McClean (1976, p207), 25 per cent by King (1971, p17), 25 per cent by Zander (1979, p108) and 54 per cent by Cutts in his 1976 study and 43 per cent in his 1981 study (Cutts, 1982, p1090). Of the 100 cases in which there was a remand in custody the police had objected to bail in only 61. Whilst the police role is clearly limited in terms of overt or active participation, in some respects it is important. Only 27 (31 per cent) of the 88 defendants whose bail was opposed by the police received bail, as against 369 (90 per cent) of the 408 defendants whose bail was unopposed. ...

One final factor to consider as regards the police role is the extent to which the court refused a request by the police for a remand in custody. This occurred in 31 per cent of the cases in which the police objected to bail. Whilst not as high as the figure of 42 per cent reported by Zander (1979, p110) it is higher than the findings of other earlier studies. Bottoms and McClean (1976, p196) reported 13 per cent, King (1971, p18) 22 per cent and Bottomley (1970, p59) only 4 per cent. ...

Prospects for reform in bail decision-making

Whilst it is clear that the bail rate has increased over the last 25 years the basic problem of the bail system remains. The nature of the system inhibits rather than guarantees informed and consistent decisions; as is clear from the Bail Act criteria for refusing bail, it is expected to be multi-purpose. Defendants can be remanded in custody if it is thought that they may fail to appear at the next hearing and also, for example, if they might commit further offences or obstruct the course of justice. At some point the risk of one or more of these may become unacceptable and a remand in custody is ordered. The necessity of having regard to several matters makes for complexity in bail decision-making,

which is increased by the fact that in relation to each and all of them numerous factors may have to be taken into account. In our study, in the 77 cases in which the police gave reasons for opposing bail, they made use of 21 different reasons and on average suggested two reasons per case. They concentrated their attention on the defendant's past and potential criminality and the needs of the criminal justice system. In the 89 cases in which defendant's representatives gave reasons as to why bail should be granted they presented an average of three reasons per defendant. They used a total of 24 different reasons which referred to factors broadly similar to those used by the police but with a greater emphasis on the defendant's circumstances.

The difficulties caused by the complexity of decision-making are compounded in several ways. The lay magistrates who make many of the bail decisions are amateurs who receive only limited training. Also, the nature of the proceedings is problematic. One of the most striking features of the operation of the courts was the rapidity of decision-making. Information was gathered on the amount of time spent on bail decisions in 209 (42 per cent) of the cases in the study. It was found that 62 per cent of the hearings lasted less than two minutes and 96 per cent less than ten minutes. There was a tendency for more time to be spent on the decision when bail was refused than when it was granted. But even in these cases 38 per cent were dealt with in less than two minutes and 87 per cent in less than ten minutes. The main reason for such speed was that the courts had a heavy work-load, dealing with an average of 60 cases between them each day. Also the participants in the court proceedings (magistrates, clerks of the court, solicitors, police officers and probation officers) would often have other responsibilities that required their attention. The court proceedings are designed to ensure that cases are dealt with quickly and there is an expectation that the participants in the process will assist in this. ...

In a situation where there is an expectation that cases are dealt with quickly, often in a non-adversarial fashion, it is perhaps not surprising that only limited information of a low quality is made available to the courts. The police and defendant's representatives are the main sources of information. Whilst, as mentioned earlier, they suggest reasons for the granting or refusing of bail these assertions are rarely scrutinised. The result is that decision-makers, often amateurs with limited training who are working under a time-pressure, have to make subjective decisions on the basis of limited unsubstantiated information. The quality of decision making must thus be regarded as suspect with consequent problems of the type outlined in the introduction to this paper. Such a situation is far from ideal. To attempt to attain the ideal would require the introduction of a standardised system, in which good-quality information of as objective a character as possible would be scrutinised by well-trained decision-makers. The operators of the system would themselves require scrutiny and probably further guidance, so as to ensure the reasonable consistency of decisions.

Bibliography

Bottomley A K (1970) *Prison Before Trial*, London: Bell.

Bottoms A and McClean J (1976) *Defendants in the Criminal Process*, London: Routledge and Kegan Paul.

Cutts L (1982) 'Has the Bail Act Made Any Difference?', *New Law Journal*, 132, 1089.

King M (1971) *Bail or Custody*, London: Cobden Trust.

Zander M (1979) 'Operation of the Bail Act in London Magistrates' Courts', *New Law Journal*, 129, 108.

The Woolf report expressed concern about the lack of information in the bail system and the consequences for both the defendant and the prison system. For the defendant custody may mean the loss of a job which would be a negative factor in relation to any eventual sentence. For the prison system the remand population not only consumes scarce prison places but also the turnover of prisoners is disruptive to the regime.

Home Office (1991) *Prison Disturbances* (Woolf Report), 10.82–10.84

Magistrates would not regularly, if ever, sentence a defendant to imprisonment on the limited information which is usually available on a bail application. Yet frequently the question of whether or not to refuse bail has an important influence on the sentence which is eventually passed. The refusal of bail can result in a defendant, for example, losing his employment or his accommodation, both of which may be important considerations in determining his ultimate disposal. We propose, therefore, that there should be a clear expectation that magistrates should not make a final decision to remand a defendant in custody until they have received at least the information which will be available to the Crown Prosecution Service in those areas where a bail information scheme is in operation. We would expect magistrates to insist on more information than that which is made available at the present time to the Crown Prosecution Service where there is no bail scheme in operation. They should develop the practice of requiring a report on the community ties which the prisoner has. In addition, we propose that magistrates should attach considerable significance to whether or not the offence which the defendant is alleged to have committed is one which, if proved, would justify a sentence of imprisonment. While it is in order to grant bail irrespective of the likely sentence, to remand a defendant in custody for an offence for which he would never be sentenced to imprisonment can be questionable, unless there is some reasonable justification such as possible interference with justice or a persistent failure to surrender to his bail or to comply with its terms.

Morgan and Jones provide an account of and commentary upon the Woolf Report analysis of, and proposals for, the remand system. What becomes apparent upon reading this is that the bail system faces not only the dilemma of imprisoning people before trial, but also that decisions to remand in custody can put considerable strain upon the prison system itself.

Morgan R and Jones S (1992) 'Bail or Jail', in Stockdale E and Casale S (eds), *Criminal Justice under Stress*, pp54–56

Woolf realised that, whatever the view of the prison authorities in the past, remand prisoners have the capacity to cause serious problems. However, that did not mean the Prison Service had failed to subject remand prisoners to sufficiently secure conditions. Woolf found no single cause for the riots and no simple solution that would prevent them. He suggested that the stability of prisons is based on management paying sufficient attention to the elements of security, control and justice, and there being a balance struck between those three elements (Woolf 1991, pp225–226). In the case of remand prisoners there was imbalance. They were the object of excessive security, and the control measures to which they were subject were inappropriate. Moreover, they suffered a grave deficiency of justice. Woolf also doubted if so many remand prisoners need be held in custody for so long (ibid, p223).

As his terms of reference were limited, Woolf had to be circumspect about the use made of remands in custody by the courts. His inclinations were clearly reductionist, but he approached the question by considering the decision-making process. He pointed out that, in procedural terms, the question of bail is dealt with by the courts more casually than sentencing. Decisions are sometimes made hurriedly, without adequate information, by one or two, rather than three, magistrates, and

without the benefit of High Court guidelines (ibid, p251). Meanwhile, he commended current government initiatives designed to increase the use of bail, or shorten the period that remands spend in custody (ibid, 251–253). In addition, his proposed Criminal Justice Consultative Council, together with parallel local committees, would be a mechanism ideally suited to develop initiatives designed to reduce the remand population.

Woolf's use of the terms 'security' and 'control' was relatively straightforward. 'Security' referred to the Prison Service's primary obligation to keep people committed to prison until they are due to be released. For remand prisoners, that meant until the time of their trial or sentence, unless granted bail in the interim. Control referred to orderliness within prison, a lack of which may spell the loss of security for other prisoners. A failure of control may sometimes lead to a breach of perimeter security.

Woolf's ideas of accommodation units for no more than 50–70 prisoners and secure 'firebreaks' between such units apply as much to remand as sentenced prisoners. However, they have a particular significance for the remand population because of his re-emphasis on separating the convicted from the unconvicted and the great importance he attached to accommodating prisoners as close as possible to their community ties in what he refers to as 'community prisons'. Woolf found that remand prisoners are currently subject 'to a degree of security and control which is frequently unnecessary' (ibid, p327), and proposed that they be treated, unless there is good reason to do otherwise, as the equivalent of security category C rather than B, their present classification. He also suggested that in the same way that the police, the CPS, the probation service and the courts co-operate to decide on the appropriate level of control needed over defendants granted bail, so those same agencies might assist the prison service by identifying defendants refused bail who may need to be subject to a higher security category (ibid, p327).

However, Woolf's use of the term 'justice' is more complex. It refers to the 'obligation' to treat prisoners with humanity and fairness and to prepare them for their return to the community in a way which makes it less likely that they will reoffend (ibid, p226). This definition is geared to the convicted but Woolf elsewhere balances this by proposing that there be a separate body of prison rules for the untried. It is clear from the body of his report that his notion of justice involves more than both fairness and due process (ibid, p412). His recommendations that there be more active regimes for prisoners, access to sanitation at all times, properly paid work, education programmes, improved contact between prisoners and their families, and better clothing indicate that for him justice covers what Dilulio (1987) has more accurately described *as amenity* and *service*.

The amenities and services available to untried prisoners should be different from those for convicted and sentenced prisoners. For example, the untried, subject to the presumption of innocence, should not be compelled to work. On the other hand, there is no case for denying them access to programmes on the ground that they have not been convicted of an offence. The vast majority of persons denied bail are seriously disadvantaged socially and economically. Many have a long record of previous convictions; that is often why they are denied bail. However, that is also why they 'should suffer no greater loss of liberty, both in duration and degree, than is necessary to secure the course of justice' (Morgan and Barclay, 1989, p23) and why, according to Woolf, it must 'be part of the task of the Prison Service to enable the remand prisoner to spend his time in custody in as constructive a manner as possible' (Woolf 1991, p247).

Bibliography
Dilulio J (1987) *Governing Prisons*, New York: Free Press.

Morgan R and Barclay A (1989) 'Remands in Custody: Problems and Prospects for Change', *Prison Service Journal*, 74: 13.

Woolf L J (1991) *Prison Disturbances April 1990: Report of an Inquiry*, London: HMSO.

The report concentrates on the issue of how unsentenced prisoners are handled by the prison system. It is a sorry tale in which the irony of the unconvicted receiving worse conditions than the guilty is spelt out. The report ends by providing a series of suggestions for reform of the system.

HM Chief Inspector of Prisons (2000) *Unjust deserts*, pp3–4, 123–125

Many of the strongest criticisms of the treatment of and conditions for prisoners – adult or young, male or female – which I have made in the past are those contained in the published reports of inspections of local prisons and remand centres. I have highlighted repeatedly the gap between the treatment and conditions for sentenced and unsentenced prisoners, the balance of advantage lying invariably with the sentenced. Logically those still presumed innocent should expect to be treated better than those proved guilty, and those awaiting sentence to be treated better than those serving a custodial sentence as punishment. But for years, despite all the evidence and all the criticism, outcomes have continued to defy this logic. This review is therefore not the first time that attention has been drawn to the unsatisfactory treatment of unsentenced prisoners, and in this respect I am in the company of politicians, judges and many others concerned with penal affairs.

Unfortunately none of these previous criticisms has impelled Ministers to drive through the sustained programme of improvement that is, I believe, urgently required if this unjust and unjustified situation is to be corrected. ...

Inspection reports have highlighted a lack of consistency and accountability in the standard of provision for unsentenced prisoners. The disgraceful conditions disclosed in the reports on HMP Wormwood Scrubs, HMP Wandsworth, HMP Chelmsford, HMP Birmingham, HMP Holloway, HMYOI and RC Feltham contrast starkly with the good practice that we have reported at HMP Altcourse, HMP Holme House, and in the most recent inspection reports of HMP Low Newton, HMP Brockhill and HMYOI and RC Werrington. My inspections of these and other establishments have led me to conclude that the outcomes for unsentenced prisoners are a lottery, depending on the size of the establishment, its design, the numbers of courts it serves, the facilities that are available, the proportion of unsentenced prisoners in its population, the size of its budget and whether it is privately or directly managed. ...

Conclusions

This review has revealed a startling gap between what the public might reasonably expect to be in place for unsentenced prisoners and what is actually in place. More worryingly however, it also identifies a gap between the official understanding of what is being delivered as described in the replies from the Governors' survey and the actual experience of unsentenced prisoners; a gap largely supported by our own observations from fieldwork and inspections.

The following factors seem to be relevant to this state of affairs:

1. *Local prisons are overcrowded.* The Prison Service has endeavoured, quite rightly, to keep the rising numbers of prisoners sent to them by the courts as close as possible to where they are to appear for trial. Also, for entirely understandable and sensible reasons the Prison Service has chosen to protect training prisons from overcrowding by concentrating this pressure on local prisons. This has resulted in the latter holding a rising number of sentenced prisoners, both short term, who increasingly serve their whole sentences in local prisons, and longer term, who can wait for extended periods to be transferred to training prisons. The sheer pressure of

numbers has therefore thwarted the development of proper regimes for unsentenced prisoners.

2. *Prisoners in local prisons are generally compliant.* Most prisoners prefer to be held in local prisons where they are closer to their homes, friends and families than in more distant training prisons. Indeed this has been such a priority for most prisoners that they have been prepared to put up with poor conditions in order to take advantage of being able to stay in their local area. The rate of turnover in the population is also such that most prisoners tolerate their conditions on the basis that they will not have to do so for a long time. Apart from the riots of the early nineties, unsentenced prisoners have not posed serious control problems. Complaints from unsentenced prisoners themselves have not therefore provided a stimulus for change.

3. *The diversity of prisoner needs presents difficult challenges for staff.* All offenders entering the prison system do so through local prisons. Any of these establishments might hold remands awaiting trial, convicted unsentenced and sentenced prisoners, debtors, civil prisoners, deportees or immigration detainees and those on overcrowding drafts from other local prisons. Sentenced prisoners may be short or longer sentenced and include life sentence prisoners both newly sentenced, recalled from training prisons or licence revoked. Among this mixture of prisoners will be those with violent tendencies, those who are vulnerable to attack from others, those who are mentally unwell, those who are drug misusers, those who are drug dealers, those who are depressed and suicidal and, of course those who are subsequently found not guilty. Although some may be familiar to staff from previous periods in custody, many will be unknown and the uncertainty and risk inherent in this mix creates one of the biggest challenges for managers and staff.

4. *Local prisons have inadequate physical facilities.* Many of the old local prisons were constructed for the penal policies of a different age and lack the facilities that are required to support healthy prison regimes. Until some 20 years ago when finances for the maintenance of prison buildings became more readily available, all were in a wretched condition. Improvements have been made, notably in the abolition of 'slopping out', but most are still in need of large capital investment to make them fit for their purpose. For example, in many of the cells designed for one person but used to accommodate two, there is no suitable screen between the toilet and the living space. The Director General and his colleagues are aware of these deficiencies and are as keen as anyone else to rectify them, but do not have the necessary finance to carry out the work.

5. *Local prisons have a culture of disengagement with prisoners.* For many decades the unspoken but unmistakable message to staff from senior Prison Service managers has been that their job is to serve the courts by taking as many prisoners as necessary, and to avoid escapes and disturbances. Given the risks associated with these tasks and the limited resources to manage them, a culture of disengagement with prisoners and risk avoidance has become established.

6. *Local prisons are able to resist change.* The staff of local prisons become the culture carriers as they are longer serving than either the prisoners or their managers. The former pass through on short periods of remand, short sentences or on to training prisons, and the latter pass through on relatively short tours of duty as they build their careers. In these circumstances staff become disproportionately influential and without training, management and leadership for their role in a modern Prison Service, their prime motivation becomes one of making life as comfortable as pos-

sible for themselves and their colleagues, and their allegiance and commitment to the Prison Service's Statement of Purpose becomes hard to find. In such prisons there is an absence of justice and fairness in dealing with legitimate requests and complaints from prisoners, governors appear powerless to introduce even the simplest of changes without disputes, and progress becomes impossible without a clear mandate for change from Ministers and the Prisons Board.

The way forward

At any time there are well over 30,000 people held in 53 local prisons and remand centres in England and Wales. Some of the establishments in which they are held treat unsentenced prisoners with humanity and try to meet their individual needs; the five contracted out local prisons, for example, and most local prisons for women. Few of the suggestions for improvement in this review are entirely original in that many reflect examples of good, indeed outstanding current practice in both directly managed and contracted out establishments. One such example is the recommendation to replace the policy of separating unconvicted from convicted prisoners with an integrated approach that is based on safety and respect which has been tried and tested by at least one former governor of a local directly managed prison. What is missing, however, is a clear unifying vision for unsentenced prisoners which details how they should be treated and the conditions in which they should be held, and a management system which ensures consistent delivery in all local prisons and remand centres. The senior management of the Prison Service has tended to believe that the answer lies in finding capable governors to take command of these prisons. It is true that without strong leadership nothing will change, but far more than the personal qualities of individual governors are needed if lasting change is to be achieved. I must emphasise that responsibility for this state of affairs does not lie with the current Prisons Board. Indeed,

I believe that it is because of the leadership already demonstrated by the Director General that there is now a real opportunity to tackle the culture of those establishments that have been producing poor, and in some cases, unacceptable treatment and conditions for prisoners, including those held on remand, for too many years. There is every reason to be optimistic that staff in the Prison Service will respond positively to the challenge of providing a healthy and needs based regime for unsentenced prisoners as they have done successfully in other parts of the prison estate, notably high security prisons. However, they will need re-training as well as strong leadership if they are to operate in a radically different way. Many, for example, will need help to understand the needs and rights of unsentenced prisoners and the proper role of local prisons within a joined up criminal justice system. They will also need to understand the complex mental health problems of unsentenced prisoners and the importance of ensuring that they have access to due process.

Recommendations

I have detailed throughout this review a number of areas where change needs to be made, and a number of recommendations are included in the text. However, I have two over-riding strategic recommendations which I detail here. Firstly, in view of the physical inadequacy of the facilities and buildings within which many unsentenced prisoners are held, I recommend that the cost of the work required to ensure that all local prisons and remand centres have the necessary facilities to hold prisoners in decent conditions should be published, and that the finance to carry it out should be provided within a five-year programme. In view of the enormity of the challenge which faces the Prison Service in bringing about cultural change in many of the establishments holding unsentenced prisoners, I recommend that a strategy is introduced by the Prisons Board, with the full support of Ministers, for a two year programme of change to identify and deliver agreed prisoner

focused outcomes as detailed in this review, for all unsentenced prisoners in local prisons and remand centres. This strategy should contain a clear sense of direction for local prisons and remand centres, detail the elements of work which they should undertake, and include costed service delivery agreements. The strategy should include the introduction of a mandatory and comprehensive initial and ongoing training programme for new staff and an immediate programme to re-educate current staff. There should also be a remedial element to the strategy to identify those prisons needing to achieve fundamental change in the way that unsentenced prisoners are treated. This information can be readily gathered from inspection reports over recent years. Such identified prisons should be set clear targets, based on the delivery of agreed outcomes for unsentenced prisoners. They should also be given suitable senior managers to carry out this work, which might include nominated 'change managers' with a clear briefing and training for what is to be achieved, and time in post to carry through the required changes. Such senior management teams should also be given both practical and personal support from senior functional managers in Prison Service headquarters, and opportunities for the regular exchange of experiences through meetings with colleagues in other similar establishments. I intend to carry out a follow-up to this review in two years' time, and will continue to monitor the treatment and conditions of unsentenced prisoners within my ongoing inspection programme. I look forward to witnessing the improvements which I am confident that the Prison Service can deliver, with the full backing of Ministers.

Research was carried out in five court areas in the period 1992–1994 to explore how the problems that exist in relation to the provision of information could be remedied and specifically to be better able to assess the risk of offending by defendants who are released on bail.

Remand Decisions and Offending on Bail: Evaluation of the Bail Process Project (1998), Home Office Research Study No 184, pp43–47, 57–60

An important reason for carrying out research into offending on bail is to assist magistrates in their assessment of risk. The aim is to identify which defendants are likely to be poor bail risks by studying characteristics of those who were granted bail and who committed offences while they were on bail. In this chapter, the case tracking data collected as part of the Bail Process Project is used for this purpose. No distinction is made between the 1993 and 1994 cases so that larger samples are obtained and hence the inter-relationships of several characteristics can be studied.

Method used

The five police forces who took part in the Bail Process Project recorded details of the bail/custody decision made for each defendant charged with an imprisonable offence during three months of 1993 and three months of 1994. The appropriate CPS branches and magistrates' courts recorded their recommendation/decisions on bail or custody for the same defendants until either the defendant was dealt with, or a second court hearing had been held, whichever was the earlier; the recording forms were then returned to the Home Office. From these records, it was possible to select defendants who were given police bail after charge, or given court bail at the first hearing, or remanded in custody at the first hearing and given court bail at the second hearing. The date on which the case was finally dealt with (and hence the end of any period on court bail) was not recorded. The reasons for the termination of the recording after the second hearing were, first, to limit the extra work imposed on the CPS and courts to manageable proportions, and also to ensure that details of all cases were returned within a reasonable period after the end of the three months.

In 1995 and early 1996, researchers searched the criminal records at the National Identification Service at Scotland Yard (NIS) for, first, the dates on which the cases were finally dealt with by the courts and, second, for details of any offences that were committed during the time the defendants were on police or court bail. This method had an important consequence for the measures of offending on bail that were used. It is sufficient to say here that the measure of offending on court bail in this study is based on defendants who were found guilty of the offence for which bail was granted (which meant that the date of conviction/sentence could be found on the criminal record), unlike the measure used in the earlier Home Office and the Metropolitan Police research. In the earlier studies, all defendants who were given bail in the selected cases were followed up for offending on bail. This problem did not apply to offending while on police bail.

Offending on bail rates in 1993 and 1994

Table 1 shows the proportions of defendants granted bail by the court in the five areas who were charged with an offence allegedly committed while they were on bail, and the proportion who were found guilty of such an offence. Out of more than 2,300 defendants granted bail by the five courts who were followed up at NIS, 21 per cent were charged with an offence and 17 per cent were found guilty of such an offence. Out of nearly 4,000 defendants granted bail after charge by the police in the five areas who were followed up at NIS, 11 per cent were charged with an offence and 9 per cent were found guilty of such an offence.

TABLE 1
POLICE AND COURT BAIL: RATES OF OFFENDING ON BAIL IN 1993 AND 1994

	Court bail	Police bail
Percentage granted bail who were charged with an offence committed while on bail	21%	11%
Percentage granted bail who were convicted of an offence committed while on bail	17%	9%
Number of defendants	2,343	3,798

The rest of this chapter will be concerned with convictions only. The term 'offending on bail' will be used as a shorthand for 'found guilty of at least one offence committed while on bail'.

Court bail: offending rates and related factors

Statistical analyses have identified the factors that were most highly related to the rates of offending on bail. Table 2 shows these factors, taken one at a time, and the corresponding offending on bail rates. The factor which was shown to be most important in explaining the offending on bail rates was the waiting time between first court appearance and trial or sentence; the offending on bail rate increased with this waiting time. (In most cases, this will have been the length of time that the defendants were on court bail. However, some defendants will have spent part of this period in custody).

Amongst the factors shown to be important, the highest offending on bail rates were found for:

1. persons with no fixed abode (42 per cent offended on bail), although the number of such defendants was small (only 97 defendants or 4 per cent of the whole sample)
2. those who waited more than six months before trial or sentence (32 per cent offended on bail)
3. those charged with theft of cars or unauthorised taking (32 per cent), burglary (29 per cent), or robbery (23 per cent)
4. those with at least one previous breach of bail (27 per cent), ie, they had failed to appear at court in the past, had breached bail conditions in the past, or were on bail when charged with the current offence.
5. those who had served a previous custodial sentence (28 per cent)
6. those under 18 (29 per cent)
7. those who were unemployed or were not in the workforce (ie, at school, retired etc) (21 per cent).

The lowest rates of offending on bail were found for:

1. persons who waited less than one month before trial or sentence (4 per cent)
2. those who were employed (7 per cent)
3. those charged with sex offences (6 per cent), assault (7 per cent) or fraud (8 per cent).

TABLE 2
COURT BAIL: FACTORS ASSOCIATED WITH HIGHER OR LOWER RATES OF OFFENDING ON BAIL

Factor		Percentage who offended on bail	Number in category
Address status	No fixed abode	42%	97
	Had address	16%	2,246
Charged with:	Car theft	32%	157
	Burglary	29%	284
	Robbery	23%	57
	Theft	20%	545
	Fraud	8%	204
	Assault	7%	392
	Sex	6%	33
Age	17 and under	29%	373
	18–20	24%	411
	21 and over	13%	1,549
Criminal record			
Had served a previous custodial sentence		28%	529
None known		14%	1,762
Previous bail history			
Had record of breaches		27%	781
None known		12%	1,510
Employment status			
Unemployed		21%	1,690
Employed		7%	564
Waiting time			
Over 6 months		32%	419
Over 3 and up to 6 months		24%	620
Over 2 and up to 3 months		17%	348
Over 1 and up to 2 months		10%	517
Up to 1 month		4%	439

Offending on bail rates, for combinations of factors, that are shown to be related to higher or lower rates of offending on bail, were sought. For example, in relation to the 32 defendants who had no fixed abode and who were charged with the offences of burglary, robbery or car theft, nearly two-thirds (63 per cent) offended on bail. This is the highest rate of offending on bail found in the study and is the only one that is greater than 50 per cent. Sixty-five defendants had no fixed abode and were charged with offences other than burglary, robbery or car theft. Of these, about one-third offended while on bail. Of those who had an address, the highest rates of offending were found for those who had a previous bail history, had served a previous custodial sentence, and who were charged with burglary, robbery or car theft. Of the 73 persons who fell into this category, 44 per cent offended on bail. The lowest rates of offending on bail were found for defendants who had a fixed address, who had no previous bail history and who had not served a custodial sentence, and who were charged with offences other than burglary, robbery or car theft. The offending on bail rate was six per cent for the 760 adult defendants who met these criteria, and four per cent for the 357 employed defendants who met these criteria.

Some of the rates discovered are very high, but these apply to small groups of defendants. Just over a fifth of the defendants studied fell into groups with offending on bail rates of 25 per cent or higher; nearly half of the defendants fell into groups with offending on bail rates between 11 per cent and 25 per cent, and around a third fell into the group with an offending rate of six per cent or less. The problem that magistrates face is how to target those defendants who will offend on bail from the groups shown. When the offending rate is as high as 44 per cent, the probability that these defendants will offend on bail is roughly the same as the probability that they will not so offend. An offending rate of six per cent means that there is a chance of around one in 16 that the defendants will offend on

bail. It may be that other details available (eg, of the circumstances of the current offence and the pattern of previous convictions) will make it possible for magistrates to refine their decisions within the categories given, or it may be that there is a degree of randomness in offending on bail which it is extremely difficult to predict.'

This report is based on a study of persons admitted to bail by Magistrates' Courts in Northern Ireland. It draws on two separate sets of data. The first considers those granted bail at Belfast Magistrates' Court in 1991; the second provides a more extended and contemporary picture of the use of bail across Northern Ireland in 1996. A total of over 2,500 records were analysed including data on types of offences, numbers of charges, amounts and conditions of bail, as well as numbers who were convicted of further offences committed whilst on Magistrates' Court bail.

Northern Ireland Office (1998)
The Use of Bail and Levels of Offending on Bail in Northern Ireland

This study is based upon the tracing of defendants on bail through criminal records. The approach has been to identify offenders disposed of in a given period who have spent some or all of their case processing time on court bail. Details of each defendant, their bailed offence, key dates and their court outcome, were recorded. The defendant was then traced on the police criminal records database and any convictions for offences committed during the bail study period were identified. Only official convictions were used. Offences were specifically tied to bail periods and were not based on hearsay evidence. What such an approach cannot measure is any level of undetected criminal activity during the bail period – and it has been claimed that around two-thirds of all crime

remains undetected. Only an offender interview approach could begin to address the area
of undetected crime and even this would be
subject to major weaknesses. The NIO study
has therefore been based on the official record
of the court. Two sets of specially collected
data were analysed – one a retrospective study
of records pertaining to bail granted in 1991;
and the other a much more contemporary look
at what has been happening during 1996. By
using two such sources some trend analysis
was possible. A total of approximately 2,500
bail records was used in this analysis.

Around one quarter of defendants were
convicted of offences committed whilst on
bail. 24 per cent of those on bail in 1996 and
20 per cent of those on bail in 1991 were so
convicted. In both years, males (23 per cent)
were almost twice as likely than were females
(12 per cent) to offend on bail. Younger defendants were also more likely than older defendants to so offend. The 562 defendants who
offended on bail across both survey periods
committed a total of 2,878 offences – an
average of 5.1 offences per offender [4.2 in
1991; 5.6 in 1996]. Thirty-nine per cent of
those offending on bail accounted for 77 per
cent of all offences committed.

Offending on bail
Overall 181 defendants – 20 per cent of the
total – were convicted of an offence committed whilst on bail. Of the 820 males granted
bail during the period of this study, 169 (21
per cent) offended whilst on bail. This male
offending rate was almost double that of
females (11 per cent). Only 12 out of 106
females offended on bail. The average number
of initial offences for male non-offenders was
2.2 compared to 3.4 for those who offended on
bail. Of the females who offended whilst on
bail, 83 per cent were initially charged with
one or two offences whilst 24 per cent of
males were charged with five or more
offences. A larger proportion of males who
offended on bail were convicted of more than
one charge (70 per cent) compared to those
who did not offend (49 per cent). Of those

who offended on bail most (62 per cent) were
charged with three or less offences committed on bail. The number of female bail offenders was so small (12) that the behaviour of a
single individual has a pronounced effect on
proportions. Only two females (17 per cent)
were charged with committing more than four
offences whilst on bail compared to 49 males
(29 per cent of their total).

Bail offences
The number of offences committed whilst on
bail totalled over 750. The average number of
offences on bail for men was 4.2 and for
women was 3.6.

Nature of offences
Theft was the most frequently committed
offence category for both men (38 per cent)
and women (67 per cent) whilst on bail, followed by burglary and robbery for men, and
by fraud/forgery and criminal damage for
women. This pattern largely mirrors that for
those granted bail – theft, burglary and
robbery being the largest categories of offence
for men, and theft, fraud and criminal damage
the largest for women. There is therefore some
evidence of persons granted bail repeating
similar offences to those with which they were
originally charged. Another significant area of
male offending was in violence against the
person, which was absent from the female
offending pattern.

Neither amounts of bail, nor levels of
surety appeared to have any significant impact
on rate of offending on bail. Conditions
attached to bail were infrequently used and
had varying impacts on subsequent offending
rates. Conditions which required defendants to
avoid people (14 per cent) or places (19 per
cent) resulted in lower rates than any other
condition. The longer a defendant spent on
bail the greater the likelihood of subsequent
offending.

The new millennium arrives and official
reports are still noting that there is a problem

with the quality of information available for bail decisions. Perhaps the answer is to do something about it rather than to talk about it. The golden rule of the criminal justice system is however that of course you can have rights and liberties so long as they do not involve expenditure.

Home Office (2001) *Criminal Justice: The Way Ahead*, pp56–57

Reducing the risk of offending on bail

Of the two million people who appear in magistrates' courts every year, about a quarter (over half a million) are remanded on bail. A further 100,000 are remanded in custody. Since 1997, the number of defendants remanded in custody annually has increased by 16,000. Magistrates have the power to deny bail and remand to custody, or to attach a wide range of conditions. These may include things like residing at bail hostel; remaining indoors at night; or staying away from a particular place or person. Under the Bail Act 1976, a person accused of an offence must be granted bail unless the court is satisfied that there are substantial grounds for believing that, if released on bail, the accused would abscond, commit an offence, interfere with witnesses or otherwise obstruct the course of justice. The court must take into account the behaviour of defendants when previously granted bail. They lose the presumption to bail if they commit a serious offence while on current bail, or are arrested for breaking bail conditions and the court is satisfied those conditions have been broken. But not every defendant who breaches bail is remanded in custody, and it can be greatly troubling to alleged victims where bail is granted to defendants who have previously breached bail conditions, or have a history of offending on bail, and who then go on to breach their conditions again or commit further offences. The Government will consider creating presumptions of custody in relation to certain breaches of bail. More needs to be done to reduce the risk of further offending on bail. Given the extent of drug-related crime, we will be increasing the number of places at approved premises where defendants most likely to commit drug-related crimes on bail can receive drug treatment.

Sound bail decisions are dependent on the quality of information available to the court. Lists of previous convictions are presented to courts, which ought to show which were committed on bail. But, like other information given to the courts, these are not always accurate or up to date. Action is being taken on a number of fronts to remedy these information deficiencies. For example, the police are speeding up the entry of convictions and other data onto the Police National Computer and courts will have more information through drug testing of arrestees in police stations. The Government has invited the Trials Issues Group to devise practical ways of improving the standard of information made available to courts. This should include reliable comparative information so that courts can see for themselves how successful they have been in securing the objectives of the bail legislation. Probation services operate court-based bail information schemes to verify information that may be relevant to the court's remand decision. The provision of bail information in courts has been patchy but it is an objective of the Probation Service to increase their coverage to all areas. In addition, the quality and usefulness of bail information reports is improving. The reports are now required to include any negative information about risk – the emphasis is on ensuring the court has all the information it needs to make a properly informed decision.

The Government will amend the criteria for bail for young defendants so that the courts can refuse bail to those with a history of committing or being charged with imprisonable offences. Courts will also have the option of requiring defendants to be electronically monitored as a condition of bail. A provision in the current Criminal Justice and Police Bill will require courts to give reasons if they grant bail in a case where the prosecutor has applied for a remand in custody. This should lead to greater transparency in courts' decision-making, helping the police and CPS to raise objections where they feel concerned, and enhancing public confidence. The CPS already has the power to appeal against certain bail decisions and make use of it in appropriate cases. Except in the most straightforward cases the grant of bail involves a risk assessment. In the light of the growth in drug related crime and of the availability to the courts of evidence from drug tests on defendants, the Government will consider whether there is a case for changing the law to help courts give proper weight to such factors.

11 Trial and Sentence

In the following extract the recommendations of the recent major review of the criminal courts under the auspices of Auld LJ are presented. This covered a large range of issues including codification, the pre-trial stage, decriminalisation and alternatives to conventional trial, a unified criminal court, judges, magistrates, juries, the procedure at trial and appeals.

Auld LJ Report (2001) *A Review of the Criminal Courts in England and Wales*

The criminal law should be codified under the general oversight of a new Criminal Justice Council and by or with the support as necessary of the Law Commission. There should be codes of offences, procedure, evidence and sentencing.

The criminal justice system

A national Criminal Justice Board should replace all the existing national planning and 'operational' bodies, including the Strategic Planning Group, and the Trial Issues Group. The new board should be the means by which the criminal justice departments and agencies provide over-all direction of the criminal justice system. It should have an independent chairman and include senior departmental representatives and chief executives of the main criminal justice agencies (including the Youth Justice Board) and a small number of non-executive members. At local level, Local Criminal Justice Boards should be responsible for giving effect to the national board's directions and objectives and for management of the criminal justice system in their areas. Both the national and local boards should be supported by a centrally managed secretariat and

should consult regularly with the judiciary. The national board should be responsible for introducing an integrated technology system for the whole of the criminal justice system based upon a common language and common electronic case files, the implementation and maintenance of which should be the task of a Criminal Case Management Agency accountable to the board. A Criminal Justice Council, chaired by the Lord Chief Justice or senior Lord Justice of Appeal, should be established to replace existing advisory and consultative bodies, including the Criminal Justice Consultative Council and the Area Strategy Committees. It should have a statutory power and duty to keep the criminal justice system under review, to advise the Government on all proposed reforms, to make proposals for reform and to exercise general oversight of codification of the criminal law. The council should be supported by a properly resourced secretariat and research staff.

A unified Criminal Court

The Crown Court and magistrates' courts should be replaced by a unified Criminal Court consisting of three Divisions: the Crown Division, constituted as the Crown Court now is, to exercise jurisdiction over all indictable-only matters and the more serious 'either-way' offences allocated to it; the District Division, constituted by a judge, normally a District Judge or Recorder, and at least two magistrates, to exercise jurisdiction over a mid-range of 'either-way' matters of sufficient seriousness to merit up to two years' custody; and the Magistrates' Division, constituted by a District Judge or magistrates, as magistrates' courts now are, to exercise their present jurisdiction over all summary matters and the less serious 'either-way' cases allocated to them.

tials are: strong and independent prosecutors; efficient and properly paid defence lawyers; ready access by defence lawyers to their clients in custody; and a modern communications system. All public prosecutions should take the form of a charge, issued without reference to the courts but for which the prosecutor in all but minor, routine or urgent cases, would have initial responsibility. It should remain the basis of the case against a defendant regardless of the court which ultimately deals with his case, thus replacing the present mix of charges, summonses and indictments. A graduated scheme of sentencing discounts should be introduced so that the earlier the plea of guilty the higher the discount for it. This should be coupled with a system of advance indication of sentence for a defendant considering pleading guilty. The scheme of mutual disclosure established by the Criminal Procedure and Investigations Act 1996 should remain, but subject to the following reforms: its expression in a single and simply expressed instrument; a single and simple test of materiality for both stages of prosecution disclosure; automatic prosecution disclosure of certain documents; removal from the police to the prosecutor of such responsibility as the police have for identifying all potentially disclosable material; and encouragement, through professional conduct rules and otherwise, of the provision of adequate defence statements. There should be a new statutory scheme for third party disclosure and for instruction by the court of special independent counsel in public interest immunity cases where the court considers prosecution applications in the absence of the defendant. In the preparation for trial in all criminal courts, there should be a move away from plea and directions hearings and other forms of pre-trial hearings to cooperation between the parties according to standard time-tables, wherever necessary, seeking written directions from the court. In the Crown and District Divisions and, where necessary, in the Magistrates' Division, there should then be a written or electronic 'pre-trial assessment' by the court

of the parties' readiness for trial. Only if the court or the parties are unable to resolve all matters in this way should there be a pre-trial hearing before or at the stage of the pre-trial assessment. The courts should have a general power to give binding directions and rulings either in writing or at pre-trial hearings. In the Crown and District Divisions and, where necessary, in the Magistrates' Division, following the pre-trial assessment and in good time before hearing, the parties should prepare, for the approval of the judge and use by him, them, and the jury in the hearing, a written case and issues summary setting out in brief the substances of charge(s) and the issues to be resolved by the court.

The trial: procedures and evidence

In trials by judge and jury, the judge, by reference to the case and issues summary, copies of which should be provided to the jury, should give them a fuller introduction to the case than is now conventional. The trial should broadly take the same form as at present, though with greater use of electronic aids in appropriate cases. The judge should sum up and direct the jury, making reference as appropriate to the case and issues summary. So far as possible, he should 'filter out' the law and fashion factual questions to the issues and the law as he knows it to be. Where he considers it appropriate, he should require the jury publicly to answer each of the questions and to declare a verdict in accordance with those answers. In trials by judge and magistrates in the District Division, the judge should be the sole judge of law, but he and the magistrates should together be the judges of fact, each having an equal vote. The order of proceedings would be broadly the same as in the Crown Division. The judge should rule on matters of law, procedure and inadmissibility of evidence in the absence of the magistrates where it would be potentially unfair to the defendant to do so in their presence. The judge should not sum up the case to the magistrates, but should retire with them to consider the court's decision, which he would give and publicly reason as a judgment of the court. The judge should be solely responsible for sentence. There should be a comprehensive review of the law of criminal evidence to identify and establish over-all and coherent principles and to make it an efficient and simple agent for securing justice. Subject to such review, I consider that the law should, in general, move away from technical rules of inadmissibility to trusting judicial and lay fact finders to give relevant evidence the weight it deserves. In particular, consideration should be given to the reform of the rules as to refreshing memory, the use of witness statements, hearsay, unfair evidence, previous misconduct of the defendant, similar fact evidence and the evidence of children. There should be reforms to strengthen the quality and objectivity of expert evidence and improve the manner of its presentation both from the point of view of the court and experts, following in some respects reforms made in the civil sphere by the Civil Procedure Rules. Urgent steps should be taken to increase the numbers and strengthen the quality of interpreters serving the criminal courts and to improve their working conditions. There are a number of ways in which the facilities and procedures of the courts should or could be modernised and better serve the public. The criminal courts should be equipped with an on-line sentencing information system.

Appeals

There should be the same tests for appeal against conviction and sentence respectively at all levels of appeal, namely those applicable for appeal to the Court of Appeal. There should be a single line of appeal from the Magistrates' Division (Magistrates' Courts) and above to the Court of Appeal in all criminal matters. This would involve: 1) abolition of appeal from magistrates' courts to the Crown Court by way of rehearing and its replacement by an appeal to the Crown Division (Crown Court) constituted by a judge alone; and 2) abolition of appeal from magistrates' courts and/or the Crown Court to the

High Court by way of a case stated or claim for judicial review and their replacement by appeal to the Court of Appeal under its general appellate jurisdiction enlarged if and to the extent necessary. I support the general thrust of the Law Commission's recommendations for the introduction of statutory exceptions to the double jeopardy rule, save that a prosecutor's right of appeal against acquittal should not be limited to cases of murder and allied offences, but should extend to other grave offences punishable with life or long terms of imprisonment. There should be provision for appeal by the defence or the prosecution against a special verdict of a jury which on its terms is perverse. The Court of Appeal should be reconstituted and its procedures should be improved to enable it to deal more efficiently with, on the one hand appeals involving matters of general public importance or of particular complexity and, on the other, with 'straightforward' appeals. The law should be amended: to widen the remit of the Sentencing Advisory Panel to include general principles of sentencing, regardless of the category of offence; and to enable the Court of Appeal to issue guidelines without having to tie them to a specific appeal before it.

The pre-trial stage involves events that for many will mean that there is no need for a trial at all. Whatever the law in the books might be, it is clear that the law in action involves pressure to plead guilty being exerted upon defendants. Research by Baldwin provides evidence of this.

Baldwin J (1985) *Pre-Trial Justice*, pp30–31

Case 20 [specific offer made to a youth charged initially with rape]: The barrister intimated that I should plead guilty. I was angry but he pointed one or two things out, but I still said I wanted to fight it. Then he went away and had a word with the judge. He came back and said there wasn't sufficient evidence of rape and they would alter the charge to indecent assault. He suggested that I plead guilty to that. He said we didn't want this poor girl to have to go into the witness box. I asked him if I would go to prison. He disappeared again and came back and said he'd spoken to the judge who intimated that he would fine me. He said, 'Are you agreeable to that?' I said, 'Yes, I am.'

Case 24 [a general offer]: The barrister said he didn't fancy my chances if I pleaded not guilty. He said 'If I can get the charge reduced and the judge to agree not to send you away, will you plead guilty?' He then talked to the judge and the prosecution. I agreed to plead guilty to assault. The barrister said the judge didn't actually say I wouldn't go to prison but he said 'Clearly prison is no good for this man, he needs something else.'

Case 61 [a specific offer made to a defendant charged with wounding and carrying an offensive weapon]: The solicitor and barrister were involved together. The solicitor contacted the barrister and they went to see the judge. They advised me to plead guilty to carrying an offensive weapon and I was actually given the choice of a fine or a suspended sentence. I chose the fine – I didn't like a suspended sentence hanging over my head.

Case 132 [a specific offer]: The trial went on for a week. The judge went out and then the lawyers. Then they came back and my barrister whispered to me that the judge would be very lenient if I pleaded guilty – a three years conditional discharge. I was pretty down, fed up with it by that time, so I changed to guilty to get it over with.

In each of these situations, the defendant seemed involved in a plea bargain in the full sense of the term. Offers of a relatively precise nature were made to the defendant – often on a 'take-it-or-leave-it' basis.

Within the criminal justice system many defendants will be guilty as a result of their own plea of guilty. As Sanders and Young indicate there are forces at work that may lead to some innocent people pleading guilty.

Sanders A and Young R (2000) *Criminal Justice*, pp473–477

Do the innocent plead guilty?

Many people would perhaps be prepared to tolerate charge bargaining, sentence discounts and sentence bargains if the net result was more convictions of the guilty and no corresponding increase in convictions of the innocent. The ends would be sufficiently desirable to render the means acceptable. This half-way house between due process and crime control may appear attractive, but in practice no guarantee can be given that the innocent will not be made to suffer as a result of striking such a compromise. This is despite the ostensible concern of the appellate courts to ensure that the innocent are not induced to plead guilty by charge bargains and the sentencing discount. ...

The danger that the factually innocent will be induced to plead guilty is exacerbated by the law providing that, the weaker the evidence against a defendant, the greater the discount given for a plea of guilty should be. One would expect that it would be harder for the police to construct strong cases against the innocent than against the guilty. The option of contesting a case should thus be more attractive to the innocent, since they stand a better chance of success before a jury. Yet the effect of this aspect of the discount principle is to make that option less attractive to the innocent, since the costs of failure before a jury are, in effect, increased. They have more discount to lose than the guilty in contesting their cases.

To some, it might seem as if the strongest safeguard against miscarriages of justice arising out of plea bargaining and related practices is the axiomatic truth that no innocent person would ever claim guilt. But just as innocent people sometimes 'confess' to the police under interrogation, so too, it seems (and often in consequence of having 'confessed' at an earlier stage) do innocent people plead guilty. Nearly half of the late plea changers in Baldwin and McConville's study made substantial and credible claims of innocence (1). ...

Baldwin and McConville acknowledged that they had no way of telling whether defendants were in fact innocent or not. But in a substantial number of these guilty plea cases, independent assessors judged the evidence against the defendant to be weak (2). Similarly, the Crown Court study by Zander and Henderson included a number of 'cracked trials' in which the CPS said that, had they gone to trial, the defendant would have stood a 'good' or 'fairly good' chance of acquittal. On an annual basis, this would total over 600 cracked trials where the defendant would have stood a good chance of acquittal and over 2,000 such cases with a fairly good chance of acquittal. Defendants in these cases may not all be factually innocent, of course, but they may well have emerged from a contested trial legally innocent.

References
1. Baldwin J and McConville M (1977) *Negotiated Justice*, Oxford: Martin Robertson, pp 62–63.
2. Ibid, p66.

In contrast with the view of Sanders and Young the Royal Commission saw less dangers in the use of sentencing discounts for guilty pleas.

Report of the Royal Commission on Criminal Justice (1993), pp110–114

41 For many decades defendants who plead guilty in the Crown Court have been regarded by the Court of Appeal as usually entitled to a discount or reduction in their sentence. The usual range of discount is 25 per cent to 30 per cent. The primary reason for the sentence discount is to encourage defendants who know themselves to be guilty to plead accordingly and so enable the resources which would be expended in a contested case to be saved. A subsidiary reason, applicable in some types of cases, is to recognise that the defendant by

pleading guilty has spared witnesses the trauma of having to give evidence at court.

42 Provided that the defendant is in fact guilty and has received competent legal advice about his or her position, there can be no serious objection to a system of inducements designed to encourage him or her so to plead. Such a system is, however, sometimes held to encourage defendants who are not guilty of the offence charged to plead guilty to it nevertheless. One reason for this is that some defendants may believe that they are likely to be convicted and that, if they are, they will receive a custodial sentence if found guilty after a contested trial but will avoid such a sentence if they plead guilty. The risk cannot be wholly avoided and although there can be no certainty as to the precise numbers it would be naive to suppose that innocent persons never plead guilty because of the prospect of the sentence discount.

43 In the Crown Court Study defence barristers were asked: 'An innocent defendant sometimes decides to plead guilty to achieve a sentence discount or reduction in the indictment. Were you concerned that this was such a case?' In 53 cases the defence barristers answered 'Yes'. Since the Crown Court Study was conducted over two weeks this appeared at first sight to mean that there were some 1,400 possibly innocent persons pleading guilty every year. Closer examination of these 53 cases showed, however, that there was little if any evidence that persons who were innocent of all the charges brought against them had pleaded guilty to one or more of these charges because of the sentence discount. It was clear that in many instances the defence barristers had misunderstood the thrust of the question they were asked. Thus in some cases the defendants were said to be not guilty only to one of several charges. In some cases, too, the barristers made it clear that they did not think that the client was innocent only that he or she was claiming to be, sometimes in the face of considerable evidence to the contrary.

44 The position of the defence barrister is dealt with in the Bar's Code of Conduct as follows:

'Where a defendant tells his counsel that he did not commit the offence with which he is charged but nevertheless insists on pleading guilty to it for reasons of his own, counsel must continue to represent him, but only after he has advised what the consequences will be and that what can be submitted in mitigation can only be on the basis that the client is guilty.'

Defence barristers should, and normally do, advise clients that they should not plead guilty if they are not guilty, but that the decision is one for them.

45 Against the risk that defendants may be tempted to plead guilty to charges of which they are not guilty must be weighed the benefits to the system and to defendants of encouraging those who are in fact guilty to plead guilty. We believe that the system of sentence discounts should remain. But we do see reason to make the system more effective. In particular we believe that a clearer system of graduated discounts would help to alleviate the problem of 'cracked' trials. The Crown Court Study showed that 'cracked' trials were 26 per cent of all cases or 43 per cent of cases other than those listed as guilty pleas.' 'Cracked' trials create serious problems, principally for all the thousands of witnesses each year – police officers experts and ordinary citizens – who come to court expecting a trial only to find that there is no trial because the defendant has decided to plead guilty at the last minute. This causes, in particular, unnecessary anxiety for victims whose evidence has, up to that point, been disputed.

46 At present the sentence discount is available at any stage until the beginning of the trial but the Court of Appeal has stated in terms that, other things being equal, an earlier plea ought to attract a higher discount and that late tactical pleas should not attract the same discount:

'This court has long said that discounts on sentence are appropriate, but everything depends upon the circumstances of each case. If a man is arrested and at once tells the police that he is guilty and co-operates

with them in the recovery of property and the identification of others concerned in the offence, he can expect to get a substantial discount. But if a man is arrested in circumstances in which he cannot hope to put forward a defence of not guilty, he cannot expect much by way of a discount. In between come this kind of case, where the court has been put to considerable trouble as a result of a tactical plea. The sooner it is appreciated that defendants are not going to get a full discount for pleas of guilty in these sorts of circumstances, the better it will be for the administration of justice' (1).

47 We agree with the view expressed by the Court of Appeal that, other things being equal, the earlier the plea the higher the discount. In broad terms, solicitors and barristers should advise their clients to that effect. Judges must, however, retain their discretion to deal appropriately with the particular circumstances of the individual case. Subject to these points, a system of graduated discounts might work broadly as follows:

1. The most generous discount should be available to the defendant who indicates a guilty plea in response to the service of the case disclosed by the prosecution.
2. The next most generous discount should be available to the defendant who indicates a guilty plea in sufficient time to avoid full preparation for trial. The discount might be less if the plea were entered only after a preparatory hearing.
3. At the bottom of the scale should come the discount for a guilty plea entered on the day of the trial itself. Since resources would be saved by avoiding a contested trial even at this late stage, we think that some discount should continue to be available. But it should be appreciably smaller than for a guilty plea offered at one of the earlier stages.

We do not think that clearer articulation of the long accepted principle that there should be greater sentence discounts for earlier pleas will increase the risk that defendants may plead guilty to offences which they did not commit. We would on the other hand expect that it would lead some who would at present plead guilty to do so earlier.

48 We believe, however, that still more could be done to reduce the incidence of 'cracked' trials. As the Seebrook Committee argued, the most common reason for defendants delaying a plea of guilty until the last minute is a reluctance to face the facts until they are at the door of the court. It is often said too that a defendant has a considerable incentive to behave in this way. The longer the delay, the more the likelihood of witnesses being intimidated or forgetting to turn up or disappearing. And, if the defendant is remanded in custody, he or she will continue to enjoy the privileges of an unconvicted remand prisoner whereas once a guilty plea has been entered, the prisoner enters the category of convicted/unsentenced and loses those privileges. Although this last disincentive can be removed, as we recommend below, the problem of last minute changes of plea can never be completely eradicated. We believe, however, that a significant number of those who now plead guilty at the last minute would be more ready to declare their hand at an earlier stage if they were given a reliable early indication of the maximum sentence that they would face if found guilty.

49 The defendant will be interested not so much in the discount on sentence that he or she might receive as the actual sentence and, in particular, whether it will be custodial or not. It used to be possible for defence counsel to ask the judge for an indication of the sentence that his or her client might receive if found guilty after a contested trial, as opposed to the sentence that might be passed if the plea were changed to guilty. But the discussion of likely sentences with judges is now severely constrained by the Court of Appeal's judgment in *R* v *Turner* (2). According to this, judges may say that, whether the accused pleads guilty or not guilty, the sentence will or will not take a particular form. They must not, however, state that on a plea of guilty they would impose one sentence while on convic-

tion following a plea of not guilty they would impose a severer sentence. The court took the view that this would be placing undue pressure on defendants, depriving them of that complete freedom of choice which is essential.

50 Many witnesses, particularly from the judiciary and the Bar, urged on us the desirability of reverting, in essence, to the system as it applied before the judgment in the case of *Turner*. The Crown Court Study also showed that, among the judges and barristers who responded, there was overwhelming support for change. We do not support a total reversal of the judgment in *Turner,* since we agree that to face defendants with a choice between what they might get on an immediate plea of guilty and what they might get if found guilty by the jury does amount to unacceptable pressure. But the effect of *Turner* and related judgments appears to have been to make judges reluctant to discuss sentence with counsel at all. We think that there is a case for a change of approach. We recommend that, at the request of defence counsel on instructions from the defendant, judges should be able to indicate the highest sentence that they would impose at that point on the basis of the facts as put to them. A request for such an indication might be made at a preparatory hearing, at a hearing called specially for this purpose, or at the trial itself.

51 We envisage that the procedure which we recommend would be initiated solely by, and for the benefit of, defendants who wish to exercise a right to be told the consequences of a decision which is theirs alone. Where a defendant would need the protection of an appropriate adult during inquiries carried out at a police station the system must be operated with particular care. The sentence 'canvass', as we have called it, should normally take place in the judge's chambers with both sides being represented by counsel. A shorthand writer should also be present. If none is available a member of the court staff should take a note to be agreed immediately by the judge and both counsel. The judge may give the answer to the question: 'What would

be the maximum sentence if my client were to plead guilty at this stage?', but to no other. The judge's indication should be based on brief statements from prosecution and defence of all the relevant circumstances, which should include details of the defendant's previous convictions, if any, and, if available, any pre-sentence report required by the Criminal Justice Act 1991. ...

56 The availability of a sentence discount for a guilty plea and the practice of asking the judge to give an indication of the possible maximum sentence should not be confused with the discussions that commonly took place between the prosecution and the defence over charge. This is what is normally described as 'plea bargaining', although it might be more accurate to call it 'charge bargaining'; the defence may offer to plead guilty to a lesser charge than the one brought by the prosecution or the prosecution may offer to accept a plea of guilty to a lesser charge. We see no objection to such discussions, but the earlier they take place the better; consultation between counsel before the trial would often avoid the need for the case to be listed as a contested trial.

57 As we have previously noted, it may be a disincentive to remand prisoners to plead guilty that, by doing so, they lose the privileges enjoyed by unconvicted prisoners. We recommend that the additional privileges enjoyed by unconvicted prisoners be extended to convicted prisoners awaiting sentence. We understand that this reform is already under consideration by the Prison Service.

58 We are also aware that Roger Hood's research provides evidence that the current system of sentence discounts, combined with the greater tendency of members of certain ethnic minority communities to maintain a plea of not guilty, puts black and other ethnic minority offenders at a greater risk of being sentenced to custody and serving longer sentences. We therefore support the recommendation made by Hood that the policy of offering sentence discounts should be kept under review. This means that it is essential for the

Crown Court to monitor the ethnic origin of everyone who appears there. Only with information on all sentences, analysed by ethnic origin, would it be possible to detect whether sentencing patterns are being established which might be unfavourable to particular minority groups. The Home Office is exploring with the Lord Chancellor's Department the feasibility of introducing ethnic monitoring of all court outcomes and we welcome this development.

References
1. *R* v *Hollingworth and Emmens* (1986) 82 Cr App R 281.
2. [1972] WLR 1093.

The authors provide an interesting account of the role of guilty pleas and their relationship with philosophies of sentencing.

Dingwall G and Harding C (1998) *Diversion in the Criminal Process*, pp156–157

In sum, the diversionary effect of guilty pleas is of enormous practical benefit to the criminal process and compensating a guilty plea with a concrete reward to the defendant in the guise of a reduced sentence greatly facilitates the operation of criminal justice in England and Wales. Its pragmatic appeals are obvious not just to an economist but to anyone concerned with the need to manage the criminal process in an efficient manner. As has been recognised earlier it is more problematic (though not wholly impossible) to justify a reduction in sentence for a guilty plea from a principled theoretical position and, more particularly under the retributivist principle of 'just deserts' currently in penological vogue. The traditional theoretical justification, namely that a guilty pleader deserves credit due to his recognition and acknowledgement of the wrong that he committed, is unduly deterministic; many defendants plead guilty not out of altruism but because they face no realistic chance of an acquittal. A guilty plea is often little more than a pragmatic response to a pragmatic offer.

Yet a desert theorist can legitimately claim that a sentence reduction is warranted if by pleading guilty the resultant harm caused by the offence is reduced in that victims and/or witnesses are spared the anxiety, inconvenience and expense of testifying at trial (a justification which is obviously more difficult to maintain in the case of so-called victimless offences). Given these attractions, it is easy to see why policy makers in most adversarial jurisdictions have sought to encourage this form of diversion. What is the benefit of a criminal trial if the majority of defendants don't appear to want one, it costs the state a considerable amount of money, and it is traumatic to most of the lay participants?

There clearly is little benefit to a trial if the defendant, assuming he has been fully and fairly apprised of the situation, elects to forfeit his right to have one. However, as has been documented in this chapter, defendants are highly reliant upon the advice that they receive from their legal advisers, and empirical research suggests that this advice may be, for a variety of reasons, slanted towards a guilty plea. It has been suggested (McConville

et al (1994)) that defence lawyers play a key pivotal role in the process, serving more to transmit to the client the system's imperatives (p281), one of which is to secure a timely guilty plea. It would also appear to be the case that, on occasion, the advice is given in such a manner that the defendant feels that he has no free choice in the matter, even though the barrister may have acted in full compliance with the relevant case law.

The right to legal advice can be rendered largely illusory in so far as defendants are the victims of various ploys on the part of the police which are designed to undermine the potential for legal advice materialising.

Sanders A and Bridges L (1993) 'The Right to Legal Advice' in Walker C and Starmer K, *Justice in Error*, pp42–43

We observed one or more ploys being used in 41.4 per cent of cases, and two or more in 9.3 per cent. All of our 10 stations used these ploys, though some did so more than others.

TYPES OF PLOY

Ploy	Frequency (Principal ploy only)	
1. Rights told too quickly/incomprehensibly/ incompletely	142	(42.9%)
2. Suspect query answered unhelpfully/incorrectly	5	(1.5%)
3. Inability of suspect to name own solicitor	2	(0.6%)
4. 'It's not a very serious charge'	1	(0:3%)
5. 'You'll have to wait in the cells until the solicitor gets here'	13	(3.9%)
6. 'You don't have to make up your mind now. You can have one later if you want to'	27	(82%)
7. 'You're only going to be here a short time'	25	(7.6%)
8. 'You're only here to be charged/interviewed'	14	(4.2%)
9. (To juvenile) 'You'll have to [or 'do you want to'] wait until an adult gets here'	18	(5.4%)
10. (To adult) '[Juvenile] has said he doesn't want one'	8	(2.4%)
11. Combination of 9 and 10	4	(1.2%)
12. 'We won't be able to get a solicitor at this time/none of them will come out/he won't be in his office'	6	(1.8%)
13. 'You don't need one for this type of offence'	2	(0.6%)
14. 'Sign here, here and here' (no information given)	7	(2.1%)
15. 'You don't have to have one'	4	(1.2 %)
16. 'You're being transferred to another station – wait until you get there'	6	(1.8%)
17. Custody officer interprets indecision/silence as refusal	9	(2.7%)
18. 'You're not going to be interviewed/charged'	1	(03%)
19. 'You can go and see a solicitor when you get out/at court'	9	(2.7%)
20. 'You're (probably) going to get bail'	6	(1.8%)
21. Gives suspects Solicitors' Directory or list of solicitors without explanation/assistance	3	(0.9%)
22. Other	19	(5.7%)
TOTAL	331	(100.0%)

The idea of an adversatorial system with the defence lawyer as the champion of the accused has been shown to be an illusory idea by a number of researchers. The following is one of the better examples.

Baldwin J and McConville M (1977) *Negotiated Justice*, pp88–89

Defence solicitor (at the outset of the pre-trial review): I want some ammunition ... What we want is really, if you could supply it, some information about whether to lean on him. Have you got lots of nice verbals?

Prosecuting solicitor: Right – I don't know about particularly nice verbals.

(He then reads out the statements of two police officers who saw a group of youths threatening to attack a man in the city centre.

He gives the defence solicitor a copy of the defendant's statement made to the police and this strongly implicates him in the offence.)

Prosecuting solicitor: I think that should give you some of the necessary information to go back to him. . . Do you think you've now got sufficient to get a plea?

Defence solicitor: Yes.

Prosecuting solicitor: Great! Another all-day not guilty [court] bites the dust.

A clear point to emerge in at least some of these cases was that defence and prosecution lawyers, eschewing an adversarial stance, were jointly engaged upon the same enterprise. The final case cited above, where the defence solicitor sought 'ammunition' from the prosecutor in order to facilitate his discussions with his client, is merely a striking example of this. In such cases, it seemed that defence lawyers were often more concerned to resolve matters expeditiously and amicably than to appear to be pressing willy-nilly the interests of their clients. Few of the defence solicitors interviewed in the present study said that they would anticipate serious difficulties in persuading a client to plead guilty when they considered it to be in his best interests to

do so. Most assumed that their clients would accept their advice on the basis that the lawyer knows best. As is commonly acknowledged, clients are on the whole ignorant of legal procedures and inevitably in a position of dependence upon their lawyers. In this situation, they tend very much to do what they are told.

The Court of Appeal gave a judicial view of the role of plea bargaining in the criminal justice system in the Turner case. The defendant pleaded not guilty at his trial on a charge of theft. He had previous convictions, and during an adjournment he was advised by his counsel in strong terms to change the plea; after having spoken to the trial judge, as the defendant knew, counsel advised that in his opinion a non-custodial sentence would be imposed if the defendant changed his plea, whereas, if he persisted with the plea of not guilty, with an attack being made on police witnesses, and the jury convicted him, there was a real possibility of a sentence of imprisonment being passed. Repeated statements were made to him that the ultimate choice of plea was his. He thought that counsel's views were those of the trial judge; nothing happened to show that they were not and the defendant changed his plea with the result that a formal verdict of guilty was returned. What came next was an appeal against conviction, on the ground that the defendant did not have a free choice in retracting the plea of not guilty and pleading guilty.

R v *Turner* [1970] 2 All ER 281 at 281–285 Court of Appeal (Lord Parker CJ, Widgery LJ and Bean J)

Lord Parker CJ

On January 26, 1970, at North East London Quarter Sessions, Mr Turner, to whom the court has now granted leave to appeal and accordingly he will be referred to as the appellant, pleaded not guilty to the theft of a car. On January 27, he retracted the plea of not guilty and pleaded guilty, whereupon a formal verdict was taken from the jury and he was fined £50, with four months' imprisonment in default of payment within four months, his licence was endorsed, and he was ordered to pay £75 towards the cost of the prosecution.

It is in some ways a curious case, because this car was his own car, and to a layman no doubt that raises a curious conception. But what had happened was, on the prosecution's case (because in the light of the plea of guilty no evidence was, of course, called for the defence), the appellant had left his car at a garage run by a father and son of the name of Brown. He had left it some time in February, 1969, asking for new piston rings to be fitted. It was the prosecution's case that after a discussion there was an agreement that the engine should be reconditioned for a cost of £65. The work was begun, and was completed on March 7. On that day, and this, it is always to be remembered, is the prosecution's case, the appellant called at the garage and said that he would come the next day to collect the car. I should have added that when the car was left, rather naturally so was the ignition key. The garage not having very much space, parked the car, when the repairs were completed, in the street, and by 6.30 pm on March 7, the garage found that the car had been taken away from the place in the street where it had been parked. The garage still had the key, and so the police were rung up. However, the next thing that happened was that on March 16 Mr Arthur Brown found this car parked in the very street where the appellant lived, and, I suppose rather indignantly, took the car back to the garage, took the engine out, and then towed the car, less engine, back to the place in the street where it had been found. The matter then got into the hands of the police, and in the end a prosecution was commenced at the instigation of the Browns.

It was the prosecution case that there had been an interview on March 16 when inquiries were made of the appellant as to his car, when he told an admitted lie, because he said he had never taken the car to the garage at all. The very next day, however, in answer to Detective-Sergeant Thompson, the appellant acknowledged that had been a lie. He then said that he had gone and taken the car away but that he had taken it with the full consent of the Browns who had handed back the key to him, the prosecution's case being that Mr Brown still had the key.

In those circumstances there clearly was, as the deputy chairman ruled, a case to go to the jury of theft of his own car, because there was evidence from which the jury could find that the Browns had a proprietary interest, namely a lien on the car, and that by reason of the alleged lies that had been told to the police, the taking had been done dishonestly. I should add that the appellant is 46, that he lives with a Miss Nelson, by whom he has two children, and that he has three findings of guilt, 14 previous convictions and, in his favour, that he seemed, under the influence possibly of Miss Nelson, to be turning over a new leaf in that his last conviction was in 1966.

Pausing there, there is really nothing to inquire into. But, of course, the matter does not end there, because this case has attracted considerable publicity as a result of what the appellant is said to have said to his solicitor the next day, and as a result of what the solicitor has made extremely public throughout the country. What is said now, in the amended grounds of appeal which have been put in, is that the appellant did not have an opportunity of exercising a free choice in retracting his plea of not guilty and pleading guilty, and that, as it were, his mind did not go with the plea of guilty. Accordingly, it was in those circumstances, as indeed it was in the Dulwich picture case, *R v Hall* [1968] 2 QB 788, for the court to look into the matter, to hear evidence in regard to it in order to see, as was stated (1968) 52 Cr App R 528, 534, whether the prisoner in the circumstances had a free choice, since the election must be his, and the responsibility his, to plead guilty or not guilty.

The uncontested facts are that by the luncheon adjournment on the second day, the prosecution witnesses had been called, in effect, the two Browns but not the police evidence, and up to that stage at any rate it could be said that things were going very well for the appellant. Indeed the Browns were saying in effect that they thought that they were suing for their money, that it was a civil case. At any rate, the time had come when the police were going to give evidence. The appellant was represented by Mr Ronald Grey of counsel, and he very rightly was worried in the matter, because he had instructions not merely to challenge the police and suggest that they had misunderstood the appellant's answers or had failed to remember what he had said, or anything of that sort, but his direct instructions were to attack the police, accusing them of complete fabrication in conjunction with the two Browns. Naturally he was faced with this, that if he observed those instructions it would be almost certain that the jury would have put before them the appellant's previous convictions.

Accordingly he did what it is the duty of every counsel to do, to give the best advice he can in the interests of the accused. Having explained the legal position, how this could amount to a theft assuming that the lien was proved, he went on to ask the appellant seriously to consider changing his plea to one of guilty. He did that quite openly in the presence of Mr Laity, the solicitor, and he went on, on more than one occasion, putting it in strong words, that on a plea of guilty it might well be a non-custodial sentence, but if he went on and these convictions came out, the appellant ran the risk of going to prison.

There were long discussions beginning at about 1.50 pm in the interview room in the courts, and they went on to something like 3.30 pm. Part of the time Miss Nelson, with whom the appellant lived, was there, and part of the time his sister, a Mrs Crowe, was there. There was also the solicitor, Mr Laity, and his clerk, Mr Blake, and of course Mr Grey of counsel. But quite clearly none of those persons, except the appellant, was there for all the time. In particular Mr Grey was not

there all the time. The time came when he said that he wanted to discuss the matter with the deputy chairman. He went, and when he came back he gave what the court accepts was his own personal opinion. His own personal opinion in the matter, and I take this from the evidence of Mr Laity who appeared before us, was this:

> 'There is a very real possibility that if you are convicted by the jury and an attack has been made on the police officers, with your 16 previous convictions, you may receive a sentence of imprisonment. If at this stage you plead guilty, you must take my word for it, you will receive a fine or some other sentence which will not involve imprisonment.'

Those were Mr Grey's views, and as I have said the court accepts that he was passing on his own views.

The interview continued and, throughout, the appellant adhered to his view that he was going to fight, he was not going to retract his plea of not guilty. By about 3.30 pm it was intimated to the court that it would continue to be a fight, and Mr Grey and the appellant left the interview room to go back into court. A further interview took place, as to what happened at that there is some dispute, in the cell adjoining or below the dock. It was only for a minute or two, but at the end of that discussion the appellant said that he was going to retract his plea, and accordingly when everybody assembled in court the indictment was put to him again, he pleaded guilty, and the formal verdict of the jury was taken.

The first point taken by Mr Hawser is that Mr Grey exercised such pressure on the appellant, undue pressure, something beyond the bounds of his duty as counsel, so as to make the appellant feel that he must retract his plea, that he had no free choice in the matter. The court would like to say that it is a very extravagant proposition, and one which would only be acceded to in a very extreme case. The court would like to say, with emphasis, that they can find no evidence here that Mr Grey exceeded his duty in the way he presented advice to the appellant. He did it in strong terms. It is perfectly right that counsel should be able to do it in strong terms, provided always that it is made clear that the ultimate choice and a free choice is in the accused person. The one thing that is clear here from all the evidence is that at every stage of these proceedings, certainly up to the interview in the cell, it was impressed upon the appellant by Mr Grey, by Mr Laity, by Miss Nelson herself, that the choice was open to him, and in so far as it rests upon undue influence by counsel, the court is quite satisfied it wholly fails.

The matter, however, does not end there, because albeit it may be sufficient in the majority of cases if it is made clear to a prisoner that the final decision is his, however forcibly counsel may put it, the position is different if the advice is conveyed as the advice of someone who has seen the judge, and has given the impression that he is repeating the judge's views in the matter. As I have said, the court is quite satisfied Mr Grey was giving his own views and not the judge's at all. But it had been conveyed to the appellant that Mr Grey had just returned from seeing the deputy chairman. What was said gave Mr Laity the impression that those were the judge's views, and Mr Grey very frankly said that in the circumstances the appellant might well have got the impression that they were the judge's views. Accordingly one asks: was he ever disabused of that, did anything happen to show that these were not the judge's views on the case?

Apparently a time came, when the discussion had been going on for a long time, when Mr MacKenzie Ross, the acting temporary clerk of the court, came down to inform counsel (although he does not remember it, I think it must be right) that the judge could not allow much longer time. He saw Mr Batt, who was the prosecuting counsel, in the robing room and conveyed this to him, and he went into the interview room and said something to Mr Grey. Mr MacKenzie Ross is quite satisfied in his own mind that what he said was that he was authorised to say that whatever hap-

pened, that is, whether there was a plea of guilty or whether the plea of not guilty stood, the result would be the same, it would not be a term of imprisonment, and of course if that were so that was really the end of the matter. There was absolutely no reason whatever for the appellant to alter his plea, he would be no worse off if he kept to his plea of not guilty.

Mr Grey at any rate did not get that impression. Mr Grey got the impression from Mr MacKenzie Ross that the message that he was authorised to give was that if at this stage there was a plea, it would be a fine, and of course that would, if true, really bear out the impression which the appellant already had.

This court is quite satisfied that Mr MacKenzie Ross must be wrong in his recollection here – no doubt he was not asked about this until some time after the event – because we should not be here today if that really had happened. Accordingly nothing was conveyed by the clerk to the court which could have disabused the appellant of the impression which he had received earlier. Indeed, it may well have confirmed it. True, as I have said, he was warned that the choice was his, but once he felt that this was an intimation emanating from the judge, it is really idle in the opinion of this court to think that he really had a free choice in the matter.

Accordingly, though not without some doubt, the court feels that this appeal must succeed. I say 'with some doubt' because despite all that I have said, the appellant drafted grounds of appeal himself originally, and really there is nothing of this in those grounds. However, Mr Laity says he was informed of this point the day after the trial, and in all the circumstances of the case the court feels that the proper course will be to treat the plea that was given as a nullity, with the result that the trial that had taken place is a mistrial, and that there should be an order for a venire de novo.

Before leaving this case, which has brought out into the open the vexed question of so-called 'plea-bargaining,' the court would like to make some observations which may be of help to judges and to counsel and, indeed, solicitors. They are these:

1. Counsel must be completely free to do what is his duty, namely to give the accused the best advice he can and if need be advice in strong terms. This will often include advice that a plea of guilty, showing an element of remorse, is a mitigating factor which may well enable the court to give a lesser sentence than would otherwise be the case. Counsel of course will emphasise that the accused must not plead guilty unless he has committed the acts constituting the offence charged.
2. The accused, having considered counsel's advice, must have a complete freedom of choice whether to plead guilty or not guilty.
3. There must be freedom of access between counsel and judge. Any discussion, however, which takes place must be between the judge and both counsel for the defence and counsel for the prosecution. If a solicitor representing the accused is in the court he should be allowed to attend the discussion if he so desires. This freedom of access is important because there may be matters calling for communication or discussion, which are of such a nature that counsel cannot in the interests of his client mention them in open court. Purely by way of example, counsel for the defence may by way of mitigation wish to tell the judge that the accused has not long to live, is suffering maybe from cancer, of which he is and should remain ignorant. Again, counsel on both sides may wish to discuss with the judge whether it would be proper, in a particular case, for the prosecution to accept a plea to a lesser offence. It is of course imperative that so far as possible justice must be administered in open court. Counsel should, therefore, only ask to see the judge when it is felt to be really necessary, and the judge must be careful only to treat such communications as private where, in fairness to the accused person, this is necessary.
4. The judge should, subject to the one exception referred to hereafter, never indicate the sentence which he is minded to impose. A statement that on a plea of guilty he would impose one sentence but that on a conviction following a plea of not guilty he would impose a severer sentence is one which should never be made. This could be taken to be undue pressure on the accused, thus depriving him of that complete freedom of choice which is essential. Such cases, however, are in the experience of the court happily rare. What on occasions does appear to happen however is that a judge will tell counsel that, having read the depositions and the antecedents, he can safely say that on a plea of guilty he will for instance, make a probation order, something which may be helpful to counsel in advising the accused. The judge in such a case is no doubt careful not to mention what he would do if the accused were convicted following a plea of not guilty. Even so, the accused may well get the impression that the judge is intimating that in that event a severer sentence, maybe a custodial sentence, would result, so that again he may feel under pressure. This accordingly must also not be done. The only exception to this rule is that it should be permissible for a judge to say, if it be the case, that whatever happens, whether the accused pleads guilty or not guilty, the sentence will or will not take a particular form, eg, a probation order or a fine, or a custodial sentence. Finally, where any such discussion on sentence has taken place between judge and counsel, counsel for the defence should disclose this to the accused and inform him of what took place.

Whatever the legal position might be, there are, as the following examples demonstrate, strong hints of the phenomenon of plea bargaining to be found in the criminal justice system.

Baldwin J and McConville M (1976) *Defendants in the Criminal Process*, pp126–127

Case 7034 T was a company director, aged 47. He was active in his social life, a Freemason (he complained that one prosecution witness gave evidence 'in Masonic form, to lend more credibility to his answers'), and lived in a comfortable suburb. He faced 15 counts alleging theft, forgery of cheques and falsification of records, part of a complicated series of steps involving tax evasion, false accounts, deception of shareholders in his company, etc His first interviews with the police were five months before his first appearance in court; he was not tried in the Crown Court until a further 11 months had elapsed. On the morning of the Crown Court appearance he was offered what he described as a 'deal': if he would plead guilty to two counts, 13 would be dropped. He refused – 'I wasn't prepared to do any deal and I told my counsel so.' He was convicted (after a five-day trial) on 13 charges, and received a total of 21 months' imprisonment; he subsequently thought that if he had accepted the deal he might have got a suspended sentence.

Case 4042 W was charged with (i) burglary, (ii) assault occasioning actual bodily harm and (iii) an alternative charge of assault. Right up to the morning of the Crown Court trial (ie ten weeks from his first appearance) he had every intention of pleading not guilty to the second and third charges on the grounds of self-defence. Just before the trial, his barrister came into the cell and according to W said he 'had to' plead guilty: 'your statement says you are technically guilty and there's no point in pleading self-defence.' W agreed, reluctantly; the prosecution then dropped the 'actual bodily harm' charge and W pleaded guilty to the lesser charge of common assault.

Case 4041 The defendant was charged with theft of steel, and obtaining by deception, both charges being in respect of mismanagement of his own business affairs. His barrister came to see him a week before the trial and said he would make a bad witness, there was not enough evidence, and he should plead guilty and 'cut his losses'. He saw him again just before the trial and said 'if you plead guilty you will get 18 months, if you plead not guilty you're bound to be found guilty and will get three years'. In sentencing the defendant to a total 18 months imprisonment, the judge said, 'You are a wise man to plead guilty and have been soundly advised. If you had been convicted by a jury you would serve your suspended sentence (12 months) plus two years. But I take heavily into account your plea of guilty ...' The defendant noted that the barrister's and the judge's statements were identical and strongly believed that his trial was 'a charade, with plea and sentence already decided'. He noted that although he had not finally decided on a guilty plea until 10 am on the morning of the trial, no prosecution witnesses seemed to be available, and one such witness who had previously been his employee said that he had not been called.'

The Royal Commission gathered a wide range of empirical and academic views in relation to the role of the confession in the criminal justice system.

Royal Commission on Criminal Procedure (1981) *Police Interrogation*, Research Studies 3 and 4, pp12–13

Confession as a basis of a conviction

Even if evidence is strong, its treatment in court by the defence makes a signed confession invaluable to the prosecution (Lewis, 1976). Not only does a confession help convince the jury, it also 'simplifies proceedings and avoids the attendance of witnesses who may be inconvenienced, embarrassed, or even threatened by the accused's associates' (Franklin 1970, p93).

Lord Devlin (1960) writes: '... the accused's statement to the police officer plays a great part in the prosecution's case. There can be no doubt of that and I should emphasise it. In any study of the inquiry into crime it would be far less important than it is to examine police methods of interrogation if it were not true to say that the evidence which such interrogation produces is often decisive. The high degree of proof which the English legal system requires – proof beyond reasonable doubt – often could not be achieved by the prosecution without the assistance of the accused's own statement' (p.48).

Laurie (1970), basing his views on data collected by Martin and Wilson (1969), expresses the view that 'every contested case involves a detective in an average of two weeks' extra work'. This is because it involves finding and persuading witnesses, taking two sets of statements, report writing, the completion of numerous forms, dealing with recovered property, and appearing in court on a number of occasions to ask for a remand. Laurie comments: 'Every plea of not guilty is a threat to the detective's precariously balanced work load'.

In a study by McCabe and Purves (1972a) the authors report: 'While there were occasional, sometimes glaring, exceptions to this rule, it was generally correct to say that the acquittal of a defendant was attributable to a single cause – the failure of the prosecution (normally the police) to provide enough information or to present it in court in a way that would convince both judge and jury of the defendant's guilt (p11). In a subsequent study these researchers (1972) comment: 'To secure a conviction the prosecution must hurdle without fail all the obstacles placed before it in the discharge of its heavy burden of proof, and must do it to the satisfaction of the jury – a jury which seems often to be as critical of the prosecution performance as it is credulous of the defendant's explanations for his activities' (p20). In the United States, Weisberg (1961) refers to what he calls 'a subtle corruption of the jury traceable to interrogation practices'. He argues that so long as the search for confessions remains so important in police work, and so many prosecutions rely on them, juries

may come to feel that a charge unsupported by a confession is weaker than it really is (p35).

Discussions with lawyers and police officers in this country indicate widespread agreement concerning the advantages of a confession, and certainly there is some support for this view in the United States (see, for example, Kuh, 1966). However, the opposite view emerges from empirical studies carried out in the United States dealing with the relationship between interrogation and confession; these conclude that the value of confessions has been grossly exaggerated, and several authors agree that most cases can be solved by other investigative techniques.

Apart from the studies by McCabe and Purves (where the question was touched upon but was not central to the research) no one in this country appears to have examined the truth of the statement that it is difficult to obtain a conviction based on evidence unsupported by a confession. If it is indeed true, then it would be important to know in what ways it is problematical. By focusing solely on confessions, almost all existing studies (and they are mainly American) have neglected to examine cases where evidence is available, but no confession; nor have there been satisfactory studies which consider whether other methods of investigation would have produced sufficient conclusive evidence, without reliance on confessions. It would therefore seem important to find out the precise nature of the problems arising from the use of alternatives to interrogation, and which nevertheless result in adequate evidence being available, since these must be weighed in the balance against any loss of individual rights experienced by suspects under interrogation.

In the New Haven Study the authors say: 'The amount of evidence to convince a jury is not entirely predictable. Several law enforcement officials have suggested to us that considerably less evidence is often needed to convict a suspect than an observer would think, especially if the defendant had a prior record.' However, they note that others have expressed contrary opinions: 'there is always a seed of doubt that remains until the defendant... rises and admits his guilt'. Despite this uncertainty as to how much evidence is required, the authors claim that in a sample of 90 cases, interrogation was successful in producing a confession or incriminating statement in 49 cases, but only necessary to the solution of four of the 49. 'In all other cases where information was obtained there was enough evidence prior to the questioning to convict the suspect' (p1589).

As mentioned above, discussions with police officers in this country suggest that apart from the uncertainty relating to evidential material (and the belief in the personal advantage to be gained by high clearance rates), the primary reason for 'needing' a confession is to save time; as one officer put it: 'Two hours spent getting a confession can save you five in court.'

Whilst various forms of safeguard have been provided for suspects, as the following examples demonstrate they may not always be effective. These are good examples of the police being motivated by crime control rather than due process considerations.

McConville M, Sanders A and Leng R (1991) *The Case for the Prosecution*, pp57–59

CE-AO1S – The officer in the case explained that he could 'get round' the requirement of contemporaneous interview notes:

> 'by trying to have a few words that aren't on the record, ie on the way in [to the police station, in the car, on the way to the cell – give them something to think about – or before the start of an interview.'

One detective, reflecting the views of many we spoke to, told us that defendants were spoken to 'off the record' and that if the suspect did want to talk in these circumstances 'no policemen who did his job is going to say no' (CE-A046).

In other cases, the custody officer is complicitous in the creation of an off-the-record interview by permitting the case officer to visit the suspect in the cells or by authorising the suspect's release to the interview room without any record being made for the purposes of the custody sheet.

CC-A048

Res: 'How do you find the custody officers, do you find that you can work with them?'

Police: 'Some of them are more strict than others. But I can get on with them all anyway. But some are really all PACE, PACE, PACE, PACE. Some will just bend a little bit, if you want a quick word with them to see you know, if somebody wants a solicitor and you haven't had a chance to chat and don't want him to have a solicitor yet.'

Res: 'So they'll help you, some of them will?'

Police: 'Some of them, for just a quick word with them, yes.'

Res: 'Has that changed a bit from the old Station Sergeant or did you have the same there?'

Police: 'No, you could always have a quick word with a juvenile before his parents come.'

Res: 'Just to get to know them, to get the picture?'

Police: 'The facts, to get the facts.'

Res: 'The facts?'

Police: 'Yes. But now you can't talk to a juvenile until his parents are there, or you aren't supposed to!' (laughs)

These practices are dependent upon the individual custody officer, the relationship between the case officer and the custody officer, and the police determination of how 'necessary' it is that the suspect should be seen informally. Even so, there are other ways of interrogating suspects informally, such as in the car on the way to the station.

There need be nothing sinister in these off-the-record exchanges, whatever the official, legal, position is. A powerful element of police culture is 'knowing your suspect', learning the suspect's habits and lifestyle, problems and worries, hopes and fears. This is believed to be useful not as criminal intelligence in any real or direct sense but as an essential strategy for 'getting under the skin' of the suspect, reading the suspect's mind, finding out what makes the suspect tick. The clinical system of contemporaneous notes or tape-recording is seen as inimical to this process.

A large scale literature review in relation to the jury system was carried out on behalf of the Auld Commission. This investigated a whole range of factors that may influence jury verdicts, including age, sex, race and socio-economic background.

Darbyshire P, Maughan A and Stewart A (2001) *What Can the English Legal System Learn from Jury Research Published up to 2001?* (Report prepared for Auld LJ Report (2001) *A Review of the Criminal Courts in England and Wales*), pp10–20

Do jurors' characteristics affect their vote in the verdict? The shortcomings of research methods

As research in England and Wales is limited, it has been necessary to examine studies in the United States. Due to the sanctity of the jury room, researchers have been prevented from assessing deliberations of real trials. Thus research has taken a number of forms: mock and shadow juries, interviews with other participants in the trials (eg professionals such as judges and lawyers) to gain a comprehensive view of each verdict, comparative statistical analysis of jury verdicts and, of course, interviews with actual jurors. Before considering the results of the research, it is worth looking at the limitations and benefits of the research methods used. Mock juries have been used in a number of studies and consist of either recordings of a trial being played to the jury,

actors re-enacting a trial, or subjects reading a case. A potential drawback to this method of research and that of shadow juries, who copy a real jury throughout a trial, is that the defendant's future is not at risk. The gravity and implications of jurors' decisions may not be fully accounted for. Further, Baldwin and McConville point out that jury equity in simulated trials may not be practised or accurately reproduced in mock jury experiments where the fate of the defendant in question is not at issue. The presentation of simulated evidence may differ from that of a real trial. Researchers have, however, reported that mock jurors take their tasks seriously. Despite the limitations, a laboratory setting has some value, notably in disentangling complex variables (such as the types of crime committed, the appearance, attractiveness, age, race and sex of the defendant or victim and the performance, race and age of counsel) from juror characteristics. Interviews with other professionals as a method of evaluating verdicts include studies such as *The American Jury* and *Jury Trials* but this research also has limitations. Baldwin and McConville point out that the assumption that jurors ought to be deciding cases in ways lawyers would decide them is questionable. Further, caution should be exercised in relation to possible inferences drawn by researchers from questionnaires and any biases those responding to questionnaires may hold.

Thanks to the elaborate American system of jury selection, called voir dire, a trial support industry has grown up which profits from advising attorneys on jury selection and, in some trials, providing shadow juries whose deliberations are observed, to found advice to attorneys on the conduct of the trial. A great deal of money has been expended on scientific jury selection (SJS) but it is generally received with cynicism in the academic community. This method of determining how potential jurors may vote is often limited to the jurisdiction and the particular facts of a trial. Saks and Hastie point out that key attitudes change not only with geography but with the passage of time or the rise of a new case to activate new issues. Further, as Hans and Vidmar state, a good juror in one jurisdiction might well be a bad juror in a different jurisdiction, even for very similar trials. Additionally, there are a number of trial manuals written to advise attorneys that are contradictory and described as often based on plain old-fashioned stereotypes and conflicting or outdated ones at that. For completeness, these methods have been mentioned but this paper will not focus on these aspects of selection.

The effect of jurors' characteristics: the research findings

The most important finding agreed on by many researchers is that the main factor that influences a jury verdict is the evidence. Bridgeman and Marlow in their study of 65 actual jurors in 10 felony cases indicate that with 59 per cent of jurors the opportunity to engage in a review of the evidence was the most influential post trial factor. Beyond that, there would appear to be a lack of consensus among commentators as to whether demographic characteristics of jurors affect verdicts. Visher states that research suggests that jurors' personal characteristics are substantially insignificant in affecting trial outcomes. Ellsworth points out, however, that different jurors draw different conclusions about the right verdict on the basis of exactly the same evidence. This being the case, it would appear that individual differences among jurors make a difference. She points out that individual differences need not be differences in character or philosophy of life. Other influences such as length of trial, juror inattentiveness or unpredictable external events may affect the juror's decision-making process. Nevertheless, some research does substantiate the proposition that certain characteristics are significant in affecting a juror's verdict.

SEX OF THE JUROR
In their study of 276 trials in Birmingham, Baldwin and McConville concluded that in cases where four or more women were sitting,

although their conviction rate was lower than that of all-male juries, their acquittal rate corresponded to the city average. Additionally, there were no significant variations regarding questionable verdicts that could be attributed to the numbers of women sitting on juries. Sealy and Cornish found in a mock rape trial that women were significantly more likely to convict on circumstantial evidence. Accounting for this finding, however, they state that in the other three situations there appeared no probability that the sex of the juror explains his or her verdict. Some studies do indicate that a juror's sex may be a factor in their decision making. For example, Mills and Bohannon analysed data from returned questionnaires received from 117 females and 80 males randomly selected from the Baltimore jury panels. They tested for statistical significance between two variables and used multivariate analysis to examine the multiple contributions of four variables: race, sex, age and education. Multiple regression analysis indicated that from 10 per cent to 16 per cent of variance in verdict could be accounted for by a combination of the four demographic variables. They found that females gave more initial guilty verdicts for rape (78 per cent) and murder cases (71 per cent) as opposed to males (53 per cent rape; 50 per cent murder). After further analysing the data by race, they found the largest sex difference was for blacks, with black females reporting a significantly higher percentage of initial guilty verdicts (73 per cent) than black males (50 per cent). No significant differences were found between white males and females. The report notes that although the majority of jurors' personal decisions originally agreed with the final group decision, a significant sex difference was found for the amount of agreement between personal and group decisions. The personal decision of 67.5 per cent of the males and 81 per cent of females agreed with the final group decision. The report points out that only 5 per cent of the female jurors reported changing their initial decisions from not guilty to guilty, whereas 10 per cent of male jurors did so. Further, a higher proportion of females' initial guilty decisions matched with the final group guilty verdicts. Only 26 per cent of female jurors felt responsible for changing other jurors' decisions as opposed to 43 per cent of males. The researchers also examined the relationship between gender and three personality variables: empathy, autonomy and socialisation. They found that for males, guilty verdicts were associated with high socialisation, low empathy and low autonomy scores. For females, guilty verdicts were associated with low socialisation and low autonomy scores. In another study in Florida, Moran and Comfort compared their findings to those of Mills and Bohannon. They found there were no sex effects for verdict or pre-deliberation verdict. Additionally, they doubted that either sex is more likely to convict in felony trials in general, although such finding is conceivable for specific felonies such as rape or robbery. In their study, however, there was an interactive effect between the sex of the juror and other variables. Their analysis showed that male jurors who convicted had more children and a lower income. Further, male jurors who were pre-deliberationally inclined to convict, not only had more children (or a higher interest in having a family), but also higher Gough socialisation scores. They also found female jurors who convicted had a stronger belief in retributive justice. Penrod and Hastie state that the safest generalisation that can be made from all research on gender differences is that female students are more likely than male students to regard the defendant in a rape case as guilty and that males participate at higher rates of deliberation than females. Research would appear to substantiate the hypothesis that males do participate in the deliberation process more than females but the indications are that gender may also have an interactive effect with other factors. Additionally, there is evidence that jurors may find it easier to empathise with a same-sex defendant. The effect of gender on jury decision making is a complex one, not necessarily confined to the juror's sex but potentially linked to many factors in the trial process.

AGE

As with other characteristics, studies as to whether the age of a juror is linked to verdict have produced inconsistent results. Sealy and Cornish noted that in their London research a significant relationship between age and verdict emerged, the most consistent feature being that higher proportions of not guilty verdicts occur amongst the youngest groups. Mills and Bohannon found jurors' guilty verdicts generally increased with age, particularly for rape cases where the strongest relationship between age and the number of guilty verdicts were found. They reported that guilty verdicts amongst females remained fairly high and constant. Male guilty verdicts were lowest, however, in the 18 to 25 age group. Moran and Comfort found age un-correlated with verdict in undifferentiated felony trials. Likewise, Baldwin and McConville, in England, found the age structure of juries had no effect whatsoever on the outcome of cases. In Reed's study of approximately 240 jurors in Louisiana, he found no associations of significance between age and verdict. It would appear that the hypothesis that a younger juror is more likely to acquit because he/she may identify with a younger defendant may be unsupported. Nevertheless, Penrod and Hastie point out that there seem to be certain differences regarding age during deliberations. In their study, there was a clear relationship between age and recall of the judge's instructions and recall of case facts; the oldest group of jurors displayed markedly poorer performance than younger jurors. Age, however, did not appear to have affected jurors' assessment of deliberation thoroughness. Likewise, belief in their own correct decisions or persuasive pressure from other jurors seemed unaffected.

SOCIO-ECONOMIC STATUS

The relationship between socio-economic status and verdict preferences appears to be uncertain and contradictory. Sealy and Cornish, in London, indicated that manual workers were the most ready to convict when the evidence against the accused is very substantial. Reed reported, however, that the higher the status of the individual, measured by education and occupation, the more likely they were to convict. Other studies of actual jurors such as that conducted by Moran and Comfort suggested that males who were on lower incomes were more prone to convict. In Mills and Bohannon's study, they found that as male education level increased so did acquittals. Bridgeman and Marlowe, however, found in their study that demographic characteristics were largely unrelated to both procedural and outcome variables. There is evidence that occupation and education do affect performance during deliberation. Penrod and Hastie found occupation-recall results closely paralleled the results obtained for education. Jurors with lowest educational levels had only a 48 per cent recall for facts from testimony, compared with 70 per cent by those with the highest level of education. Additionally, in a sub-sample of 269 jurors, a number of factors such as residence in a wealthy suburb, attitude towards someone who causes another's death, newspaper read and marital status accounted for 11 per cent of variance in verdict preference. Thus, like age and gender, the effect of socio-economic juror characteristics on verdict seems uncertain. With all three, however, an impact on the deliberation process is evident.

RACE

Does the race of a juror affect verdict? The OJ Simpson trials and that of the four white police officers acquitted by a state jury with no black members in the first Rodney King police brutality trial would indicate that race is a factor influencing a juror's decisions. These and other notorious trials have, at the very least, focused attention on this sensitive issue. England and Wales were re-alerted to potential racism among jurors in 2000, when the European Court of Human Rights determined that a Crown Court judge had not acted sufficiently robustly where racist remarks had been made in the jury room. In a recent case, a judge dismissed a jury after allegations of racism were made. The racial structure of English and Welsh juries may become a political issue which will prove impossible to ignore. In an early study, Broeder reported findings of the University of Chicago Jury Project that Negroes and persons of Slavic and Italian descent were more likely to vote for acquittal. Interestingly, as Van Dyke pointed out, in Baltimore in 1969 when jury commissioners switched from selecting jurors from property lists to randomly selecting them from the voter registration list, the composition of juries changed from 70 per cent white to 43.7 per cent black by 1973. The conviction rate also dropped from 83.6 per cent in 1969 to an average of 70 per cent in the next few years. Laboratory findings would appear to support the theory that racial bias affects the determination of guilt. The problems regarding mock juries have been discussed but Johnson adds that there is always a risk for example, [that] the condition of being observed might cause the subjects to conceal their racial bias. Her article eloquently argues that none of the ordinary sources of concern about external validity seriously threatens the significance of the laboratory findings on race and guilt attribution. Ugwuegbu's two studies of 256 white undergraduates and 196 black undergraduates systematically varied the defendant's and victim's race and the strength of evidence pointing towards guilt. Results revealed that white subjects rated a black defendant more culpable than a white defendant. It was found, however, that when the evidence is not strong enough for conviction a white juror gives the benefit of the doubt to a white defendant but not a black defendant. The second study revealed that black subjects rated the black defendant as significantly less culpable than the white defendant but interestingly tended to grant the black defendant the benefit of the doubt not only when the evidence was doubtful but even when there was strong evidence against him. King points out that attempts to measure the relationship between verdicts and juror race demonstrate that, whenever a connection exists, it is likely to be the specific kind of connection often predicted by judges: white jurors are harsher with black defendants and more lenient with those charged with crimes against black victims than black jurors. Further studies using mock juries reveal definite racial bias. One study of 896 Alabama citizens in 1979 found the black defendant to be judged much more culpable than the white defendant. In order to substantiate findings of mock jury research, it is useful to consider data from real trials to ascertain if there are particular racial trends that emerge. One comprehensive study in New York State took place over a 10-year period between 1986 and 1995. It examined a total of 35,595 criminal verdicts in 27 counties analysing the relationship between racial make-up and jury acquittal rates. The study found a close relationship between racial demography and jury behaviour. Bronx County had the highest jury acquittal rate but also the highest black and Hispanic population. Conversely, Ontario County had the lowest acquittal rate and second to lowest population of blacks and Hispanics. The researchers questioned whether strong and weak prosecutions were similar across jurisdictions but with an independent control of trial rate – ie those cases actually going to trial – the data strongly suggests it is, indeed, the presence of black and Hispanic jurors that spells the difference in jury conviction rates from county to county. It is widely assumed in the United States that the ethnic diversity of modern juries has caused the acknowledged increase in hung juries. Klein and Klastorin use statistical analysis to argue that diversity is an insignificant cause of hung juries and eliminating it would only reduce the rate by three per cent. In England and Wales in 1995, 382,000 crimes were considered by the victim to be racially motivated. The evidence that racism exists is irrefutable. Peter Herbert makes the point that the reliability of the common man must seriously be in question if one considers the extent of racism in Britain. As has been discussed, randomness is not the same as representative-

ness. Further, representatives of the local community may not be the peers of a defendant. An employed, predominantly white jury may not be viewed as peers of an unemployed black defendant. Van Dyke points out that a jury that includes a cross-section of the community provides a modern definition of peer. All people are represented on a jury panel ensuring their impartiality and independence. He points out that people have different perspectives resulting from different life experiences that need to be balanced to achieve impartiality. It is often, however, the way hidden biased attitudes might affect impartiality that is in issue, a situation less likely to prevail if a portion of the jury is of a similar ethnic background or gender to the defendant. In 1989, the Court of Appeal in *Royston Ford* held that a trial judge had no power to construct a multi-racial jury; a judge's power was limited to jurors' competency to serve. Prior to this there were a number cases where the judiciary exercised discretion to ensure a representation of minorities on a jury trying a minority defendant. For over five centuries, until 1870, members of minorities such as Jews, Germans and Italians had the right to be tried by a jury comprised half of foreigners. It was called the jury de mediate linguae. This right was abolished on the ground that no foreigner need fear for a fair trial in England. Given the trial data, reported cases and research findings, can we in England and Wales believe this to be true now? It has been argued that one serious consequence of the abolition of the peremptory challenge is the loss of a potential means to ensure a racially mixed jury. In England and Wales there is virtually no mechanism to ensure that juror bias may be removed. Certainly there remains challenge for cause but the defence are given no facts about jurors upon which to base a challenge. Thus, short of a juror having a swastika tattoo in full view of the court, challenge for cause is practically redundant. Lawyers and defendants have little access to information about jurors. The point is well made that in certain cases, such as mercy killings, members of pro-life, euthanasia societies and certain religious groups should be excluded from the jury. The court, however, would probably be unaware of such associations and beliefs. As Richard May points out, in the United States, being able to question jurors about their past experience has the advantage of dispensing with those who may be thought unlikely to come to a fair and impartial verdict. Certainly there are many difficulties with their system. The process can be lengthy and expensive, with more potential jurors needing to be summoned to take the places of those challenged and dismissed. Nevertheless, the argument that peremptory challenge causes the rigging of juries has yet to be substantiated. There are arguments against racially structuring juries. If one type of defendant, for example, an Afro-Caribbean, is entitled to stipulate the kind of jury that will try him, then this would open the floodgates to other minorities. Homosexuals, alcoholics and militant feminists could argue they also should be afforded the same treatment. Further, structuring a jury would interfere with randomness that appears to be important in the English concept of a fairly structured jury. The Runciman Commission suggested that in exceptional cases, three ethnically similar jurors to the victim or defendant could be included, on the judge's order, following a request by the prosecution or defence. Research indicates that unless there is a minimum of three minority jurors, they may not withstand group pressure. Commenting on this recommendation, the New Zealand writers consider such judicial tinkering would be undesirable, as compromising the integrity of the jury. They argue that juries should be selected so as to achieve representativeness in all cases, not just where the accused is a minority (in that case a Maori). Bootham criticises the Royal Commission's recommendation, that the mixed jury should only be ordered in exceptional cases, as unlikely to inspire much confidence among ethnic minority defendants. Sanders and Young expand on this criticism as the RCCJ's recommendation

ignores the evidence that race plays a much broader role within the operation of the criminal process than this. Nevertheless, if potential bias towards a defendant or victim has been identified, is there not a duty to reduce or eliminate it so that he or she may receive a fair and impartial trial? With the abolition of the peremptory challenge and the decision in *Ford*, there is now virtually no mechanism to achieve this. Johnson points out that in structuring a jury, the aim should be to prevent a wrong rather than make a victim whole. Further, potential hostility towards an ethnic minority would not increase, for unlike some affirmative action plans, those in question are not being given, rather than earning, a benefit that is not afforded to white persons. Research in Santa Cruz indicated that only 28.3 per cent of those with postgraduate education and 36 per cent of men as opposed to 51.8 per cent of women and 60 per cent of blacks are likely to favour mandated racial quotas to create racially mixed juries. This is an interesting finding if one considers that decision-makers within societies are predominantly educated and male. The report does state, however, that 70.7 per cent of all those questioned agreed that, in criminal trials, African-American jurors should be included when the defendant was African-American.

Comment

It appears that the racial composition of the jury can affect its verdict. We might consider permitting the trial judge to draw three or more black or Asian jurors (whichever is appropriate) from the pool to place them on a jury in a racially sensitive case, or where a defendant or victim requests this. Such a facility must apply to victims as well as defendants, since we must remember that the first Rodney King beatings trial, in 1992, was seen as unfair because the all-white jury acquitted in the face of overwhelming evidence of a vicious assault by white police officers on a black victim. The jury were undoubtedly the peers of the four defendants and representative of their community. We would add a word of caution. The allegation is sometimes made that Irish defendants accused of terrorist crimes do not have the benefit of an impartial jury when tried in England and Wales and some of the most notorious miscarriages of justice in English legal history have involved Irish defendants. We have strong unpublished evidence of discrimination against Irish defendants at every level of the English criminal process. Our suggestion will not solve this problem, but we are alarmed to read Helena Kennedy's comment, when interviewed by Grove, that in IRA trials in England it is routine to *excuse* Irish jurors.

The Court of Appeal considered whether or not a judge was wrong in refusing a request for a multiracial jury in relation to an ethnic minority defendant. They decided that he was not wrong in that he would have had no power to grant such a request. Lord Lane delivered the judgement on behalf of the court.

R v *Ford (Royston)* [1989] 3 All ER 445 at 446–450 Court of Appeal (Lord Lane CJ, Rose LJ and Sir Bernard Caulfield)

Lord Lane CJ

We deal first of all with the fact that the judge refused the application for a multiracial jury. This is a problem which has arisen more than once in recent months, and it is likely to be a problem that will arise again. Consequently it seems to us that it is necessary to give careful thought to the way in which a judge should approach the problem.

At common law a judge has a residual discretion to discharge a particular juror who ought not to be serving on the jury. This is part of the judge's duty to ensure that there is a fair trial. It is based on the duty of a judge expressed by Lord Campbell CJ in *R* v *Mansell* (1857) 8 E & B 54 as a duty 'to prevent scandal and the perversion of justice'. A judge must achieve that, for example, by preventing a juryman from serving who is

completely deaf or blind or otherwise incompetent to give a verdict.

It is important to stress, however, that that is to be exercised to prevent individual jurors who are not competent from serving. It has never been held to include a discretion to discharge a competent juror or jurors in an attempt to secure a jury drawn from particular sections of the community, or otherwise to influence the overall composition of the jury. For this latter purpose the law provides that 'fairness' is achieved by the principle of random selection.

The way in which random selection should take place is a matter not for the judge but for the Lord Chancellor, as we endeavoured to point out in the course of argument to Mr Herbert by citing the relevant portion of the Juries Act 1974, which is section 5(1). That provides:

'The arrangements to be made by the Lord Chancellor under this Act shall include the preparation of lists (called panels) of persons summoned as jurors, and the information to be included in panels, the court sittings for which they are prepared, their division into parts or sets (whether according to the day of first attendance or otherwise), their enlargement or amendment, and all other matters relating to the contents and form of the panels shall be such as the Lord Chancellor may from time to time direct.'

There are several cases which give examples of this residual discretion. It may be exercised even in the absence of any objection by any of the parties. The basic position is that a juror may be discharged on grounds that would found a challenge for cause. In addition jurors who are not likely to be willing or able properly to perform their duties may also be discharged.

Those grounds are again set out in the judgment of Lord Campbell CJ in *R* v *Mansell* when he said, at pp80–81:

'If a juryman were completely deaf, or blind, or afflicted with bodily disease which rendered it impossible for him to continue in the jury box without danger to his life, or were insane, or drunk, or with his mind so occupied by the impending death of a near relation that he could not duly attend to the evidence ...'

That was repeated in different words by Lawton LJ in *R* v *Mason* [1981] QB 881, 887. Lawton LJ gave as an example of common judicial intervention exclusion from the jury of a member of the panel who is infirm, has difficulty in hearing, or one for whom taking part in a long trial would be unusually burdensome.

That discretion has now been confirmed by express statutory provision in the Juries Act 1974, section 10; and *Practice Direction (Jury Service: Excusal)* [1988] 1 WLR 1162 expressly provides for excusal of jurors at the court's discretion on grounds of 'personal hardship or conscientious objection to jury service'. It does not however envisage excusal on more general grounds such as race, religion or political beliefs.

On occasion however, as Mr Herbert has pointed out to us by citing certain cases, in particular *R* v *Binns* [1982] Crim LR 522, trial judges have been invited to exercise their discretion not merely to remove an individual juror, but to go further and use the power of discretionary discharge to alter the composition of the panel or of a particular jury. The most common cases in which this question has arisen have involved questions of ethnic groups where it has been suggested that the jury should consist partly or wholly of members of that same ethnic group. Those applications provide particular difficulty for the judge and the present case is a very good example. They arise without warning and are usually argued without any reference to authority, as indeed was very largely the case in the present instance.

There have been occasions on which it has been accepted that such a discretion exists, most notably *R* v *Thomas* (1989) 88 Cr App R 370, where the prosecution conceded, and the judge accepted, that such a discretion did exist, albeit, it was added, that it was only to be exercised sparingly and in very exceptional

circumstances. In the judgment of this court that concession made in *R* v *Thomas* was not correct. The trial judge had no discretion to interfere in that way with the composition of the panel or of an individual jury. It is important to note the nature of the objection to the juries in question, and of the discretion that is supposed to meet that objection. The racial composition of a particular panel or part panel would not be grounds for challenge to the array. A challenge to the array is a challenge to the whole panel on the ground of some irregularity in their summoning by the officer responsible.

In *R* v *Danvers* [1982] Crim LR 680, an application was made to challenge the array at the trial of a defendant of West Indian origin, when all members of the jury panel were found to be white. The application was made on the ground that the jury panel did not reflect the ethnic composition of the community, and on the further ground that an all-white jury could not understand the mental and emotional atmosphere in which black families live, so that a black defendant could not have unreserved confidence in an all-white jury. Not surprisingly, due to the fact that the challenge contained no allegation that the all-white jury panel was the result of bias or improper conduct on the part of the summoning officer, the challenge failed. It was held that there is no requirement in law that there should be a black member on a jury or jury panel.

It has never been suggested that the judge has a discretion to discharge a whole panel or part panel on grounds that would not found a valid challenge. Similarly, in the absence of evidence of specific bias, ethnic origins could not found a valid ground for challenge to an individual juror. The alleged discretion of the judge to intervene in the selection of the jury does not therefore fall within any acknowledged category of judicial power or discretion.

There are, moreover, strong reasons why such a discretion should not be recognised. The whole essence of the jury system is random selection, as the passage from *R v Sheffield Crown Court, ex parte Brownlow* [1980] QB 530, from Lord Denning's judgment cited in the course of argument, shows. He said, at p541:

'Our philosophy is that the jury should be selected at random – from a panel of persons who are nominated at random. We believe that 12 persons selected at random are likely to be a cross-section of the people as a whole – and thus represent the views of the common man. ... The parties must take them as they come.'

The judgment was supported by Shaw LJ, sitting with Lord Denning MR. Secondly, it is worth noting that on occasions in the past when it has been thought desirable that the court should have a power of this kind, it has been expressly granted by statute and equally subsequently abolished by statute. Thirdly, such an application is in effect a request to the judge either to give directions as to the constitution of the panel or to order some individual jurors to be replaced without assigning a cause, that is, peremptorily. It is true that in *R v Bansal* [1985] Crim LR 151, in response to an application of this type, Woolf J did give directions that the jury panel should be selected from a particular area known to contain members of the Asian community, but the judge does not appear to have had the benefit of full argument on the point. Responsibility for the summoning of jurors to attend for service in the Crown Court and the High Court is by statute clearly laid upon the Lord Chancellor. That is clear from ss2 and 5 of the Juries Act 1974 which has already been cited in this judgment. It is not the function of the judge to alter the composition of the panel or to give any directions about the district from which it is to be drawn. The summoning of panels is not a judicial function, but it is specifically conferred by statute on an administrative officer. That fact may not have been drawn to the attention of the court in the cases we have cited and others which have suggested that the judge has power to give directions as to the composition of the panel of jurors.

It should also be remembered that the mere fact that a juror is, for instance, of a particular race or holds a particular religious belief, cannot be made the basis for a challenge for cause on the grounds of bias or on any other grounds. If therefore a judge were to exercise his discretion to remove a juror on either of these grounds, he would be assuming bias where none was proved. Such a course is not only unjustified in law, but also indeed might be thought to be seriously derogatory of the particular juror. Further, any attempt to influence the composition of the jury on these grounds would conflict with the requirement that the jury to try an issue before a court shall be selected by ballot in open court from the panel as summoned: see Juries Act 1974 section 11.

In *R v Chandler (No 2)* [1964] 2 QB 322, Lord Parker CJ held that earlier authorities that had been cited did not establish that the defendant in the particular case of a trial for misdemeanour had a right comparable to that of the Crown to ask a juror to stand by, but he did add, at p337:

'That, of course, is not to say that in an exceptional case, whether felony or misdemeanour, a judge cannot in his discretion, himself stand by a juror or allow a defendant to do so.'

That was either a slip of the tongue or else it may be that Lord Parker CJ had in mind what was stated in *R v Mansell* 8 E & B 57, 81 in relation to individual, incompetent jurors, because *Mansell* (and the judgment of Lord Campbell CJ) was cited to the court in that case, *R v Chandler*.

We have been referred among other cases to *R v Binns* [1982] Crim LR 522. It is important to recollect and to note that in Binns the original report in the Criminal Law Review was supplemented by a corrigendum at p 823, which puts the case in a very different light. In so far as *R v Binns* conflicts with the principles which we have endeavoured already to state in this judgment, the opinion expressed in *R v Binns* must be said to have been wrong. The conclusion is that, however well-intentioned the judge's motive might be, the judge has no power to influence the composition of the jury, and that it is wrong for him to attempt to do so. If it should ever become desirable that the principle of random selection should be altered, that will have to be done by way of statute and cannot be done by any judicial decision.

We wish to make two final further points. It appears to have been suggested in some of the cases that there is a 'principle' that a jury should be racially balanced. One of those cases to which Mr Herbert has referred us is *R* v *Frazer* [1987] Crim LR 418. There was a similar suggestion in *R* v *Bansal* [1985] Crim LR 151 already referred to. The existence of any such principle however was denied in a case which escaped the attention of Mr Herbert, *R* v *McCalla* [1986] Crim LR 335. No authority is cited by those who have argued for the existence of the principle. In our judgment such a principle cannot be correct, for it would depend on an underlying premise that jurors of a particular racial origin or holding particular religious beliefs are incapable of giving an impartial verdict in accordance with the evidence.

Secondly, the principles we have already set out apply not only where it is argued that a jury of a particular composition ought to be empanelled because of the nature of the particular case or particular defendants, but also where complaint is made that the panel was not truly 'random' – for instance, that the population of a particular area contained 20 per cent of persons of West Indian origin, but that only a much lower percentage of such persons was to be found on the panel. For the judge to entertain any such application would equally involve his seeking to investigate the composition of the panel in a manner which, for reasons already indicated, lies outside his jurisdiction, and lies within the jurisdiction of the Lord Chancellor.

So far as the mode of summoning the panel is concerned, the judge is limited, we repeat, to considering, in a challenge for cause, whether the summoning officer has dis-

played bias or other impropriety. If that cannot be established, the judge has no power to review or take action in respect of any procedures that are alleged to have led to the panel not being in fact 'random.' Any such complaint would be a complaint of administrative error and has to be tackled by means other than the judge's action. If the officer concerned is in fact not performing his duties properly, in circumstances that fall short of his displaying bias or impropriety, he must be corrected, in other words, by administrative means.

As emphasised above, action could certainly not take the form of directions by the judge as to how the task of selection should in fact be performed. That being the case, in the present instance, although the judge was not given the opportunity of argument on this point to any extent, he was right in the upshot to come to the conclusion that he should not order a multiracial jury to be empanelled, because he had no power so to do.

Sections 1–11 make provision in relation to powers that are exercisable before sentence. This includes the possibility of the sentence being deferred and the transfer of individuals to other courts for sentencing purposes.

Powers of Criminal Courts (Sentencing) Act 2000, ss1–11

PART I
POWERS EXERCISABLE BEFORE SENTENCE
Section 1

 delay

Deferment of sentence

1 (1) The Crown Court or a magistrates' court may defer passing sentence on an offender for the purpose of enabling the court, or any other court to which it falls to deal with him, to have regard in dealing with him to –

> (a) his conduct after conviction (including, where appropriate, the making by him of reparation for his offence); or

(b) any change in his circumstances; but this is subject to subsections (2) and (3) below.

(2) The power conferred by subsection (1) above shall be exercisable only if –

(a) the offender consents; and

(b) the court is satisfied, having regard to the nature of the offence and the character and circumstances of the offender, that it would be in the interests of justice to exercise the power.

(3) Any deferment under this section shall be until such date as may be specified by the court, not being more than six months after the date on which the deferment is announced by the court; and, subject to section 2(7) below, where the passing of sentence has been deferred under this section it shall not be further so deferred.

(4) Notwithstanding any enactment, a court which under this section defers passing sentence on an offender shall not on the same occasion remand him. *cannot remand him to custody*

(5) Where the passing of sentence on an offender has been deferred by a court under this section, the court's power under this section to deal with the offender at the end of the period of deferment –

(a) is power to deal with him, in respect of the offence for which passing of sentence has been deferred, in any way in which it could have dealt with him if it had not deferred passing sentence; and

(b) without prejudice to the generality of paragraph (a) above, in the case of a magistrates' court includes the power conferred by section 3 below to commit him to the Crown Court for sentence.

(6) Nothing in this section or section 2 below shall affect –

(a) the power of the Crown Court to bind over an offender to come up for judgment when called upon; or

(b) the power of any court to defer passing sentence for any purpose for which it may lawfully do so apart from this section.

Section 2
Further powers of courts where sentence deferred under section 1

2 (1) A court which under section 1 above has deferred passing sentence on an offender may deal with him before the end of the period of deferment if during that period he is convicted in Great Britain of any offence.

(2) Subsection (3) below applies where a court has under section 1 above deferred passing sentence on an offender in respect of one or more offences and during the period of deferment the offender is convicted in England or Wales of any offence ('the later offence').

(3) Where this subsection applies, then (without prejudice to subsection (1) above and whether or not the offender is sentenced for the later offence during the period of deferment), the court which passes sentence on him for the later offence may also, if this has not already been done, deal with him for the offence or offences for which passing of sentence has been deferred, except that –

(a) the power conferred by this subsection shall not be exercised by a magistrates' court if the court which deferred passing sentence was the Crown Court; and

(b) the Crown Court, in exercising that power in a case in which the court which deferred passing sentence was a magistrates' court, shall not pass any sentence which could not have been passed by a magistrates' court in exercising that power.

(4) Where –

(a) a court which under section 1 above has deferred passing sentence on an offender proposes to deal with him, whether on the date originally specified by the court or by virtue of subsection (1) above before that date, or

(b) the offender does not appear on the date so specified, the court may issue a summons requiring him to appear before the court, or may issue a warrant for his arrest.

(5) In deferring the passing of sentence under section 1 above a magistrates' court shall be regarded as exercising the power of adjourning the trial conferred by section 10(1) of the Magistrates' Courts Act 1980, and accordingly sections 11(1) and 13(1) to (3A) and (5) of that Act (non-appearance of the accused) apply (without prejudice to subsection (4) above) if the offender does not appear on the date specified under section 1(3) above.

(6) Any power of a court under this section to deal with an offender in a case where the passing of sentence has been deferred under section 1 above –

(a) is power to deal with him, in respect of the offence for which passing of sentence has been deferred, in any way in which the court which deferred passing sentence could have dealt with him; and

(b) without prejudice to the generality of paragraph (a) above, in the case of a magistrates' court includes the power conferred by section 3 below to commit him to the Crown Court for sentence.

(7) Where –

(a) the passing of sentence on an offender in respect of one or more offences has been deferred under section 1 above, and

(b) a magistrates' court deals with him in respect of the offence or any of the offences by committing him to the Crown Court under section 3 below, the power of the Crown Court to deal with him includes the same power to defer passing sentence on him as if he had just been convicted of the offence or offences on indictment before the court.

Section 3
Committal to Crown Court for sentence
Committal for sentence on summary trial of offence triable either way

3 (1) Subject to subsection (4) below, this section applies where on the summary trial of an offence triable either way a person aged 18 or over is convicted of the offence.

(2) If the court is of the opinion –

(a) that the offence or the combination of the offence and one or more offences associated with it was so serious that greater punishment should be inflicted for the offence than the court has power to impose, or

(b) in the case of a violent or sexual offence, that a custodial sentence for a term longer than the court has power to impose is necessary to protect the public from serious harm from him, the court may commit the offender in custody or on bail to the Crown Court for sentence in accordance with section 5(1) below.

(3) Where the court commits a person under subsection (2) above, section 6 below (which enables a magistrates' court, where it commits a person under this section in respect of an offence, also to commit him to the Crown Court to be dealt with in respect of certain other offences) shall apply accordingly.

(4) This section does not apply in relation to an offence as regards which this section is excluded by section 33 of the Magistrates' Courts Act 1980 (certain offences where value involved is small).

(5) The preceding provisions of this section shall apply in relation to a corporation as if –

(a) the corporation were an individual aged 18 or over; and

(b) in subsection (2) above, paragraph (b) and the words 'in custody or on bail' were omitted.

Section 4
Committal for sentence on indication of guilty plea to offence triable either way

4 (1) This section applies where –

(a) a person aged 18 or over appears or is brought before a magistrates' court ('the court') on an information charging him with an offence triable either way ('the offence');

(b) he or his representative indicates that

he would plead guilty if the offence were to proceed to trial; and

(c) proceeding as if section 9(1) of the Magistrates' Courts Act 1980 were complied with and he pleaded guilty under it, the court convicts him of the offence.

(2) If the court has committed the offender to the Crown Court for trial for one or more related offences, that is to say, one or more offences which, in its opinion, are related to the offence, it may commit him in custody or on bail to the Crown Court to be dealt with in respect of the offence in accordance with section 5(1) below.

(3) If the power conferred by subsection (2) above is not exercisable but the court is still to inquire, as examining justices, into one or more related offences –

(a) it shall adjourn the proceedings relating to the offence until after the conclusion of its inquiries; and

(b) if it commits the offender to the Crown Court for trial for one or more related offences, it may then exercise that power.

(4) Where the court –

(a) under subsection (2) above commits the offender to the Crown Court to be dealt with in respect of the offence, and

(b) does not state that, in its opinion, it also has power so to commit him under section 3(2) above, section 5(1) below shall not apply unless he is convicted before the Crown Court of one or more of the related offences.

(5) Where section 5(1) below does not apply, the Crown Court may deal with the offender in respect of the offence in any way in which the magistrates' court could deal with him if it had just convicted him of the offence.

(6) Where the court commits a person under subsection (2) above, section 6 below (which enables a magistrates' court, where it commits a person under this section in respect of an offence, also to commit him to the Crown Court to be dealt with in respect of certain other offences) shall apply accordingly.

(7) For the purposes of this section one offence is related to another if, were they both to be prosecuted on indictment, the charges for them could be joined in the same indictment.

Section 5
Power of Crown Court on committal for sentence under sections 3 and 4

5 (1) Where an offender is committed by a magistrates' court for sentence under section 3 or 4 above, the Crown Court shall inquire into the circumstances of the case and may deal with the offender in any way in which it could deal with him if he had just been convicted of the offence on indictment before the court.

(2) In relation to committals under section 4 above, subsection (1) above has effect subject to section 4(4) and (5) above.

Section 6
Committal for sentence in certain cases where offender committed in respect of another offence

6 (1) This section applies where a magistrates' court ('the committing court') commits a person in custody or on bail to the Crown Court under any enactment mentioned in subsection (4) below to be sentenced or otherwise dealt with in respect of an offence ('the relevant offence').

(2) Where this section applies and the relevant offence is an indictable offence, the committing court may also commit the offender, in custody or on bail as the case may require, to the Crown Court to be dealt with in respect of any other offence whatsoever in respect of which the committing court has power to deal with him (being an offence of which he has been convicted by that or any other court).

(3) Where this section applies and the relevant offence is a summary offence, the committing court may commit the offender, in custody or on bail as the case may require, to the Crown Court to be dealt with in respect of –

(a) any other offence of which the committing court has convicted him, being either –

    (i) an offence punishable with imprisonment; or

    (ii) an offence in respect of which the committing court has a power or duty to order him to be disqualified under section 34, 35 or 36 of the Road Traffic Offenders Act 1988 (disqualification for certain motoring offences); or

(b) any suspended sentence in respect of which the committing court has under section 120 (1) below power to deal with him.

(4) The enactments referred to in subsection (1) above are –

    (a) the Vagrancy Act 1824 (incorrigible rogues);

    (b) sections 3 and 4 above (committal for sentence for offences triable either way);

    (c) section 13(5) below (conditionally discharged person convicted of further offence);

    (d) section 116(3)(b) below (offender convicted of offence committed

during currency of original sentence); and

    (e) section 120(2) below (offender convicted during operational period of suspended sentence).

Section 7
Crown Court on committal for sentence under section 6

7 (1) Where under section 6 above a magistrates' court commits a person to be dealt with by the Crown Court in respect of an offence, the Crown Court may after inquiring into the circumstances of the case deal with him in any way in which the magistrates' court could deal with him if it had just convicted him of the offence.

(2) Subsection (1) above does not apply where under section 6 above a magistrates' court commits a person to be dealt with by the

Crown Court in respect of a suspended sentence, but in such a case the powers under section 119 below (power of court to deal with suspended sentence) shall be exercisable by the Crown Court.

(3) Without prejudice to subsections (1) and(2) above, where under section 6 above or any enactment mentioned in subsection (4) of that section a magistrates' court commits a person to be dealt with by the Crown Court, any duty or power which, apart from this subsection, would fall to be discharged or exercised by the magistrates' court, shall not be discharged or exercised by that court but shall instead be discharged or may instead be exercised by the Crown Court.

(4) Where under section 6 above a magistrates' court commits a person to be dealt with by the Crown Court in respect of an offence triable only on indictment in the case of an adult (being an offence which was tried summarily because of the offender's being under 18 years of age), the Crown Court's powers under subsection (1) above in respect of the offender after he attains the age of 18 shall be powers to do either or both of the following –

    (a) to impose a fine not exceeding £5,000;

    (b) to deal with the offender in respect of the offence in any way in which the magistrates' court could deal with him if it had just convicted him of an offence punishable with imprisonment for a term not exceeding six months.

Section 8
Remission for sentence: young offenders etc
Power and duty to remit young offenders to youth courts for sentence

8 (1) Subsection (2) below applies where a child or young person (that is to say, any person aged under 18) is convicted by or before any court of an offence other than homicide.

(2) The court may and, if it is not a youth court, shall unless satisfied that it would be undesirable to do so, remit the case –

(a) if the offender was committed for trial or sent to the Crown Court for trial under section 51 of the Crime and Disorder Act 1998, to a youth court acting for the place where he was committed for trial or sent to the Crown Court for trial;

(b) in any other case, to a youth court acting either for the same place as the remitting court or for the place where the offender habitually resides; but in relation to a magistrates' court other than a youth court this subsection has effect subject to subsection (6) below.

(3) Where a case is remitted under subsection (2) above, the offender shall be brought before a youth court accordingly, and that court may deal with him in any way in which it might have dealt with him if he had been tried and convicted by that court.

(4) A court by which an order remitting a case to a youth court is made under subsection (2) above –

(a) may, subject to section 25 of the Criminal Justice and Public Order Act 1994 (restrictions on granting bail), give such directions as appear to be necessary with respect to the custody of the offender or for his release on bail until he can be brought before the youth court; and

(b) shall cause to be transmitted to the justices' chief executive for the youth court a certificate setting out the nature of the offence and stating –

(i) that the offender has been convicted of the offence; and

(ii) that the case has been remitted for the purpose of being dealt with under the preceding provisions of this section.

(5) Where a case is remitted under subsection (2) above, the offender shall have no right of appeal against the order of remission, but shall have the same right of appeal against any order of the court to which the case is remitted as if he had been convicted by that court.

(6) Without prejudice to the power to remit any case to a youth court which is conferred on a magistrates' court other than a youth court by subsections (1) and (2) above, where such a magistrates' court convicts a child or young person of an offence it must exercise that power unless the case falls within subsection (7) or (8) below.

(7) The case falls within this subsection if the court would, were it not so to remit the case, be required by section 16(2) below to refer the offender to a youth offender panel(in which event the court may, but need not, so remit the case).

(8) The case falls within this subsection if it does not fall within subsection (7) above but the court is of the opinion that the case is one which can properly be dealt with by means of –

(a) an order discharging the offender absolutely or conditionally, or

(b) an order for the payment of a fine, or

(c) an order (under section 150 below) requiring the offender's parent or guardian to enter into a recognizance to take proper care of him and exercise proper control over him, with or without any other order that the court has power to make when absolutely or conditionally discharging an offender.

(9) In subsection (8) above 'care' and 'control' shall be construed in accordance with section 150(11) below.

(10) A document purporting to be a copy of an order made by a court under this section shall, if it purports to be certified as a true copy by the justices' chief executive for the court, be evidence of the order.

Section 9
Power of youth court to remit offender who attains age of 18 to magistrates' court other than youth court for sentence

9 (1) Where a person who appears or is brought before a youth court charged with an offence subsequently attains the age of 18, the

youth court may, at any time after conviction and before sentence, remit him for sentence to a magistrates' court (other than a youth court) acting for the same petty sessions area as the youth court.

(2) Where an offender is remitted under subsection (1) above, the youth court shall adjourn proceedings in relation to the offence, and –

(a) section 128 of the Magistrates' Courts Act 1980 (remand in custody or on bail) and all other enactments, whenever passed, relating to remand or the granting of bail in criminal proceedings shall have effect, in relation to the youth court's power or duty to remand the offender on that adjournment, as if any reference to the court to or before which the person remanded is to be brought or appear after remand were a reference to the court to which he is being remitted; and

(b) subject to subsection (3) below, the court to which the offender is remitted ('the other court') may deal with the case in any way in which it would have power to deal with it if all proceedings relating to the offence which took place before the youth court had taken place before the other court.

(3) Where an offender is remitted under subsection (1) above, section 8(6) above (duty of adult magistrates' court to remit young offenders to youth court for sentence) shall not apply to the court to which he is remitted.

(4) Where an offender is remitted under subsection (1) above he shall have no right of appeal against the order of remission (but without prejudice to any right of appeal against an order made in respect of the offence by the court to which he is remitted).

(5) In this section –

(a) 'enactment' includes an enactment contained in any order, regulation or other instrument having effect by virtue of an Act; and

(b) 'bail in criminal proceedings' has the same meaning as in the Bail Act 1976.

Section 10
Power of magistrates' court to remit case to another magistrates' court for sentence

10 (1) Where a person aged 18 or over ('the offender') has been convicted by a magistrates' court ('the convicting court') of an offence to which this section applies ('the instant offence') and –

(a) it appears to the convicting court that some other magistrates' court ('the other court') has convicted him of another such offence in respect of which the other court has neither passed sentence on him nor committed him to the Crown Court for sentence nor dealt with him in any other way, and

(b) the other court consents to his being remitted under this section to the other court, the convicting court may remit him to the other court to be dealt with in respect of the instant offence by the other court instead of by the convicting court.

(2) This section applies to –

(a) any offence punishable with imprisonment; and

(b) any offence in respect of which the convicting court has a power or duty to order the offender to be disqualified under section 34, 35 or 36 of the Road Traffic Offenders Act 1988 (disqualification for certain motoring offences).

(3) Where the convicting court remits the offender to the other court under this section, it shall adjourn the trial of the information charging him with the instant offence, and –

(a) section 128 of the Magistrates' Courts Act 1980 (remand in custody or on bail) and all other enactments, whenever passed, relating to remand or the granting of bail in criminal proceedings shall have effect, in relation to the convicting court's power or duty to remand the offender on that adjournment, as if any reference to the court to or before which the person remanded is to be brought or appear after remand were a reference to the court to which he is being remitted; and

(b) subject to subsection (7) below, the other court may deal with the case in any way in which it would have power to deal with it if all proceedings relating to the instant offence which took place before the convicting court had taken place before the other court.

(4) The power conferred on the other court by subsection (3) (b) above includes, where applicable, the power to remit the offender under this section to another magistrates' court in respect of the instant offence.

(5) Where the convicting court has remitted the offender under this section to the other court, the other court may remit him back to the convicting court; and the provisions of subsections (3) and (4) above (so far as applicable) shall apply with the necessary modifications in relation to any remission under this subsection.

(6) The offender, if remitted under this section, shall have no right of appeal against the order of remission (but without prejudice to any right of appeal against any other order made in respect of the instant offence by the court to which he is remitted).

(7) Nothing in this section shall preclude the convicting court from making any order which it has power to make under section 148 below (restitution orders) by virtue of the offender's conviction of the instant offence.

(8) In this section –

(a) 'conviction' includes a finding under section 11(1) below (remand for medical examination) that the person in question did the act or made the omission charged, and 'convicted' shall be construed accordingly;

(b) 'enactment' includes an enactment contained in any order, regulation or other instrument having effect by virtue of an Act; and

(c) 'bail in criminal proceedings' has the same meaning as in the Bail Act 1976.

Section 11
Remand by magistrates' court for medical examination

11 (1) If, on the trial by a magistrates' court of an offence punishable on summary conviction with imprisonment, the court –

(a) is satisfied that the accused did the act or made the omission charged, but

(b) is of the opinion that an inquiry ought to be made into his physical or mental condition before the method of dealing with him is determined, the court shall adjourn the case to enable a medical examination and report to be made, and shall remand him.

(2) An adjournment under subsection (1) above shall not be for more than three weeks at a time where the court remands the accused in custody, nor for more than four weeks at a time where it remands him on bail.

(3) Where on an adjournment under subsection (1) above the accused is remanded on bail, the court shall impose conditions under paragraph (d) of section 3(6) of the Bail Act 1976 and the requirements imposed as conditions under that paragraph shall be or shall include requirements that the accused –

(a) undergo medical examination by a registered medical practitioner or, where the inquiry is into his mental condition and the court so directs, two such practitioners; and

(b) for that purpose attend such an institution or place, or on such practitioner, as the court directs and, where the inquiry is into his mental condition, comply with any other directions which may be given to him for that purpose by any person specified by the court or by a person of any class so specified.

The extract from Toby is valuable as a source of a whole variety of ideas in relation to punishment and principles of sentencing in general.

Toby J (1964) 'Is Punishment Necessary?', *Journal of Criminal Law, Criminology and Police Science*, pp333–337

The urge to punish

Many crimes have identifiable victims. In the case of crimes against the person, physical or psychic injuries have been visited upon the victim. In the case of crimes against property, someone's property has been stolen or destroyed. In pressing charges against the offender, the victim may express hostility against the person who injured him in a socially acceptable way. Those who identify with the victim – not only his friends and family but those who can imagine the same injury being done to them – may join with him in clamouring for the punishment of the offender. If, as has been argued, the norm of reciprocity is fundamental to human interaction, this hostility of the victim constituency toward offenders is an obstacle to the elimination of punishment from social life. Of course, the size of the group constituted by victims and those who identify with victims may be small. Empirical study would probably show that it varies by offence. Thus, it is possible that nearly everyone identifies with the victim of a murderer but relatively few people with the victim of a blackmailer. The greater the size of the victim constituency, the greater the opposition to a non-punitive reaction to the offender.

It would be interesting indeed to measure the size and the composition of the victim constituencies for various crimes. Take rape as an illustration. Since the victims of rape are females, we might hypothesise that *women* would express greater punitiveness toward rapists than men and that degrees of hostility would correspond to real or imaginary exposure to rape. Thus, pretty young girls might express more punitiveness toward rapists than homely women. Among males, we might predict that greater punitiveness would be expressed by those with more reason to identify with the victims. Thus, males having sisters or daughters in the late teens or early twenties might express more punitiveness toward rapists than males lacking vulnerable 'hostages to fortune'.

Such a study might throw considerable light on the wellsprings of punitive motivation, particularly if victimisation reactions were distinguished from other reasons for punitiveness. One way to explore such motivation would be to ask the same respondents to express their punitive predispositions toward offences which do not involve victims at all, eg, gambling, or which involve victims of a quite different kind. Thus, rape might be balanced by an offence the victims of which are largely male. Survey research of this type is capable of ascertaining the opposition to milder penalties for various offences. It would incidentally throw light on the comparatively gentle societal reaction to white-collar crime. Perhaps the explanation lies in the difficulty of identifying with the victims of patent infringement or watered hams.

The social control functions of punishment

Conformists who identify with the *victim* are motivated to punish the offender out of some combination of rage and fear. Conformists who identify with the *offender,* albeit unconsciously, may wish to punish him for quite different reasons. Whatever the basis for the motivation to punish, the existence of punitive reactions to deviance is an obstacle to the abolition of punishment. However, it is by no means the sole obstacle. Even though a negligible segment of society felt punitive toward offenders, it might still not be feasible to eliminate punishment if the social control of deviance depended on it. Let us consider, therefore, the consequences of punishing offenders for (a) preventing crime, (b) sustaining the morale of conformists, and (c) rehabilitating offenders.

Punishment as a means of crime prevention

Durkheim (1) defined punishment as an act of

vengeance. 'What we avenge, what the criminal expiates, is the outrage to morality.' But why is vengeance necessary? Not because of the need to deter the bulk of the population from doing likewise. The socialisation process prevents most deviant behaviour. Those who have introduced the moral norms of their society cannot commit crimes because their self – concepts will not permit them to do so. Only the unsocialised (and therefore amoral) individual fits the model of classical criminology and is deterred from expressing deviant impulses by a nice calculation of pleasures and punishments. Other things being equal, the anticipation of punishment would seem to have more deterrent value for inadequately socialised members of the group. It is difficult to investigate this proposition empirically because other motivationally relevant factors are usually varying simultaneously, eg, the situational temptations confronting various individuals, their optimism about the chances of escaping detection, and the differential impact of the same punishment on individuals of different status. Clearly, though, the deterrent effect of anticipated punishments is a complex empirical problem, and Durkheim was not interested in it. Feeling as he did that *some* crime is normal in every society, he apparently decided that the crime prevention function of punishment is not crucial. He pointed out that minute gradation in punishment would not be necessary if punishment were simply a means of deterring the potential offender (crime prevention). 'Robbers are as strongly inclined to rob as murderers are to murder; the resistance offered by the former is not less than that of the latter, and consequently, to control it, we would have recourse to the same means.' Durkheim was factually correct; the offences punished most severely are not necessarily the ones which present the greatest problem of social defence. Thus, quantitatively speaking, murder is an unimportant cause of death; in the United States it claims only half as many lives annually as does suicide and only one-fifth the toll of automobile accidents. Furthermore, criminologists have been unable to demonstrate a relationship between the murder rate of a community and its use or lack of use of capital punishment.

Most contemporary sociologists would agree with Durkheim that the anticipation of punishment is not the first line of defence against crime. The socialisation process keeps most people law abiding, not the police – if for no other reason than the police are not able to catch every offender. This does not mean, however, that the police could be disbanded. During World War II, the Nazis deported all of Denmark's police force, thus providing a natural experiment testing the deterrent efficacy of formal sanctions. Crime increased greatly. Even though punishment is uncertain, especially under contemporary urban conditions, the possibility of punishment keeps some conformists law-abiding. The empirical question is: How many conformists would become deviants if they did not fear punishment?

Punishment as a means of sustaining the morale of conformists

Durkheim considered punishment indispensable as a means of containing the demoralising consequences of the crimes that could not be prevented. Punishment was not for Durkheim mere vindictiveness. Without punishment Durkheim anticipated the demoralisation of 'upright people' in the face of defiance of the collective conscience. He believed that unpunished deviance tends to demoralise the conformist and therefore he talked about punishment as a means of repairing 'the wounds made upon collective sentiments'. Durkheim was not entirely clear; he expressed his ideas in metaphorical language. Nonetheless, we can identify the hypothesis that the punishment of offenders promotes the solidarity of conformists.

Durkheim anticipated psychoanalytic thinking as the following reformulation of his argument shows: One who resists the temptation to do what the group prohibits, to drive his car at 80 miles per hour, to beat up an enemy, to take what he wants without paying for it, would like to feel that these self-imposed abnegations have some meaning. When he sees others defy rules without untoward consequences, he needs some reassurance that his sacrifices were made in a good cause. If 'the good die young and the wicked flourish as the green bay tree', the moral scruples which enable conformists to restrain their own deviant inclinations lack social validation. The social significance of punishing offenders is that deviance is thereby defined as unsuccessful in the eyes of conformists, thus making the inhibition or repression of their own deviant impulses seem worthwhile. Righteous indignation is collectively sanctioned reaction formation. The law-abiding person who unconsciously resents restraining his desire to steal and murder has an opportunity, by identifying with the police and the courts, to affect the precarious balance within his own personality between internal controls and the temptation to deviate. A bizarre example of this pschological mechanism is the man who seeks out homosexuals and beats them up mercilessly. Such pathological hostility toward homosexuals is due to the sadist's anxiety over his own sex-role identification. By 'punishing' the homosexual, he denies the latent homosexuality in his own psyche. No doubt, some of the persons involved in the administration of punishment are sadistically motivated. But Durkheim hypothesised that the psychic equilibrium of the *ordinary* member of the group may be threatened by violation of norms; Durkheim was not concerned about psychopathological punitiveness.

Whatever the practical difficulties, Durkheim's hypothesis is, in principle, testable. It should be possible to estimate the demoralising impact of nonconformity on conformists. Clearly, though, this is no simple matter. The extent of demoralisation resulting from the failure to punish may vary with type of crime. The unpunished traffic violator may cause more demoralisation than the unpunished exhibitionist – depending on whether or not outwardly conforming members of society are more tempted to exceed the speed limit than to expose themselves. The extent of demoralisation may also vary with position in the social structure occupied by the conformist. Thus, Ranulf suggested that the middle class was especially vulnerable: 'The disinterested tendency to inflict punishment is a distinctive characteristic of the lower middle class, that is, of a social class living under conditions which force its members to an extraordinarily high degree of self-restraint and subject them to much frustration of natural desires. If a psychological interpretation is to be put on this correlation of facts, it can hardly be to any other effect than that moral indignation is a kind of resentment caused by the repression of instincts.' (2)

Once the facts on the rate and the incidence of moral indignation are known, it will become possible to determine whether something must be done to the offender in order to prevent the demoralisation of conformists. Suppose that research revealed that a very large proportion of conformists react with moral indignation *to most* violations of the criminal laws. Does this imply that punishment is a functional necessity? Durkheim apparently thought so, but he might have been less dogmatic in his approach to punishment had he specified the functional problem more clearly: making the nonconformist unattractive as a role model. If the norm violation can be defined as unenviable through some other process than by inflicting suffering upon him, punishment is not required by the exigencies of social control.

Punishment can be discussed on three distinct levels: (a) in terms of the motivations of the societal agents administering it, (b) in terms of the definition of the situation on the part of the person being punished, and (c) in terms of its impact on conformists. At this point I am chiefly concerned with the third level, the impact on conformists. Note that punishment of offenders sustains the morale of conformists only under certain conditions. The first has already been discussed, namely that conformists unconsciously wish to violate the rules themselves. The second is that conformists implicitly assume that the nonconformity is a result *of deliberate defiance* of society's norms. For some conformists, this second condition is not met. Under the guidance of psychiatric thinking, some conformists assume that norm violation is the result of illness rather than wickedness. For such conformists, punishment of the offender does not contribute to their morale. Since they assume that the nonconformity is an involuntary symptom of a disordered personality, the offender is automatically unenviable because illness is (by definition) undesirable. Of course, it is an empirical question as to the relative proportions of the conforming members of society who make the 'wicked' or the 'sick' assumption about the motivation of the offender, but this can be discovered by investigation.

In Western industrial societies, there is increasing tendency to call contemporary methods of dealing with offenders 'treatment' rather than 'punishment'. Perhaps this means that increasing proportions of the population are willing to accept the 'sick' theory of nonconformity. Note, however, that the emphasis on 'treatment' may be more a matter of symbolism than of substance. Although the definition of the situation as treatment rather than punishment tends to be humanising – both to the offender and to the persons who must deal with him – there are still kind guards and cruel nurses. Furthermore, it would be an error to suppose that punishment is invariably experienced as painful by the criminal whereas treatment is always experienced as pleasant by the psychopathological offender. Some gang delinquents consider a reformatory sentence an opportunity to renew old acquaintances and to learn new delinquent skills; they resist fiercely the degrading suggestion that they need the services of the 'nut doctor'. Some mental patients are terrified by shock treatment and embarrassed by group therapy.

What then is the significance of the increasing emphasis on 'treatment'? Why call an institution for the criminally insane a 'hospital' although it bears a closer resemblance to a prison than to a hospital for the physically ill'? In my opinion, the increased emphasis on treatment in penological thinking and practice reflects the existence of a large group of conformists who are undecided as between the 'wicked' and the 'sick' theories of nonconformity. When they observe that the offender is placed in 'treatment', their provisional diagnosis of illness is confirmed, and therefore they do not feel that he has 'gotten away with it'. Note that 'treatment' has the capacity to make the offender unenviable to conformists whether or not it is effective in rehabilitating him and whether or not he experiences it as pleasant. Those old-fashioned conformists who are not persuaded by official diagnoses of illness will not be satisfied by 'treatment'; they will prefer to see an attempt made to visit physical suffering or mental anguish on the offender. For them, punishment is necessary to prevent demoralisation.

Punishment as a means of reforming the offender

Rehabilitation of offenders swells the number of conformists and therefore is regarded both by humanitarians and by scientifically minded penologists as more constructive than punishment. Most of the arguments against imprisonment and other forms of punishment in the correctional literature boil down to the assertion that punishment is incompatible with rehabilitation. The high rate of recidivism for prisons and reformatories is cited as evidence of the irrationality of punishment. What sense is there in subjecting offenders to the frustrations of incarceration? If rehabilitative programmes are designed to help the offender cope with frustrations in his life situation, which presumably were responsible for his nonconformity, imprisoning him hardly seems a good way to begin. To generalise the argument, the status degradation inherent in punishment makes it more difficult to induce the offender to play a legitimate role instead of a nonconforming one. Whatever the offender's original motivations for nonconformity, punishment adds to them by neutralising his fear of losing the respect of the community; he has already lost it.

Plausible though this argument is, empirical research has not yet verified it. The superior rehabilitative efficacy of 'enlightened' prisons is a humanitarian assumption, but brutal correctional systems have, so far as is known, comparable recidivism rates to 'enlightened' systems. True, the recidivism rate of offenders who are fined or placed on probation is less than the recidivism rate of offenders who are incarcerated, but this comparison is not merely one of varying degrees of punishment. Presumably, more severe punishment is meted out to criminals who are more deeply committed to a deviant way of life. Until it is demonstrated that the recidivism rates of strictly comparable populations of deviants differ depending on the degree of punitiveness with which they are treated, the empirical incompatibility of punishment and rehabilitation will remain an open question.

Even on theoretical grounds, however, the incompatibility, of punishment and rehabilitation can be questioned once it is recognised that one may precede the other. Perhaps some types of deviants become willing to change only if the bankruptcy of their way of life is conclusively demonstrated to them. On this assumption, punishment may be a necessary preliminary to a rehabilitative programme in much the same way that shock treatment makes certain types of psychotics accessible to psychotherapy.

It seems to me that the compatibility of punishment and rehabilitation could be clarified (although not settled) if it were considered from the point of view of the *meaning of* punishment to the offender. Those offenders who regard punishment as a deserved deprivation resulting from their own misbehaviour are qualitatively different from offenders who regard punishment as a misfortune bearing no relationship to morality. Thus, a child who is spanked by his father and the member of a bopping gang who is jailed for carrying concealed weapons are both 'punished'. But one accepts the deprivation as legitimate, and the other bows before superior force. I would hypothesise that punishment has rehabilitative significance only for the former. If this is so, correctional officials must convince the prisoner that his punishment is just before they can motivate him to change. This is no simple task. It is difficult for several reasons:

1. It is obvious to convicted offenders, if not to correctional officials, that some so called 'criminals' are being punished disproportionately for trifling offences whereas some predatory business men and politicians enjoy prosperity and freedom. To deny that injustices occur confirms the cynical in their belief that 'legitimate' people are not only as predatory as criminals but hypocritical to boot. When correctional officials act as though there were no intermediate position between asserting that perfect justice characterises our society and that it is a jungle, they make it more difficult to persuade persons undergoing punishment that the best approximation of justice is available that imperfect human beings can manage.

2. Of course, the more cases of injustice known to offenders, the harder it is to argue that the contemporary approximation of justice is the best that can be managed. It is difficult to persuade Negro inmates that their incarceration has moral significance if their life experience has demonstrated to them that the police and the courts are less scrupulous *of their* rights than of the rights of white persons. It is difficult to persuade an indigent inmate that his incarceration has moral significance if his poverty resulted in inadequate legal representation.

3. Finally, the major form of punishment for serious offenders (imprisonment) tends to generate a contraculture which denies that justice has anything to do with legal penalties. That is to say, it is too costly to confine large numbers of people in isolation from one another, yet congregate confine-

ment results in the mutual reinforcement of self-justifications. Even those who enter prison feeling contrite are influenced by the self-righteous inmate climate; this may be part of the reason recidivism rates rise with each successive commitment.

In view of the foregoing considerations, I hypothesise that punishment – as it is now practised in Western societies – is usually an obstacle to rehabilitation. Some exceptions to this generalisation should be noted. A few small treatment institutions have not only prevented the development of a self-righteous contra-culture but have managed to establish an inmate climate supportive of changed values. In such institutions punishment has rehabilitative significance for the same reason it has educational significance in the normal family: it is legitimate.

To sum up: The social control functions of punishment include crime prevention, sustaining the morale of conformists, and the rehabilitation of offenders. All of the empirical evidence is not in, but it is quite possible that punishment contributes to some of these and interferes with others. Suppose, for example, that punishment is necessary for crime prevention and to maintain the morale of conformists but is generally an obstacle to the rehabilitation of offenders. Since the proportion of deviants is small in any viable system as compared with the proportion of conformists, the failure to rehabilitate them will not jeopardise the social order. Therefore, under these assumptions, sociological counsel would favour the continued employment of punishment.

Conclusion

A member of a social system who violates its cherished rules threatens the stability of that system. Conformists who identify with the victim are motivated to punish the criminal in order to feel safe. Conformists who unconsciously identify with the criminal fear their own ambivalence. If norm violation is defined by conformists as wilful, visiting upon the offender some injury or degradation will make

him unenviable. If his behaviour is defined by conformists as a symptom of pathology they are delighted not to share, putting him into treatment validates their diagnosis of undesirable illness. Whether he is 'punished' or 'treated', however, the disruptive consequence of his deviance is contained. Thus, from the viewpoint of social control, the alternative outcomes of the punishment or treatment processes, rehabilitation or recidivism, are less important than the deviant's neutralisation as a possible role model. Whether punishment is or is not necessary rests ultimately on empirical questions: (1) the extent to which identification with the victim occurs, (2) the extent to which nonconformity is prevented by the anticipation of punishment, (3) what the consequences are for the morale of conformists of punishing the deviant or of treating his imputed pathology, and (4) the compatibility between punishment and rehabilitation.

References
1. Durkheim E (1933) *The Division of Labour in Society*, Illinois: Free Press.
2. Ranulf (1938) *Moral Indignation and Middle Class Psychology*.
   Item 99

The idea of the punishment to fit the crime seems attractive as a principle of sentencing and this is the basis of the desert model, which is explored by von Hirsch. It can claim to be fair in terms of its proportionality. It is also clear that it looks to the past rather than the future and of course in many respects it is the future that we are mainly concerned with.

Von Hirsch A (1985) *Past or Future Crimes*, pp10–11

The central organising principle of sentencing, on this rationale, is that of 'commensurate deserts'. Sentences, according to this principle, are to be proportionate in their severity to the gravity of the defendant's criminal conduct. The criterion for deciding the quantum of punishment is retrospective: the seriousness of the violation the defendant has committed. Future-oriented considerations – the offender's need for treatment, his likelihood of offending again, the deterrent effect of his punishment on others – do not determine the comparative severity of penalties. In such a system, imprisonment, because of its severity, is visited only upon those convicted of serious felonies. For non-serious crimes, penalties less severe than imprisonment are to be used. The degree of intrusiveness of these non-prison sanctions is determined not by rehabilitative or predictive considerations but, again, by the degree of gravity of the criminal conduct. Warnings, limited deprivations of leisure time, and fines are among the sanctions that could be used.

Advocates of the desert model opposed the use of individual prediction in sentencing as a matter of principle, not merely because of such forecasts' tendency to error. Their objection to predictive sentencing was simply that it led to undeserved punishments and would do so even if the false-positive rate could be reduced. The use of predictions, accurate or not, meant that those identified as future recidivists would be treated more severely than those not so identified, not because of differences in the blameworthiness of their past conduct, but because of crimes they supposedly would commit in future. It was felt that punishment, as a blaming institution, was warranted only for past culpable choices and could not justly be levied for future conduct. Unless the person actually made the wrongful choice he was predicted to make, he ought not to be condemned for that choice – and hence should not suffer punishment for it.

The difficulties of justifying retribution are explored further in this extract. Clearly reductionism is not available as a justification and arguments such as the annulment of the offence or the repayment of a debt to society have their own difficulties.

Walker N and Padfield N (1996) *Sentencing Theory, Law and Practice*, pp112–113

Why must offending be penalised? The 'reducer' has little difficulty in answering this: the hope of reducing the frequency of future offences has so obvious a point that it can be questioned only by arguing that in fact penalties never or seldom fulfil this hope. The 'punisher' however, is in a more awkward position, for he is expected to explain what is meant by 'deserving' a penalty irrespective of its future utility. He must explain, that is, why the infliction of hardship or inconvenience on an offender is the morally right response to his offence even when it can lead to no benefit. This seems to be difficult for punishers. It is not too difficult to explain why so many people feel that a penalty is an appropriate response. This is the way they were brought up, and this is one of the assumptions of their culture. That, however, is an answer to another sort of question, a question for social psychologists. What punishers must also provide is a justifying *explanation*, which would help people from a non-retributive culture to see why there is something right about the transaction known as punishing, irrespective of any of its benefits.

Most attempts to do this are suspect because they could be true only in a metaphorical sense. For example –

1. The penalty 'annuls' the offence: ie achieves a state of affairs in which it is as if the offence had not been committed. Note that it is necessary to say 'as if'. It is sometimes literally possible to undo the harm done by an offence, and sometimes possible to approximate this by making the offender pay compensation: but that is reparation, not retribution, and it cannot usually undo all the harm. One cannot be unmurdered or unraped.

2. By undergoing the penalty the offender pays a debt to society. In fact there is no literal debt to pay, only a fiction that

society is owed compensation for the breach of its rules or its peace.

Paternalism is examined in the next extract. The approach suggests that punishment is of value in helping people to understand the difference between right and wrong and that it can assist in our moral development. So rather as with a parent and a child the guidance is given for the offender's own good.

Morris H (1993) 'A Paternalistic Theory of Punishment', in Duff A and Garland G (eds), *A Reader on Punishment*, p110

I have claimed that to have as one's aim in punishing the good of the wrongdoer counts strongly in favour of the moral legitimacy of punishing. I do not claim, of course, that this is the sole justification for punishment, though I do believe that what it seeks to promote is among the most important, if not the most important, of human goods. The practice of punishment is complex and any justification proposed as an exclusive one must, in my judgment, be met with scepticism, if not scorn. There is, too, as I earlier briefly noted, a significant logical overlapping of this theory with retributivism, though at a certain point, when one considers types of punishment, they diverge. A paternalistic theory, given the good as defined, would support principles that are familiar dictates of retributivism – that only the guilty may be punished, that the guilty must be, and that the punishment inflicted reflect the degree of guilt. Failure to comply with the demands of retributivism would preclude realisation of the paternalist's goal. I have also, however, suggested that retributivism needs supplementing if it is to meet our intuitions of what is morally permissible punishment. But, of course, this overlapping of justifications for punishment includes as well some form of utilitarianism, for if our goal is as I have defined it, and punishments are

threatened and imposed, deterrent values are also furthered. I do not question the rich over-determination of goods promoted by the practice of punishment. I do urge that weight be given, and on the issue of restrictions on punishment, determinative weight, to paternalistic ends.

Duff and Garland warn us that we should not expect too much in finding total coherence in terms of sentencing philosophy. In particular it is clear that criminal justice systems are going to be driven by pragmatic considerations.

Duff A and Garland G (1994) 'Introduction', in Duff A and Garland G (eds), *A Reader on Punishment*, p19

... how far should we even hope, or aim, for a penal system which is structured by just one coherent normative theory of punishment? Should we not rather recognise that punishment is inevitably a locus both of conflicting principles, and of conflicts between principles and more pragmatic considerations? Von Hirsch (1993) argues, for instance, that the principle of proportionality should be the primary guide to sentencing; legislators, policy-makers, and sentencers should strive to ensure that each offender receives a sentence whose severity is proportionate to the seriousness of the crime, in order that the punishment can express the appropriate degree of censure. Critics have objected, first, that we cannot in practice hope to achieve a proper proportionality between crime and punishment; second, that there are other principles such as that of parsimony in punishment which may conflict with the demands of proportionality; and third that an undue emphasis on strict proportionality stands in the way of making effective use of the wide range of intermediate sanctions (such as intensive probation or supervision, substantial fines, and community service, which fall between imprisonment and traditional probation) which are finding favour amongst penal policy-makers.

The ideas of restorative justice have been promoted in a number of jurisdictions including Canada. In the following extract the meaning attributed to the notion in Nova Scotia is explained. The role of the victim is viewed as being important, as indeed is the need for the offender to take responsibility for their actions. A face-to-face meeting between the victim, offender and community is one means of achieving this. This can be contrasted with other systems in a number of ways; for example, financial recompense to the victim as a form of reparation would be resorted to rather than a financial penalty which would have been designed to act as a punishment.

Nova Scotia Department of Justice (1998) *Restorative Justice*, p9

In the current criminal justice system, victims frequently feel frustrated and left out of their own cases, except perhaps for being witnesses. Restorative justice recognises that victims have many needs. They need an opportunity to speak about their feelings and to have the power restored to them that has been taken away by the experience of the offence; they need recognition of the pain and suffering they have endured; and they also need to understand the offender's motivation for committing a crime. Restorative justice recognises these needs, and allows for victim involvement in determining how those needs can best be met. Restorative justice also provides community members with an opportunity to voice their feelings and concerns, show disapproval of the offender's behaviour without branding them an outcast, and be actively involved in a process which holds offenders accountable and repairs the harm caused to the victim and the community.

In the conventional criminal justice system, offenders usually focus on avoiding punishment. The general fixation on punishment as the principal tool for correcting behaviour drives offender responsibility underground. If the only option available for offenders is a potentially harmful period of incarceration, non-acceptance of responsibility will be the standard response. It is socially more valuable to have offenders acknowledge the harm their actions have caused and right their wrong. Restorative justice requires offenders to take responsibility for their conduct, and then take action to repair the harm their offence has caused to the victim and the community. Restorative programmes place a high value on a face-to-face meeting between the victim, offender and community. During the course of that meeting, each party is given an opportunity to tell the story of the crime from their own perspective, and talk about their concerns and feelings. The meeting helps the parties develop an understanding of the crime, of the other parties, and of the steps needed to make amends. The meeting concludes with an agreement outlining how the offender will make reparation. Reparation can include monetary payment, service to the victim, community service or any other outcome agreed upon in the process. Terms of the agreement can be personalised to take into consideration the individual circumstances of the offender. In the application of restorative justice, it will be necessary to assess each case based on its merits and the circumstances of the victim and the offender. Restorative justice is only available when offenders are prepared to accept responsibility for their actions. Furthermore, for the more serious offences, an offender may still be required to go to jail after participating in a restorative justice forum.

The following extract makes an attempt at stating fundamental principles for restorative justice. The stress is very much upon building relationships and community and could be contrasted with other models of the criminal justice system.

Claassen R (1996) *Restorative Justice – Fundamental Principles*

1. Crime is primarily an offence against human relationships, and secondarily a violation of a law (since laws are written to protect safety and fairness in human relationships).

2. Restorative justice recognises that crime (violation of persons and relationships) is wrong and should not occur, and also recognises that after it does there are dangers and opportunities. The danger is that the community, victim(s), and/or offender emerge from the response further alienated, more damaged, disrespected, disempowered, feeling less safe and less cooperative with society. The opportunity is that injustice is recognised, the equity is restored (restitution and grace), and the future is clarified so that participants are safer, more respectful, and more empowered and cooperative with each other and society.

3. Restorative justice is a process to 'make things as right as possible' which includes: attending to needs created by the offence such as safety and repair of injuries to relationships and physical damage resulting from the offence; and attending to needs related to the cause of the offence (addictions, lack of social or employment skills or resources, lack of moral or ethical base, etc).

4. The primary victim(s) of a crime is/are the one(s) most impacted by the offence. The secondary victims are others impacted by the crime and might include family members, friends, witnesses, criminal justice officials, community, etc.

5. As soon as immediate victim, community, and offender safety concerns are satisfied, restorative justice views the situation as a teachable moment for the offender; an opportunity to encourage the offender to learn new ways of acting and being in community.

6. Restorative justice prefers responding to the crime at the earliest point possible and with the maximum amount of voluntary cooperation and minimum coercion, since healing in relationships and new learning are voluntary and cooperative processes.

7. Restorative justice prefers that most crimes are handled using a cooperative structure, including those impacted by the offence, as a community to provide support and accountability. This might include primary and secondary victims and family (or substitutes if they choose not to participate), the offender and family, community representatives, government representatives, faith community representatives, school representatives, etc.

8. Restorative justice recognises that not all offenders will choose to be cooperative. Therefore there is a need for outside authority to make decisions for the offender who is not cooperative. The actions of the authorities and the consequences imposed should be tested by whether they are reasonable, restorative, and respectful (for victim(s), offender, and community).

9. Restorative justice prefers that offenders who pose significant safety risks and are not yet cooperative be placed in settings where the emphasis is on safety, values, ethics, responsibility, accountability, and civility. They should be exposed to the impact of their crime(s) on victims, invited to learn empathy, and offered learning opportunities to become better equipped with skills to be a productive member of society. They should continually be invited (not coerced) to become cooperative with the community and be given the opportunity to demonstrate this in appropriate settings as soon as possible.

10. Restorative justice requires follow-up and accountability structures utilising the natural community as much as possible, since keeping agreements is the key to building a trusting community.

11. Restorative justice recognises and encourages the role of community institutions,

including the religious/faith community, in teaching and establishing the moral and ethical standards which build up the community.

Printed by permission

The role that reparation could play in the principles of sentencing is explored in the following extract. A reparative schema would demand the abandonment of culpability of the offender as the central focus of sentencing and, in its place, pay much closer attention to the issue of harm delivered to victims, society and perhaps also offenders. Restoring individual damage and repairing social bonds rather than inflicting pain on the offender is the aim. In this we would, as a society, invite (or perhaps demand) the involvement of the community in the process of restoration.

Zedner L (1998) 'Reparation and Retribution: Reconcilable?', in Von Hirsch A and Ashworth A (eds), *Principled Sentencing*, p337

What is reparative justice?

'Reparation' is not synonymous with restitution, still less does it suggest a straightforward importation of civil into criminal law. Reparation should properly connote a wider set of aims. It involves more than 'making good' the damage done to property, body or psyche. It must also entail recognition of the harm done to the social relationship between offender and victim, and the damage done to the victim's social rights in his or her property or person. According to Davis, reparation 'should not be seen as residing solely in the offer of restitution; adequate reparation must also include some attempt to make amends for the victim's loss of the presumption of security in his or her rights'. This way of thinking echoes, consciously or not, the concept of 'dominion' developed by Braithwaite and Pettit. For dominion to be restored, what is sought is some evidence of a change in attitude, some expression of remorse that indi-

cates that the victim's rights will be respected in the future. Achieving such a change in attitude may entail the offender agreeing to undergo training, counselling or therapy and, as such, these may all be seen as part of reparative justice. A forced apology or obligatory payment of compensation will not suffice; indeed, it may even be counter-productive in eliciting a genuine change of attitude in the offender. But is 'symbolic reparation' alone sufficient? According to Braithwaite, if reparation is not to come too cheap it must be backed up by material compensation.

Von Hirsch and Ashworth make the point, in relation to restorative justice, that whilst the recognition of the victim is important, this needs to be rationalised in terms of the idea that the crime belongs to the state.

Von Hirsch A and Ashworth A (1998) Introduction to Chapter 7 'Restorative Justice', in Von Hirsch A and Ashworth A (eds), *Principled Sentencing*, p303

This readiness of modern restorative theorists to recognise the wider community's interests in crime should not, however, deflect attention from the question of the nature of the victim's interest. Is it not arguable that one key element in modern states is that the state takes over the responsibility for government and law; that it does so in order to ensure efficiency and consistency, and especially to displace vigilantism and to prevent people from 'taking the law into their own hands'; that therefore the state ought to control adjudication and sentencing; but that its doing so ought not to deprive victims of their right to compensation (as happened for some centuries, and happens in some cases now)? It may be true that one of the driving forces behind modern restorativism is dissatisfaction with the 'conventional' punishment paradigm, as developed in many criminal justice systems. But the question is whether what is wrong is the paradigm or the way in which it has been developed. How convincing are Christie's (1977) arguments that 'conflicts' should be taken back from the state and returned to the victim and her or his community? To what extent does Pettit and Braithwaite's (1993) conception of dominion, in the context of their wider republican theory, imply that the particular victim has an interest going beyond compensation and 'recognition', and do they accept that it is the state's function to decide on the measure and form of 'recognition, recompense and reassurance'?

The criminal justice system makes use of a number of sentences and orders that could be viewed as having restorative elements. The following statutory provisions provide the basis for compensation orders and restitution orders. There are also powers to deprive offenders of property used for the purposes of crime and such property can then be used as a means of providing recompense to the victim.

Powers of Criminal Courts (Sentencing) Act 2000, ss130–134, 143, 145 and 148–149

Section 130
Compensation orders against convicted persons

130 (1) A court by or before which a person is convicted of an offence, instead of or in addition to dealing with him in any other way, may, on application or otherwise, make an order (in this Act referred to as a 'compensation order') requiring him –

(a) to pay compensation for any personal injury, loss or damage resulting from that offence or any other offence which is taken into consideration by the court in determining sentence; or

(b) to make payments for funeral expenses or bereavement in respect of a death resulting from any such offence, other than a death due to an accident arising out

of the presence of a motor vehicle on a road;

but this is subject to the following provisions of this section and to section 131 below.

(2) Where the person is convicted of an offence the sentence for which is fixed by law or falls to be imposed under section 109(2), 110(2) or 111(2) above, subsection (1) above shall have effect as if the words 'instead of or' were omitted.

(3) A court shall give reasons, on passing sentence, if it does not make a compensation order in a case where this section empowers it to do so.

(4) Compensation under subsection (1) above shall be of such amount as the court considers appropriate, having regard to any evidence and to any representations that are made by or on behalf of the accused or the prosecutor.

(5) In the case of an offence under the Theft Act 1968, where the property in question is recovered, any damage to the property occurring while it was out of the owner's possession shall be treated for the purposes of subsection (1) above as having resulted from the offence, however and by whomever the damage was caused.

(6) A compensation order may only be made in respect of injury, loss or damage (other than loss suffered by a person's dependants in consequence of his death) which was due to an accident arising out of the presence of a motor vehicle on a road, if –

(a) it is in respect of damage which is treated by subsection (5) above as resulting from an offence under the Theft Act 1968; or

(b) it is in respect of injury, loss or damage as respects which –

(i) the offender is uninsured in relation to the use of the vehicle; and

(ii) compensation is not payable under any arrangements to which the Secretary of State is a party.

(7) Where a compensation order is made in

respect of injury, loss or damage due to an accident arising out of the presence of a motor vehicle on a road, the amount to be paid may include an amount representing the whole or part of any loss of or reduction in preferential rates of insurance attributable to the accident.

(8) A vehicle the use of which is exempted from insurance by section 144 of the Road Traffic Act 1988 is not uninsured for the purposes of subsection (6) above.

(9) A compensation order in respect of funeral expenses may be made for the benefit of anyone who incurred the expenses.

(10) A compensation order in respect of bereavement may be made only for the benefit of a person for whose benefit a claim for damages for bereavement could be made under section 1A of the Fatal Accidents Act 1976; and the amount of compensation in respect of bereavement shall not exceed the amount for the time being specified in section 1A(3) of that Act.

(11) In determining whether to make a compensation order against any person, and in determining the amount to be paid by any person under such an order, the court shall have regard to his means so far as they appear or are known to the court.

(12) Where the court considers –

(a) that it would be appropriate both to impose a fine and to make a compensation order, but

(b) that the offender has insufficient means to pay both an appropriate fine and appropriate compensation, the court shall give preference to compensation (though it may impose a fine as well).

Section 131
Limit on amount payable under compensation order of magistrates' court

131 (1) The compensation to be paid under a compensation order made by a magistrates' court in respect of any offence of which the court has convicted the offender shall not exceed £5,000.

(2) The compensation or total compensation to be paid under a compensation order or compensation orders made by a magistrates' court in respect of any offence or offences taken into consideration in determining sentence shall not exceed the difference (if any) between –

(a) the amount or total amount which under subsection (1) above is the maximum for the offence or offences of which the offender has been convicted; and

(b) the amount or total amounts (if any) which are in fact ordered to be paid in respect of that offence or those offences.

Section 132
Compensation orders: appeals etc

132 (1) A person in whose favour a compensation order is made shall not be entitled to receive the amount due to him until (disregarding any power of a court to grant leave to appeal out of time) there is no further possibility of an appeal on which the order could be varied or set aside.

(2) Rules under section 144 of the Magistrates' Courts Act 1980 may make provision regarding the way in which the magistrates' court for the time being having functions (by virtue of section 41(1) of the Administration of Justice Act 1970) in relation to the enforcement of a compensation order is to deal with money paid in satisfaction of the order where the entitlement of the person in whose favour it was made is suspended.

(3) The Court of Appeal may by order annul or vary any compensation order made by the court of trial, although the conviction is not quashed; and the order, if annulled, shall not take effect and, if varied, shall take effect as varied.

(4) Where the House of Lords restores a conviction, it may make any compensation order which the court of trial could have made.

(5) Where a compensation order has been made against any person in respect of an

offence taken into consideration in determining his sentence –

(a) the order shall cease to have effect if he successfully appeals against his conviction of the offence or, if more than one, all the offences, of which he was convicted in the proceedings in which the order was made;

(b) he may appeal against the order as if it were part of the sentence imposed in respect of the offence or, if more than one, any of the offences, of which he was so convicted.

Section 133
Review of compensation orders

133 (1) The magistrates' court for the time being having functions in relation to the enforcement of a compensation order (in this section referred to as 'the appropriate court') may, on the application of the person against whom the compensation order was made, discharge the order or reduce the amount which remains to be paid; but this is subject to subsections (2) to (4) below.

(2) The appropriate court may exercise a power conferred by subsection (1) above only –

(a) at a time when (disregarding any power of a court to grant leave to appeal out of time) there is no further possibility of an appeal on which the compensation order could be varied or set aside; and

(b) at a time before the person against whom the compensation order was made has paid into court the whole of the compensation which the order requires him to pay.

(3) The appropriate court may exercise a power conferred by subsection (1) above only if it appears to the court –

(a) that the injury, loss or damage in respect of which the compensation order was made has been held in civil proceedings to be less than it was taken to be for the purposes of the order; or

(b) in the case of a compensation order in respect of the loss of any property, that the property has been recovered by the person in whose favour the order was made; or

(c) that the means of the person against whom the compensation order was made are insufficient to satisfy in full both the order and a confiscation order under Part VI of the Criminal Justice Act 1988 made against him in the same proceedings; or

(d) that the person against whom the compensation order was made has suffered a substantial reduction in his means which was unexpected at the time when the order was made, and that his means seem unlikely to increase for a considerable period.

(4) Where the compensation order was made by the Crown Court, the appropriate court shall not exercise any power conferred by subsection (1) above in a case where it is satisfied as mentioned in paragraph (c) or (d) of subsection (3) above unless it has first obtained the consent of the Crown Court.

(5) Where a compensation order has been made on appeal, for the purposes of subsection (4) above it shall be deemed –

(a) if it was made on an appeal brought from a magistrates' court, to have been made by that magistrates' court;

(b) if it was made on an appeal brought from the Crown Court or from the criminal division of the Court of Appeal, to have been made by the Crown Court.

Section 134
Effect of compensation order on subsequent award of damages in civil proceedings

134 (1) This section shall have effect where a compensation order, or a service compensation order or award, has been made in favour of any person in respect of any injury, loss or damage and a claim by him in civil proceedings for damages in respect of the injury, loss or damage subsequently falls to be determined.

(2) The damages in the civil proceedings shall be assessed without regard to the order or award, but the plaintiff may only recover an amount equal to the aggregate of the following –

(a) any amount by which they exceed the compensation; and

(b) a sum equal to any portion of the compensation which he fails to recover, and may not enforce the judgment, so far as it relates to a sum such as is mentioned in paragraph (b) above, without the leave of the court.

(3) In this section a 'service compensation order or award' means –

(a) an order requiring the payment of compensation under paragraph 11 of Schedule 5A to the Army Act 1955, of Schedule 5A to the Air Force Act 1955 or of Schedule 4A to the Naval Discipline Act 1957; or

(b) an award of stoppages payable by way of compensation under any of those Acts.

PART VII: FURTHER POWERS OF COURTS
Section 143
Powers to deprive offender of property used etc for purposes of crime

143 (1) Where a person is convicted of an offence and the court by or before which he is convicted is satisfied that any property which has been lawfully seized from him, or which was in his possession or under his control at the time when he was apprehended for the offence or when a summons in respect of it was issued –

(a) has been used for the purpose of committing, or facilitating the commission of, any offence, or

(b) was intended by him to be used for that purpose, the court may (subject to subsection (5) below) make an order under this section in respect of that property.

(2) Where a person is convicted of an offence and the offence, or an offence which the court has taken into consideration in determining his sentence, consists of unlawful possession of property which –

(a) has been lawfully seized from him, or

(b) was in his possession or under his control at the time when he was apprehended for the offence of which he has been convicted or when a summons in respect of that offence was issued, the court may (subject to subsection (5) below) make an order under this section in respect of that property.

(3) An order under this section shall operate to deprive the offender of his rights, if any, in the property to which it relates, and the property shall (if not already in their possession) be taken into the possession of the police.

(4) Any power conferred on a court by subsection (1) or (2) above may be exercised –

(a) whether or not the court also deals with the offender in any other way in respect of the offence of which he has been convicted; and

(b) without regard to any restrictions on forfeiture in any enactment contained in an Act passed before 29 July 1988.

(5) In considering whether to make an order under this section in respect of any property, a court shall have regard –

(a) to the value of the property; and

(b) to the likely financial and other effects on the offender of the making of the order (taken together with any other order that the court contemplates making).

(6) Where a person commits an offence to which this subsection applies by –

(a) driving, attempting to drive, or being in charge of a vehicle, or

(b) failing to comply with a requirement made under section 7 of the Road Traffic Act 1988 (failure to provide specimen for analysis or laboratory test) in the course of an investigation into whether the offender had committed an offence while driving, attempting to drive or being in charge of a vehicle, or

(c) failing, as the driver of a vehicle, to comply with subsection (2) or (3) of section 170 of the Road Traffic Act 1988 (duty to stop and give information or report accident), the vehicle shall be regarded for the purposes of subsection (1) above (and section 144(1)(b) below) as used for the purpose of committing the offence (and for the purpose of committing any offence of aiding, abetting, counselling or procuring the commission of the offence).

(7) Subsection (6) above applies to –

(a) an offence under the Road Traffic Act 1988 which is punishable with imprisonment;

(b) an offence of manslaughter; and

(c) an offence under section 35 of the Offences Against the Person Act 1861 (wanton and furious driving).

(8) Facilitating the commission of an offence shall be taken for the purposes of subsection (1) above to include the taking of any steps after it has been committed for the purpose of disposing of any property to which it relates or of avoiding apprehension or detection.

Section 145
Application of proceeds of forfeited property

145 (1) Where a court makes an order under section 143 above in a case where –

(a) the offender has been convicted of an offence which has resulted in a person suffering personal injury, loss or damage, or

(b) any such offence is taken into consideration by the court in determining sentence,

the court may also make an order that any proceeds which arise from the disposal of the property and which do not exceed a sum specified by the court shall be paid to that person.

(2) The court may make an order under this section only if it is satisfied that but for the inadequacy of the offender's means it would

have made a compensation order under which the offender would have been required to pay compensation of an amount not less than the specified amount.

(3) An order under this section has no effect –

(a) before the end of the period specified in section 144(1)(a) above; or

(b) if a successful application under section 1(1) of the Police (Property) Act 1897 has been made.

Section 148
Restitution orders

148 (1) This section applies where goods have been stolen, and either –

(a) a person is convicted of any offence with reference to the theft (whether or not the stealing is the gist of his offence); or

(b) a person is convicted of any other offence, but such an offence as is mentioned in paragraph (a) above is taken into consideration in determining his sentence.

(2) Where this section applies, the court by or before which the offender is convicted may on the conviction (whether or not the passing of sentence is in other respects deferred) exercise any of the following powers –

(a) the court may order anyone having possession or control of the stolen goods to restore them to any person entitled to recover them from him; or

(b) on the application of a person entitled to recover from the person convicted any other goods directly or indirectly representing the stolen goods (as being the proceeds of any disposal or realisation of the whole or part of them or of goods so representing them), the court may order those other goods to be delivered or transferred to the applicant; or

(c) the court may order that a sum not exceeding the value of the stolen goods shall be paid, out of any money of the person convicted which was taken out of his possession on his apprehension, to any person who, if those goods were in the possession of the person convicted, would be entitled to recover them from him;

and in this subsection 'the stolen goods' means the goods referred to in subsection (1) above.

(3) Where the court has power on a person's conviction to make an order against him both under paragraph (b) and under paragraph (c) of subsection (2) above with reference to the stealing of the same goods, the court may make orders under both paragraphs provided that the person in whose favour the orders are made does not thereby recover more than the value of those goods.

(4) Where the court on a person's conviction makes an order under subsection (2)(a) above for the restoration of any goods, and it appears to the court that the person convicted –

(a) has sold the goods to a person acting in good faith, or

(b) has borrowed money on the security of them from a person so acting, the court may order that there shall be paid to the purchaser or lender, out of any money of the person convicted which was taken out of his possession on his apprehension, a sum not exceeding the amount paid for the purchase by the purchaser or, as the case may be, the amount owed to the lender in respect of the loan.

(5) The court shall not exercise the powers conferred by this section unless in the opinion of the court the relevant facts sufficiently appear from evidence given at the trial or the available documents, together with admissions made by or on behalf of any person in connection with any proposed exercise of the powers.

(6) In subsection (5) above 'the available documents' means –

(a) any written statements or admissions which were made for use, and would have been admissible, as evidence at the trial; and

(b) such written statements, depositions and other documents as were tendered by or on behalf of the prosecutor at any committal proceedings.

(7) Any order under this section shall be treated as an order for the restitution of property within the meaning of section 30 of the Criminal Appeal Act 1968 (which relates to the effect on such orders of appeals).

(8) Subject to subsection (9) below, references in this section to stealing shall be construed in accordance with section 1(1) of the Theft Act 1968 (read with the provisions of that Act relating to the construction of section 1(1)).

(9) Subsections (1) and (4) of section 24 of that Act (interpretation of certain provisions) shall also apply in relation to this section as they apply in relation to the provisions of that Act relating to goods which have been stolen.

(10) In this section and section 149 below, 'goods', except in so far as the context otherwise requires, includes money and every other description of property (within the meaning of the Theft Act 1968) except land, and includes things severed from the land by stealing.

(11) An order may be made under this section in respect of money owed by the Crown.

Section 149
Restitution orders: supplementary

149 (1) The following provisions of this section shall have effect with respect to section 148 above.

(2) The powers conferred by subsections (2) (c) and (4) of that section shall be exercisable without any application being made in that behalf or on the application of any person appearing to the court to be interested in the property concerned.

(3) Where an order is made under that section against any person in respect of an offence taken into consideration in determining his sentence –

(a) the order shall cease to have effect if he successfully appeals against his conviction of the offence or, if more than one, all the offences, of which he was convicted in the proceedings in which the order was made;

(b) he may appeal against the order as if it were part of the sentence imposed in respect of the offence or, if more than one, any of the offences, of which he was so convicted.

(4) Any order under that section made by a magistrates' court shall be suspended –

(a) in any case until the end of the period for the time being prescribed by law for the giving of notice of appeal against a decision of a magistrates' court;

(b) where notice of appeal is given within the period so prescribed, until the determination of the appeal; but this subsection shall not apply where the order is made under section 148(2)(a) or (b) and the court so directs, being of the opinion that the title to the goods to be restored or, as the case may be, delivered or transferred under the order is not in dispute.

A number of different forms of diversion are explored in this article and the extract provides an account of two contrasting forms of diversion in the United Kingdom, these being the Juvenile Liasion Bureaus and Adult Reparation Bureaus.

Hughes G, Pilkington A and Leisten R (1998) 'Diversion in a Culture of Severity', *Howard Journal*, pp19–20

The key aims of the Juvenile Liasion Bureau throughout the decade of the 1980s were as follows:

1. To divert young people where possible from penal and welfare intervention systems into informal networks of control, support and care;
2. to avoid the imposition of those forms of penalties and welfare intervention which

tend to aggravate the very problem they seek to reduce;
3. to enable agencies to respond to delinquent behaviour in ways which may reduce offending and enable young people to become more responsible adults;
4. to encourage normal institutions of society to respond constructively to adolescent behaviour. ...

The Adult Reparation Bureau was based in Kettering between 1986 and 1991 and then expanded to the county from 1991 to 1993. The Adult Reparation Bureau dealt with adult offenders who were referred to it from the police. It had six formal aims, namely:

1. to facilitate offenders undertaking reparation work relating to their offences;
2. to divert offenders from the formal criminal justice system where alternative forms of resolution are available and considered beneficial;
3. to facilitate offenders apologising to victims and facing up to the consequences of their offences;
4. to facilitate victims of crime having the means to receive reparation from offenders;
5. to facilitate victims of crime being able to meet offenders to help them overcome the adverse effects of their experiences as victims;
6. to provide an opportunity for post-court disposal.

The use of reintegrative ideas in Auckland which are derived from Maori practices are explored by Braithwaite and Mugford. The ideas are not presented as a criminological utopia, because that is an unattainable dream, but rather as an alternative that seems to offer some attractive prospects.

Braithwaite J and Mugford S (1994) 'Conditions of Successful Reintegration Ceremonies', *British Journal of Criminology*, p168

There are no criminal justice utopias to be

found, just better and worse directions to head in. The New Zealand Maori have shown a direction for making reintegration ceremonies work in multicultural metropolises such as Auckland, a city that faces deeper problems of recession, homelessness, and gang violence than many cities in Western Europe. Implementation of these ideas by the white New Zealand authorities has been riddled with imperfection, re-professionalisation, patriarchy, ritualistic proceduralism that loses sight of objectives, and inappropriate net-widening. The important thing, however, is that the general direction of change is away from these pathologies; it is deprofessionalising, empowering of women, oriented to flexible community problem-solving and, for the most part, narrowing nets of state control. Most critically, it shows that the conditions of successful reintegration ceremonies that criminologists identify when in high theory mode can be given practical content for implementation by police and citizens.

As both Max Scheler and Garfinkel point out: 'There is no society that does not provide in the very features of its organisation the conditions sufficient for inducing shame.' (Garfinkel 1956: 420). The question is what sort of balance societies will have between degradation ceremonies as a 'secular form of communion' and reintegration ceremonies as a rather different communion. Garfinkel showed that there was a practical programme of communication tactics that will get the work of status degradation done. We hope to have shown that equally there is a practical programme of communication tactics that can accomplish reintegration.

This extract provides data in relation to the experiences of victims in family group conferences. This procedure was introduced in New Zealand in 1989 and clearly it incorporates aspects of restorative justice. The system is used as a response to crime that has been committed by young people. A meeting would be held at which the following could be present – the young person and members of their family, the victim and a support person for the victim or a representative for the victim, a representative from the police and a mediator who would be an employee of the Department of Social Welfare. A lawyer and a social worker could also participate.

Morris A and Maxwell G (1998) 'Restorative Justice in New Zealand: Family Group Conferences as a Case Study', *Western Criminology Review*, p7

Family group conferences and victims

Victims can also feel involved in conferences by being present at the conference. Though our research (Maxwell and Morris 1993) indicated that victims attended only about half of the family group conferences, the reasons for this were related primarily to poor practice: they were not invited, the time was unsuitable for them, or they were given inadequate notice of the family group conference. Good practice suggests that victims should be consulted about the time and venue of conferences and informed of them in good time. There will always be a minority of victims who choose not to participate in conferencing, but our research found that only 6 per cent of victims, when asked, said that they did not wish to meet the offender. This is a clear indicator of victims' willingness, indeed desire, to be involved in these processes.

Our research also showed that, when victims were involved in conferencing, many found it a positive process. About 60 per cent of the victims interviewed described the family group conference they attended as helpful, positive, and rewarding. Generally, they said that they were effectively involved in the process and felt better as a result of participating. Victims also commented on two other specific benefits for them. First, it provided them with a voice in determining appropriate outcomes. Second, they were able to meet the offender and the offender's family face-to-face, so that they could assess their attitude, understand better why the offence had occurred, and assess the likelihood of its recurring.

About a quarter of the victims said that they felt worse as a result of attending the family group conference. There were a variety of reasons for this. The most frequent and perhaps the most important was that the victim did not feel that the young person and/or his or her family were truly sorry. Other less common reasons included the inability of the family and young person to make reparation, the victims' inability to express themselves adequately, the difficulty of communicating cross-culturally, a lack of support for them in contrast to the support given to offenders, feeling that their concerns had not been adequately listened to and feeling that other participants were interested in or unsympathetic to them. These findings point again to the need for good practice guidelines. Most of the concerns expressed by victims can be addressed through briefing the participants about what to expect at a conference and training the managers of the process to be effective mediators. The concerns raised were not fundamental objections to conferencing per se.

A youth justice conferencing scheme in Australia was created under the New South Wales Young Offenders Act. In the following piece of research, the views of participants (both offenders and victims) were sought as part of an evaluation of this Australian initiative.

New South Wales Attorney General's Department Bureau of Crime Statistics and Research, Press Release (12 June 2000) *Youth Justice Conferencing*

Both victims and offenders were positive in their views and this can be contrasted with the largely negative response engendered by more traditional versions of criminal justice systems. Youth Justice conferences are an alternative to court for juvenile offenders who have not committed certain kinds of violent offences or certain other serious kinds of crime. Under the scheme, juvenile offenders who plead guilty can elect to go before a Youth justice conference instead of court. At the conference the victim is given an opportunity to explain the impact of the crime. Offenders, on the other hand, are encouraged to provide some form of restoration to the victim. The findings were as follows.

Participants were asked to rate various aspects of the scheme, such as its fairness. The survey responses indicated that:

- at least 87 per cent were either 'quite satisfied' or 'very satisfied' with the arrangements made for them to get to the conference;
- at least 92 per cent stated that they understood what was going on in the conference;
- at least 95 per cent believed that the conference was either 'somewhat fair' or 'very fair' to the offender;
- at least 91 per cent believed that the conference was either 'somewhat fair' or 'very fair' to the victim;
- at least 92 per cent perceived that they had been treated with respect during the conference;
- at least 91 per cent felt that they had had the opportunity to express their views in the conference;
- at least 89 per cent felt that the conference had taken account of what they had said in deciding what should be done;
- at least 78 per cent perceived that the outcome of the conference was 'fair' for the offender;
- at least 89 per cent perceived that the outcome plan was either 'somewhat fair' or 'very fair' for the victim; and,
- at least 79 per cent were satisfied with the way their case had been handled by the justice system.

Examples are provided in the next extract of the variety of different forms of restorative justice that have been developed. The first case is an example of victim-offender mediation in North America. The second example describes a typical conclusion of a family group conference in New Zealand. The third scenario describes a Circle Sentencing conference in Canada, an updated version of the traditional sanctioning and healing practices of Canadian Aboriginal peoples. Finally, the fourth case is from the Reparative Probation Programme as practised in Vermont.

Bazemore G and Griffiths C (1997) *Conferences, Circles, Boards and Mediations*

Case 1 – After approximately two hours of at times heated and emotional dialogue, the mediator felt that the offender and victim had heard each other's story and had learned something important about the impact of the crime and about each other. They had agreed that the offender, a 14 year old, would pay $200 in restitution to cover the cost of damages to the victim's home resulting from a break-in. In addition, he would be required to reimburse the victims for the cost of a VCR he had stolen estimated at $150. A payment schedule would be worked out in the remaining time allowed for the meeting. The offender had also made several apologies to the victim and agreed to complete community service hours working in a food bank sponsored by the victim's church. The victim, a middle-aged neighbour of the offender, said that she felt less angry and fearful after learning more about the offender and the details of the crime and thanked the mediator for allowing the mediation to be held in her church basement.

Case 2 – After the offender, his mother and grandfather, the victim and the local police officer who had made the arrest had spoken about the offence and its impact, the Youth Justice Coordinator asked for any additional input from other members of the group of about 10 citizens assembled in the local school (the group included two of the offender's teachers, two friends of the victim,

and a few others). The coordinator then asked for input into what should be done by the offender to pay back the victim, a teacher who had been injured and had a pair of glasses broken in an altercation with the offender, and pay back the community for the damage caused by his crime. In the remaining half hour of the approximately hour-long conference, the group suggested that restitution to the victim was in order to cover medical expenses and the costs of a new pair of glasses and that community service work on the school grounds would be appropriate.

Case 3 – The victim, the wife of the offender who had admitted to physically abusing her during two recent drunken episodes, spoke about the pain and embarrassment her husband had caused to her and her family. After she had finished, the ceremonial feather (used to signify who would be allowed to speak next) was passed to the next person in the circle, a young man who spoke about the contributions the offender had made to the community, the kindness he had shown toward the elders by sharing fish and game with them and his willingness to help others with home repairs. An elder then took the feather and spoke about the shame the offender's behaviour had caused to his clan— noting than in the old days, he would have been required to pay the woman's family a substantial compensation as a result. Having heard all this, the judge confirmed that the victim still felt that she wanted to try to work it out with her estranged husband and that she was receiving help from her own support group (including a victim's advocate). Summarising the case by again stressing the seriousness of the offence and repeating the Crown Counsel's opening remarks that a jail sentence was required, he then proposed to delay sentencing for six weeks until the time of the next circuit court hearing. If during that time the offender had met the requirements presented earlier by a friend of the offender who had agreed to lead a support group and had met with the community justice committee to work out an alcohol and anger management treatment plan; fulfilled the expectations of the victim and her support group; and completed 40 hours of service to be supervised by the group, he would forgo the jail sentence. After a prayer in which the entire group held hands, the circle disbanded and everyone retreated to the kitchen area of the community centre for refreshments.

Case 4 – The young offender, a 19 year old caught driving with an open can of beer in his pick-up truck, sat nervously awaiting the conclusion of a deliberation of the Reparative Board. He had been sentenced by a judge to reparative probation and did not know whether to expect something tougher or much easier than regular probation. About a half hour earlier prior to retreating for their deliberation, the citizen members of the board had asked the offender several simple and straightforward questions. At 3 pm the chairperson explained the four conditions of the offender's contract: 1) begin work to pay off his traffic tickets; 2) complete a state police defensive driving course 3) undergo an alcohol assessment; and 4) write a three-page paper on how alcohol had negatively affected his life. After the offender had signed the contract, the chairperson adjourned the meeting.

If alternatives to the courts are to be used then it is of course important that there will be procedural protections for all parties concerned. The extract provides a protocol that could be used in relation to meetings between an offender and a victim of the offence.

American Bar Association (1994) *Endorsement of Victim-Offender Mediation/Dialogue Programmes*, pp3–4

Victim-Offender Mediation/Dialogue Programme requirements:

1. Participation in a programme by both the offender and victim must be voluntary.
2. Programme goals are specified in writing

and procedures are established to meet those goals.
3. A plan exists for ongoing evaluation and review of goals and the steps taken to reach such goals.
4. Before participating in such programmes, victims and offenders are appropriately screened on a case-by-case basis, are fully informed orally and in writing about the mediation/dialogue process, procedures and goals, and are specifically told that their participation in the process is voluntary.
5. Refusal to participate in a programme in no way adversely affects an offender, and procedural safeguards are established to ensure that there are no systemic negative repercussions because of an offender's refusal to participate in the programme.
6. A face-to-face meeting is encouraged.
7. When agreements are reached between victims and offenders, which may include restitution, a process is established to monitor and follow up on the agreements reached.
8. The statements made by victims and offenders and documents and other materials produced during the mediation/dialogue process are inadmissible in criminal or civil court proceedings.
9. Properly trained mediator-facilitators are used in the mediation/dialogue process.
10. The programmes are adequately funded and staffed.
11. Mediator-facilitators are selected from a cross-section of the community to ensure that they reflect the diversity of their community in terms of race, ethnicity and gender.
12. Criminal justice professionals and the public are educated about these programmes, and these programmes are fully integrated with other components of the criminal justice system.
13. Participation in a programmes that occurs prior to an adjudication of guilt takes place only with the consent of the prosecutor and with the victim's and offender's informed consent, obtained in writing, or

orally in court. If the offender is represented by an attorney, the offender's consent should be given only after the offender has had the chance to discuss with the attorney the advisability of participating in the victim-offender mediation/dialogue programme. Participation in a programme that occurs after an adjudication of guilt takes place only after notification to the prosecutor and defence attorney, if any.

The following item is the text of the leaflet that is provided for guidance to the victims of crime in England and Wales. It explains the process and the role of the various agencies that could be involved including victim support if required. Details are also provided as regards the various means by which compensation may be obtained.

Home Office (1999) *Victims of Crime*

This leaflet explains what will happen now you have reported a crime to the police. It tells you:

1. what help is available;
2. how the crime will be investigated and what you will need to do to help the police with the investigation;
3. how you may be able to get compensation if you have been injured or if your property has been stolen or damaged;
4. what will happen if you have to go to court;
5. who you can contact for help and advice.

The police

If you need to talk to the police about the crime you should contact the officer dealing with your case or, where there is one, the crime desk. The numbers are:

1. Police force:
2. Police station:
3. Telephone number:
4. Officer dealing with your case:
5. Name:
6. Rank and number:

7. Telephone number of crime desk (where relevant):
8. Date:

Whenever you complain to the police about a criminal offence they make enquiries to try to solve the crime. Wherever possible you should:

1. give them as much information as you can about the offence;
2. tell them if you are worried about your (or your family's) safety so they can give you appropriate advice. If, for instance, you are worried about the suspect being granted bail they will pass your concern to the Crown Prosecution Service;
3. tell the police if you change your address or phone number so that they can tell you if someone has been arrested, charged or cautioned in connection with the offence;
4. tell them of any other changes: for example, you may have noticed further losses or damage since you first reported the offence, or you may be suffering further effects from an injury caused by the crime.

What happens next?

The police will try to catch the criminal but they may not always succeed. If they do have a suspect, there may not be enough evidence to charge the person or, if the suspect is young or mentally disordered, and the offence is not too serious, the police may decide to caution him or her instead. In some cases the suspect may be facing more serious charges for other offences and may be prosecuted for those offences instead. If the police decide to charge someone the case is taken over by the Crown Prosecution Service (CPS), an independent authority which prosecutes in the name of the Queen. They decide whether there is enough evidence to provide a realistic prospect of conviction and whether prosecution would be in the public interest. The CPS does not act directly on behalf of individual victims or represent them in criminal proceedings, but it does carefully consider the interests of victims when deciding where the public interest lies.

The press

The press can play an important role in tackling crime. For the purposes of investigating an offence, catching criminals or for crime prevention, the police may release details of a case to the press. If you are concerned about this happening, tell the police officer dealing with your case.

Going to court

For the reasons mentioned above many cases never reach court. Of those which do the great majority are dealt with by magistrates' courts. The most serious cases have to be sent to the Crown Court for trial by jury.

If your case goes to court and you are needed as a witness:

1. You will be sent a copy of the leaflet *Witness in Court* which will explain what is likely to happen.
2. You should let the police know if there are any days you could not manage to attend court – for instance, because of important job or professional commitments, or because you have a holiday booked. If possible, these dates will then be avoided although there may be times when the case has to go ahead even though this may not be convenient for individual witnesses.
3. The aim is that prosecution witnesses do not have to wait more than two hours before being called to give evidence.
4. Arrangements will be made to provide an interpreter if you are called to give evidence and are unable to give it in English.

If you are not needed as a witness the police will try to keep you informed about hearing dates (there could be several such dates if, for example, cases are delayed or postponed). They will also try to keep you informed of the results of cases.

Compensation

If you have been injured or your property has been damaged or stolen as a result of a crime you may be able to get compensation in a number of different ways. If you think you may qualify for compensation

WRITE DOWN

Any extra expenses that you have had as a result of the offence, for example medical expenses or the cost of repairing or replacing your property.

Any loss of earnings you have suffered.

Any income that you have received as a result of the offence (for example DSS benefits).

KEEP

Any receipts, estimates or other documents about any of these

Compensation from the offender

If someone is caught and convicted the criminal court may order the offender to pay you compensation for any injury, loss or damage which you have suffered because of the offence. You cannot apply for a compensation order yourself so it is important that you tell the police if you would like to receive compensation. You should give them accurate details of your losses with documentary evidence (for example receipts) where possible. The police will then pass this information on to the CPS who will make sure that the court knows about it.

You can be compensated for personal injury; losses because of theft of, or damage to, property; losses because of fraud; loss of earnings while off work; medical expenses; travelling expenses; pain and suffering; loss, damage or injury caused to or by a stolen vehicle. The dependants of a victim who has died (other than as the result of a road traffic incident) may also receive compensation (for example, through the courts or from the Criminal Injuries Compensation Scheme – see further on).

The role of the court

The court has to consider compensation in every appropriate case and decide whether to order an offender to pay compensation, and if so, how much. The court must take account of the offender's circumstances and ability to pay. So if the court does decide to make an order it may not be for the full amount of your loss. If the court decides to make an order against the offender he or she will be required to pay the money to the court who will pass it on to you. If the offender has enough money the compensation will normally be paid in a lump sum. In most cases, however the court will allow time for the offender to pay, or may allow the offender to pay by instalments. It is the job of the court to make sure that the offender pays the compensation. So if you have any questions about the compensation order or the way it will be paid to you, you should contact the clerk of the court. Do not contact the offender direct.

Criminal Injuries Compensation Scheme

If you have been injured because of a crime of violence you can apply for compensation under the Criminal Injuries Compensation Scheme. It does not matter whether the offender has been caught, but there are other rules which will determine whether or not you receive compensation. You can find out more from the leaflet *Victims of Crimes of Violence, a guide to the Criminal Injuries Compensation Scheme* which is available from the police, Victim Support schemes, your Citizens Advice Bureau or from:

The Criminal Injuries Compensation Authority,
Tay House,
300 Bath Street,
Glasgow G2 4JR.

Civil proceedings

Whether or not the offender is convicted in the criminal courts, you can sue him or her for damages in a civil court. You can find out more about this at your Citizens Advice Bureau or by asking a solicitor.

Motor Insurers Bureau

If you suffer injury or loss or damage to property as a result of a road traffic incident, compensation will normally be payable under insurance arrangements. Where the offender is

untraced or uninsured, compensation may be available from:

Motor Insurers' Bureau
152 Silbury Boulevard,
Central Milton Keynes,MK9 1NG.
Tel: 0908 830001.

If you should succeed in getting compensation in two or more ways, for example from a criminal court and through the Criminal Injuries Compensation Scheme or the Motor Insurers' Bureau, the award may be reduced to avoid double payment. You can't get compensation twice for the same thing from public funds.

Check-list for action

If you report a crime to the police you can expect:

1. the police to investigate the crime;
2. in most cases, to be contacted by Victim Support – unless you ask the police not to pass on your details;
3. to be told by the police if someone is charged with, or cautioned for, the offence;
4. if you are needed as a witness, to be given the Witness in Court leaflet, and told the date of the trial;
5. if the case goes to court, consideration to be given to making a compensation order in your favour;
6. to be told the results of the court case;
7. to be given advice about applying for compensation from the Criminal Injuries Compensation Authority; and
8. to be given crime prevention advice by the police if you ask for it.

To help make this possible, you should:

1. report the crime to the police promptly;
2. give the police full details of your injury or loss;
3. tell the police if you want compensation;
4. tell the police if you fear for your (or your family's) safety;
5. tell the police if you do not want them to tell Victim Support or the press;
6. tell the police of any change of address while the case remains unresolved; and

7. contact Victim Support directly if you want to.

Protecting yourself against crime
There may be things which you can do to reduce the risk of becoming a victim of crime again. The police are able to offer you crime prevention advice. Ask your local police about this.

You may also find useful the Home Office crime prevention guide, *Your Practical Guide to Crime Prevention*. It gives details of simple precautions which you can take to protect yourself, your family and your property. Copies are available from your local police station. They can also be obtained from the Home Office, Crack Crime, PO Box 999, Sudbury, Suffolk CO10 6FS. It is also available on audio tape and in Arabic, Bengali, Chinese, Gujarati, Hindi, Punjabi, Urdu and Welsh. If there is a local Neighbourhood Watch scheme, you may want to join it. If there is no scheme in your area you might want to talk to your local crime prevention officer about starting one – there may be other people in your area who would be interested.

Remember
If you are not sure about anything mentioned in this leaflet, ask your local police for advice. Victim Support are also willing to help whenever they can.

Further help
VICTIM SUPPORT SCHEMES
You may be feeling shocked, sad, distressed, or angry, following the crime you have just reported. These feelings are common. Victim Support volunteers are specially trained to help you through this experience and to provide you with practical help and information. The police *automatically* tell Victim Support about all cases of burglary, theft, criminal damage, arson, assault (other than domestic violence), and racial harassment. If you don't want this to happen, tell the police officer dealing with your case. If you have suffered other violent crimes (including sexual crimes or domestic violence), you will be asked if you wish to be referred to Victim Support. You can contact them yourself at a later date if you prefer. Because resources are limited, victims whose cars are stolen or vandalised will not normally be referred to Victim Support. If you need help, tell the police officer in your case or contact Victim Support direct.

Flood-Page C and Mackie A (1998)
Sentencing during the Nineties

Research was conducted on 3,000 cases heard at 25 magistrates courts in 1994–1995 and also 1,800 cases at 18 Crown court centres so as to reveal how the Criminal Justice Act 1991 was operating. The Act gave more emphasis to the offence and less to the offender. It lays down basic rules for the use of custody, community sentences, fines and discharges. Information for the study was gathered through court observation, from court records and from interviews with magistrates and justices' clerks. The following were the most important of the findings:

a) offenders who pleaded guilty had their sentences reduced by around a third at the Crown Court;
b) women were less likely than men to receive a prison sentence when other factors were taken into account and were also less likely to be fined;
c) magistrates were enthusiastic about combination orders and liked being able to tailor probation orders to the offender's circumstances;
d) offenders in breach of a court order or with previous convictions were more likely to get custody;
e) stipendary magistrates sentenced a higher proportion of offenders to custody than lay magistrates after allowing for other factors;
f) there was no evidence that black or Asian offenders were more or less likely than whites to receive a custodial sentence

when other factors were taken into account.

Home Office (2001) *Criminal Justice: The Way Ahead*, pp41–48

A new sentencing philosophy

Judges, magistrates, court staff and the prison and probation services invest huge skill and effort in sentencing and then supervising offenders. But the current framework, set by the Criminal Justice Act 1991, does not always assist them in preventing reoffending. Of those sentenced to custody or community penalties 56 per cent are reconvicted within two years. The current sentencing framework is too narrowly focused on the specific offence for which the offender is before the court – though this may be just the latest in a series of similar crimes. Since the 100,000 most persistent offenders account for about half of all crime, we need greater consistency, with a presumption that repeat offending will lead to more severe punishment. The present framework does not do enough to tackle re-offending: sentencers do not get routine feedback about the effectiveness of different punishments which they have handed down, so they have little evidence of what works to tackle offending nor if whether their judgment about an offender's future behaviour have been borne out by events. Currently, only prisoners serving longer sentences are supervised following their release. Resettlement in the community, which can help to reduce reoffending, should be given more priority, especially for short sentence prisoners. The procedures available today for enforcement and 'sentence management' are complex, inefficient and insufficiently effective. We are still well below consistent enforcement for breaches of community sentences or non-payment of fines. There is a sharp division of roles between sentencers, who confine themselves to the immediate offences and surrounding circumstances, and the prison and probation services who implement sentences passed. There is no requirement to work collectively

in managing the sentences as a whole, nor to take account of the offender's progress during sentence. And for offenders on community sentences, there is little incentive to work to address their offending behaviour. Finally, the current sentencing framework is not transparent to the victim and society about the reasons for different sentences or their actual content. This can also fuel a perception of racial bias in the system. Nor does the existing framework do enough to encourage reparation to the individual victim or the community.

To respond to these problems the Government has commissioned a major review of our sentencing framework that is expected to report in May 2001. The review still has work to do. Already, however, what is emerging is:

1. A new sentencing philosophy based on the offender not just the offence, which pays more attention to sentence outcomes such as crime reduction and reparation.
2. A clear presumption that the severity of punishment should increase for persistent offenders. Since 100,000 most persistent offenders commit almost half of crime, recent and relevant previous convictions should lead to more intensive penalties – and persistent offenders should know this.
3. A new armoury of non-custodial and custodial sentences based on continuous assessment of needs and risks to prevent re-offending.
4. More rigorous sentence implementation and enforcement and fast, effective means of sending back to custody, where appropriate, offenders who break their conditions.

In the recent reforms of the youth justice system, the emphasis on a single outcome – preventing offending – has helped focus minds and effort. The Government wants to extend this emphasis on outcomes to the wider sentencing arena. We also want to make it plain to offenders that the onus is on them to change their ways – they will be offered help and incentives to tackle the problems underlying their offending, but strict enforcement and sanctions will follow if they fail. As it considers the outcome of the sentencing review, the Government will pursue three key objectives:

1. A focus on high risk, high rate offenders, with intensive criminal justice supervision throughout the entire duration of their sentences.
2. Tackling the underlying causes of criminal behaviour through and during sentence, based on 'what works for whom'.
3. Maximum transparency to the public, victims and witnesses about the content of sentences.

More flexible and effective community sentences

In terms of more flexible and effective community sentences, the new National Probation Service will be focused on delivering a five per cent reduction in re-convictions by people under its supervision – by putting 30,000 offenders through programmes by 2004 it is estimated 200,000 offences might be avoided every year. As well as improving probation performance, the Government wants to give courts a more effective choice of community penalties. The Government is therefore considering introducing a more flexible community sentence. This would provide courts with a menu of options to choose from, providing elements of punishment, crime reduction and reparation, to fit both the offender and the offence. Courts would also have the power to make offenders come back to court at specified intervals to report on the progress they were making on their community sentences. For example, an offender might be ordered to stay off drugs and undergo regular drug tests. If the offender failed to comply with the drug testing requirements, testing intensity might be increased. If the offender was drug free, the frequency of test might be reduced. The DTTO provides a good model of the type of community sentence the Government wants to adopt more widely:

1. It is linked to the causes of offending, requiring the offender to deal with those causes.
2. It gives probation officers and the courts effective sanctions for breach.
3. It gives courts feedback on how the sentence is working.

More effective short prison sentences

Each year the Prison Service discharges about 90,000 prisoners into the community. Of these in 1999 over 42,000 adult males (47 per cent of total discharges) and around 4,000 adult female prisoners (four per cent of total discharges) were sentenced to prison terms of less than 12 months and so would under the current sentencing framework have received no follow up supervision after their release (although all released young prisoners get a minimum of three months supervision post-release). And few of these short sentence prisoners will have had the opportunity of rehabilitation programmes whilst in custody. The Government wishes to improve the supervision and support of short sentence prisoners after their release from prison. Starting from the general principle that in future every offender released from prison who needs it should have follow up support or supervision, the Government thinks that a new 'Custody Plus' sentence might be more effective than the existing short prison sentences, and in the long run, by reducing conviction rates, more cost effective too. Custody Plus would consist of a fixed period in prison, followed by a further period under an enforced programme in the community. Those breaching the conditions of the community element of the sentence would automatically be returned to prison to serve out the remainder of their sentence. A similar split custody and community sentence for young offenders – the Detention and Training Order – has been in operation since April 2000 and appears to be an effective way of combating re-offending behaviour.

Providing more intense punishment for persistent offenders

It is seen as desirable that the courts must be empowered to get to grips with persistent offending and its causes – since the most persistent offenders commit such a large proportion of crime. The sentencing framework should make it clear to prolific offenders that if they persist in their crimes, they will face increasingly more severe punishment. For example, under the current framework for motoring offences, penalty points are accumulated until an individual loses his or her driving licence. A different and more sophisticated system would clearly be needed to sentence a non-motoring offender and achieve a just outcome in the light of the circumstances of the case. The Government will explore ways of achieving the desired result – predictably more severe sentences for persistent offenders with recent and relevant previous convictions.

We will ensure that sentences are rigorously supervised and enforced

Improving the sentencing options available to the court is merely the starting point of creating a framework for punishment and rehabilitation that works. Sentences must be completed in the way intended, requiring proper supervision and rigorous enforcement. The current framework for enforcing community sentences is cumbersome and ineffective. There are often significant delays in getting offenders back to court if they breach the conditions of their sentence and only a limited range of punishments for breach. Over the past four years the prison and probation services – with the Youth Justice Board, YOTs, the police, the Parole Board and electronic monitoring contractors – have been developing a more robust and seamless approach to sentence supervision. This is yielding positive results:

1. The correct enforcement of breach procedures for community sentences has improved significantly.
2. A joint prison-probation system for assessing offenders (OASys) has been developed. The aim is to have a common, evidence-based approach to the assessment of offenders underpinning work to manage and reduce risks to the public.
3. The new Detention and Training Order is ensuring a seamless transition from custody to planned release and community supervision for young offenders.
4. Home Detention Curfew has allowed a more controlled return to the community for many short or medium term prisoners. Through electronic monitoring, curfew conditions have been enforced rigorously and speedily – and offenders promptly returned to prison if they breach the conditions.

We have also reformed the system for execution of warrants to bring defaulting offenders (both for community sentences and financial orders) back before the courts. In the past this has been a low priority for the police. We have now transferred lead responsibility to the courts themselves, who will employ their own enforcement staff or contract out the function to approved agencies. We will set rigorous targets to ensure that defaulters are dealt with rapidly. Powers in the Criminal Justice and Court Services Act 2000 provide tougher enforcement for breaches of community sentences. When an offender is returned to court following a breach, the courts will have to consider whether it is likely the offender will comply with the order if it remains in force. If not – other than in exceptional circumstances – the court must impose a prison sentence. The Government has provided the resources needed to make rigorous enforcement of community sentences a reality. The Probation Service will be able to take on 1,450 new probation officers and 3,000 other staff over the next three years and we are funding an additional 2,660 prison places. Financial orders, too, will be enforced rigorously. It is our intention that everyone who can pay, will pay their fine or compensation order. A new system for tracing defaulters' addresses will be introduced from April 2001. We will establish a countrywide programme of improvement in enforcement methods, based on proven successes and bring forward proposals for rationalising and streamlining the existing powers and structures. Rigorous enforcement is crucial to demonstrate to offenders and the public that the courts' order cannot be evaded with impunity. Enforcement also matters to ensure that sentences have their desired effect in reducing crime. Specialist *review hearings* in courts might help to improve enforcement – giving sentencers a greater active role in overseeing sentences, to tailor them to the response of the individual offender. Offenders' own behaviour might determine in part whether their sentence gets more or less intense – the review hearings would take account of progress in varying the level of intensity of supervision.

A review hearing might:

1. Review progress on community sentences.
2. If a community sentence were breached, increase the intensity of supervision – within limits set by the original sentencing court – or re-sentence the offender to custody, if appropriate.
3. Reduce the intensity of a community sentence or supervision – within limits set by the original sentencing court – in response to good progress.
4. Hear appeals against recall to prison.
5. Re-sentence for non-payment of fines.

Some review hearings might focus on certain categories of offence, for example drug hearings or domestic violence, requiring further specialisation. Sentence reviewers would need to develop close working links with the prison and probation services.

Making prison work
Custodial sentences are an essential sanction for the courts. But custodial sentences should not only be there as a punishment and incapacitation but also should help prisoners to lead law-abiding lives after release. To discharge prisoners with the same problems and attitudes as when they went in and with no monitoring of their behaviour afterwards does

little to prevent crime or to turn lives around. So we are investing to make prison work better to prevent re-offending. This requires decent, humane regimes and adequate and appropriate training and employment programmes. Conditions in some prisons are very poor and must be improved. Through the 2000 Spending Review, the Government has provided an additional £689 million for the Prison Service over the next three years. Of this additional funding, some £211 million will be directed to preventing reoffending. The new resources will deliver:

1. An increase in prison capacity by 2,660 places.
2. More prisons drug programmes, reducing the risk of re-offending.
3. More basic educational and vocational training through a new partnership with the DfEE. At present, about three fifths of prisoners have poor literacy skills and two thirds have poor numeracy skills.73 By 2004 we aim to increase by 50 per cent the number of qualifications gained by prisoners while they are inside.
4. A new three-year strategy to prevent suicide and self-harm by prisoners. Prisoners most at risk will be better identified and cared for by better trained and supported staff.
5. A £5 million a year programme at five local prisons and five Young Offender Institutions to improve regimes with a focus on preparing prisoners for work. This is part of a new £30 million Custody to Work programme. As well as improving conditions, the Prison Service is examining the scope for a long-term programme to replace old, run-down and remote prisons with new, purpose-designed and more accessible ones.

Work after release to prevent re-offending
We know that for ex-prisoners, unemployment doubles the chances of reconviction and homelessness increases the likelihood by two and a half times. Almost three-fifths of those

sent to prison are unemployed when sentenced; and up to 90 per cent are estimated to leave prison without a job. About a third of prisoners lose their homes while in prison; two-fifths will be homeless on release. To protect society from further crime from ex-prisoners, it makes sense to invest more time and care in resettling them in the community. The Prison Service is establishing a new £30 million Custody to Work programme to double by 2004 the number of prisoners going into jobs when they leave prison and improve their chance of getting accommodation. The programme will include gearing prison industries and workshops to prepare prisoners more effectively for jobs and working more closely with employers to meet their needs and priorities. We will ensure that prisoners have appropriate documentation when they leave prison to enable them more effectively to take up education, training and employment and access any other help they need. The Social Exclusion Unit is also examining the scope for reducing re-offending by ex-prisoners. It is due to report to the Prime Minister in spring 2001. Already a range of practical issues is emerging, such as:

1. Whether the low levels of financial support for prisoners immediately following release encourage crime.
2. Whether more could be done to suspend housing tenancies upon imprisonment, to prevent prisoners running up substantial rent arrears.
3. Whether better and more systematic links with employers could make prison education and training provision more responsive to the needs of the modern labour market.
4. Whether the present lack of compulsory supervision of short term prisoners has contributed to higher levels of re-offending.

Improving the supervision of longer custodial sentences

The current sentencing framework for longer sentence prisoners is overcomplicated and confusing. Different release conditions apply to sentences under and over four years. For the last quarter of each sentence, an offender receives no supervision at all in the community – no matter how little they may have cooperated whilst in prison. In the light of the findings of the Sentencing Review, the Government will look at ways of ensuring that all offenders are supervised right up to the end of their sentence, and that they complete in the community the work started in prison to prevent re-offending. This might be achieved through review hearings before a prisoner is released on licence, to specify what conditions should be applied after release up to the end of the sentence. The conditions would reflect what was needed to prevent re-offending, in the light of progress made while in custody. Offenders who breached the conditions of their release into the community should be recalled immediately to custody by executive action. They would have a right of appeal – to a review hearing – against this executive recall, but would exercise that right from within prison.

Home Office (2001) *Overview of John Halliday's Report of a Review of the Sentencing Framework for England and Wales, 'Making Punishments Work'*, pp1–5

The Review by John Halliday has examined whether the sentencing framework for England and Wales can be changed to improve results, especially by reducing crime, at justifiable expense.

The review has looked at:

1. the types of sentence that should be available to the courts, with the aim of designing more flexible sentences that work effectively, whether the offender is in prison or in the community;
2. the ways in which sentences are enforced;
3. the systems that govern release from prison;
4. the role of the courts in decision making while the sentence is in force;

5. judicial discretion in sentencing and the guidelines governing its use;
6. the framework of statute law;
7. costs and benefits of the recommendations and the factors critical for successful implementation.

1. The case for change

The report points out that although the present framework has much in its favour, it also has limitations and is problematic. In particular, the unclear and unpredictable approach to persistent offenders, who commit a disproportionate amount of crime, and the fact that prison sentences of less than 12 months have little meaningful impact on criminal behaviour. There are also new opportunities to improve outcomes. The most important of these are the recent advances towards reducing re-offending through work with offenders under sentence, and the prison and probation services' developing ability to work in more integrated ways to that end. There is growing awareness of the contributions that reparation and 'restorative justice' schemes can make. The framework could do more to exploit these developing opportunities, within a clearer sense of common purpose. It could increase public confidence if it was more transparent, accessible and accountable. The report points out that the purposes of sentencing are not only punishment but also crime reduction and reparation. It is therefore important to establish how much sentencing can be expected to contribute to crime reduction.

2. The principles of sentencing

The principle that severity of sentence should be 'proportionate' to the seriousness of criminal conduct and that imprisonment should be reserved for cases in which no other sentence will do remains valid. However, this should take clearer and more predictable account of previous convictions. There should be a new presumption that severity of sentence will increase as a result of any recent and relevant convictions that show a continuing course of criminal conduct. To do this, it is recommended that:

- guidelines will be needed to help sentencers match sentence severity with the seriousness of offences, and to show the ranges within which previous convictions may impact on sentence severity, otherwise the effect of this new presumption on sentencing practice would be unpredictable and disproportionately severe sentences could result;
- sentencing decisions should be structured so that if a prison sentence of 12 months or more were not necessary to meet the needs of punishment, sentencers would consider whether a non-custodial sentence would meet the needs of crime reduction, punishment and reparation.

Consistency in sentencing should be a continuing goal measured by uniformity of approach rather than of outcomes. The transparency of the framework and understanding among the public of how it is supposed to work should be improved.

3. Short sentences

One of the most serious failures of the present system is seen in prison sentences of under 12 months. The report points out that only half of this time is served, less with a home detention curfew, and the remainder is not subject to any conditions. The Prison Service has little opportunity to tackle criminal behaviour as the time served in custody is so limited – yet these sentences are used for large numbers of persistent offenders who are likely to re-offend. A structured framework is needed for the large number of offenders who persist in the type of criminality that does not require longer prison sentences. Under a new sentence of 'custody plus', this could be done by requiring those who serve short prison sentences to undertake supervised programmes after release, under conditions, which – if breached – could result in swift return to custody. The initial period in custody could be between two weeks and three months, and the period of supervision could last between (a minimum) of six months and whatever would take the sentence as whole to less than 12 months. Such a sentence would be potentially more punitive in its effect on offenders who breached their conditions than any existing prison sentence of under 12 months. For those small numbers of offenders for whom post custody supervision is not needed, a sentence of ordinary custody, of up to three months, would be available. All short-term prison sentences would then mean what they said, in terms of time served.

4. Prison sentences of 12 months or more

At present half of an existing prison sentence of 12 months or more has to be served in custody, at which point the prisoner is released on licence (except for earlier releases under home detention curfew). If the sentence is over four years, release has to be authorised by the Parole Board and can be delayed until two thirds of the way through the sentence. Prisoners released from these sentences are subject to conditions until three-quarters of the sentence has passed. At this point the offender is free of conditions, although the remaining part of the sentence can be re-activated on conviction of a further offence. Special provisions apply to violent and sexual offenders, for whom supervision can be extended.

Under the proposals, the supervisory period would run until the end of the total sentence, making these sentences more 'real' and increasing opportunities for crime reduction through work with offenders in the second half. To achieve these goals, all sentences of 12 months or more should be served in full, half in custody and half in the community, the second half being subject to conditions whose breach could result in recall to prison. Before an offender is released, the prison and probation services should design a package of measures required of the offender after release. The conditions would be geared to public protection, rehabilitation and resettlement and would run until the end of the sentence. The package would be subject to review in a criminal court before release. Discretionary release would be reserved for 'dangerous' offenders (convicted of specified violent or sexual offences) likely to re-offend and/or to cause serious harm. For these offenders there would be a special sentence, with release during the second half at the discretion of the Parole Board. In addition, the court could order an extended period of supervision of up to 10 years for sexual offences and five years for violent offences. Instead of the existing discretionary early release scheme (home detention curfew), it would be possible to include curfews and electronic monitoring in post-release conditions for all custodial sentences.

5. Intermediate sanctions

Two new sentences were examined by John Halliday's report. One was 'intermittent custody' to allow the offender to spend part of a custodial sentence out of prison. The other, 'suspended sentence plus', would combine a community sentence with a suspended sentence of imprisonment, which could be activated if the offender failed to comply with the conditions of the non-custodial sentence. The Prison Service believes, with its existing establishments, it would be unable to manage a sentence of intermittent custody, other than through release on temporary licence schemes, which it already operates. Those schemes are important in resettlement, but are not a real alternative to a new sentence incorporating temporary release from the outset. The Prison Service should consider how the prison estate could accommodate intermittent forms of custody for certain offenders, in prison close to their communities. In parallel, a review of hostels, probation and attendance centres could help optimise the use of such facilities, strengthening the possibilities for 'containment in the community' in a non-custodial sentence. In looking at suspended sentences, no grounds were found for removing the current restrictions on their use. When a prison sentence has to be passed, suspending it entirely, as long as another conviction is not received, should continue to be possible only in exceptional circumstances. For imprisonable offences, when a non-custodial sentence is passed, there would be benefit in making clear to offenders the 'conditional' nature of the sentence – if the offender does not comply to agreed conditions, a custodial sentence may be passed instead. The sentencing court should be able to indicate a starting point for any such custodial sentence.

6. Non-custodial sentences

To ensure that a non-custodial sentence reduces the likelihood of re-offending, courts should have the power to impose a single, non-custodial penalty made up of specific elements – which would replace all existing community sentences. These elements would include:

- treatment for substance abuse or mental illness;
- curfew and exclusion orders;
- electronic monitoring;
- reparation to victims and communities;
- compulsory work;
- attendance at offending behaviour programmes.

Supervision in all cases would be geared towards managing and enforcing the sentence, and supporting resettlement. The court would consider the aims of punishment, reparation and prevention of re-offending in deciding on the elements of the sentence. The 'punitive weight' should reflect the seriousness of offences, subject to any increased severity required for previous convictions. Under the new framework:

- financial penalties would be available at all levels of seriousness, both in isolation and in combination with non-custodial penalties;
- a new interim review order, strengthening the existing power to defer sentences would be available when a court found reasons for allowing time for an offender to meet commitments voluntarily, such as reparation, voluntary attendance at drug/alcohol treatment programmes, or participation in restorative justice schemes, before being sentenced.

7. Sentence management

Sentence management issues – such as sentence calculation and enforcement – have been very difficult. Enforcement mechanisms, in particular, are complicated and not transparent. Procedures for enforcing sentences and penalties for breach of conditions vary greatly. There is also a sharp division of roles between sentencers who confine themselves to the immediate offences and sentencing decision, and the prison and probation services who implement the sentences passed. Unless sentencers request progress reports, there is no procedure through which they can receive feedback from the outcomes and implications of their decisions, or take account of an offender's progress or otherwise, during the sentence – other than for drug treatment and testing orders. Under the new framework all non-custodial sentences would be enforced by the court, which could, if the terms of the sentence were breached, replace the community sentence by a custodial one. In cases where there was a high risk of re-offending and swift action was required, the probation service should make more use of their power to apply for an arrest warrant which could lead to remand in custody, pending a full court hearing. All custodial sentences would be enforced administratively on breach of requirements, subject to a right of appeal to a court.

Courts should have a more active role in determining what is needed throughout the course of a sentence. With better information about the outcomes of their decisions, they could develop and provide a 'sentence review' capacity. This would deal with breaches of community sentences, hear appeals against recall to prison, authorise pre-release plans, and review progress during community sentences or the community part of custodial sentences. Visible involvement of the court for the duration of the sentence would exert additional leverage over the sentenced offender, especially at the crucial stage of release from prison, but also during periods in the community, whether after release from prison, or under a community sentence. Offenders would realise that when they were under sentence in the community, whether they stayed there or faced return to prison would depend on their own good behaviour and compliance. This would also be transparent to the public.

8. The shape of the framework: guidelines and legislation

For a new framework, the report says that an Act of Parliament should:

- set out the general principles;
- specify the newly designed sentences;
- provide for review hearings;
- prescribe enforcement procedures;
- require guidelines to be drawn up.

The Act should make provision for a Penal Code, which would be continuously updated.

The general principles should include:

- the severity of the sentence should reflect the seriousness of the relevant offences, and the offender's criminal history;
- the seriousness of the offence should reflect the harm caused, threatened or risked, and the offender's degree of blame in committing the offence;
- the severity of the sentence should increase as a consequence of sufficiently recent and relevant previous convictions;
- a prison sentence should be imposed only when no other sentence would be adequate to reflect the need for punishment;
- non-custodial sentences (including financial penalties) should be used, when they are adequately punitive, in ways designed to reduce the risk of re-offending and protect the public.

New guidelines for the use of judicial discretion will be an essential part of the new framework to avoid unpredictable consequences, such as in the sentencing of persistent offenders. These could be set out in a separate code

that would apply to all criminal courts. The guidelines would:

- specify graded levels of seriousness of offence;
- provide 'entry points' of sentence severity in relation to each level of seriousness;
- set out how severity of sentence should increase in relation to numbers and types of previous convictions;
- explain other possible grounds for mitigation and aggravation.

Responsibility for producing, monitoring, revising and accounting for the guidelines should be placed on an independent judicial body. This could be either the Court of Appeal (Criminal Division) sitting in a new capacity, with the Sentencing Advisory Panel in an expanded remit providing a resource to the court; a new judicial body set up for the purpose, which would be independent of the Court of Appeal but under strong judicial leadership complemented by professionals and academics – the Sentencing Advisory Panel could be subsumed within this body – or an independent body with a more mixed membership, not necessarily judicially dominated and into which the Sentencing Advisory Panel would be subsumed.

9. Costs and benefits

The effect of the framework proposed in the report by John Halliday on public expenditure, the size of the prison population, and the workload of the courts and probation services, will depend very much on how it is used. For instance, based on changes in length of prison sentences, increases or decreases in the custody rates, and diversion either way from under 12 months to over 12 months sentences, the proposed reforms (once established) could require additional annual public expenditure of between £300m and £650m. The prison population could see a decrease of 1500 or an increase of up to 9500, and the probation service would be working at any one time with up to 80,000 more offenders.

But these of course are not the necessary or only possible consequences of a reformed framework.

10. Implementation

10.1 Several conditions must be met for successful implementation of any new framework.

These include:

- a shared understanding of, and commitment to it among all those involved in its implementation, and a wider public;
- an adequate infrastructure of systems and processes to enable the new arrangements to work as intended;
- adequate resources, especially programmes for offenders, to meet the needs of staff and services;
- legislation and guidelines that are clear and intelligible to all concerned.

A framework that will last needs firm foundations. Benefits would not materialise if the framework proved short-lived, and the necessary transitional costs would be wasted. A challenging timetable will be necessary, but one that allows sufficient time for all the necessary work to be completed. A target date should be set as soon as all the necessary tasks have been identified, but should be contingent on the required resources being available in time.

A project team will need to work closely with all interested parties in creating a comprehensive implementation plan, subject to direction from a high level steering group and full consultation with all concerned.

The probation service or social workers would prepare a pre-sentence report when it was required or requested. National standards as to the preparation of pre-sentence reports have been introduced and the 2000 Standards are presented.

Home Office (2000) *The 2000 National Standards for Pre-Sentence Reports*

The purpose of a pre-sentence report is to provide information to the sentencing court about the offender and the offence(s) committed and to assist the court to decide on suitable sentence.

The requirements for a pre-sentence report:

a) to be objective, impartial, free from discriminatory language and stereotype, balanced, verified and factually accurate;

b) to be based on the use of the Offender Assessment System (OASys), when implemented to provide a systematic assessment of the nature and the causes of the defendant's offending behaviour, the risk the defendant poses to the public and the action which can be taken to reduce the likelihood of re-offending;

c) to be based on at least one face-to-face interview with the offender;

d) to specify information available from the CPS, any hostel placement or from any other relevant source;

e) to be written, and a copy provided to the court, the defence, the offender and (where required by the Crime (Sentences) Act 1997) the prosecution; and

f) to be prepared within, at most, 15 working days of request; or such shorter timescale as has been agreed in protocols with the court;

Offence analysis

Every pre-sentence report has to contain an offence analysis which has the following tasks:

a) an analysis of the offence(s) before the court, highlighting the key features in respect of the nature and circumstances of offences;

b) to assess the offender's culpability and level of premeditation;

c) to assess the consequences of the offence, including what is known of the impact on any victim, either from the CPS papers or from a victim statement where available;

d) to assess the offender's attitude to the offence and awareness of its consequences, including to any victim;

e) to indicate whether or not any positive action has been taken by the offender to make reparation or address offending behaviour since the offence was committed.

Offender assessment

Every pre-sentence report must also contain an offender assessment which has to:

a) state the offender's status in relation to literacy and numeracy, accommodation and employment;

b) assess the implications of any special circumstances, eg family crisis, substance abuse or mental illness, which were directly relevant to the offending;

c) evaluate any patterns of offending including reasons for offending and assess the outcome of any earlier court interventions, including the offender's response to previous supervision;

d) where substance misuse is relevant, provide details of the nature of the misuse and the offender's response to previous or current treatment;

e) give consideration to the impact of racism on the offender's behaviour where directly relevant to the offence;

f) include any relevant personal background which may have contributed to the offender's motive for committing the offence.

Risk factors

Pre-sentence reports also have to contain an assessment of the offender's likelihood of reoffending based on the current offence, attitude to it, and other relevant information, contain an assessment of the offender's risk of causing serious harm to the public and identify any risks of self harm.

Conclusion

This is also required in a pre-sentence report and it must have a content that:

a) evaluates the offender's motivation and ability to change and identifies, where relevant action required to improve motivation;

b) explicitly states whether or not an offender is suitable for a community sentence;

c) makes a clear and realistic proposal for sentence designed to protect the public and reduce reoffending, including for custody where this is necessary;

d) where the proposal is for a probation order or combination order, include an outline supervision plan containing a description of the purposes and desired outcomes of the proposed sentence, the methods envisaged and interventions likely to be undertaken, including attendance at accredited programmes where appropriate, the level of supervision envisaged (which for offenders at high risk of causing serious harm to the public is likely to be higher than the minimum required by the Standards);

e) where a specific condition is proposed, sets out the requirement precisely as it is proposed to appear in any order, and gives a likely start date;

f) where the proposal is for a curfew order, include details of the suitability of the proposed curfew address and its likely effects on others living at the offender's address;

g) for all serious sexual or violent offences, provide advice on the appropriateness of extended supervision;

h) where custody is a likely option, identify any anticipated effects on the offender's family circumstances, current employment or education.

Research was carried out in relation to the issue of consistency in the sentencing practices of magistrates. The extract demonstrates that this was not at the forefront of their minds. The factors that had produced this situation were not easy to uncover and perhaps worryingly were based on largely inarticulated perceptions.

Parker H, Sumner M and Jarvis G (1989) *Unmasking the Magistrates*, pp82–83

It seems that differences in perceptions of local crime are important in explaining sentencing variation. The question which arises, however, is how these perceptions and beliefs and the sentencing patterns associated with them are sustained. One possible explanation might be the existence of locally adopted bench policies, such as clampdowns on specific types of offence. Our respondents did indeed refer to such policies. Thus Yellowtown magistrates said that there was a policy of thinking about custody in cases involving drug related burglary, while Greytown respondents considered the taking of motor vehicles as a particular problem. Bluetown benches were concerned about inter-school gang fights and in Redtown the bench felt it had to clamp down on 'town centre trouble'. But it was also clear that these policies were not always adhered to and that actually neither their own nor their colleagues' previous sentencing decisions had very much impact on magistrates' sentencing of the sample cases. Intra-bench consistency was no more of an issue for most magistrates than inter-court consistency.

A few of the panels interviewed (11.12 per cent), particularly those in Yellowtown, said that they thought their bench was already consistent. But a number of Yellowtown magistrates, perhaps because of the size of the Bench there, said that they did not know enough about their colleagues' sentencing to answer or said that they had not given the matter any thought. The vast majority of magistrates in all the courts did not believe that they were consistent and only a minority (6.6 per cent) thought that they should be. Consistency was seen as a salient issue only in

respect of the fines imposed on motoring offenders. The largest single response, from almost a third of the benches interviewed, was that some framework of consistency was needed but in the end it is more important to judge every case on its merits. Altogether, three-fifths of the respondents stressed the individuality of each case. The following were typical replies:

Magistrates get a lot of criticism for not being consistent. Consistency is important but it never ought to be a case of looking up the offence in a book in order to fix the penalty. (Magistrate, Redtown)

It's rough and ready justice I suppose, but you can't standardise it without making it so rigid it becomes unfair. (Magistrate, Greytown)

Sentencing is a very personal thing. It has to be directed to the individual. (Magistrate, Yellowtown)

Consistency need not, of course, imply rigidity, but this equation was one which many magistrates seemed to make. Decisions taken by colleagues even in their own court were largely discounted.

The research by Hood provides an account of the impact of race as a factor in sentencing decisions in the Crown Court. It is well known that the rate of custody is higher for some groups than others. The important issue, and the one that Hood tackles, is whether or not this can be explained in terms of characteristics of the offence and of the offender. Taking such factors into account does remove some of the differences in custody rates but some still remain. So it seems that a person's race can on the face of it be an operative variable.

Hood R (1992) *Race and Sentencing*, pp194–199

The impetus for the research in this book was the over-representation of Afro-Caribbeans in prisons and young offender institutions. The research was carried out in order to investigate the possibility of a racial factor in sentencing. Crown Court records for 1989 in a variety of courts in the West Midlands provided a major source of the material used in the book. A total of 1,441 ethnic minority males went through the courts in the period and a sample of 1,443 white males was drawn for comparative purposes.

Ethnic minority defendants accounted for 28 per cent of the males sentenced at the West Midlands Crown Courts in 1989. This was two-and-a-half times greater than their proportion in the population at large, which was about 11 per cent. This was because Afro-Caribbeans were generally over represented, making up 21 per cent of the those found guilty at Birmingham and 15 per cent at the Dudley courts (which sat in court rooms at Dudley, Wolverhampton and Birmingham) although they accounted for less than 4 per cent of the general male population in the age range of 16 to 64. Asian males, on the other hand, were convicted in the Crown Court only slightly more often than would be expected from their number in the population at large.

Any differences in the sentences imposed on ethnic minorities as compared with whites have to be set in the general context of a considerable amount of variation, irrespective of race, in the percentage of males sentenced to custody (including imprisonment, a partially suspended sentence, and detention in a young offenders' institution). This varied from 61 per cent of these dealt with at Coventry to 46 per cent of the men sentenced at Birmingham.

Differences in the proportions of each ethnic category – white, black or Asian – given a custodial sentence were marked. Taking the sample as a whole, the proportion of blacks sentenced to custody was just over eight percentage points higher than for whites (56.6 per cent v 48.4 per cent). Asians, on the other hand, were sentenced to custody less often than either whites or blacks (39.6 per cent).

Variations between the proportions of ethnic minorities sentenced to custody at the different Crown Court centres were even larger. The black:white 'custody ratio' was particularly high for those sentenced by the Dudley courts, amounting to a difference of 17 percentage points (65 per cent v 48 per cent). There was a similar high black:white ratio at Warwick and Stafford, although the numbers dealt with there were much smaller. Only at Coventry were more whites and Asians sentenced to custody than blacks.

It was possible to examine the pattern of sentences of 18 judges (17 Circuit Judges and one Recorder), each of whom had dealt with at least 45 cases in the sample, and who, between them, had sentenced over half of all the cases. They varied a great deal in their overall use of custody (ie for all cases irrespective of race) ranging from one judge who had sentenced 29 per cent of the cases he dealt with to custody to another who sentenced 69 per cent. As regards race, three judges had sentenced considerably fewer blacks to custody than whites, eight appeared to be relatively even-handed, and five sentenced a much higher proportion of blacks than whites to custody: the difference ranging from 11 to 42 percentage points, equivalent to a greater proportion of black offenders getting a custodial sentence of between 41 and 111 per cent. When judges were ranked in order of their severity (measured by proportion to custody) for each ethnic group, there was a very low level of concordance between them. In other words, they appeared to vary a great deal in their relative severity on defendants of different ethnic backgrounds.

To what extent could these disparities be accounted for by variability in the nature of the cases dealt with by these judges at the various courts covered by the study? A comparison was first made of the nature and circumstances of the offences and the legally relevant characteristics of the defendants in each ethnic group. This showed that, although more black offenders had appeared at the Crown Court charged with offences which could only be tried on indictment at such a court, there were no significant differences in the proportions of blacks and whites convicted of the most serious crimes of personal violence. More blacks were, however, charged with and convicted of robbery and of supplying drugs (mostly cannabis), although there were proportionately fewer sentenced for housebreaking, theft or fraud. Their modus operandi for illegally obtaining money was clearly often different. As far as social characteristics were concerned, more blacks were unemployed and in receipt of welfare benefits, but it appeared that fewer had an unsettled or disrupted social life or were impaired by alcohol at the time of the offence. Although fewer blacks had no prior convictions a higher proportion of whites had eight or more. The pattern of these convictions differed somewhat, the black offenders being more likely to have a record for robbery or a drugs offence. Nevertheless, a smaller proportion of them had been convicted in the past of the same broad type of offence as that of which they had currently been convicted. It was particularly noticeable that more of the blacks pleaded not guilty and contested the case against them before a jury. As a consequence of this a considerably smaller proportion had a Social Inquiry Report (SIR) prepared about them by the probation service.

When the cases involving Asians were examined there was much to suggest that the lower proportion of them sentenced to custody was largely due to the fact that they were less involved in criminal acts than either whites or blacks. Although more had been charged with indictable only offences, fewer had more than one indictment laid against them and fewer had multiple charges or other offences taken into consideration. A much lower proportion had been previously convicted or had already served a custodial sentence. Furthermore, considerably fewer were unemployed or came from obviously unsettled backgrounds. They, too, had more often pleaded not guilty than had whites, and they too less often had an SIR.

In order to test whether the observed differences could be explained by the combination of factors in each case and the weighting given to them, a statistical method was used to 'match' cases as closely as possible in terms

of those variables which were shown to have had the most significant impact on whether an offender was committed to custody or not. This was done by using standard multivariate statistical techniques to calculate a 'probability of custody' score for each case, a score which summarised the probability of an offender with that particular combination of attributes getting a custodial sentence. In deriving this score more than 80 variables were analysed and 15 chosen which described 50 legally relevant attributes of the offence and the offender's criminal record. These variables correctly predicted whether an offender would receive custody or not in 75 per cent of cases. To what extent did the observed race differences in the proportion of blacks, whites and Asians sentenced to custody disappear when their probability of custody, as determined by these other factors, was taken into account?

A higher proportion of blacks than whites did fall into the category with the highest risk of custody, and fewer in the category with the lowest probability of receiving such a sentence. Asian offenders, on the other hand, were much less likely to be in the highest risk of custody group and were much more frequently in the lowest.

When this was taken into account the black-white difference in the sample as a whole of 8.2 percentage points in the proportion sentenced to custody was reduced to a difference of about 2.5 percentage points. Given the fact that the white custody rate was just under 50 per cent this amounts to a 5 per cent greater probability of a male black defendant being sentenced to custody than a white male. When a comparison was made on the basis of a probability of custody score derived only from the black defendants the difference was rather larger: whites being 7.6 per cent less likely to get a custodial sentence. Five per cent is not as large a 'residual race difference' as many commentators have suggested, but in a sample of this size it can be estimated that the number of blacks who received a custodial sentence would, if race had had no effect at all, have been 479 rather than 503 in the year 1989. It is important to bear in mind that this does not refer to any particular cases, only to the aggregate difference between the observed and expected probability of receiving a custodial sentence.

The substantially lower proportion of Asian males sentenced to custody was largely explained by the less serious nature of the cases. Even so, it was still a little lower than expected.

The black:white difference in the proportion sent to custody was at its greatest in the band of cases which could he described as of medium seriousness (with a probability of custody ranging from 45 to 80 per cent). Here the 68 per cent custody rate for blacks was significantly higher than the 60 per cent rate for whites: a difference which amounts to a 13 per cent greater probability of a black offender receiving a custodial sentence than a white in the range of cases.

An example of the work of the Sentencing Advisory Panel is provided. The extract concentrates on their examination of the offence of rape in circumstances where there is a relationship between offender and victim.

Sentencing Advisory Panel (2001) *Sentencing Guidelines on Rape: Consultation Paper*, paras 1–2 and 35–55

The Sentencing Advisory Panel has decided to propose that the Court of Appeal should revise its sentencing guidelines for the offence of rape. Before submitting such a proposal to the Court of Appeal, the panel is required by section 81 of the Crime and Disorder Act 1998 to obtain and consider the views of interested organisations and individuals, including those who are designated for this purpose by the Lord Chancellor.

As the attached consultation paper explains, there have been a number of changes in the law which suggest that the Court of

Appeal's current guideline judgment, in *Billam* (1986) 8 Cr App R (S) 48, may be in need of revision. The panel also believes that any new guidelines on rape should specifically address the relevance (if any) to sentencing of a previous relationship between offender and victim. In order to explore these issues in more detail, the panel has commissioned Surrey Social and Market Research to carry out a qualitative survey of people's views on the relative seriousness of 'stranger rape', 'date rape' and 'relationship rape'. The panel intends to consider the findings from the survey in parallel with responses to the present consultation exercise, before submitting its advice to the Court of Appeal. We invite comments from all interested parties, whether on the specific questions summarised at the end of the consultation paper, or on any other relevant matter which consultees think the panel should take into account.

Introduction

1. The Sentencing Advisory Panel has decided to propose to the Court of Appeal that it should revise its sentencing guideline on rape. There are two main reasons for suggesting that the current guideline, in *Billam* (1986) 8 Cr App R (S) 48, is in need of revision. First, there have been a number of changes in the law since 1986:

   a) a provision in the Sexual Offences Act 1993 allowing boys under 14 to be charged with rape;

   b) the recognition of marital rape as an offence (through the House of Lords ruling in *R* v *R* [1991] 4 All ER 481, which was placed on a statutory footing by the Criminal Justice and Public Order Act 1994);

   c) the recognition of male rape as an offence (in section 142 of the Criminal Justice and Public Order Act 1994); and

   d) the provision in section 2 of the Crime (Sentences) Act 1997, which came into force in October 1997, that a second conviction for a serious offence (including rape or attempted rape) will, unless there are exceptional circumstances, attract an automatic sentence of life imprisonment.

2. Apart from these legislative changes, the most significant development since the 1980s is the rise in the number of reported rapes where the victim and the offender were known to each other before the offence took place. The proportion of recorded cases categorised as 'stranger' rapes dropped from 30 per cent in 1985 to 12 per cent in 1996. The number of stranger rapes did not change significantly, but the change is explained by a large increase in the number of 'acquaintance' and 'intimate' rapes. Although the effect of the *Billam* guidelines appears to have been an overall increase in the severity of sentencing for rape, sentences have continued to be generally lower when the offence is committed by an acquaintance or intimate of the victim, rather than a stranger. The implications of this, and the issues it raises, are examined in greater detail below. ...

Relationship between offender and victim

35. The fact that the offender had a pre-existing relationship with the victim (whether sexual or otherwise) is not mentioned in *Billam* as a factor that should affect the level of sentence. In practice, there is evidence that overall sentencing levels are lower in cases where the victim and offender were known to each other before the rape, and in some cases, at least, the courts appear to have explicitly treated such a relationship as a mitigating factor.

36. A Home Office research project compared the nature of rape offences leading to a conviction in 1973 with those leading to such a conviction in 1985. (The cases covered in this study thus pre-dated both the *Billam* guidelines and the statutory recognition of marital rape.) The researchers found that in both years stranger rapists received a much

larger proportion of prison sentences over five years than acquaintances or intimates. Even when consideration was confined to cases where the attack was very serious and the victim badly injured, stranger rapists seemed to receive longer sentences than non-strangers. This was against the background that the proportion of cases in which the convicted rapist was a stranger to the victim fell from 47 per cent in 1973 to 39 per cent in 1985.

37. The 1992 sweep of the British Crime Survey (BCS) included a sentencing exercise, completed by a 50 per cent sub-sample, which involved 10 vignettes designed to elicit the public's attitude to punishment. The questionnaire was designed, in particular, to focus on crimes 'whose illegality or gravity was a matter of public controversy', including date rape, marital rape, drunk driving and possession of cannabis for personal use. The rape offences in the vignettes were both committed by a 25-year-old offender, with no mention of a previous criminal record in either case. Exactly half the sample favoured a custodial sentence for the date rapist, and 29 per cent in the case of marital rape. Of the remaining respondents, the majority (41 per cent for marital rape and 22 per cent for date rape) thought the offender should be let off with a warning by the police or the court.

38. Although the BCS study was not designed to focus specifically on rape, this suggests that a significant percentage of the public is prepared to be much more lenient than the courts in relation to marital rape and date rape: in practice, the issue for the sentencer is almost always the length of a custodial sentence, rather than the choice between a custodial and non-custodial sentence.

39. The possibility of creating a separate offence of 'date rape' or 'acquaintance rape', with a lower maximum sentence, was considered more recently by the Home Office review of sex offences. In *Setting the boundaries*, the review concludes that rape 'should not be subdivided into lesser or more serious offences'. It points out that, in the absence of research into juries' deliberations, there is no firm evi-

dence for the argument that juries would be more willing to convict if there were lower sentences for 'lesser' offences. More fundamentally, it questions whether rape by an acquaintance or intimate genuinely is a less serious offence than rape by a stranger:

> 'Some research indicates that the level of violence in partner/ex-partner rape is second only to stranger rape. We were told by those who counsel victims/survivors that those raped by friends or family often find it much harder to recover and may take longer to do so. In addition to these powerful arguments, it is hard to see how degrees of rape could be defined – when does a stranger become an acquaintance or a friend? The crime of rape is so serious that it needs to be considered in its totality rather than being constrained by any relationship between the parties.'

40. On the issue of sentencing, the review concluded that: 'Rape is a very serious crime but sentences can, and should, reflect the seriousness of each individual case within an overall maximum. Gradation of the seriousness of a particular offence is best reflected in the sentence finally imposed rather than creating separate offences.'

41. Before making a proposal to the Court of Appeal for a revised sentencing guideline on rape, the panel would like to find out more about people's attitudes to the relative seriousness of a rape committed by someone who was already known to the victim, and by a stranger. The panel has therefore commissioned Surrey Social and Market Research to conduct research into public opinion on this particular issue, at the same time as the present consultation exercise which covers the wider issues relating to sentencing of this offence.

The Court of Appeal's approach to 'marital rape' and 'acquaintance rape'

42. Although it is not a guideline case, *Berry* (1988) 10 Cr App R (S) 13 has been treated as an authority on the principles to be adopted in sentencing rape cases where the victim and offender have previously had a sexual relationship. The facts of this case were that the defendant and his partner had a child, but she moved away after starting a relationship with another man. The offender visited his former partner and their child, and their sexual relationship continued on an occasional basis. On one such visit the offender lost his temper, kicked in the latch of the victim's back door, and raped her after an argument which turned into a fight. Considerable violence was used, although she suffered no serious harm. On being arrested the offender, who had no previous convictions, immediately admitted what he had done; he expressed regret, and pleaded guilty in court. He was sentenced in the Crown Court to six years' imprisonment.

43. In reducing the six year sentence to four years, the Court of Appeal commented: 'These facts show that this case is far from those in which, for example, a woman walking home has been set upon by a total stranger and violated.' As a general observation, the court said:

> 'The rape of a former wife or mistress *may* have exceptional features which make it a less serious offence than otherwise it would be ... To our mind ... *in some instances* the violation of the person and defilement that are inevitable features where a stranger rapes a woman are not always present to the same degree when the offender and the victim had previously had a longstanding sexual relationship.' [Italics added]

44. This approach was endorsed in *Thornton* (1990) 12 Cr App R (S) 1 (*Attorney-General's Reference (No 7 of 1989)*), a contested case where the offender had used some violence in raping a former cohabitant. In increasing the sentence from two years to four and a half, the court said:

> 'The mere fact that the parties have over a period of nearly two years – 20 months – been living together and having regular sexual intercourse obviously does not license the man once that cohabitation or sexual intercourse has ceased to have sexual intercourse with the girl willy-nilly. It is

however a factor to which some weight can be given by the sentencing court for the reasons which Mustill LJ set out in [*Berry*].'

45. The idea that the 'worst' kind of rape is always one committed by a stranger also occurs in cases where the victim and offender had been known to each other before the offence, although they had not had a sexual relationship. In *Harvey* (1987) 9 Cr App R (S) 124, where the only aggravating feature was the defendant's previous convictions for sex offences, Lord Lane CJ said:

'There was no unnecessary violence: by that I mean violence beyond that which is necessarily involved in the commission of the crime of rape. There were no sexual indignities as unhappily one all too frequently finds in these cases nowadays imposed upon a girl. There was no weapon used or threatened. *The parties were known to each other.* There were no physical injuries suffered by the girl – that was the doctor's evidence ...' [Italics added]

46. In this case, the victim was a friend of the offender's cousin, and had known the offender himself for about a year. The offence took place when she went to his home on Christmas Day to look for her friend. It is not clear from the Court of Appeal's remarks exactly what significance was attached, for sentencing purposes, to her prior acquaintance with the offender.

47. In *M* (1995) 16 Cr App R (S) 770, the Court of Appeal (per Lord Taylor CJ) made a further distinction between cases of marital rape where the parties were estranged, and those where they were still living together:

'In the present case we would point out that there is a distinction between a husband who is estranged from his wife and is parted from her and returns to the house as an intruder either by forcing his way in or by worming his way in through some device and then rapes her, and a case where, as here, the husband is still living in the same house, and, indeed, with consent occupying the same bed as his wife. We do not consider

that this class of case is as grave as the former class.'

48. Here, the court reduced a sentence of three years to 18 months, pointing out that the offender had not used violence or undue force, was previously of good character, made an immediate admission, and showed genuine remorse.

49. In other cases, especially those involving a considerable degree of violence, the Court of Appeal has said that less importance should be attached by sentencers to the existence of a previous sexual relationship. The application of the *Billam* guidelines to cases of marital rape was explicitly discussed by Lord Taylor CJ in *W* (1993) 14 Cr App R (S) 256:

'In our judgment, it should not be thought that a different and lower scale of sentencing attaches automatically to rape by a husband as against that set out in *Billam*. All will depend on the circumstances of the individual case. Where the parties were cohabiting normally at the time and the husband insisted on intercourse against his wife's will, but without violence or threats, the consideration identified in *Berry* and approved in *Thornton* ... will no doubt be an important factor in reducing the level of sentencing. Where, however, the conduct is gross and does involve threats or violence, the facts of the marriage, of long cohabitation and that the defendant is no stranger will be of little significance. Clearly between those two extremes there will be many intermediate degrees of gravity which judges will have to consider case by case. The present case falls at the grave end of the scale.'

50. Similarly, in *Workman* [1998] 10 Cr App R (S) 329, the court said:

'We have been referred to ... the case of *Berry*, where it was said by this court that rape is perhaps a less serious offence when the victim is not a total stranger but someone known to the defendant, and particularly someone whom the defendant had previously had sexual relations with. But one cannot carry that doctrine too far. One cannot say that if the victim is someone who is known to the defendant in a sexual context he thereby has a licence to rape, or at any rate gets a significant advantage in terms of sentence, now that she has shown herself unwilling to have anything more to do with him.'

51. In that case, the Court of Appeal upheld a sentence of five years for the rape of a former cohabitant; although the defendant pleaded guilty, the offence involved some degree of violence, considerable humiliation to the victim, and an unwelcome intrusion into her home in the middle of the night.

52. Again, in *H* [1997] 2 Cr App R (S) 339, the court said:

'This was, it is right to say, an offence of rape committed by a husband on his wife. That does not in any way make it more excusable. Its only relevance, so far as mitigation is concerned, is that the consequences of rape, grave indeed though they are likely to be, and are in this case, *may* not be as grave as when a woman is raped by a stranger' [Italics added]. '...There can be little doubt that in the instant case the conduct was gross, and it certainly did involve threats of violence. . . . The appellant raped his wife on three occasions and subjected her to other very unpleasant sexual indignities. It was a planned attack. She suffered injuries and very considerable emotional and psychological disturbance. These are all aggravating factors in this case.'

53. In upholding a custodial sentence of five years in this case, the court observed that the sentence would have been 'well in excess' of this but for the mitigating factors of the offender's guilty plea and previous good character.

54. The Court of Appeal's approach in *Berry* and subsequent cases has been criticised by some commentators, who claim that the distinction between 'stranger' and other rape leads to sentences significantly lower than those suggested by *Billam*, and is not supported by research on the experience of rape victims. It has been suggested that the breach of trust involved in rape by an intimate should be explicitly identified as an aggravating factor.

55. From the cases cited at paragraphs 42–54 above, it appears that a previous relationship between the offender and victim is generally treated by the Court of Appeal as a mitigating factor, but one for which credit may be reduced or lost in cases where serious aggravating factors (especially violence) are present.

The next material provides statistical information on the operation of the Criminal Cases Review Commission.

Criminal Cases Review Commission (2001) *Provisional Figures to 31 July 2001*, Website press release

Since 31 March 1997, the Commission has received over 4,301 applications and 3,321 cases have been completed. Convictions are referred to the appellate courts if the commission believes that there is a real possibility that they will be found to be unsafe. A high proportion of applications involve only simple points of fact or law, and can be reviewed within a month or two. Where there are complex issues to investigate, the review may take a year or more. There have been 139 referrals of which the Court of Appeal have made decisions in 73 cases – in 55 of these cases the sentence was quashed.

12 Juvenile and Young Adult Offenders

The statistics provide an account of the amount of crime recorded as having being carried out by young people. It is a very great amount and to a large extent the crime problem is a problem of young people.

Home Office (2001) *Criminal Statistics 1999*

INDICTABLE OFFENCES IN 1999 (THOUSANDS)
Males

	All ages	10–14	15–17	18–20
Cautioned	126.1	22.0	28.7	22.7
Found guilty	291.7	8.9	35.1	52.6
Total	417.8	30.9	63.8	75.2

Females

	All ages	10–14	15–17	18–20
Cautioned	44.5	9.9	9.3	5.7
Found guilty	49.0	1.4	5.2	7.6
Total	93.5	11.3	14.5	13.3

The Government's ideas on youth justice reform are presented in the next extract. This includes analysis of a number of recent initiatives such as the Intensive Supervision and Surveillance Programme, Bail Supervision and Support Schemes, Drug Treatment and Testing Orders and Referral Orders.

Home Office (2001) *Criminal Justice: The Way Ahead*, pp32–33

Youth justice reform

For the more persistent young offenders who are already involved with the CJS, the Government is investing £45 million over three years from April 2001 in a new Intensive

265

Supervision and Surveillance Programme (ISSP) to deal with 2,500 of the most difficult cases. There has been a concerted drive to reduce offending by young people on bail through the new Bail Supervision and Support Schemes linked to national standards. The new DTTO – part custody, part community sentence – has a strong emphasis on constructive regimes in custody and better resettlement in the community. A separate juvenile secure estate has been created with improved accommodation and we will amend the criteria for bail for offenders so that the courts can refuse bail to youngsters with a history of committing or being charged with imprisonable offences. For young offenders in custody, we will be making a determined effort to break the pattern of offending behaviour by providing active programmes including 30 hours a week education, training or similar development work. We also plan over the next five years to build 400 additional secure training centre places, providing intensive supervision and high quality programmes for young people in custody. As far as possible, these places will be near to offenders' home areas so that effective links can be made with education and other services which will deal with them after release. This will remove young women from adult prisons and many younger boys from prison accommodation. In 2002 new referral orders will be implemented, under which young offenders appearing in court for the first time will be referred to Youth Offender Panels chaired by a local person. The panel will negotiate with the offender, their family and the victim (if the victim agrees) and set out a programme to tackle the factors which led to the offending. If this fails, the offender will go back to court for normal sentencing. Referral orders are already being piloted in 11 areas.

The question of what to do about the misbehaviour of youngsters has produced a variety of different answers over the years. A particular focus has been the competing claims of the welfare model and the justice model. The following extracts from the Black Committee (1979) Report on the system in Northern Ireland provide an account of these models.

Black Report (1979) *Report of the Children and Young Persons Review Group* (in Stewart G and Tutt N (1987) *Control without Custody*, pp91–92)

The assumptions of the welfare model:

a) delinquent, dependent and neglected children are all products of an adverse environment which at its worse is characterised by multiple deprivation. Social, economic and physical disadvantage, including poor parental care, are all relevant considerations;

b) delinquency is a pathological condition; a presenting sympton of some deeper maladjustment out of the control of the individual concerned;

c) since a person has no control over the multiplicity of casual factors dictating his delinquency he cannot be considered responsible for his actions or held accountable for them. Considerations of guilt or innocence are, therefore, irrelevant and punishment is not only inappropriate but is contrary to the rules of natural justice;

d) all children in trouble (both offenders and non-offenders) are basically the same and can be effectively dealt with through a single unified system designed to identify and meet the needs of children;

e) the needs or underlying disorders, of which delinquency is symptomatic, are capable of identification and hence treatment and control are possible;

f) informality is necessary if the child's needs are to be accurately determined and his best interests served. Strict rules of procedure or standards of proof not only hinder the identification of need but are unnecessary in proceedings conducted in the child's best interests;

g) inasmuch as need is highly individualised, flexibility of response is vital. Wide discretion is necessary in the determination and variation of treatment measures;

h) voluntary treatment is possible and is not punishment. Treatment has no harmful side effects;

i) the child and his welfare are paramount though considerations of public protection cannot be ignored. In any event, a system designed to meet the needs of the child will in turn protect the community and serve the best interests of society;

j) prevention of neglect and alleviation of disadvantage will lead to prevention of delinquency.

The assumptions of the justice model:

a) delinquency per se is a matter of opportunity and choice – other factors may combine to bring a child to the point of delinquency, but unless there is evidence to the contrary, the act as such is a manifestation of the rational decision to that effect;

b) insofar as a person is responsible for his actions he should also be accountable. This is qualified in respect of children by the doctrine of criminal responsibility as originally evolved under common law and now endorsed by statue;

c) proof of commission of an offence should be the sole justification for intervention and the sole basis of punishment;

d) society has the right to re-assert the norms and standards of behaviour both as an expression of society's disapproval and as an individual and general deterrent to future similar behaviour;

e) sanctions and controls are valid responses to deviant behaviour both as an expression of society's disapproval and as an individual and general deterrent to similar behaviour;

f) behaviour attracting legal intervention and associated sanctions available under the law should be specifically defined to avoid uncertainty;

g) the power to interfere with a person's freedom and in particular that of a child should be subject to the most rigorous standard of proof which traditionally is found in a court of law. Individual rights are most effectively safeguarded under the judicial process;

h) there should be equality before the law; like cases should be treated alike;

i) there should be proportionality between the seriousness of the delinquent or criminal behaviour warranting intervention and the community's response; between the offence and the sentence given.

The government report, *Preventing Children Offending*, contains a wealth of detail on recent developments in the field, with a summary of what measures are currently available. Factors that can be linked to both the cause and prevention of offending are isolated. Also provided is an account of some thinking for the future, including an analysis of the particular problems posed by persistent and serious young offenders. The importance of early intervention is stressed.

Preventing Children Offending (1997), pp6–17, 23–24

Chapter 1. Government action to tackle juvenile crime

The Government has introduced a comprehensive set of measures to tackle juvenile crime, including:

– preventive measures aimed at stopping children and young people from being drawn into crime;

– measures to encourage those who have committed one or two offences to lead law-abiding lives; and

– measures to deal with the small but significant number of persistent and serious offenders.

CRIME PREVENTION

The Government has committed significant resources to help children and young people avoid turning to crime:

- Phase 1 of the Safer Cities programme funded some 800 schemes in England and Wales aimed at young people with grants totalling around £4.2 million;
- Phase 2 of the programme, administered by the Department of the Environment since April 1994, has provided additional grants of £4 million to 800 crime prevention schemes in 1994/95 and 1995/96. Many of these are targeted at young people;
- under the Grants for Education Support and Training (GEST) programme, the Department for Education and Employment has supported expenditure of over £10 million on the Youth Action Scheme over the period 1993–96. The scheme was designed to help young people at risk of drifting into crime to plan, organise and participate in programmes of challenging activities to develop their self-esteem and sense of responsibility to themselves and the wider community;
- proceeds from the National Lottery amounting to £174 million have been paid to 1,149 organisations which are engaged in constructive activities with children, such as the arts, sport and community work;
- the Government pays an annual grant of £750,000 to the organisation Crime Concern, and encourages it to take a particular interest in youth crime prevention in England and Wales. Examples of Crime Concern's work are:
  - the carrying out of youth crime audits or surveys on behalf of local authorities;
  - providing education in parenting, to tackle some of the factors affecting families which may contribute to juvenile offending; and
  - the development of *Youth Action Groups*. Crime Concern and the Prudential Corporation launched a five-year strategy in 1993, costing about £1.5 million, to develop Youth Action Groups in secondary schools

across the country. They tackle problems such as bullying, personal safety, vandalism, graffiti and drug abuse; increase young people's interest in crime prevention and encourage a sense of social responsibility.

Crime Concern's strategy for youth crime prevention recognises the value of programmes which are designed to address the risk factors associated with offending. This paper builds on that idea in considering how a framework for preventing children offending might be developed.

A different approach to crime prevention is by attaching conditions to police bail. Section 27 of the Criminal Justice and Public Order Act 1994 gives the police power to attach conditions to bail when a person has been charged, where this is necessary to prevent that person from committing an offence. The Government has been interested to see the use made of this power by the Metropolitan Police in Catford. In response to disorderly behaviour by gangs of young people in the area, the police began to impose curfews on those arrested for an offence. The curfew was tailored to the offence so that, for example, a child arrested for shoplifting at 7pm might be ordered to keep off the streets between the hours of 6pm and 6am. The Government understands that the police officers who made the arrests would be present in court when the case was heard, and that the court invariably agreed to re-impose the curfew restriction as a condition of bail. The Government notes that the firm approach taken by the police appears to have gained widespread support in the area and to have been successful in dealing with a difficult public older problem.

CAUTIONING
The great majority of children and young who offend do so only once or twice. For them, a caution or informal warning administered by the police is sufficient to prevent further offending. A caution can only be administered where the offence is admitted, and it is not a conviction, but it may be mentioned in court if

the person appears in court for a subsequent offence.

Around 80 per cent of offenders who are cautioned for the first time do not re-offend within two years of the caution. Subsequent cautions have been shown to be progressively less effective, however, and guidelines issued to the police in 1994 (Home Office Circular 18/1994) emphasised that a caution should not be given where there is no reasonable expectation that it will curb offending:

> '... *cautions should not be administered to an offender in circumstances where there can be no reasonable expectation that this will curb his offending. It is only in the following circumstances that more than one caution should be considered:*
> *– where the subsequent offence is trivial; or*
> *– where there has been a sufficient lapse of time since the first conviction to suggest that it had some effect.*'

The Government has noted with interest the development, in a number of areas, of *caution plus or supported caution* schemes. These offer programmes tailored to the individual needs of offenders. For example, the aim of the Milton Keynes Retail Theft Initiative is to work with young offenders to educate them to realise that shop theft is not a victimless crime, to appreciate the consequences of their actions for themselves, the shops and others, and to learn how to resist the temptation to re-offend. All offenders receive a formal caution on completion of the scheme. Because the scheme is voluntary, it is not possible to discount the effect of self-selection, but Home Office research (McCulloch, 1996) has shown, over the period of the study, a re-offending rate of 3 per cent for first-time offenders attending the scheme, compared with 35 per cent for first-time offenders dealt with in other ways, and a 50 per cent reduction in the amount of police time spent dealing with shop thieves.

Some schemes of this kind involve an element of reparation. For example, the HALT scheme in The Netherlands is a diversion scheme in which offenders sign agreements admitting their guilt, and pay a fine or undertake some form of community work, such as cleaning up graffiti or repairing damage caused. In some cases victims are compensated.

The report *Review of Delay in the Criminal Justice System*, published in February 1997, recommended that the Youth Court should be given the power to issue a court caution on an admission of guilt by the defendant, and if appropriate attach the kind of conditions currently included in a caution plus scheme. As the report explains, a court-based caution plus offers a number of advantages over existing schemes, not least that if the offender failed to comply with the conditions attached to it he could be returned to court and sentenced for the original offence.

COURT POWERS TO DEAL WITH JUVENILE CRIME

Parents have a responsibility to ensure that their children do not break the law. Courts therefore have powers to involve parents in their children's court proceedings and punishment. The Courts can require parents:

– to attend court with their children;
– to pay their children's fines; and
– to be bound over to exercise control over their children properly and to ensure their child's compliance with a community sentence (unreasonable refusal to agree to a bindover, or failure to comply with it, can result in a fine or the forfeiture of up to £1,000).

The Government believes that it is important for parents to be both willing and able to exercise control over their children. How they might be encourage to do so is explored in more detail later in this paper.

The courts have a range of powers to deal with young offenders in the community:

– children can be fined up to £250 on conviction in a magistrates' court, if they are aged 10–13 and up to £1,000 if they are aged 14–17;
– parents generally have to pay the fine if

the child is under 16, and may be ordered to pay if he is aged 16–17;

– children (or their parents) may be ordered to pay compensation of up to £5,000;

– children aged 10–15 may be placed under the supervision of the local authority (and those aged 16–17 under the supervision of the local authority or a probation officer). Courts can attach conditions to the order, for example a night restriction or a school attendance requirements;

– children aged 10–20 can be ordered to go to an attendance centre (normally for 12 hours, but for up to 24 hours if they are aged 10–15 and up to 36 if they are aged 16–20);

– children aged 16–17 may be sentenced to community service for between 40 and 240 hours;

– children aged 16–17 may be placed on probation for between six months and three years. The probation order may impose conditions, for example attending treatment programmes for drug or alcohol misuse;

– pilot trials of electronic monitoring are currently taking place in three areas, where the courts may make an offender aged 16 or over subject to a curfew for up to 12 hours a day.

Community sentences – supervision, probation, community service, combination order and attendance centre orders – are subject to National Standards which set out what should happen when they are imposed. The National Standards should help to ensure that these sentences are realistic and effective forms of punishment as well as a means of helping to reduce the risk of further offending.

PERSISTENT AND SERIOUS YOUNG OFFENDERS
Despite all these efforts, there is a small number of young offenders who are responsible for a disproportionate amount of crime in England and Wales. In 1990, for example, 1 per cent of male offenders aged 17 accounted for around 60 per cent of all the convictions of' persons of that age. Similarly, a survey

undertaken by the Home Office in 1993 suggested that, on average, persistent juvenile offenders committed around 17 offences each. Figures for 1995 show that 10–15 year olds account for around 14 per cent of all known offenders and 10–17 year olds for around 26 per cent. The Government believes that firm action is needed to deal with these particularly disruptive young people.

The Government has introduced a series of measures to strengthen the courts' powers to deal with persistent and serious young offenders:

– it has extended existing legislation so that any child aged 10 or over who commits an offence for which an adult could be sentenced to 14 years or more, or life imprisonment, can be sentenced to long periods of detention;

– it has extended from one to two years the maximum period for which a 15–17 year old may be sentenced to detention in a young offender institution;

– it is introducing a new sentence of detention – the secure training order – which will enable the courts to deal more effectively with persistent young offenders aged 12–14. The order will be for between six months and two years – half to be spent in detention, and half under supervision in the community. The order will be implemented once the new secure training centres are available; and

– it is bringing arrangements for juveniles into line with measures being introduced to ensure that the time served by offenders in prison matches much more closely the sentence passed by the court.

The Government has also recently announced two new initiatives to tackle persistent offending by children and young people:

– the extension of electronic monitoring of a curfew order to include those aged 10–15. The power is currently available for those aged 16 or over in three pilot areas: Berkshire, Greater Manchester and Norfolk. Under the order, offenders may be confined to a specific place or places for between 2 and 12 a day, for example a curfew to be at home during football matches; and

– the extension of the youth court's discretion to allow juveniles who have been convicted of an offence to be identified, where this will help to protect the public or to prevent crime. At present, the court may to be identified only if it is in their interest, or if juveniles charged with or convicted of a serious offence are unlawfully at large.

PREVENTING CHILDREN FROM BECOMING OFFENDERS

Firm action must be taken to tackle persistent offending when it occurs. But it would clearly be more desirable if, instead of developing into persistent criminals, this group of children could be diverted from their criminal careers at an earlier age, and before they enter the criminal justice system. What is needed is a dual approach which offers support to children at risk of offending, backed by sanctions for parents who will not face up to their responsibilities. The rest of this paper examines in detail how this approach would work.

Chapter 2. Early intervention with children at risk of offending

WHY CHILDREN COMMIT CRIME

People are influenced throughout their lives – but especially as they grow up – by a variety of factors which may lead them towards, or away from, crime. Through experiences in the family, at school, in the community and at leisure, children can learn the benefits of obeying the law and the costs of not doing so.

Research cannot provide definitive answers to why some people become offenders and others do not, but it does indicate which of a wide range of factors appear to be most influential. Recent Home Office research (Graham and Bowling, 1995) has confirmed that key factors related to criminality are:

– being male;
– being brought up by a criminal parent or parents;

– living in a family with multiple problems;
– experiencing poor parenting and a lack of supervision;
– poor discipline in the family and at school;
– playing truant;
– associating with delinquent friends; and
– having brothers and sisters who offend.

On the whole, the personalities of many young offenders are indistinguishable from those of non-offenders. But *persistent and serious offenders* are more likely, as young children, to have been aggressive, dishonest, cruel, impulsive, selfish and inconsiderate, and to have had difficulty seeing things from another's point of view and thinking through the consequences of their actions.

Although anti-social behaviour during childhood is a powerful predictor of adult offending, not all children who display anti-social behaviour end up as anti-social adults. A number of factors affect the way in which children develop.

THE FAMILY

The single most important influence on a child's development is that of the family. Those children who show signs of criminal behaviour at an early age are those who are most likely to end up as serious or persistent offenders. Such children often come from communities and families which are unstable, chaotic and suffer from a number of problems. Their parents are likely to have criminal records, to neglect their children, or to exercise low levels of supervision and harsh and erratic discipline, and themselves to come from similar families. Children who are exposed to abuse and neglect within a climate of hostility at home are particularly at risk of becoming violent offenders.

Research (Utting et al, 1993; Graham and Bowling, 1995) has shown that children who live in a single-parent or step-parent family are more at risk of offending than those who live with both natural parents. This is not a direct result of the family structure itself; single or step parents may, for a whole variety of reasons, find it more difficult to supervise their children or exercise consistent discipline, and family relationships may be more difficult in situations where one parent is not present.

Research has also shown that where children are brought up in a stable environment, and have a good relationship with their parents, they are less likely to display delinquent behaviour. The capacity and willingness of the parent or parents to supervise their children and exercise fair and consistent discipline is crucial.

THE SCHOOL
There is evidence to suggest that to an appreciable extent, children's behaviour and attitudes are shaped and influenced by their experiences at school. The capacity of schools to motivate and integrate their pupils, and offer them a sense of achievement, may help to prevent delinquent behaviour. Research shows that children who offend are also more likely than others to fail at school, to play truant persistently, to behave disruptively or be permanently excluded from school (Graham, 1989; Graham and Bowling, 1995).

Research also suggests that the characteristics of the school – relationships between pupils and staff, levels of staff and pupil motivation and commitment, the system of rules and how they are enforced – can play an important part in helping children to stay out of trouble. Schools which have a good relationship between staff and pupils, provide clear and consistently enforced rules, and ensure pupils are offered a wide range of opportunities for achieving success, are most likely to make a positive contribution to preventing criminality.

The inclusion of pupil absence data in the school performance tables published by the Department for Education and Employment has done much to focus attention on the problem of truancy. The DfEE has also provided direct, practical help to schools and education authorities through its grant-aid for locally-devised projects costing some £70 million over five years under the Truancy and Disaffected Pupils category of the Grants for Education Support and Training (GEST) pro-

gramme. Provisions in the Bill currently before Parliament will require authorities to publish new behaviour support plans outlining the arrangements made in relation to pupils with behaviour problems, including both for schools in tackling those problems and provision for pupils who have been excluded from school.

The Government also attaches great importance to allowing all children to have a good start to their educational lives. The nursery education scheme, which will be introduced throughout England and Wales from 1 April 1997, offers the parents of four-year-olds vouchers which will – over time – allow them to choose a good quality place before the start of compulsory school. Also, the Government is supporting, through the GEST programme, the extension over the next few years of Family Literacy Programmes to all local education authorities. These help both children and parents with literacy difficulties to acquire essential basic skills in reading and writing.

LEISURE USE AND PEER GROUPS
Juvenile offenders often commit offences with others. The use of leisure time, and peer pressure, can influence the likelihood of offending. For example, offending by boys is associated with the amount of time they spend away from home and with their friends. Those who spend their leisure time in unstructured and unsupervised activity on the streets are more at risk of offending. There is also evidence that those whose friends engage in delinquent activity are more likely to do so themselves than those whose friends do not.

Young people who are out on the streets may obtain alcohol, get drunk and vandalise property, and cause mischief in other ways. The Government published a consultation paper *Under–Aged Drinking in Public* in September 1996 with proposals to tackle this problem by giving the police new powers to confiscate alcohol from under age drinkers in public places. The proposals are now contained in the Confiscation of Alcohol (Young Persons) Bill currently before Parliament. The

Bill enables the police to confiscate any alcohol in the possession of a person aged under 18 who is in a public place; to confiscate any alcohol from a person of any age in a public place that the police believe that the alcohol will be passed on to an under aged person who will drink it in a public place; and to request the name and address of any person from whom alcohol has been confiscated under these powers. Anyone who refused to surrender the alcohol to the police or to give his name and address would be committing an offence and could be fined up to £500.

In contrast, participation in the arts and sports enables young people to use their leisure time in a constructive way. Group activities such as team games can promote a sense of community and pride in achievement which lead to a heightened awareness of the obligations of citizenship. Competitive sport teaches valuable lessons such as fair play, self-discipline and respect for others. The policy paper, *Sport: Raising the Game*, which was published in July 1995, set out the Government's blueprint for revitalising sport at all levels, with a particular emphasis on putting sport back at the heart of school life.

There is also a wide range of volunteering opportunities for young people, which not only helps them to forge close links with their communities but also provides them with skills and experience to benefit them in later life. The Government's strategy for encouraging more young people to volunteer set out in the document *Young People Make a Difference*, which was published in February 1997.

RISK AND PROTECTIVE FACTORS

These risk factors often coincide and interact. Although it is not possible to predict with any degree of certainty who will become an offender on the basis of the level of risk to which they are exposed, it is known that children exposed to multiple risks are disproportionately likely to end up as serious or persistent offenders.

Of course, not all children exposed to high levels of risk end up as criminals. Some are resilient and cope with disruption and upheaval more readily; others are particularly intelligent, or learn to adapt to risks in a constructive way. An anchor in the life of all children is important. They may be helped by a particularly committed adult (for example, a member of the family, a teacher with whom they have a especially good relationship with or a close friend). They may come from families with strong religious or moral beliefs. They may find some way to succeed at school, against the odds, or excel at some form of sporting activity. Above all, they may enjoy strong, warm and consistent relationships with one or both of their parents. Preventing children from becoming offenders is therefore also about finding ways to increase these protective factors as well as decreasing the risks.

THE EFFECTIVENESS OF EARLY INTERVENTION

The Government believes that it is essential to intervene with children at risk of becoming offenders as early as possible. It is also essential to develop strategies for intervention on the basis of sound knowledge about what works.

Currently, most evidence for the effectiveness of early intervention comes from the USA, where a number of initiatives have been independently evaluated (see Graham and Bennett, 1995). For example, the Syracuse Family Development programme, which provided pre-natal and post-natal advice and support to mothers of children up to the age of five, showed that, by the age of 15, the children in families who received such support had offended less, and less seriously, than children not on the programme (Lally et al, 1988). Encouraging results were also achieved in the USA by the LIFT programme (Linking Interests of Families and Teachers), which was set up in Oregon to discourage anti-social behaviour at home and school through parent training, social skills classes for children, measures to improve behaviour and supervision in the playground, and the use of a school-to-home telephone line on which teachers and parents could leave and receive messages. Initial findings suggest that LIFT has reduced aggressive and antisocial behaviour in the short-term (Reid et al, 1994).

One of the best-known examples of early intervention is the Perry Pre-School project (USA). It was set up with the explicit object-ive of reducing the risk of delinquency. The project placed a number of black children from low socio-economic families either in a pre-school child development programme or in a control group for a period of, in most cases, two years at the age of three. The child development programme involved pre-school supervision of children by teachers, and weekly home visits to mothers and children by teachers. Over a period of 16 years, informa-tion was collected on all the children involved in the project. The information included data on, for example, school performance, atti-tudes, employment record and self and police-reported delinquency. The study found that those children who attended the pre-school programme performed better in school and adult education and were more likely to grad-uate and get employment. Teenage pregnancy rates were much lower (about half), and arrest rates were 40 per cent lower than for children in the control groups at the age of 19. By the age of 27, about one in three of the control group had been arrested five or more times compared with about one in 14 of those who had attended the pre-school programme (Schweinhart and Weikart, 1993).

A cost-benefit analysis, of the project (Schweinhart, 1987) found that it cost in the region of $5,000 per child each year. The anal-ysis showed that, for every $1 invested, $6 was saved in future public expenditure. On that basis, early intervention to prevent chil-dren offending makes sound financial sense.

A number of initiatives similar to the Perry Pre-School project have been introduced in the United Kingdom. So far, there is very little hard evidence in this country to demonstrate the impact of early intervention on later offending. But these initiatives do seem to have an impact on the risk factors known to be associated with anti-social behaviour and offending, such as child abuse and neglect,

early behavioural problems at home and at school, school failure, bullying and persistent non-attendance in school. *Reducing Criminality among Young People*, a research study which was carried out for the Home Office by David Utting in 1996, and which is being published with this paper, evaluates a number of promising British approaches.

Some of the programmes or projects which Utting describes and which the Government believes are of value are as follows:

Home start: this is a network of nearly 200 home visiting schemes across the country, supported by a national consultancy. It uses trained volunteers, who are themselves experi-enced parents, to offer friendship, practical advice and support to families with pre-school children. It works alongside the statutory health and social services, accepting referrals from doctors, teachers and other profession-als as well as from voluntary organisations such as RELATE. The families that Home Start works with may be in difficulty because of domestic violence, suspected child abuse, debt, children's behavioural problems or other reasons. Volunteers aim to share their practi-cal experience as parents; to encourage parents to become more confident in their own abilities; and to reassure then that it is not unusual to encounter problems in bringing up children. Visits usually take place once or twice a week, but may be more frequent in times of crisis. The Home Office has recently offered Home Start a grant of £23,000 a year for three years to support two projects in Castleford and Wycombe. Ten other Home Start projects have between them received some £397,000 in the third round of grants by the National Lottery Charities Board (Health, Disability and Care Grants).

Parent network: a parent education pro-gramme, offering a 13-week Parent Link course with a published curriculum. An esti-mated 10,000 parents have attended courses in the past ten years. The programme aims to improve the quality of family life and reduce the likelihood of family breakdown or divorce. Questionnaires completed by participants before and after a course funded by the London Borough of Waltham Forest found that parents thought the programme had helped them to manage their children's behaviour more effectively. An external evaluation of Parent Link by Professor Hilton Davies of the Bloomfield Centre of Guy's hospital found that over 70 per cent of parents said they had observed significant improvements in their children's behaviour.

Dorset Healthy Alliance Project: an experimental project sponsored by the Home Office Programme Development Unit, which promoted closer parent-school links tackling a range of behavioural problems, including disruptive behaviour, truancy and bullying. An education welfare officer based at a primary school in Bournemouth was able to launch a number of initiatives, including home visits to encourage attendance at school parents' evenings; anti-bullying campaigns; and preventing exclusions and truancy by enlisting the active support of parents in setting targets for pupils to improve their behaviour.

There are other approaches. For example, some schemes bring together children at risk of offending with trained mentors. Although further research is needed before firm conclusions can be drawn about the value of mentoring, anecdotal evidence from schemes in this country suggests that there may be some benefits.

The *Dalston Youth Project* in Hackney works with children aged 11 to 15 and includes devising tailored programmes which among other things confront motives for offending. The scheme is an extension of a previous project which focused on those aged 15 to 19 and which won the 'Make a difference' award in 1995.

The *CHANCE Project* in Islington provides programmes which include mentoring for children aged five to ten who are deemed to be at risk. The project, like the Dalston Youth

Project, is funded and will be evaluated by the Home Office Programme Development Unit.

The *Milton Keynes Young People's Befriender Scheme* pairs up young people who have been in some trouble with trained mentors. The scheme has not been independently evaluated, but records kept by the scheme co-ordinator in liaison with the police show that at least 80 per cent of those involved in the scheme have not re-offended within one year.

These are some examples of a range of programmes which may help to prevent children offending. The Government believes that these provide a basis for developing a targeted and systematic response locally to children who are at risk of offending. The next chapter examines how this might be done.

Chapter 3. A new framework for preventing offending

INTRODUCTION

Given the extent of juvenile crime, it should be a priority to identify children who are at risk of offending. They should be identified before they start to offend, and as early as possible. They and their parents should be offered the support they need to try to ensure that these children do not turn to crime.

The right way to approach this task is for local agencies to work together, as they currently do for a range of other purposes such as case conferences and planning children's services. The principle of inter-agency co-operation to prevent children offending is not new. But no existing inter-agency group has the specific and sole aim of targeting children at risk of offending and referring them to local programmes which may reduce the risk.

The Government proposes the establishment of a new local organisation, with both operational and supervisory functions. The Government proposes that this should be known as a Child Crime Team, but it would welcome alternative suggestions.

The *operational team* would:

– maintain a register of local programmes

and services of the kind described in the previous chapter;

- identify children who are at risk of offending; and
- refer these children, and their parents if appropriate, to a suitable scheme which may reduce the risk of children offending.

The *supervisory team* would:

- encourage the development of suitable programmes and services, in the light of an assessment of what is needed locally;
- allocate resources for the work of the operational team; and
- monitor the work of the operational team and evaluate its effectiveness. ...

Chapter 5. Making parents face up to their responsibilities

Parents have the primary responsibility for ensuring that children know the difference between right and wrong and are brought up to respect the law. The Government recognises that most parents would be concerned at the prospect of their children turning to crime. It believes that most parents would want to take up the offer of a referral to a suitable scheme if that reduced the risk of their children offending.

However, the Government also notes with concern that a small minority of parents not only fail to exercise adequate control over their children but also fail to respond to the support that is offered. Their children may continue to behave in a way suggesting that they are likely to offend, or may actually commit an offence.

A NEW COURT POWER: THE PARENTAL CONTROL ORDER

The Government accordingly proposes to give the courts a new power, to be called a parental control order, for use in these circumstances. The Government expects that it would generally be used where previous attempts to ensure that parents faced up to their responsibilities had failed. It could be imposed either in its own right where no offence had yet been committed, or instead of a parental bindover where

a child had been convicted of an offence. In the latter case, the order could be imposed in addition to any penalty imposed on the child for the offence. Given that, as explained below, the order would fulfil all the functions of the existing parental bindover in cases where the child had been convicted, and would provide the court with additional powers, it is for consideration whether any useful purpose would be served by retaining the bindover.

Where the child had been convicted, the court would be able to impose the order of its own motion. Where a child was at risk of offending but had not come before a court, the Government envisages that either the police or a social services department would be able to apply for the order.

The order would be available in respect of children aged 16 and under. It would require parents to exercise proper care and control over their child in cases where the court was satisfied that the child had demonstrated behaviour which:

- was likely to lead to offending, or
- had resulted in conviction of an offence;
- this behaviour had resulted from a lack of parental care and control;
- and the new order would be effective in tackling that lack of care and control.

Where the child was aged under ten, the test of demonstrating behaviour which was likely to lead to offending would include doing something which could be charged as an offence if the child was aged ten or over.

In considering whether to make an order, the court would be able to take into account whether the parents had accepted a referral of themselves or their child to a programme offered by the child crime team. The court would also want to consider the ability of the parents to exercise proper care and control, taking into account, for example, the age of the child, and the relationship between the parents and the child. The Government accordingly proposes that before making a parental control order, the court should be able to obtain and consider information about the family circumstances of the child and the likely effect of the order on those circumstances.

In making the order, the court would explain to the parents what they needed to do to comply with it. This would be in the form of conditions attached to the order. These might include attending a suitable programme, or ensuring that the child was at home during certain hours or attending school. This need not entail the parents themselves staying at home, as long as they were able to make suitable alternative arrangements for ensuring that the child was at home.

Bibliography
Graham J (1989) *Families, Parenting Skills and Delinquency*, London: Home Office Research and Statistics Department.

Graham J and Bowling B (1995) *Young People and Crime*, London: Home Office Research and Statistics Directorate.

Lally J R, Mangione P L, Honig A S and Wittner D S (1988) 'More Pride, Less Delinquency: Findings from the Ten Year Follow-up Study of the Syracuse University Family Development Research Program', *Zero-to-three*, vol 8, no 4, 13–18.

McCulloch H (1996) *Shop Theft: Improving the Police Response*, Police Research Group, London: Home Office Police Policy Directorate.

Reid J B, Eddy M, Bank L and Tetrow R (1994) 'A Universal Prevention Strategy for Conduct Disorder: Some Preliminary Findings', paper presented to SRCAP Conference, June 1994, London.

Schweinhart L J (1987) 'Can Pre-school Programmes Help Prevent Delinquency?', in J Q Wilson and G C Loury (eds), *Families, Schools and Delinquency Prevention*, vol III of *From Children to Citizens*, New York: Springer Verlag.

Schweinhart L J and Weikhart D P (1993) *A Summary of Significant Benefits: The High/Scope Perry Pre-School Study through Age 27*, Ypsilanti/Michigan: High/Scope Press.

Utting D et al (1993) *Crime and the Family*, Occasional Paper 16, London: Family Policy Studies Centre.

Pointers are provided for strategies of intervention in relation to young offenders and those at risk of becoming young offenders. A key factor is identified as being the need for early intervention. This can be at a very early age as in the provision of pre-school programmes in disadvantaged neighbourhoods. These have been shown to reduce criminality in later life.

Utting D (1999) *Catching Them Early: What Works in the United Kingdom?*, pp3–4

The risk factors include poor parental supervision, family conflict, family attitudes favourable to antisocial behaviour, low family income and a parent or sibling with a criminal record. At to schooling, going to a poorly organised school, a lack of personal commitment, poor school performance and aggressive behaviour are risk factors. Community risk factors are a disadvantaged neighbourhood, community disorganisation and neglect, the availability of drugs and high turnover and lack of neighbourhood attachment. In terms of friends and peers, the risk factors are alienation and lack of social commitment, attitudes that condone criminal behaviour and involvement in criminal behaviour.

A promising approach is home visiting schemes, which have succeeded in strengthening the bonds of affection between family members. Also successful are family literacy schemes and reading recovery programmes in schools that tackle low educational achievement. The Sheffield anti-bullying initiative is a specific example of a programme that delivered good results. This was evaluated in 23 Sheffield primary and secondary schools. Schools were encouraged to tackle aggressive behaviour and bullying which are known risk factors for violent and criminal behaviour in adolescence and adulthood. This included the creation of a whole school ethos as well as work with individuals. The schools were expected to produce clear and enforceable anti-bullying policies and procedures that were endorsed by governors, staff, parents and pupils. In addition to describing disciplinary measures, schools took steps that included the use of anti-bullying material in the curriculum, classes teaching problem-solving skills, assertiveness training as well as innovative 'no blame' techniques for dealing with bullies. Evaluation a year after the programme was implemented showed a positive impact, with schools that had put the most effort into their strategies generally achieving the best results. Compared with a number of control schools, project schools saw an increase in the number of pupils saying they had not been bullied and a significant decrease in the frequency of bullying, which was most evident in primary schools. An increase in pupils' willingness to take bullying problems to their teachers was most evident in secondary schools.

More generally, cognitive and behavioural approaches seem to offer the most potential. These are characterised as being concerned with behaviour modification; (consistently rewarding socially acceptable behaviour, and ensuring consequences for unacceptable behaviour), social skills training; (teaching new skills for dealing with other people in different settings), problem solving; (seeking to improve problem awareness, ability to foresee likely consequences of antisocial behaviour and ability to work out and negotiate more acceptable solutions), anger management; (improving self-regulation and the ability to relax) and moral reasoning (tackling immature understanding of moral issues, including the effects of crime on victims). These are factors that were identified by Vennard et al (1997), 'The Use of Cognitive-Behavioural Approaches with Offenders: Messages from the Research', Home Office Research Study 171.

An example of such an approach is the Inverclyde Intensive Probation Unit pro-

gramme for 16 to 21-year-olds. Young offenders at serious risk of custody were offered the opportunity, on a voluntary basis, to deal with the problems contributing to their offending behaviour and to learn new social and problem solving skills. Different modules enabled packages to be assembled that were tailored to the individual offender's risk profile needs which are systematically assessed. A study of reconvictions, 18 months after the programme, found that 33 per cent of participants who completed the course had not been reconvicted. This was significantly lower than the reconviction rate for similar high tariff offenders who were referred for assessment but received a custodial sentence or other disposal. Also identified are strategies that do not work and these include general counselling and therapy sessions, corporal punishment, suspension from school and fear arousal.

This Practice Direction, which is concerned with arrangements for the trial of children and young persons, was issued as a response to the recent judgment of the European Court of Human Rights in *V* v *United Kingdom*; *T* v *United Kingdom* (The Times 17 December 1999). During the case the arrangements for the trial of young defendants in the Crown Court were criticised. The case concerned the juvenile killers of James Bulger in 1993.

Practice Direction (Crown Court: Trial of Children and Young Persons) (2000) The Times 17 February Lord Chief Justice's Court (Lord Bingham of Cornhill CJ and Klevan J)

The steps taken in any given case should have regard to the age, maturity and development (intellectual and emotional) of the young defendant on trial and all other circumstances of the case. Some young defendants accused of committing serious crimes might be very young and very immature when standing trial in the Crown Court. The purpose of a trial is to determine guilt (if that was in issue) and to decide the appropriate sentence if the young defendant pleaded guilty or was convicted. The trial process should not itself expose the young defendant to avoidable intimidation, humiliation or distress. All possible steps were to be taken to assist a young defendant to understand and participate in the proceedings. The ordinary trial process should so far as is necessary be adapted to meet those ends. Regard should be had to the welfare of the young defendant as required by s44 of the Children and Young Persons Act 1933.

Before trial

If a young defendant was indicted jointly with an adult defendant, the court should consider at the plea and directions hearing whether the young defendant should be tried on his own. It should normally order this unless a joint trial would be in the interests of justice and would not be unduly prejudicial to the welfare of the young defendant. If a young defendant was tried jointly with an adult the ordinary procedures would apply subject to such modifications (if any) as the court might see fit to order. At the plea and directions hearing before the trial of a young defendant, the court should consider and so far as practicable give directions on the matters noted below. It might be appropriate to arrange a private visit to the court in advance of the trial. Arrangements should be made to try to ensure protection from hostile members of the public and a direction should be made as to the control of pre-trial publicity.

The trial

The trial should, if practicable, be held in a courtroom in which all the participants were on the same or almost the same level. A young defendant should normally, if he wished, be free to sit with members of his family or others in a like relationship and in a place which permitted easy, informal communication with his legal representatives and others with whom he wanted or needed to communicate. The court should explain the proceedings to a young defendant in terms he could understand and remind those representing a young defendant to act in the same manner. The trial should be conducted according to a timetable that took full account of a young defendant's inability to concentrate for long periods. Robes and wigs should not normally be worn. Police officers would similarly normally be in plain clothes. The court should be prepared to restrict attendance, perhaps limited to some of those with an immediate and direct interest in the outcome of the trial. Facilities for reporting the trial should be available but may need to be restricted. A separate audio and perhaps video link for reporters would be a suitable alternative for those not admitted.

An account is provided of the main statutory provisions that relate to young offenders. Sections 16–27 of the Powers of Criminal Courts (Sentencing) Act 2000 makes provision for the system of referral orders, the operation of youth offender panels and a system to provide for youth offender contracts. Sections 63–68 provide for supervision orders, 69–72 action plan orders and 73–75 reparation orders. Sections 89–95 provide rules restricting the use of imprisonment to those over 21 but allow the detention of those who are younger by a system of detention at her majesty's pleasure. Further systems of detention are permitted by ss96–99 (detention in a young offender institution) and ss100–107 (detention and training orders). Sections 135–138 and 150 provide for financial measures in a number of different circumstances. Whether they will be applied to the offender or his parents or guardians depends on the circumstances.

Powers of Criminal Courts (Sentencing) Act 2000, ss16–27, 63–66, 69–75, 89–107, 135–138 and 150

PART III
MANDATORY AND DISCRE-TIONARY REFERRAL OF YOUNG OFFENDERS
Section 16
Referral orders
Duty and power to refer certain young offenders to youth offender panels
16 (1) This section applies where a youth court or other magistrates' court is dealing with a person aged under 18 for an offence and –

(a) neither the offence nor any connected offence is one for which the sentence is fixed by law;

(b) the court is not, in respect of the offence or any connected offence, proposing to impose a custodial sentence on the offender or make a hospital order (within the meaning of the Mental Health Act 1983) in his case; and

(c) the court is not proposing to discharge him absolutely in respect of the offence.

(2) If –

(a) the compulsory referral conditions are satisfied in accordance with s17 below, and

(b) referral is available to the court, the court shall sentence the offender for the offence by ordering him to be referred to a youth offender panel.

(3) If –

(a) the discretionary referral conditions are satisfied in accordance with s17 below, and

(b) referral is available to the court, the court may sentence the offender for the offence by ordering him to be referred to a youth offender panel.

(4) For the purposes of this Part an offence is connected with another if the offender falls to be dealt with for it at the same time as he is dealt with for the other offence (whether or not he is convicted of the offences at the same time or by or before the same court).

(5) For the purposes of this section referral is available to a court if –

(a) the court has been notified by the Secretary of State that arrangements for the implementation of referral orders are available in the area in which it appears to the court that the offender resides or will reside; and

(b) the notice has not been withdrawn.

(6) An order under subs(2) or (3) above is in this Act referred to as a 'referral order'.

(7) No referral order may be made in respect of any offence committed before the commencement of s1 of the Youth Justice and Criminal Evidence Act 1999.

Section 17
The referral conditions
17 (1) For the purposes of s16(2) above the compulsory referral conditions are satisfied in relation to an offence if the offender –

(a) pleaded guilty to the offence and to any connected offence;

(b) has never been convicted by or before a court in the United Kingdom of any offence other than the offence and any connected offence; and

(c) has never been bound over in criminal proceedings in England and Wales or Northern Ireland to keep the peace or to be of good behaviour.

(2) For the purposes of s16(3) above the discretionary referral conditions are satisfied in relation to an offence if –

(a) the offender is being dealt with by the court for the offence and one or more connected offences;

(b) although he pleaded guilty to at least one of the offences mentioned in paragraph (a) above, he also pleaded not guilty to at least one of them;

(c) he has never been convicted by or before a court in the United Kingdom of any offence other than the offences mentioned in paragraph (a) above; and

(d) he has never been bound over in criminal proceedings in England and Wales or Northern Ireland to keep the peace or to be of good behaviour.

(3) The Secretary of State may by regulations make such amendments of this section as he considers appropriate for altering in any way the descriptions of offenders in the case of which the compulsory referral conditions or the discretionary referral conditions fall to be satisfied for the purposes of s16(2) or (3) above (as the case may be).

(4) Any description of offender having effect for those purposes by virtue of such regulations may be framed by reference to such matters as the Secretary of State considers appropriate, including (in particular) one or more of the following –

(a) the offender's age;

(b) how the offender has pleaded;

(c) the offence (or offences) of which the offender has been convicted;

(d) the offender's previous convictions (if any);

(e) how (if at all) the offender has been previously punished or otherwise dealt with by any court; and

(f) any characteristics or behaviour of, or circumstances relating to, any person who has at any time been charged in the same proceedings as the offender (whether or not in respect of the same offence).

(5) For the purposes of this section an offender who has been convicted of an offence in respect of which he was conditionally discharged (whether by a court in England and Wales or in Northern Ireland) shall be treated, despite –

(a) section 14(1) above (conviction of offence for which offender so discharged deemed not a conviction), or

(b) Article 6(1) of the Criminal Justice (Northern Ireland) Order 1996 (corresponding provision for Northern Ireland), as having been convicted of that offence.

Section 18
Making of referral orders: general

18 (1) A referral order shall –

(a) specify the youth offending team responsible for implementing the order;

(b) require the offender to attend each of the meetings of a youth offender panel to be established by the team for the offender; and

(c) specify the period for which any youth offender contract taking effect between the offender and the panel under s23 below is to have effect (which must not be less than three nor more than 12 months).

(2) The youth offending team specified under subs(1)(a) above shall be the team having the function of implementing referral orders in the area in which it appears to the court that the offender resides or will reside.

(3) On making a referral order the court shall explain to the offender in ordinary language –

(a) the effect of the order; and

(b) the consequences which may follow –

(i) if no youth offender contract takes effect between the offender and the panel under s23 below; or

(ii) if the offender breaches any of the terms of any such contract.

(4) Subsections (5) to (7) below apply where, in dealing with an offender for two or more connected offences, a court makes a referral order in respect of each, or each of two or more, of the offences.

(5) The orders shall have the effect of referring the offender to a single youth offender panel; and the provision made by them under subs(1)

above shall accordingly be the same in each case, except that the periods specified under subs(1)(c) may be different.

(6) The court may direct that the period so specified in either or any of the orders is to run concurrently with or be additional to that specified in the other or any of the others; but in exercising its power under this subsection the court must ensure that the total period for which such a contract as is mentioned in subs(1)(c) above is to have effect does not exceed 12 months.

(7) Each of the orders mentioned in subs(4) above shall, for the purposes of this Part, be treated as associated with the other or each of the others.

Section 19
Making of referral orders: effect on court's other sentencing powers

19 (1) Subsections (2) to (5) below apply where a court makes a referral order in respect of an offence.

(2) The court may not deal with the offender for the offence in any of the prohibited ways.

(3) The court –

(a) shall, in respect of any connected offence, either sentence the offender by making a referral order or make an order discharging him absolutely; and

(b) may not deal with the offender for any such offence in any of the prohibited ways.

(4) For the purposes of subs(2) and (3) above the prohibited ways are –

(a) imposing a community sentence on the offender;

(b) ordering him to pay a fine;

(c) making a reparation order in respect of him; and

(d) making an order discharging him conditionally.

(5) The court may not make, in connection with the conviction of the offender for the offence or any connected offence –

(a) an order binding him over to keep the peace or to be of good behaviour;

(b) an order under s150 below (binding over of parent or guardian); or

(c) a parenting order under s8 of the Crime and Disorder Act 1998.

(6) Subsections (2), (3) and (5) above do not affect the exercise of any power to deal with the offender conferred by paragraph 5 (offender referred back to court by panel) or paragraph 14 (powers of a court where offender convicted while subject to referral) of Schedule 1 to this Act.

(7) Where s16(2) above requires a court to make a referral order, the court may not under s1 above defer passing sentence on him, but s16(2) and subs(3)(a) above do not affect any power or duty of a magistrates' court under –

(a) section 8 above (remission to youth court, or another such court, for sentence);

(b) section 10(3) of the Magistrates' Courts Act 1980 (adjournment for inquiries); or

(c) section 35, 38, 43 or 44 of the Mental Health Act 1983 (remand for reports, interim hospital orders and committal to Crown Court for restriction order).

Section 20
Making of referral orders: attendance of parents etc

20 (1) A court making a referral order may make an order requiring –

(a) the appropriate person, or

(b) in a case where there are two or more appropriate persons, any one or more of them, to attend the meetings of the youth offender panel.

(2) Where an offender is aged under 16 when a court makes a referral order in his case –

(a) the court shall exercise its power under subs(1) above so as to require at least one appropriate person to attend meetings of the youth offender panel; and

(b) if the offender falls within subs(6)

below, the person or persons so required to attend those meetings shall be or include a representative of the local authority mentioned in that subsection.

(3) The court shall not under this section make an order requiring a person to attend meetings of the youth offender panel –

(a) if the court is satisfied that it would be unreasonable to do so; or

(b) to an extent which the court is satisfied would be unreasonable.

(4) Except where the offender falls within subs(6) below, each person who is a parent or guardian of the offender is an 'appropriate person' for the purposes of this section.

(5) Where the offender falls within subs(6) below, each of the following is an 'appropriate person' for the purposes of this section –

(a) a representative of the local authority mentioned in that subsection; and

(b) each person who is a parent or guardian of the offender with whom the offender is allowed to live.

(6) An offender falls within this subsection if he is (within the meaning of the Children Act 1989) a child who is looked after by a local authority.

(7) If, at the time when a court makes an order under this section –

(a) a person who is required by the order to attend meetings of a youth offender panel is not present in court, or

(b) a local authority whose representative is so required to attend such meetings is not represented in court, the court must send him or (as the case may be) the authority a copy of the order forthwith.

Section 21
Youth offender panels
Establishment of panels

21 (1) Where a referral order has been made in respect of an offender (or two or more associated referral orders have been so made), it is the duty of the youth offending team specified in the order (or orders) –

(a) to establish a youth offender panel for the offender;

(b) to arrange for the first meeting of the panel to be held for the purposes of s23 below; and

(c) subsequently to arrange for the holding of any further meetings of the panel required by virtue of s25 below (in addition to those required by virtue of any other provision of this Part).

(2) A youth offender panel shall –

(a) be constituted,

(b) conduct its proceedings, and

(c) discharge its functions under this Part (and in particular those arising under s23 below), in accordance with guidance given from time to time by the Secretary of State.

(3) At each of its meetings a panel shall, however, consist of at least –

(a) one member appointed by the youth offending team from among its members; and

(b) two members so appointed who are not members of the team.

(4) The Secretary of State may by regulations make provision requiring persons appointed as members of a youth offender panel to have such qualifications, or satisfy such other criteria, as are specified in the regulations.

(5) Where it appears to the court which made a referral order that, by reason of either a change or a prospective change in the offender's place or intended place of residence, the youth offending team for the time being specified in the order ('the current team') either does not or will not have the function of implementing referral orders in the area in which the offender resides or will reside, the court may amend the order so that it instead specifies the team which has the func-

tion of implementing such orders in that area ('the new team').

(6) Where a court so amends a referral order –

(a) subsection (1)(a) above shall apply to the new team in any event;

(b) subsection (1)(b) above shall apply to the new team if no youth offender contract has (or has under paragraph (c) below been treated as having) taken effect under s23 below between the offender and a youth offender panel established by the current team;

(c) if such a contract has (or has previously under this paragraph been treated as having) so taken effect, it shall (after the amendment) be treated as if it were a contract which had taken effect under s23 below between the offender and the panel being established for the offender by the new team.

(7) References in this Part to the meetings of a youth offender panel (or any such meeting) are to the following meetings of the panel (or any of them) –

(a) the first meeting held in pursuance of subs(1)(b) above;

(b) any further meetings held in pursuance of s25 below;

(c) any progress meeting held under s26 below; and

(d) the final meeting held under s27 below.

Section 22
Attendance at panel meetings

22 (1) The specified team shall, in the case of each meeting of the panel established for the offender, notify –

(a) the offender, and

(b) any person to whom an order under s20 above applies, of the time and place at which he is required to attend that meeting.

(2) If the offender fails to attend any part of such a meeting the panel may –

(a) adjourn the meeting to such time and place as it may specify; or

(b) end the meeting and refer the offender back to the appropriate court; and subs(1) above shall apply in relation to any such adjourned meeting.

(3) One person aged 18 or over chosen by the offender, with the agreement of the panel, shall be entitled to accompany the offender to any meeting of the panel (and it need not be the same person who accompanies him to every meeting).

(4) The panel may allow to attend any such meeting –

(a) any person who appears to the panel to be a victim of, or otherwise affected by, the offence, or any of the offences, in respect of which the offender was referred to the panel;

(b) any person who appears to the panel to be someone capable of having a good influence on the offender.

(5) Where the panel allows any such person as is mentioned in subs(4)(a) above ('the victim') to attend a meeting of the panel, the panel may allow the victim to be accompanied to the meeting by one person chosen by the victim with the agreement of the panel.

Section 23
Youth offender contracts
First meeting: agreement of contract with offender

23 (1) At the first meeting of the youth offender panel established for an offender the panel shall seek to reach agreement with the offender on a programme of behaviour the aim (or principal aim) of which is the prevention of re-offending by the offender.

(2) The terms of the programme may, in particular, include provision for any of the following –

(a) the offender to make financial or other reparation to any person who appears to the panel to be a victim of, or otherwise affected by, the offence, or any of the offences, for which the offender was referred to the panel;

(b) the offender to attend mediation sessions with any such victim or other person;

(c) the offender to carry out unpaid work or service in or for the community;

(d) the offender to be at home at times specified in or determined under the programme;

(e) attendance by the offender at a school or other educational establishment or at a place of work;

(f) the offender to participate in specified activities (such as those designed to address offending behaviour, those offering education or training or those assisting with the rehabilitation of persons dependent on, or having a propensity to misuse, alcohol or drugs);

(g) the offender to present himself to specified persons at times and places specified in or determined under the programme;

(h) the offender to stay away from specified places or persons (or both);

(i) enabling the offender's compliance with the programme to be supervised and recorded.

(3) The programme may not, however, provide –

(a) for the electronic monitoring of the offender's whereabouts; or

(b) for the offender to have imposed on him any physical restriction on his movements.

(4) No term which provides for anything to be done to or with any such victim or other affected person as is mentioned in subs(2)(a) above may be included in the programme without the consent of that person.

(5) Where a programme is agreed between the offender and the panel, the panel shall cause a written record of the programme to be produced forthwith –

(a) in language capable of being readily understood by, or explained to, the offender; and

(b) for signature by him.

(6) Once the record has been signed –

(a) by the offender, and

(b) by a member of the panel on behalf of the panel, the terms of the programme, as set out in the record, take effect as the terms of a 'youth offender contract' between the offender and the panel; and the panel shall cause a copy of the record to be given or sent to the offender.

Section 24
First meeting: duration of contract

24 (1) This section applies where a youth offender contract has taken effect under s23 above between an offender and a youth offender panel.

(2) The day on which the contract so takes effect shall be the first day of the period for which it has effect.

(3) Where the panel was established in pursuance of a single referral order, the length of the period for which the contract has effect shall be that of the period specified under s18(1) (c) above in the referral order.

(4) Where the panel was established in pursuance of two or more associated referral orders, the length of the period for which the contract has effect shall be that resulting from the court's directions under s18(6) above.

(5) Subsections (3) and (4) above have effect subject to –

(a) any order under paragraph 11 or 12 of Schedule 1 to this Act extending the length of the period for which the contract has effect; and

(b) subs(6) below.

(6) If the referral order, or each of the associated referral orders, is revoked (whether under paragraph 5(2) of Schedule 1 to this Act or by virtue of paragraph 14(2) of that Schedule),

the period for which the contract has effect expires at the time when the order or orders is or are revoked unless it has already expired.

Section 25

First meeting: failure to agree contract

25 (1) Where it appears to a youth offender panel to be appropriate to do so, the panel may –

(a) end the first meeting (or any further meeting held in pursuance of paragraph (b) below) without having reached agreement with the offender on a programme of behaviour of the kind mentioned in s23(1) above; and

(b) resume consideration of the offender's case at a further meeting of the panel.

(2) If, however, it appears to the panel at the first meeting or any such further meeting that there is no prospect of agreement being reached with the offender within a reasonable period after the making of the referral order (or orders) –

(a) subsection (1)(b) above shall not apply; and

(b) instead the panel shall refer the offender back to the appropriate court.

(3) If at a meeting of the panel –

(a) agreement is reached with the offender but he does not sign the record produced in pursuance of s23(5) above, and

(b) his failure to do so appears to the panel to be unreasonable, the panel shall end the meeting and refer the offender back to the appropriate court.

Section 26

Progress meetings

26 (1) At any time –

(a) after a youth offender contract has taken effect under s23 above, but

(b) before the end of the period for which the contract has effect, the specified team shall, if so requested by the panel, arrange

for the holding of a meeting of the panel under this section ('a progress meeting').

(2) The panel may make a request under subs(1) above if it appears to the panel to be expedient to review –

(a) the offender's progress in implementing the programme of behaviour contained in the contract; or

(b) any other matter arising in connection with the contract.

(3) The panel shall make such a request if –

(a) the offender has notified the panel that –

(i) he wishes to seek the panel's agreement to a variation in the terms of the contract; or

(ii) he wishes the panel to refer him back to the appropriate court with a view to the referral order (or orders) being revoked on account of a significant change in his circumstances (such as his being taken to live abroad) making compliance with any youth offender contract impractical; or

(b) it appears to the panel that the offender is in breach of any of the terms of the contract.

(4) At a progress meeting the panel shall do such one or more of the following things as it considers appropriate in the circumstances, namely –

(a) review the offender's progress or any such other matter as is mentioned in subsection (2) above;

(b) discuss with the offender any breach of the terms of the contract which it appears to the panel that he has committed;

(c) consider any variation in the terms of the contract sought by the offender or which it appears to the panel to be expedient to make in the light of any such review or discussion;

(d) consider whether to accede to any request by the offender that he be referred back to the appropriate court.

(5) Where the panel has discussed with the

offender such a breach as is mentioned in subs(4)(b) above –

(a) the panel and the offender may agree that the offender is to continue to be required to comply with the contract (either in its original form or with any agreed variation in its terms) without being referred back to the appropriate court; or

(b) the panel may decide to end the meeting and refer the offender back to that court.

(6) Where a variation in the terms of the contract is agreed between the offender and the panel, the panel shall cause a written record of the variation to be produced forthwith –

(a) in language capable of being readily understood by, or explained to, the offender; and

(b) for signature by him.

(7) Any such variation shall take effect once the record has been signed –

(a) by the offender; and

(b) by a member of the panel on behalf of the panel; and the panel shall cause a copy of the record to be given or sent to the offender.

(8) If at a progress meeting –

(a) any such variation is agreed but the offender does not sign the record produced in pursuance of subs(6) above, and

(b) his failure to do so appears to the panel to be unreasonable, the panel may end the meeting and refer the offender back to the appropriate court.

(9) Section 23(2) to (4) above shall apply in connection with what may be provided for by the terms of the contract as varied under this section as they apply in connection with what may be provided for by the terms of a programme of behaviour of the kind mentioned in s23(1).

(10) Where the panel has discussed with the offender such a request as is mentioned in subs(4) (d) above, the panel may, if it is satis-fied that there is (or is soon to be) such a change in circumstances as is mentioned in subs(3)(a)(ii) above, decide to end the meeting and refer the offender back to the appropriate court.

Section 27
Final meeting

27 (1) Where the compliance period in the case of a youth offender contract is due to expire, the specified team shall arrange for the holding, before the end of that period, of a meeting of the panel under this section ('the final meeting').

(2) At the final meeting the panel shall –

(a) review the extent of the offender's compliance to date with the terms of the contract; and

(b) decide, in the light of that review, whether his compliance with those terms has been such as to justify the conclusion that, by the time the compliance period expires, he will have satisfactorily completed the contract; and the panel shall give the offender written confirmation of its decision.

(3) Where the panel decides that the offender's compliance with the terms of the contract has been such as to justify that conclusion, the panel's decision shall have the effect of discharging the referral order (or orders) as from the end of the compliance period.

(4) Otherwise the panel shall refer the offender back to the appropriate court.

(5) Nothing in s22(2) above prevents the panel from making the decision mentioned in subs(3) above in the offender's absence if it appears to the panel to be appropriate to do that instead of exercising either of its powers under s22(2).

(6) Section 22(2)(a) above does not permit the final meeting to be adjourned (or re-adjourned) to a time falling after the end of the compliance period.

(7) In this section 'the compliance period', in

relation to a youth offender contract, means the period for which the contract has effect in accordance with s24 above.

CHAPTER V COMMUNITY ORDERS AVAILABLE ONLY WHERE OFFENDER AGED UNDER 18
Section 63
Supervision orders

63 (1) Where a child or young person (that is to say, any person aged under 18) is convicted of an offence, the court by or before which he is convicted may (subject to ss34 to 36 above) make an order placing him under the supervision of –

(a) a local authority designated by the order;

(b) a probation officer; or

(c) a member of a youth offending team.

(2) An order under subs(1) above is in this Act referred to as a 'supervision order'.

(3) In this Act 'supervisor', in relation to a supervision order, means the person under whose supervision the offender is placed or to be placed by the order.

(4) Schedule 6 to this Act (which specifies requirements that may be included in supervision orders) shall have effect.

(5) A court shall not make a supervision order unless it is satisfied that the offender resides or will reside in the area of a local authority; and a court shall be entitled to be satisfied that the offender will so reside if he is to be required so to reside by a provision to be included in the order in pursuance of paragraph 1 of Schedule 6 to this Act.

(6) A supervision order –

(a) shall name the area of the local authority and the petty sessions area in which it appears to the court making the order (or to the court amending under Schedule 7 to this Act any provision included in the order in pursuance of this paragraph) that the offender resides or will reside; and

(b) may contain such prescribed provi-sions as the court making the order (or amending it under that Schedule) considers appropriate for facilitating the performance by the supervisor of his functions under s64(4) below, including any prescribed provisions for requiring visits to be made by the offender to the supervisor; and in paragraph (b) above 'prescribed' means prescribed by rules under s144 of the Magistrates' Courts Act 1980.

(7) A supervision order shall, unless it has previously been revoked, cease to have effect at the end of the period of three years, or such shorter period as may be specified in the order, beginning with the date on which the order was originally made.

(8) A court which makes a supervision order shall forthwith send a copy of its order –

(a) to the offender and, if the offender is aged under 14, to his parent or guardian;

(b) to the supervisor;

(c) to any local authority who are not entitled by virtue of paragraph (b) above to such a copy and whose area is named in the supervision order in pursuance of subs(6) above;

(d) where the offender is required by the order to reside with an individual or to undergo treatment by or under the direction of an individual or at any place, to the individual or the person in charge of that place; and

(e) where a petty sessions area named in the order in pursuance of subs(6) above is not that for which the court acts, to the justices' chief executive for the petty sessions area so named; and, in a case falling within paragraph (e) above, shall also send to the justices' chief executive in question such documents and information relating to the case as the court considers likely to be of assistance to them.

(9) If a court makes a supervision order while another such order made by any court is in force in respect of the offender, the court making the new order may revoke the earlier

order (and paragraph 10 of Schedule 7 to this Act (supplementary provision) shall apply to the revocation).

Section 64
Selection and duty of supervisor and certain expenditure of his

64 (1) A court shall not designate a local authority as the supervisor by a provision of a supervision order unless –

(a) the authority agree; or

(b) it appears to the court that the offender resides or will reside in the area of the authority.

(2) Where a provision of a supervision order places the offender under the supervision of a probation officer, the supervisor shall be a probation officer appointed for or assigned to the petty sessions area named in the order in pursuance of s63(6) above and selected under arrangements made under s4(1)(d) of the Probation Service Act 1993 (arrangements made by probation committee).

(3) Where a provision of a supervision order places the offender under the supervision of a member of a youth offending team, the supervisor shall be a member of a team established by the local authority within whose area it appears to the court that the offender resides or will reside.

(4) While a supervision order is in force, the supervisor shall advise, assist and befriend the offender.

(5) Where a supervision order –

(a) requires compliance with directions given by virtue of paragraph 2(1) of Schedule 6 to this Act, or

(b) includes by virtue of paragraph 3(2) of that Schedule a requirement which involves the use of facilities for the time being specified in a scheme in force under s66 below for an area in which the offender resides or will reside,

any expenditure incurred by the supervisor for the purposes of the directions or requirements

shall be defrayed by the local authority whose area is named in the order in pursuance of s63 (6) above.

Section 65
Breach, revocation and amendment of supervision orders

65 Schedule 7 to this Act (which makes provision for dealing with failures to comply with supervision orders and for revoking and amending such orders) shall have effect.

Section 66
Facilities for implementing supervision orders

66 (1) A local authority shall, acting either individually or in association with other local authorities, make arrangements with such persons as appear to them to be appropriate for the provision by those persons of facilities for enabling –

(a) directions given by virtue of paragraph 2(1) of Schedule 6 to this Act to persons resident in their area, and

(b) requirements that (because of paragraph 3(7) of that Schedule) may only be included in a supervision order by virtue of paragraph 3(2) of that Schedule if they are for the time being specified in a scheme, to be carried out effectively.

(2) The authority or authorities making any arrangements in accordance with subs(1) above shall consult each relevant probation committee as to the arrangements.

(3) Any such arrangements shall be specified in a scheme made by the authority or authorities making them.

(4) A scheme shall come into force on a date to be specified in it.

(5) The authority or authorities making a scheme shall send copies of it to the justices' chief executive for each petty sessions area of which any part is included in the area to which the scheme relates.

(6) A copy of the scheme shall be kept avail-

able at the principal office of every authority who are a party to it for inspection by members of the public at all reasonable hours; and any such authority shall on demand by any person supply him with a copy of the scheme free of charge.

(7) The authority or authorities who made a scheme may at any time make a further scheme altering the arrangements or specifying arrangements to be substituted for those previously specified.

(8) A scheme which specifies arrangements to be substituted for those specified in a previous scheme shall revoke the previous scheme.

(9) The powers conferred by subs(7) above shall not be exercisable by an authority or authorities unless they have first consulted each relevant probation committee.

(10) The authority or authorities who made a scheme shall send to the justices' chief executive for each petty sessions area of which any part is included in the area for which arrangements under this section have been specified in the scheme notice of any exercise of a power conferred by subs(7) above, specifying the date for the coming into force, and giving details of the effect, of the new or altered arrangements; and the new or altered arrangements shall come into force on that date.

(11) Arrangements shall not be made under this section for the provision of any facilities unless the facilities are approved or are of a kind approved by the Secretary of State for the purposes of this section.

(12) In this section 'relevant probation committee' means a probation committee for an area of which any part is included in the area to which a scheme under this section relates.

Section 69
Action plan orders

69 (1) Where a child or young person (that is to say, any person aged under 18) is convicted of an offence and the court by or before which he is convicted is of the opinion mentioned in subs(3) below, the court may (subject to ss34 to 36 above) make an order which –

(a) requires the offender, for a period of three months beginning with the date of the order, to comply with an action plan, that is to say, a series of requirements with respect to his actions and whereabouts during that period;

(b) places the offender for that period under the supervision of the responsible officer; and

(c) requires the offender to comply with any directions given by the responsible officer with a view to the implementation of that plan; and the requirements included in the order, and any directions given by the responsible officer, may include requirements authorised by s70 below.

(2) An order under subs(1) above is in this Act referred to as an 'action plan order'.

(3) The opinion referred to in subs(1) above is that the making of an action plan order is desirable in the interests of –

(a) securing the rehabilitation of the offender; or

(b) preventing the commission by him of further offences.

(4) In this Act 'responsible officer', in relation to an offender subject to an action plan order, means one of the following who is specified in the order, namely –

(a) a probation officer;

(b) a social worker of a local authority social services department;

(c) a member of a youth offending team.

(5) The court shall not make an action plan order in respect of the offender if –

(a) he is already the subject of such an order; or

(b) the court proposes to pass on him a custodial sentence or to make in respect of him a probation order, a community service order, a combination order, an attendance centre order, a supervision order or a referral order.

(6) Before making an action plan order, the court shall obtain and consider –

(a) a written report by a probation officer, a social worker of a local authority social services department or a member of a youth offending team indicating –

(i) the requirements proposed by that person to be included in the order;

(ii) the benefits to the offender that the proposed requirements are designed to achieve; and

(iii) the attitude of a parent or guardian of the offender to the proposed requirements; and

(b) where the offender is aged under 16, information about the offender's family circumstances and the likely effect of the order on those circumstances.

(7) The court shall not make an action plan order unless it has been notified by the Secretary of State that arrangements for implementing such orders are available in the area proposed to be named in the order under subs(8) below and the notice has not been withdrawn.

(8) An action plan order shall name the petty sessions area in which it appears to the court making the order (or to the court amending under Schedule 8 to this Act any provision included in the order in pursuance of this subsection) that the offender resides or will reside.

(9) Where an action plan order specifies a probation officer under subs(4) above, the officer specified must be an officer appointed for or assigned to the petty sessions area named in the order.

(10) Where an action plan order specifies under that subsection –

(a) a social worker of a local authority social services department, or

(b) a member of a youth offending team, the social worker or member specified must be a social worker of, or a member of a youth offending team established by, the local authority within whose area it appears to the court that the offender resides or will reside.

(11) Before making an action plan order, the court shall explain to the offender in ordinary language –

(a) the effect of the order and of the requirements proposed to be included in it;

(b) the consequences which may follow (under Schedule 8 to this Act) if he fails to comply with any of those requirements; and

(c) that the court has power (under that Schedule) to review the order on the application either of the offender or of the responsible officer.

Section 70
Requirements which may be included in action plan orders and directions

70 (1) Requirements included in an action plan order, or directions given by a responsible officer, may require the offender to do all or any of the following things, namely –

(a) to participate in activities specified in the requirements or directions at a time or times so specified;

(b) to present himself to a person or persons specified in the requirements or directions at a place or places and at a time or times so specified;

(c) subject to subs(2) below, to attend at an attendance centre specified in the requirements or directions for a number of hours so specified;

(d) to stay away from a place or places specified in the requirements or directions;

(e) to comply with any arrangements for his education specified in the requirements or directions;

(f) to make reparation specified in the requirements or directions to a person or persons so specified or to the community at large; and

(g) to attend any hearing fixed by the court under s71 below.

(2) Subsection (1)(c) above applies only where the offence committed by the offender is an offence punishable with imprisonment.

(3) In subsection (1)(f) above 'make reparation', in relation to an offender, means make reparation for the offence otherwise than by the payment of compensation.

(4) A person shall not be specified in requirements or directions under subs(1)(f) above unless –

>   (a) he is identified by the court or (as the case may be) the responsible officer as a victim of the offence or a person otherwise affected by it; and

>   (b) he consents to the reparation being made.

(5) Requirements included in an action plan order and directions given by a responsible officer shall, as far as practicable, be such as to avoid –

>   (a) any conflict with the offender's religious beliefs or with the requirements of any other community order to which he may be subject; and

>   (b) any interference with the times, if any, at which he normally works or attends school or any other educational establishment.

Section 71
Action plan orders: power to fix further hearings

71 (1) Immediately after making an action plan order, a court may –

>   (a) fix a further hearing for a date not more than 21 days after the making of the order; and

>   (b) direct the responsible officer to make, at that hearing, a report as to the effectiveness of the order and the extent to which it has been implemented.

(2) At a hearing fixed under subs(1) above, the court –

>   (a) shall consider the responsible officer's report; and

>   (b) may, on the application of the responsible officer or the offender, amend the order –

>   >   (i) by cancelling any provision included in it; or

>   >   (ii) by inserting in it (either in addition to or in substitution for any of its provisions) any provision that the court could originally have included in it.

Section 72
Breach, revocation and amendment of action plan orders

72 Schedule 8 to this Act (which makes provision for dealing with failures to comply with action plan orders and reparation orders and for revoking and amending such orders) shall have effect so far as relating to action plan orders.

CHAPTER VI REPARATION ORDERS FOR YOUNG OFFENDERS
Section 73
Reparation orders

73 (1) Where a child or young person (that is to say, any person aged under 18) is convicted of an offence other than one for which the sentence is fixed by law, the court by or before which he is convicted may make an order requiring him to make reparation specified in the order –

>   (a) to a person or persons so specified; or

>   (b) to the community at large; and any person so specified must be a person identified by the court as a victim of the offence or a person otherwise affected by it.

(2) An order under subs(1) above is in this Act referred to as a 'reparation order'.

(3) In this section and s74 below 'make reparation', in relation to an offender, means make reparation for the offence otherwise than by the payment of compensation; and the requirements that may be specified in a reparation order are subject to s74(1) to (3).

(4) The court shall not make a reparation order in respect of the offender if it proposes –

(a) to pass on him a custodial sentence; or

(b) to make in respect of him a community service order, a combination order, a supervision order which includes requirements authorised by Schedule 6 to this Act, an action plan order or a referral order.

(5) Before making a reparation order, a court shall obtain and consider a written report by a probation officer, a social worker of a local authority social services department or a member of a youth offending team indicating –

(a) the type of work that is suitable for the offender; and

(b) the attitude of the victim or victims to the requirements proposed to be included in the order.

(6) The court shall not make a reparation order unless it has been notified by the Secretary of State that arrangements for implementing such orders are available in the area proposed to be named in the order under s74(4) below and the notice has not been withdrawn.

(7) Before making a reparation order, the court shall explain to the offender in ordinary language –

(a) the effect of the order and of the requirements proposed to be included in it;

(b) the consequences which may follow (under Schedule 8 to this Act) if he fails to comply with any of those requirements; and

(c) that the court has power (under that Schedule) to review the order on the application either of the offender or of the responsible officer; and 'responsible officer' here has the meaning given by s74(5) below.

(8) The court shall give reasons if it does not make a reparation order in a case where it has power to do so.

Section 74
Requirements and provisions of reparation order, and obligations of person subject to it

74 (1) A reparation order shall not require the offender –

(a) to work for more than 24 hours in aggregate; or

(b) to make reparation to any person without the consent of that person.

(2) Subject to subs(1) above, requirements specified in a reparation order shall be such as in the opinion of the court are commensurate with the seriousness of the offence, or the combination of the offence and one or more offences associated with it.

(3) Requirements so specified shall, as far as practicable, be such as to avoid –

(a) any conflict with the offender's religious beliefs or with the requirements of any community order to which he may be subject; and

(b) any interference with the times, if any, at which he normally works or attends school or any other educational establishment.

(4) A reparation order shall name the petty sessions area in which it appears to the court making the order (or to the court amending under Schedule 8 to this Act any provision included in the order in pursuance of this subsection) that the offender resides or will reside.

(5) In this Act 'responsible officer', in relation to an offender subject to a reparation order, means one of the following who is specified in the order, namely –

(a) a probation officer;

(b) a social worker of a local authority social services department;

(c) a member of a youth offending team.

(6) Where a reparation order specifies a probation officer under subs(5) above, the officer specified must be an officer appointed for or

assigned to the petty sessions area named in the order.

(7) Where a reparation order specifies under that subsection –

(a) a social worker of a local authority social services department, or

(b) a member of a youth offending team, the social worker or member specified must be a social worker of, or a member of a youth offending team established by, the local authority within whose area it appears to the court that the offender resides or will reside.

(8) Any reparation required by a reparation order –

(a) shall be made under the supervision of the responsible officer; and

(b) shall be made within a period of three months from the date of the making of the order.

Section 75
Breach, revocation and amendment of reparation orders

75 Schedule 8 to this Act (which makes provision for dealing with failures to comply with action plan orders and reparation orders and for revoking and amending such orders) shall have effect so far as relating to reparation orders.

CHAPTER II DETENTION AND CUSTODY OF YOUNG OFFENDERS
Section 89
Restriction on imposing imprisonment on persons under 21

89 (1) Subject to subs(2) below, no court shall –

(a) pass a sentence of imprisonment on a person for an offence if he is aged under 21 when convicted of the offence; or

(b) commit a person aged under 21 to prison for any reason.

(2) Nothing in subs(1) above shall prevent the committal to prison of a person aged under 21 who is –

(a) remanded in custody;

(b) committed in custody for trial or sentence; or

(c) sent in custody for trial under s51 of the Crime and Disorder Act 1998.

Section 90
Offenders who commit murder when under 18: duty to detain at Her Majesty's pleasure

90 Where a person convicted of murder appears to the court to have been aged under 18 at the time the offence was committed, the court shall (notwithstanding anything in this or any other Act) sentence him to be detained during Her Majesty's pleasure.

Section 91
Offenders under 18 convicted of certain serious offences: power to detain for specified period

91 (1) Subsection (3) below applies where a person aged under 18 is convicted on indictment of –

(a) an offence punishable in the case of a person aged 21 or over with imprisonment for 14 years or more, not being an offence the sentence for which is fixed by law; or

(b) an offence under s14 of the Sexual Offences Act 1956 (indecent assault on a woman); or

(c) an offence under s15 of that Act (indecent assault on a man) committed after 30th September 1997.

(2) Subsection (3) below also applies where a person aged at least 14 but under 18 is convicted of an offence under –

(a) section 1 of the Road Traffic Act 1988 (causing death by dangerous driving); or

(b) section 3A of that Act (causing death by careless driving while under influence of drink or drugs).

(3) If the court is of the opinion that none of the other methods in which the case may legally be dealt with is suitable, the court may sentence the offender to be detained for such period, not exceeding the maximum term of imprisonment with which the offence is punishable in the case of a person aged 21 or over, as may be specified in the sentence.

(4) Subsection (3) above is subject to (in particular) ss79 and 80 above.

Section 92
Detention under sections 90 and 91: place of detention etc

92 (1) A person sentenced to be detained under s90 or 91 above shall be liable to be detained in such place and under such conditions –

(a) as the Secretary of State may direct; or

(b) as the Secretary of State may arrange with any person.

(2) A person detained pursuant to the directions or arrangements made by the Secretary of State under this section shall be deemed to be in legal custody.

(3) A direction of the Secretary of State under this section may be signified only –

(a) under the hand of the Secretary of State or an Under-Secretary of State or an Assistant Under-Secretary; or

(b) under the hand of an authorised officer; and arrangements of the Secretary of State under this section may be signified only as mentioned in paragraph (a) above.

Section 93
Duty to impose custody for life in certain cases where offender under 21

93 Where a person aged under 21 is convicted of murder or any other offence the sentence for which is fixed by law as imprisonment for life, the court shall sentence him to custody for life unless he is liable to be detained under s90 above.

Section 94
Power to impose custody for life in certain other cases where offender at least 18 but under 21

94 (1) Where a person aged at least 18 but under 21 is convicted of an offence –

(a) for which the sentence is not fixed by law, but

(b) for which a person aged 21 or over would be liable to imprisonment for life, the court shall, if it considers that a sentence for life would be appropriate, sentence him to custody for life.

(2) Subsection (1) above is subject to (in particular) ss79 and 80 above, but this subsection does not apply in relation to a sentence which falls to be imposed under s109(2) below.

Section 95
Custody for life: place of detention

95 (1) Subject to s22(2)(b) of the Prison Act 1952 (removal to hospital etc), an offender sentenced to custody for life shall be detained in a young offender institution unless a direction under subs(2) below is in force in relation to him.

(2) The Secretary of State may from time to time direct that an offender sentenced to custody for life shall be detained in a prison or remand centre instead of a young offender institution.

Section 96
Detention in a young offender institution for other cases where offender at least 18 but under 21

96 Subject to ss90, 93 and 94 above, where –

(a) a person aged at least 18 but under 21 is convicted of an offence which is punishable with imprisonment in the case of a person aged 21 or over, and

(b) the court is of the opinion that either or both of paragraphs (a) and (b) of s79(2) above apply or the case falls within s79(3), the sentence that the court is to pass is a sentence of detention in a young offender institution.

Section 97
Term of detention in a young offender institution, and consecutive sentences

97 (1) The maximum term of detention in a young offender institution that a court may impose for an offence is the same as the maximum term of imprisonment that it may impose for that offence.

(2) Subject to subs(3) below, a court shall not pass a sentence for an offender's detention in a young offender institution for less than 21 days.

(3) A court may pass a sentence of detention in a young offender institution for less than 21 days for an offence under s65(6) of the Criminal Justice Act 1991 (breach of requirement imposed on young offender on his release from detention).

(4) Where –

    (a) an offender is convicted of more than one offence for which he is liable to a sentence of detention in a young offender institution, or

    (b) an offender who is serving a sentence of detention in a young offender institution is convicted of one or more further offences for which he is liable to such a sentence,

the court shall have the same power to pass consecutive sentences of detention in a young offender institution as if they were sentences of imprisonment.

(5) Subject to s84 above (restriction on consecutive sentences for released prisoners), where an offender who –

    (a) is serving a sentence of detention in a young offender institution, and

    (b) is aged 21 or over, is convicted of one or more further offences for which he is liable to imprisonment, the court shall have the power to pass one or more sentences of imprisonment to run consecu-

tively upon the sentence of detention in a young offender institution.

Section 98
Detention in a young offender institution: place of detention

98 (1) Subject to s22(2)(b) of the Prison Act 1952 (removal to hospital etc), an offender sentenced to detention in a young offender institution shall be detained in such an institution unless a direction under subs(2) below is in force in relation to him.

(2) The Secretary of State may from time to time direct that an offender sentenced to detention in a young offender institution shall be detained in a prison or remand centre instead of a young offender institution.

Section 99
Conversion of sentence of detention or custody to sentence of imprisonment

99 (1) Subject to the following provisions of this section, where an offender has been sentenced to a term of detention in a young offender institution and either –

    (a) he has attained the age of 21, or

    (b) he has attained the age of 18 and has been reported to the Secretary of State by the board of visitors of the institution in which he is detained as exercising a bad influence on the other inmates of the institution or as behaving in a disruptive manner to the detriment of those inmates, the Secretary of State may direct that he shall be treated as if he had been sentenced to imprisonment for the same term.

(2) An offender who by virtue of this section falls to be treated as if he had been sentenced to imprisonment instead of detention in a young offender institution shall not be so treated for the purposes of s65 of the Criminal Justice Act 1991 (supervision of young offenders after release).

(3) Where the Secretary of State gives a direction under subs(1) above in relation to an offender, the portion of the term of detention

in a young offender institution imposed by the sentence of detention in a young offender institution which he has already served shall be deemed to have been a portion of a term of imprisonment.

(4) Rules under s47 of the Prison Act 1952 may provide that any award for an offence against discipline made in respect of an offender serving a sentence of detention in a young offender institution shall continue to have effect after a direction under subs(1) above has been given in relation to him.

(5) This section applies to a person –

(a) who is detained under s90 or 91 above, or

(b) who is serving a sentence of custody for life, as it applies to a person serving a sentence of detention in a young offender institution.

Section 100
Offenders under 18: detention and training orders

100 (1) Subject to ss90, 91 and 93 above and subs(2) below, where –

(a) a child or young person (that is to say, any person aged under 18) is convicted of an offence which is punishable with imprisonment in the case of a person aged 21 or over, and

(b) the court is of the opinion that either or both of paragraphs (a) and (b) of s79(2) above apply or the case falls within s79(3), the sentence that the court is to pass is a detention and training order.

(2) A court shall not make a detention and training order –

(a) in the case of an offender under the age of 15 at the time of the conviction, unless it is of the opinion that he is a persistent offender;

(b) in the case of an offender under the age of 12 at that time, unless –

(i) it is of the opinion that only a custodial sentence would be adequate to

protect the public from further offending by him; and

(ii) the offence was committed on or after such date as the Secretary of State may by order appoint.

(3) A detention and training order is an order that the offender in respect of whom it is made shall be subject, for the term specified in the order, to a period of detention and training followed by a period of supervision.

(4) On making a detention and training order in a case where subs(2) above applies, it shall be the duty of the court (in addition to the duty imposed by s79(4) above) to state in open court that it is of the opinion mentioned in paragraph (a) or, as the case may be, paragraphs (a) and (b) (i) of that subsection.

Section 101
Term of order, consecutive terms and taking account of remands

101 (1) Subject to subs(2) below, the term of a detention and training order made in respect of an offence (whether by a magistrates' court or otherwise) shall be 4, 6, 8, 10, 12, 18 or 24 months.

(2) The term of a detention and training order may not exceed the maximum term of imprisonment that the Crown Court could (in the case of an offender aged 21 or over) impose for the offence.

(3) Subject to subs(4) and (6) below, a court making a detention and training order may order that its term shall commence on the expiry of the term of any other detention and training order made by that or any other court.

(4) A court shall not make in respect of an offender a detention and training order the effect of which would be that he would be subject to detention and training orders for a term which exceeds 24 months.

(5) Where the term of the detention and training orders to which an offender would otherwise be subject exceeds 24 months, the excess shall be treated as remitted.

(6) A court making a detention and training

order shall not order that its term shall commence on the expiry of the term of a detention and training order under which the period of supervision has already begun (under s103(1) below).

(7) Where a detention and training order ('the new order') is made in respect of an offender who is subject to a detention and training order under which the period of supervision has begun ('the old order'), the old order shall be disregarded in determining –

(a) for the purposes of subs(4) above whether the effect of the new order would be that the offender would be subject to detention and training orders for a term which exceeds 24 months; and

(b) for the purposes of subs(5) above whether the term of the detention and training orders to which the offender would (apart from that subsection) be subject exceeds 24 months.

(8) In determining the term of a detention and training order for an offence, the court shall take account of any period for which the offender has been remanded in custody in connection with the offence, or any other offence the charge for which was founded on the same facts or evidence.

(9) Where a court proposes to make detention and training orders in respect of an offender for two or more offences –

(a) subsection (8) above shall not apply; but

(b) in determining the total term of the detention and training orders it proposes to make in respect of the offender, the court shall take account of the total period (if any) for which he has been remanded in custody in connection with any of those offences, or any other offence the charge for which was founded on the same facts or evidence.

(10) Once a period of remand has, under subs(8) or (9) above, been taken account of in relation to a detention and training order made in respect of an offender for any offence or

offences, it shall not subsequently be taken account of (under either of those subsections) in relation to such an order made in respect of the offender for any other offence or offences.

(11) Any reference in subs(8) or (9) above to an offender's being remanded in custody is a reference to his being –

(a) held in police detention;

(b) remanded in or committed to custody by an order of a court;

(c) remanded or committed to local authority accommodation under s23 of the Children and Young Persons Act 1969 and placed and kept in secure accommodation; or

(d) remanded, admitted or removed to hospital under ss35, 36, 38 or 48 of the Mental Health Act 1983.

(12) A person is in police detention for the purposes of subs(11) above –

(a) at any time when he is in police detention for the purposes of the Police and Criminal Evidence Act 1984; and

(b) at any time when he is detained under s14 of the Prevention of Terrorism (Temporary Provisions) Act 1989; and in that subsection 'secure accommodation' has the same meaning as in s23 of the Children and Young Persons Act 1969.

(13) For the purpose of any reference in ss102 to 105 below to the term of a detention and training order, consecutive terms of such orders and terms of such orders which are wholly or partly concurrent shall be treated as a single term if –

(a) the orders were made on the same occasion; or

(b) where they were made on different occasions, the offender has not been released (by virtue of subs(2), (3), (4) or (5) of s102 below) at any time during the period beginning with the first and ending with the last of those occasions.

Section 102
The period of detention and training

102 (1) An offender shall serve the period of detention and training under a detention and training order in such secure accommodation as may be determined by the Secretary of State or by such other person as may be authorised by him for that purpose.

(2) Subject to subs(3) to (5) below, the period of detention and training under a detention and training order shall be one-half of the term of the order.

(3) The Secretary of State may at any time release the offender if he is satisfied that exceptional circumstances exist which justify the offender's release on compassionate grounds.

(4) The Secretary of State may release the offender –

(a) in the case of an order for a term of 8 months or more but less than 18 months, one month before the half-way point of the term of the order; and

(b) in the case of an order for a term of 18 months or more, one month or two months before that point.

(5) If a youth court so orders on an application made by the Secretary of State for the purpose, the Secretary of State shall release the offender –

(a) in the case of an order for a term of 8 months or more but less than 18 months, one month after the half-way point of the term of the order; and

(b) in the case of an order for a term of 18 months or more, one month or two months after that point.

(6) An offender detained in pursuance of a detention and training order shall be deemed to be in legal custody.

Section 103
The period of supervision

103 (1) The period of supervision of an offender who is subject to a detention and training order –

(a) shall begin with the offender's release, whether at the half-way point of the term of the order or otherwise; and

(b) subject to subs(2) below, shall end when the term of the order ends.

(2) The Secretary of State may by order provide that the period of supervision shall end at such point during the term of a detention and training order as may be specified in the order under this subsection.

(3) During the period of supervision, the offender shall be under the supervision of –

(a) a probation officer;

(b) a social worker of a local authority social services department; or

(c) a member of a youth offending team; and the category of person to supervise the offender shall be determined from time to time by the Secretary of State.

(4) Where the supervision is to be provided by a probation officer, the probation officer shall be an officer appointed for or assigned to the petty sessions area within which the offender resides for the time being.

(5) Where the supervision is to be provided by –

(a) a social worker of a local authority social services department, or

(b) a member of a youth offending team, the social worker or member shall be a social worker of, or a member of a youth offending team established by, the local authority within whose area the offender resides for the time being.

(6) The offender shall be given a notice from the Secretary of State specifying –

(a) the category of person for the time being responsible for his supervision; and

(b) any requirements with which he must for the time being comply.

(7) A notice under subs(6) above shall be given to the offender –

(a) before the commencement of the period of supervision; and

(b) before any alteration in the matters specified in subs(6)(a) or (b) above comes into effect.

Section 104
Breach of supervision requirements

104 (1) Where a detention and training order is in force in respect of an offender and it appears on information to a justice of the peace acting for a relevant petty sessions area that the offender has failed to comply with requirements under s103(6) (b) above, the justice –

(a) may issue a summons requiring the offender to appear at the place and time specified in the summons before a youth court acting for the area; or

(b) if the information is in writing and on oath, may issue a warrant for the offender's arrest requiring him to be brought before such a court.

(2) For the purposes of this section a petty sessions area is a relevant petty sessions area in relation to a detention and training order if –

(a) the order was made by a youth court acting for it; or

(b) the offender resides in it for the time being.

(3) If it is proved to the satisfaction of the youth court before which an offender appears or is brought under this section that he has failed to comply with requirements under s103(6) (b) above, that court may –

(a) order the offender to be detained, in such secure accommodation as the Secretary of State may determine, for such period, not exceeding the shorter of three months or the remainder of the term of the detention and training order, as the court may specify; or

(b) impose on the offender a fine not exceeding level 3 on the standard scale.

(4) An offender detained in pursuance of an order under subs(3)(a) above shall be deemed to be in legal custody.

(5) A fine imposed under subs(3)(b) above shall be deemed, for the purposes of any enactment, to be a sum adjudged to be paid by a conviction.

(6) An offender may appeal to the Crown Court against any order made under subs(3)(a) or (b) above.

Section 105
Offences during currency of order

105 (1) This section applies to a person subject to a detention and training order if –

(a) after his release and before the date on which the term of the order ends, he commits an offence punishable with imprisonment in the case of a person aged 21 or over ('the new offence'); and

(b) whether before or after that date, he is convicted of the new offence.

(2) Subject to s8(6) above (duty of adult magistrates' court to remit young offenders to youth court for sentence), the court by or before which a person to whom this section applies is convicted of the new offence may, whether or not it passes any other sentence on him, order him to be detained in such secure accommodation as the Secretary of State may determine for the whole or any part of the period which –

(a) begins with the date of the court's order; and

(b) is equal in length to the period between the date on which the new offence was committed and the date mentioned in subs(1) above.

(3) The period for which a person to whom this section applies is ordered under subs(2) above to be detained in secure accommodation –

(a) shall, as the court may direct, either be served before and be followed by, or be served concurrently with, any sentence imposed for the new offence; and

(b) in either case, shall be disregarded in determining the appropriate length of that sentence.

(4) Where the new offence is found to have been committed over a period of two or more days, or at some time during a period of two or more days, it shall be taken for the purposes of this section to have been committed on the last of those days.

(5) A person detained in pursuance of an order under subs(2) above shall be deemed to be in legal custody.

Section 106
Interaction with sentences of detention in a young offender institution

106 (1) Where a court passes a sentence of detention in a young offender institution in the case of an offender who is subject to a detention and training order, the sentence shall take effect as follows –

(a) if the offender has been released by virtue of subs(2), (3), (4) or (5) of s102 above, at the beginning of the day on which it is passed;

(b) if not, either as mentioned in paragraph (a) above or, if the court so orders, at the time when the offender would otherwise be released by virtue of subs(2), (3), (4) or (5) of s102.

(2) Where a court makes a detention and training order in the case of an offender who is subject to a sentence of detention in a young offender institution, the order shall take effect as follows –

(a) if the offender has been released under Part II of the Criminal Justice Act 1991 (early release of prisoners), at the beginning of the day on which it is made;

(b) if not, either as mentioned in paragraph (a) above or, if the court so orders, at the time when the offender would otherwise be released under that Part.

(3) Subsection (1)(a) above has effect subject to s105(3) (a) above and subs(2) (a) above has effect subject to s116(6) (b) below.

(4) Subject to subsection (5) below, where at any time an offender is subject concurrently –

(a) to a detention and training order, and

(b) to a sentence of detention in a young offender institution, he shall be treated for the purposes of ss102 to 105 above and of s98 above (place of detention), Chapter IV of this Part (return to detention) and Part II of the Criminal Justice Act 1991 (early release) as if he were subject only to the one of them that was imposed on the later occasion.

(5) Nothing in subs (4) above shall require the offender to be released in respect of either the order or the sentence unless and until he is required to be released in respect of each of them.

(6) Where, by virtue of any enactment giving a court power to deal with a person in a way in which a court on a previous occasion could have dealt with him, a detention and training order for any term is made in the case of a person who has attained the age of 18, the person shall be treated as if he had been sentenced to detention in a young offender institution for the same term.

Section 107
Meaning of 'secure accommodation' and references to terms

107 (1) In ss102, 104 and 105 above 'secure accommodation' means –

(a) a secure training centre;

(b) a young offender institution;

(c) accommodation provided by a local authority for the purpose of restricting the liberty of children and young persons;

(d) accommodation provided for that purpose under subs(5) of s82 of the Children Act 1989 (financial support by the Secretary of State); or

(e) such other accommodation provided for the purpose of restricting liberty as the Secretary of State may direct.

(2) In ss102 to 105 above references to the term of a detention and training order shall be construed in accordance with s101(13) above.

Section 135
Limit on fines imposed by magistrates' courts in respect of young offenders

135 (1) Where a person aged under 18 is found guilty by a magistrates' court of an offence for which, apart from this section, the court would have power to impose a fine of an amount exceeding £1,000, the amount of any fine imposed by the court shall not exceed £1,000.

(2) In relation to a person aged under 14, subs(1) above shall have effect as if for '£1,000', in both places where it occurs, there were substituted '£250'.

Section 136
Power to order statement as to financial circumstances of parent or guardian

136 (1) Before exercising its powers under s137 below (power to order parent or guardian to pay fine, costs or compensation) against the parent or guardian of an individual who has been convicted of an offence, the court may make a financial circumstances order with respect to the parent or (as the case may be) guardian.

(2) In this section 'financial circumstances order' has the meaning given by subs(3) of s126 above, and subs(4) to (6) of that section shall apply in relation to a financial circumstances order made under this section as they apply in relation to such an order made under that section.

Section 137
Power to order parent or guardian to pay fine, costs or compensation

137 (1) Where –

(a) a child or young person (that is to say, any person aged under 18) is convicted of any offence for the commission of which a fine or costs may be imposed or a compensation order may be made, and

(b) the court is of the opinion that the case would best be met by the imposition of a fine or costs or the making of such an order, whether with or without any other punishment, the court shall order that the fine, compensation or costs awarded be paid by the parent or guardian of the child or young person instead of by the child or young person himself, unless the court is satisfied –

(i) that the parent or guardian cannot be found; or

(ii) that it would be unreasonable to make an order for payment, having regard to the circumstances of the case.

(2) Where but for this subsection a court would impose a fine on a child or young person under –

(a) paragraph 4(1)(a) or 5(1)(a) of Schedule 3 to this Act (breach of curfew, probation, community service, combination or drug treatment and testing order),

(b) paragraph 2(1)(a) of Schedule 5 to this Act (breach of attendance centre order or attendance centre rules),

(c) paragraph 2(2)(a) of Schedule 7 to this Act (breach of supervision order),

(d) paragraph 2(2)(a) of Schedule 8 to this Act (breach of action plan order or reparation order),

(e) section 104(3)(b) above (breach of requirements of supervision under a detention and training order), or

(f) section 4(3)(b) of the Criminal Justice and Public Order Act 1994 (breach of requirements of supervision under a secure training order), the court shall order that the fine be paid by the parent or guardian of the child or young person instead of by the child or young person himself, unless the court is satisfied –

(i) that the parent or guardian cannot be found; or

(ii) that it would be unreasonable to make an order for payment, having regard to the circumstances of the case.

(3) In the case of a young person aged 16 or over, subs(1) and (2) above shall have effect as if, instead of imposing a duty, they conferred a power to make such an order as is mentioned in those subsections.

(4) Subject to subs(5) below, no order shall be made under this section without giving the parent or guardian an opportunity of being heard.

(5) An order under this section may be made against a parent or guardian who, having been required to attend, has failed to do so.

(6) A parent or guardian may appeal to the Crown Court against an order under this section made by a magistrates' court.

(7) A parent or guardian may appeal to the Court of Appeal against an order under this section made by the Crown Court, as if he had been convicted on indictment and the order were a sentence passed on his conviction.

(8) In relation to a child or young person for whom a local authority have parental responsibility and who –

(a) is in their care, or

(b) is provided with accommodation by them in the exercise of any functions (in particular those under the Children Act 1989) which stand referred to their social services committee under the Local Authority Social Services Act 1970, references in this section to his parent or guardian shall be construed as references to that authority.

(9) In subsection (8) above 'local authority' and 'parental responsibility' have the same meanings as in the Children Act 1989.

Section 138
Fixing of fine or compensation to be paid by parent or guardian

138 (1) For the purposes of any order under s137 above made against the parent or guardian of a child or young person –

(a) section 128 above (fixing of fines) shall have effect as if any reference in

subs(1) to (4) to the financial circumstances of the offender were a reference to the financial circumstances of the parent or guardian, and as if subs(5) were omitted;

(b) section 130(11) above (determination of compensation order) shall have effect as if any reference to the means of the person against whom the compensation order is made were a reference to the financial circumstances of the parent or guardian; and

(c) section 130(12) above (preference to be given to compensation if insufficient means to pay both compensation and a fine) shall have effect as if the reference to the offender were a reference to the parent or guardian; but in relation to an order under s137 made against a local authority this subsection has effect subject to subs(2) below.

(2) For the purposes of any order under s137 above made against a local authority, subs128 (1) (duty to inquire into financial circumstances) and 130(11) above shall not apply.

(3) For the purposes of any order under s137 above, where the parent or guardian of an offender who is a child or young person –

(a) has failed to comply with an order under s136 above, or

(b) has otherwise failed to co-operate with the court in its inquiry into his financial circumstances, and the court considers that it has insufficient information to make a proper determination of the parent's or guardian's financial circumstances, it may make such determination as it thinks fit.

(4) Where a court has, in fixing the amount of a fine, determined the financial circumstances of a parent or guardian under subs(3) above, subs(2) to (4) of s129 above (remission of fines) shall (so far as applicable) have effect as they have effect in the case mentioned in s129(1), but as if the reference in s129(2) to the offender's financial circumstances were a reference to the financial circumstances of the parent or guardian.

(5) In this section 'local authority' has the same meaning as in the Children Act 1989.

Section 150
Young offenders: Binding over of parent or guardian

150 (1) Where a child or young person (that is to say, any person aged under 18) is convicted of an offence, the powers conferred by this section shall be exercisable by the court by which he is sentenced for that offence, and where the offender is aged under 16 when sentenced it shall be the duty of that court –

(a) to exercise those powers if it is satisfied, having regard to the circumstances of the case, that their exercise would be desirable in the interests of preventing the commission by him of further offences; and

(b) if it does not exercise them, to state in open court that it is not satisfied as mentioned in paragraph (a) above and why it is not so satisfied;

but this subsection has effect subject to s19(5) above and paragraph 13(5) of Schedule 1 to this Act (cases where referral orders made or extended).

(2) The powers conferred by this section are as follows –

(a) with the consent of the offender's parent or guardian, to order the parent or guardian to enter into a recognizance to take proper care of him and exercise proper control over him; and

(b) if the parent or guardian refuses consent and the court considers the refusal unreasonable, to order the parent or guardian to pay a fine not exceeding £1,000; and where the court has passed a community sentence on the offender, it may include in the recognizance a provision that the offender's parent or guardian ensure that the offender complies with the requirements of that sentence.

(3) An order under this section shall not require the parent or guardian to enter into a recognizance for an amount exceeding £1,000.

(4) An order under this section shall not require the parent or guardian to enter into a recognizance –

(a) for a period exceeding three years; or

(b) where the offender will attain the age of 18 in a period shorter than three years, for a period exceeding that shorter period.

(5) Section 120 of the Magistrates' Courts Act 1980 (forfeiture of recognizances) shall apply in relation to a recognizance entered into in pursuance of an order under this section as it applies in relation to a recognizance to keep the peace.

(6) A fine imposed under subs(2)(b) above shall be deemed, for the purposes of any enactment, to be a sum adjudged to be paid by a conviction.

(7) In fixing the amount of a recognizance under this section, the court shall take into account among other things the means of the parent or guardian so far as they appear or are known to the court; and this subsection applies whether taking into account the means of the parent or guardian has the effect of increasing or reducing the amount of the recognizance.

(8) A parent or guardian may appeal to the Crown Court against an order under this section made by a magistrates' court.

(9) A parent or guardian may appeal to the Court of Appeal against an order under this section made by the Crown Court, as if he had been convicted on indictment and the order were a sentence passed on his conviction.

(10) A court may vary or revoke an order made by it under this section if, on the application of the parent or guardian, it appears to the court, having regard to any change in the circumstances since the order was made, to be in the interests of justice to do so.

(11) For the purposes of this section, taking 'care' of a person includes giving him protection and guidance and 'control' includes discipline.

The Youth Justice and Criminal Evidence Act 1999 introduced a new primary sentencing disposal, the referral order – for 10–17 year olds pleading guilty and convicted for the first time by the courts. The disposal involves referring the young offender to a youth offender panel (YOP). The work of YOPs is to be governed by the principles underlying the concept of restorative justice, defined as restoration, reintegration and responsibility. This research provides an account of its initial use on a pilot basis.

Newburn T et al (2001) *The Introduction of Referral Orders into the Youth Justice System: Second Interim Report*, ppv–ix

The pilots
Referral orders are currently being piloted in 11 areas: Blackburn with Darwen, Cardiff, Nottingham, Nottinghamshire, Oxfordshire, Swindon, Suffolk, Wiltshire, Hammersmith and Fulham, Kensington and Chelsea, and Westminster. The introduction of referral orders was staggered across the pilot areas over the summer of 2000. National roll-out of referral orders will begin on 1 April 2002. The pilots are being overseen by an inter-agency referral order steering group chaired by the Youth Justice Board and incorporating representation from the Home Office, Youth Justice Board, Lord Chancellor's Department, Department of Education and Employment, Judicial Studies Board, evaluation team, police, youth offending teams (YOTs), Victim Support, NACRO and the Restorative Justice Consortium.

The evaluation
An evaluation of the introduction of referral orders in the youth justice system is being undertaken by a consortium from Goldsmiths College and the Universities of Kent and Leeds. The pilots are being evaluated over a period of 18 months, which commenced in March 2000 when the pilots began to set up

their operations. The first interim report was published in March 2001. This is the second interim report. A final report will be published in early 2002.

This report
This report concentrates on the first nine months of operation of referral orders. In particular it presents data on the operation of YOPs, and of the experience and views of some of the key actors in this new development in youth justice – offenders, YOT staff and Community Panel Members (CPMs).

Methods
Data in this report are drawn from a broad range of sources:

- a survey of YOT staff
- analysis of YOT records
- survey of CPMs
- observation of YOP meetings
- assessment forms completed by CPMs at YOP meetings not observed by the evaluation team
- interviews with young offenders.

Results
REFERRAL ORDERS AND YOUTH OFFENDER PANELS

Three major sources of data were used to collect information on progress so far in relation to the use of referral orders and the operation of youth offender panels: summary data from YOT records; data from monitoring forms completed by CPMs; and data drawn from panels observed by the evaluation team.

Summary data
1,107 referral orders were made in the 11 pilot sites before April 1 2001. The most striking feature is the very low number of orders made in the West London sites.

Offenders are predominantly male (over 80 per cent), white (87 per cent) and aged between 15 and 17 (70 per cent).

Four-fifths of orders are for six months or less. Over one-third are for acquisitive offences (35 per cent) and one-fifth (20 per cent) for vehicle offences. As a mandatory sentence, there have been concerns that referral orders might be made for very minor offences. The evidence is that this concerns only a small minority of cases.

In approximately one-quarter (27 per cent) of the 371 cases 'closed' by the end of March 2001 the young person had been convicted of a further offence during the lifetime of the order. In just under one-fifth of all closed orders (18 per cent) the young person was re-sentenced by the court.

In 69 per cent of the 'closed cases' for which there are panel data the young person is recorded as having completed the contract they signed.

Monitoring data
Monitoring data were collected for 737 initial, progress or final panels.

Almost all panels (98 per cent) were held with single offenders. Very few young people appeared not to attend panels (3 per cent).

One-fifth (21 per cent) of offenders appearing before panels were female. Almost nine-tenths (87 per cent) were white; 8 per cent were black, 3 per cent Asian and 2 per cent other.

Over two-thirds (71 per cent) of panels considered a single offence, 17 per cent considered two, and 7 per cent considered three.

One-third (34 per cent) of panels took place within the national standard of 15 working days. Over four-fifths (84 per cent) took place within 30 working days.

Almost two-thirds (62 per cent) of panels were held after 5pm, with over a third (36 per cent) of all panels scheduled to begin between 6pm and 7pm.

The majority of initial panel meetings (56 per cent) lasted between 45 and 90 minutes. A little under 10 per cent lasted longer than this. However, 60 per cent of progress panel meetings and 86 per cent of final panel meetings lasted under 30 minutes.

The vast majority (86 per cent) of panels sat with the minimum of three panel members, 4 per cent sat with fewer, and 10 per cent with more.

CPMs are predominantly white females (62 per cent of panel leaders and 66 per cent of second panel members). YOT advisers are evenly split (male 51 per cent, and female 49 per cent).

Young people attended panels with one other person in over two-thirds of cases (70 per cent) – usually their mother (41 per cent). They attended with two 'supporters' in 16 per cent of cases and alone in 13 per cent of cases.

A victim or victims attended in only 36 of the 566 initial panels on which data were collected.

The overwhelming majority (97 per cent) of young people who attend initial panels agreed a contract. Two-thirds (68 per cent) of contracts had either two (30 per cent) or three (38 per cent) items in them. Few (13 per cent) contracts contained any voluntary elements.

Over four-fifths (84 per cent) of contracts contained an element of reparation – most commonly community reparation (44 per cent of all reparation elements) and written apologies (34 per cent). Referrals to mediation or direct work for victims were uncommon (4 per cent).

Progress panel meetings predominantly considered the progress made by young people to be satisfactory (88 per cent). Contracts were varied in 9 per cent of cases, and the young person returned to court for resentencing in only 3 per cent of cases.

Four-fifths (82 per cent) of final panels considered the young person to have successfully completed their contract. Only one young person who reached a final panel was returned to court for failing to complete their contract.

Observation data
Between August 2000 and May 2001 members of the evaluation team attended a total of 144 panels. Of these, 120 proceeded. The majority were initial panels.

On average, initial panel meetings lasted approximately 50 minutes, progress panels 26 minutes and final panel meetings 16 minutes.

In preparation for the meetings 90 per cent of the CPMs had received a YOT-prepared report for the meeting. In one of the pilot areas CPMs received a copy of ASSET.

Pre-panel discussions focused on the respective roles of the panel members, information about the offender and the offence, information about victims, discussion of reparation activities, proportionality and content of contracts, as well as procedural matters on a wide range of other issues.

The composition of the panel was fully explained to the young person in the vast majority (87 per cent) of cases.

The purpose of the panel meeting was fully explained in three-quarters (77 per cent) of cases and partly explained in 19 per cent of cases.

Ground rules for panel meetings were fully explained in three-fifths (61 per cent) of meetings. In 88 per cent of meetings, the ground rules were fully observed by all those attending.

The vast majority of young people did appear to engage with the process and made a full or reasonably full verbal contribution to the meetings.

Almost two-thirds (63 per cent) of young people acknowledged full responsibility for all their offending.

The victim's perspective was not fully reflected in all panels. In 25 per cent of the panels, no mention was made of the victim's perspective.

Victim contact and victim input

The experience of the pilots to date illustrates some of the difficulties of identifying victims and, more particularly, in encouraging 'corporate victims' to attend panel meetings.

Contact by telephone, rather than by letter, appears more personal and effective. 'Opt in' letters appear the least effective.

The evidence from the study to date suggests clear thought needs to be given to providing victims with alternative means of input to YOPs.

At the present there appears to be a tension between the requirements of informed consent and the aim of involving as many victims as possible in the referral order process.

Most pilot sites did not have a clear or formal set of criteria to guide the assessment of victims' suitability to attend a panel.

In the absence of significant victim attendance there are obvious concerns that victims' issues are insufficiently represented.

In most areas victims only appear to be kept informed of progress when, and if, they specifically request this.

The experience of the pilots reinforces the understanding that victim contact work is labour-intensive and requires significant resources, time, commitment and training.

Offenders' views

Interviews were conducted with 40 offenders. Offenders were generally very nervous about going to court, but understood what was going on and felt that the court dealt with them fairly.

The majority of offenders interviewed had received satisfactory information about the referral order and panels prior to the initial panel meeting. However, there were obvious inconsistencies in the quality and amount of information received by individual respondents.

Interviewees were considerably less nervous about attending the initial panel meeting than they were about attending court. The majority of respondents also felt that the panel meeting was clearly explained and conducted fairly and with respect.

Most respondents felt that the main purpose of the initial panel meeting was to help them get on with their lives.

Although a significant minority of interviewees felt that they had little say in the contents of the contract, only two offenders interviewed felt that the contract they had received was too harsh.

Just under three-quarters of those interviewed also felt that the contract had helped them to stay out of trouble.

Only three respondents had attended an initial panel meeting with a victim present, and all of them agreed that it was right that the victim was there and that having the victim present had made them think about things differently.

However, very few of the interviewees who had attended the initial panel meeting without a victim present said that they would have liked the victim to be there.

The majority of all interviewees felt that the initial panel meeting had made them more aware of the consequences of their offending, regardless of whether the victim was in attendance at the panel.

All interviewed offenders who expressed an opinion felt more at ease at subsequent panel meetings than they had at the initial panel meeting.

The views of YOT staff

A survey of YOT staff in the 11 pilot areas was conducted in January 2001. It will be repeated in August and September 2001. A total of 187 responses were received (a response rate of 56 per cent).

YOT staff were overwhelmingly supportive (92 per cent) of the introduction of a restorative approach to dealing with young people in trouble with the law.

Four-fifths (82 per cent) 'agreed' or 'strongly agreed' with the statement that 'referral orders offer a 'new and positive way of responding to youth crime'.

The idea that referral orders would encourage greater community involvement was endorsed by almost two-thirds (64 per cent) of YOT staff.

YOT staff, like magistrates and youth court clerks (Newburn et al, 2001) were somewhat more sceptical of the idea that referral orders would speed up responses to youth crime. They appeared confident, however, that referral orders would not lead magistrates to precipitous use of custody, and two-thirds reported having positive or very positive relationships with magistrates. The most strongly held view among YOT staff on the impact of referral orders was that they would lead to 'a significant increase in the workload of the YOT (79 per cent 'agreed' or 'strongly agreed').

A minority of YOT staff raised concerns about proportionality, both in terms of the length of referral orders and the nature of the contracts agreed.

Concern for the viability of victim involvement in referral orders was expressed by several respondents. There was particular concern about the time constraints and resource implications.

The views of Community Panel Members

A survey of CPMs was conducted in April 2001; 218 responses were received (a response rate of approximately 60 per cent). Most CPMs were white (91 per cent), female (69 per cent), over 40 years of age (68 per cent) and employed in professional or managerial occupations (50 per cent). The most common reason for becoming a CPM was interest in the issues of young people and crime (66 per cent) and a desire to give something back to the community (52 per cent). Asked about their skills, three-fifths of CPMs (61 per cent) felt that a broad range of social and life experiences gave them skills that informed their work. Relationships with YOT staff were positive, with over three-fifths (62 per cent) saying they had a 'very good' working relationship with YOT panel members, and almost a further third (32 per cent) saying it was 'reasonably good'. A majority of CPMs (57 per cent) felt at least reasonably confident when sitting on their first panel. Once again, we found that timeliness of the provision of reports was important in influencing the extent to which CPMs felt able to contribute to panels. Over three-fifths of CPMs 'agreed' or 'strongly agreed' with the statement that 'panels are more informal than expected'. Three-quarters (76 per cent) of CPMs 'agreed' or 'strongly agreed' that 'CPMs determine the direction of meetings'. Their views were also generally positive about the contribution made by young people and their family members at panel meetings. Particular concerns were raised, once again, about the low level of victim involvement.

However, those CPMs that had had experience of panels at which victims had attended suggested that their presence significantly altered the dynamics of the panel, most often in a progressive manner. Other concerns cited included perceived insufficient programmes of reparation and lack of resources/programmes of activity for young people. Nearly all concerns highlighted by CPMs related to problems of implementation rather than the general principles underlying referral orders.

Sentencing guidelines for juvenile offenders were provided by the Court of Appeal in 2000 in the case of *R* v *G*.

R v *G (Stephen) (A Juvenile)* (2000) The Times 7 June Court of Appeal (Criminal Division) (Rose LJ, Silber and Sullivan JJ)

G, a juvenile offender, was appealing against a sentence of 18 months' detention for grievous bodily harm. The court allowed the appeal and substituted a detention and training order. They applied the provisions of the Crime and Disorder Act 1998 s73 to s79, which related to detention and training orders for offenders under the age of 18. The Court of Appeal was, by virtue of the Criminal Appeal Act 1995 s11 (3)(b), empowered, when passing a different sentence from that imposed in the court below, to pass a sentence which the court below had power to pass. The court was under a duty, under the Crime and Disorder Act 1998 (Commencement No 6) Order 1999 para 4, when considering the sentence that might or could have been imposed in the court below, to presume that s73 to s79 of the 1998 Act, which came into force on April 1, 2000, had been in force. Detention in young offender institutions and secure training orders had been abolished under s73(7) of the 1998 Act and were replaced by detention and training orders under s73(1). Such orders constituted custodial sentences within the Criminal Justice Act 1991 Part 1, and accordingly it was

necessary that the requirements of s1(2)(a) or (b) of the 1991 Act were met. Where a defendant was under the age of 15 at the time of conviction, a detention and training order should not be made unless that person was a persistent offender. Similarly, such an order should not be made where an offender was below the age of 12 unless a custodial sentence was the only means of preventing further offences, and the offence had been committed on or after a day to be appointed. The court could not impose terms of less than four months consecutively so as to result in a total sentence of four months, *R* v *Dover Youth Court, ex parte K* [1999] 1 WLR 27 considered. The term imposed should not exceed the maximum available to the Crown Court in relation to an offender over the age of 21. The power to impose detention under the Children and Young Persons Act 1933 s53(3) remained unaffected. Equally the principles relating to such a sentence and the undesirability of long periods of detention under the age of 18 continued to apply, *R* v *M (Aaron Shaun)* [1998] 1 WLR 363 considered. Time spent in custody on remand was not to be deducted from the period to be served under a detention and training order, although it was to be considered by the sentencer. However, the court should have regard when dealing, on the same occasion, with offenders both above and below the age of 18, to the fact that time in custody on remand would automatically be deducted from the sentence imposed on the older offender.

The reports by Her Majesty's Chief Inspector of Prisons are an excellent source of information in relation to the system of custodial detention. In this case the report deals with a remand centre which mainly holds young prisoners and the facility also in part operates as a young offender institution.

HM Chief Inspector of Prisons (2001) *Report of an Inspection of HM Remand Centre and YOI Northallerton*, pp3–5

Uncertainty is the word that immediately comes to mind when describing HMRC and YOI Northallerton. Housed in the oldest Prison Service buildings in continuous penal use, it contains largely unsentenced young prisoners, and therefore is much more of a remand centre than a young offender institution. However, its future role is uncertain, although, at the time of the inspection, £2 million was being spent on putting a security wall around the establishment, altering the traffic circulation through the town in the process. Its main building contains some of the smallest cells, fitted with integral sanitation, that I have ever seen, the majority of which hold two young prisoners in conditions which, to my mind, are in breach of human rights, as is described in Chapter 3. Certainly they are in breach of the cell certification conditions that have recently been endorsed by the Prisons Board, and are to become fully operative in September of this year. The current CNA of 152 is much nearer the actual capacity of the establishment than the operational capacity that is currently said to be 298. The uncertainty over capacity is compounded by the fact that the current CNA certificate permits 268, and in excess of 200 young prisoners were held shortly before our inspection, at which time the population stood at 165.

Looked at objectively it would seem that the world has passed Northallerton by for a number of years. Starved of capital resources, workshops and outside physical education facilities, the staff have stuck to their perceived role, and, as the report spells out, developed some really good practice. Much of this stems from the fact that the vast majority of staff clearly like working with this age group, and have sympathy for the problems that they face in making their way through adolescence. This makes up for the absence of structures to ensure that the practices will

continue whoever is in a particular post, such as allocation and progressive transfer which, in the case of sentenced young prisoners, is commendably swift. In passing I must register my surprise that PE provision, without any outside facilities, achieved a 'superior' audit grading. I agree that the staff are doing an excellent job, but they are hampered by the lack of appropriate facilities for this age group, which should be brought to the attention of those responsible for their provision.

I also applaud the way in which outside agencies are being used to provide admirable support for young prisoners. The linkage between the health care centre and local NHS providers has been established for a number of years, and is an example of what will, I hope, become common practice everywhere. I am glad to see full and proper mention of the work of the Senior Probation Officer, supported as she clearly is by her colleagues in relevant probation areas, because I believe that more use of her expertise could usefully be made. I particularly liked the Job Centre initiative, funded by the local Employment Service. I have never seen better, and this is an example not just of good but of best practice that I hope that the Prison Service will install in every prison in the country.

I hope too that attention will be paid to the very detailed comments about education and its provision, because they spell out some very important pointers for the future regarding this age group in particular. The co-ordinator told me that, on assessment, over 80 per cent of all new receptions were found to be performing at level 1 or below, 35 per cent at entry level or below. A constant 65–70 per cent have been excluded from school for one reason or another. Therefore they present a group of young people who have developed different ways of avoiding any demonstration of their educational inadequacy, while, at the same time, being thoroughly disaffected in regard to education per se. Therefore the principal aim of education staff should be to encourage and foster a return to learning. This is not best done by repeating a solely class-room based approach that they have already rejected, but by a widely based curriculum in which education is introduced as a life skill, including such programmes as that being developed with the PE staff at Northallerton. Taken alongside the revelations of other deficiencies disclosed by the speech therapist who came with us to HMYOI Swinfen Hall, I believe that there is clear evidence of the need for educational provision for this age group to be reconsidered and recast. Certainly the current level 2 KPI is inappropriate as an indicator of the resources that are needed to ensure that the opportunity presented by a period of imprisonment is not lost. With only 31 other employment places in the establishment, the importance of education in Northallerton cannot be overstated.

But to return to uncertainty. Visits are a very important part of the regime, particularly for young prisoners undergoing their first experience of imprisonment. The visits room is rightly described as awful – stark, out-of-date and unwelcoming. It, together with the inadequate Gate Lodge and the lack of a visitor's centre, is another representation of the world rather having passed Northallerton by. But, until the future role and size of the establishment is confirmed, it is difficult to be precise about what needs to be done, other than the obvious of changing the furniture and the internal arrangements to make them more appropriate for the reception of Visitors.

There is much on which the new governor can build, using the platform not only of this report, but also the work that has already been put in hand by his predecessor and the staff that he has inherited, supported by the area manager. I have no doubt that, given a clear indication of what is required of them, and provided with suitable conditions in which to treat the needs of young prisoners, the staff at HMRC and YOI Northallerton have a significant contribution to make in the young prisoner estate in the north east part of the country. To say more would be to add to conjecture, and so increase, rather than decrease, the uncertainty from which I hope that all

those, who are doing so much good work in adverse conditions, will soon be relieved.

This report offers an indictment of Feltham in relation to its work with young adult prisoners between the ages of 18 and 21. It is difficult to know which of the many unacceptable features is the most worrying. In many ways it is perhaps the attitude of both the prison officers that work there and those who have failed to respond to similar reports on the same institution in the past.

HM Chief Inspector of Prisons (2001) *Report of an Inspection of HM Prison and YOI Feltham*, pp2–6

I am forced to conclude from this, my fourth inspection of HMYOI and RC Feltham in four years, that Feltham B – that part of the establishment that now holds young adult prisoners between the ages of 18 and 21 – should no longer be allowed to operate as a Prison Service run Young Offender Institution. I say this because, despite all the recommendations that I have made, all the plans made and formulated and all the additional financial resources allocated by Ministers and the Director General since my second report – which showed that nothing had been done to action the recommendations in my first – little or nothing appears to have been done to resolve the very serious failings in the treatment of and conditions for young adult prisoners that I, and others such as the very active Board of Visitors, have identified in this and many other previous reports.

In contrast, while, at the time of my inspection, much still remained to be done to provide a proper environment for unconvicted and convicted children held in Feltham A, I am pleased to report considerable progress in developing sound foundations on which a suitable regime for them can be provided and delivered. I know too that there have been a number of further developments since the

312 Criminology Sourcebook

inspection, which is encouraging, and in stark contrast to Feltham B.

I am entirely at a loss to know what more I can do to draw attention to the wholly unacceptable conditions in which young adult prisoners, and those children who have to be held there while accommodation in Feltham A is refurbished, continue to be held. I find it utterly disgraceful that, despite the efforts of some heroic staff who were trying to make a difference, there had been virtually no change in the way that the majority of young people were treated since my first report:

- Feltham B was dirty.
- The environment for young prisoners was not safe.
- The regime was failing to address the needs of the population.
- Too many young people spent most of the day confined to their cells, with no purposeful activity to occupy them.
- The staff culture remained predominantly and profoundly negative.
- The establishment lacked consistent leadership – the incoming governor was the seventh in five years.
- There were no signs of any strategic plan to provide a better future.

Over the course of the previous 12 months there had been:

- The suicide of yet another young person.
- The murder of a young man by his racist cell companion.
- A serious disturbance in one of the residential units, occasioned by frustration at yet further short notice cancellation of physical exercise and/or association, leading to damage costing many thousands of pounds.
- Five different governing governors, two of them admittedly as temporary stand-ins.

I know that the Director General is personally committed to putting Feltham right, but, arising from the above I find myself asking the following three questions:

1. What further evidence do I need to provide to prove that the treatment of and condi-

tions for young people held in Feltham B is unacceptable?
2. For how much longer can Ministers allow Feltham B to remain a consistently failing establishment, and when is something going to be done about it?
3. Does the will and commitment to improve the treatment of and conditions for those aged between 18 and 21, match the will and commitment of the YJB and the Prison Service to improve the treatment of and conditions for the smaller number of those aged between 15 and 18, actually exist?

In asking these questions I must, however, mention one contributory factor to the situation, which can and must be eliminated. On a number of occasions I have drawn attention to the malign influence of individual members of the Prison Officers Association (POA) in an establishment, who mount ritual and continuous challenge to legitimate management and present a consistent obstacle to planned and essential improvements to the treatment of and conditions for prisoners. Nowhere has this been more apparent or reprehensible than in Feltham, where, over the years, certain members of the POA have prided themselves on their negative attitude to the responsibility of management to manage, and the duty of care that all staff have towards those committed to their charge. I challenge them to state publicly whether or not they would be happy for their sons, or the sons of their friends or relations, to be submitted to the regime that they seem to think it appropriate to impose on vulnerable and impressionable young people.

There still is, as there has been for years, a powerful staff culture in Feltham which is supportive neither of management, change nor any structured attempt to deliver a decent regime for young prisoners. This was expressed to inspectors most obviously in the inflexible insistence on conditions determining when evening association could be provided, an inflexibility that leads to frequent short notice cancellation, a major cause of the disturbance mentioned above. Management has reluctantly had to agree to a motion from the POA which quite clearly puts the impact of evening working on its members before the needs of young prisoners, and which must be re-examined. The culture is expressed through the actions of the POA Committee whose constant demand for more staff and more overtime is no more than public exposure of the refusal to be realistic and work with management. Even during our inspection we witnessed an inordinate amount of management time being taken up by a trivial issue about the amount of paid duty time that locally elected POA officials claimed that they should be allowed to spend on POA matters, that was nothing to do with the needs of the establishment and impacted on the delivery of the daily regime for young prisoners. This continuous manifestation of the determination of the POA Committee at Feltham to regard and present itself as an alternative management, is a distortion of the real role of a responsible staff association. The Home Secretary and the Director General have spoken publicly about the need for partnership. The attitude and behaviour of some members of the POA at Feltham is far removed from a spirit of partnership, and the responsible and constructive attitude that the association, in general, claims to be its approach – and which it practises in the vast majority of other prisons. It endorses all the negative views that people have about the POA, for which reason alone I would have expected it to be condemned by the national executive committee, which itself claims to be responsible and constructive. It is also far removed from the approach to their task of the vast majority of decent staff, who want to have no part in this behaviour. It has long been the main obstacle to all those who seek progress, and are determined to set Feltham on the right path. I sympathise with the Governor and the Director General in their frustration over this, and must suggest that those members of the POA who are not prepared to change their ways should get out of the Prison Service now. I can see no valid reason why they should remain on the public payroll.

Following previous inspections of Feltham and other establishments also holding a mix of children and young adults, I have pleaded with the Director General to appoint a senior manger, possibly at board director level, to be responsible and accountable for this part of the service's task, in the same way that it was deemed essential to do so for high security prisons following the escapes from Whitemoor and Parkhurst. That person was able to instil consistency into the way in which such prisoners were held, and eliminate the management and staff incompetence that had so publicly been exploited by prisoners. I contend that exactly the same approach is needed in the treatment of and conditions for young prisoners, whom the Director General has acknowledged publicly, on a number of occasions, to be in need of urgent care and attention. I, and many who know far more about the subject than I do, freely acknowledge that establishments such as Feltham are very difficult to manage effectively, because of the need to develop regimes capable of holding difficult, vulnerable and impressionable young people securely, safely and decently, while making determined efforts to challenge their offending behaviour and prevent future victims. The potential for providing such leadership exists in the Prison Service. But I remain seriously concerned that the frequently identified unsatisfactory treatment of and conditions for young prisoners remains unaltered, while such remedial action, together with the processing of the literally hundreds of recommendations and suggestions that I have made consistently over the past five years, have neither been openly endorsed by Ministers nor implemented following instructions by the Director General.

The bulk of this report is specifically about Feltham B, but action is needed now in all other establishments in which this age group is held, in which I have reported similar degrees of neglect and deprivation. The reason why conditions for juveniles in Feltham A are improving is because the Prison Service has had to respond to the contracted demands of the Youth Justice Board (YJB), which has laid down how children should be treated in all custodial establishments. The YJB has funded structured improvement in both physical conditions and staff resources. In addition the Director General has, at last, appointed an operational manager for this age group, which is bound to lead to the consistency in regime delivery that I have been calling for for so long. However, no similar initiative exists for young adult prisoners, and I find it distressing that all I can do is, yet again, report that the problems to which I have so often, and so consistently, drawn attention over the past five years, remain as bad as, if not worse than, they ever did. Resources have been committed, and more are promised. But, because I see no evidence that these resources are yet being put to best effect by those to whom they have been given, I have to recommend to Ministers that unless they are, by the end of 2001 at the latest, responsibility for the custody of young prisoners in Feltham B should be withdrawn from the Prison Service and passed to the private sector.

13 Non-Custodial Dispositions

The numerical importance of the fine is evident from the statistics provided. The data on the last five items, which of course are custodial dispositions, is provided for comparative purposes.

Home Office (2001) *Criminal Statistics 1999*

SENTENCES AND ORDERS 1998 AND 1999 (THOUSANDS)

	1998	1999
Absolute discharge	17.8	15.9
Conditional discharge	114.7	114.1
Fine	1060.7	993.3
Probation order	58.2	58.4
Supervision order	12.4	12.7
Community service order	48.6	49.6
Curfew order	1.0	1.6
Attendance centre order	8.1	8.7
Combination order	21.2	20.8
Secure training order	0.1	0.2
Young offender institution	23.5	24.9
Immediate prison	76.3	79.7
Suspended sentence	3.4	3.2
Section 53, Children and Young Persons Act 1933	0.6	0.6

This government report provides a number of different types of information in relation to community penalties. A considerable amount of information is provided in relation to the probation service, new initiatives such as electronic monitoring are noted and the Green Paper *Strengthening Punishment in the Community* (1995) is analysed.

Protecting the Public (1996), pp36–38

Community sentencing

The Government's aim is to ensure that community sentences are effective forms of punishment and to reduce the risk of further crime. They are available for offences which are so serious that a financial penalty will not suffice, but not so serious that only a prison sentence is justified. Offenders have to undergo physically, mentally or emotionally challenging programmes, and are required to conform to a structured regime. The courts may specify any additional requirement in the interests of securing the rehabilitation of the offender or protecting the public from harm or further crime – for example, a requirement for drug or alcohol treatment, or to reside in a specified place, or not to approach or contact the victim.

The punishment also includes the prospect of a prompt return to court if the offender fails to comply with the requirements of supervision, so that the court can decide the appropriate course of action. This may mean a prison sentence if the original offence or offences attracted the possibility of custody.

It is the probation service's responsibility to supervise adult offenders in the community, so that they lead law abiding lives, in a way which minimises risk to the public. The 54 local probation services in England and Wales provide a wide range of community service placements providing unpaid work for the benefit of the community and a wide range of demanding and constructive activities and other forms of supervision. Supervision will include work to confront offending behaviour, so that offenders are aware of the impact of their crimes on their victims and the community and work to instil a greater sense of personal responsibility and discipline, aiding re-integration as a law abiding member of society.

The Government sets priorities for the probation service on the basis of a rolling three-year plan. The Home Secretary's priorities for the probation service are:

– to ensure that community sentences provide a tough and demanding punishment which is effective in reducing crime;
– making community supervision safer for the public by enhanced risk assessment, enforcement and management; and
– improving both the quality of service delivery and the use of resources.

Her Majesty's Inspectorate of Probation undertakes a rolling programme of local area quality and effectiveness inspections, as well as regular thematic inspections into specific areas of service delivery.

The Government published the first National Standards for the work of probation services and social services departments in 1992. After a comprehensive review, revised National Standards were published jointly by the Home Office, the Department of Health and the Welsh Office in March 1995. The new standards improve and strengthen the supervision of offenders.

The 1995 National Standards for the supervision of offenders in the community are the required standards of practice for probation services and social services departments in England and Wales, in relation to the supervision of offenders in the community and in providing services to the courts. The revised National Standards ensure that community sentences are demanding as punishments, that supervision is rigorous and that offenders are returned to court promptly if they fail to comply with the requirements of supervision, for the courts to consider appropriate action. The standards:

– protect the public from further offending by requiring effective supervision of offenders;
– make clear to the private and voluntary sector partners with whom probation and social services work how they are expected to meet these standards;
– provide a framework for good practice and a basis for demonstrating accountability for probation staff and local authority social workers;
– provide clear guidance on the preparation of reports, supervision of offenders and how to proceed when offenders behave unacceptably; and
– make it clear to offenders what is expected of them and what action will be taken if they fail to comply with the requirements of the standards.

The courts have powers to bind over the

parents of young offenders, to require their attendance at court, and to order them to pay any fines or compensation arising from the child's offending behaviour. The Government has taken steps to strengthen these powers and included new provisions in the Criminal Justice and Public Order Act 1994 which allow the courts, in passing a community sentence, to bind over the child's parents to ensure compliance with the sentence. The provisions are aimed at those parents who might not otherwise give their children the support that is needed. Failure to comply with the binding over order can lead to a fine of up to £1,000.

The Criminal Justice and Public Order Act 1994 allows trials of electronic monitoring of curfew orders to take place in selected areas. This new community sentence was established on a national basis in section 12 of the Criminal Justice Act 1991. Pilot trials of electronic monitoring commenced in July 1995 at three locations: Manchester, Reading and the County of Norfolk. The area of the trials was subsequently extended in November 1995 to include the whole of Greater Manchester and Berkshire.

The objectives of the trials were:

– to establish the technical and practical arrangements necessary to support the electronic monitoring of curfew orders;
– to ascertain the likely cost and effectiveness of curfew orders in relation to court sentences; and
– to evaluate the scope for introducing electronic monitoring of curfew orders on a selective or national basis.

It is too early to make a final evaluation of the trials so far, but they have already proved the potential value of electronic monitoring as a highly flexible, restrictive community sentence with a part to play in punishing offenders and reducing crime. The curfew order is a significant restriction of liberty with the courts empowered to sentence for up to 2,000 hours over a period of six months. The technology has so far proved successful in monitoring offenders whom the courts want

off the streets, and has ensured that the courts' sentences cannot be evaded without serious consequences. The slightest breach of a curfew order or attempt to tamper with the equipment is detected, and investigated by the contractors immediately. No violations are ignored, with warnings given for the most minor infringement. Offenders who continue not to comply are returned to court.

The courts are keen to test the new curfew order fully, but the Magistrates' Association has pointed to the need for more time for magistrates to get used to the sentence and has suggested that more courts might be involved. In the light of these views, the trials have been extended until April 1997, and powers have been extended for more courts in the trial areas to use the sentence. The Government is also carefully considering the scope for wider application of electronic monitoring.

The Government published a Green Paper *Strengthening Punishment in the Community* in March 1995 seeking views on proposals designed to improve understanding and confidence in community sentences.

The current range of community orders (the probation order, the community service order, the combination order, the curfew order, the attendance centre order and the supervision order) provide the courts with a variety of sentencing disposals, taking into account the seriousness of the offence, suitability, the degree of restriction of liberty imposed and the age of the offender. The present array of community orders have been established over several years and do not provide sentencers with the widest possible choice of sentencing options.

Despite recent initiatives to reinforce rigorous standards for the supervision of offenders, community sentences are often portrayed as a 'soft option' and perceived as such by the public. The Green Paper *Strengthening Punishment in the Community* recognised the need to address this perception by strengthening the hand of sentencers in passing a community sentence. It proposed that there should be more choice and flexibility in sentencing options, and that the purpose and content of community sentences should be made clear at the point of sentence, thus increasing public understanding of supervision in the community.

The Green Paper proposed:

- the introduction of a single integrated sentence replacing and incorporating the present range of community orders in the adult court;
- the matching of sentence elements to the three principal purposes of punishment in the community: restriction of liberty; reparation; and the prevention of re-offending;
- the court's role should be to address these purposes of punishment; to decide whether one or more should be met in the sentence passed: and to determine the balance between a wider range of sentence elements to match the punishment;
- the courts should have increased discretion to determine the content of community sentences in individual cases, either singly or in combination and increased choice and flexibility in the range of supervisory or reparative activities provided by the probation service;
- the courts should also have more consistent access to information on the progress and outcome of community sentences; and
- the present requirement that offenders consent to community orders should be removed.

Comments on the proposals in the Green Paper ... revealed general support for the further development of community sentences, greater clarity about the content of community sentences at the time they are passed by the courts, a wider range of sentencing options and more information for the courts. However, some respondents considered that a single integrated community sentence was unnecessary because the current community orders already provided a sufficient range of options.

The 2000 Act makes provision for suspended sentences and suspended sentence supervision orders in ss118–124. I have taken the positive view in treating them as non-custodial dispositions.

Powers of Criminal Courts (Sentencing) Act 2000, ss118–124

Section 118
Suspended sentences of imprisonment

118 (1) A court which passes a sentence of imprisonment for a term of not more than two years for an offence may (subject to subs(4) below) order that the sentence shall not take effect unless, during a period specified in the order, the offender commits in Great Britain another offence punishable with imprisonment and thereafter a court having power to do so orders under s119 below that the original sentence shall take effect.

(2) The period specified in an order under subs(1) above must be a period of not less than one year nor more than two years beginning with the date of the order.

(3) In this Act –

'suspended sentence' means a sentence to which an order under subs(1) above relates; and

'operational period', in relation to such a sentence, means the period specified in the order under subs(1).

(4) A court shall not deal with an offender by means of a suspended sentence unless it is of the opinion –

(a) that the case is one in which a sentence of imprisonment would have been appropriate even without the power to suspend the sentence; and

(b) that the exercise of that power can be justified by the exceptional circumstances of the case.

(5) A court which passes a suspended sentence on any person for an offence shall consider whether the circumstances of the case are such as to warrant in addition the imposition of a fine or the making of a compensation order.

(6) A court which passes a suspended sentence

on any person for an offence shall not impose a community sentence in his case in respect of that offence or any other offence of which he is convicted by or before the court or for which he is dealt with by the court.

(7) On passing a suspended sentence the court shall explain to the offender in ordinary language his liability under s119 below if during the operational period he commits an offence punishable with imprisonment.

(8) Subject to any provision to the contrary contained in the Criminal Justice Act 1967, this Act or any other enactment passed or instrument made under any enactment after 31 December 1967 –

> (a) a suspended sentence which has not taken effect under s119 below shall be treated as a sentence of imprisonment for the purposes of all enactments and instruments made under enactments except any enactment or instrument which provides for disqualification for or loss of office, or forfeiture of pensions, of persons sentenced to imprisonment; and

> (b) where a suspended sentence has taken effect under s119, the offender shall be treated for the purposes of the enactments and instruments excepted by paragraph (a) above as having been convicted on the ordinary date on which the period allowed for making an appeal against an order under that section expires or, if such an appeal is made, the date on which it is finally disposed of or abandoned or fails for non-prosecution.

Section 119
Power of court on conviction of further offence to deal with suspended sentence

119 (1) Where an offender is convicted of an offence punishable with imprisonment committed during the operational period of a suspended sentence and either he is so convicted by or before a court having power under s120 below to deal with him in respect of the suspended sentence or he subsequently appears or is brought before such a court, then, unless the sentence has already taken effect, that court shall consider his case and deal with him by one of the following methods –

> (a) the court may order that the suspended sentence shall take effect with the original term unaltered;

> (b) the court may order that the sentence shall take effect with the substitution of a lesser term for the original term;

> (c) the court may by order vary the original order under s118(1) above by substituting for the period specified in that order a period ending not later than two years from the date of the variation; or

> (d) the court may make no order with respect to the suspended sentence.

(2) The court shall make an order under paragraph (a) of subs(1) above unless it is of the opinion that it would be unjust to do so in view of all the circumstances, including the facts of the subsequent offence; and where it is of that opinion the court shall state its reasons.

(3) Where a court orders that a suspended sentence shall take effect, with or without any variation of the original term, the court may order that that sentence shall take effect immediately or that the term of that sentence shall commence on the expiry of another term of imprisonment passed on the offender by that or another court.

(4) The power to make an order under subs(3) above has effect subject to s84 above (restriction on consecutive sentences for released prisoners).

(5) In proceedings for dealing with an offender in respect of a suspended sentence which take place before the Crown Court, any question whether the offender has been convicted of an offence punishable with imprisonment committed during the operational period of the suspended sentence shall be determined by the court and not by the verdict of a jury.

(6) Where a court deals with an offender under this section in respect of a suspended sentence, the appropriate officer of the court shall notify

the appropriate officer of the court which passed the sentence of the method adopted.

(7) Where on consideration of the case of an offender a court makes no order with respect to a suspended sentence, the appropriate officer of the court shall record that fact.

(8) For the purposes of any enactment conferring rights of appeal in criminal cases, any order made by a court with respect to a suspended sentence shall be treated as a sentence passed on the offender by that court for the offence for which the suspended sentence was passed.

Section 120
Court by which suspended sentence may be dealt with

120 (1) An offender may be dealt with in respect of a suspended sentence by the Crown Court or, where the sentence was passed by a magistrates' court, by any magistrates' court before which he appears or is brought.

(2) Where an offender is convicted by a magistrates' court of an offence punishable with imprisonment and the court is satisfied that the offence was committed during the operational period of a suspended sentence passed by the Crown Court –

(a) the court may, if it thinks fit, commit him in custody or on bail to the Crown Court; and

(b) if it does not, shall give written notice of the conviction to the appropriate officer of the Crown Court.

(3) For the purposes of this section and of s121 below, a suspended sentence passed on an offender on appeal shall be treated as having been passed by the court by which he was originally sentenced.

Section 121
Procedure where court convicting of further offence does not deal with suspended sentence

121 (1) If it appears to the Crown Court, where that court has jurisdiction in accordance with subs(2) below, or to a justice of the peace having jurisdiction in accordance with that subsection –

(a) that an offender has been convicted in Great Britain of an offence punishable with imprisonment committed during the operational period of a suspended sentence, and

(b) that he has not been dealt with in respect of the suspended sentence,

that court or justice may, subject to the following provisions of this section, issue a summons requiring the offender to appear at the place and time specified in it, or a warrant for his arrest.

(2) Jurisdiction for the purposes of subs(1) above may be exercised –

(a) if the suspended sentence was passed by the Crown Court, by that court;

(b) if it was passed by a magistrates' court, by a justice acting for the area for which that court acted.

(3) Where –

(a) an offender is convicted by a court in Scotland of an offence punishable with imprisonment, and

(b) the court is informed that the offence was committed during the operational period of a suspended sentence passed in England or Wales, the court shall give written notice of the conviction to the appropriate officer of the court by which the suspended sentence was passed.

(4) Unless he is acting in consequence of a notice under subs(3) above, a justice of the peace shall not issue a summons under this section except on information and shall not issue a warrant under this section except on information in writing and on oath.

(5) A summons or warrant issued under this section shall direct the offender to appear or to be brought before the court by which the suspended sentence was passed.

(6) In relation to a suspended sentence passed on appeal, this section is to be construed in accordance with s120(3) above.

Section 122
Suspended sentence supervision orders

122 (1) Where a court passes on an offender a suspended sentence for a term of more than six months for a single offence, the court may make a suspended sentence supervision order, that is to say, an order placing the offender under the supervision of a supervising officer for a period which is specified in the order and does not exceed the operational period of the suspended sentence.

(2) A suspended sentence supervision order shall specify the petty sessions area in which the offender resides or will reside; and the supervising officer shall be a probation officer appointed for or assigned to the area for the time being specified in the order (whether under this subsection by virtue of s124(3) below (power to amend order)).

(3) An offender in respect of whom a suspended sentence supervision order is in force shall keep in touch with the supervising officer in accordance with such instructions as he may from time to time be given by that officer and shall notify him of any change of address.

(4) On making a suspended sentence supervision order, the court shall explain its effect to the offender in ordinary language.

(5) The court by which a suspended sentence supervision order is made shall forthwith give copies of the order to a probation officer assigned to the court, and he shall give a copy to the offender and to the supervising officer.

(6) The court by which such an order is made shall also, except where it itself acts for the petty sessions area specified in the order, send to the justices' chief executive for that area –

(a) a copy of the order; and

(b) such documents and information relating to the case as it considers likely to be of assistance to a court acting for that area

in the exercise of its functions in relation to the order.

(7) The Secretary of State may by order –

(a) direct that subs(1) above be amended by substituting, for the number of months specified in that subsection as originally enacted or as previously amended under this paragraph, such other number (not more than six) as the order may specify; or

(b) make in that subsection the repeals necessary to enable a court to make a suspended sentence supervision order in the case of any suspended sentence, whatever the length of the term.

(8) Where under s119 above a court deals with an offender in respect of a suspended sentence by varying the operational period of the sentence or by making no order with respect to the sentence, the court may make a suspended sentence supervision order in respect of the offender –

(a) in place of any such order made when the suspended sentence was passed; or

(b) if the court which passed the sentence could have made such an order but did not do so; or

(c) if that court could not then have made such an order but would have had power to do so if subs(1) above had then had effect as it has effect at the time when the offender is dealt with under s119.

Section 123
Breach of requirement of suspended sentence supervision order

123 (1) If, at any time while a suspended sentence supervision order is in force in respect of an offender, it appears on information to a justice of the peace acting for the petty sessions area for the time being specified in the order that the offender has failed to comply with any of the requirements of s122(3) above, the justice may –

(a) issue a summons requiring the offender to appear at the place and time specified in it; or

(b) if the information is in writing and on oath, issue a warrant for his arrest.

(2) Any summons or warrant issued under this section shall direct the offender to appear or be brought before a magistrates' court acting for the petty sessions area for the time being specified in the suspended sentence supervision order.

(3) If it is proved to the satisfaction of the court before which an offender appears or is brought under this section that he has failed without reasonable cause to comply with any of the requirements of s122(3) above, the court may, without prejudice to the continuance of the order, impose on him a fine not exceeding £1000.

(4) A fine imposed under subs(3) above shall be deemed, for the purposes of any enactment, to be a sum adjudged to be paid by a conviction.

Section 124
Suspended sentence supervision orders: revocation, amendment and cessation

124 (1) A suspended sentence supervision order may be revoked on the application of the supervising officer or the offender –

(a) if it was made by the Crown Court and includes a direction reserving the power of revoking it to that court, by the Crown Court;

(b) in any other case, by a magistrates' court acting for the petty sessions area for the time being specified in the order.

(2) Where a suspended sentence supervision order has been made on appeal, for the purposes of subs(1) above it shall be deemed –

(a) if it was made on an appeal brought from a magistrates' court, to have been made by that magistrates' court;

(b) if it was made on an appeal brought from the Crown Court or from the criminal division of the Court of Appeal, to have been made by the Crown Court.

(3) If a magistrates' court acting for the petty

sessions area for the time being specified in a suspended sentence supervision order is satisfied that the offender proposes to change, or has changed, his residence from that petty sessions area to another petty sessions area, the court may, and on the application of the supervising officer shall, amend the order by substituting the other petty sessions area for the area specified in the order.

(4) Where a suspended sentence supervision order is amended by a court under subs(3) above, the court shall send to the justices' chief executive for the new area specified in the order a copy of the order, together with such documents and information relating to the case as it considers likely to be of assistance to a court acting for that area in the exercise of its functions in relation to the order.

(5) A suspended sentence supervision order shall cease to have effect if before the end of the period specified in it –

(a) a court orders under s119 above that a suspended sentence passed in the proceedings in which the order was made shall have effect; or

(b) the order is revoked under subs(1) above or replaced under s122(8) above.

―――――――――

The workings of the suspended sentence since the implementation of the Criminal Justice Act 1991 is examined in this extract. The Act did have a dramatic effect as the disposal was used for 24,700 indictable cases in 1988 but only 2,300 in 1993. By 1996 the figure had increased again, but only to 3,400 cases and by 1999 it was down to 3,200.

Stone N (1994) 'The Suspended Sentence since the Criminal Justice Act 1991', *Criminal Law Review*, pp399 and 408

Speculation about the fate of the suspended sentence of imprisonment has so far centred on the handful of Court of Appeal decisions which have illustrated the presence or absence of 'exceptional circumstances' justifying such a sentence under s22(2)(b) of Powers of Criminal Courts Act 1973. In his commentary on one of the most recently reported cases, *Ullah Khan* (1) (in which a fraudulent solicitor's serious health problems were considered sufficiently exceptional) David Thomas considers it 'unlikely that a consistent approach will be found to the meaning of the new restriction' and suggests that 'inconsistency in the use of suspended sentences will be inevitable'. He concludes that 'either this restriction ... should be repealed or the suspended sentence itself should be abolished'. Writing from his perspective as liaison probation officer at the Court of Appeal, David Foot is less troubled by this diversity and individuality of approach and feels that it can be left 'to the good sense of magistrates and judges to determine whether, on the facts before them in a particular case, such (exceptional) circumstances exist' (2).

To gain a better understanding of how that 'good sense' is actually being exercised in the daily world of sentencing practice, I examined the residual use of the suspended sentence during the first operational year of the 1991 Act, October 1992–September 1993, in one shire county. It has not been possible to obtain the statistical returns of the courts (including two Crown Court centres) which sit in that county but I was able to use the data held by the local probation service on sentences passed following the preparation of pre-sentence reports by its staff.

Few and far between?

In the view of the Lord Chief Justice in *Robinson* (3) 'the instances in which a suspended sentence will be appropriate will be few and far between'. On the strength of this, commentators have concluded that 'for all practical purposes, the suspended sentence has been abolished except for a tiny number of extraordinary cases'. The evidence of this admittedly small study is to the contrary, suggesting that the measure retains an enduring pragmatic appeal and has not been completely marginalised by the 1991 Act.

The courts in this sample clearly wished to mark the offence with a custodial sentence without requiring the offender to incur the pains of imprisonment. This sentencing tactic was sometimes observable even in the absence of any of the exceptional factors identified above, for example in dealing with breach of a regulatory court order (such as keeping a dog whilst disqualified or being involved in the management of a company while an undischarged bankrupt). Here the court perhaps hoped to leave the offender in no doubt of the unacceptability of such behaviour while holding back from the ultimate sanction. In other instances the court seemed simply very reluctant to send the offender to prison and thus seized upon the suspended sentence as a convenient route of retreat with dignity. For example, in sentencing a woman (aged 28) convicted of cruelty to a child, described in the pre-sentence report as reluctant to take responsibility for her behaviour and very preoccupied with her own emotional needs and drug dependency, the judge justified suspension of sentence by referring to her guilty plea, the fact that the case had been pending for over a year, the unlikelihood that she would resume care of the child in the immediate future and the 'lamentable lack of support and advice' from her mother during the critical period. ...

Few if any of the cases resulting in a suspended sentence in this study would have satisfied the stringent approach of the Court of Appeal demonstrated in *Lowery* and *Robinson*. However, only 2 per cent of offenders sentenced to suspended sentences at Crown Court in 1992 appealed against sentence (4) and that appeal rate is now likely to be even smaller. As a consequence, although 'exceptional circumstances' may seem a somewhat questionable or even spurious concept, it is likely that courts will continue to opt for an exceptional course of sentence for a variety of familiar reasons. Furthermore, the more recent Court of Appeal decisions finding exceptionality may signal greater flexibility and bolster the courts' reluctance to 'kill off' the suspended sentence.

References
1. [1993] Crim LR 982.
2. 'The Use of Suspended Sentences' (1993) 157 *Justice of the Peace* 565–567.
3. *Robinson* (1992) 14 Cr App R (S) 559.
4. *Criminal Appeals, England and Wales, 1992*, Home Office Statistical Bulletin, London: Home Office. The appeal rate against fully suspended imprisonment from magistrates' courts to the Crown Court was 1 per cent.

Sections 12–13 provide for absolute and conditional discharges whilst ss33–51 and 59–62 provide for the following community sentences and orders: curfew orders, probation orders, community service orders, combination orders, drug treatment and testing orders, attendance centre orders, supervision orders and action plan orders.

Powers of Criminal Courts (Sentencing) Act 2000, ss12–14, 33–51 and 59–62

PART II
ABSOLUTE AND CONDITIONAL DISCHARGE
Section 12
Absolute and conditional discharge

12 (1) Where a court by or before which a person is convicted of an offence (not being an offence the sentence for which is fixed by law or falls to be imposed under s109(2), 110(2) or 111(2) below) is of the opinion, having regard to the circumstances including the nature of the offence and the character of the offender, that it is inexpedient to inflict punishment, the court may make an order either –

(a) discharging him absolutely; or

(b) if the court thinks fit, discharging him subject to the condition that he commits no offence during such period, not exceeding three years from the date of the order, as may be specified in the order.

(2) Subsection (1)(b) above has effect subject to s66(4) of the Crime and Disorder Act 1998 (effect of reprimands and warnings).

(3) An order discharging a person subject to such a condition as is mentioned in subs(1)(b) above is in this Act referred to as an 'order for conditional discharge'; and the period specified in any such order is in this Act referred to as 'the period of conditional discharge'.

(4) Before making an order for conditional discharge, the court shall explain to the offender in ordinary language that if he commits another offence during the period of conditional discharge he will be liable to be sentenced for the original offence.

(5) If (by virtue of s13 below) a person conditionally discharged under this section is sentenced for the offence in respect of which the order for conditional discharge was made, that order shall cease to have effect.

(6) On making an order for conditional discharge, the court may, if it thinks it expedient for the purpose of the offender's reformation, allow any person who consents to do so to give security for the good behaviour of the offender.

(7) Nothing in this section shall be construed as preventing a court, on discharging an offender absolutely or conditionally in respect of any offence, from making an order for costs against the offender or imposing any disqualification on him or from making in respect of the offence an order under s130, 143 or 148 below (compensation orders, deprivation orders and restitution orders).

Section 13
Commission of further offence by person conditionally discharged

13 (1) If it appears to the Crown Court, where that court has jurisdiction in accordance with subs(2) below, or to a justice of the peace having jurisdiction in accordance with that subsection, that a person in whose case an order for conditional discharge has been made –

(a) has been convicted by a court in Great Britain of an offence committed during the period of conditional discharge, and

(b) has been dealt with in respect of that offence, that court or justice may, subject to subs(3) below, issue a summons requiring that person to appear at the place and time specified in it or a warrant for his arrest.

(2) Jurisdiction for the purposes of subs(1) above may be exercised –

(a) if the order for conditional discharge was made by the Crown Court, by that court;

(b) if the order was made by a magistrates' court, by a justice acting for the petty sessions area for which that court acts.

(3) A justice of the peace shall not issue a summons under this section except on information and shall not issue a warrant under this section except on information in writing and on oath.

(4) A summons or warrant issued under this section shall direct the person to whom it relates to appear or to be brought before the court by which the order for conditional discharge was made.

(5) If a person in whose case an order for conditional discharge has been made by the Crown Court is convicted by a magistrates' court of an offence committed during the period of conditional discharge, the magistrates' court –

(a) may commit him to custody or release him on bail until he can be brought or appear before the Crown Court; and

(b) if it does so, shall send to the Crown Court a copy of the minute or memorandum of the conviction entered in the register, signed by the justices' chief executive by whom the register is kept.

(6) Where it is proved to the satisfaction of the court by which an order for conditional discharge was made that the person in whose case the order was made has been convicted of an offence committed during the period of conditional discharge, the court may deal with him, for the offence for which the order was made, in any way in which it could deal with

him if he had just been convicted by or before that court of that offence.

(7) If a person in whose case an order for conditional discharge has been made by a magistrates' court –

(a) is convicted before the Crown Court of an offence committed during the period of conditional discharge, or

(b) is dealt with by the Crown Court for any such offence in respect of which he was committed for sentence to the Crown Court, the Crown Court may deal with him, for the offence for which the order was made, in any way in which the magistrates' court could deal with him if it had just convicted him of that offence.

(8) If a person in whose case an order for conditional discharge has been made by a magistrates' court is convicted by another magistrates' court of any offence committed during the period of conditional discharge, that other court may, with the consent of the court which made the order, deal with him, for the offence for which the order was made, in any way in which the court could deal with him if it had just convicted him of that offence.

(9) Where an order for conditional discharge has been made by a magistrates' court in the case of an offender under 18 years of age in respect of an offence triable only on indictment in the case of an adult, any powers exercisable under subs(6), (7) or (8) above by that or any other court in respect of the offender after he attains the age of 18 shall be powers to do either or both of the following –

(a) to impose a fine not exceeding £5,000 for the offence in respect of which the order was made;

(b) to deal with the offender for that offence in any way in which a magistrates' court could deal with him if it had just convicted him of an offence punishable with imprisonment for a term not exceeding six months.

(10) The reference in subs(6) above to a person's having been convicted of an offence

committed during the period of conditional discharge is a reference to his having been so convicted by a court in Great Britain.

Section 14

14 (1) Subject to subs(2) below, a conviction of an offence for which an order is made under s12 above discharging the offender absolutely or conditionally shall be deemed not to be a conviction for any purpose other than the purposes of the proceedings in which the order is made and of any subsequent proceedings which may be taken against the offender under s13 above.

(2) Where the offender was aged 18 or over at the time of his conviction of the offence in question and is subsequently sentenced (under s13 above) for that offence, subs(1) above shall cease to apply to the conviction.

(3) Without prejudice to subs(1) and (2) above, the conviction of an offender who is discharged absolutely or conditionally under s12 above shall in any event be disregarded for the purposes of any enactment or instrument which –

(a) imposes any disqualification or disability upon convicted persons; or

(b) authorises or requires the imposition of any such disqualification or disability.

(4) Subsections (1) to (3) above shall not affect –

(a) any right of an offender discharged absolutely or conditionally under s12 above to rely on his conviction in bar of any subsequent proceedings for the same offence;

(b) the restoration of any property in consequence of the conviction of any such offender; or

(c) the operation, in relation to any such offender, of any enactment or instrument in force on 1 July 1974 which is expressed to extend to persons dealt with under s11) of the Probation of Offenders Act 1907 as well as to convicted persons.

(5) In subs(3) and (4) above –

'enactment' includes an enactment contained in a local Act; and

'instrument' means an instrument having effect by virtue of an Act.

(6) Subsection (1) above has effect subject to s50(1A) of the Criminal Appeal Act 1968 and s108 (1A) of the Magistrates' Courts Act 1980 (rights of appeal); and this subsection shall not be taken to prejudice any other enactment that excludes the effect of subs(1) or (3) above for particular purposes.

(7) Without prejudice to paragraph 1(3) of Schedule 11 to this Act (references to provisions of this Act to be construed as including references to corresponding old enactments), in this section –

(a) any reference to an order made under s12 above discharging an offender absolutely or conditionally includes a reference to an order which was made under any provision of Part I of the Powers of Criminal Courts Act 1973 (whether or not reproduced in this Act) discharging the offender absolutely or conditionally;

(b) any reference to an offender who is discharged absolutely or conditionally under s12 includes a reference to an offender who was discharged absolutely or conditionally under any such provision.

PART IV COMMUNITY ORDERS AND REPARATION ORDERS
CHAPTER I COMMUNITY ORDERS: GENERAL PROVISIONS
Section 33
Meaning of 'community order' and 'community sentence'

33 (1) In this Act, 'community order' means any of the following orders –

(a) a curfew order;

(b) a probation order;

(c) a community service order;

(d) a combination order;

(e) a drug treatment and testing order;

(f) an attendance centre order;

(g) a supervision order;

(h) an action plan order.

(2) In this Act, 'community sentence' means a sentence which consists of or includes one or more community orders.

Section 34
Community orders not available where sentence fixed by law etc

34 None of the powers to make community orders which are conferred by this Part is exercisable in respect of an offence for which the sentence –

(a) is fixed by law; or

(b) falls to be imposed under s109(2), 110(2) or 111(2) below (requirement to impose custodial sentences for certain repeated offences committed by offenders aged 18 or over).

Section 35
Restrictions on imposing community sentences

35 (1) A court shall not pass a community sentence on an offender unless it is of the opinion that the offence, or the combination of the offence and one or more offences associated with it, was serious enough to warrant such a sentence.

(2) In consequence of the provision made by s51 below with respect to combination orders, a community sentence shall not consist of or include both a probation order and a community service order.

(3) Subject to subs(2) above and to s69(5) below (which limits the community orders that may be combined with an action plan order), where a court passes a community sentence –

(a) the particular order or orders comprising or forming part of the sentence shall be such as in the opinion of the court is, or taken together are, the most suitable for the offender; and

(b) the restrictions on liberty imposed by the order or orders shall be such as in the opinion of the court are commensurate with the seriousness of the offence, or the combination of the offence and one or more offences associated with it.

(4) Subsections (1) and (3) (b) above have effect subject to s59 below (curfew orders and community service orders for persistent petty offenders).

Section 36
Procedural requirements for community sentences: pre-sentence reports etc

36 (1) In forming any such opinion as is mentioned in subs(1) or (3)(b) of s35 above, a court shall take into account all such information as is available to it about the circumstances of the offence or (as the case may be) of the offence and the offence or offences associated with it, including any aggravating or mitigating factors.

(2) In forming any such opinion as is mentioned in subs(3)(a) of that section, a court may take into account any information about the offender which is before it.

(3) The following provisions of this section apply in relation to –

(a) a probation order which includes additional requirements authorised by Schedule 2 to this Act;

(b) a community service order;

(c) a combination order;

(d) a drug treatment and testing order;

(e) a supervision order which includes requirements authorised by Schedule 6 to this Act.

(4) Subject to subs(5) below, a court shall obtain and consider a pre-sentence report before forming an opinion as to the suitability for the offender of one or more of the orders mentioned in subs(3) above.

(5) Subsection (4) above does not apply if, in the circumstances of the case, the court is of the opinion that it is unnecessary to obtain a pre-sentence report.

(6) In a case where the offender is aged under 18 and the offence is not triable only on indictment and there is no other offence associated with it that is triable only on indictment, the court shall not form such an opinion as is mentioned in subs(5) above unless –

(a) there exists a previous pre-sentence report obtained in respect of the offender; and

(b) the court has had regard to the information contained in that report, or, if there is more than one such report, the most recent report.

(7) No community sentence which consists of or includes such an order as is mentioned in subs(3) above shall be invalidated by the failure of a court to obtain and consider a pre-sentence report before forming an opinion as to the suitability of the order for the offender, but any court on an appeal against such a sentence –

(a) shall, subject to subs(8) below, obtain a pre-sentence report if none was obtained by the court below; and

(b) shall consider any such report obtained by it or by that court.

(8) Subsection (7)(a) above does not apply if the court is of the opinion –

(a) that the court below was justified in forming an opinion that it was unnecessary to obtain a pre-sentence report; or

(b) that, although the court below was not justified in forming that opinion, in the circumstances of the case at the time it is before the court, it is unnecessary to obtain a pre-sentence report.

(9) In a case where the offender is aged under 18 and the offence is not triable only on indictment and there is no other offence associated with it that is triable only on indictment, the court shall not form such an opinion as is mentioned in subs(8) above unless –

(a) there exists a previous pre-sentence report obtained in respect of the offender; and

(b) the court has had regard to the information contained in that report, or, if there is more than one such report, the most recent report.

(10) Section 156 below (disclosure of pre-sentence report to offender etc) applies to any pre-sentence report obtained in pursuance of this section.

CHAPTER II
COMMUNITY ORDERS AVAILABLE FOR OFFENDERS OF ANY AGE
Section 37
Curfew orders

37 (1) Where a person is convicted of an offence, the court by or before which he is convicted may (subject to ss34 to 36 above) make an order requiring him to remain, for periods specified in the order, at a place so specified.

(2) An order under subs(1) above is in this Act referred to as a 'curfew order'.

(3) A curfew order may specify different places or different periods for different days, but shall not specify –

(a) periods which fall outside the period of six months beginning with the day on which it is made; or

(b) periods which amount to less than two hours or more than 12 hours in any one day.

(4) In relation to an offender aged under 16 on conviction, subs(3)(a) above shall have effect as if the reference to six months were a reference to three months.

(5) The requirements in a curfew order shall, as far as practicable, be such as to avoid –

(a) any conflict with the offender's religious beliefs or with the requirements of any other community order to which he may be subject; and

(b) any interference with the times, if any, at which he normally works or attends school or any other educational establishment.

(6) A curfew order shall include provision for making a person responsible for monitoring the offender's whereabouts during the curfew periods specified in the order; and a person who is made so responsible shall be of a description specified in an order made by the Secretary of State.

(7) A court shall not make a curfew order unless the court has been notified by the Secretary of State that arrangements for monitoring the offender's whereabouts are available in the area in which the place proposed to be specified in the order is situated and the notice has not been withdrawn.

(8) Before making a curfew order, the court shall obtain and consider information about the place proposed to be specified in the order (including information as to the attitude of persons likely to be affected by the enforced presence there of the offender).

(9) Before making a curfew order in respect of an offender who on conviction is under 16, the court shall obtain and consider information about his family circumstances and the likely effect of such an order on those circumstances.

(10) Before making a curfew order, the court shall explain to the offender in ordinary language –

(a) the effect of the order (including any additional requirements proposed to be included in the order in accordance with s38 below (electronic monitoring));

(b) the consequences which may follow (under Part II of Schedule 3 to this Act) if he fails to comply with any of the requirements of the order; and

(c) that the court has power (under Parts III and IV of that Schedule) to review the order on the application either of the offender or of the responsible officer.

(11) The court by which a curfew order is made shall give a copy of the order to the offender and to the responsible officer.

(12) In this Act, 'responsible officer', in relation to an offender subject to a curfew order, means the person who is responsible for monitoring the offender's whereabouts during the curfew periods specified in the order.

Section 38
Electronic monitoring of curfew orders

38 (1) Subject to subs(2) below, a curfew order may in addition include requirements for securing the electronic monitoring of the offender's whereabouts during the curfew periods specified in the order.

(2) A court shall not make a curfew order which includes such requirements unless the court –

(a) has been notified by the Secretary of State that electronic monitoring arrangements are available in the area in which the place proposed to be specified in the order is situated; and

(b) is satisfied that the necessary provision can be made under those arrangements.

(3) Electronic monitoring arrangements made by the Secretary of State under this section may include entering into contracts with other persons for the electronic monitoring by them of offenders' whereabouts.

Section 39
Breach, revocation and amendment of curfew orders

39 Schedule 3 to this Act (which makes provision for dealing with failures to comply with the requirements of certain community orders, for revoking such orders with or without the substitution of other sentences and for amending such orders) shall have effect so far as relating to curfew orders.

Section 40
Curfew orders: supplementary

40 (1) The Secretary of State may make rules for regulating –

(a) the monitoring of the whereabouts of persons who are subject to curfew orders (including electronic monitoring in cases where arrangements for such monitoring are available); and

(b) without prejudice to the generality of paragraph (a) above, the functions of the responsible officers of persons who are subject to curfew orders.

(2) The Secretary of State may by order direct –

(a) that subs(3) of s37 above shall have effect with the substitution, for any period there specified, of such period as may be specified in the order; or

(b) that subs(5) of that section shall have effect with such additional restrictions as may be so specified.

CHAPTER III
COMMUNITY ORDERS AVAILABLE ONLY WHERE OFFENDER AGED 16 OR OVER
Section 41
Probation orders

41 (1) Where a person aged 16 or over is convicted of an offence and the court by or before which he is convicted is of the opinion that his supervision is desirable in the interests of –

(a) securing his rehabilitation, or

(b) protecting the public from harm from him or preventing the commission by him of further offences, the court may (subject to ss34 to 36 above) make an order requiring him to be under supervision for a period specified in the order of not less than six months nor more than three years.

(2) An order under subs(1) above is in this Act referred to as a 'probation order'.

(3) A probation order shall specify the petty sessions area in which the offender resides or will reside.

(4) If the offender is aged 18 or over at the time when the probation order is made, he shall, subject to paragraph 18 of Schedule 3 to this Act (offender's change of area), be required to be under the supervision of a probation officer appointed for or assigned to the petty sessions area specified in the order.

(5) If the offender is aged under 18 at that time, he shall, subject to paragraph 18 of Schedule 3, be required to be under the supervision of –

(a) a probation officer appointed for or assigned to the petty sessions area specified in the order; or

(b) a member of a youth offending team established by a local authority specified in the order; and if an order specifies a local authority for the purposes of paragraph (b) above, the authority specified must be the local authority within whose area it appears to the court that the offender resides or will reside.

(6) In this Act, 'responsible officer', in relation to an offender who is subject to a probation order, means the probation officer or member of a youth offending team responsible for his supervision.

(7) Before making a probation order, the court shall explain to the offender in ordinary language –

(a) the effect of the order (including any additional requirements proposed to be included in the order in accordance with s42 below);

(b) the consequences which may follow (under Part II of Schedule 3 to this Act) if he fails to comply with any of the requirements of the order; and

(c) that the court has power (under Parts III and IV of that Schedule) to review the order on the application either of the offender or of the responsible officer.

(8) On making a probation order, the court may, if it thinks it expedient for the purpose of the offender's reformation, allow any person who consents to do so to give security for the good behaviour of the offender.

(9) The court by which a probation order is made shall forthwith give copies of the order to –

(a) if the offender is aged 18 or over, a probation officer assigned to the court, or

(b) if the offender is aged under 18, a probation officer or member of a youth offending team so assigned, and he shall give a copy to the offender, to the responsible officer and to the person in charge of any institution in which the offender is required by the order to reside.

(10) The court by which such an order is made shall also, except where it itself acts for the petty sessions area specified in the order, send to the clerk to the justices for that area –

(a) a copy of the order; and

(b) such documents and information relating to the case as it considers likely to be of assistance to a court acting for that area in the exercise of its functions in relation to the order.

(11) An offender in respect of whom a probation order is made shall keep in touch with the responsible officer in accordance with such instructions as he may from time to time be given by that officer, and shall notify him of any change of address.

Section 42
Additional requirements which may be included in probation orders

42 (1) Subject to subs(3) below, a probation order may in addition require the offender to comply during the whole or any part of the probation period with such requirements as the court, having regard to the circumstances of the case, considers desirable in the interests of –

(a) securing the rehabilitation of the offender; or

(b) protecting the public from harm from him or preventing the commission by him of further offences.

(2) Without prejudice to the generality of subs(1) above, the additional requirements which may be included in a probation order shall include the requirements which are authorised by Schedule 2 to this Act.

(3) Without prejudice to the power of the court under s130 below to make a compensation order, the payment of sums by way of

damages for injury or compensation for loss shall not be included among the additional requirements of a probation order.

Section 43
Breach, revocation and amendment of probation orders

43 Schedule 3 to this Act (which makes provision for dealing with failures to comply with the requirements of certain community orders, for revoking such orders with or without the substitution of other sentences and for amending such orders) shall have effect so far as relating to probation orders.

Section 44
Offenders residing in Scotland or Northern Ireland

44 Schedule 4 to this Act (which makes provision for and in connection with the making and amendment in England and Wales of certain community orders relating to persons residing in Scotland or Northern Ireland) shall have effect so far as relating to probation orders.

Section 45
Probation orders: supplementary

45 (1) The Secretary of State may by order direct that subs(1) of s41 above shall be amended by substituting, for the minimum or maximum period specified in that subsection as originally enacted or as previously amended under this subsection, such period as may be specified in the order.

(2) An order under subs(1) above may make in paragraph 19(2)(a) of Schedule 3 to this Act any amendment which the Secretary of State thinks necessary in consequence of any substitution made by the order.

Section 46
Community service orders

46 (1) Where a person aged 16 or over is convicted of an offence punishable with imprisonment, the court by or before which he is

convicted may (subject to ss34 to 36 above) make an order requiring him to perform unpaid work in accordance with s47 below.

(2) An order under subs(1) above is in this Act referred to as a 'community service order'.

(3) The number of hours which a person may be required to work under a community service order shall be specified in the order and shall be in the aggregate –

    (a) not less than 40; and

    (b) not more than 240.

(4) A court shall not make a community service order in respect of an offender unless, after hearing (if the court thinks it necessary) an appropriate officer, the court is satisfied that the offender is a suitable person to perform work under such an order.

(5) In subs(4) above 'an appropriate officer' means –

    (a) in the case of an offender aged 18 or over, a probation officer or social worker of a local authority social services department; and

    (b) in the case of an offender aged under 18, a probation officer, a social worker of a local authority social services department or a member of a youth offending team.

(6) A court shall not make a community service order in respect of an offender unless it is satisfied that provision for him to perform work under such an order can be made under the arrangements for persons to perform work under such orders which exist in the petty sessions area in which he resides or will reside.

(7) Subsection (6) above has effect subject to paragraphs 3 and 4 of Schedule 4 to this Act (transfer of order to Scotland or Northern Ireland).

(8) Where a court makes community service orders in respect of two or more offences of which the offender has been convicted by or before the court, the court may direct that the hours of work specified in any of those orders shall be concurrent with or additional to those specified in any other of those orders, but so that the total number of hours which are not concurrent shall not exceed the maximum specified in subs(3)(b) above.

(9) A community service order –

    (a) shall specify the petty sessions area in which the offender resides or will reside; and

    (b) where the offender is aged under 18 at the time the order is made, may also specify a local authority for the purposes of s47(5)(b) below (cases where functions are to be discharged by member of a youth offending team); and if the order specifies a local authority for those purposes, the authority specified must be the local authority within whose area it appears to the court that the offender resides or will reside.

(10) Before making a community service order, the court shall explain to the offender in ordinary language –

    (a) the purpose and effect of the order (and in particular the requirements of the order as specified in s47(1) to (3) below);

    (b) the consequences which may follow (under Part II of Schedule 3 to this Act) if he fails to comply with any of those requirements; and

    (c) that the court has power (under Parts III and IV of that Schedule) to review the order on the application either of the offender or of the responsible officer.

(11) The court by which a community service order is made shall forthwith give copies of the order to –

    (a) if the offender is aged 18 or over, a probation officer assigned to the court, or

    (b) if the offender is aged under 18, a probation officer or member of a youth offending team so assigned, and he shall give a copy to the offender and to the responsible officer.

(12) The court by which such an order is made shall also, except where it itself acts for the

petty sessions area specified in the order, send to the clerk to the justices for that area –

(a) a copy of the order; and

(b) such documents and information relating to the case as it considers likely to be of assistance to a court acting for that area in the exercise of its functions in relation to the order.

(13) In this section and Schedule 3 to this Act 'responsible officer', in relation to an offender subject to a community service order, means the person mentioned in subs(4)(a) or (b) or (5)(b) of s47 below who, as respects the order, is responsible for discharging the functions conferred by that section.

Section 47
Obligations of person subject to community service order

47 (1) An offender in respect of whom a community service order is in force shall –

(a) keep in touch with the responsible officer in accordance with such instructions as he may from time to time be given by that officer and notify him of any change of address; and

(b) perform for the number of hours specified in the order such work at such times as he may be instructed by the responsible officer.

(2) The instructions given by the responsible officer under this section shall, as far as practicable, be such as to avoid –

(a) any conflict with the offender's religious beliefs or with the requirements of any other community order to which he may be subject; and

(b) any interference with the times, if any, at which he normally works or attends school or any other educational establishment.

(3) Subject to paragraph 22 of Schedule 3 to this Act (power to extend order), the work required to be performed under a community service order shall be performed during the period of 12 months beginning with the date of the order; but, unless revoked, the order shall remain in force until the offender has worked under it for the number of hours specified in it.

(4) If the offender is aged 18 or over at the time when the order is made, the functions conferred by this section on 'the responsible officer' shall be discharged by –

(a) a probation officer appointed for or assigned to the petty sessions area specified in the order; or

(b) a person appointed for the purposes of this section by the probation committee for that area.

(5) If the offender is aged under 18 at that time, those functions shall be discharged by –

(a) a person mentioned in subs(4)(a) or (b) above; or

(b) a member of a youth offending team established by a local authority specified in the order.

(6) The reference in subs(4) above to the petty sessions area specified in the order and the reference in subs(5) above to a local authority so specified are references to the area or an authority for the time being so specified, whether under s46(9) above or by virtue of Part IV of Schedule 3 to this Act (power to amend orders).

Section 48
Breach, revocation and amendment of community service orders

48 Schedule 3 to this Act (which makes provision for dealing with failures to comply with the requirements of certain community orders, for revoking such orders with or without the substitution of other sentences and for amending such orders) shall have effect so far as relating to community service orders.

Section 49
Offenders residing in Scotland or Northern Ireland

49 Schedule 4 to this Act (which makes provision for and in connection with the making and amendment in England and Wales of certain community orders relating to persons residing in Scotland or Northern Ireland) shall have effect so far as relating to community service orders.

Section 50
Community service orders: supplementary

The Secretary of State may by order direct that subs(3) of s46 above shall be amended by substituting, for the maximum number of hours for the time being specified in paragraph (b) of that subsection, such number of hours as may be specified in the order.

Section 51
Combination orders

51 (1) Where a person aged 16 or over is convicted of an offence punishable with imprisonment and the court by or before which he is convicted is of the opinion mentioned in subs(3) below, the court may (subject to ss34 to 36 above) make an order requiring him both –

(a) to be under supervision for a period specified in the order, being not less than 12 months nor more than three years; and

(b) to perform unpaid work for a number of hours so specified, being in the aggregate not less than 40 nor more than 100.

(2) An order under subs(1) above is in this Act referred to as a 'combination order'.

(3) The opinion referred to in subs(1) above is that the making of a combination order is desirable in the interests of –

(a) securing the rehabilitation of the offender; or

(b) protecting the public from harm from him or preventing the commission by him of further offences.

(4) Subject to subs(1) above, ss41, 42, 46 and 47 above and Schedule 2 to this Act shall apply in relation to combination orders –

(a) in so far as those orders impose such a requirement as is mentioned in paragraph (a) of subs(1) above, as if they were probation orders; and

(b) in so far as they impose such a requirement as is mentioned in paragraph (b) of that subsection, as if they were community service orders.

(5) Schedule 3 to this Act (which makes provision for dealing with failures to comply with the requirements of certain community orders, for revoking such orders with or without the substitution of other sentences and for amending such orders) shall have effect so far as relating to combination orders.

(6) Schedule 4 to this Act (which makes provision for and in connection with the making and amendment in England and Wales of certain community orders relating to persons residing in Scotland or Northern Ireland) shall have effect so far as relating to combination orders.

Section 59
Curfew orders and community service orders for persistent petty offenders

59 (1) This section applies where –

(a) a person aged 16 or over is convicted of an offence;

(b) the court by or before which he is convicted is satisfied that each of the conditions mentioned in subs(2) below is fulfilled; and

(c) if it were not so satisfied, the court would be minded to impose a fine in respect of the offence.

(2) The conditions are that –

(a) one or more fines imposed on the offender in respect of one or more previous offences have not been paid; and

(b) if a fine were imposed in an amount which was commensurate with the seriousness of the offence, the offender would not have sufficient means to pay it.

(3) The court may –

(a) subject to subs(5) and (7) below, make a curfew order under s37(1) above, or

(b) subject to subs(6) and (7) below, make a community service order under s46(1) above, in respect of the offender instead of imposing a fine.

(4) Subsection (3) above applies notwithstanding anything in subs(1) and (3)(b) of s35 above (restrictions on imposing community sentences).

(5) Section 37(1) above (curfew orders) shall apply for the purposes of subs(3)(a) above as if for the words from the beginning to 'make' there were substituted 'Where s59 below applies, the court may make in respect of the offender'; and –

(a) section 37(3), (5) to (8) and (10) to (12), and

(b) so far as applicable, the other provisions of this Part relating to curfew orders,

have effect in relation to a curfew order made by virtue of this section as they have effect in relation to any other curfew order.

(6) Section 46(1) above (community service orders) shall apply for the purposes of subsection (3)(b) above as if for the words from the beginning to 'make' there were substituted 'Where s59 below applies, the court may make in respect of the offender'; and –

(a) section 46(3) and (4), and

(b) so far as applicable, the following provisions of s46 and the other provisions of this Part relating to community service orders, have effect in relation to a community service order made by virtue of this section as they have effect in relation to any other community service order.

(7) A court shall not make an order by virtue of subs(3)(a) or (b) above unless the court has been notified by the Secretary of State that arrangements for implementing orders so made are available in the relevant area and the notice has not been withdrawn.

(8) In subs(7) above 'the relevant area' means –

(a) in relation to a curfew order, the area in which the place proposed to be specified in the order is situated;

(b) in relation to a community service order, the area proposed to be specified in the order.

CHAPTER IV
ATTENDANCE CENTRE ORDERS: OFFENDERS UNDER 21 AND DEFAULTERS
Section 60
Attendance centre orders

60 (1) Where –

(a) (subject to ss34 to 36 above) a person aged under 21 is convicted by or before a court of an offence punishable with imprisonment, or

(b) a court would have power, but for s89 below (restrictions on imprisonment of young offenders and defaulters), to commit a person aged under 21 to prison in default of payment of any sum of money or for failing to do or abstain from doing anything required to be done or left undone, or

(c) a court has power to commit a person aged at least 21 but under 25 to prison in default of payment of any sum of money, the court may, if it has been notified by the Secretary of State that an attendance centre is available for the reception of persons of his description, order him to attend at such a centre, to be specified in the order, for such number of hours as may be so specified.

(2) An order under subs(1) above is in this Act referred to as an 'attendance centre order'.

(3) The aggregate number of hours for which an attendance centre order may require a person to attend at an attendance centre shall not be less than 12 except where –

(a) he is aged under 14; and

(b) the court is of the opinion that 12 hours

would be excessive, having regard to his age or any other circumstances.

(4) The aggregate number of hours shall not exceed 12 except where the court is of the opinion, having regard to all the circumstances, that 12 hours would be inadequate, and in that case –

(a) shall not exceed 24 where the person is aged under 16; and

(b) shall not exceed 36 where the person is aged 16 or over but under 21 or (where subs(1)(c) above applies) under 25.

(5) A court may make an attendance centre order in respect of a person before a previous attendance centre order made in respect of him has ceased to have effect, and may determine the number of hours to be specified in the order without regard –

(a) to the number specified in the previous order; or

(b) to the fact that that order is still in effect.

(6) An attendance centre order shall not be made unless the court is satisfied that the attendance centre to be specified in it is reasonably accessible to the person concerned, having regard to his age, the means of access available to him and any other circumstances.

(7) The times at which a person is required to attend at an attendance centre shall, as far as practicable, be such as to avoid –

(a) any conflict with his religious beliefs or with the requirements of any other community order to which he may be subject; and

(b) any interference with the times, if any, at which he normally works or attends school or any other educational establishment.

(8) The first time at which the person is required to attend at an attendance centre shall be a time at which the centre is available for his attendance in accordance with the notification of the Secretary of State, and shall be specified in the order.

(9) The subsequent times shall be fixed by the officer in charge of the centre, having regard to the person's circumstances.

(10) A person shall not be required under this section to attend at an attendance centre on more than one occasion on any day, or for more than three hours on any occasion.

(11) Where a court makes an attendance centre order, the clerk of the court shall –

(a) deliver or send a copy of the order to the officer in charge of the attendance centre specified in it; and

(b) deliver a copy of the order to the person in respect of whom it is made or send a copy by registered post or the recorded delivery service addressed to his last or usual place of abode.

(12) Where a person ('the defaulter') has been ordered to attend at an attendance centre in default of the payment of any sum of money –

(a) on payment of the whole sum to any person authorised to receive it, the attendance centre order shall cease to have effect;

(b) on payment of a part of the sum to any such person, the total number of hours for which the defaulter is required to attend at the centre shall be reduced proportionately, that is to say by such number of complete hours as bears to the total number the proportion most nearly approximating to, without exceeding, the proportion which the part bears to the whole sum.

Section 61
Breach, revocation and amendment of attendance centre orders
61 Schedule 5 to this Act (which makes provision for dealing with failures to comply with attendance centre orders, for revoking such orders with or without the substitution of other sentences and for amending such orders) shall have effect.

Section 62
Provision, regulation and management of attendance centres

62 (1) The Secretary of State may continue to provide attendance centres.

(2) In this Act 'attendance centre' means a place at which offenders aged under 21 may be required to attend and be given under supervision appropriate occupation or instruction in pursuance of attendance centre orders.

(3) The Secretary of State may make rules for the regulation and management of attendance centres.

(4) For the purpose of providing attendance centres, the Secretary of State may make arrangements with any local authority or police authority for the use of premises of that authority.

The probation statistics provide details not just of probation orders but also the wide variety of orders and sentences for which the probation service have responsibilities. An account is also provided which details their work in relation to the variety of reports that have to be produced.

Probation Statistics, England and Wales 1999 (2001)

In 1999 community sentences were imposed in 29 per cent of sentences for indictable offences, a similar percentage to 1998. However, the two types of court had different trends. In the Crown Court, the proportion has fallen from 30 per cent in 1995 to 27 per cent in 1996, and then risen to 28 per cent in 1997–1998 before falling to 27 per cent in 1999. But, in magistrates' courts, the proportion was steady at 27–28 per cent during 1994 and 1995, before increasing slightly to 29 per cent in 1996–1999. Magistrates' courts imposed 86 per cent of all community sentences in 1999. In 1999 magistrates' courts passed nearly 42 per cent of all new prison sentences for indictable offences. The proportion sentenced to probation or a community service order for indictable violence against the person offences has doubled between 1989 and 1999. For probation the proportion rose from 6 per cent to 12 per cent and for community service order from 7 per cent to 13 per cent.

Reports prepared for the courts

The estimated number of pre-sentence reports (PSRs) written in 1999 (237,500) was very similar to the number written in 1998 (236,800). Pre-sentence reports written for adult magistrates' courts rose 3 per cent in 1999 to 164,900; those written for the youth court fell by 12 per cent. In the Crown Court, the number of pre-sentence reports fell 4 per cent to 58,400. Reports following other criminal inquiries rose by 2 per cent in 1999. The number of bail information reports written has fallen back between 1998 and 1999.

Criminal court orders

The total number of people starting community sentences was about the same in 1998 as 1999 at almost 130,000. However, the types of orders given are changing, with a continuing increase in the use of community service orders and falls in the number of combination orders and money payment supervision orders.

Combination orders

Combination orders were first introduced in October 1992 by the Criminal Justice Act 1991. The number of people starting these orders increased steadily between 1993 and 1998, rising by at least 2,000 each year to peak at 21,200 in 1998. However, for the first time numbers have fallen to 20,600 in 1999.

PERSONS STARTING CRIMINAL SUPERVISION BY THE PROBATION SERVICE (THOUSANDS)

Court orders	1995	1996	1997	1998	1999
Probation order	48.3	49.1	51.5	55.5	55.6
Community service order	49.2	46.5	47.9	50.3	51.2
Combination order	14.8	17.0	19.1	21.2	20.6
Children and Young Persons Act 1969	2.8	2.9	2.8	2.6	2.2
Suspended sentence supervision order	0.4	0·5	0.6	0.5	0.5
Money payment supervision order	3.3	6.4	4.6	3.0	2.2
All court orders	112.3	115.4	119.8	126.8	126.0

Money payment supervision orders

The number of people starting a money payment supervision order rose by 94 per cent in 1996 to 6,400, having fallen each year between 1989 and 1995. The 1996 figure was the highest ever reached apart from 1989 (6,500). A judgment by the High Court in January 1996 means the courts must now consider all other methods of enforcing payment of fines before sentencing to prison for default. In spite of this judgment, the numbers fell back to 3,000 in 1998 and 2,200 in 1999. The number of fines has also fallen back.

Gender and age

There was an average of 18 men with a community service order for each woman with a community service order in 1989. This ratio has fallen to eight men for each woman with a community service order in 1999. Sentencers have become more ready to give a sentence of community service order to a woman over the period 1989–1999. Between 1989 and 1999 the numbers of probation and community service orders starting have changed little for those aged 16–20 (Includes the probation and community service elements of combination orders). In contrast, for those aged 21 or more the numbers of orders have

at least doubled over the same period. Thus in 1989 over 40 per cent of those dealt with by the probation service under the main three order types were under 21, whereas in 1999 only a little over a quarter are under age 21.

Offences

Of those commencing probation orders in 1999, theft and handling stolen goods represented the largest specific offence group at 26 per cent. This was also true of those commencing community service orders and combination orders (19 per cent and 17 per cent respectively). However, since 1995 the proportion of those commencing probation orders for theft and handling offences has decreased significantly (from 33 per cent to 26 per cent) whereas the proportion of those committing violent offences has increased from 7 per cent to 10 per cent. This pattern is also repeated across the other two main orders.

Previous criminal history

When combination orders were first introduced, the courts used almost half of them (49 per cent in 1993) for offenders who had previously served a prison sentence. However, the 1996–1999 figures suggest that there is now little difference between probation and combination orders in terms of the offender's previous criminal history. For both orders in 1999 about a third had a previous prison sentence and 23–24 per cent had no previous convictions. The courts more often give a probation or combination order, than a community service order, to an offender with a previous prison sentence. In 1999, 20 per cent of community service orders had previous custody and 42 per cent had no previous convictions. Over the last six years the proportions of the three main orders that have gone to those with no previous convictions have grown considerably. This is part of a general trend to more severe sentencing. The proportions for community service orders with no previous convictions grew from 19 per cent to 42 per cent between 1993 and 1999. (Equivalent figures for probation were 12 per cent and 24 per cent and for combination orders 10 per cent and 23 per cent.)

Orders – length and additional requirements

In 1991, 24 per cent of new probation orders had an additional requirement. This proportion rose to 34 per cent in 1998, but has fallen back marginally in 1999 to 33 per cent. The requirement to participate in a specified activity has shown steady growth for a number of years. There were 8 per cent of all probation orders with such a requirement in 1989 and 20 per cent in 1999. The proportion of all additional requirements that had a residential element declined from 20 per cent in 1989 to 8 per cent in 1999. Up to 1994 some 17 per cent of those beginning a combination order had an additional requirement. This proportion rose to 26 per cent in 1998, but has decreased to 24 per cent in 1999. Of these the largest number each year have been required to participate in specified activities; 9 per cent had such a requirement in 1992 and this proportion grew to 16 per cent in 1999. The average length of a straight probation order and that of the probation element of a combination order were similar through 1992 to 1994 as they both fell. However, since 1994 the

average length of a straight probation order has remained at 16.6–16.7 months. In contrast the length of the probation element of the combination order fell to 16.0 months in 1998, although it has risen again to 16.4 months in 1999. The average length of a community service order fell from 134.2 hours in 1989 to 120.3 hours in 1999.

The Government published the first national standards for the work of probation services and social services departments in 1992. Further sets of standards were produced in 1995 and 2000. They set the required standards of practice for probation services and social services departments in England and Wales, in relation to the supervision of offenders in the community and in providing services to the courts.

The National Standards for Probation (2000), pp2–3

Levels of contact

By way of example of the nature of the 2000 Standard, the required levels of contact and how to achieve compliance are described as follows. It states that achieving the minimum required levels of contact, and enforcing supervision rigorously, serves two main purposes – it satisfies the courts and the community that a credible level of disciplined supervision is taking place and also ensures that offenders have the opportunity to engage in effective supervision. The standards set the minimum requirements and are likely to be exceeded for offenders who pose risks of serious harm to the public, or have a higher probability of reoffending, or for those who may be subject to additional order or licence requirements. In terms of the required levels of contact, for those aged under 22 or serving 12 months or more in custody, the home probation service shall provide the offender with a supervising officer or case manager within 10 working days of sentencing. The levels and nature of contact between prisoners, prison staff and the offender's supervising (or managing) officer are not specified in these standards. Staff are expected to use their judgment to ensure that there is sufficient contact at the pre-release stage to enable the successful resettlement of the offender and the preparation of a supervision plan. Supervising officers shall ensure that they refer to, and act in accordance with, the guidance in The Lifer Manual when dealing with arrangements for offenders sentenced to life imprisonment. If an offender has spent sufficient time on remand to be released on licence direct from the court and no supervising officer has been appointed, the court duty probation officer shall give the supervising probation area as much detail as possible about the offender and the release address, and arrange for the licence to be served. The police shall be given release, licence and address information as soon as practicable and in any case within 10 working days of release. Wherever possible the date of the first appointment for those on community orders should be given to the offender either by the probation service or by the bench (acting on probation service advice) before the offender leaves court. This should be arranged to take place within five working days of the order being made.

The first meeting

The probation service shall ensure that for all offenders, at the first meeting the supervising officer shall provide written information setting out what is expected of the offender during the period of supervision and what the offender can expect from the probation service, explain to the offender and provide a copy of instructions setting out the required standards of behaviour that apply during the period of supervision, which shall prohibit:

a) further offending;
b) violent or aggressive behaviour or threats of violence;
c) other conduct or language that might reasonably give offence to probation staff, other persons on supervision or members of the public;

d) other wilful or persistent non-cooperation or behaviour designed to frustrate the purpose of the offender's or others' supervision.

They must also ensure that offenders sign their order or licence (where possible) and indicate that they understand its requirements. Appointments that count towards meeting the standard are those made in connection with the supervision plan and include appointments with partnership agencies, such as for drug counselling. All such appointments are enforceable and appropriate enforcement action must be taken if any appointment is missed.

In 1998 The Probation Inspectorate came up with the following suggestions for effective offender supervision on the part of the probation service.

HM Inspectorate of Probation, (1998) *Strategies for Effective Offender Supervision*

The following were suggested as points to adopt:

a) programmes which seek to modify offenders' patterns of thinking and behaving are generally more successful than techniques like group or individual counselling;
b) programmes need to be closely matched to the needs and learning styles of offenders;
c) consistency in programme content to allow evaluation.

Points to improve upon:

a) widen the use of structured risk assessment processes;
b) availability of a sufficient range of programmes to allow a match with offender needs;
c) dealing with non-attenders at programmes;
d) more use of community service;
e) better quality control of supervisors.

This Home Office research is an attempt to examine the work of the probation service by looking at it from the perspective of the probationer.

Mair G and May C (1997) *Offenders on Probation*, Home Office Research Study 167, ppviii, xi, 65–67

Recently there has been increasing pressure on the probation service to demonstrate its effectiveness. Assessment has concentrated on reconviction studies and sentencer satisfaction surveys, but hitherto little has been known of the impact of probation from the point of view of those supervised. The study described here surveyed a sample of offenders on probation, examining the backgrounds, their experiences of probation, and their perceptions of its helpfulness in tackling problems and stopping further offending.

Social and Community Planning Research (SCPR) conducted the survey in the first half of 1994. At this time the 1992 National Standards were in place (revised standards were introduced in 1995). The survey was restricted to those who had been sentenced to a probation or combination order, and covered 22 of the then 55 probation areas in England and Wales.

The sample of offenders in each area was drawn at random. In total the issued sample consisted of 3,300 offenders. Nearly 40 per cent of the sample could not be contacted, mainly because they had been taken into custody, their order had terminated, or they had been transferred to another area. The effective sample, after subtracting those not contactable, was 1,980. Of these, 1,213 interviews were achieved, giving a response rate of 61 per cent. It is possible that those who failed to keep survey appointments will tend to have a less favourable attitude to the probation service than those included. The possibility of bias should be kept in mind when examining the findings.

Overall, 84 per cent of the sample were currently on a probation order only, 12 per cent were on a combination order, and four per cent were on a probation order and also serving a separate community service order. For just over half of the respondents it was their first time on probation. ...

Views of and attitudes towards probation and probation officers

Offenders were asked why they thought they had been given a probation/combination order rather than another sentence. The most common response (27 per cent) was that the court had wanted the offender to benefit from the services available while on probation. No-one mentioned that they had been given their current sentence to stop them reoffending.

The most frequently given 'good point' about being on probation (mentioned by more than half) was that it gave offenders access to someone independent to talk to about problems. A third of respondents mentioned getting practical help or advice with specific problems, and about 20 per cent mentioned being helped to keep out of trouble and avoid offending. The most commonly mentioned bad point was the time taken to attend supervision sessions (24 per cent), with the inconvenience of travelling to attend (7 per cent) being next most mentioned. These criticisms help to suggest that orders are achieving the objective of restricting liberty and punishing offenders. More than half the sample did not mention any bad points at all.

Nine out of ten respondents thought that their current probation order was either fairly or very useful. Women and older offenders were more likely to see their orders as very useful.

Respondents were shown a series of statements about probation and probation officers. More than a third agreed strongly that being on probation would help them to stop offending altogether, while a further 20 per cent agreed slightly. However, fewer than half agreed strongly that being on probation kept them out of trouble. More than 60 per cent agreed strongly with two general statements about probation officers being able to help people.

There were high levels of agreement with the positive statements about probation officers and high levels of disagreement with the negative statements. Only one in twenty respondents said anything negative about their probation officer. Three-quarters of the sample felt that they could always talk to their probation officer if they were worried about something, and nearly as many said that they felt they could be completely honest and frank. More than three-quarters of the sample said that there was nothing that they would be unwilling or embarrassed to talk about with their officer.

Nearly three-quarters of respondents said that being on probation had helped them understand their offending behaviour, and almost two-thirds said that they thought being on probation would help them stay out of trouble in the future. ...

The survey, of offenders on probation reported in this study, is the first occasion on which a large sample of probationers has been asked for their views of probation and probation officers. As such, it cannot provide the depth of detail found in previous studies where small samples of offenders were interviewed (eg Day, 1981; Fielding, 1986). Instead, and as is the case for most sample surveys, this study offers a snapshot of offenders' views of probation in the early 1990s – a key time for the probation service – and this can also stand as a benchmark for future work.

In this final chapter we set out the salient findings of the survey and discuss these briefly in terms of their meaning for probation. It may be worth emphasising again that this study did not cover offenders on community service orders alone and therefore the results cannot be extrapolated to include this group (although those with combination orders were included). In addition, the probation service has been subjected to considerable change in the past ten years or so. If this continues, with, for example, changes in probation officer training, and the introduction of curfew orders with electronic monitoring, the results of this survey may become outdated quickly. These warnings are not meant in any way to diminish the results of the survey; as the first national exercise of this kind the results are important in themselves.

There is no doubt that probation supervision and probation officers are seen in a very positive light by offenders. Previous studies have found this to be the case – albeit for different reasons – and this survey provides confirmation of earlier findings. Such a finding may not please those who desire probation to be more punitive. However, offenders who see probation in a positive light are more likely to turn up for meetings with their probation officers, more willing to listen, and more likely to try to put into practice what is suggested to them. If probation were to be seen negatively offenders would be more likely to fail to appear for supervision. This would lead to increased breach action and – ultimately – increases in the custodial population.

There is little doubt that probation can become more rigorous and demanding without losing its basic character (see Mair et al, 1994 for the example of intensive probation). May (1995) has shown that sentencers also see probation positively. The appreciation of probation by offenders should not be ignored or forgotten. Nor should it be ignored that not all of those interviewed were equally positive about probation; older respondents and female respondents were generally more positive than young male offenders (and, although numbers were small, black respondents were most negative of all about probation). This suggests that probation officers may have to use a different approach for such offenders. Similarly the fact that 27 per cent of the effective sample failed to keep appointments for the survey interview should not be forgotten. It is likely that this group represents those who were not favourable towards probation and if they had been interviewed there may have been more negative comments. It cannot simply be assumed that this percentage of offenders fails to keep appointments with their probation officers regularly (though half the sample admitted to having missed sessions), but if anything approaching this proportion is failing to turn up then this not only raises serious questions about breach, but about how probation officers can possibly organise their work effectively. Further research might be usefully carried out into this issue.

Previous research has demonstrated the deprived background of those on probation (see Stewart and Stewart, 1993) and the survey provides confirmation of this. Most respondents were not working and dependent on state benefits; they had difficulty paying bills, were poorly qualified educationally and not particularly healthy. A significant minority had spent time in care as a child. There is little doubt amongst criminologists that such factors are associated with offending although the precise relationship between them remains unclear. Their presence cannot, therefore, be ignored by probation officers and much probation work is focused on trying to alleviate the problems caused by such characteristics. In terms of their background, probationers are very similar to prisoners.

For the most part National Standards seemed to be followed, but the responses of offenders suggest that in a minority of cases the 1992 Standards were not being met. How much more difficult will it be to keep to the stricter 1995 Standards? ...

What happened on probation? Offending behaviour was the most commonly discussed topic during supervision, although other matters related to the characteristics of offenders were also talked about – employment, accommodation, money, personal and family problems.

Groupwork was not uncommon, and outside agencies were used frequently. Such a picture of probation work will not be surprising to those who are familiar with the service. The key question becomes how such subjects are covered; after all, most respondents seemed to be unsure about whether probation would stop them from further offending. Thus, how different topics are introduced,

how their relevance to the offender is stressed, and how offenders understand these matters, become crucial questions for research into the effectiveness of probation.

While offending behaviour is discussed often during supervision, it is odd that no-one considered that their current sentence had been made in order to stop further offending. Perhaps the courts could emphasise this in passing sentence, and probation officers could make sure that this is mentioned repeatedly as a major aim of supervision. Most offenders considered that they understood their offending behaviour better as a result of probation supervision, yet one-third had committed further offences since being on probation. Respondents felt that prison was much more likely to stop further offending than probation or community service – a perception which is at odds with the evidence of reconviction rates (see Lloyd, Mair and Hough, 1994). How such paradoxes might be resolved – indeed, whether they can be resolved satisfactorily – is unclear, but the need for further research is obvious.

While many of the issues which have emerged from the findings of the survey have implications for work with offenders, three in particular may be worth noting. First, reasons given for offending change over time; second, the family and friends of offenders seem to be fairly heavily involved in criminal activity; and third, drugs and alcohol play a significant role in the lives of respondents. These issues need to be taken into account by probation officers in their work with offenders both at the assessment stage and as part of supervision.

Overall, the message contained in this report is a good one for the probation service; it is viewed favourably by most of those it supervises, and seems to work hard at trying to achieve its formal aims and objectives as stated in the National Standards. However, this should not lead to any sense of complacency. It is arguable that any agency which provided similar help to that provided by the probation service to the poor and unemployed would be seen in an equally positive light. The high rate of failed survey appointments almost certainly means that those most critical of probation were not included in the survey; and young male offenders, who commit most offences and reoffend most frequently, were not as satisfied with probation as other respondents.

Bibliography
Day P (1981) *Social Work and Social Control*, London: Tavistock.

Ellis T, Hedderman C and Mortimer E (1996) *Ensuring Compliance and Dealing with Breach: A Study of Enforcement in the Probation Service*, Home Office Research Study 158, London: Home Office.

Fielding N (1986) *Probation Practice: Client Support under Social Control*, Aldershot: Gower.

Lloyd C, Mair G and Hough M (1994) *Explaining Reconviction Rates: A Critical Analysis*, Home Office Research Study 136, London: Home Office.

Mair G, Lloyd C, Nee C and Sibbitt R (1994) *Intensive Probation in England and Wales: an Evaluation*, Home Office Research Study 133, London: Home Office.

May C (1995) *Measuring the Satisfaction of Courts with the Probation Service*, Home Office Research Study 144, London: Home Office.

Stewart G and Stewart J (1993) *Social Circumstances of Younger Offenders under Supervision*, London: Association of Chief Officers of Probation.

This Home Office report contains a literature review and the findings of a survey into the workings of specific forms of probation practice. Evidence is found that some forms of intervention work better than others – particularly if they are targeted at certain offender types. It is also clear that the performance of some measures are undermined in practice because of lack of rigour in the delivery of them. Also apparent was the need for better evaluation of the measures that were being used.

Mair G, Vennard J, Sugg D and Hedderman C (1997) *Changing Offenders' Attitudes and Behaviour: What Works?*, Home Office Research Study 171

Part One: Vennard J, Sugg D and Hedderman C, 'The Use of Cognitive-Behavioural Approaches with Offenders: Messages from the Research', pp33, 35

The findings from several literature reviews and meta-analytic studies of rehabilitative programmes carried out with offenders have challenged the view that 'nothing works'. Although these reviews do not identify particular programmes or techniques associated with large reductions in offending across the broad range of offenders, there is evidence of moderate reductions with selected groups of offenders. A question of central concern to the probation service in England and Wales is whether the incorporation of the messages from this literature can increase the effectiveness of the service in reducing reoffending.

One such message, consistently reported in the meta-analytic studies in the field of offender rehabilitation, is that the type of approach used to address offending behaviour matters. Programmes which draw upon cognitive skills and behavioural methods are reported as achieving higher levels of effectiveness than those which employ group or individual counselling and favour traditional non-directive therapy. The use of cognitive-behavioural methods in a multi modal programme which includes life skills and social skills training shows the most positive results with both juvenile and adult offenders. This combination of components and techniques has also shown some success when targeted on particular groups of offenders – notably, sex offenders and violent offenders – although in most such studies the assessment of effectiveness is confined to clinical outcomes.

Certain important caveats surround these seemingly promising findings. The first is that the research literature does not demonstrate that cognitive behavioural approaches, or indeed, any other type of approach, routinely produce major reductions in reoffending among a mixed population of offenders. ...

The inconclusive findings of the literature reviews and meta-analyses summarised in this report point to the need in this country for rigorous evaluation of existing and future programmes which incorporate cognitive behavioural methods and the principles of effective assessment and delivery. Well-designed and carefully evaluated small-scale studies can, of course, be informative but are no substitute for larger scale studies which are able to achieve higher standards with regard to sampling and design and have the potential for replication with a different sample in a different setting. Such studies should make use of (multivariate) statistical techniques in order to begin to distinguish which programme features and other factors (including the good practice principles, offence and offender characteristics) are most strongly associated with successful programmes. Programmes included in an evaluation should make explicit the underlying theory as to how they are expected to effect change, having regard to existing knowledge of the diverse causes of crime. Evaluations must include measurement of change in the targeted attitudes, behaviour or skills as well as in reconviction rates. More information is needed about the types of offender who are responsive to interventions which use cognitive-behavioural approaches and about the intensity of work needed to bring about a sustained effect. Although the literature suggests that the intensity of work with offenders should be based on the level of risk posed by the offender there is still much to be learnt about the optimum level of intervention for different levels of risk. Similarly, much more research is needed into the way in which programme components and

techniques can be matched to offenders needs in such a way as to achieve a long term reduction in reoffending. ...

Part Two: Hedderman C and Sugg C, 'The Influence of Cognitive Approaches: a Survey of Probation Programmes', pp39, 51, 52

In February 1996 the Offenders and Corrections Unit of the Home Office sent out a questionnaire to all probation areas asking for information about the extent to which the programmes they operated, or had access to, made use of cognitive skills training. Cognitive skills was defined for the purposes of this survey as an approach which attempted to reduce reoffending by teaching offenders to analyse and modify their thinking. ...

Thirty-nine areas provided information on 191 programmes and four areas said they did not run programmes with a cognitive skills component – a response rate of 78 per cent. Of the remaining 12 areas, two had amalgamated and were not in a position to provide information and seven were in the process of restructuring their entire system for providing programmes and were reluctant to take part in the survey. Only three areas failed to reply at all to the survey despite being sent a further two reminders. ...

Taken as a whole the survey results reveal that since the late 1980s a majority of probation areas have developed or bought programmes with a cognitive skills or cognitive-behavioural dimension. Two-thirds of the areas which ran such programmes were running between five and ten of them. The limited information provided on costs shows that such programmes do not come cheap, yet areas appear to have spent remarkably little time or effort on examining whether such programmes work. In most areas it seems that they do not even know how many people attend, who drops out and why, and who succeeds and why. While offender and staff feedback can be useful ways of examining how user-friendly such programmes are, they are a poor source of data on overall effectiveness in modifying patterns of thinking and reducing reoffending.

The survey also suggests that while the probation service has picked up on the message that 'something works' and recognise that 'cognitive skills' and 'cognitive-behaviourism' are central to this, they have not committed themselves fully to 'what works' principles. In particular, this survey shows a lack of commitment to programme integrity. This is apparent in the fact that the duration and intensity of programmes is commonly altered; and from the fact that staff training is limited or even non-existent. Programmes also seem to function without reference to risk and needs principles. Mixing offenders on parole with others subject to additional requirements and those attending voluntarily may keep programme numbers high, but is unlikely to achieve programmes which are well matched to the levels of risk, and criminogenic needs, of the offenders who attend. While sex offender programmes tend to be (comparatively) well-organised, run by well-trained staff, and able to draw on outside expertise, they too are rarely restricted to serious offenders.

Perhaps the most encouraging aspect of our findings was that respondents were far from complacent about the way programmes were operating. The frankness of their replies and the use they made of open-ended questions shows that many of those responsible for running the programmes on a day-to-day basis would welcome more training, more advice and better evaluations. They believe their programmes work, but they cannot prove it and they know that many could work even better. One obvious step which could be made would be for a more strategic approach to setting up and running programmes at senior levels – perhaps with programmes being run initially on a pilot basis and properly evaluated before being delivered on a larger scale. Another improvement might be to create a standard set of evaluation measures (which areas could add to but not amend) which would ensure that similar programmes were being compared

fairly. It could also enable the results of several small-scale evaluations to be combined, so that sample-sizes were great enough to test for statistical significance, without resorting to less reliable techniques such as meta-analysis.

Since various disposals are available it is valuable to have information as to the success rates of these various disposals. One way of obtaining such information is to carry out research which measures the reconviction rates that follow on from the use of the disposals. The Home Office research provides some new data and also examines the problems of research of this type. The research suggests that there is little to choose between straight probation, probation with requirements, community service and the use of imprisonment. Pseudo reconvictions, which are taken account of in the research, are those which were recorded in the follow-up period but which in fact were committed prior to the follow-up period.

Lloyd C, Mair G and Hough M (1994) *Explaining Reconviction Rates: A Critical Analysis*, Home Office Research Study 136, pp51–53

This study has presented both a critique and an analysis of reconviction rates. With regard to the former, the aim was to provide a clear context within which reconviction rates might be understood and used more appropriately. As for the analysis, this is the first national comparative study of reconviction rates for 15 years – which serves as its own justification. In addition, however, the analysis has attempted – by following a step-by-step approach – to set out the complex nature of reconviction studies in practice; the impact of key variables has been studied both individually and in interaction with each other. In this concluding chapter the main findings of the analysis are summarised, and the implications of these for future research are discussed.

Main findings

The key findings of this study are the comparative reconviction rates for the four disposals considered when pseudo-reconvictions have been taken into account: for prisons, 54 per cent were reconvicted within two years of release; for probation orders with a 4A/4B requirement 63 per cent were reconvicted within two years of sentence; in the case of community service orders the figure was 49 per cent; and for straight probation orders, 43 per cent were reconvicted. It is clear that there were considerable differences amongst the four disposals – with a gap of 20 per cent between the reconviction rate associated with straight probation and that associated with probation with 4A/4B requirements. This does not mean that straight probation is far more successful in terms of reconviction rates than probation with a 4A/4B requirement. What it does mean is that offenders with very different characteristics (and therefore different risks of reconviction) are being sentenced to these different disposals – as, in fact, should be the case.

More significant, therefore, is the comparison between the predicted reconviction rates for each disposal and the actual rates (after correcting for pseudo-reconvictions): for prisons the actual rate was 1 per cent higher than that predicted; for the 4A/4B group the actual rate was 3 per cent greater than that predicted; for CSOs the actual rate was 3 per cent lower than that predicted; and for straight probation the actual rate was 2 per cent lower than that predicted. A simple reading of these findings might lead us to the conclusion that straight probation and community service orders are more effective than prison and probation with 4A/4B requirements in reducing reoffending. A more cautious and more sustainable conclusion is that there is little to choose between these sentencing options in terms of their impact on reoffending – whether the impact is construed as deterrent or rehabilitative.

Several caveats should be noted in comparing the performance of the four types of sentence. In the first place, the findings reflect practice in 1987 – there have been marked changes since then in both probation and prison practice and there may have been consequent changes in effectiveness. Second, it is important to bear in mind that this study has looked at disposals in aggregate, and that there may well be significant differences among individual examples of the same sentence (see Mair and Nee, 1992). Third, this study only looked at reconviction rates in the light of offenders' age, gender, current offence and criminal history. It was impossible to take account of social variables, and indeed there may be other variables which sentencers take into account which are correlated with reconviction and which were not included in the study. And finally, the findings relate only to the impact of court sentences in preventing reoffending; they can say nothing about the other purposes which sentencing may serve, such as general deterrence, incapacitation and the declaratory function of expressing societal reaction to certain sorts of crime.

More generally, the study points to the gaps in our knowledge about what actually happens in prisons, probation centres and the like – precisely what kind of staff work in these places, what is their motivation and how do they carry out their tasks – and what kinds of regimes and programmes are delivered? It is only common-sense to assume that a carefully planned regime, based upon some considered theoretical foundation, relevant to the needs/problems of offenders, and delivered by committed, enthusiastic staff will have a more positive impact upon offenders than one which is ad hoc, irrelevant and delivered by tired, cynical workers. At present we know far too little about the content, organisation and delivery of court disposals.

On a more specific point, the fact that the 4A/4B predicted rate of reconviction is 7 per cent higher than that for prison raises some interesting questions. For example, has the probation service been too successful in diverting from custody offenders with a high risk of reconviction and thereby condemning

4A/4B programmes to a high reconviction rate. How far are sentencers aware of the possible differences between offenders who commit serious offences but who have a low risk of reconviction, and those who commit less serious offences but who have a high risk of reconviction; and how do they take account of these factors in sentencing? Such questions may be difficult to answer, but one clear conclusion from the 'Nothing Works' debate is that matching appropriate offenders to relevant sentences or programmes is likely to lead to reduced recividism – and it may be that this is not happening in the case of prison and 4A/4B programmes.

The key correlates of reconviction were found to be as previous studies have suggested – age, sex, offence, criminal history – but this may be partly to do with the fact that most reconviction studies only consider these variables. Collecting more 'social' variables would add considerably more work to an already heavy task, but it will be very important to try to establish the relative contribution of social and criminal history variables in predicting reconvictions. Teasing out the individual impact of the variables used here is not an easy matter, although it does appear that age remains a particularly strong predictor of reconviction.

The analysis also shows that wherever possible the number of previous convictions should be counted as well as the number of previous appearances with a guilty finding. And although sex becomes less powerful in predicting reconviction when other variables are taken into account, there are some interesting differences at the margins: as age increases, the female reconviction rate approaches that of males; and after eight or more previous appearances the female reconviction rate catches up with that of males.

It is worth drawing attention to the impact of pseudo-reconvictions. If these were equally distributed amongst sentences their effect would not be so important, but the analysis carried out here suggests that they have a larger effect upon community penalties,

leading to over-estimation of reconviction rates. The prison rate dropped by 2 per cent when pseudo-reconvictions were removed, while the CSO rate fell by 7 per cent, straight probation by 6 per cent, and 4A/4B orders by 5 per cent. Taking these corrected rates into account improves the performance of each of the four disposals, but especially that of probation and CSOs. In future reconviction studies it will be necessary to take account of pseudo-reconvictions; and further work is needed to assess whether or not the converse situation (where offenders commit a crime but are not dealt with until their current sentence has been completed) has an impact in the final months of a sentence.

It is clear that the bulk of reconvictions occur in the first 12 months of sentence/release, although certain types of offenders seem more likely to be reconvicted fairly quickly – notably those originally convicted of criminal damage or motor offences – while others such as sex offenders tend to take longer to be reconvicted. Those with 4A/4B requirements were more likely to be reconvicted within 12 months than those with other sentences. Prisoners tended to catch up with 4A/4B offenders by the end of the two-year period, and this raises the question of what happens after two years. More work is needed on time to reconviction; should the usual two year period remain the most appropriate or do other periods need to be used depending upon the offences involved and sentences imposed?

There was little association between offence seriousness and risk of reconviction. Indeed, many of the most serious offences were associated with low risks of reconviction. A comparison between the seriousness of the 'target' offence (for which offenders were originally sentenced to imprisonment or community disposals) with that at reconviction revealed a tendency for offending behaviour to regress to the mean. Thus, prisoners, a large proportion of whom were originally convicted of serious offences, tended to be reconvicted of less serious offences, while probationers who were originally convicted of less serious offences tended to be reconvicted of offences of similar gravity at reconviction.

———————————

Originally it was as one of the innovations of the Crime and Disorder Act 1998 that drug treatment and testing orders were introduced. It is ss52–7 of the 2000 Act that makes provision for them at the moment.

Powers of Criminal Courts (Sentencing) Act 2000, ss52–57

Section 52
Drug treatment and testing orders

52 (1) Where a person aged 16 or over is convicted of an offence, the court by or before which he is convicted may (subject to sections 34 to 36 above) make an order which –

(a) has effect for a period specified in the order of not less than six months nor more than three years ('the treatment and testing period'); and

(b) includes the requirements and provisions mentioned in sections 53 and 54 below; but this section does not apply in relation to an offence committed before 30 September 1998.

(2) An order under subs(1) above is in this Act referred to as a 'drug treatment and testing order'.

(3) A court shall not make a drug treatment and testing order in respect of an offender unless it is satisfied –

(a) that he is dependent on or has a propensity to misuse drugs; and

(b) that his dependency or propensity is such as requires and may be susceptible to treatment.

(4) For the purpose of ascertaining for the purposes of subs(3) above whether the offender has any drug in his body, the court may by order require him to provide samples of such description as it may specify; but the court shall not make such an order unless the

offender expresses his willingness to comply with its requirements.

(5) A court shall not make a drug treatment and testing order unless it has been notified by the Secretary of State that arrangements for implementing such orders are available in the area proposed to be specified in the order under s54(1) below and the notice has not been withdrawn.

(6) Before making a drug treatment and testing order, the court shall explain to the offender in ordinary language –

(a) the effect of the order and of the requirements proposed to be included in it;

(b) the consequences which may follow (under Part II of Schedule 3 to this Act) if he fails to comply with any of those requirements;

(c) that the order will be periodically reviewed at intervals as provided for in the order (by virtue of s54(6) below); and

(d) that the order may be reviewed (under Parts III and IV of Schedule 3) on the application either of the offender or of the responsible officer;

and 'responsible officer' here has the meaning given by s54(3) below.

(7) A court shall not make a drug treatment and testing order unless the offender expresses his willingness to comply with its requirements.

Section 53
The treatment and testing requirements

53 (1) A drug treatment and testing order shall include a requirement ('the treatment requirement') that the offender shall submit, during the whole of the treatment and testing period, to treatment by or under the direction of a specified person having the necessary qualifications or experience ('the treatment provider') with a view to the reduction or elimination of the offender's dependency on or propensity to misuse drugs.

(2) The required treatment for any particular period shall be –

(a) treatment as a resident in such institution or place as may be specified in the order; or

(b) treatment as a non-resident in or at such institution or place, and at such intervals, as may be so specified; but the nature of the treatment shall not be specified in the order except as mentioned in paragraph (a) or (b) above.

(3) A court shall not make a drug treatment and testing order unless it is satisfied that arrangements have been or can be made for the treatment intended to be specified in the order (including arrangements for the reception of the offender where he is to be required to submit to treatment as a resident).

(4) A drug treatment and testing order shall include a requirement ('the testing requirement') that, for the purpose of ascertaining whether he has any drug in his body during the treatment and testing period, the offender shall during that period, at such times or in such circumstances as may (subject to the provisions of the order) be determined by the treatment provider, provide samples of such description as may be so determined.

(5) The testing requirement shall specify for each month the minimum number of occasions on which samples are to be provided.

Section 54
Provisions of order as to supervision and periodic review

54 (1) A drug treatment and testing order shall include a provision specifying the petty sessions area in which it appears to the court making the order that the offender resides or will reside.

(2) A drug treatment and testing order shall provide that, for the treatment and testing period, the offender shall be under the supervision of a probation officer appointed for or assigned to the petty sessions area specified in the order.

(3) In this Act 'responsible officer', in relation to an offender who is subject to a drug treat-

ment and testing order, means the probation officer responsible for his supervision.

(4) A drug treatment and testing order shall –

(a) require the offender to keep in touch with the responsible officer in accordance with such instructions as he may from time to time be given by that officer, and to notify him of any change of address; and

(b) provide that the results of the tests carried out on the samples provided by the offender in pursuance of the testing requirement shall be communicated to the responsible officer.

(5) Supervision by the responsible officer shall be carried out to such extent only as may be necessary for the purpose of enabling him –

(a) to report on the offender's progress to the court responsible for the order;

(b) to report to that court any failure by the offender to comply with the requirements of the order; and

(c) to determine whether the circumstances are such that he should apply to that court for the revocation or amendment of the order.

(6) A drug treatment and testing order shall –

(a) provide for the order to be reviewed periodically at intervals of not less than one month;

(b) provide for each review of the order to be made, subject to s55(6) below, at a hearing held for the purpose by the court responsible for the order (a 'review hearing');

(c) require the offender to attend each review hearing;

(d) provide for the responsible officer to make to the court responsible for the order, before each review, a report in writing on the offender's progress under the order; and

(e) provide for each such report to include the test results communicated to the responsible officer under subs(4)(b) above and the views of the treatment provider as to the treatment and testing of the offender.

(7) In this section references to the court responsible for a drug treatment and testing order are references to –

(a) where a court is specified in the order in accordance with subs(8) below, that court;

(b) in any other case, the court by which the order is made.

(8) Where the area specified in a drug treatment and testing order made by a magistrates' court is not the area for which the court acts, the court may, if it thinks fit, include in the order provision specifying for the purposes of subs(7) above a magistrates' court which acts for the area specified in the order.

(9) Where a drug treatment and testing order has been made on an appeal brought from the Crown Court or from the criminal division of the Court of Appeal, for the purposes of subs(7)(b) above it shall be deemed to have been made by the Crown Court.

Section 55
Periodic reviews

55 (1) At a review hearing (within the meaning given by subs(6) of s54 above) the court may, after considering the responsible officer's report referred to in that subsection, amend any requirement or provision of the drug treatment and testing order.

(2) The court –

(a) shall not amend the treatment or testing requirement unless the offender expresses his willingness to comply with the requirement as amended;

(b) shall not amend any provision of the order so as to reduce the treatment and testing period below the minimum specified in s52(1) above, or to increase it above the maximum so specified; and

(c) except with the consent of the offender, shall not amend any requirement or provision of the order while an appeal against the order is pending.

(3) If the offender fails to express his willingness to comply with the treatment or testing requirement as proposed to be amended by the court, the court may –

(a) revoke the order; and

(b) deal with him, for the offence in respect of which the order was made, in any way in which it could deal with him if he had just been convicted by the court of the offence.

(4) In dealing with the offender under subs(3)(b) above, the court –

(a) shall take into account the extent to which the offender has complied with the requirements of the order; and

(b) may impose a custodial sentence (where the order was made in respect of an offence punishable with such a sentence) notwithstanding anything in s79(2) below.

(5) Where the order was made by a magistrates' court in the case of an offender under 18 years of age in respect of an offence triable only on indictment in the case of an adult, any powers exercisable under subs(3)(b) above in respect of the offender after he attains the age of 18 shall be powers to do either or both of the following –

(a) to impose a fine not exceeding £5,000 for the offence in respect of which the order was made;

(b) to deal with the offender for that offence in any way in which the court could deal with him if it had just convicted him of an offence punishable with imprisonment for a term not exceeding six months.

(6) If at a review hearing the court, after considering the responsible officer's report, is of the opinion that the offender's progress under the order is satisfactory, the court may so amend the order as to provide for each subsequent review to be made by the court without a hearing.

(7) If at a review without a hearing the court, after considering the responsible officer's report, is of the opinion that the offender's

progress under the order is no longer satisfactory, the court may require the offender to attend a hearing of the court at a specified time and place.

(8) At that hearing the court, after considering that report, may –

(a) exercise the powers conferred by this section as if the hearing were a review hearing; and

(b) so amend the order as to provide for each subsequent review to be made at a review hearing.

(9) In this section any reference to the court, in relation to a review without a hearing, shall be construed –

(a) in the case of the Crown Court, as a reference to a judge of the court;

(b) in the case of a magistrates' court, as a reference to a justice of the peace acting for the commission area for which the court acts.

Section 56
Breach, revocation and amendment of drug treatment and testing orders

56 Schedule 3 to this Act (which makes provision for dealing with failures to comply with the requirements of certain community orders, for revoking such orders with or without the substitution of other sentences and for amending such orders) shall have effect so far as relating to drug treatment and testing orders.

Section 57
Copies of orders

57 (1) Where a drug treatment and testing order is made, the court making the order shall (subject to subs(3) below) forthwith give copies of the order to a probation officer assigned to the court.

(2) Where such an order is amended under s55(1) above, the court amending the order shall forthwith give copies of the order as amended to a probation officer so assigned.

(3) Where a drug treatment and testing order is

made by a magistrates' court and another magistrates' court is responsible for the order (within the meaning given by s54(7) above) by virtue of being specified in the order in accordance with s54(8) –

(a) the court making the order shall not give copies of it as mentioned in subs(1) above but shall forthwith send copies of it to the court responsible for the order; and

(b) that court shall, as soon as reasonably practicable after the order is made, give copies of it to a probation officer assigned to that court.

(4) A probation officer to whom copies of an order are given under this section shall give a copy to –

(a) the offender;

(b) the treatment provider; and

(c) the responsible officer.

One of the innovations of the Crime and Disorder Act 1998 was the drug treatment and Testing Order. The research in the report provides evidence as to the working of the order in its earliest days.

Home Office (2000) *Drug Treatment and Testing Orders: Final Evaluation Report*, pp79–82

This report presents the findings of our evaluation of drug treatment and testing orders. We have examined the three pilot sites (in Croydon, Gloucestershire and Liverpool) as well as four additional projects which use probation 1 A(6) orders in ways which closely resemble drug treatment and testing orders. Our results cover the full period of the drug treatment and testing orders pilot projects, which ran from 1 October 1998 to 31 March 2000. In total 210 offenders were given drug treatment and testing orders. Gloucestershire had the highest number (100) and Croydon the lowest (42); Liverpool had 68. The pilots had differing referral and assessment strategies.

Liverpool winnowed out slightly more candidates when deciding whether or not to mount full assessments. In Liverpool the courts played a larger part in deciding who to accept and who to reject as suitable candidates for drug treatment and testing orders.

Testing

We have records of 2,555 urine tests carried out by the end of March covering 173 offenders – an average of 15 each. Just over half (53 per cent) were conducted at the Croydon site. In Liverpool and Croydon, the tests screened for all common illicit drugs except cannabis, and methadone. The Gloucestershire team was more selective. Across the three sites just over two-fifths of the tests (42 per cent) were positive for opiates and 45 per cent were positive for cocaine.

Results from our self-report interviews on drug use are broadly consistent with the urine test results. We have self-reported data on drug use covering 30-day periods, at four to six weeks after the start of the order, after six months and – where applicable – on completion. Looking only at those for whom we have test data corresponding to these periods, the majority who tested positive admitted at interview that they had used the drug in question (72 per cent). What the tests do not show, of course, is changes in level of drug use. Even though they were still using illicit drugs, most of those we interviewed reported steep reductions.

The main views from practitioners about urine testing were:

- tests work well in reinforcing good progress in stopping drug use;
- frequent testing is expensive and pointless for those who continue to use drugs;
- tests can be destructive to the motivation of those who are reducing their drug use but not managing to stop it completely.

Enforcement

The three sites had widely differing approaches to warnings, breaches and revocations. In all three sites offenders quite often failed to meet the conditions of the order. The main form of non-compliance was failure to attend, but as noted above, many continued to use illicit drugs, especially near the start of their order.

The three pilot teams had different expectations of drug-using offenders and varied in their readiness to warn or breach for non-compliance. The Gloucestershire team imposed the strictest requirements both about drug use and attendance. They had the highest revocation rate, at 60 per cent. Croydon's rate was lower, at 40 per cent, and Liverpool's much lower, at 28 per cent.

Reviews

We hold information on 413 separate review hearings for 154 offenders, an average of 2.6 hearings per offender. ... There were practical problems in arranging reviews, mainly to do with case listing in two of the three sites. More than four out of five reviews in Liverpool were heard by the judge or magistrates who originally passed sentence; in Croydon the figure was a third, and in Gloucestershire a fifth. Especially for reviews which were heard by the original sentencer, the process seemed a useful one, welcomed by staff and offenders alike as making a positive contribution to the treatment process.

Impact on offenders

We carried out 132 interviews with offenders within six weeks of receiving the order; we re-interviewed 48 of these after they had been on their order for six months; and we carried out 50 'exit interviews' with those who had completed their drug treatment and testing order successfully, nearly completed it or had it revoked. On the basis of self-report data, there were substantial reductions in drug use and offending at the start of the order. The average weekly spend on drugs fell from £400 before arrest to around £25. Polydrug use had become much less common; typically people stopped using crack or amphetamine, but continued to use opiates, albeit at a reduced level. There were commensurate reductions in acquisitive crime. As ever, one should be circumspect about self-report data,, though the picture to emerge is consistent with the urine testing results and other surveys of this kind.

The six-month interviews showed that these reductions were largely sustained over time. This implies that if drug treatment and testing orders succeed in retaining offenders within the programme, they seem likely to contain drug use and offending. We cannot say conclusively that this is the case, however. To do this we would need some form of comparison group who had not been exposed to the programmes. However the qualitative (unstructured) data collected in the course of interviews supports the view that offenders who completed their order benefited from the programme. The exit interviews were completed on two groups – those who reached (or had nearly reached) the end of their order successfully, and those who had failed. The 31 successes said they were crime-free and 27 said they were drug-free – except for their use of cannabis. At present very few orders have matured to this stage. All we can say at this stage is that an eighth of those on orders seem to have emerged drug-free. This proportion will obviously grow over time, but we cannot yet say by how much. Even the failures had reduced their drug use, and some claimed to have benefited from their experience on the order. Although we cannot be certain, we strongly suspect that we managed to contact the 'partial failures' and that there will be a disproportionate number of serious relapses amongst the remainder whom we were unable to interview.

Sections 126–9, 139–40 and 147 of the 2000 Act make provision for fines and recognizances – the former being the most commonly used disposal by the courts.

Powers of Criminal Courts (Sentencing) Act 2000, ss126–129 and 139–140

PART VI FINANCIAL PENALTIES AND ORDERS
Section 126
Powers to order statement as to offender's financial circumstances

126 (1) Where an individual has been convicted of an offence, the court may, before sentencing him, make a financial circumstances order with respect to him.

(2) Where a magistrates' court has been notified in accordance with s12(4) of the Magistrates' Courts Act 1980 that an individual desires to plead guilty without appearing before the court, the court may make a financial circumstances order with respect to him.

(3) In this section 'a financial circumstances order' means, in relation to any individual, an order requiring him to give to the court, within such period as may be specified in the order, such a statement of his financial circumstances as the court may require.

(4) An individual who without reasonable excuse fails to comply with a financial circumstances order shall be liable on summary conviction to a fine not exceeding level 3 on the standard scale.

(5) If an individual, in furnishing any statement in pursuance of a financial circumstances order –

(a) makes a statement which he knows to be false in a material particular,

(b) recklessly furnishes a statement which is false in a material particular, or

(c) knowingly fails to disclose any material fact, he shall be liable on summary conviction to imprisonment for a term not exceeding three months or a fine not exceeding level 4 on the standard scale or both.

(6) Proceedings in respect of an offence under subs(5) above may, notwithstanding anything in s127(1) of the Magistrates' Courts Act 1980

(limitation of time), be commenced at any time within two years from the date of the commission of the offence or within six months from its first discovery by the prosecutor, whichever period expires the earlier.

Fines: general
Section 127
General power of Crown Court to fine offender convicted on indictment

127 Where a person is convicted on indictment of any offence, other than an offence for which the sentence is fixed by law or falls to be imposed under s109(2), 110(2) or 111(2) above, the court, if not precluded from sentencing the offender by its exercise of some other power, may impose a fine instead of or in addition to dealing with him in any other way in which the court has power to deal with him, subject however to any enactment requiring the offender to be dealt with in a particular way.

Section 128
Fixing of fines

128 (1) Before fixing the amount of any fine to be imposed on an offender who is an individual, a court shall inquire into his financial circumstances.

(2) The amount of any fine fixed by a court shall be such as, in the opinion of the court, reflects the seriousness of the offence.

(3) In fixing the amount of any fine to be imposed on an offender (whether an individual or other person), a court shall take into account the circumstances of the case including, among other things, the financial circumstances of the offender so far as they are known, or appear, to the court.

(4) Subsection (3) above applies whether taking into account the financial circumstances of the offender has the effect of increasing or reducing the amount of the fine.

(5) Where –

(a) an offender has been convicted in his absence in pursuance of s11 or 12 of the

Magistrates' Courts Act 1980 (non-appearance of accused), or

(b) an offender –

(i) has failed to comply with an order under s126(1) above, or

(ii) has otherwise failed to cooperate with the court in its inquiry into his financial circumstances, and the court considers that it has insufficient information to make a proper determination of the financial circumstances of the offender, it may make such determination as it thinks fit.

Section 129
Remission of fines

129 (1) This section applies where a court has, in fixing the amount of a fine, determined the offender's financial circumstances under s128(5) above.

(2) If, on subsequently inquiring into the offender's financial circumstances, the court is satisfied that had it had the results of that inquiry when sentencing the offender it would –

(a) have fixed a smaller amount, or

(b) not have fined him, it may remit the whole or any part of the fine.

(3) Where under this section the court remits the whole or part of a fine after a term of imprisonment has been fixed under s139 below (powers of Crown Court in relation to fines) or s82 (5) of the Magistrates' Courts Act 1980 (magistrates' powers in relation to default), it shall reduce the term by the corresponding proportion.

(4) In calculating any reduction required by subs(3) above, any fraction of a day shall be ignored.

Section 139
Powers and duties of Crown Court in relation to fines and forfeited recognizances

139 (1) Subject to the provisions of this

section, if the Crown Court imposes a fine on any person or forfeits his recognizance, the court may make an order –

(a) allowing time for the payment of the amount of the fine or the amount due under the recognizance;

(b) directing payment of that amount by instalments of such amounts and on such dates as may be specified in the order;

(c) in the case of a recognizance, discharging the recognizance or reducing the amount due under it.

(2) Subject to the provisions of this section, if the Crown Court imposes a fine on any person or forfeits his recognizance, the court shall make an order fixing a term of imprisonment or of detention under s108 above (detention of persons aged 18 to 20 for default) which he is to undergo if any sum which he is liable to pay is not duly paid or recovered.

(3) No person shall on the occasion when a fine is imposed on him or his recognizance is forfeited by the Crown Court be committed to prison or detained in pursuance of an order under subs(2) above unless –

(a) in the case of an offence punishable with imprisonment, he appears to the court to have sufficient means to pay the sum forthwith;

(b) it appears to the court that he is unlikely to remain long enough at a place of abode in the United Kingdom to enable payment of the sum to be enforced by other methods; or

(c) on the occasion when the order is made the court sentences him to immediate imprisonment, custody for life or detention in a young offender institution for that or another offence, or so sentences him for an offence in addition to forfeiting his recognizance, or he is already serving a sentence of custody for life or a term –

(i) of imprisonment;

(ii) of detention in a young offender institution; or

(iii) of detention under s108 above.

(4) The periods set out in the second column of the following table shall be the maximum periods of imprisonment or detention under subs(2) above applicable respectively to the amounts set out opposite them.

An amount not exceeding £200	7 days
An amount exceeding £200 but not exceeding £500	14 days
An amount exceeding £500 but not exceeding £1,000	28 days
An amount exceeding £1,000 but not exceeding £2,500	45 days
An amount exceeding £2,500 but not exceeding £5,000	3 months
An amount exceeding £5,000 but not exceeding £10,000	6 months
An amount exceeding £10,000 but not exceeding £20,000	12 months
An amount exceeding £20,000 but not exceeding £50,000	18 months
An amount exceeding £50,000 but not exceeding £100,000	2 years
An amount exceeding £100,000 but not exceeding £250,000	3 years
An amount exceeding £250,000 but not exceeding £1 million	5 years
An amount exceeding £1 million	10 years

(5) Where any person liable for the payment of a fine or a sum due under a recognizance to which this section applies is sentenced by the court to, or is serving or otherwise liable to serve, a term of imprisonment or detention in a young offender institution or a term of detention under s108 above, the court may order that any term of imprisonment or detention fixed under subs(2) above shall not begin to run until after the end of the first-mentioned term.

(6) The power conferred by this section to dis-

charge a recognizance or reduce the amount due under it shall be in addition to the powers conferred by any other Act relating to the discharge, cancellation, mitigation or reduction of recognizances or sums forfeited under recognizances.

(7) Subject to subs(8) below, the powers conferred by this section shall not be taken as restricted by any enactment which authorises the Crown Court to deal with an offender in any way in which a magistrates' court might have dealt with him or could deal with him.

(8) Any term fixed under subs(2) above as respects a fine imposed in pursuance of such an enactment, that is to say a fine which the magistrates' court could have imposed, shall not exceed the period applicable to that fine (if imposed by the magistrates' court) under s149(1) of the Customs and Excise Management Act 1979 (maximum periods of imprisonment in default of payment of certain fines).

(9) This section shall not apply to a fine imposed by the Crown Court on appeal against a decision of a magistrates' court, but subs(2) to (4) above shall apply in relation to a fine imposed or recognizance forfeited by the criminal division of the Court of Appeal, or by the House of Lords on appeal from that division, as they apply in relation to a fine imposed or recognizance forfeited by the Crown Court, and the references to the Crown Court in subs(2) and (3) above shall be construed accordingly.

(10) For the purposes of any reference in this section, however expressed, to the term of imprisonment or other detention to which a person has been sentenced or which, or part of which, he has served, consecutive terms and terms which are wholly or partly concurrent shall, unless the context otherwise requires, be treated as a single term.

(11) Any reference in this section, however expressed, to a previous sentence shall be construed as a reference to a previous sentence passed by a court in Great Britain.

Section 140
Enforcement of fines imposed and recognizances forfeited by Crown Court

140 (1) Subject to subs(5) below, a fine imposed or a recognizance forfeited by the Crown Court shall be treated for the purposes of collection, enforcement and remission of the fine or other sum as having been imposed or forfeited –

(a) by a magistrates' court specified in an order made by the Crown Court, or

(b) if no such order is made, by the magistrates' court by which the offender was committed to the Crown Court to be tried or dealt with or by which he was sent to the Crown Court for trial under s51 of the Crime and Disorder Act 1998, and, in the case of a fine, as having been so imposed on conviction by the magistrates' court in question.

(2) Subsection (3) below applies where a magistrates' court issues a warrant of commitment on a default in the payment of –

(a) a fine imposed by the Crown Court; or

(b) a sum due under a recognizance forfeited by the Crown Court.

(3) In such a case, the term of imprisonment or detention under s108 above specified in the warrant of commitment as the term which the offender is liable to serve shall be –

(a) the term fixed by the Crown Court under s139(2) above, or

(b) if that term has been reduced under s79(2) of the Magistrates' Courts Act 1980 (part payment) or s85(2) of that Act (remission), that term as so reduced, notwithstanding that that term exceeds the period applicable to the case under s149(1) of the Customs and Excise Management Act 1979 (maximum periods of imprisonment in default of payment of certain fines).

(4) Subsections (1) to (3) above shall apply in relation to a fine imposed or recognizance forfeited by the criminal division of the Court of Appeal, or by the House of Lords on appeal

from that division, as they apply in relation to a fine imposed or recognizance forfeited by the Crown Court; and references in those subsections to the Crown Court (except the references in subs(1)(b)) shall be construed accordingly.

(5) A magistrates' court shall not, under ss85(1) or 120 of the Magistrates' Courts Act 1980 as applied by subs(1) above, remit the whole or any part of a fine imposed by, or sum due under a recognizance forfeited by –

    (a) the Crown Court,

    (b) the criminal division of the Court of Appeal, or

    (c) the House of Lords on appeal from that division, without the consent of the Crown Court.

(6) Any fine or other sum the payment of which is enforceable by a magistrates' court by virtue of this section shall be treated for the purposes of the Justices of the Peace Act 1997 and, in particular, s60 of that Act (application of fines and fees) as having been imposed by a magistrates' court, or as being due under a recognizance forfeited by such a court.

Research was commissioned to examine current sentencing practice in magistrates' courts and the Crown Court in more detail than that routinely provided by criminal statistics. It combines a survey of 3,000 sentenced cases in 25 magistrates' courts with interviews with 126 magistrates and almost 2,000 sentenced cases in 18 Crown Court centres. The most common sentence is the fine and it is that which is concentrated upon in the extract.

Flood-Page C and Mackie A (1998) *Sentencing Practice: An Examination of Decisions in Magistrates' Courts and the Crown Court in the mid-1990s*, pp47–53

Fines and discharges

Four-fifths of cases in magistrates' courts result in a fine. For many of the offences magistrates deal with, especially summary motoring, fines are almost invariably used. Although violent, sexual and property offences attract a much wider range of sentences, the fine has fallen in recent years. The use of the conditional discharge increased steadily until 1993, since when there has been a slight fall. Despite the relative importance of the fine and discharges they have attracted little attention from research and there is little appellate guidance. In order to be able to impose a discharge, the court must find that, having considered the nature of the offence and the character of the offender, it would be 'inexpedient to inflict punishment' (PCCA 1973 s1A).

The factors that were associated with the use of fines tended to be the obverse of the factors associated with custody: fines were given to first offenders and those convicted of less serious (mostly summary) offences – low-level motoring, possession of drugs or summary (non-motoring) offences. Factors which have previously been seen to aggravate an offence, for example, being uncooperative or aggressive to the police on arrest, being subject to a court order at the time of the offence, posing a danger to the public or having other offences taken into consideration at sentencing – made a fine less likely. Those with personal problems (eg mental illness or significant family responsibilities) were also less likely to be fined.

Fining people who are unemployed

Following the CJA 1991, the use of fines for unemployed offenders rose sharply from 30 per cent to 43 per cent of indictable offences sentenced at magistrates' courts. After the implementation of the CJA 1993 which abolished unit fines, the proportion of unemployed offenders fined fell to 32 per cent (Statistical Bulletin 20/1994). The same study also found that employed offenders were more likely to be fined. Unemployed offenders were three times as likely to receive a conditional discharge whether or not they had previous convictions. Unemployed first offenders were more likely to receive a community sentence than were first offenders with a job. Magistrates in seven of the 12 areas said that sometimes they would use conditional discharges where they felt that the offender could not afford to pay a fine. In four of these areas, magistrates regarded this as bad sentencing practice but said that they sometimes felt it was the only practical option. The Crime (Sentences) Act 1997 provided a range of new sentences for persistent petty offenders which will go some way to solving this sentencing problem.

Fixing the amount

Following the abolition of unit fines in 1993, courts have more discretion in how they set fines in relation to means. The Magistrates' Association issued revised guidelines for fines in 1993 which courts were able to vary to reflect local economic conditions. The most recent guidelines (April 1997) provide for a more structured approach to relating fines to means. Fines are set according to three income bands:

- low income – about £100 per week;
- average income – about £250 per week;
- high income – about £600 per week.

These figures have not been discounted for a guilty plea, and refer to net income. Charman et al (1996:2) examined the guidance available to magistrates in courts throughout England and Wales and found that, while 55 per cent of courts had adopted the Magistrates' Association guidelines wholesale for setting the level of fines, 28 per cent had made significant modifications to them. An informal unit fines approach was retained by 17 per cent. Four of

the 12 courts where interviews were undertaken in the present study had broadly adopted the fines recommended in the Magistrates' Association's 1993 guidelines, though three of these had adjusted the recommended fines to reflect local average income. The fourth felt that it was important to promote consistency over the country by sticking to the guidelines wherever possible.

Four courts had gone further than simply adjusting the levels of fines to reflect local average income, and had altered indicators of seriousness or 'entry levels' for different offences to take account of local factors. For example, in one court the entry point for drugs offences was 'tougher' than neighbouring jurisdictions; in another, the entry point for common assault was increased from a fine to a community penalty.

Four of the 12 courts had retained some type of informal unit fines system. One of these had continued to use a strict unit fines system so that, where the magistrates felt that a fine was appropriate, the local guidelines provide an 'entry point' in units. Sentencers then calculated the defendant's disposable weekly income within a range of £4 to a maximum of £100 as provided in the 1991 legislation. The other three courts had a less rigid formula for relating fines to weekly income. In one, guidelines suggested a range of fines depending on the income of the offender so, for example, the suggested fine for the offence of falsely obtaining electricity was within the range £120 and £300. Bench guidelines for two other courts set a norm for people on average income which could be reduced by up to half for people on low incomes or doubled for the better off.

All but one of the courts followed the recommendations of the best practice guidance issued by the Lord Chancellor's Department (1990) to obtain information about their income on means forms. (The other court relied on questions in court). The forms ask for information on income and regular outgoings. In cases where there was no information on the means of the defendant (eg because he or she pleaded guilty by letter) the court would assume that the defendant had an 'average income'.

> 'If they fail to complete the form, we assume that they can pay the going rate, whatever that may be.'

Sentencers recognised that this could result in low-income defendants being fined more than they might be but felt that it would not be practicable to adjourn in every case to obtain means information. If the offender was unable to pay the fine, it could be reassessed at a means enquiry

> 'The only thing that you can do is hope that they will be shocked enough to come into the office to sort something out.'

Fining low-income offenders – magistrates' views

Where there was no local guidance on the size of fines for people on low incomes, magistrates would often set the maximum at what they believed the defendant could afford to pay over a year. As magistrates assumed that the maximum weekly amount that a person receiving benefits could afford to pay was between £3 and £5 a week, the maximum fine for unemployed offenders was normally between £150 and £250. Fining people on low incomes for driving without insurance and not having a TV licence was felt to pose special problems. In order to create a deterrent, it was important that the offender did not benefit from the offence, so any fine had to be more than the cost of car insurance or a TV licence. However, this could lead to fines which were beyond the means of the offenders although for motor insurance cases penalty points can be an additional punishment. One magistrate said:

> 'We all resent having to fine people very low amounts for no insurance. We're all sitting in court, having paid our dues, and they are taking a chance and getting away with it. If they are on income support, how can they afford to own a car?'

Unfortunately, allowing low-income

offenders to 'get away with it' was seen as unavoidable if the court is to set fines that can be enforced. As one justices' clerk said:

> 'It might be galling that the fine is cheaper than paying for motor insurance, but, at the end of the day, you can't get blood out of a stone. If you are to have any chance at all of enforcing the fine, you have to set the level of the fine that they can pay in the first instance. That is the difficult bit.'

In contrast, magistrates sometimes regretted having to impose fines for not having a TV licence which were heavy in relation to the offender's income:

> 'By imposing the fine [for no TV licence) you are making that person into a criminal. My worry is that magistrates' courts are putting people into a situation where they are going to a loan shark to pay a fine and making a bigger problem.'

Fining the wealthy – magistrates' views

There were mixed views about increasing fines for more wealthy offenders:

> 'A fine is a punishment and someone who is very wealthy and given a small fine, it would mean nothing to them. But to someone who hasn't got much money, the same financial penalty would be a big punishment. That's why I think that we have got to be flexible.'

The fact that the wealthy received larger fines was also seen as increasing the credibility of the fine:

> 'You get footballers for example. The man in the street knows what their wages are. When they get caught speeding or drunk and disorderly the fine has to pull up the general public with a jerk so they think, "I'm not doing that".'

However, other magistrates did not support the principle of bigger fines for wealthy people:

> 'I don't think that someone is likely to be punished because he's got extra money; I think that what we're doing is imposing a realistic fine and scaling it down because of

lack of income. A wealthy person doesn't need it scaling down so he gets the realistic fine.'

These contrasting opinions meant that wealthy offenders could receive very different fines at different courts as the size of the fine imposed depends largely upon the views of the magistrates at that court.

14 Imprisonment

The data provided from the official prison statistics reveal large, increasing and over-crowded prison populations. Material is also provided so as to allow comparisons by gender.

Elkins M, Gray S and Rogers K (2001) *Prison Population Brief England and Wales: July 2001*

The prison population fell unexpectedly in the autumn of 2000, but has increased steadily since the beginning of 2001. The prison population in England and Wales in July 2001 was 67,090, a 2 per cent increase on the number in July 2000 (65,870). There were 63,290 male prisoners in July 2001, an increase of 1 per cent over the year. There were 3,800 female prisoners in July 2001, an increase of 11 per cent over the year. Young prisoners (mainly aged 15 to 20) decreased by 3 per cent, from 11,470 in July 2000 to 11,130 in July 2001. Juvenile prisoners aged 15 to 17 decreased by 3 per cent over the year to 2,430. Remand prisoners decreased by 2 per cent from 11,700 to 11,430. Sentenced prisoners increased by 2 per cent over the year from 53,520 to 54,570. Eight per cent were serving sentences of less than six months, 8 per cent were serving from six months to less than 12 months, 37 per cent were serving from 12 months to less than four years, and 38 per cent were serving sentences of four years and over (excluding life sentence prisoners). There were 4,840 life sentence prisoners in July 2001 (9 per cent of all sentenced prisoners);. 150 of these were young persons. There were 4,680 males and 160 females serving life sentences. In July 2001, the ethnic breakdown of the prison population was as follows: 79 per cent white, 14 per cent black, 3 per cent South Asian and 4 per cent Chinese and other. The prison population was 3,430 (5 per cent) higher than the certified normal accommodation (CNA) of 63,670. The numbers of prisoners held was 4,180 below the operational capacity of the prisons (71,270).

PRISON POPULATION 31 JULY 2001

	Males	Females	Total
Aged 15–17	2,330	97	2,430
On remand	430	24	450
Sentenced	1,900	73	1,980
Civil prisoners	0	0	0
Aged 18–20	8,270	430	8,700
On remand	1,830	120	1,950
Sentenced	6,420	310	6,730
Civil prisoners	19	4	23
Adult	52,690	3,270	55,960
On remand	8,350	680	9,030
Sentenced	43,320	2,560	45,870
Civil prisoners	1,030	41	1,070
Total	63,290	3,800	67,090
All remand	10,610	820	11,430
All sentenced	51,640	2,940	54,580
All civil	1,050	45	1,090

The use of rounding on totals explains the apparent arithmetical anomalies.

The next document presents the latest prison population projections for England and Wales up to the year 2008.

Gray C and Elkins M (2001)
Projections of Long Term Trends in the Prison Population to 2008

The 2000 figure of 64.8 thousand is projected to increase to 70.2 thousand in 2008 if custody rates and sentence rates remained at 2000 levels. Things rarely stay exactly as they were before and two further plausible scenarios are explored. Firstly, where it is assumed that custody rates increase at 2 per cent per year for males and 4.5 per cent for females and that sentence rates remained at 2000 levels, this gives a prison population of 76,700 in 2008. Alternatively, if custody rates increase at 4 per cent per year for males and 9 per cent for females, and sentence rates remain at 2000 levels, this gives a prison population of 83,500 in 2008.

Whilst the knowledge of the public about issues of law and order may be limited their influence is not. The call of the mob for a tough approach to crime means that sentencers and politicians will be subject to pressure. The outcome in terms of options used may not accord with the evidence in relation to those options. Our use of custody is a classic account of this phenomenon.

Dunbar I and Langdon A (1998) *Tough Justice*, p153

The truth is that the courts are using prison more freely than at any time in living memory, and they are also passing much longer sentences than would have been considered normal 20 or 30 years ago. The explosion of prison numbers is due to an absolutely extraordinary step change in sentencing norms over a very short period. To make matters worse, the remand population (which decreased by nearly 1,000 from 1994 to 1996) is now also rising steadily. It is implicit in this account that the sentencing surge has been mainly attributable to the politics of a particular situation and that sentencers have been responding to the knowledge that nobody would stand up for them if they were reviled in the media. The judges' own opinions of the causes behind shifts in sentencing are usually shrouded in mystery. On this occasion, however, the Lord Chief Justice, Lord Bingham of Cornhill, has put his views on the record in two important speeches. (Bingham, Lord, 'The Sentence of the Court', Police Foundation Lecture, 10 July 1997; and speech to the National Probation Convention 12 November 1997, both Lord Chancellor's Department Press Office.)

In Lord Bingham's opinion the higher rate of custodial sentencing and increased length of sentences cannot be explained by changes in sentencing powers and is simply due to 'the vocal expression of opinion by influential public figures that custody is an effective penalty'. Judges and magistrates had been the subject of criticism 'none the less influential because indirect – for imposing what are widely portrayed as excessively lenient sentences', and that view had been strongly supported in 'certain sections of the media'. As a result, magistrates and judges had increasingly been choosing custody in the middle rank of cases where there was a choice to be made between custody and a community punishment, and Lord Bingham was forthright in saying that he regarded this trend as 'a real

source for concern' on grounds of both justice and effectiveness.

In Lord Bingham's view the problem that the courts have in using community penalties instead of imprisonment is partly due to a lack of confidence about them in the mind of the public and the perception of the media. Probation officers should be demanding taskmasters, but they were not seen in that light by the public. This question of public perception should, he said, be vigorously addressed, though it was a political rather than a judicial task to convince the public that community punishments were not a soft option.

Sections 76–83 of the 2000 Act provide for custodial dispositions and state the criteria that have to be satisfied before custody is resorted to. Sections 109–11 deal with requirements of custody for certain offences.

Powers of Criminal Courts (Sentencing) Act 2000, ss76–83 and 109–111

PART V CUSTODIAL SENTENCES ETC CHAPTER I GENERAL PROVISIONS
Section 76
Meaning of 'custodial sentence'

76 (1) In this Act 'custodial sentence' means –

(a) a sentence of imprisonment (as to which, see s89(1) a) below);

(b) a sentence of detention under s90 or 91 below;

(c) a sentence of custody for life under s93 or 94 below;

(d) a sentence of detention in a young offender institution (under s96 below or otherwise); or

(e) a detention and training order (under s100 below).

(2) In subs(1) above 'sentence of imprisonment' does not include a committal for contempt of court or any kindred offence.

Section 77
Liability to imprisonment on conviction on indictment

77 Where a person is convicted on indictment of an offence against any enactment and is for that offence liable to be sentenced to imprisonment, but the sentence is not by any enactment either limited to a specified term or expressed to extend to imprisonment for life, the person so convicted shall be liable to imprisonment for not more than two years.

Section 78
General limit on magistrates' courts' power to impose imprisonment or detention in a young offender institution

78 (1) A magistrates' court shall not have power to impose imprisonment, or detention in a young offender institution, for more than six months in respect of any one offence.

(2) Unless expressly excluded, subs(1) above shall apply even if the offence in question is one for which a person would otherwise be liable on summary conviction to imprisonment or detention in a young offender institution for more than six months.

(3) Subsection (1) above is without prejudice to s133 of the Magistrates' Courts Act 1980 (consecutive terms of imprisonment).

(4) Any power of a magistrates' court to impose a term of imprisonment for non-payment of a fine, or for want of sufficient distress to satisfy a fine, shall not be limited by virtue of subsection (1) above.

(5) In subs(4) above 'fine' includes a pecuniary penalty but does not include a pecuniary forfeiture or pecuniary compensation.

(6) In this section 'impose imprisonment' means pass a sentence of imprisonment or fix a term of imprisonment for failure to pay any sum of money, or for want of sufficient distress to satisfy any sum of money, or for failure to do or abstain from doing anything required to be done or left undone.

(7) Section 132 of the Magistrates' Courts Act 1980 contains provision about the minimum term of imprisonment which may be imposed by a magistrates' court.

Section 79
General restrictions on imposing discretionary custodial sentences

79 (1) This section applies where a person is convicted of an offence punishable with a custodial sentence other than one –

(a) fixed by law; or

(b) falling to be imposed under s109(2), 110(2) or 111(2) below.

(2) Subject to subs(3) below, the court shall not pass a custodial sentence on the offender unless it is of the opinion –

(a) that the offence, or the combination of the offence and one or more offences associated with it, was so serious that only such a sentence can be justified for the offence; or

(b) where the offence is a violent or sexual offence, that only such a sentence would be adequate to protect the public from serious harm from him.

(3) Nothing in subs(2) above shall prevent the court from passing a custodial sentence on the offender if he fails to express his willingness to comply with –

(a) a requirement which is proposed by the court to be included in a probation order or supervision order and which requires an expression of such willingness; or

(b) a requirement which is proposed by the court to be included in a drug treatment and testing order or an order under s52(4) above (order to provide samples).

(4) Where a court passes a custodial sentence, it shall –

(a) in a case not falling within subs(3) above, state in open court that it is of the opinion that either or both of paragraphs (a) and (b) of subs(2) above apply and why it is of that opinion; and

(b) in any case, explain to the offender in open court and in ordinary language why it is passing a custodial sentence on him.

(5) A magistrates' court shall cause a reason stated by it under subs(4) above to be specified in the warrant of commitment and to be entered in the register.

Section 80
Length of discretionary custodial sentences: general provision

80 (1) This section applies where a court passes a custodial sentence other than one fixed by law or falling to be imposed under s109(2) below.

(2) Subject to sections 110(2) and 111(2) below, the custodial sentence shall be –

(a) for such term (not exceeding the permitted maximum) as in the opinion of the court is commensurate with the seriousness of the offence, or the combination of the offence and one or more offences associated with it; or

(b) where the offence is a violent or sexual offence, for such longer term (not exceeding that maximum) as in the opinion of the court is necessary to protect the public from serious harm from the offender.

(3) Where the court passes a custodial sentence for a term longer than is commensurate with the seriousness of the offence, or the combination of the offence and one or more offences associated with it, the court shall –

(a) state in open court that it is of the opinion that subs(2)(b) above applies and why it is of that opinion; and

(b) explain to the offender in open court and in ordinary language why the sentence is for such a term.

(4) A custodial sentence for an indeterminate period shall be regarded for the purposes of subsections (2) and (3) above as a custodial sentence for a term longer than any actual term.

(5) Subsection (3) above shall not apply in any case where the court passes a custodial sentence falling to be imposed under subs(2) of s110 or 111 below which is for the minimum term specified in that subsection.

Section 81
Pre-sentence reports and other requirements

81 (1) Subject to subs(2) below, a court shall obtain and consider a pre-sentence report before forming any such opinion as is mentioned in subs(2) of s79 or 80 above.

(2) Subsection (1) above does not apply if, in the circumstances of the case, the court is of the opinion that it is unnecessary to obtain a pre-sentence report.

(3) In a case where the offender is aged under 18 and the offence is not triable only on indictment and there is no other offence associated with it that is triable only on indictment, the court shall not form such an opinion as is mentioned in subs(2) above unless –

(a) there exists a previous pre-sentence report obtained in respect of the offender; and

(b) the court has had regard to the information contained in that report, or, if there is more than one such report, the most recent report.

(4) In forming any such opinion as is mentioned in subs(2) of s79 or 80 above, a court –

(a) shall take into account all such information as is available to it about the circumstances of the offence or (as the case may be) of the offence and the offence or offences associated with it, including any aggravating or mitigating factors; and

(b) in the case of any such opinion as is mentioned in paragraph (b) of that subsection, may take into account any information about the offender which is before it.

(5) No custodial sentence shall be invalidated by the failure of a court to obtain and consider a pre-sentence report before forming an opinion referred to in subs(1) above, but any court on an appeal against such a sentence –

(a) shall, subject to subs(6) below, obtain a pre-sentence report if none was obtained by the court below; and

(b) shall consider any such report obtained by it or by that court.

(6) Subsection (5)(a) above does not apply if the court is of the opinion –

(a) that the court below was justified in forming an opinion that it was unnecessary to obtain a pre-sentence report; or

(b) that, although the court below was not justified in forming that opinion, in the circumstances of the case at the time it is before the court, it is unnecessary to obtain a pre-sentence report.

(7) In a case where the offender is aged under 18 and the offence is not triable only on indictment and there is no other offence associated with it that is triable only on indictment, the court shall not form such an opinion as is mentioned in subs(6) above unless –

(a) there exists a previous pre-sentence report obtained in respect of the offender; and

(b) the court has had regard to the information contained in that report, or, if there is more than one such report, the most recent report.

(8) Section 156 below (disclosure of pre-sentence report to offender etc) applies to any pre-sentence report obtained in pursuance of this section.

Section 82
Additional requirements in case of mentally disordered offender

82 (1) Subject to subs(2) below, in any case where the offender is or appears to be mentally disordered, the court shall obtain and consider a medical report before passing a custodial sentence other than one fixed by law or falling to be imposed under s109(2) below.

(2) Subsection (1) above does not apply if, in the circumstances of the case, the court is of the opinion that it is unnecessary to obtain a medical report.

(3) Before passing a custodial sentence, other than one fixed by law or falling to be imposed under s109(2) below, on an offender who is or appears to be mentally disordered, a court shall consider –

(a) any information before it which relates to his mental condition (whether given in a medical report, a pre-sentence report or otherwise); and

(b) the likely effect of such a sentence on that condition and on any treatment which may be available for it.

(4) No custodial sentence which is passed in a case to which subs(1) above applies shall be invalidated by the failure of a court to comply with that subsection, but any court on an appeal against such a sentence –

(a) shall obtain a medical report if none was obtained by the court below; and

(b) shall consider any such report obtained by it or by that court.

(5) In this section, 'mentally disordered', in relation to any person, means suffering from a mental disorder within the meaning of the Mental Health Act 1983.

(6) In this section, 'medical report' means a report as to an offender's mental condition made or submitted orally or in writing by a registered medical practitioner who is approved for the purposes of s12 of the Mental Health Act 1983 by the Secretary of State as having special experience in the diagnosis or treatment of mental disorder.

(7) Nothing in this section shall be taken as prejudicing the generality of s81 above.

Section 83
Restriction on imposing custodial sentences on persons not legally represented

83 (1) A magistrates' court on summary conviction, or the Crown Court on committal for sentence or on conviction on indictment, shall not pass a sentence of imprisonment on a person who –

(a) is not legally represented in that court, and

(b) has not been previously sentenced to that punishment by a court in any part of the United Kingdom, unless he is a person to whom subs(3) below applies.

(2) A magistrates' court on summary conviction, or the Crown Court on committal for sentence or on conviction on indictment, shall not –

(a) pass a sentence of detention under s90 or 91 below,

(b) pass a sentence of custody for life under s93 or 94 below,

(c) pass a sentence of detention in a young offender institution, or

(d) make a detention and training order, on or in respect of a person who is not legally represented in that court unless he is a person to whom subs(3) below applies.

(3) This subsection applies to a person if either –

(a) he was granted a right to representation funded by the Legal Services Commission as part of the Criminal Defence Service but the right was withdrawn because of his conduct; or

(b) having been informed of his right to apply for such representation and having had the opportunity to do so, he refused or failed to apply.

(4) For the purposes of this section a person is to be treated as legally represented in a court if, but only if, he has the assistance of counsel or a solicitor to represent him in the proceedings in that court at some time after he is found guilty and before he is sentenced.

(5) For the purposes of subs(1)(b) above a previous sentence of imprisonment which has been suspended and which has not taken effect under s119 below or under s19 of the Treatment of Offenders Act (Northern Ireland) 1968 shall be disregarded.

(6) In this section 'sentence of imprisonment' does not include a committal for contempt of court or any kindred offence.

CHAPTER III REQUIRED CUSTODIAL SENTENCES FOR CERTAIN OFFENCES

Section 109
Life sentence for second serious offence

109 (1) This section applies where –

(a) a person is convicted of a serious offence committed after 30 September 1997; and

(b) at the time when that offence was committed, he was 18 or over and had been convicted in any part of the United Kingdom of another serious offence.

(2) The court shall impose a life sentence, that is to say –

(a) where the offender is 21 or over when convicted of the offence mentioned in subs(1)(a) above, a sentence of imprisonment for life,

(b) where he is under 21 at that time, a sentence of custody for life under s94 above, unless the court is of the opinion that there are exceptional circumstances relating to either of the offences or to the offender which justify its not doing so.

(3) Where the court does not impose a life sentence, it shall state in open court that it is of that opinion and what the exceptional circumstances are.

(4) An offence the sentence for which is imposed under subs(2) above shall not be regarded as an offence the sentence for which is fixed by law.

(5) An offence committed in England and Wales is a serious offence for the purposes of this section if it is any of the following, namely –

(a) an attempt to commit murder, a conspiracy to commit murder or an incitement to murder;

(b) an offence under s4 of the Offences Against the Person Act 1861 (soliciting murder);

(c) manslaughter;

(d) an offence under s18 of the Offences

Against the Person Act 1861 (wounding, or causing grievous bodily harm, with intent);

(e) rape or an attempt to commit rape;

(f) an offence under s5 of the Sexual Offences Act 1956 (intercourse with a girl under 13);

(g) an offence under s16 (possession of a firearm with intent to injure), s17 (use of a firearm to resist arrest) or s18 (carrying a firearm with criminal intent) of the Firearms Act 1968; and

(h) robbery where, at some time during the commission of the offence, the offender had in his possession a firearm or imitation firearm within the meaning of that Act.

(6) An offence committed in Scotland is a serious offence for the purposes of this section if the conviction for it was obtained on indictment in the High Court of Justiciary and it is any of the following, namely –

(a) culpable homicide;

(b) attempted murder, incitement to commit murder or conspiracy to commit murder;

(c) rape or attempted rape;

(d) clandestine injury to women or an attempt to cause such injury;

(e) sodomy, or an attempt to commit sodomy, where the complainer, that is to say, the person against whom the offence was committed, did not consent;

(f) assault where the assault –

(i) is aggravated because it was carried out to the victim's severe injury or the danger of the victim's life; or

(ii) was carried out with an intention to rape or to ravish the victim;

(g) robbery where, at some time during the commission of the offence, the offender had in his possession a firearm or imitation firearm within the meaning of the Firearms Act 1968;

(h) an offence under s16 (possession of a

firearm with intent to injure), s17 (use of a firearm to resist arrest) or s18 (carrying a firearm with criminal intent) of that Act;

(i) lewd, libidinous or indecent behaviour or practices; and

(j) an offence under s5(1) of the Criminal Law (Consolidation) (Scotland) Act 1995 (unlawful intercourse with a girl under 13).

(7) An offence committed in Northern Ireland is a serious offence for the purposes of this section if it is any of the following, namely –

(a) an offence falling within any of paragraphs (a) to (e) of subs(5) above;

(b) an offence under s4 of the Criminal Law Amendment Act 1885 (intercourse with a girl under 14);

(c) an offence under art 17 (possession of a firearm with intent to injure), art 18(1) (use of a firearm to resist arrest) or art 19 (carrying a firearm with criminal intent) of the Firearms (Northern Ireland) Order 1981; and

(d) robbery where, at some time during the commission of the offence, the offender had in his possession a firearm or imitation firearm within the meaning of that Order.

Section 110
Minimum of seven years for third class A drug trafficking offence

110 (1) This section applies where –

(a) a person is convicted of a class A drug trafficking offence committed after 30 September 1997;

(b) at the time when that offence was committed, he was 18 or over and had been convicted in any part of the United Kingdom of two other class A drug trafficking offences; and

(c) one of those other offences was committed after he had been convicted of the other.

(2) The court shall impose an appropriate custodial sentence for a term of at least seven

years except where the court is of the opinion that there are particular circumstances which –

(a) relate to any of the offences or to the offender; and

(b) would make it unjust to do so in all the circumstances.

(3) Where the court does not impose such a sentence, it shall state in open court that it is of that opinion and what the particular circumstances are.

(4) Where –

(a) a person is charged with a class A drug trafficking offence (which, apart from this subsection, would be triable either way), and

(b) the circumstances are such that, if he were convicted of the offence, he could be sentenced for it under subs(2) above, the offence shall be triable only on indictment.

Section 111
Minimum of three years for third domestic burglary

111 (1) This section applies where –

(a) a person is convicted of a domestic burglary committed after 30 November 1999;

(b) at the time when that burglary was committed, he was 18 or over and had been convicted in England and Wales of two other domestic burglaries; and

(c) one of those other burglaries was committed after he had been convicted of the other, and both of them were committed after 30 November 1999.

(2) The court shall impose an appropriate custodial sentence for a term of at least three years except where the court is of the opinion that there are particular circumstances which –

(a) relate to any of the offences or to the offender; and

(b) would make it unjust to do so in all the circumstances.

(3) Where the court does not impose such a

sentence, it shall state in open court that it is of that opinion and what the particular circumstances are.

(4) Where –

(a) a person is charged with a domestic burglary which, apart from this subsection, would be triable either way, and

(b) the circumstances are such that, if he were convicted of the burglary, he could be sentenced for it under subs(2) above, the burglary shall be triable only on indictment.

(5) In this section 'domestic burglary' means a burglary committed in respect of a building or part of a building which is a dwelling.

The Court of Appeal Criminal Division considered aspects of the system of mandatory sentencing under the Crime (Sentences) Act 1997 in the *Buckland* case.

R v Buckland [2000] 1 All ER 907 at 909–914 Court of Appeal (Lord Bingham CJ, Garland and Nelson JJ)

Lord Bingham of Cornhill CJ:

At about 4.40 pm on Thursday, 11 June, 1998 the appellant, who is now aged 31, entered a branch of Barclays Bank in Stockport. There were a few customers in the bank as he joined the queue for the customer service desk, a desk where advice was given. When his turn came he handed the clerk an envelope on which he had written 'This is a robbery, give us the money, I have a gun'. This message was written by the appellant in his own handwriting and signed by him in his correct name. The envelope had been addressed to the appellant and bore his typed name and address on the reverse. The appellant had made no attempt to disguise himself, and produced no gun. But the clerk took the note seriously and told the appellant he needed the counter. The appellant replied 'You better go and get it. I want £100,000'.

The clerk activated an alarm which summoned the police. Meanwhile the appellant sat quietly and waited at the customer service desk. At one point he walked to a cashier's window, tapped on the glass and said 'Where is he? He's gone to get me some money and I haven't got all day'. He was told to sit down and obediently did so.

When the police arrived they walked straight past the appellant, who was still sitting and waiting. He was pointed out, and arrested without a struggle. He was searched and a blue plastic imitation handgun costing £1.50 was found in his tracksuit pocket. When asked for his occupation by the custody sergeant he gave it as 'Saving Planet Earth'. After being charged and cautioned he replied 'Nuclear'.

The appellant was indicted on two counts. The first count charged him with attempted robbery, contrary to s1(1) of the Criminal Attempts Act 1981, the particulars alleging that on the date in question he had attempted to rob an employee of Barclays Bank of £100,000. The second count charged him with possessing a firearm upon arrest, contrary to s17(2) of the Firearms Act 1968, the particulars alleging that on the date in question and at the time of committing an offence specified in Schedule 1 to the Firearms Act, namely theft, he had in his possession a firearm, namely an imitation handgun. (It does not appear to have been pointed out that the relevant Schedule 1 offence committed by the appellant was not theft but attempted robbery, perhaps because it would have made no difference.)

The appellant pleaded not guilty to both counts but was convicted in February 1999. In March he was sentenced on both counts to concurrent terms of life imprisonment. The sentencing court specified a term of two years and nine months for the purposes of s28(2)(b) of the Crime (Sentences) Act 1997.

This was, on the facts, an almost farcical caricature of a professional bank hold-up. Although obviously distressing to the staff of the bank, it was scarcely an offence calling for the most severe sentence which the court can impose. But the judge held himself bound by s2 of the 1997 Act to impose such a sentence, and found no exceptional circumstances to justify him in not doing so. The single judge refused leave to appeal against sentence, and so at first did the full court. But the full court changed its mind, and on October 22, 1999 granted leave to appeal against sentence. On the hearing of this appeal we have had the benefit of submissions not only from Mr Goldstone QC on behalf of the appellant but also from Dr David Thomas, whom the Attorney-General helpfully instructed as an *amicus*.

Section 2 of the 1997 Act obliges the court to impose a life sentence on a defendant convicted of a 'serious offence' as defined in the section committed after the commencement of the section if, when committing that offence, the defendant was aged 18 or more and had previously been convicted anywhere in the United Kingdom of another 'serious offence' as defined. The court is relieved of this duty only if it is of the opinion that there are exceptional circumstances relating to either of the offences or to the offender which justify its not doing so.

The appellant's record shows him to have been a persistent but relatively minor offender. One of his previous convictions, however, is central to this appeal. In November 1993, for having an imitation firearm with intent to resist arrest, contrary to s18(1) of the Firearms Act 1968, he was sentenced to four years' imprisonment. We understand the facts of that offence to be these. On Christmas night in 1992 the appellant had been drinking alcohol and also taking a cocktail of soft drugs. He was in a friend's house in Stockport and picked up a starting pistol (or something similar) which fired caps. At about midnight, he was on his way to another house when he was stopped by the police for boisterous and drunken behaviour (which included firing the pistol). He ran off and, whilst running away, turned and fired the pistol once. He was arrested in January 1993. It is this conviction which has been treated as triggering the operation of s2 of the 1997 Act.

On the submissions made to us, five questions arise for decision.

1. Is the appellant's 1993 conviction under s18(1) of the Firearms Act of a 'serious offence' as defined in s2 of the 1997 Act? Section 2(5) of the 1997 Act provides that an offence shall be a serious offence if it is:

> '... (g) an offence under s16 (possession of a firearm with intent to injure), s17 (use of a firearm to resist arrest) or section18 (carrying a firearm with criminal intent) of the Firearms Act 1968; ...'.

It is argued for the appellant, supported by the *amicus*, that the appellant's 1993 offence does not fall within s2(5) because it involved an imitation firearm. The 1968 Act distinguishes between firearms and imitation firearms, but the reference to s18 of that Act in s2(5)(g) makes no reference to imitation firearms, in contrast with s2(5)(h), to which we will come, where such reference is made. The parenthetical summary of the effect of s18 in s2(5)(g) should, it is argued, be taken to limit its scope for purposes of s2 to firearms only, excluding imitation firearms.

In our judgment this is not a tenable construction. Section 2(5)(g) makes reference to 'an', which must mean 'any', offence under the three Firearms Act sections. These are referred to by number, followed by the printed section heading (with the addition of the indefinite article). None of the section headings purports to convey the full effect of the section. Section 16, for instance, headed 'Possession of firearm with intent to injure' makes it an offence 'for a person to have in his possession any firearm or ammunition with intent by means thereof to endanger life ... or enable another person by means thereof to endanger life'. Section 17 is headed 'Use of firearm to resist arrest', and makes it an offence in (1) 'to make or attempt to make any use whatsoever of a firearm or imitation firearm with intent to resist or

prevent the lawful arrest or detention of himself or another person'. It is in our view plain that the parenthetical references in s2(5)(g) are not intended to limit the applicable scope of those sections, but simply to convey their effect by reference to the section heading. It would be little short of absurd if a conviction based on a part of any of these sections not comprised in the section heading were held to fall outside s2(5)(g). It is readily understandable that the draftsman made reference to imitation firearms in s2(5)(h) because in that case he had no section to refer to.

2. Is the appellant's 1999 conviction of attempted robbery a 'serious offence' as defined in s2? Section 2(5) of the 1997 Act provides that an offence shall be a serious offence if it is:

> '... (h) robbery where, at some time during the commission of the offence, the offender had in his possession a firearm or imitation firearm within the meaning of that [the Firearms] Act.'

It is submitted that the appellant's conviction of attempted robbery does not fall within this provision, since it makes no reference to attempts. When the draftsman intended to cover attempts, as in the case of murder (s2(5)(a)) or rape (s2(5)(e)) he did so expressly. It must be inferred that the draftsman intended to include robbery, but not the lesser offence of attempted robbery.

We consider this argument to be plainly correct. It is not quite clear whether the sentencing judge regarded the attempted robbery conviction as triggering the operation of s2 (which in his judgment was triggered by the firearm conviction anyway), but if he did we think he was wrong. The appellant should have been sentenced for attempted robbery on ordinary sentencing principles.

Dr Thomas advanced a further argument, in reliance on *R* v *Courtie* (1984) 78 Cr App R 292, [1984] AC 463, that the absence of particulars relating to the firearm in the statement of offence of the attempted robbery count precluded the court from relying on that ingredient of the offence to impose a life sentence. Since we are satisfied that attempted robbery is not covered by s2(5)(h), we need not address that argument.

3. Is the appellant's 1999 conviction under s17(2) of the Firearms Act a 'serious offence' as defined in s2?

So far as material, s17 of the 1968 Act reads:

> 'Use of firearm to resist arrest
>
> (1) It is an offence for a person to make or attempt to make any use whatsoever of a firearm or imitation firearm with intent to resist or prevent the lawful arrest or detention of himself or another person. (2) If a person, at the time of his committing or being arrested for an offence specified in Schedule 1 to this Act, has in his possession a firearm or imitation firearm, he shall be guilty of an offence unless he shows that he had it in his possession for a lawful object.'

The appellant, supported by Dr Thomas, submits that his recent conviction under s17(2) does not fall within s2(5)(g) (quoted above) because the offence does not fall within the parenthetical summary of s17 there given. This is essentially the same argument that we have already considered and rejected with regard to s18, and we reject it in this context also. It is, however, submitted further that the reference to s17 in s2(5)(g) should be read as referring to s17(1) only and not 17(2) also. This submission is based on the absence in s2 (5) (g) of any reference to Schedule 1 offences, on the very wide range of offences covered by Schedule 1 and on the suggestion that Parliament could not have intended all offences under s17(2) to carry such potentially severe penal consequences.

Much as we would like to accept this last argument, we are unable to do so. By no process of construction can 'an offence under ... s17' be read to mean 'an offence under ... s17(1)'. Had the draftsman intended his reference to be to s17(1) only, he would have been bound to say so specifically. This is what was done in s2(6)(j) where reference was made to s5(1) of the Criminal Law (Consolidation) Scotland Act 1995; a lesser offence in s5 (2) of that Act was deliberately excluded. The same technique was adopted in s2(7)(c) where reference was made to article 18(1) of the Firearms (Northern Ireland) Order 1981; the effect of this reference was to include the Northern Irish equivalent of s17(1) within the scope of s2 but exclude the Northern Irish equivalent of s17(2). Why the Northern Irish situation should have been differentiated in that way we do not know, although it is possible to think of reasons. What is impermissible in our view is to treat the reference to s17 in s2(5)(g) as a reference to s17(1) only when that is not what it says and there is nothing whatever to suggest that Parliament intended the reference to be limited in that way.

4. Was the judge wrong to hold that there were no exceptional circumstances which justified him in not imposing a life sentence pursuant to s2 on the appellant's conviction under s17(2)?

Where the conditions set out in s2 are met, the court must impose a life sentence unless it is 'of the opinion that there are exceptional circumstances relating to either of the offences or to the offender which justify its not doing so'. As this court pointed out in *Kelly* [1999] 2 WLR 1100 at 1107, [1999] 2 Cr App R (S) 176 at 182, two conditions must be met:

> 'First, that the court is of the opinion that there are exceptional circumstances relating to either of the relevant offences or to the offender; and secondly, that the court is of the opinion that those exceptional circumstances justify the court in not imposing a life sentence.'

It is unnecessary to repeat what the court there said about the meaning of 'exceptional' in this context. But the judgment whether exceptional circumstances exist is not quantitative only, but may be qualitative also. It may, to take an example from quite another field, be far from exceptional for a candidate to obtain five A grades at A level, but highly exceptional for this to be achieved by a candidate who is deaf and dumb, or who has only spoken English for a year. In judging whether, if exceptional circumstances are found to exist, they justify the court in not imposing a life sentence, the court must bear in mind the rationale of the section. The section is founded on an assumption that those who have been convicted of two qualifying serious offences present such a serious and continuing danger to the safety of the public that they should be liable to indefinite incarceration and, if released, should be liable indefinitely to recall to prison. In any case where, on all the evidence, it appears that such a danger does or may exist, it is hard to see how the court can consider itself justified in not imposing the statutory penalty, even if exceptional circumstances are found to exist. But if exceptional circumstances are found, and the evidence suggests that an offender does not present a serious and continuing danger to the safety of the public, the court may be justified in imposing a lesser penalty.

It is not unprecedented, but it is certainly very unusual, for a bank robbery to be carried out with the incompetence and lack of aggression shown by the appellant on June 11, 1998. No physical injury was, or could ever have been, caused. The appellant never produced his blue plastic imitation firearm. Any distress to the bank staff must have been very far from extreme. The appellant made no gain and was never likely to do so. In our opinion the circumstances of this offence can fairly be described as exceptional. We consider

that the judge was wrong to hold otherwise. We cannot describe the circumstances of the 1993 conviction as exceptional. But we note that, on the facts as we understand them, it was an offence adventitiously committed, no injury was or could have been caused, and it was far from the most serious of firearms offences.

A pre-sentence report dated February 25, 1999 describes the drug-induced psychosis from which the appellant has intermittently suffered. His potential to cause harm was recognised as a significant factor. A psychiatric report dated 14 October 1998 suggests that psychotic symptoms from which the appellant was suffering on 11 June 1998 were an important factor in the offence. His psychotic symptoms had resolved in custody while the appellant had abstained from amphetamines. The report was broadly positive. An educational report from the prison spoke of the appellant in glowing terms. This is in our judgment a case in which, on all the evidence, it is safe to conclude that the appellant does not present a serious and continuing danger to the public such as could justify the imposition of a life sentence, and we accordingly conclude that the exceptional circumstances (already summarised) relating to the June 1998 offence were such as to justify the court in not imposing a life sentence. In all the circumstances we consider that such a sentence should not have been imposed.

To this question we accordingly give an affirmative answer.

5. What term should the appellant be ordered to serve?

The sentencing judge gave loyal effect to the decision of this court in *Marklew and Lambert* [1999] 1 WLR 485, [1999] 1 Cr App R (S) 6. He held that the appropriate determinate sentence on each count would have been one of seven years; he took half of that sentence, three and a half years; he made allowance for the period of nine months the appellant had spent in custody; and he specified the term of two years and nine months for purposes of s28 on each count. On behalf of the appellant it is argued that the judge took too high a starting point, and that seven years was in all the circumstances too long on the special and unusual facts of this case. We agree. It is true that the appellant pleaded not guilty to both counts, although perhaps understandably. His self-induced psychotic state affords no excuse. We accept that sentences for offences of this kind must have a very clear deterrent element. But we consider that seven years was too high a starting point for these particular offences.

In the result, we allow the appeal, set aside the judge's order and substitute a sentence of four and a half years' imprisonment on each count concurrently. The appellant will be eligible for parole after serving half this term, and entitled to it after serving two-thirds. He will be subject to supervision until three-quarters of the term of the sentence has elapsed. He will receive credit for the time he has already spent in custody.

The May Report in 1979 was a famous attempt to examine and report upon the prison system. It suggested that the purpose of prison should be to provide positive custody. It also made valuable suggestions as to how the prison population could be reduced.

Report of a Committee of Inquiry into the UK Prison Services (1979) Cmnd 7673, pp276–278 (The May Report)

Summary of principal conclusions and recommendations

INTRODUCTION

Although the Inquiry was set up as a result of some particular pay and allowance disputes, the real causes of deteriorating industrial relations over a long period were more fundamental. They included dissatisfaction with the way the services were run, the state of the buildings, and the physical conditions for staff and inmates.

The terms of reference have been interpreted as necessitating an examination of the criminal justice background to imprisonment in order to make worthwhile recommendations on resources. For similar reasons, the report spells out what it is thought modern penal objectives should be.

The pace of work has made some omissions unavoidable and detailed recommendations have not been offered in every case except where appropriate.

The recommendations should be seen and treated as a whole. The fact that an Inquiry has been necessary into what has gone wrong should not be taken to mean that nothing is right. The UK is fortunate in the men and women it has secured to run its penal establishments. They deserve all necessary support from the public. If we turn our backs on our prisons, we turn our backs on our society and our values.

THE PRISON POPULATIONS

Current populations

All the prison populations have risen since the War. Apart from the special circumstances in Northern Ireland, the main cause of the increase has been the rise in crime. Until recently, in England and Wales, this has been matched by the tendency of the courts to send proportionately fewer offenders to prison.

Overcrowding is worst in England. and Wales, and is least in Scotland.

The inmates have generally become more criminally sophisticated and represent greater problems of control.

All inmate population forecasts show upward trends. Successful attempts to reduce inmate populations in Holland and Sweden suggest that UK practices, especially sentencing policy, require re-examination.

The scope for reduction

Every effort should continue to be made to reduce the inmate populations.

It is wrong both in principle and in practice to imprison mentally disordered offenders and the DHSS should take urgent steps to ensure that the NHS lives up to its proper responsibilities in respect of them.

Prison should be avoided wherever possible for fine and maintenance defaulters as well as for drunkenness. More determination should be shown in dealing with alcoholism, and local voluntary schemes should be encouraged where appropriate, with government grants, both to start and maintain them.

Petty persistent offenders represent a series of intractable problems which require continuing effort to find solutions, not only to keep such people out of prison but also to keep them out of the criminal justice system as a whole.

Non-custodial disposals should continue to be developed wherever possible though there seem to be difficulties in the way of expanding some of them.

Executive intervention through remission schemes and parole should be kept under consideration.

There should be continuing vigilance over the number and lengths of remands in custody. Alternatives to custodial remand should be encouraged and defendants remanded in custody should be brought to trial as soon as possible.

However, in general none of these possible developments singly or together will absolve society from the need to support for the foreseeable future a substantial penal population.

OBJECTIVES AND REGIMES

Objectives

Whilst the first objective must be secure custody, that alone is not enough.

There is a need for restating modern objectives because the language, if not all the practical content, of Rule 1 has become overtaken by various developments.

Little systematic or precise evidence on objectives was received. Although 'humane containment' seems to enjoy some support, both it and 'treatment and training' should be rejected as sole objectives in favour of a new Rule 1 centred on 'positive custody'.

Regimes

Regimes should continue to be based on useful work but greater efforts should be made to establish a full working week and improve managerial performance.

Rigorous education of all kinds should be expanded where possible, including on a full-time basis.

The facilities for remand prisoners should be improved.

POSITIVE CUSTODY

'Positive custody' should become the guiding aim and penal establishments should therefore be as hopeful and purposive communities as possible. Amongst other things 'positive custody' means that the management of penal establishments should be consistently characterised by an openness of approach and mind not only to the staff but to all public requirements as well as to the interests of the inmates.

The Woolf Report followed on from a series of prison disturbances and its recommendations were portrayed as providing an agenda for the future of the prison service.

Report of an Inquiry into Prison Disturbances in April 1990 (1991) Cmnd 1456, pp19–20 (The Woolf Report)

Twelve central recommendations

These are that there should be:

1. closer co-operation between the different parts of the criminal justice system. For this purpose a national forum and local committees should be established;
2. more visible leadership of the Prison Service by a Director-General who is and is seen to be the operational head and in

day to day charge of the Service. To achieve this there should be a published 'compact' or 'contract' given by ministers to the Director-General of the Prison Service who should be responsible for the performance of that 'contract' and publicly answerable for the day-to-day operations of the Prison Service;

3. increased delegation of responsibility to governors of establishments;

4. an enhanced role for prison officers;

5. a 'compact' or 'contract' for each prisoner setting out the prisoner's expectations and responsibilities in the prison in which he or she is held;

6. a national system of accredited standards, with which, in time, each prison establishment would be required to comply;

7. a new prison rule that no establishment should hold more prisoners than is provided for in its certified normal level of accommodation, with provisions for Parliament to be informed if exceptionally there is to be a material departure from that rule;

8. a public commitment from ministers setting a timetable to provide access to sanitation for all inmates at the earliest practicable date not later than February 1996;

9. better prospects for prisoners to maintain their links with families and the community through more visits and home leaves and through being located in community prisons as near to their homes as possible;

10. a division of prison establishments into small and more manageable and secure units;

11. a separate statement of purpose, separate conditions and generally a lower security categorisation for remand prisoners;

12. improved standards of justice within prisons involving the giving of reasons to a prisoner for any decision which materially and adversely affects him; a grievance procedure and disciplinary proceedings which ensure that the governor deals with most matters under his present powers;

relieving boards of visitors of their adjudicatory role; and providing for final access to an independent complaints adjudicator.

Stern provides a useful insight into the types of people and tasks that prisons have to cope with, and the variations in what the experience of prison can be for inmates.

Stern V (1987) *Bricks of Shame*, pp31–35

It holds the untried, the unsentenced, the civil prisoners. It acts as a social service, a hospital, a place where reports are written, ... a nursery for mothers and their babies, a maternity hospital and a drug-rehabilitation facility. It contains prisoners whom many other prisoners would like to injure because of the nature of their offences, and prisoners who want to injure or kill themselves ... spending time in prison can mean many different experiences – being locked up with two other young men in a smelly cell for most of the day, waiting seven weeks to go to court for trial and then being released and given a community service order, bringing up a newborn baby in the mother and baby unit at Holloway, coping with mental illness in a prison hospital, working in the green houses of an open prison and sharing a dormitory with the most middle-class elements of the population ... or settling down for a long spell in an electronically controlled not over-crowded, top-security prison on the Isle of Wight.

The possibilities of alternatives to mainstream prisons are demonstrated by the special unit at Barlinnie Prison in Scotland. The unit was closed in 1995. Jimmy Boyle was one of the prisoners in this special unit and he describes his experiences of it. The three extracts that follow this one are also concerned with the special unit. The material in relation to the unit is most effectively portrayed when contrasted with other provisions made for long-term prisoners in Scotland. After a violent criminal past

Jimmy Boyle was sentenced to life imprisonment for murder in 1967. Within the Scotttish prison system there were a number of prisoners who in effect had nothing to lose and who protested against their conditions and the brutality that was used against them. For this they were punished, which led to further incidents in which people were being seriously injured. Boyle tells well his experience of Inverness Prison.

Boyle J (1984) *The Pain of Confinement*, pp3–5

I found myself connecting with other prisoners who were in the same boat. We had a lot in common and built up personal relationships when in solitary through an archaic ventilator system that was linked to each cell. In this way we began to plan and co-ordinate our actions. We soon learned that the system which copes well with individual troublemakers doesn't when these same individuals begin to organise and co-operate with each other.

In response to this the authorities became more reactionary and oppressive in their measures to contain us. After a succession of fights, riots and demonstrations five of us found ourselves held in the cages in Inverness prison.

These were iron-barred cage fronts that sub-divided a prison cell; reminiscent of those used to hold animals in a travelling circus. We were, at times, kept naked and given one book per week to read. The decor and structure of the whole block was built for sensory deprivation. The rules – blatantly plastered on the wall – stated that no prisoner would be kept in the cages for less than two months or more than six. This was flagrantly abused.

Having taken us to the ultimate in official punishment the authorities had in fact played their last card. They were now helpless in the face of our rebellion. In a strange sort of way we had been set free. I was aware of having an unpretentious naked truth and dignity in that cage. The authorities would publicly portray us as monsters and animals, but pri-

vately we knew that the degree of brutal violence exerted on us by gangs of prison officers was no different to that for which we were convicted. It was condoned by people turning a blind eye to it and the public not wanting to know. In essence, it was an unconscious, unspoken collusion that was rooted in revenge. The underlying belief that acts of physical violence have an instant 'cure' in the exercise of a more powerful physical violence. In fact, it made all of us worse.

The climax of this downward spiral took the form of a bloody riot in the cages. Many prison officers and prisoners were injured. The doctors announced that I wasn't expected to last the night. Four of us were eventually charged with the attempted murder of six prison officers. It made no difference to any of us. I simply worked my body back to physical fitness in preparation for the next bloody occasion. I thought there was no alternative.

Behind the scenes, outwith our sphere of knowledge, the authorities were stretched to the limit. A number of prison officers in Inverness resigned from the Service in the aftermath of the riot. Prison staff in other prisons were saying they wouldn't have the hard core of us back. The pressure was on to get the special unit opened.

As regards the special unit at Barlinnie, MacDonald and Sim provide the following account.

MacDonald D and Sim J (1977) *Scottish Prisons and the Special Unit*, pp26–27

Due mainly to the efforts of its staff and prisoners the special unit has evolved over its five years into a self-styled therapeutic community. In terms of physical conditions and personal relationships between prisoners and the staff the unit had progressed away from the traditional authoritarian non-relationships and spartan conditions that the majority of long-term prisoners in Scotland face. There is a great deal of freedom, responsibility and personal choice given to prisoners within the confines of the unit.

The men wear their own clothes rather than prison uniform. They can decorate their own cells and keep books and record players. They can cook their own food, supplementing prison rations with food bought with their own money. Their mail, unlike that of prisoners in the traditional system, is unrestricted and uncensored. Access to visitors is also unrestricted except when the men are locked up at night.

Each prisoner plans his own routine for the day and democratic community meetings take place weekly to discuss any issues that may have arisen. Any member of the community – either staff or prisoner – who 'lets the side down' by breaking the rules, can end up in the 'hot-seat' where his actions are discussed, criticised and chastised by the other members of the community, again whether staff or prisoner.

These weekly meetings function as a place where people learn to talk out any problems they might have in an open and objective way – something which is impossible in the traditional system. When a decision affecting domestic issues has to be made, each man, staff or prisoner, has one vote. One of the earliest and most symbolic taken was to remove the door of the punishment cell, which meant that reliance on the old method of punishing an individual by locking him up in solitary confinement was abandoned in favour of the new community based 'hot-seat'. This, according to both the staff and the inmates, is a much more effective means of control than the measures used in the traditional system, measures which, in the majority of cases, serve only to make the prisoner more resentful and bitter.

Ultimately, it is this ability to make democratic decisions and the positive staff-prisoner relationships, together with the physical environment far removed from the obsolete conditions of the majority of prison buildings, which makes the special unit unique.

There were problems at Barlinnie including violence and the death of a prisoner from a drug over-dose. But clearly it was a very different system to that which operated elsewhere in the Scottish prison system. The following report of a prison governor on Boyle prior to his transfer to the special unit is instructive. Such clientelle did not offer the special unit an easy ride. Eventually Boyle was released from prison and has had success as an author and sculptor and made a useful contribution in terms of an involvement with both grassroots social problems and as a commentator upon social issues. The key seems to be humanity.

Boyle J (1984) *The Pain of Confinement*, p2

I am firmly of the opinion that this man is so dangerous that he should never, under any circumstances, be liberated from prison and further, despite the assaults and incidents in which he has been involved in the past, he is still, even at this moment, planning further assaults and further incidents. He is liable at any time if given the slightest opportunity, to attack and kill anybody with whom he is liable to come in contact.

Boyle relates one of the experiences of his first day in the special unit at Barlinnie as follows. Given that Boyle was facing trial for six charges of attempted murder on prison staff it was certainly an optimistic approach. Suffice to say that the lessons of such experiences have not been adopted by the prison system.

Boyle J (1977) *A Sense of Freedom*, p230

I was then 'asked' by the screw if I would come round and sort out my personal property with him. I went, and while we opened the parcels containing old clothing he did something that to him was so natural but to me was something that had never been done before. He turned to me and handed me a pair of scissors and asked me to cut open some of them. He then went about his business. I was absolutely stunned. This was the first thing that made me feel human again. It was the completely natural way that it was done. This simple gesture made me think. In my other world, the penal system in general, such a thing would never happen.

The Prison Service's system of Close Supervision Centres, for the management of disruptive prisoners, was introduced in February 1998 to replace the former network of special units established in the late 1980s, following the recommendations of the Control Review Committee (1984), and generally known as CRC units. The Close Supervision Centres were also intended to take prisoners previously placed on the Continuous Assessment Scheme. The present research is an evaluation of their operation.

Clare E and Bottomley A et al (2001) *Evaluation of Close Supervision Centres*

The original role of the centres was to operate as part of a national management strategy which aims to secure the return of problematic or disruptive prisoners to a settled and acceptable pattern of institutional behaviour. To this end it has the following functions:

a) to remove the most seriously disruptive prisoners from mainstream dispersal or training prisons.
b) to contain highly dangerous or disruptive individuals in small highly supervised units with safety for staff and prisoners.
c) to provide the opportunity for individuals to address their anti-social disruptive behaviour in a controlled environment.
d) to stabilise behaviour and prepare for a return to the mainstream with minimum disruption.
e) the long term containment of those who continue to pose a serious threat to the safety of staff and prisoners.

The researchers in this report argue that the Close Supervision Centres' central underlying principle of prisoner progression, through a variety of incentives and earned privileges, is seriously flawed with respect to the management of these particular prisoners and that their management should be based on a set of rather different operational principles and processes. The key elements should include:

a) a comprehensive assessment process which includes substantial and integrated clinical input from forensic psychiatric services and others, in order to identify personality disorder and mental illness, and to assess risk.
b) the establishment of differential regimes with safe and humane conditions in which the minimum threshold should be standards and conditions that at least equate to those found in dispersal segregation units.
c) the long-term containment of a small number of high risk prisoners whom it would be unsafe to return to normal location, even when they have spent many years in the Close Supervision Centres system and have progressed to the top level.

Downes, in a comparison of the system in England and Wales with that of The Netherlands, notes the comments of prisoners in both systems. Such comparisons make it clear that there are alternatives to the regimes operating in parts of the prison system in England and Wales.

Downes D (1988) *Contrasts in Tolerance: Post-War Penal Policy in The Netherlands and England and Wales*, p163

They treat you like a human being. They say 'Enjoy your meal', 'Good morning'. They treat you like a man, they let you do things the way you like, they're not always looking up your arse for drugs, they don't guard you to see the governor, with two warders either side. Even when you go to solitary, you take yourself there. You think 'It can't be true, there must be a catch' but there isn't. I just can't believe they don't despise you because you're a criminal. In England they punish you for being a criminal. Then they punish you while they're punishing you. Then you're punished for the rest of your life. (English prisoner in a Dutch closed prison.)

Dutch prisons are much better, especially at thinking how to bring prisoners back to the normal life. There is home leave every weekend or so – here there is no way you can get that experience. If they realise that you are not a thoroughgoing criminal, they will do their best to re-establish you in society. Here there is no real attempt to do that, and for the English prisoners this is very bad. He goes out to nothing, so he goes back to crime … (Dutch prisoner in English training prison).

This report on Wormwood Scrubs could be interpreted in a number of ways. It details numerous ways in which the prison has improved, but it must be remembered that previous reports had highlighted very poor conditions so there is still some way to go.

HM Chief Inspector of Prisons (2000) *Report of an Inspection of HMP Wormwood Scrubs*, Preface and Executive Summary

In the report of our unannounced inspection of HMP Wormwood Scrubs in March 1999, I highlighted a number of very serious deficiencies in the treatment of and conditions for prisoners, many of which had remained unactioned since our previous inspection in September 1996. I listed these in the Preface to the report, and reproduce them, as a reminder, at Appendix 3.

Following that, the area manager and the governor, with the authority of the Director General, produced a strategic action plan for the prison, part of which was made public at

the time of the publication of our report. This plan was designed to cover a three-year period and included many initiatives to be implemented in the first six months. The purpose of the follow-up inspection, which this report covers, was to evaluate the remedial action taken, and, in particular, to see whether the action plan had resulted in significant improvements in the treatment of and conditions for prisoners. We did not inspect the action plan itself, nor simply check on progress in the actioning of our recommendations, but conducted a thorough scrutiny of the whole establishment, to test the extent of improvements and confirm that they were soundly based.

Our March 1999 inspection had revealed a culture amongst too many prison officer grades that openly challenged the authority of management and suborned the day to day routines for prisoners to meet their own ends. The efforts of conscientious staff and managers were stifled. (A full description of the culture that can develop within Prison Service establishments is contained in my 1999 Annual Report). Quite rightly, in my opinion, the Director General, senior managers in the Prison Service and the governor decided that the most significant and urgent action required was the restoration of legitimate authority in the prison, because all further developments depended on that being unquestioned. With that in mind the action plan had been designed with two immediate aims:

Firstly the introduction of a totally new shift system and staff profile, on 3 October 1999, to restore the authority of managers, and give staffs a clear set of tasks within the new shift arrangements.

Secondly to ensure that residential units were properly run and published routines fully implemented.

Quite understandably we detected considerable nervousness and tension on the part of most staff about our follow-up inspection, who were concerned that we might not find sufficiently positive change to enable them to proceed with their planning as designed. But, to their credit, and reflecting their growing confidence that the new way was the right one, this did not in any way inhibit the open manner in which they received and spoke to inspectors. This was in stark contrast to their attitude in March 1999, when too many were obviously concerned about the reaction of those who regarded themselves as being in control of being seen talking to us.

At the time of this inspection the prison had a population of only 640 compared with 890 in March 1999 – an essential prerequisite to change – and, in assessing the quality of what had been achieved, it must be remembered that staffs were only dealing with half the potential population of the prison. In my previous report I outlined a number of possible solutions to the Wormwood Scrubs situation, of which Option 4 – Partial closure and Staff Retraining – could be said to have been selected. I said that this could only work if there was a significant reduction in the prisoner population, which should be initiated without delay. It was, and, as at HMP Brixton in the past, it appears to have worked so far, which renders all the other options, including market testing, obsolete, at least for the present. I hope so, because Option 4 requires the governor to retain influence over his staff, through involvement with a retraining programme. When the two refurbished wings are ready – the first of which will be reoccupied in March 2000 – the population will return to the level on which we reported in September 1996. It is only when that has happened that the effectiveness of the changes that have taken place will be fully tested, and can be fully confirmed.

I acknowledge that only a certain amount could be expected to have been undertaken and achieved within such a comparatively short period, including tackling the old culture of staff largely determining how prisoners were treated. But we found ample evidence that the Prison Service, area manager, governor and managers in the establishment had accepted, very seriously, the need to undertake fundamental changes in order to improve the treatment and conditions of prisoners. Most of the staff had clearly accepted the need for change, and their attitude, along with the new shift system, represented a watershed in the history of the establishment. Despite continuing problems of so many staff suspensions, and uncertainty over the outcome of outstanding criminal investigations and disciplinary proceedings, most staff were clearly prepared to 'knuckle down' and determined to make the place work.

Staff rarely mentioned the time before 3 October 1999, every discussion starting from the introduction of the new shift pattern. That this had been an essential was confirmed by the fact that 55 separate shift patterns were discovered in the old system, many designed solely for the benefit of particular staff. However it must not be assumed that everyone is now signed up to the new arrangements. During our meeting with middle managers, a member of the POA Committee complained that the new shift pattern had been designed to satisfy the needs of prisoners rather than staff. As I said in the report on our March 1999 inspection, it is essential that those with such attitudes be removed from the prison and the Prison Service, in which there is no room for them.

Change had taken place and life for prisoners on the residential units had improved, as is described in the report. Basic and fundamental tasks had been reintroduced and were regularly provided. Prisoners felt safer, and their relationships with staff were better. Even in stable conditions, such changes are not easily achieved. It is therefore to the credit of all involved that legitimate authority has returned to managers.

Positive action had also taken place in a number of non-residential areas. Visits had been transformed. Health care was radically improved, helped by the fact that there is now a health care strategy for all London prisons. Education had been expanded and, together with employment, could attract most prisoners into purposeful activity. These three examples alone demonstrate the ability of managers to achieve good standards and bode well for the success of other developments.

I believe that the strategy for the next chosen period should be firstly to consolidate what has been achieved, and then to press on with progress in other areas. This is because the new way has first to encompass the re-opening of a third wing, for whose prisoners activities are required. Support and further training for managers, especially senior officers, is crucial. This is a general weakness right across the Prison Service, and not confined to Wormwood Scrubs, but senior officers are an essential part of any management structure, particularly in large establishments, and must be selected and trained for their tasks. Prison officers should be trained to give them the confidence to undertake a full range of activities, including the vital role of personal officer. Care for vulnerable prisoners must be improved. Throughcare and pre-release arrangements must be fully developed, so that those who are about to be released have suitable preparation and support. The psychology unit needs redirection in order to produce needs analyses, throughcare and support for management. The governor knows all this, and our detailed recommendations are spelled out in the report.

This will take time, but there has been a promising start and we have no reason to believe that the momentum of change and improvement cannot continue. A member of staff commented to us that Wormwood Scrubs had been asked to do in six months what had taken 10 years to achieve in other establishments. He forgot to say that the reason why staff were being required to do so much in six months was that they were 10 years behind most of the Prison Service, and had to catch up fast. It is one thing to have plans; it is another to make them work, and yet another to oversee their implementation to ensure their continued and consistent application. This is not something that the Prison Service is particularly good at, and it will require a determined effort, by all concerned, to reach the next levels of achievement.

But the period under review has been marked by a number of pluses. Firstly, of course, the determination of the vast majority of staff, and those who work in the prison, to see HMP Wormwood Scrubs restored to a place of excellence, known for the high quality of the treatment of and conditions for its prisoners. Secondly the determination of the governor and his team that the old culture should be eliminated once and for all, and that legitimate authority should be restored. Thirdly the support of the area manager, which has been as determined as it has been positive and encouraging.

For the strategic plan to succeed, the same degree of determination, and the same degree of continuing active support from Prison Service headquarters will be essential. There is much to be done but, tackled in the same spirit as that disclosed in this report, I have no doubt that my next inspection, in a year's time, will confirm that progress has been maintained, and so the treatment of and conditions for prisoners yet further enhanced

Executive summary

1. There was a clear improvement in the treatment of prisoners on the residential units. There was significantly more time out of cell and, for the most part, routines were taking place on time. Prisoners told us that they felt safe and when they approached staff, they were being accorded a greater level of respect. We are able to say therefore that the action plan developed by the Prison Service has started to improve conditions for prisoners.

2. Principal officers told us that their authority had been considerably enhanced, they were being backed by senior management and had a clear understanding of what was expected of them and how to take matters forward. Most of their time was engaged in ensuring that essential routines were completed and that the new approach to the treatment of prisoners was being implemented. Day to day management of

wing business properly fell to senior officers. However it was clear to us that generally prisoners did not regard them as
authoritative nor did they themselves feel
that they were managers with responsibilities and power. Some senior officers
recognised that they had to enforce new
procedures and that they could no longer
ostensibly operate as an officer grade.
Both they and the officers were finding the
transition difficult and there continued to
be some resistance to change. Senior officers in particular, required training to help
them understand how they could be more
effective in their role and their part in the
plans for improvement.

3. Although the personal officer scheme had
started it had yet to make a substantial difference to the treatment of most prisoners.
Staff were uncertain of their full responsibilities in this area. Senior officers needed
to give more active leadership to their staff
in this challenging task. Work with lifers
needed to improve especially when
helping prisoners to accept and come to
terms with their offences. The whole area
of throughcare, especially in sentence
management and preparation for release,
needed to be strengthened.

4. The following conclusions and main recommendations are based upon the tests of
a healthy prison taken from Chapter 7 of
the Thematic Review 'Suicide is
Everyone's Concern', published by HM
Inspectorate of Prisons in May 1999.

Test 1 – All prisoners are safe

5. In marked contrast to the last inspection,
control of prisoners was being achieved
through the exercise of proper authority
by prison officers, the maintenance of
regular and active routines and through
relationships between staff and prisoners.
Prisoners stated that they felt safer and that
most staff were more approachable. The
use of force to control prisoners and
recourse to the segregation unit were low.
Although some prisoner questionnaires

stated that they felt less safe than on earlier
occasions, this could be attributed to more
time out of cell and greater exposure to
other prisoners. We did not think that the
incentives scheme was encouraging good
behaviour, as differences in privileges
between those on the standard and
enhanced levels were minimal.

6. The reception and induction of new prisoners were satisfactory although there
were delays in getting prisoners onto the
wings because of the waiting time to see
the doctor. However, first night arrangements for those new to custody were still
unsatisfactory and needed urgent improvement. A new scheme had been introduced
which was yet to be fully understood by
staff. We considered that prisoners on
their first night at Wormwood Scrubs were
unnecessarily vulnerable.

Recommendations
*   The frequent use of questionnaires to
assess prisoners' perceptions should
continue.
*   The incentives and earned privileges
scheme should encourage prisoners to
improve their behaviour by providing
more effective rewards.
*   Medical assessment of those prisoners
newly received into the establishment
should not delay their transfer to
wings.
*   First night arrangements should ensure
that prisoners are properly informed
of what is happening to them and that
their immediate problems are
addressed.

Test 2 – Prisoners are treated with respect

7. It is an important task for every prison to
assess the needs of its prisoners. This had
been carried out in the Education
Department, but understanding of the
extent to which new prisoners had drug
problems was not evident. Most prisoners
told us that staff were treating them with
more respect and this was evident from

our own observations. Senior officers needed to show more leadership in encouraging personal officers to take the initiative in getting to know prisoners. Some prisoners were still reluctant to present problems to staff because they feared ridicule. Personal officer work was in its infancy and it had some considerable way to go before influencing life for prisoners. Overall, the early stages of the scheme had started to bed in, but most officers were unaware of what was expected of them in the role. Written comments on wing history sheets for example were inadequate.

8. Health care had vastly improved and was providing a good level of care that had been properly developed in association with local health authorities. Those identified as being at risk of self-harm were receiving reasonable support as detailed in Prison Service Guidelines. More work needed to be done to encourage 'at risk' prisoners in distress to approach staff at an early stage. The treatment of foreign nationals had improved.

Recommendations
• The personal officer scheme should be made more effective.
• The needs of prisoners with drug problems should be accurately assessed and addressed.

Test 3 – Purposeful activity
9. Most purposeful activity places were in education. This department was generally well run, with a developing syllabus prioritising classes in basic skills. There was a need for more classes to meet the wider educational needs of prisoners. Although filling education places on a daily basis had improved we were disappointed to find vacancies on classes. We were also disappointed with the lack of punctuality for classes starting in the daytime and in the evenings. It was good to find many more prisoners taking part in purposeful activities but basic systems needed to operate more effectively to get value from education and employment. There was a need for more employment opportunities providing practical skills for prisoners.

Recommendations
• Skills training should be introduced in workshops.
• Prisoners should arrive on time at activities.

Test 4 – Family links and preparation for release
10. We were very pleased to find that there had been significant improvements in visiting arrangements. Visitors told us that they felt welcome on arrival and that the environment in the visits room was more conducive to a relaxed visit. Prisoners endorsed this.

11. Little work had been undertaken to improve throughcare and preparation for release. A new throughcare department had been introduced but sentence planning was severely hampered by the fact that staff who should have been involved were often re-deployed. A significant number of prisoners are released directly into the community from this prison and many have spent several months there. There is an opportunity therefore for Wormwood Scrubs to challenge offending behaviour and assist prisoners to prepare for release.

12. The psychology department needed to be more active in conducting needs analyses, designing programmes for release and tackling offending behaviour. There had been improvements for lifers requiring assessment and provision of services. But risk assessments for lifers were undertaken far too late and more effective intervention were required to help lifers come to terms with their offence. We were delighted to find a greater sense of direction in the Max Glatt Centre.

Recommendations
• The psychology department should be more effective.

- The diversion of staff from through-care work should stop.
- Programmes to prepare prisoners discharged from Wormwood Scrubs should be introduced.
- Offending behaviour programmes should be introduced.
- Sentence management should become a more significant part of the work of staff and integrated into the personal officer scheme.
- Regime provision to enable lifers to come to terms with their offence should be provided.
- Risk assessments for lifers should be more timely.

13. Much had been done to create a prison that was far healthier than described in the last report. But consolidation and further development of new routines and policies needed to be vigorously pursued. The leadership of managers has to continue to push forward the planned developments. Staff, especially officers and senior officers, require more training, supervision and support. Those who resist progress should be challenged and requested to work as part of the team. It was clear that most staff had begun to show a greater flexibility in their approach and a growing understanding of what was required from them to create a healthier prison. This report acknowledges significant improvements but the task of turning Wormwood Scrubs into a prison in which prisoners are safe, are treated with respect, take part in purposeful activities and are helped to resettle into society without offending has a long way to go.

This report on Doncaster is a reminder that there are good prisons and it can also be noted that this is a private sector establishment. The finding that there was a continued high standard of staff/prisoner relationships, based on the all-important ethos of people treating each other with respect as fellow human beings, can be contrasted with the accounts of other institutions that were presented earlier.

HM Chief Inspector of Prisons (2001) *Report of an Inspection of HMP and YOI Doncaster*, pp2–4

When we first inspected Doncaster in March 1996 we reported it to be a good prison, well able to cater for its designed population of 771 prisoners, with the exception of the provision of suitable numbers of activity places. This time it was still a good prison, not so well able to cater for the 1,100 prisoners for which it now has to cater, not least because of the continued lack of sufficient activity places. The many examples of good practice are a tribute in particular to the sustained contribution of the director, who has been in charge of Doncaster since it opened. In particular I must commend the continued high standard of staff/prisoner relationships, based on the all-important ethos of people treating each other with respect as fellow human beings. I suspect that Doncaster will be one of the prisons whose CNA will have to be reconsidered when the revised cell certification procedures come into force on 1 September. Many of the cells are too small for two people, and will be unable to contain two beds, two tables, two chairs and two lockers, the minimum requirement if overcrowding conditions are not to apply. On the subject of the CNA I must recommend, yet again, that beds in the health care centre, which are provided for 24-hour in-patient care, should be removed from the CNA of prisons. They could well contain seriously mentally disturbed or ill patients, making them totally unsuitable for normal prisoners, particularly those experiencing their first night in prison. On the subject of health care I must commend that partnership with the local health authority which has resulted in working in the prison being accepted as part of the approved training programme for specialist forensic psychiatric registrars. This boosts the skill complement in the health care centre, while recognising the relevance of the experience of working in a prison. In the same breath however I must recommend a re-examination of the detoxification procedures, to ensure that they conform to laid down practice.

One of the original requirements of local prisons was that they should provide resettlement arrangements for local prisoners, who would return to the prison at the end of their sentence for that purpose. Bearing in mind how many of them are located in the inner city areas from which so many prisoners come, this would seem to be a task that should be re-established. It is quite clear that preparation for release and resettlement are taken very seriously at Doncaster, witness the admirable initiatives of the well-named community re-entry team and the premier information and counselling support. Although it is still early days, I have no doubt that both will make a significant contribution to this very important work.

There is much else that is good, such as sentence planning and the system for monitoring self harm, but I remain concerned at the lack of purposeful activity. The obsession with meeting targets that so dominates Prison Service management procedures has affected an honest admission that meeting the target of 20 hours purposeful activity per prisoner per week, in terms of the total number of hours worked, hides the fact that some of that work is not very purposeful, and some 400 prisoners are getting no work at all. The Prison Service required Doncaster to increase its role by 500 prisoners and, in equity, should have provided funding to provide 500 workspaces in which they could be occupied. This did not happen, and so it is unfair to blame the prison. But, instead of presenting figures designed to show that it is meeting its target, it would be better if it declared how many prisoners were in receipt of a 20-hour working week, so that appropriate action to provide for the remainder could be considered.

I also recommend that it is time that the practice of not allowing directors to conduct adjudications was reviewed. The reasons why it was introduced go back to the time when the controller was called the controller, because it was envisaged that he or she would assume control if that was lost by the director. Private sector prisons have proved their worth for more than 10 years, and directors have exactly the same responsibilities, and are subject to exactly the same inspection and audit arrangements, as public sector prisons. They tend to be more experienced than the controllers, to whom adjudication responsibility is delegated, and I believe that this practice is now illogical. There are sufficient checks and balances, including the presence of the Board of Visitors, to ensure that any irregularity can be identified quickly and appropriate remedial action taken.

So Doncaster remains a good and healthy prison, and I am glad that its contract has been renewed for 10 years, as opposed to the shorter terms that had become the norm, so that considered investment can be made in the future as well as the present.

All staff can take satisfaction from this, as can the citizens of Doncaster in the standard of its prison.

This report on Winchester prison gives insight into the operation of local prisons. In particular the perennial problems such as inadequate induction programmes; lack of criminogenic or social needs assessments; lack of programmes for short sentenced prisoners; inadequate work or education places; undeveloped personal officer schemes and ambivalence over anti-bullying programmes.

HM Chief Inspector of Prisons (2001) *Report of an Inspection of HMP Winchester*, pp3–4

The key paragraph in this report is the last, in which mention is made of a new sense of direction in HMP Winchester, which gives grounds for optimism. This is reinforced by the impressive degree of commitment by managers and staff to bring about fundamental change, encouraged by being part of two

Prison Service pilot schemes 'Safer Custody' and 'Custody to Work' which seem set to improve some aspects of the regime provided in local prisons in particular. That said, it is always disappointing to read of prisons that have not made expected progress, or have gone back in some respects, since previous inspections. The burst of energy following our previous inspection is recorded, which included recognition that the women's wing was an entity in its own right, now dignified by the name West Hill. But this seems to have diminished over time, until arrested by the new governor. With his Grendon Underwood background he is well suited to consider the possibility of West Hill becoming a therapeutic unit for women. But the same depressingly familiar litany of problems that beset far too many local prisons still remain – inadequate induction programmes; lack of criminogenic or social needs assessments; lack of programmes for short sentenced prisoners; inadequate work or education places; undeveloped personal officer schemes; ambivalence over anti-bullying programmes; too many life sentenced prisoners without an appropriate regime; inadequate provision of offending behaviour programmes for high risk Schedule 1 or registered sex offenders; inadequate arrangements for foreign national prisoners or immigration detainees; reported staff shortages following imposed financial 'efficiency savings', in this case affecting all important nursing staff in particular; health care beds inappropriately included in an overcrowded certified normal accommodation (CNA) figure, with the likelihood that this may result in new arrivals being placed beside severely mentally disordered prisoners; inadequate physical facilities in need of capital investment, in this case arrangements for visitors in particular, and so on. I have lost count of the number of times I have mentioned some or all of these issues in other reports, and still they remain untackled. The similarity of this list was one of the reasons for our recently published thematic review of the treatment of and conditions for unsentenced prisoners, Unjust

Deserts. It remains the reason why I continue to advocate for the Prison Service to accept that consistency is best ensured by making someone responsible for consistent delivery, however hard they fight against that proven reality.

I hope that this report will help the new governor to harness the commitment that I mention above, but, like all the other prisons faced with similar problems, real improvements depend on Prison Service assistance. Above all I believe that the annual round of so-called 'efficiency savings' must be challenged by Ministers. If such reductions are made because there is spare capacity, gross inefficiency or waste in a prison, then they could be both understood and justified. But, as our reports on prisons such as HMP Winchester show, this is simply not the case, and they seem to be based more on financial than prisoner treatment-based reasoning. It is all very well providing additional ring-fenced money for promising pilot schemes, or drug treatment programmes. But, if this provision is only made at the expense of the basic essentials of tackling re-offending – in other words treatment and conditions designed to help prisoners to live useful and law-abiding lives in prison and on release – then, far from being efficient, the required savings undermine rather than enhance the purpose of imprisonment. I cannot say this strongly or often enough, and, in order to obtain relief, do so directly to Ministers on behalf of the Prison Service as a whole. I also do so to try to ensure that the Governor and staff of HMP Winchester are given the means to do what the report demonstrates that they are keen to do, namely to contribute to public protection by providing treatment of and conditions for their prisoners that is designed to prevent crime and recidivism.

In this article Walker looked at the possibilities of unwanted side-effects of prison, such as damage to physical and mental health.

Walker N (1983) 'Side-effects of Incarceration', *British Journal of Criminology*[1], vol 23, no 1, pp61–71

One of the unfortunate results of ambitious and costly efforts to use imprisonment to achieve positive improvement in prisoners' characters has been the way in which these distracted attention from the unwanted effects of incarceration. Now that positive improvement is seen to be infrequent and precarious, more emphasis is being laid on the unintended harm which incarceration is believed to inflict. Another lesson, however, which has still to be learned from the collapse of therapeutic optimism is that beliefs about effects of any kind, good or bad, need critical examination. For example, one of the remarkable features of nearly everything that has been written about unwanted side-effects of incarceration is the assumption that any side-effect which can be demonstrated or hypothesised must be permanent. Yet the writers who assume this are also capable of pointing out that one reason why custodial institutions are unlikely to have lasting reformative or deterrent effects is that the social environment into which inmates are discharged is a more immediate and powerful influence than the carceral experience.

Damage to physical health

Undoubtedly this happens in some prison systems, as a result of malnutrition, insanitary conditions, cold, heat, excessively hard labour or inhumane disciplinary measures. What is very doubtful is whether the English prison system is such as to threaten the physical health of reasonably healthy inmates. Those whose health was impaired before admission will be mentioned later.

Malnutrition is most unlikely. The Prison Department (Home Office, 1977, p32) claim that the diet compares 'not unfavourably with that in hospitals and other institutions; in other words, the worst that can be said is that it is

[1] Copyright © 1983 *British Journal of Criminology* and Walker N. Used by permission.

cheap, not very exciting, sometimes not very well cooked, and often tepid rather than hot when it reaches the palate. Special diets can be authorised 'when needed on medical or religious grounds'. Prisoners say that food sent in by friends outside sometimes does not reach them; but that does not mean deprivation of what is essential to health. They also say that they tend to put on unhealthy fat as a result of the diet; but since few prisoners are on an ideal diet in outside life this is more likely to be a result of insufficient exercise, which is usually limited to one hour a day in the open air if weather permits (if it does not permit, there is sometimes no indoor alternative, although many prisons have indoor gymnasia where prisoners can at least take evening classes in PE). Even outdoor exercise may be limited, in the larger locals, to walking round a yard. From the medical point of view, it is the exercise rather than the diet which needs improvement.

The Prison Medical Service has not yet, however, made any scientific effort to determine the effect of imprisonment on physical health. To be fair, the only research project known to me which attempted this showed how difficult it is. In Tennessee, David Jones (1976) compared the medical records of men on probation, on parole and in prison. He wisely excluded chronic conditions, since these might well have begun before probation, imprisonment or parole, and took into account only acute disorders or injuries. Even so, he excluded prisoners who had served less than six months, in order to eliminate most if not all disorders likely to have begun before they went inside. He found that the per capita rate of recorded acute disorders of most kinds was higher amongst his prisoners than amongst his parolees and probationers, and also higher than that of the US male population for the comparable age-groups. The exception was respiratory disorders, which seemed to have a slightly lower incidence amongst his prisoners than amongst US males. What was odd, however, was that it was lower still amongst his parolees and probationers. The explanation is probably that his parolees and probationers were the most under-privileged as regards access to and use of medical services, while his prisoners had the readiest access of all the groups, and reporting sick has many attractions for prisoners. (This is not to suggest that prisoners are able to fake acute physical disorders: rather that many outsiders suffer from unreported acute disorders.) It would be going too far, however, to say that this explains away the high rates of digestive ailments and infectious or parasitic conditions amongst his prisoners: markedly higher than that of US males. All that can be said is that his 'controls' were not very good ones. In short, the study was not a very rigorous test of the hypothesis that prisoners suffer more from acute disorders. Even in a country with a fairly accessible National Health Service a study of this design would not be a good test. It is much easier and tempting to report sick in prison than to go to a gp's surgery when one is free, even if one is really ill.

A problem of a different sort is the prisoner who is already ill when admitted. In some cases admission is good for his health: the alcoholic dosser, suffering from malnutrition, bronchitic from sleeping rough, sometimes infested, is dried out, fed properly, disinfected and ejected a few weeks later with his expectation of life slightly increased. Occasionally admission to prison leads to medical treatment which was overdue. Every prisoner must be medically examined within 24 hours of reception, although many prisoners say that the examination is not very thorough. On the other hand, prisoners suffering from some disorder requiring regular self-medication, such as diabetics, find that they are not allowed to keep their own drugs with them in their cells. Because of the strict precautions against the misuse of drugs by prisoners, they have to get their insulin – even their aspirin – from a hospital officer. Sleeping pills, too, are not readily forthcoming, and because of the lack of exercise and stimulation many prisoners find it hard to sleep. A prisoner who is a bed case is put into the hospital wing, or into one of the

prison hospitals, which have surgical units. If he needs major surgery or intensive care he is transferred to a National Health Service hospital, under escort if he is an escape-risk. Pregnant prisoners are always transferred to NHS maternity hospitals shortly before the birth of their babies, in order to save the child the stigma of being born in prison.

What prisons do expose their inmates to is the risk of assault by other inmates and to a lesser extent by prison officers. Homosexual rape which is said to be frequent in American custodial institutions, is rare in English ones. It is ordinary violence which both male and female prisoners have to fear, and especially if they belong to one of four groups:

a) those believed to have sexually molested or ill-treated children;

b) those believed to be 'grasses' (ie informers);

c) those involved in frauds;

d) those who do not pay debts incurred in gambling or trafficking in tobacco or drugs within the prison.

The use of Rule 43 to protect prisoners from assault by other inmates is well documented. Case law says that the prison authorities have 'a common law duty ... to take reasonable care for the safety of prisoners' (*Ellis* v *Home Office* [1953] All ER 149 (CA)). It is true that as *Ellis* and other cases have demonstrated it is not easy for plaintiffs to convince courts that this reasonable care has not been taken, but at least one plaintiff has succeeded in doing so: *Darcy* v *Prison Commissioners* (1955) Times Law Reports, 15 November.

Nowadays when a prisoner known to be a likely target for violence is received from outside or on transfer staff are alerted to the need to keep an eye on him, and he is supervised at work and other places where he associates with prisoners. Special care is taken when allocating him to shared cells, dormitories or working parties. Transfer schemes encourage staff to identify inmates who are likely to be attacked because of their offences or past behaviour in prison. A move to one of the special units at Gloucester, Maidstone or

Wakefield is not a Rule 43 matter, and allows the prisoner to live in association with others for most of the day.

Mental health

It is widely believed that imprisonment impairs mental health. To what extent is this true of the English system? It is necessary to distinguish two suppositions. One is that imprisonment causes some mental disorders; the other is that it leads to what is loosely called 'institutionalisation'. The notion that it causes mental disorder in mentally healthy prisoners rests on no sound evidence. Certainly there are many impaired, psychopathic, hypomanic, schizophrenic, overanxious prisoners. Equally certainly impairment, mania, psychopathy, schizophrenia are not caused by events such as imprisonment, although they may come to official notice as a result of observation in prison. Most prisoners suffering from such disorders turn out to have histories of special care or treatment before their first imprisonment. Manic-depressive prisoners, too, are likely to have had episodes of mania and depression before admission.

What is true is that many prisoners become very depressed on first admission, especially during the process of trial and sentence; and this seems to be especially true of young adults in remand centres, where attempts at suicide are not uncommon. It has to be realised, however, that some of these prisoners were of a depressive temperament in their ordinary lives: this is especially likely to be true of the heavy drinkers, whose depression can no longer be concealed when they are deprived of alcohol. In some other cases the depression is an understandable reaction to the prospect of conviction, stigma, loss of job, rejection by one's family and deprivation of liberty: in other words it is a natural response to the situation rather than a product of the regime.

Yet if the English prison regime cannot be accused of causing mental disorder, the possibility that it leads to what is called 'institu-

tionalisation' or 'prisonisation' must be taken seriously. This condition was first 'diagnosed' in long-term mental hospital patients; and it was only later that the possibility of a similar effect in other types of institution was mooted. It is attributed to long continuous periods of detention, coupled with monotony, lack of autonomy and loss of contact with the world outside. In England the average time actually served by a male prisoner is slightly under six months (four months for women). It is only a minority of prisoners (about one in seven of those received under sentence) who are destined to spend more than 12 months inside, although many of the short-sentence men spend considerable fractions of their adult lives inside, with intervals of liberty. At the other extreme, roughly 1,000 men, plus a few women, enter prison each year with sentences of more than four years; and although many can expect to be paroled after two or three years their psychological fate is not unimportant.

There is evidence and pseudo-evidence. The best-known example of pseudo-evidence is the very influential book by Stan Cohen and Laurie Taylor, *Psychological Survival*. This was based on their discussions with long-term prisoners in the high-security wing of Durham from 1968 to 1971, while they were supposed to be providing the prisoners with classes in sociology, but were in fact holding 'unprogrammed discussions' and moving into the role of research workers (1932, p72). What they describe in their book is not so much the deterioration which the prisoners were suffering as the prisoners' fears of deterioration, some at least of which must have been stimulated or reinforced by the discussions and by the books with which Cohen and Taylor supplied them. *Psychological Survival* is a fascinating and insightful description of what went on in the minds of MacVicar and his fellow-inmates, and also of the real frustrations which they had to endure; but it is not evidence of actual deterioration.

Unfortunately few investigators have tried to measure this in nonsubjective ways, and most of those who have were more interested in special conditions than in ordinary prison life: for example in the effects of short periods of solitary confinement (1), or death-cell experiences. A thorough review of studies published in English was completed in 1979 by Bukstel and Kilmann (1980), who found that most had serious methodological shortcomings. If these are disregarded, we are left with a few studies which bear on the following aspects of psychological deterioration:

Intellectual performance

Bolton et al (1976) tested and retested, after about 20 months, 154 long-term male prisoners and, for comparison, 30 adult male non-prisoners. Using well-developed types of test, they found no evidence of intellectual deterioration. Indeed verbal ability seemed to have improved (perhaps because prisoners spend so much time talking). It is worth noting that many of their subjects were in the same prison as that described by Cohen and Taylor, and that the two investigations were more or less contemporary (2).

Aspects of personality

Using the MMPI, Steininger (1959) (3) studied 'first offenders' adjustment to prison life, finding that they experienced a strong 'distress syndrome' which lasted several months (ie they were unhappy). They were at first anxious to create a good impression and therefore behaved fairly well. Later their behaviour deteriorated and their distress abated, but worsened towards the end of the year of study. Jacobs (1974) (4) found that during their first year inmates became less anxious and concerned about others' evaluation of them, more manipulative, and more paranoid. As they neared release their anxiety increased again. As regards hostility towards others and oneself, the findings of various investigators conflict with each other, perhaps because different personality types were not adequately distinguished.

Problems

In an English prison for lifers and long-sentence men, Richards (1978) developed a list of 20 problems which seemed to sample the areas of psychological stress experienced during longer periods of incarceration. His subjects were 11 men who were in their first 18 months of sentence (the Early Group) matched for age, types of offence and type of sentence with 11 who had served at least eight years (the Late Group). The two groups, however, did not seem to differ in their ratings of the relative frequency and intensity of the 20 problems. The five most severe problems were: missing somebody; feeling that your life is being wasted; feeling sexually frustrated; missing little 'luxuries'; missing social life. Interestingly, although these problems are essentially deprivations of the perquisites of freedom, it was the men who had served at least eight years who were more preoccupied with them: a finding which contradicts the usual picture of 'prisonisation'. Even more interesting were the five problems which they rated as least severe: losing your self confidence; feeling angry with the world; being afraid of dying before you get out; being afraid of going mad; feeling suicidal. This, and the prisoners' emphasis on their capacity for self reliance, does not support the gloomier descriptions of the state of mind of long-term inmates.

Richards concedes that the prison in which this study was done had the reputation of an 'easy nick'. It is possible that the findings in a 'tough nick' would have been more discouraging; and, as we shall see, lifers in particular do have to fear certain things. What the study does suggest is that in one of the better English prisons long-sentence men are less likely to become psychological casualties than Goffman or Cohen and Taylor believe. It is often forgotten that the personal experience on which Goffman based *Asylums* (1961) was acquired in mental hospitals, although he draws on the literature of prisons, concentration camps, boarding schools, borstals nunneries, barracks, in order to support a number of generalisations about 'total institutions'. The reader is led to believe, by implication rather than direct statement, that the degradation of a concentration camp and the somewhat spartan life in Orwell's Eton do similar damage.

On the other hand, it is possible that a life sentence, with its uncertainty about eventual release, has more undesirable effects than a long determinate one. Most of Richards's subjects knew that they would be released or paroled on or before a definite date. Sapsford (1978) took as his subjects 60 homicidal lifers in a different prison, with conditions of maximum security: 26 had just begun their sentences; 24 had served about six years and had not yet been reviewed for parole by their local review committee; ten were men who had spent longer than the average lifer inside (ie more than about nine years) and must thus have realised that they might be in for many years yet. His sample was what is known as a 'cross-section', and did not involve following up the same men, which would obviously have been sounder, but would have taken a very long time. Sapsford did, however, manage to match some of the third-stage men with others in the earlier groups at least so far as age at conviction, victim-type and psychiatric reports were concerned, and he made allowances for the age factor. He did not find the decline in interest in the outside world which some people predict as a result of time served, but did find

a) that wives and girl-friends had ceased to be in contact by visits or letters by about the seventh year. In contrast, parents, brothers and sisters kept up regular visits, even with the long-term group;

b) the long-term group tended to talk about the past rather than the future;

c) the longer a man had been inside the less interested he was in social activities and 'outgoing behaviour';

d) the longer a man had been inside the more dependent he was on routine and the less he took decisions for himself.

Either Sapsford's technique was more sensitive than Richards's, or being a lifer is more likely to have such effects than serving a long determinate sentence.

What Sapsford himself points out is that we do not know whether changes such as (b), (c) or (d) persist after release, or whether the ex-prisoner recovers, in which case these side-effects would be a matter of less concern. There is no doubt that long-term prisoners experience a difficult period of adjustment when they come out: but that does not mean that they remain institutionalised. We have no real evidence about this at the moment.

Schools for crime?

Obviously one of the most important questions is whether detention in the company of offenders, most of them recidivists, makes prisoners less law abiding in their attitudes. The traditional criticism – Sidney Smith's, for example – is that prisons are schools for crime: that prisoners acquire from each other ideas, techniques and personal contacts which lead them into subsequent offences. This may well be so: the most encouraging reservation that can be made is that these ideas, techniques and contacts come from the less successful offenders, are already well known to police or security staff, and are likely to lead to petty, incompetent thefts, burglaries and robberies, with a high risk of reconviction.

A more interesting question, but much more difficult to answer, is whether an offender whose orientation is on the whole law-abiding when he enters prison is likely to be less so when he leaves. Sociologists have carried out numerous studies of the ways in which prisoners become adapted to 'the subculture of prison', with wide differences in their findings. Wheeler's pioneering report (1961) that in the early stage of their sentence prisoners' values were not very different from those of their guards, but later approximated to those of their fellow-inmates, and in the final stage reverted almost, but not fully, to their earlier values, was soon found to be an oversimplification (5). The so-called 'subculture of prison' is to a considerable extent imported from the subculture of petty crime outside. Whether a prisoner is assimilated to it depends on his own subcultural background and personality. It also depends on the extent to which the regime allows the prisoners to be dominated by powerful prisoners, on the frequency of contacts which prisoners are able to maintain with outsiders of their own choice, and, last but not least, on the length of time which they spend in any one prison. The shortness of most English sentences means that it is a minority of prisoners who, if they were law-abiding when they entered, are at risk of being turned into 'enemies of society'.

A finding which needs more investigation, however, is that the more custodial sentences a man or youth has served the more likely he is to be reconvicted, even when allowances are made for previous convictions and other predictors (see, for example, Nuttall et al, 1977, and Mannheim and Wilkins, 1955). It is conceivable that sentencers are selecting reconviction prone men for custodial sentences with a high degree of discriminatory skill; but it seems more likely that there is something about long or frequent periods of custody which increases a man's likelihood of being reconvicted. What we need to know is whether this is simply because ex-prisoners are more easily detected in their crimes than ex-finees or ex-probationers (perhaps police pay more attention to them; perhaps they learn incompetent techniques or acquire incompetent accomplices); or because they really have been rendered more crime-prone by their custodial experience. ...

Families

What happens to marital relations during and after prison sentences has been studied by Pauline Morris, first in interviews with the wives of 588 prisoners, some serving their first sentences ('stars'), some undergoing the latest in a series of prison terms (1965); more recently in interviews with nearly 100 men before and some months after release from two prisons (1975). In the sample from the 1960s only about one in four married stars but

about one in two married recidivists had not been living with their wives. Among the wives of the unseparated stars nearly three in four said they were happy about their marriages, or even that they were stronger than ever: an impression which seemed to be confirmed by most of the parolees in the later sample. All the wives of the white-collar prisoners, and four in five of the stars' wives expressed willingness to have their husbands back, even when their crimes were homicidal or sexual: and from the later sample it seemed that if a prisoner expected to be taken back by his wife he nearly always was. Some men even claimed that the tensions of trial and imprisonment had brought them closer to their wives. The marriages of recidivists and 'professional' criminals were more likely to become casualties. On the whole it seemed that if a marriage was reasonably harmonious before a prison sentence, and if the wife was not alienated by the offence itself (which she seldom was), only a very long sentence, or a succession of sentences, was likely to break it up.

On the other hand whatever the length of sentence many prisoners worry about the fidelity of their wives and are vulnerable to malicious gossip. Both husbands and wives, being young, suffer from sexual deprivation during the sentence. There is no evidence, however, that this causes psychological damage: it certainly does not turn heterosexual men into homosexuals, whatever may have happened to them inside.

What must not be ignored is the hardship often experienced by prisoners' families. The absence of some fathers can be a relief, and permanent separation may sometimes be in the long-term interests of the rest of the family; but in most cases wives and children suffer emotionally. In most cases, too, they suffer financially. In Morris's (1965) survey, three out of four stars' wives and four out of five recidivists' wives were receiving state assistance, and many were also getting help from relatives and voluntary agencies. In some cases this meant that they were better off than when the husband was free, because he would then misuse whatever money the family was receiving. At that time, in the early 1960s, only one in five of her stars and two in five of her recidivists were unemployed when detected in their offences; nowadays the percentages would be higher. On the other hand, the stigma of having a husband in prison seemed to be only a temporary worry. Many of the wives admitted that they had friends who had been in trouble, and fear of gossip quickly wore off.

Pauline Morris did not study the effects on prisoners' children. I know of only two English investigations which have attempted this: one by a research student of mine in the 1960s (Monger J, 1970), the other by Monger M et al (1981) based on social workers' reports of their visits to the homes of 102 children whose Nottingham fathers were in prison. The most interesting observations were that some wives pretended to children that their fathers were 'abroad', or 'in hospital' or away at work; but that few children were deceived and that most wanted to visit their fathers. Some of the Nottingham children's problems were attributable to their father's absences; but these families were not compared with any whose fathers were absent for other reasons.

Conclusion

Imprisonment is almost always boring, irksome and humiliating; in some prisons it is also squalid, and some prisoners suffer from grievances or anxieties. Condemnation of prison conditions is so universal that even to ask how serious is the harm they cause sounds heretical. Yet it does seem possible to exaggerate the harms. Exaggeration can take the form of attributing to all prisons the evils of the worst kinds of total institution; of attributing to short sentences effects which have been demonstrated only in some long sentence men; or simply of accepting (to say nothing of encouraging) prisoners' beliefs about their own deterioration. The most remarkable omission, however, in the literature of unwanted effects is any attempt to find out to what extent

the harm in question is permanent or lasting. This is particularly so where psychological harm is concerned; and it is even more remarkable when it is set alongside the scepticism about the psychological benefits of imprisonment. The more evidence there is to undermine any optimism about the likelihood of beneficial changes in prisoners' personalities, the more critically should we look at the assumption that detrimental effects are lasting, especially when the assumption is not merely unsupported by evidence but completely unexplored. The one exception is the finding that reconviction rates increase with length or frequency of custody; yet this too requires much more investigation before we can interpret it.

References
1. Which did not seem to be more stressful than ordinary prison life, according to Ecclestone et al, 1974.
2. Cohen and Taylor devoted a whole appendix of *Psychological Survival* to criticisms of this research, which, though not then complete, seemed likely to contradict some of their impressions.
3. As summarised by Bukstel and Kilmann: the theses remain unpublished.
4. Since their average age was about 30, and they were all in reasonable health, this is not surprising.
5. It was in any case based on samples of different prisoners from the early, middle and late stages of sentence, whereas only a follow-through of the same prisoners for the whole of their sentences would have been convincing. It was done in a single, high-security penitentiary in the United States; and studies of men serving shorter sentences in prisons with different regimes in the United States, Scandinavia and elsewhere often yielded different findings.

Bibliography
Bolton N et al (1976) 'Psychological Correlates of Long-term Imprisonment', *British Journal of Criminology*, 16: 38.
Bukstel L H and Kilmann, P R (1980)

'Psychological Effects of Imprisonment on Confined Individuals', *Psychological Bulletin*, 88: 469.

Cohen S and Taylor L (1972), *Psychological Survival*, Harmondsworth: Penguin.

Ecclestone G E et al (1974) 'Solitary Confinement of Prisoners: an Assessment of Its Effects on Inmates' Personal Activity', *Canadian Journal of Behavioral Science*, 6: 178.

Goffman E (1961) *Asylums*, New York: Doubleday and Co Inc.

Home Office (1977) *Prisons and the Prisoner*, London: HMSO.

Jones D (1976) *The Health Risks of Imprisonment*, Lexington: Lexington Books.

Mannheim H and Wilkins L T (1958) *Prediction Methods in Relation to Borstal Training*, London: HMSO.

Monger J (1970) 'Prisoners' Children: A Descriptive Study of Some of the Effects on Children of their Fathers' Imprisonment', unpublished thesis in the Library of Barnett House, Oxford and Institute of Criminology, Cambridge.

Monger M et al (1981) *Through-care with Prisoners' Families* (Social Work Studies No 9), Nottingham: University of Nottingham, Department of Social Administration and Social Work.

Morris P (1965) *Prisoners and Their Families*, London: Allen and Unwin.

Morris P (1975) *On Licence: A Study of Parole*, London: John Wiley and Sons.

Nuttall C P et al (1977) *Parole in England and Wales*, Home Office Research Study 38, London: Home Office.

Prison Department (of Home Office), *Annual Reports*, London: HMSO.

Richards B (1978) 'The Experience of Long-term Imprisonment', *British Journal of Criminology*, 18: 162.

Sapsford R J (1978) 'Life Sentence Prisoners: Psychological Changes during Sentence', *British Journal of Criminology*, 18: 128.

Wheeler S (1961) 'Socialisation in Correctional Communities', *American Sociological Review,* 26: 697.

The message to be derived from the evidence in this report is that imprisonment and indeed other sentences fail in terms of preventing recidivism.

Kershaw C, Goodman J and White S (1999) *Reconvictions of Offenders Sentenced or Discharged from Prison in 1995*

On a two-year follow up, the reconviction rate was 58 per cent for sentences of imprisonment and 56 per cent for community penalties. For conditional discharge, it was 44 per cent, 43 per cent for fines, probation 59 per cent, community service 52 per cent and combination orders 60 per cent. Some of the differences can be accounted for by such as offender variables and some categories of offender are just bad risks regardless of the disposal used. For some offences the chances of reconviction are much higher than for others – burglary has a 77 per cent rate whilst sex offences have an 18 per cent rate. Of the sex offenders reconvicted, only 9 per cent were reconvicted for a sex offence. For young males, generally 77 per cent will re-offend whereas for adult males the figure is 53 per cent. Reconviction rates were lower where the sentence length was longer, but of course the longer sentence would have increased their age upon release. Another important variable in recidivism was having previous convictions and even more so the larger the amount of previous convictions. Amongst the adult males who were released, 30 per cent received a custodial sentence within two years of release.

PERCENTAGE RECONVICTED BY GENDER AND DISPOSAL

	Male	Female
Probation	62	44
Community service	52	38
Combination order	62	41
All community penalties	58	42
Immediate custody	58	47

Murray, the famous American writer on the underclass, suggests that prison works so long as you use it correctly. By this he means with sufficient ruthlessness. By way of comment it has to be said that it makes for a plausible argument. It is certainly another point of view. But treat these ideas with some suspicion. There is too much evidence suggesting that severe penalties will not deter. This has been seen in relation to capital punishment for murder and indeed, for a whole range of offences, in the past. For deterrence to operate, the potential offender needs to have the penalty in mind at the time that the offence is about to be committed. The reality is that most offenders do not have penalties in mind at that stage.

Murray C (1997) 'The Ruthless Truth: Prison Works', *Sunday Times*, 12 January

Prison would deter shoplifters, if all shoplifters who were convicted were sentenced to a year in prison. Shoplifting would become exceedingly rare. Deterrence fails only because the odds of being caught and imprisoned are not high enough, or because the sentence is not harsh enough. Can imprisonment prevent people from committing crimes? Of course it can. The technical term is incapacitation. Burglars who are locked up do not commit burglaries. Lessons are to be learnt

from the United States. Like Britain it first tried a sustained, large-scale reduction in the use of prison. It then embarked on a large scale increase in the use of prison, that has lasted much longer and been much more massive, than Britain's recent shift in prison policy. During the period of reduction the crime rate was rising. In 1974 things changed in the United States. The courts began sending criminals to prison in wholesale lots. The number of prisoners in state and federal prisons in 1974 stood at 218,205. It reached 300,000 five years later. It took four more years to reach 400,000 three more to reach 500,000 in 1986. Since then, the United States has been adding about 100,000 prisoners every two years. As of 1995 there were more than one million people in American prisons. Does this mean that prison does not work? It would appear so given that there is still a high crime rate there. Such an approach shows a failure to understand what happened in the United States. It is the risk of going to prison that matters. In the United States, starting in 1961, the risk fell by 64 per cent in just 10 years, because the American crime rate shot up. At the same time the policy was to reduce the use of imprisonment. By the time the United States started increasing the number of people in prison in the mid-1970s, huge increases were required just to make the risk of imprisonment keep up with the continuing increases in crime. Only in the past few years, with more than 1 million in prison, has the ratio of prisoners to crimes reached the level that prevailed in 1961. Britain would have to quintuple the prison population to get back to 1954 risk levels.

Prison can stop a rising crime rate and then begin to push it down. The American crime rate hit its peak in 1980, a few years after the risk of imprisonment had bottomed out. Since then, with only a few exceptions, rates for the various serious crimes have generally been returning to the levels of 20 years ago. The academics are still arguing about how much of this is because of prison. Levitt, a Harvard economist, concluded that a 1,000 inmate increase prevents about four murders, 53 rapes, 1,200 assaults, 1,100 robberies, 2,600 burglaries and 9,200 thefts. Academics can reach such conclusions by comparing offenders who are left on the streets with offenders who are imprisoned. More than 60 per cent of American defendants accused of violent crimes are released while awaiting trial. Some will not receive a custodial sentence and some prisoners will be released early. For example, a federal study of state prisoners found that 45 per cent of them were in prison for a crime they had committed while on probation or parole. Most of those on probation had never been in prison (one cannot invoke the 'prison only makes them worse' argument to explain their behaviour). It is possible to work out how many offences they commit during periods that they could otherwise have been in custody. Such an analysis would not of course have taken into account the extra undetected crimes.

It is true that crime in America has receded during the 1980s and 1990s, but it is still extremely high compared with the 1950s. Prison has stopped the rot. It will not defeat crime in itself. If you are looking for a return to 1950s crime levels through increased use of prison you are going to be disappointed. Raising the imprisonment rate does not affect many of the 'root causes' of crime. Incarcerating people will not, by itself, solve the crime problem. But an intelligent approach

to prison does not require that it does so. You must ask what do we want prison to accomplish? John Dilulio, a leading American criminologist, weary of hearing the critics of prison repeat that 'incarceration is not the answer' got to the heart of the matter: 'If incarceration is not the answer,' he wrote, 'what, precisely, is the question?' If the question is 'how can we restore the fabric of family life and socialise a new generation of young males to civilised behaviour?' then prison is not the answer. If the question is: 'how can we make unemployable youths employable?' prison is not the answer. If the question is 'how can we rehabilitate habitual criminals so that they become law-abiding citizens?', prison is only rarely the answer. But if the question is 'how can we deter people from committing crimes?' then prison is an indispensable part of the answer. If the question is 'how can we restrain known, convicted criminals from murdering, raping, assaulting and thieving?', prison is just about the perfect answer.

Morgan provides a short reminder that there is much to praise in British prisons and that talk of crisis has been overdone.

Morgan R (1997) 'Imprisonment: Current Concerns', in Maguire M et al (eds), *The Oxford Handbook of Criminology*, 2nd ed, pp1183–1187

Over two decades the British prison services have perennially been said by commentators to be in crisis (see, for example, Evans, 1980; Shaw, 1992) – a crisis of order, of legitimacy, of staff morale. Use of the word crisis represents dramatic licence. The British prison services fulfill their intrinsically difficult mandate relatively efficiently most of the time, and they do so in a manner which is publicly a good deal more accountable than most systems in Europe (Morgan, 1993). They are remarkably free from corruption. In spite of the high security lapses of 1994–5 the number of escapes by prisoners who pose a genuine threat to the public is small and declining (Prison Service, 1996a: 11–12). Following the disturbances in 1990 there had, by the end of 1996, been only one major subsequent disturbance – that at Wymott in 1993. And though there is of course violence, and fear of violence, in British prisons, no prisoner has been killed in a British prison, by either staff or fellow prisoners, for over ten years (King and McDermott, 1995: chapter 3), and no officer has died while on duty at the hands of prisoners in recent memory. Moreover, the material conditions in which most prisoners now live are undoubtedly better in 1997 than for many years. There is only modest overcrowding, the indignities of slopping out are largely a thing of the past and most prisoners are able today to receive visits more frequently in accommodation more pleasant than ever previously known. These improvements in prisoners' living conditions have been matched by improved industrial relations and staff working conditions. The long overtime hours worked until the 1980s have gone and staff turnover is low and declining (Prison Service, 1996: 27).

Yet though our prisons can by no stretch of the imagination be said to be in crisis – on the verge of breakdown – their problems are many and the gains of recent years are at grave risk of being lost. The recent massive surge in the prison population, a surge which no reputable commentator has been able to justify in terms of public protection, threatens the stability of the system. The background to the surge, and the mechanics of its production, are discussed in Ashworth and Downes and Morgan, this volume. It has politically been talked into being – the rhetoric of 'prison works' – and engineered by judicial decisions taken without crime preventive justification. Space does not permit analysis of how the prison population could without prejudice to public safety be reduced, but at various points in this chapter indications have been given. The recent growth in the number of juvenile prisoners who, it is generally agreed, should not be held in prison. The large number of

mentally disordered prisoners who similarly do not belong. The explosion in the number of women prisoners the characteristics of whom suggest that many need not have been confined.

Bibliography

Ashworth A (1997) 'Sentencing', in M Maguire et al (eds), *The Oxford Handbook of Criminology*, Oxford: Clarendon Press, 2nd ed.

Downes D and Rock P (1997) 'Dumping the "Hostages to Fortune"? The Politics of Law and Order in Post-war Britain', in M Maguire et al (eds), *The Oxford Handbook of Criminology*, Oxford: Clarendon Press, 2nd ed.

Evans P (1980) *Prison Crisis*, London: Allen and Unwin.

King R D and McDermott K (1995) *The State of Our Prisons*, Oxford: Clarendon Press.

Morgan R (1993) 'Prisons Accountability Revisited', *Public Law*, 314–332.

Prison Service (1996) *Corporate Plan 1996–9*, London: Prison Service.

Shaw S (1992) 'Prisons', in E Stockdale and S Casale (eds), *Criminal Justice under Stress,* London: Blackstone.

Newman, writing in the context of the United States, made points that are pertinent to England and Wales at the present time. These are quite simply that we have a definite need for prisons for some categories of offender but not for others.

Newman D (1974) 'In Defence of Prison', in Johnston N and Savitz L (1982), *Legal Process and Corrections*, p340

In summary, any significant moves in the direction of diversion and decarceration, as attractive as they sound, have a long way to go and numerous obstacles to overcome. No-one, myself included, is in favour of present-day prisons, but until feasible and effective alternatives which meet all the needs of crime control and which respect all its safeguards are developed, then to simply postulate decarceration is not only foolish but dangerous. Prisons need not and should not be human warehouses, nor ugly and brutalising. Nor should they be used to chill political dissent or sincere efforts to change our social order in the direction of a more equitable, just and crime-free culture. Neither should they be used cosmetically, to remove 'nuisances' from our streets, to hold the inept, unpleasant or unemployed who present no real physical danger to others. But until the millennium when the crime-producing factors in our world have been eliminated, incarceration of the dangerous and the deliberate – the violent, the professional, the organised and the wilful, persistent offender – is not only necessary but is itself an alternative to worse choices.

This research looks at one of the schemes that can operate in relation to released prisoners. The Home Detention Curfew scheme was introduced on 28 January 1999 across the whole of England and Wales. Most prisoners sentenced to at least three months but less than four years are eligible for release up to 60 days early on an electronically monitored curfew provided that they pass a risk assessment and have a suitable address. Data is provided here in relation to the first 16 months of the scheme.

Dodgson K et al (2001) *Electronic Monitoring of Released Prisoners: An Evaluation of the Home Detention Curfew Scheme*

Prison and probation staff make an assessment of the suitability of an inmate for home detention curfew and also consider the suitability of his/her proposed address. Of the 72,400 prisoners eligible for the scheme in the first 16 months, 30 per cent were granted early release on home detention curfew following this risk assessment process.

Over the first 16 months of the scheme, over 21,000 inmates (an average of over 1,300 per month) were released on home detention curfew to spend the last part of their custodial sentence on curfew in the community. At any one time, an average of just under 2,000 prisoners have been on home detention curfew. Of those released in this period, only five per cent were recalled to prison following a breakdown in their curfew. The main reasons for recall were breach of the curfew conditions (68 per cent of recalls) or a change of circumstances (25 per cent). Only eight curfewees (less than 1 per cent of all recalls) were returned to custody because they represented a risk of serious harm to the public.

Data Covering The First Sixteen Months of the Order

Numbers eligible to be considered for home detention curfew	72,400
Numbers released on home detention curfew	21,400
Release rate (as percentage of those eligible)	30 per cent
Number recalled to prison	1,100
Recall rate	5 per cent
Average number on curfew at any one time	2,000

Variations in release and recall rates

Release rates vary considerably between different types of establishment and prisoner. Most of these differences appear to be related to risk of re-conviction and re-imprisonment for the inmate population of particular establishments. Sub-groups of the prison population that are granted home detention curfew less often than average tend to have higher than average risk scores, suggesting that the risk assessment process is working largely as planned. However, it is also possible that some variation is as a result of the different approaches to home detention curfew implementation and assessment taken by Prison Service area managers and local governors. There is less variation in rates of recall to prison. Women are more likely to be granted home detention curfew than men (40 per cent of eligible prisoners compared with 29 per cent for male prisoners), reflecting their lower average risk of reoffending and re-imprisonment. In general, older prisoners are more likely to be granted home detention curfew than younger ones. Black prisoners are marginally more likely than white to be granted home detention curfew (31 per cent compared to 29 per cent), but South Asian (51 per cent) and Chinese and other (39 per cent) inmates are much more likely to be released early onto the scheme. Again, these release rates are closely linked to actuarial risk assessments and reflect what also happens in parole decisions.

Recalls

The rate of recall to prison from home detention curfew has remained more or less constant over the first 16 months of the scheme, at around five per cent. There is no clear link between establishments, release rates and recall rates – that is, those prisons that release a higher proportion of eligible inmates onto home detention curfew are not associated with higher levels of recall following a breakdown of the curfew. Recalls were highest for those convicted of burglary (10 per cent) compared

to just 2 per cent for those convicted of fraud and forgery.

The views of curfewees

The generally successful operation of home detention curfew was confirmed by the survey of curfewees, family members and supervising probation officers, suggesting that the scheme has had some success in achieving its aim of easing the transition from custody into the community. Curfewees were very positive about the scheme, with only two per cent saying that they would have preferred to spend the time in prison rather than on home detention curfew. Prior to release, over a third of prisoners (37 per cent) said that the prospect of being granted home detention curfew influenced their behaviour in prison. Other household members were also very positive about the scheme. While the majority of curfewees interviewed (83 per cent) remembered being given something in writing with the rules of the scheme, less than one in three (29 per cent) had seen the video about the scheme. Almost half (49 per cent) felt that they were quite, or very poorly, informed about the scheme prior to release. According to the curfewees themselves, the main advantages of the scheme were being out of prison (82 per cent) and meeting up with family. Other household members said that the main advantages were having the curfewee back home (72 per cent) and no more need for prison visits (69 per cent). Neither group mentioned many disadvantages, although 41 per cent of curfewees cited the curfew restrictions as a disadvantage. At the time of interview, one-third of curfewees were in work (28 per cent full-time, 6 per cent part-time), with a further 36 per cent seeking work. This latter group was most likely to cite advantages (such as developing a routine and enabling them to look for work) and also more likely than others to cite disadvantages (such as the difficulty of finding a job because of the curfew restrictions and the inconvenience of the curfew hours for other household members).

Unannotated Cracknell's Statutes for use in Examinations

New Editions of Cracknell's Statutes

£11.95 due 2002

Cracknell's Statutes provide a comprehensive series of essential statutory provisions for each subject. Amendments are consolidated, avoiding the need to cross-refer to amending legislation. Unannotated, they are suitable for use in examinations, and provide the precise wording of vital Acts of Parliament for the diligent student.

Commercial Law
ISBN: 1 85836 472 8

European Community Legislation
ISBN: 1 85836 470 1

Conflict of Laws
ISBN: 1 85836 473 6

Family Law
ISBN: 1 85836 471 X

Criminal Law
ISBN: 1 85836 474 4

Public International Law
ISBN: 1 85836 476 0

Employment Law
ISBN: 1 85836 475 2

For further information on contents or to place an order, please contact:

Mail Order
Old Bailey Press
at Holborn College
Woolwich Road
Charlton
London
SE7 8LN

Telephone No: 020 7381 7407
Fax No: 020 7386 0952
Website: www.oldbaileypress.co.uk

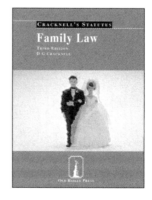

Suggested Solutions to Past Examination Questions 2000–2001

The Suggested Solutions series provides examples of full answers to the questions regularly set by examiners. Each suggested solution has been broken down into three stages: general comment, skeleton solution and suggested solution. The examination questions included within the text are taken from past examination papers set by the London University. The full opinion answers will undoubtedly assist you with your research and further your understanding and appreciation of the subject in question.

Only £6.95 Due December 2002

Constitutional Law
ISBN: 1 85836 478 7

Criminal Law
ISBN: 1 85836 479 5

English Legal System
ISBN: 1 85836 482 5

Elements of the Law of Contract
ISBN: 1 85836 480 9

Jurisprudence and Legal Theory
ISBN: 1 85836 484 1

Land Law
ISBN: 1 85836 481 7

Law of Tort
ISBN: 1 85836 483 3

For further information on contents or to place an order, please contact:

Mail Order
Old Bailey Press
at Holborn College
Woolwich Road
Charlton
London
SE7 8LN

Telephone No: 020 7381 7407
Fax No: 020 7386 0952
Website: www.oldbaileypress.co.uk

Old Bailey Press

The Old Bailey Press integrated student law library is tailor-made to help you at every stage of your studies from the preliminaries of each subject through to the final examination. The series of Textbooks, Revision WorkBooks, 150 Leading Cases and Cracknell's Statutes are interrelated to provide you with a comprehensive set of study materials.

You can buy Old Bailey Press books from your University Bookshop, your local Bookshop, direct using this form, or you can order a free catalogue of our titles from the address shown overleaf.

The following subjects each have a Textbook, 150 Leading Cases/Casebook, Revision WorkBook and Cracknell's Statutes unless otherwise stated.

Administrative Law
Commercial Law
Company Law
Conflict of Laws
Constitutional Law
Conveyancing (Textbook and 150 Leading Cases)
Criminal Law
Criminology (Textbook and Sourcebook)
Employment Law (Textbook and Cracknell's Statutes)
English and European Legal Systems
Equity and Trusts
Evidence
Family Law
Jurisprudence: The Philosophy of Law (Textbook, Sourcebook and Revision WorkBook)
Land: The Law of Real Property
Law of International Trade
Law of the European Union
Legal Skills and System (Textbook)
Obligations: Contract Law
Obligations: The Law of Tort
Public International Law
Revenue Law (Textbook, Revision WorkBook and Cracknell's Statutes)
Succession

Mail order prices:	
Textbook	£14.95
150 Leading Cases	£11.95
Revision WorkBook	£9.95
Cracknell's Statutes	£11.95
Suggested Solutions 1998–1999	£6.95
Suggested Solutions 1999–2000	£6.95
Suggested Solutions 2000–2001	£6.95
Law Update 2002	£9.95
Law Update 2003	£10.95

Please note details and prices are subject to alteration.

To complete your order, please fill in the form below:

Module	Books required	Quantity	Price	Cost
		Postage		
		TOTAL		

For Europe, add 15% postage and packing (£20 maximum).
For the rest of the world, add 40% for airmail.

ORDERING

By telephone to Mail Order at 020 7381 7407, with your credit card to hand.

By fax to 020 7386 0952 (giving your credit card details).

Website: www.oldbaileypress.co.uk

By post to: Mail Order, Old Bailey Press at Holborn College, Woolwich Road, Charlton, London, SE7 8LN.

When ordering by post, please enclose full payment by cheque or banker's draft, or complete the credit card details below. You may also order a free catalogue of our complete range of titles from this address.

We aim to despatch your books within 3 working days of receiving your order.

Name

Address

Postcode   Telephone

Total value of order, including postage: £

I enclose a cheque/banker's draft for the above sum, or

charge my   ☐ Access/Mastercard   ☐ Visa   ☐ American Express

Card number

☐☐☐☐ ☐☐☐☐ · ☐☐☐☐ ☐☐☐☐

Expiry date   ☐☐☐☐

Signature: ....Date: ....